W. F. DEEDES

Words and Deedes

SELECTED JOURNALISM 1931–2006

PAN BOOKS

First published 2006 by Macmillan

First published in paperback 2007 by Pan Books
This edition published 2013 by Pan Books
an imprint of Pan Macmillan, a division of Macmillan Publishers Limited
Pan Macmillan, 20 New Wharf Road, London N1 9RR
Basingstoke and Oxford
Associated companies throughout the world
www.panmacmillan.com

ISBN 978-1-4472-6274-9

A CIP catalogue record for this book is available from
the British Library.

Typeset by SetSystems Ltd, Saffron Walden, Essex
Printed and bound by CPI Group (UK) Ltd, Croydon, CR0 4YY

Contents

A national newspaper reporter shares that bench along with the coach, the physios and the substitutes which stands right on the edge of the field of play. From there, he sometimes sees more of the game than they do from the directors' box in the grandstand.

W. F. Deedes, 2006

SECOND WORLD WAR

I ENTERED JOURNALISM in 1931 when we were wondering whether we had let our guard down too far after the First World War and were thinking of rebuilding our defences. In the early part of the 1930s this concern became more pronounced, particularly after the advent of Hitler in Germany in 1933, and it led to all sorts of openings for journalism – the condition of our territorial army, the way we had let things slide, and our failure to match Germany's advancements in the air. The subject of rearmament became of great interest and I found it a very good journalistic outlet.

When I moved over to the *Daily Telegraph* in 1937, the subject of precautions against air raids had become uppermost. Stanley Baldwin had said, 'The bomber will always get through.' The question was: what would the bomber bring with it? I spent much of 1937, 1938 and the first half of 1939 studying the possibilities. It involved introducing myself to certain gases, which were never used in the war, flying through blackouts over various parts of England and looking at the deficiencies in our forces. I found this a very worthwhile occupation.

Britain then began to turn to the likelihood of war, which led to Munich, and I was a part witness to this because I saw Neville Chamberlain off on one of his voyages to Germany. I've always been a supporter of Munich because the time that Neville Chamberlain bought was so important to our defences, particularly in the air. At the time most people were sceptical and we had to report that. Good friends fell out with each other on the subject.

When war came, we found that, on balance, we were better prepared for it than the French. I contracted out of journalism for a while and put on a uniform, and therefore saw no more of the war as a journalist until after the peace in 1945.

I've always felt that the two world wars took a much heavier toll of our national strength than most people believe. Every time I go back to Normandy and other parts of France and look at the war graves, it does come home to me how much we had to sacrifice for those two victories.

Quite recently, I went over the battle lines from Normandy to Hanover that we took in 1944–5, and was reminded of what an amazing achievement our re-entry into Europe in 1944 and our conquest of the German army thereafter had been.

On the sixtieth anniversary of our victory, I looked back still thinking that we do not make enough allowance for the losses we incurred in treasure and in blood. As far as I am concerned, as one born on the eve of the First World War, our lives have been more altered by those two events than by any other occurrence.

LONDON'S DUTY TO ITS TERRITORIALS

To Fill Depleted Ranks

NEED TO STIR UP EMPLOYERS

In this, the concluding article of the series on the position and needs of the Territorial Army in London, our Special Representative sums up and suggests some ways in which recruiting could be stimulated

The Territorial Army in London, indeed, throughout the country, can never attain the strength and standard which England requires of it, nor occupy its rightful place in the scheme of national defence, until a radical change is brought about in the minds of those English men and women whom it seeks to defend.

Personnel is low because the people of this country refuse to believe, or are too ignorant to appreciate, how necessary the Territorial Army is to their safety, to the security of their homes, to the defence of all they should most care for.

Personnel is low because people do not mind sufficiently whether the Territorial Army exists or not. Personnel is low because these same people are not prepared to demand, as they only can demand, that the men needed for the Territorial Army are found, and found quickly.

Equipment essential for training is lacking in quality and quantity because insufficient men have been found to use the guns, searchlights and motor vehicles which otherwise would have to be made available. Accommodation is poor because the pressure of manpower from within the Territorial Army is not strong enough to force the hand of authority into providing money for rebuilding, renovation and expansion.

MORE PRESTIGE

So first, London must become more jealous for the name and prestige of its Territorial Army. Five years ago a "Buy British" campaign was successfully organised in this country, because the public were persuaded that the purchase of more British goods was essential for England's survival from an economic blizzard. Then, to some extent, a firm's reputation depended upon its ability to supply British goods, to conceal the wares of foreign competitors.

To-day, employers could be similarly persuaded into helping the Territorial Army if the public were prepared to satisfy itself that those from whom goods were purchased, those with whom business must be done and those who stood to gain from public support were all actively and positively assisting the Territorial Army.

If Regiments could safely leave the problem of recruiting in the hands of the public, less valuable time would be wasted by hard-worked adjutants and officers with inadequate permanent staffs in searching and bargaining for men.

In any case, the way would be better paved for these officers in search of recruits if a printed letter, signed by the Secretary of State for War, were addressed to principal employers, emphasising the need for helping the Territorial Army, and requesting that any officer who might call on the subject of recruiting be considered an accredited representative of the Secretary of State himself in this matter, and accordingly be received with courtesy and respect.

It must be assumed that most employers in London, if only better acquainted with the needs of the situation, would require no such pressure from public opinion. But unfortunately they are not so acquainted. How many know the number of men in their employ who are members of the Territorial Army? How many have taken the trouble to inquire?

Facilities for Service

There must be no suggestion that the member of a firm who is in the Territorial Army should directly receive preferential treatment; for such action might lead to an undesirable and dangerous form of private conscription which must inevitably reflect upon the voluntary spirit of the Territorial system.

But those who are prepared to serve their country in an hour of need, should at least be granted the necessary time and facilities to prepare for this service; and steps ought to be taken to ensure that such men do not lose either financially or by departmental victimisation.

Too few employers realise that by giving even a week with full pay, over and above the usual domestic holiday, they are enabling a Territorial soldier to partake in the most vital and valuable part of his training; to share in the climax and epitome of a Regiment's annual work.

It should not be necessary for the Commanding Officer of a certain London Regiment to preface the circular letter sent to all employers in such terms are these: "May I first of all say that I am most anxious that nothing in this letter shall prejudice the employment of this man, who, I believe, is on your staff." Many such letters have been sent out this year—and have remained unanswered.

It has been suggested that employers might share or even supplement the Government contribution towards Territorial pay. This ought not to be necessary, but at least the Government should take steps to ascertain, by inquiry among the proper authorities, whether or not the rates of pay are adequate.

TOO LITTLE FOR DRILLS

At present a proficiency grant of £3 is paid to all men who on October 31 have attended camp and have performed the required number of drills. (Obligatory drills are almost invariably 40 for recruits in their first year, and 20 in each subsequent year.) A weapon training grant of 10s. is paid to each man who has qualified in musketry.

As from November 1 of this year, a further grant of one shilling is to be made for each drill performed in excess of proficiency grant drills, up to a total of 30 drills each year. The maximum amount which can be earned in this way is therefore £5 per annum. Specialists are able to supplement this.

During camp minimum pay fluctuates between 6s. per day for a sergeant and 2s. for a private. Marriage allowance for a married man without child is only 7s. per week, rising to 17s. per week for a man with three children. There are bitter, not unjustified complaints among Territorial soldiers that these allowances are totally insufficient, particularly for men who must take their fortnight's leave in camp without salary.

It seems clear that a weakness in the present payment for drill system lies in the fact that still too little is done towards encouraging men to perform more than their obligatory drills. One shilling for every extra drill up to 30 after the first 20 is a bare inducement.

Those who conscientiously perform every drill are insufficiently rewarded. In many cases it is questionable whether these shillings fulfil their first and most important object, which is to ensure that no Territorial soldier is out of pocket in travelling and other minor expenses.

Vicious Circle

Enough has already been said on the subject of equipment to indicate the immediate need for a vast improvement in all directions, and this must obviously be entirely the responsibility of the authorities.

It is a national disgrace that Territorial units should be unwilling to accept urgently needed personnel because equipment and accommodation are lacking to meet increased demand. The vicious circle of insufficient men to warrant more equipment; insufficient accommodation to store additional equipment; insufficient equipment and accommodation to justify recruiting must be broken.

Admittedly the Government are experiencing some difficulty at this time in organising the manufacture of equipment to satisfy the current needs of the Regular Army, Navy, and Air Force. No doubt these difficulties will soon be overcome. But the Territorial Army suspects, not without very good reason, that they will be last served in the distribution of new material.

For the Field Army this procedure is inevitable and justifiable. There can, however, be no question that the Anti-Aircraft Division, which in emergency would be needed as soon as any national force, is entitled to expect treatment on a parallel with the Regular Services.

Hard-pressed manufacturers cannot be held an excuse for the present state of the Territorial Army's accommodation; nor for the delay in putting approved plans for building and expansion into operation; nor for suppression of minor improvement schemes suggested by individual units.

Apart from the requirements of training, premises must be made more attractive and more comfortable for the men themselves. Exteriors must be brightened up, and must carry proper advertisements to attract the public attention, to arouse public interest. Inside there should be canteens of better quality than public bars in cheap hostelries.

WHERE FAULT LIES

These shortcomings cannot be laid at the door of the County of London Territorial Association, which, with the City of London Territorial Association, is doing all within its power to obtain better treatment for the Territorial Army in London. Nor can the War Office be blamed.

Fault lies with those responsible for the administration of national finance, for their apparent inability to appreciate the real dangers of the present situation.

Above all, today the Territorial Army requires a lead from the top. From the highest possible source the public must be told the truth and asked for help. The miserable spirit of contempt for the Territorial Army, which is still far too prevalent in some places, must be beaten down and lost for ever.

Whatever the merits or drawbacks of the system, very great responsibilities which are vital to the defence of this country have been entrusted to the Territorial Army. It is not too much to say that England might stand or fall by the manner in which these responsibilities were carried out.

In the recent words of the Secretary of State for War: "The Territorial Army is a unique possession. No other country possesses anything similar. We should be very proud of this, our heritage, and prove our pride by being worthy of it."

CLOSING UP LOOPHOLES IN A.R.P. ORGANISATION

Voluntary Efforts must be better Co-ordinated

Defects Due to Delays in Whitehall Policy

Next Monday afternoon the Home Secretary will meet representatives of all local authorities to discuss Air Raid Precautions and the possibility of accelerating the home defence programme.

One month has gone since, at the time of the Austrian crisis, he called for 1,000,000 volunteers, and overnight changed A.R.P. from a subject of leisurely discussion into a matter for immediate action.

It is a good moment to take stock of the situation. How strong are the country's passive defences now? There is only one honest answer: If peace could be guaranteed until the end of 1939—some 20 months hence—we could afford to view the rate of progress with equanimity; but for any emergency which might arise, say, before the end of this year, the whole of the civilian population, and London in particular, is still highly vulnerable.

What has been accomplished? Perhaps a fifth of the immense task which involves the training and detailed organisation of at least 1,500,000 men and women by 2,000 local authorities, the education of some 20,000,000 adults and the expenditure of £15,000,000 in the current year alone.

CALL FOR VOLUNTEERS

In the past month the Government have achieved their first object, which was to arouse among all local authorities a sense of their responsibilities. The local government system, which is the foundation and framework of the whole plan, is being subjected to a tremendous strain. The frame is creaking and groaning, in some places splintering a little, but slowly and surely there is a united movement forward.

Progress, of course, is uneven. Some councils, the biggest among them, have brought their A.R.P. plans up to date, recruited three-quarters of their personnel, trained, perhaps, half of this total and are ready for practical tests. Others—unhappily the majority—have just set up special committees, are still without A.R.P. advisers, have only one-tenth of the volunteers needed—few of them trained—and are making heavy weather of the Home Office instructions.

It is difficult to estimate accurately the numbers enrolled. The Home Secretary asked for 1,000,000, but that was before his department advised the training of reserves, and the total needed is now probably nearer 2,000,000. At a rough and generous guess, there are between 300,000 and 350,000 volunteers enrolled throughout the country, of which about one-third are trained and another third in training.

GAS MASK PRODUCTION

Although Britain is still behind France and Germany in general A.R.P. preparedness, it is some satisfaction to know that we lead the world in the production of gas masks. More than 30,000,000 are ready, and comprehensive plans exist for their storage in conditions which will preserve their effectiveness indefinitely, and for their complete distribution in eight hours.

All the necessary transport, as for most other requirements of internal defence, has been registered; but local authorities have to find 1,200 storage depots and earmark 10,000 suitable distributing centres before we can call the scheme complete.

How is the public reacting to these developments? In a few districts, mainly rural areas, the response is admirable. There is a spirit of busy enthusiasm usual among small communities. But this enthusiasm flags in the big, sprawling urban areas, where relationships between authority and the individual are weak and distant.

In the cities there is still indifference, apathy, even defeatism and a specious belief that the job can be safely left to others. Too many people are saying: "I'd like to help, but I shall have more important things to do in the next war." Except for members of the Services, that is a fallacious argument. The Government do not imagine that everyone who passes through A.R.P. training will be available for active duty in emergency. That is why they want twice or three times as many volunteers as will actually be needed to work the machine.

The value of every man to the community will be increased by a

course of training, now, in one of the A.R.P. services. There is no
limit to the number who should be trained.

Many Months Wasted

And the second familiar theme is: "I suppose one should do something. But everything seems in a state of muddle. I cannot find out
what I ought to do."

It is true that there has been some muddling; that informative
propaganda, centrally and locally, is inadequate; that hundreds of
local authorities are resentful of the apparently ruthless way in which
the Home Office are giving out a succession of drastic instructions,
and that sometimes enthusiastic volunteers find themselves treated in
a way which appears discouraging.

But on the public's side there seems to be insufficient appreci-
ation of the difficulties of improvising the biggest scheme of peacetime civilian organisation ever conceived in this country.

Critics would do well to consider that up till the autumn of last
year scarcely any practical moves had been made. Months had been
wasted in a wrangle between the Home Office and local authorities
on finance.

There is still much to be done in Whitehall too. Policy on air
raid shelters, for instance, is vague, and in this respect we lag far
behind Paris and Berlin. Orders for a survey of underground space
available to precede construction came too late. Many local bodies
had already begun to put their plans into operation, and are now
busily digging and building without any national standard of strategy,
strength or cost to guide them.

Shelters and Rates

Industrialists are dissatisfied with the finanical terms offered them by
the Government. The question as to whether or not the private
construction of shelters adds to the rateable value of property should
be settled quickly.

Again, there has been delay in the production of regulations to
minimise air raid risks in the erection of new buildings. Elementary
precautions have been observed in most European cities for some
time, but the Home Office only recently began to consult the Royal
Institute of British Architects.

There is a serious shortage of instructors. Whole districts are without a single qualified expert. Thousands who have volunteered recently are waiting to be trained.

Propaganda and the distribution of instructive literature, one might repeat, have been very inadequate, and are only slowly improving. Not one person in a hundred knows what A.R.P. will involve. Four out of five men and women have no idea precisely what they are wanted for. Almost as many still do not know that they should apply direct to their local council at the Town Hall for enrolment.

Incidentally, there is a widespread misconception, particularly among women, that all branches of A.R.P. mean great physical exertion, and that age is a drawback. This is generally incorrect. Air Raid Wardens, for whom there is by far the greatest demand, are valued for their intelligence and ability to inspire confidence, not for their agility.

To some extent the mass meetings now being organised all over the country are helping to increase public knowledge, but indoor gatherings are not going to be popular between now and October, and other means will have to be found. The Churches have been asked to assist, and a great deal may be accomplished by their help. The cinema, too, offers immense propaganda resources as yet untapped.

A.R.P. must be made more attractive in working-class areas, where recruiting generally is weak. The difficulties are obvious. Men and women are too preoccupied with their daily work; insufficient time can be spared for training; it is hard to find good leaders; many feel vaguely that they ought to be paid for their work.

The Training Problem

The wisest authorities in these areas are concentrating on the shopkeepers, who live and work in the same district and whose premises make good local strategic centres. Even so, it is obvious that a fresh approach will have to be made in the poorer and densely populated districts.

Arising indirectly from this problem it seems that in London, at any rate, too little use is being made of the police. In the provinces the Chief Constable is often in charge of the local scheme, and the police are valuable contacts with the public, as well as providing a solid nucleus of disciplined men on which to train and organise civilians. In London practically no use is being made of the Metropolitan Police Force.

Training is a big problem, and will become more difficult as summer draws on and outdoor interests increase. Many who work for their living all day are unwilling to give a proportion of their hard-earned leisure to training.

Understandable reticence is being shown by the authorities on the subject of civilian evacuation from London and the more densely populated areas. Evacuation is an ugly, disquieting word, and the Government want no needless alarms raised in this direction.

Test for Democracy

Nevertheless, whatever the problems involved, future policy will have to be declared soon. Here, again, we are far behind the French, who have already decided to evacuate 2,500,000 people from Paris and have earmarked all the necessary transport for the task.

These are some of the outstanding problems. They do not detract from the remarkable achievements of that much-maligned Air Raid Precautions department of the Home Office, on whose shoulders overwhelming responsibility has been thrust.

The Home Secretary has well said that A.R.P. is a crucial test for our democracy. Can we, voluntarily, achieve as much as the countries in which civilian organisation is compulsory? So far there is no serious reason to doubt that we can. It rests with each individual to make sure that such doubts shall never arise.

PREMIER REPORTS ON HIS MISSION

"EACH OF US UNDERSTANDS THE OTHER'S MIND"

AUDIENCE OF KING LAST NIGHT: CABINET TO-DAY

MR. CHAMBERLAIN CONFERS WITH LORD RUNCIMAN

The Prime Minister returned to England by air from Germany last evening and was immediately engaged in discussions with members of the Cabinet on the outcome of his conversations with Herr Hitler.

Last night Mr. Chamberlain was received in audience by the King at Buckingham Palace. This morning at 11 o'clock the Cabinet will meet to consider his report on his mission.

Both at Heston airport on his arrival and in Downing-street, the Prime Minister was given an ovation from crowds which gathered to greet him. He received a letter of personal congratulation from the King.

In a statement on his mission, Mr. Chamberlain said: "I had a long talk with Herr Hitler. It was a frank talk, but it was a friendly one, and I feel satisfied, now, that each of us fully understands what is in the mind of the other."

Early in the evening Viscount Runciman, head of the unofficial mediation mission, had an interview with the Prime Minister, at whose request he had returned by air from Prague.

It was reported from Paris last night that the French Premier, M. Daladier, may come to London to meet Mr. Chamberlain before the further meeting with Herr Hitler takes place. This is expected to be on Tuesday at Godesberg, in the Rhineland.

CONGRATULATIONS FROM THE KING

Within a few minutes of his arrival by 'plane at Heston airport from Berchtesgaden last evening, Mr. Chamberlain went to a microphone and made the following statement on his visit to Herr Hitler:

"I have come back again rather quicker than I expected, after a journey which, if I had not been so preoccupied, I should have found thoroughly enjoyable.

"Yesterday afternoon I had a long talk with Herr Hitler. It was a frank talk; it was a friendly one, and I feel satisfied now that each of us fully understands what is in the mind of the other.

"You won't, of course, expect me to discuss now what may be the results of that talk. What I have got to do now is to discuss them with my colleagues, and I would advise you not to accept prematurely any unauthorised account of what took place in the conversation.

NEXT HITLER TALK

"Half Way to Meet Me"

"But I shall be discussing them tonight with my colleagues and with others, especially with Lord Runciman, and later on—perhaps in a few days—I am going to have another talk with Herr Hitler.

"Only this time he has told me that it is his intention to come half way to meet me. He wishes to spare an old man another such long journey."

Laughter and cheers from the large crowd which had gathered to greet the Prime Minister marked his jocular reference to the Fuehrer coming "half way to meet me."

Mr. Chamberlain, who appeared to be in excellent spirits, was given an enthusiastic welcome.

As soon as he stepped from the British Airways machine which had taken him to and from Munich he was handed an envelope, black-edged and sealed, by his private secretary.

It was a three-page letter of congratulations upon his mission from the King, written in his Majesty's own hand.

Before moving forward Mr. Chamberlain slit the envelope and slowly read the letter through. Then he replaced it in the envelope and handed it to Sir Horace Wilson, his chief Civil Service adviser, who, with Mr. William Strang, of the Foreign Office, had accompanied him to Berchtesgaden.

Turning with a broad smile to the waiting crowd, the Prime Minister received warm handshakes and words of congratulation from the many prominent personalities waiting to greet him.

Asked how he had enjoyed his journey, he admitted jovially that his first experience of air travel at the age of 69 showed it to be far pleasanter than he had ever believed possible.

German Envoy's Hope

"Won Our People's Hearts"

Half an hour before Mr. Chamberlain's aeroplane was due to land Viscount Halifax, Foreign Secretary, had arrived at Heston. Lord Halifax immediately went over and shook hands with Dr. Kordt, German Chargé d'Affaires, and Baron von Selzam, First Secretary at the German Embassy in London, who reached the airport some time earlier.

Dr. Kordt was first to greet Mr. Chamberlain. Shaking him warmly by the hand, he said: "I hope you feel you were successful. At any rate, you have conquered the hearts of my countrymen."

So great was the press of news reporters, cameramen and airport officials that Lord Halifax was unable to reach the Prime Minister for some minutes.

While Mr. Chamberlain was reading the letter from the King and speaking to Dr. Kordt, the Foreign Secretary crouched, bent almost double, beneath one of the aeroplane's wings.

Suddenly the Prime Minister espied him and, with a smile, stepped forward and shook him by the hand. "I had an excellent journey," he remarked: "they were all very kind indeed to me."

Crowd on Roof

Woman Cries "Well Done"

Crowds on the roof of the airport offices and on the edge of the flying-field raised a tremendous cheer as Mr. Chamberlain stepped to the microphones. From the roof came a woman's single cry: "Well done, Chamberlain!" The Premier looked up towards the woman, raised his hat, and smiled cheerfully.

As soon as he had delivered the broadcast message Mr. Chamberlain walked over with Lord Halifax to the car which was waiting to take him back to 10, Downing-street. As he was entering a messenger ran up carrying a sheaf of official telegrams and messages.

Lord Halifax and Mr. Chamberlain motored back to London together. As they reached the airport gates the biggest cheer of all came from the thousands lining the route, far into the Great West-road, who had seen little or nothing of the aeroplane's arrival. The Premier waved his acknowledgement.

Whitehall Scenes

Mrs. Chamberlain's Greeting

Another vast crowd waited for the Premier in Whitehall and Downing-street, and gave him a thunderous reception. Among them was Sir Thomas Inskip, Minister for the Co-ordination of Defence, who waved as Mr. Chamberlain's car went by.

Crowds surged round the entrance to No. 10 as the Prime Minister stepped from his car. Mrs. Chamberlain, who had waited in the hall for some little time, was the first to greet her husband.

Side by side, and arm in arm, both smiling happily, they stood on the steps of No. 10 and faced a battery of photographers and cinema operators, who took picture after picture.

Even in Downing-street, where journalists and large numbers of police were gathered, there were cheers, which were taken up by some onlookers from the high windows of Government offices.

Inside No. 10 Sir John Simon and Sir Samuel Hoare were waiting with Sir Robert Vansittart, Chief Diplomatic Adviser to the Government, and Sir Alexander Cadogan, Permanent Under-Secretary to the Foreign Office.

Even after Mr. Chamberlain had gone in, repeated efforts were made by hundreds of people in Whitehall to pass the police into Downing-street, with a view to staging a cheering demonstration outside No. 10. Police, reinforced by mounted men, insisted on their remaining in Whitehall.

February 1939

TIME V. SECURITY IN PROVISION OF AIR RAID SHELTERS

Pros and Cons of the Government's Short-term Policy

*By W. F. Deedes, who has made a special study of the progress of
Air Raid Precautions since their inception*

No part of the Government's defence programme is rousing more controversy, and consequent uneasiness in the public mind, than the provision of air raid shelter for the civil population.

From the mass of conflicting, confusing and rather inconclusive ideas so far expressed on the subject, the issue seems to emerge quite plainly:

Does the Government's short-term policy of protecting the population by means of dispersal and surface shelters—trenches, reinforced basements, steel shelters and so on—provide adequate security?

How far is it desirable or practicable to supplement this immediate policy by construction of deep bomb-proof shelters or tunnels?

Fundamentally, it is an issue of Time versus Security. The short-term policy, as the Government admit frankly, can only provide part-protection against blast and splinter of bombs, less protection against gas and fire, and no protection at all against direct hits from bombs. It is not good, but, as its description of "short-term" implies, it can—and must—be executed within a period of months.

Bomb-proof shelters, it is claimed on the other hand, would give nearly 100 per cent protection against all aspects of the air menace. But it is a solution involving at least two years of work.

One thing is certain. The absolute confidence of the civilian population is vital to the success of this particular aspect of the Government's defence programme. At present it is perfectly clear from all that is being said and written on the subject that the public is far from feeling such confidence. How far is this uneasiness justified?

Six Chief Points

The Government's plans have been announced at irregular intervals, and for many reasons it has not been possible to present the public with the whole picture at one time. Here, briefly, are the six main heads of the official short-term policy, which, if they are to be called inadequate, must in fairness be viewed as a whole:

1. Evacuation, whereby about 3,000,000 children, expectant and nursing mothers, aged and infirm persons will be taken from vulnerable areas and dispersed over the countryside in private houses and Government camps.
2. Trenches, designed to shelter about one-tenth of the urban population—say, 2,000,000 persons, though it is doubtful whether anything approaching the number of trenches required for this purpose has yet been or will be dug.
3. Sectional steel shelters for about 10,000,000 people in urban areas who live in two-storeyed houses and have garden or yard space in which to erect the shelter.
4. Basements reinforced with steel plates and props, not only for the inhabitants of this type of house, about 10,000,000, but for those who may be caught in the streets.
5. An obligation—not yet law—on all employers to provide improvised shelter accommodation during the working day for at least 14,000,000 of the insured population, and some millions more who work in offices.
6. A decision—it is no more yet—to compel the inclusion of shelter in many types of new houses, offices and public buildings.

Five Years Lost

This is essentially a short-term policy, which could be carried out within a few months from now. It is comprehensive. At least 90 per cent of the urban population will find themselves covered by one or more of these heads.

It has been observed that the Government have had to choose an unconvincing way of announcing this policy. But this does not wholly account for public apprehension. Apart altogether from expert criticism of their defensive value, which will be summarised later, there have been disquieting administrative faults in these proposals which cannot be overlooked. To appreciate Sir John Anderson's difficulties it is essential to know the background from which he is working.

To take the last item first, it is surely extraordinary that no less than five years after the genesis of A.R.P. the fundamental precaution of including good shelters in all new buildings should still be a matter for future legislation. For five years builders have been allowed to ignore the obvious need. Tens of thousands of houses and thousands of big offices and public buildings have been constructed. Now it is proposed to provide the necessary compulsory powers in a bill which cannot be fully effective for at least six months.

BASEMENTS SURVEY

Almost as bad, from the administrative point of view, is the history of action taken in regard to basements—a plain story of muddle and delay. Many months ago local authorities were told to survey all basement accommodation. Some did the work; others ignored the request. The result of their labours is of small consequence, since it was apparently overlooked that such a survey of space available is useless unless undertaken by engineers and architects, who would know how far structures of varying age and types would permit safe reinforcement of their basements.

To-day the Government are back where they started on this, probably the biggest, item in their short-term policy. Now architects and engineers all over the country are to be mobilised to start the survey again. No one doubts Sir John Anderson's ability to compress this survey into a few weeks; but he cannot recover lost months.

The story of Britain's trenches is too well known to need repetition. But after much administrative muddling and delay, when these trenches are at last being made permanent at great expense, the Government experts are beginning openly to question their value.

The best of the programme is the third item, for which Sir John Anderson has been mainly responsible. He received a report recommending this type of shelter on Dec. 20, announced his plans in the House of Commons on Dec. 21, placed the first order for one-tenth of the quantity on Jan. 16, and issued plans for distribution on Feb. 8.

FACTORY EQUIPMENT

It is not possible to say how far the Government have persuaded employers to carry out their obligations properly. By all accounts, progress is uneven; many factories are superbly equipped; far more business houses in dangerous areas are badly behind with preparations.

Compulsion from the Government is coming very late in the day, and it is difficult to understand why this was not included in the A.R.P. Bill of 1935.

All this is hardly an impressive record, but though presenting ample justification for public anxiety it does not in itself reflect on the technical soundness of the proposals. Critics of the defensive values of the Government's plans are chiefly concerned with only three of the items given above—trenches, sectional steel shelters and reinforced basements.

Many types of trenches have been designed, but most of them have been exposed to the same objection: First, having been dug in parks and open spaces, too often remote from congested neighbour-hoods, they fail to meet one of the first principles for which they are designed, the need for surface accommodation to be near at hand for all. Again, the official quota of space allotted (3.5 square feet) is said to be inadequate, and in practice it will clearly be impossible to distribute crowds equably.

It is urged, not without reason, that in a moment of panic thousands might try to storm a section of trenches where there is space only for hundreds. It is hard to envisage how any form of policing can meet this danger.

AT MERCY OF GAS

Furthermore, there is no real protection in trenches against gas, nor can those who are already contaminated be kept out during a rush to enter. There are no proper sanitary or first-aid services at hand, and fainting or infirm persons would receive no adequate attention. Finally, trenches are specially vulnerable to direct hits, which might easily involve immense casualties.

Sectional steel shelters are open to many fewer objections, but certain points against them are justified. All will be situated very near houses, and though they are said to be capable of resisting a two-ton fall of masonry, occupants whose shelters are involved in the collapse of buildings may remain trapped and unseen for hours. The shelters are not gas-proof, nor are they designed to give protection against heavy bombs dropped nearer than 20ft. They cannot be guaranteed to resist big splinters from an even greater distance.

Reinforced basements share many of the technical objections advanced against trenches and the steel shelter. Few buildings with basements are constructed to resist the lateral forces of bombs. Through direct hit or blast, they may collapse and smother the basement. There is little protection against gas or fire which would lead to death by suffocation. Gas, water and drain pipes are sources of great danger. Rarely are there sufficient exits from a household basement.

To meet even the minor objections, most basements must undergo substantial structural alterations, the cost of which would be far beyond the means of most householders. In a phrase, critics describe reinforced basements in all but steel-framed buildings as potential death-traps.

EVACUATION CAMPS

Evacuation can hardly be examined from the point of view of defence values. The Government have now decided to supplement billeting by building a number of experimental camps, but for a long time their plans are bound to depend largely on the co-operation and goodwill of private householders in rural areas. Strategically, these plans are beyond criticism. Socially, they are said to raise a number of difficulties—none of them insuperable; and many, it has to be admitted, inspired by selfish considerations.

There, briefly, is the critics' case. For immediate purposes it is entirely destructive. No one has been able to produce better alternatives capable of execution in the time which the Government allow themselves. There is no answer to the Government's question: What else can be done quickly at reasonable cost?

Ignoring the factors of time, finance, labour and materials, the critics insist that deep shelters or tunnels for all remain the only sound and reasonable solution. Before passing judgment, it is necessary to examine their proposals in detail.

March 1939

TWO BABIES TEST GAS HELMETS

ONE WAS BORED AND WENT TO SLEEP

DEVICE PERFECTED AFTER TWO YEARS

Winifred Margaret Baker, aged three weeks, and James Pochetty, aged eight weeks, performed their first acts of National Service yesterday by spending ten minutes inside the Government's new gas helmets for babies.

Winifred kicked and cried half-heartedly for a few seconds after the hood had been belted round her waist. Then her eyes focused on her mother's face through the window, and she remained perfectly contented.

James did not cry at all. In a very few seconds he grew tired of staring back at reporters and went to sleep.

They were the last and youngest of the many babies who, with their mothers, have been helping the Government for two years to find the perfect baby's respirator by undergoing innumerable tests. These, it was disclosed, included entry by a mother and her baby into a lethal chamber, the child in a helmet and the mother in a civilian respirator.

Yesterday's demonstration by Winifred and James and others of their generation at the Holborn Town Hall was the culmination of these experiments.

1,400,000 REQUIRED

Production of the 1,400,000 helmets required is now proceeding rapidly, and every mother with a child under two years of age will receive the device free of charge—though it will remain the property of the Home Office.

The device consists of a big rubber hood, made of gas-proof material, and fitted with a large window of cellulose acetate. It covers the baby down to the waist, where it is secured by tape.

This means that the infant has full use of its arms inside the hood, and can put its finger in its mouth—an act which the Government experts consider essential to its comfort and well-being.

On the underside the hood is padded. On the right side, rubber bellows are fitted, which supply a constant stream of filtered air to the baby.

No Fright or Discomfort

A slow and steady rate of pumping of about 40 strokes a minute is enough to keep out gas and provide sufficient air. There is sufficient air space inside the hood to allow pumping to stop for several minutes if necessary.

The hood is fitted to a metal frame, which is to be painted in bright colours. Frame and hood together weigh 6lb, can be easily carried, placed in a pram, or rest on the mother's knee.

It was apparent from yesterday's demonstration that the helmet causes baby no fright or discomfort.

LIFE IN LONDON IN EVENT OF WAR

Planning to Transfer Big Business from Centre to Circumference

By William Deedes, who has made a special study of A.R.P. for
"The Daily Telegraph"

Of all the home defence problems before the Government, none is bigger and more complex than the maintenance of London's commercial, administrative and domestic life in time of war. It is a subject on which remarkably little has been heard so far, but an immense amount of hard thought has been given to it, and we are likely to be told a good deal more in the near future.

So vast a question, involving 8,000,000 people and 600 square miles of property and business, is not resolved by defence measures alone. Even if there were so many 'planes, anti-aircraft guns, balloons and air raid shelters that the life of the individual could be counted relatively safe, the life of the capital in a modern war would not be assured.

How far could "business as usual" be expected in London during war? Until hostilities began there could be no final answer, even if the Government made their plans public. But by piecing together what is already known on the subject, one can form a clearer picture than most Londoners have in their minds at the present moment.

Removing the "City"

Damage and loss of life, though they might reach considerable proportions through air raids, are not the greatest dangers. Dislocation is potentially a more serious factor, and it is against such a contingency that the authorities are most actively taking precautions. It is met chiefly in two ways: by decentralisation and by duplication. For both, plans are well advanced.

Decentralisation, for example, will help to preserve two of London's most important nerve centres: the City of London, heart of commerce, and Whitehall, administrative heart of the Empire.

The City of London, as we know it to-day, would cease to exist in wartime. Plans are being kept secret, but there is reason to think that such great institutions as the Bank of England, the Stock Exchange, Leadenhall and Smithfield markets, and headquarters of the banks, shipping and insurance companies would be found elsewhere during war.

Preparations for the transfer of this essential business, to be carried on with skeleton staffs in safer zones, have been in progress for a long time. On the tremendous reorganisation which the evacuation would involve the biggest commercial houses have concentrated their attention for many months. Clerks have been working late, duplicating necessary books and papers. The significance of such decentralisation may be judged by the fact that the City's night-time population of 11,000 becomes nearly 500,000 by day.

DAILY TREK TO WORK

Whitehall, too, would cease to be the real centre of Government. Doubtless small staffs would remain in the underground fortresses which the Office of Works has been busily constructing under the Whitehall Ministries; and the extent of Civil Service evacuation may depend to some extent on the effectiveness of the first air raids. But generally, civil departments and their staffs would be evacuated, mainly to the western side of London.

Certain other big concerns centred in London have similar plans, calculated to disperse their business from the centre to the circumference of London's giant circle. Thus London would resemble a slice of pineapple. The circumference would be bigger, and would form a larger target, but the City and Whitehall could no longer be destroyed by a single destructive blow.

At once there arises a huge problem of communications. People have no idea as yet how they might travel to and from business. For many it might well become a daily outward or parallel movement from suburban home to work, instead of an inward movement from home as it is to-day. Therefore transport arrangements would have to be drastically adapted.

Private cars would be off the roads, to conserve petrol supplies for the R.A.F. If London Transport carries on under Government control, as the railways will, it might be expected that the underground system, which runs on home-made power, would be used as far as possible in preference to omnibuses. There would almost certainly be a boom in bicycles.

With "key" commerce and administration decentralised and dispersed to new and strange locations, telephones become of vital importance, though their use would certainly be drastically restricted for civil defence purposes. Unobtrusively the Post Office has been doing a tremendous amount of work to counteract possible breakdowns.

Here, as with the nation's utilities which supply water, gas and electricity, the policy of duplication comes into operation.

If a telephone cable or even an exchange is blown up, the Post Office must be in a position swiftly to restore communications by a roundabout route. London exchanges are intercommunicating, so that a quick transfer could nearly always be made. We can assume that the International Telephone Exchange and the Central Telegraph Office would be transferred to a safer district than London, E.C.

Evacuation Problems

Greater London's total population must shrink to a 19th-century level. Apart from those who might be away on active service, we know that at least 500,000 school-children and another 500,000 young children with mothers can leave at once for the country. During September it was proposed to evacuate under Government control up to 2,000,000 non-essential civilians, after the children, in addition to at least 250,000 people who could find their own way out to homes of relatives and friends in the country.

At present London's evacuation plans, beyond the million children and mothers, are vague. Sir John Anderson believes that able-bodied civilians should stay at their posts. Yet this is not incompatible with the removal of many more civilians who would have no essential industrial or defence posts at which to stay.

If they remain, these civilians will have to be fed in more difficult circumstances, and given far more extensive and expensive shelter than they need in rural areas. It would not be surprising if the Government eventually decided that a large measure of controlled adult evacuation was the simplest solution to the shelter and maintenance problem.

What of the River Thames which, as anyone who has flown over

London will agree, forms not only a fine guide to airmen, but runs through a series of important targets? There can be little doubt that London's docks and warehouses, the six big road and rail bridges, and the vast network of the Southern Railway system from London Bridge, Cannon-street, Charing Cross and Victoria would be a first objective of enemy aircraft. And around these targets, on the East and South, are packed hundreds of thousands of London's poorer population. If controlled evacuation begins, after the children have gone, it must surely start from the river banks.

From 'Phone to Siren

One cannot leave the subject of dislocation, which affects not only railways, roads, communications and administration, but also people at work, without reference to the air raid warning system, as it would affect London. It is perhaps not sufficiently realised how this essential system, operating as far as the public are concerned from telephone exchanges to the sirens, may influence daily existence.

It is certainly one of the major factors which have influenced the Government experts against deep shelters, which would require several minutes to reach; but its implications go deeper. For every raid actually carried out, a London borough might well receive a dozen alarms, which must be heeded. It is not hard to imagine an astute enemy seriously interfering with essential work by causing constant movement of citizens to and from shelter.

This is also a problem for the industrial areas in the Midlands and North, but they would receive relatively fewer alarms than London. One wonders how far it would be possible to maintain the great area of industry, much of it engaged in vital war production, which is centred in North and West London.

Closing of Cinemas

If there were to be constant alarms over London, the fewer non-essential citizens there were to swell the crowds, to increase the dangers of chaos and panic, and to fill the hospitals, the better. When London has been stripped of its non-essential population, the task of providing adequate shelter, transport and food for those who have to carry on becomes a good deal simplified.

But there would be very little relaxation for those who remained in London. Already, we have been warned that cinemas and theatres would have to close, because the concentration of crowds, unable to dissipate in the maximum of five minutes, must be avoided. Even museums and picture galleries would be closed, for they have planned the swift evacuation of their treasures on the first threat of hostilities.

Clearly, therefore, there would be no business or pleasure as usual in London during war time, and though much might depend on the initial successes of enemy aircraft, and the confidence or apprehension created thereby, drastic reorganisation of business, commerce and the day-to-day life of millions would be inevitable. To meet such reorganisation, planning is essential and much of it must remain secret.

IDENTITY CARD AND NUMBER FOR ALL IN WAR-TIME

PLANS TO REGISTER NATION COMPLETE

65,000 ENUMERATORS AND FORMS READY

BABY SMITH MAY BE KPHT-297-6

Everything is now ready for the completion of a National Register of every man, woman and child in the country within a fortnight if an emergency arises.

The Registrar-General's department announced yesterday that all the necessary forms and documents have been printed and either stored or distributed to enumerators and other officials.

The forms to be filled in by householders go into greater detail than any census schedules. They will be exchanged for identity cards for each individual, bearing name and number.

The official announcement states that the scheme provided for:

Recruitment of 65,000 enumerators, compared with 49,000 for the 1931 Census; and

Division of the country into 65,000 districts and the allocation to each enumerator of between 200 and 300 households.

Most of the preparations, whereby the authorities could complete a National Register within a fortnight of an emergency, have been made in the eight months since Sir John Anderson, Lord Privy Seal, announced the Government policy on the subject on Dec. 2 last.

GOVERNMENT'S POLICY

This policy was that no register for war-time use could be up to date unless it was compiled when war broke out; but that machinery for the 1941 Census should be made ready so that the register could, if necessary, be started at a moment's notice.

Everyone, including foreigners resident in this country, would be included. Clerks of every local authority have been appointed National Registration Officers. They would supervise the compilation of the register.

Forms are more comprehensive than census schedules. In addition to age, sex, marital condition, occupation and the usual particulars, they would show the individual's occupation, if any, in National Service.

Enumerators will have nothing to do until the register is ordered, but they must give two months' notice of resignation. A substantial reserve is being built up. Most of them are insurance agents, or men and women experienced in this type of work.

It is thought that each could distribute forms to 200 or 300 households within a week, perhaps less. When collecting the returns, an identity card would be filled and issued for each member of every household. This would bear the individual's name and number.

How it Will Work

The numbers are in three serials. First, each of the 65,000 districts is registered under four letters. One district of two or three streets might be KPHT.

Secondly, the forms to be distributed in one district are numbered from one to 200, or whatever it may be.

Thirdly, each line on the form for a separate member of the household is numbered. The baby in the household of Mr. and Mrs. Smith might thus become KPHT-297-6.

It is admitted that execution of this scheme might be very difficult after the outbreak of war. The difficulties of carrying on the work under bombardment, it is emphasised, have not been underestimated.

Moreover, it is recognised that the movement of population might have begun before the start of the register.

In these circumstances husbands and wives might have to give particulars from separate addresses. The important point would be that one or other parent would be allocated a number similar to those of the children. Husbands and wives already parted would exchange numbers by post as soon as possible.

Keeping in Touch

If evacuation had begun, registration of the children would be organised by schools. Arrangements have been completed to carry out this work.

The number system is thought to have great uses. Wide dispersal of the population in war-time, it is believed, would create grave danger of children losing their families and individual members of families losing touch. The identity card system would provide an invisible net holding the population together.

Again, if carried on cards or discs, the numbers would facilitate identification of civilian casualties. They would also be linked up with the food-rationing scheme. Numbers might have special uses as proofs of identity for those claiming payments or allowances under war schemes.

If the cards were lost they would be replaced by cards of a slightly different colour, with a small alteration in the numbering. This would effectively counter attempts at misrepresentation. A number of secret devices have been considered by the authorities to prevent misuse of the cards.

Work of Maintenance

In addition, the card would have to be produced for all purposes concerning the maintenance of the register, and for all persons authorised to inspect it.

Unlike Census preparations, the plans have had to cover the subsequent maintenance and working of a register.

There would be a system of central and local schedules. The latter would be kept up to date by the Registration Officer. Removals would be recorded locally and notified to the Central Index.

Complete arrangements have been made for recording deaths, births, discharges from the Services, arrivals in this country, and similar changes.

July 1939

BILLETING 3,000,000 CHILDREN
IN TIME OF WAR

DOOR-TO-DOOR CENSUS TO BE TAKEN

An immediate house-to-house census is to be undertaken by local authorities and completed within two months, to find suitable accommodation for children who may be evacuated from London and other big cities in time of war.

I understand that a total of about 3,000,000 children, who will have to be moved and given priority, including 1,000,000 in London alone, is envisaged by the Ministry of Health, the department responsible for the inquiry.

Thousands of visitors are to be recruited at once by the authorities. They will be under the charge of local Government officers. Equipped with identity cards and record sheets, these voluntary workers are to visit every dwelling house in the country outside the urban areas, whence those to be evacuated will be drawn. Visitors must ascertain from all householders:

> The number of habitable rooms and the number of persons living in the house;
> Where a surplus is revealed, whether the home conditions are suitable for unaccompanied children;
> Whether the householder elects, in the event of emergency, to receive and care for unaccompanied children up to the standard of one person per habitable room.

In a special note to householders, Mr. Walter Elliot, Minister of Health, states that householders who provide homes will be paid by the Government at the rate of 10s 6d a week where one child is taken, and 8s 6d a week for each additional child.

PAYMENT FOR LODGING

"Children under school age," he adds, "will be accompanied by their mothers or some other person, who will be responsible for looking

34

after them. In these cases the householder will only be asked to provide lodging, not board, and payment will be made at the rate of 5s a week for each adult and 3s a week for each child.

"Payment at the rate of 5s a week will be made by the Government where the householder provides lodging for a teacher or helper accompanying a party of school children. Arrangements for the necessary transport and for increased supplies of food to be made available for shopkeepers will be made by the Government."

Empty houses, other buildings and camps will be considered for the purpose, but the Ministry make it clear that for reasons of health and comfort "the main prospective source of supply of suitable homes can only be found in the use of existing occupied houses." Hotels and boarding houses will be included.

CASES FOR EXEMPTION

It is indicated that householders able to convince visitors that they are planning to receive relatives in emergency will probably be exempted. It is not yet clear, however, how far this exemption will be allowed to go in respect of friends and acquaintances.

No hint is given by the Ministry as to where the dividing line falls between areas to be evacuated and areas to receive refugees. Some guidance on this point is offered, however, by the appendix to the Anderson Committee's Report, completed last July.

A rough survey of England and Scotland showed that on the standard of one person to one room about 5,500,000 persons could be accommodated outside industrial areas. In view of the special requirements of children, this number will almost certainly be greatly reduced by this current survey.

In advising local authorities on the course of procedure, the Ministry emphasise the need for tact and discretion by visitors. All the information obtained must be regarded as secret.

Choice of visitors is left to the authority, but it is suggested that "a judicious combination of skilled official personnel and of voluntary effort" would be best.

Health visitors, housing officers, teachers, school attendance officers and sanitary inspectors are mentioned as forming a good nucleus.

"There will be a number of persons," the Ministry state, "who, though not unwilling to play their part, are not capable of undertaking the care of children. Instances to be anticipated are: Aged and infirm people living alone and not capable of doing more than look after themselves; houses where there is a confirmed invalid; persons living alone whose employment requires them to be absent all day.

Plans for Farms

"In some such cases the householder may be willing to take in children on the understanding that a teacher or other helper will be accommodated with them, and that some arrangement for care outside school hours can be made, e.g., communal recreation, feeding, laundry and other facilities. The making of such arrangements would be a field for the operation of local voluntary effort."

Farms must receive special consideration. In wartime, it is pointed out, the Government will increase home production. These arrangements must allow for housing additional labour.

The Board of Education is about to address local education authorities on the subject of continuing the education of children who have been evacuated.

Full cost of the inquiry is to be borne by the Government.

June 1949

NORMANDY TO-DAY:
THE COST OF LIBERATION

Today is the fifth anniversary of the Normandy landing. Mr. Deedes, who served with the K.R.R.C. in Normandy, has been revisiting the Battlefields

BAYEUX, SUNDAY

In Normandy now the deep green fields and orchards look much as one imagines they did five years ago to-day, on the eve of invasion. The towns and villages are still distressingly as one remembers them in the late summer of 1944, after the Allied armies had swept east.

To visit Normandy again, five years after it became a battlefield, is to see more clearly than most of us did at the time the cost of liberation.

The litter has been swept up, except for rusty smudges in out-of-the-way places. Now you can reckon the final cost. The Normans, it is clear, face a task to be measured in terms not of years but of decades.

From the mouth of the Orne west along the seaboard, "Sword," "Juno" and "Gold" beaches are now clear of iron and scrap and infernal devices—but not yet of the Atlantic Wall, which is too massive for local resources.

PORT WINSTON

At Arromanches—Port Winston, as they call it now—you can view the remains of Mulberry from a new promenade, Quai Admiral Sir Bertram Ramsay. That small quay, raised in our honour, with its tablet to Winston Churchill, is the most ambitious piece of reconstruction within sight.

The rest is desolate. In stretches, ragged lines of wrecked villas, houses with sightless windows and battered defences stand apparently untouched since the day they were hit.

Inside what became known as the Normandy bridgehead the achievements of four and a half years only emphasise the immensity

37

of the task ahead. One becomes painfully aware of the absence of a concerted plan.

Tilly-sur-Seulles, Evrecy, Villers Bocage and many more consist mainly to-day of temporary chalets, stacks of stone and single rooms salvaged out of partially demolished dwellings.

Faith and Patience

The churches are first. If masons are anywhere you will find them there, as I did at Norrey. There a dozen are working on a superb 13th-century church—and nowhere else.

If little else is standing in a village you will probably find the church tower in rudimentary scaffolding, rising foot by foot. As far east as Lisieux the great white cathedral of St. Pierre, apparently restored, shines above a town two-thirds demolished in the bombing of June 6 and 7, 1944.

A visitor knowing little about the Normandy battles can still follow their course and measure their intensity by the level of the village walls. Tilly, he could guess without difficulty, was, as the Michelin guide says, "dans un secteur très disputé."

There, however, as in many villages in the Orne and Odon valleys, he would have to look carefully, because with each year the grass and weeds grow longer and the foundations harder to find. It is not easy now to see where all of Tilly was.

Caen, pivot of the Normandy battles, epitomises the material cost of liberation. To stress the havoc there is not to disparage the immense, individual exertions being made to build again and to build nobly. "Renaissance de Caen," as one builder's board describes it.

Caen, it can be seen, will rise again—but not within the lifetime of most of us. In a steel and concrete age most of this work is being done by hand. To grasp the problem you must realise that much of Normandy's renaissance is being tackled as it might have been 400 years ago. Single masons toil where a hundred with modern machinery would find work for a decade.

In such patience and apparent faith that in time, though not in a lifetime, all will rise again there is the spirit of another age, which created great architecture. It is impressive, even inspiring, but it does not ease a modern housing problem.

Undiminished Glory

You might think that the Normans would be embittered by five years of this, by what they see about them and before them. That is not so. In many villages last week they were stringing up flags and bunting and coloured bulbs between the ruins. "Fête de la Libération," they said. The fifth anniversary of annihilation was not to pass without full honours.

In Normandy you cannot altogether judge the price of liberation by material standards. To those who live there, perhaps more than to those who fought there, this fertile province and its ancient walls stand a little apart from the rest of France.

To them these battlefields are not ordinary soil. So you will find the road which led 3 Division and the Canadians from the beaches to Caen called La Voie Sacrée. The shadow of the advancing armies has not diminished. Nor to some of the inhabitants of Normandy has their glory.

The War Cemeteries

At a score of chosen places in the bridgehead area are established another part of the price of liberation, the war cemeteries, now in the capable hands of the Imperial War Graves Commission.

They are surmounting difficulties with skill. Happily, perhaps, there are no vast cemeteries. In the largest, outside Bayeux, there are 6,000 graves. In the smallest, at Jerusalem, there are less than 50.

Many in XXI Army Group will remember Jerusalem, a disagreeable, bitterly contested crossroads, four miles south of Bayeux. Jerusalem cemetery is now the essence of an English memorial.

It lies in a green hollow beside the road, screened on two sides by a belt of high, shell-battered trees, where in England there would be rooks; and on the third side by a long, grey Norman barn. The grass is level and trim. It is most peaceful. Of the 48 headstones 25 bear the crest of the Durham Light Infantry, 50 Division.

Not Foreign Fields

I visited 12 of the British cemeteries in Northern France. One must do this to understand how faithfully the work has been done, first by the Army and now by the Commission.

These cemeteries are concentrations of single graves, scattered across the battlefields. The plots in which they lie have been given by France in perpetuity, so they are not foreign fields.

The Army founded them, concentrated the graves and marked them with metal crosses, painted white and briefly inscribed. On these foundations the Imperial War Graves Commission now builds, with French labour under English direction.

From England small headstones of Portland stone, bearing the regimental crest (or a maple leaf for all Canadians), the name of the soldier and an inscription chosen by his next of kin, are coming slowly to replace the white crosses.

Eventually all these cemeteries will be on lawns, their headstones set in long narrow beds, planted with English flowers. Some of the Commission working here have come from Flanders and the North of France. They brought with them the seeds of flowers which grow at Ypres. So the battlefields are linked.

The French, understandably, are in two minds about these arrangements. Under the Army's régime they were able to adopt graves and plant flowers of their own choice. Under the tidier administration of the Commission this is not desirable. None can doubt, after studying the Commission's handiwork, that this is a right and wise decision. But it has to be implemented with tact.

It may be 10 years before these cemeteries are as the English gardeners envisage them. Their situations vary and not all were chosen with a gardener's eye.

FLOWERS ALL SUMMER

At Brouay the graves lie on a sheltered and fertile slope, surrounded by trees and close to the village church. Hermanville beach cemetery is surrounded by tall trees and Fontenay is sheltered by a wood. At St. Manvieu, at Ranville and at Douvres the cemeteries lie on open ground.

Bény cemetery, where the Canadians lie, stands on open ground on the highest part of the ridge behind Courseulles. From there, looking north, you can see the way they came from the beaches three miles away and the sea beyond; and, looking south, the unattained dark green hills far beyond the bridgehead.

Each cemetery has a nursery garden, so that the graves will never be without flowers in the summer time. A rose tree, which will always be in bloom about this time of year, has been planted between every other grave. Each grave has its own flower.

Hedges, shrubs and saplings are being grown to replace the fences and to make avenues. In each cemetery there will eventually be a memorial to the missing.

A Bond of Friendship

These cemeteries, I think, account for the feeling here that the cost of liberation has been shared. That is a bond. That explains partly why tomorrow in Normandy will be treated as a Festival, an occasion for thanksgiving.

The Normans, as we found in 1944, are a slow-moving, phlegmatic people. Yet they have other qualities. Among a predominantly peasant population the heavy material losses, the need to sow again, create no bitterness, no recriminations.

Perhaps the return of their fat cattle—slain in thousands in 1944 and now back in abundance—consoles them. Perhaps their way of life gives them more patience and comprehension. None can be certain about these things.

At any rate, in this corner of France the cost of liberation, theirs and ours, will tomorrow be commemorated in a spirit of amity and understanding. That in Europe to-day makes it a memorable anniversary.

WATCHING WAR AND PEACE OVER CHURCHILL'S SHOULDER

The Fringes of Power: Downing Street Diaries 1939–1955
By John Colville (Hodder & Stoughton)

Friday, May 10 (1940). Rode at Richmond in summer heat. As I dismounted the groom told me that Holland and Belgium had been invaded.

A Private Secretary to the Prime Minister, particularly Winston Churchill, ought to have a touch of style. On the night before he rode in Richmond Park John Colville had dined fashionably with Mrs Henley, daughter of Lord Stanley of Alderley, and gone on to a dance at the Savoy.

There he sat next to Mary Churchill, whom he thought rather supercilious. "The Savoy was stuffy and I felt jaded, devitalised and utterly uninteresting."

It is to be hoped the ride did him good, because later that same day, Churchill, after seeing the King, took over at No. 10 from Neville Chamberlain. The private secretaries must have had a full day. Colville, at 24 and on a salary of £400 p.a., was in the thick of it.

From then on he became increasingly close to Churchill and his family (including Mary) and, but for his insistence on joining the R.A.F. in October 1941 for long enough to train and taste action, would have served at No. 10 throughout the war.

The family summoned him back (in R.A.F. uniform) in December 1943 when Churchill was taken ill at Carthage. He wangled another short break from No. 10 to go into action as a pilot in the critical months May–August 1944.

It is well to bring that into it. No girl would have sent a white feather to a man who had served on Churchill's inner treadmill throughout the war. But it puts a stamp on the character of the author of some extraordinary diaries.

The World in a Dozen Oysters

They are extraordinary because even after the millions of words written about the last war, the memoirs and the histories and Churchill's own enormous work, they come like a dozen oysters (if you like oysters). They cost about the same but take much longer to consume.

They are also extraordinary because, although superficially they appear to be the daily jottings of someone with a gift for clean prose who was close to Churchill and had a fashionable circle of friends, they give the reader insight not only into the four years of war but the past 40 years as well.

They convey faithfully, usually through Churchill's visionary asides, how certain events at that time led us to where we are now.

> Tuesday, January 23. When going to bed P.M. said to me;
> "Make no mistake, all the Balkans, except Greece, are going to
> be Bolshevised; and there is nothing I can do to prevent it.
> There is nothing I can do for poor Poland either."

Here is a tale of the human tragedy. No sooner did dawn break for the Allies after long night; no sooner did victory in the West beckon, than it became apparent that West and East were fighting together for totally different aims.

In February 1945 Churchill is talking to Colville of "the shadow of victory." In 1940 (he said) he could see what was to be done. But when Harris had finished his destruction of Germany, "what will lie between the white snows of Russia and the white cliffs of Dover?"

A day or two later he is moved to talk of a small lion talking between a huge Russian bear and a great American elephant. All this while, aside from fighting, Russia was being insistent about the future of Rumania.

Churchill was under no illusion. Yet he could do nothing, he told Colville. Russia had let us go our way in Greece; she would insist on imposing her will on Rumania and Bulgaria. As they went to bed at 2 a.m., he added: "I have not the slightest intention of being cheated over Poland, not even if we go to the verge of war with Russia."

Now here was the ultimate irony. For Nazi Germany's Goebbels and his satraps were keeping at the centre of their dying message the theme that when the Allies had destroyed them, there would be nothing between the Allies and the Soviet Union.

All this emerges from these diaries, not as Colville's opinions which are sparing, but through scraps of conversation with the Prime Minister, harsh telegrams from Stalin and Molotov—and evidence of relentless pressure.

There emerges, too, the tragedy of Roosevelt's frailty. Staunch when the tide of war ran heavily against us, he played no supportive role to Churchill in laying the foundations of the peace that was lost.

Colville's diaries are an enormous quarry out of which different people will dig their own aggregates. Much will be made of Churchill's severe illness in 1954 and the part played by Colville and others in covering it up.

There is not much useful substance to be got out of that because it is not likely to happen again.

These diaries have one other main virtue, so obvious that it will be overlooked unless one mentions it. They remind us that winning that war was stupendously difficult.

So much has appeared since, bringing to our notice with hindsight how it might have been so much better done; how this loss and that disgrace might have readily been avoided, that a generation not living in those years might suppose that we blundered our way to victory.

One might suppose from some latter day accounts that Churchill conducted the war in a pretty high-handed style. So at times he did. But through the diaries are scattered many private admissions of his own shortcomings.

Thursday, December 12 (1940). Remarking that tomorrow was Friday, 13th, I said that last year, on Friday, November 13 the B.B.C. had gloated over the date as having been a bad one for German submarines. Four hours later the Royal Oak was sunk. "I wrote that communique," replied Winston laconically. I subsided.

A TASTE FOR LATE-NIGHT CHAT

It does not follow that the portrait of Churchill which emerges is all *couleur de rose*. The diaries recall the old aphorism that no man is a hero to his valet.

Churchill's foibles and virtues, strengths and weaknesses—and all his maddening habits appear in the day to day entries. His most maddening habit was keeping a captive audience out of bed until

2 a.m., 3 a.m. or even 4 a.m. Not for work—the boxes were often neglected—but for chat.

Most of Colville's entries seem to have been made between those hours and getting his own head on to the pillow. The irritation comes across.

A SENTIMENTAL LOOK AT MUNICH

W. F. Deedes, a reporter with The Daily Telegraph in 1938, relives the comings and goings of Neville Chamberlain

In the Cabinet War Rooms, where they have put on a melancholy exhibition to mark the 50th anniversary of Munich and which I have just visited for sentimental reasons, there is on display one particularly incriminating document. It is not the piece of paper I saw Chamberlain wave about on his return—though that is also on view. It is the German minutes, 12 pages of them, of a conference that Hitler held with his senior political and military advisers on November 5, 1937.

At this meeting Hitler announced his intention to annexe Austria and to dismember Czechoslovakia. His Military Adjutant, Col Friedrich Hossbach, wrote the minutes. They were destroyed. An illicitly typed copy was found by the Allies in 1945. This also disappeared—but not before it had been photographed.

So much for Neville Chamberlain's belief that Hitler was a man with whom he could deal. So much for his foolish delusion that he wrung from Hitler after their last and most crucial of three meetings a promise of "peace for our time".

So much, you might add, for those who strive to be fair to Chamberlain, among whom I am one.

There is an unbridgeable gulf between the state of mind in this country at the time of Munich and the mental picture people have formed of Chamberlain, with his Homburg hat, umbrella and earnest intentions, dealing with Hitler as we came to know him. Appearances are all against Chamberlain. So, for that matter, was his voice—which they reproduce on tape at the Cabinet War Room exhibition, alternating it with Hitler's ranting.

I can still hear that precise, rather prim voice delivering into a primitive microphone at Heston airport, before his second visit to Hitler on September 22, a little homily about "try, try, try again".

"When I get back," he went on, "I hope I may be able to say as

Hotspur in Henry IV, 'out of this nettle, danger, we pluck this flower, safety'." All this at 8.30 am but I wrote it down and still possess a copy of my report.

Our national state of mind at the time is much harder to recapture and convey. Among those still alive from those days there is a clear—and, alas, quite false—recollection that we thought Chamberlain was wrong; that we knew in our hearts, as Churchill put it pungently, there had been a choice between war and dishonour; we had chosen dishonour—and would get war. We knew nothing of the kind.

As someone who was then reporting for this newspaper on defence against the air, I had a fairly clear picture of how we stood. I shared the view of several Cabinet Ministers, that to embark on war in the autumn of 1938 would have been to expose our urban populations to aerial warfare with totally insufficient anti-aircraft defences. We could have suffered a massacre. Some historians have since sought to prove that a year later Hitler had actually increased his air superiority over us. That does not alter what Chamberlain had to consider when he embarked on these German expeditions.

The mood that pervaded all but a few—and all honour to them— when Chamberlain got back for the last time was one of profound relief. I went up one day in 1938 to watch workmen forlornly digging trenches in the London parks. Everyone could see pictures of that, and most of them knew what it portended.

Now what is it we say today? We say, first of all, that our defences should never have fallen into such neglect and for that Baldwin, Chamberlain and Co were wholly to blame. That is dishonest. This democracy had shown itself deeply reluctant to rearm. I quoted last week, elsewhere in this newspaper, the indifferent attitude of employers towards the Territorial Army.

Our second charge is that Chamberlain betrayed a small country, Czechoslovakia, in order to save our own skins. There is no question: our pressure on the Czechs to satisfy Hitler's demands was cruel. There can be only one defence for it: if we believed that to fight Hitler's demands at the time of Munich could well lead to a war which both we and the Czechs would lose, then Chamberlain took the only way open to him.

In recent weeks my remote connections with Munich have produced a great many letters. The vehemence of some of them has surprised me. Some of the old war wounds have healed—but not Munich. The feeling runs very deep. So I am aware that any defence of Chamberlain will not only be resisted by many, it will be resented. It is always well to know when differences are ineradicable.

December 1989

THE HARD ROAD IN DEFENCE
OF HONOUR

Whatever the damages, there are no real winners in libel actions such as Lord Aldington's, argues W. F. Deedes. Even so, he was right to go ahead

A little earlier this year, suing for libel looked an easy road to a large fortune. There was Jeffrey Archer's £500,000, Sonia Sutcliffe's £600,000 (since reduced by agreement to £60,000), Elton John's settlement with the *Sun* for £1 million, and sundry other awards in the five- to six-figure range, mostly against newspapers. With damages of £1.5 million, Toby Aldington has received more than any of them—but on anything but an easy road.

He went to court, not seeking a fortune but to defend his honour. That has taken almost nine weeks and cost at least £1 million. But most expensive of all, for the past three years his peace of mind has been destroyed.

Let us recall the sworn testimony of his wife, Araminta, on October 18. She was discussing the effect on her husband of the pamphlet circulated 2½ years ago, while he was Warden of Winchester College. From that point onwards, she said, her husband became increasingly involved in the affair and spent several hours every evening in his office, sorting paper. He had no time to play cards with her.

"He was, at this point," she went on, "getting extremely fragile and very . . . well every wife I think will know what I mean. Nothing one says is absolutely correct, whatever one says is not absolutely right and it is very difficult to live with someone like that. He is 75 but I never thought of him as 75 before. I am sure he will bob back, but it has undermined his health."

As a contemporary as well as a close neighbour of Lord Aldington, who has followed this business since the first communication from Watts circulated our village in 1985, I think it hard to exaggerate the peace-of-mind factor. Given reasonable health, a man past 70 can work hard, play two rounds of golf a day (as we both do) and

49

sleep soundly at night; but more than at any time in his life he counts on peace of mind. The weight of worry multiplies once you have passed a certain age.

So on the face of it, Toby Aldington has paid an exceedingly high price to defend his honour, which no amount of damages can restore. Happiness stolen from youth may eventually be regained; tranquillity stolen from old age is much harder to retrieve.

In my own mind I have no doubt that Toby Aldington was right to proceed as he did. For one thing, to shrug it off would have left a shadow over future generations of his family. "I forget what happened, but wasn't her grandfather once accused of . . .?" And if a great school appoints you to be head of its affairs, the defence of your good name ceases to be wholly a matter for yourself.

I doubt, with hindsight, whether most people would take this line; indeed I doubt whether, if it came to the point, I would have the courage to take it myself. What will get home to the majority who have followed this interminable case is that there can be no winners in such actions. A consequence of the Aldington case, paradoxically, is a signal that to defame a man's honour is much safer than it was, because there will be deeper reluctance to go to court.

Such a conclusion, in my view, will be injurious. If actions for defamation are made to appear unreachable, in the light of Aldington's ordeal, then a valuable section of English law will fall into disuse. Worse—and we can count on it—Government will eventually feel the need to do something instead. My Tory beliefs lead me always to prefer the long-established law of the land to knee-jerk remedial interventions by Government.

In my submission, the Aldington case was outside the general run of actions for defamation. Thus it would be wrong to see it as holding a mirror to our law on libel.

The case was exceptional in that the two defendants, Nigel Watts and Count Nikolai Tolstoy, had embarked on their actionable courses with different motives; but that is not the important distinction. What set this case apart was the gulf between those who had shared some of Aldington's wartime experiences and therefore comprehended them, and those who by no effort of imagination could visualise Europe in 1945, and what it demanded of soldiers fighting a total war which must end in unconditional surrender.

Even those of us who were not Brigadiers General Staff had dirty work to do. In the summer of 1945, to make good the frontier agreed with the Soviet Union, I was ordered with my rifle company, as part of a brigade operation, to hand over a slice of Germany—and all the occupants—to the Russian Army. All I now recall of the episode was that the riflemen swapped watches for Russian revolvers. What became of the unhappy German families involved in this transaction I did not pause to think. The date? I could not even tell you which month it was.

At one point in his testimony in court (November 3), Tolstoy declared that Aldington had handed the Cossacks over to the Red Army because he had his "eye on the main chance" and did not wish to jeopardise his budding political career. In these easygoing times, 44 years from these events, it may well be argued that an officer who disapproved of orders should have argued the toss with his superiors.

But it needs firmly to be entered that, after five years of war, even those of us who had enlisted as amateurs via the Territorial Army (as Aldington did himself), had learnt not to treat lawful military commands as a basis for discussion.

For the certain—and in war, proper—consequence of conscientiously disobeying such a command would be a court martial for the disobedient officer, and his replacement by someone willing to carry it out. It would not have entered my head to jib at the command to hand over Germans to Russian soldiers, nor to question their fate. Many of us, particularly in the aftermath of that war, did things for which we later had reason to feel sorry.

There is no way to bridge the gulf between those who experienced conditions in Europe at the time and those who did not. It was difficult to distinguish friend from foe. Soldiers were tired and prone to lower their guard. What seemed of great urgency was to clean up the death camps and to retrieve British prisoners of war from the chaos. And for some of these dealings we were dependent on Stalin's, not Gorbachev's, Russia.

In the early summer of 1945, I persuaded my commanding officer to let me travel south across Germany to the Klagenfurt area in Austria, where one of our regular battalions was wrestling with the consequences of peace. Here were to be found most of the conditions with which Aldington in Eighth Army was struggling.

What most British soldiers had uppermost in their minds was the date of their demobilisation and their chances of starting a fresh life. What many still-combatant European partisans had in mind was pursuing the struggle, by force of arms if necessary, until the political end they desired had been reached. Thus, while much of the world was preparing to turn swords into ploughshares, some ruthlessness had to be shown by occupying forces.

Lord Aldington has private misgivings lest his action has the effect of bringing discredit on Sixth Army and its senior commanders. Such fears, I think, are misplaced. It is well that people should be reminded occasionally what the rigours of total war demanded of people. It is open to anyone to declare that total war is therefore evil. It is not open to accuse of wickedness those who in course of such a war have to obey lawful commands. Soldiers in total war are not afforded the latitude of employees in, say, British Rail or the Post Office.

For, as the Roman Centurion told us long ago, "I am a man under authority, having soldiers under me: and I say to this man, Go and he goeth; and to another, Come, and he cometh; and to my servant, Do this, and he doeth it." He was commended for his faith.

With every year that passes it becomes less likely that another case like this enormously costly action will ever be fought in our courts again. We should not allow the stunning sums of money at stake to lead us into wrong-headed conclusions about the worth of our libel laws.

D-DAY STRANDED BY THE DOCKERS

W. F. Deedes was all set to go to war, but the London dockers would not lift a finger unless they were paid the rate for the job

For 27th Independent Armoured Brigade, on the day, it was a brilliant feat of arms. For our battalion, 12th King's Royal Rifle Corps, it was a disappointment. For my B company, it culminated in ignominy. For most of those involved, D-Day was a day of mixed fortunes. It had first entered my inner consciousness with the return of our colonel to dinner in the Mess some time in May, after a long day at the War Office. He had, he confessed, head in hands, failed to get us a place on a D-Day landing craft.

All officers at the dinner table wore suitably disappointed looks, though I concealed a secret feeling of relief. We would, the colonel reassured us, be only a day or so behind. "We" were a motor battalion, kitted out with a rare breed of semi-armoured car, called the White, and made in America. Our task was to work with and ease the way for the three armoured regiments in our brigade, also armed by America with special Sherman tanks.

On D-Day these "swimming" tanks were foremost among our secret weapons. They were equipped with an engine that could drive a propellor, but reverted to driving tracks on dry land. They were fitted with a rigid canvas screen 4–5 feet high which on D-Day kept the tank afloat, though most of it was under water. When dry land was reached, the screen was collapsed, and the tank reverted to its normal role.

27th Independent Armoured Brigade, as it was then called, commanded by Brigadier Errol Prior-Palmer of the 9th Lancers, was allotted these tanks because it had a crucial role to play. Dropped off landing craft, some two miles out to sea, they were to "swim" to Sword Beach to destroy the German guns in heavily fortified emplacements at both ends of the beach. These guns would have crippled any landing force, and had to be neutralised.

Prior-Palmer's tanks were meticulously trained to fire directly into the slits of the heavily fortified gun emplacements. This became known in the Brigade as "posting a letter." All but two tanks from the three armoured regiments, 13/18 Hussars, 4/7 Dragoon Guards, Nottinghamshire Yeomanry, reached the beach. The operation was brilliantly successful. When the infantry landed at H hour, the German guns were silent and many lives were saved. In this, alas, we of the 12 KRRC had had no active part to play.

We sat with our vehicles and disconsolate colonel somewhere in the London docklands, waiting for our ship. On the night before we sailed, the very first V1 fell not far away in east London. When we learned what it was next morning, it heightened our depression. Not only would we arrive late on the beaches, we would seem to be retreating from danger in the homeland. In charge of our battalion's departure was Major Fred Coleridge, battalion second-in-command, already a considerable figure at Eton, subsequently to be a revered house master and then Vice-Provost. We had been sharing a Nissen hut.

Around noon, on our scheduled day of departure, he called me from the docks.

"We have a problem here," he said. "Join me."

On arrival at our berth, my eye met a confused scene. All our vehicles were still on the quayside. The ship stood empty. "The dockers," said Coleridge, "say they can't handle it." He urged me to reason with them.

"Trouble is, mate," the dockers replied in the friendliest terms, "we haven't got the rate."

"The rate?"

"That's right, the rate for loading these 'ere vehicles. Never seen 'em before."

Coleridge and I pleaded with them for a while. He then urged me to try a speech on the lines of "Friends, Romans, countrymen . . ."

Look, I said to the dockers, some of the men in the Normandy bridgehead are possibly sons, nephews, relatives of yours. They are hanging on by their eyebrows. Surely you want us there to back them up. The dockers nodded enthusiastically. "Abso-ruddy-lutely," they said. "Sooner you get there the better but, you see, we haven't got the rate."

After a long spell of this we reached a compromise. The riflemen would be permitted to load our vehicles, and a retired docker would be permitted to advise. Loading took a very long time, and the outcome was predictable. All our cars had been waterproofed, so that they could move through about three feet of sea water. In inexpert hands, they went into the ship's holds like falling leaves. The waterproofing suffered irreparable damage. When the cars were lugged out, off the Normandy shore, they suffered further damage. So it came about that roughly a quarter of my Company's scout cars sank shortly after taking to the water. Nobody drowned, but it took a lot of work to get sea water out of the cars' systems. They were late into battle.

Nor was that the ultimate humiliation. As we struggled ashore, I observed a party of VIPs on the beach casting an eye over the scene and observing our progress. They included Generals Eisenhower and Montgomery.

Later—much later—I persuaded myself to see the performance of the dockers as a blessing in disguise. Burdened with the prospect of losing up to a third of my company, I had no scope left to worry about the battle itself. The Normandy bridgehead had been established. We had no fighting to do immediately on landing. But, they warned, there are snipers all the way down the road to Bayeux. Snipers barely entered my head. What would the Colonel have to say to an officer who had drowned a quarter of his company? That was the urgent question. It is impossible, I learned, to be frightened and preoccupied at one and the same time.

Gradually, our fortunes improved. Our vehicles were dried out and returned to us. We became 8th Armoured Brigade and, under the forceful command of Brigadier Errol Prior-Palmer, led 30 Corps out of the bridgehead and through much of Europe. "B" company, 12 KRRC, became the first British unit to link up with the American 9th Army on the Lower Rhine. We were the first—unavailingly alas—to reach the Airborne at Arnhem. Thus memory of the indignity suffered in the hands of the London dockers gradually faded from the mind.

IT'S CHRISTMAS: DIG IN

*W. F. Deedes recalls a memorable dinner interrupted by
the Battle of the Bulge*

Our Christmas of 1944 was scrubbed. We spent it digging in the snow, or rather digging into frozen ground under snow, which is harder. For those of us spending a sixth Christmas in uniform, it was a disappointment. Field Marshal von Rundstedt, a formidable German general, had chosen Tuesday, December 16, to launch Germany's last desperate offensive of the Second World War.

News of the attack reached me—not, as I would have wished, in the front line—but over a delicious dinner in an expensive Brussels restaurant, before which I had drunk a bottle of Veuve Cliquot. This apparent lapse from duty stemmed from the unsatisfactory position in which the Allied armies then found themselves. After our narrow failure in XXX Corps to link up with the Airborne at Arnhem, we were committed to a winter of stalemate. We sat uneasily on the Dutch/German frontier waiting, as so many armies in history had done before, for the Spring offensive.

Because of this, there was virtually no home leave, though as a consolation we could take it in turn to spend two and a bit days on the binge in Brussels. So it came about that on December 16, Major F. J. R. Coleridge, second in command of our battalion, 12 King's Royal Rifle Corps (KRRC), and I embarked on this spree. It was, incidentally, the day that the American bandleader Glenn Miller vanished over the English Channel.

Coleridge and I were friends because, not long before D-Day, he had suggested we showed our faith in the future by my putting down a newly born son for his prospective house at Eton. "Preferential terms for penitent Old Harrovians," he said. It created a bond.

Time must not be wasted during a short outing like that, so within an hour of reaching Brussels we had taken hot baths and shared two bottles of the best. In optimistic mood, we set off for the

Grand' Place in the city centre. (A couple of years ago, while in the square, I looked in vain for the restaurant where we dined that night. *Tout casse, tout lasse, tout passe*, as they say.)

After giving the menu serious attention, we chose a fillet of beef which turned out to be beyond all previous human experience. There came with it, I recall, a *sauce béarnaise* that set the taste buds dancing. Then, as I raised a glass of red wine to my lips, a third presence suddenly made itself felt. It was an officer vaguely known to both of us, who was something not very much on the military staff in Brussels.

He had been charged with the unrewarding task of going round the Brussels nightspots to tell people like Fred Coleridge and me that the Germans had just charged into the Ardennes, that all we held dear lay in the balance, that all leave had been cancelled, and we must return to our units forthwith. I was reminded of Waterloo—"There was a sound of revelry by night . . ."

We were still engaged on the first third of our fillet. In such situations I am useless. I panic easily. Coleridge was altogether steadier. "And how," he asked the officer, forking in a mouthful of steak, "are we expected to return to our units tonight? There is transport for us?" We munched on for a bit. "You know," said Coleridge, "I really think we shall get back quickest if we start in the morning." "You are my superior officer," I said meekly. "I know my company is in good hands."

So there was time for fruit, cheese and a glass of brandy. Then, to ease our conscience, we rang up a very senior member of another black-button regiment, Major-General Bobby Erskine, who happened to be military boss of Brussels. "The morning will do fine," he said.

We returned, however, to no joy at all. Rundstedt had conjured up some 24 divisions, 10 of them armoured, and had hurled them at the weakest point of the Allied line. He took the same line of advance through the Ardennes forest as the German armies had done in 1940. We were caught on the hop. It was a brilliant stroke, falling between Montgomery's 21 Army Group and Patton's Third Army. This made overall command difficult. It led to bitter Anglo-American recriminations with which, when I came to know Montgomery well after the war, I became fully acquainted.

What became known as the Battle of the Bulge was more dangerous than we thought at the time. "Give your all to one last effort,"

Rundstedt had told his soldiers. They got 30 miles into Belgium towards the Meuse before they were stopped. Had we thought about it, which we did not, there was also an ominous parallel with the great German offensive of March 1918 which routed our Fifth Army, came close to the gates of Amiens and, when it seemed all was lost, inspired Haig's famous order of the day " . . . with our backs to the wall and believing in the justice of our cause . . ."

We were spending that winter of 1944 in a town called Heerlerheide, which I remember because it was the first time I had slept under a feather duvet. British troops were thin on the ground. We were on our boundary with the Americans and guarding the approaches to Maastricht. As XXX Corps reserve, we were ordered to spend our Christmas preparing for possible German attacks.

We had to be ready to move with one regiment of tanks and one infantry battalion to one of eight different defensive positions. So digging was urgent and extensive. When one position had been dug, we moved to another. All Christmas festivities were cancelled. We stuck to it until all eight positions were ready. It was a white Christmas, and the ground hard. The cold was intense, and I remember feeling my duvet was the only friend I had.

The Germans could not sustain their offensive, so we were not unduly troubled. We celebrated Christmas on New Year's Day, when we were even colder but a degree safer—the most dangerous German divisions had moved south. We were by then warmly housed in the mining town of Brunssum, whose inhabitants were wonderfully kind.

From time to time I think back on that hard decision Coleridge and I had to make in that wonderful restaurant, now gone with the wind, as we tucked into our steak. Did we let our country down? If we did, then I have to say we paid the price for it. We lost the Christmas of half a century ago. We had to live with, and keep some semblance of military order among, riflemen who were also missing Christmas for the first time in their young lives, while digging into ground like rock.

May 1995

TOMORROW . . . THE HOPES
AND THE FEARS

W. F. Deedes ended his war in Germany guarding PoWs and V2 fuel tanks and then returned to a homeland that was changed for ever. Britain was broke. No one was grateful to Winston Churchill

We marked the end of a hard war in Europe by sending our three-ton lorries over to France to collect what was left of the champagne. Krug non-vintage for supper every night was heady stuff on which to contemplate one's chances in the post-war world. It failed to raise my spirits very high.

Most of us were wearier than we realised. There were 16 million displaced people roaming Europe, for some of whom I suddenly became responsible. My rifle company's duties in Hanover were two fold: to guard 2,000 German prisoners-of-war; and to patrol a store of the fluid which flew Germany's V2s. It was almost pure alcohol, and the vagrants who dodged my riflemen and drank it died.

The end of battle created new disciplinary problems. "Fraternisation" was forbidden. But hungry German girls, anxious to offer favours in return for the unexpired portion of our ample rations, posed problems. At some point, under the peace settlement, I had to hand over a portion of Germany to Russia. Riflemen cheerfully swapped their watches for Russian revolvers. So next day I had a company armed to the teeth but unable to tell the time.

Against this sombre background I reflected on my future. Labour's election victory later in the summer left me not much surprised. I was called on to give talks on "Current Affairs". The riflemen had made their feelings plain to me. In any case, as a political reporter before the war, I knew the track record of the so-called National Government which under an astonishing variety of leaders had lasted from 1931 until 1945. I had also discovered there is no gratitude in politics—even for Winston Churchill. At that point, the prospect of Labour in charge made no great impact on me.

Nor, curiously, did it at first make much impact on anyone else. Refreshing my memory from our files of what the papers said at the time, I find astonishingly little during the last half of 1945 on the new Labour Government.

We were wholly preoccupied with the dire consequences of a global war—and, until Japan's surrender at midnight August 15, with its further prosecution. Churchill's plea to Labour to keep the coalition going until the end of the Japanese war was sensible. Labour, rejecting it as a Tory ploy to improve its crumpled organisation, won office on July 26 with 393 seats against the Tories' 213.

I recall hearing that Churchill had declared in the election campaign that Labour would fall back on some sort of Gestapo, and reckoning he had put his foot on it. Orwell and Professor Hayek, whose *The Road to Serfdom* had become a book to read, were fine authors, but dangerous to mix with electioneering.

War's aftermath apart, what troubled Britain during the months after Labour's victory lay mainly outside Westminster. In October the dockers stopped work, squeezing the country's tenuous supplies even tighter and giving a foretaste of the demands to come from the labour front.

Labour's plans to nationalise railways, ports, road haulage and coal mines attracted notice. But we heard far more from loved ones in Britain about the meat ration—cut from 1s 2d a week to 1s in January 1946—and the talk of bread rationing. As winter set in, power failed, Britain froze and Buckingham Palace was lit by candles. There were 700,000 houses in London alone in need of repairs.

It slowly sank in that we were broke, heavily dependent on American charity. In August 1945, Attlee warned the nation that we were in dead trouble over the abrupt end to Lease Lend. By December, we had negotiated a fresh US loan for £1,100,000,000. On the same day, Churchill assailed Socialist follies in a debate (which he lost by 381 votes to 197), but much of his heat was directed against "uniformed unemployment", in other words slowness of demobilisation.

Troubled by the fall in fertility—this was before the post-war baby boom—the Royal Commission on Population sent a questionnaire to 1,500,000 wives, 10 per cent of the total, seeking intimate particulars. In what was plainly the saddest failure of post-war planning, we carried a headline on October 31, 1945, "Britain to Train Girls as Housewives". Behind this lay a proposal in R A

Butler's Education Act of 1944 for county colleges to provide, for one hour a week, compulsory part-time education of 1,500,000 in the 15–18 age group. The aim was to help young people to live a healthy life, develop their knowledge and understanding, their character and "a balanced outlook on life". The idea came to naught; our resources would not run to it.

This was the background against which I would shortly set about rebuilding my future, for which I felt ill-prepared. In return for willingness sometimes to chance your arm, a Service like the Army is wonderfully supportive. It undertakes to provide you with accommodation, regular meals, transport and health care which can be bothersome in everyday life. It saves you thinking about insurance rates, the car licence, putting back tiles after a storm, or being let down by British Rail. These and other responsibilities, I reflected, now returned to me.

With childhood recollections of the First World War's aftermath, and Lloyd George's flawed promise of "a land fit for heroes" my expectations from a grateful public were low. At 32, I was old enough to realise that we would be returning to a world radically different from the one we had left in 1939. The effect of a world war is like pressing the forward button on the video flicker. We would be poorer—and much changed.

Translation from civilian life to military discipline at the start of a war, which many of us had experienced in 1939, tears up all your roots. Putting them down again in different, impoverished soil is difficult; and no amount of Krug could alter that. My wife had just bought a house in the North Riding of Yorkshire, where her family lived. While contemplating the prospects of finding a livelihood up there, I received a letter from Arthur Watson, then editor of this newspaper. There was a chronic shortage of staff, he wrote crossly. How soon could he count on my services?

Even that failed to lift my heart. At roughly the same time I was offered command of a battalion which would invade Japan. It was tempting. I felt more confident as a soldier than as a journalist. Luckily, the bomb on Hiroshima settled it. Eventually I wrote humbly to our editor giving the date of my demobilisation, requesting a fortnight to visit the bereaved, but otherwise signifying my willingness to buckle down.

In theory, we were far better prepared for the peace than we had been in 1918. During the war, Churchill had turned senior ministers on to post-war planning—though by May 1945 some of these plans bore little relationship to the resources available. I failed to anticipate how wartime controls and rationing, which prevailed long after the war, would complicate resettlement. You needed a licence to procure the timber to mend a hole in the roof.

What little we knew about United Nations looked a better bet than the old League of Nations. On the other hand, I recall an uneasy feeling that the Russians had beaten us to it. If only some of us had contrived to pull it off at Arnhem during those last fraught hours, I reflected, and had ended the war in the autumn of 1944 instead of the spring of 1945, our position would be sounder. The Russian soldiers I had met during our exchange of territory struck me as belonging to another world. I had no sense of returning to a more stable world, only a badly battered one.

I recalled nostalgically the last year or so before the war, when life had seemed so carefree, with long, inexpensive suppers with friends at the Café Royal and dancing in London to Joe Loss and the Savoy Orpheans. I thought of an exceptionally jolly day at the Oval just before the call-up in August 1939, when I sat with a girlfriend watching the West Indians make hay in the sunshine. Those joyful days were past, I felt. No champagne in the world could conquer that kind of thinking.

Having had responsibility for censoring the riflemen's letters to loved ones, I had a rough picture of their domestic circumstances. SWALK, they wrote on the back of the envelopes, meaning "sealed with a loving kiss". I felt that under the strain of resettlement some of them would find the marriage bed less warm than they hoped.

For some reason I became mildly obsessed by this thought. I wrote to a distinguished relative, suggesting that the Queen might consider a sympathetic broadcast, gently warning Service wives that the man returning to them might not be the same man who had departed for the war and urging patience. Nothing came of this but I was not far wide of the mark. In May 1945, there were 50,000 Service divorces outstanding in the courts; in November we reported a tidal wave of divorce sweeping the country. I recalled the anguished letters I had had to read. It was not only bombs that destroyed homes.

I had no inkling of the rate of post-war inflation but it seemed unlikely that money would buy as much as it had in pre-war days, and now I had a wife and son to consider. My mother wrote expressing faint disappointment that a local parliamentary seat had fallen vacant and that I had not been available. I should have been pleased by this expression of maternal confidence. Instead, I felt irritated by an expectation so far removed from what I then felt would be possible.

When eventually I was demobbed with my smart new suit and stout shoes and had visited parents who had lost their sons, such feelings underwent a change. One or two of these families had lost an only son. All the hopes they had for him were gone for ever. Much of my life lay ahead and depended on what I chose to make of it. I returned for a talk with Arthur Watson, who had been a gunner in the First World War and understood these things. He proposed that I reinforce the solitary figure who throughout the war had produced the Peterborough column. He welcomed me. Things started to look up.

IT LOOKS AS THOUGH ONLY A MIRACLE CAN HALT SLIDE INTO WAR

Evacuations, blackouts, mobilisations—the impact of the impending conflict was growing as Britain entered September 1939. In the latest of his recollections using letters and his personal archive, W. F. Deedes captures the atmosphere leading up to the declaration of war

Arthur Watson, editor of *The Daily Telegraph*, has been on the telephone to me at Caxton Street. He is alarmed at the sudden loss of so many of the newspaper's sub editors. They have been summoned by our battalion headquarters to join the actor/journalist company. We have to get the paper out, Watson explains reasonably. Can I arrange to have one or two of them exempted and sent back?

Ever since I joined the paper in 1937 I have regarded Watty, as he is known in the reporters' room, with respect bordering on awe. He became editor in 1928 when Lord Camrose bought the paper. Before any major assignment I had listened to his advice, always sound. Now he was asking the impossible of me.

Watson had been a gunner in the first war and had won a DSO. It occurred to me he ought to know better than to make such a request. During our conversation I realised suddenly that my umbilical cord with the *Telegraph* had been severed. We were preparing for war. The editor's wishes were no longer paramount.

At the same time, I am left feeling uneasy. For it was I who had encouraged most of these people to join 2nd Queen's Westminsters. The morning hours of drill appealed particularly to sub editors. There had been the makings of an office row about it. I was summoned by Lord Burnham, whose family had owned the *Telegraph* before Camrose bought it and who was now managing director.

He foresaw problems for the newspaper, he explained, if war came and suggested I stopped being a recruiting sergeant. This, I considered at the time, to be pot calling kettle black. Lord Burnham was a senior, distinguished and decorated Territorial Army officer.

Later on, he helped to steady things on Dunkirk beaches. He rose to the rank of major general.

At a convenient moment I mention Watson's request to Colonel Savill, but mercifully in a lighthearted fashion. He looked about to have apoplexy. I perceived we had passed the point of no return.

In theory, it is pay day for some of the men. Two of us walk to a bank in Victoria Street with a cheque from the battalion which, much to my surprise, is cashed without question. Nobody is going to get anything like £1 for their work, yet the men don't grumble. Walking behind our headquarters, I suddenly encounter A G Macdonell, novelist and author of the classic *England their England*. A resident of this district, he is wearing the steel helmet of an ARP warden and looking acutely unhappy.

We exchange a few words about the outlook. He strikes me as a lonely figure. To be alone, with war looming! Not for the first or last time, I reflect on the value of companionship in war.

Macdonell murmurs something about his duties with evacuees. The evacuation of three million people starts today. We have now ordered complete naval mobilisation. Poland has rejected Hitler's terms. It really does look as if it will take a miracle to stop the slide to war. Reading my letters home at this time, I am surprised by my fatalism. In recent weeks I seem never to have expected any other outcome.

My close association with Victor Gordon Lennox and Helen Kirkpatrick in the *Telegraph* office may have had something to do with it. He was our diplomatic correspondent, whom I sometimes assisted. Both of us came under the spell of Kirkpatrick, a young American with a brilliant academic record who was working in our office for the *Chicago Daily News*. Early in 1939, she had written a book for English readers called *This Terrible Peace*. She left me in no doubt about the inevitability of it all. Later, she joined the ranks of influential American war correspondents.

I am also having a depressing exchange of correspondence with my father. Something of a political eccentric with Left-wing inclinations, he lays all the blame on our rulers. I differ, seeing the punitive terms of the Treaty of Versailles in 1919 as the cause of all present trouble.

"You remember the country's attitude then?" I write to my father. "The outcome at Versailles did not carry 'the peace against Germany' any further than the country demanded ... It's too easy now with all we have learned in 20 years saying that Lloyd George and Co lacked vision. This country in 1919 didn't want vision. It wanted revenge . . . Well they got revenge—full and juicy revenge did the statesmen from England and France exact *in response* to hysterical cries from this country to hang the Kaiser, starve the German people out, etc."

Versailles and its consequences for Germany sought by our democracy, I argued, had left Neville Chamberlain with very few cards.

But this sense of the inevitable is widely shared. The public mood is wholly different from that of August 1914. Then, we seemed taken by surprise. Now we are ready and braced.

This evening I set off to dine at the club with another officer. In the gloaming just outside the Junior Carlton, we encounter the jaunty figure of Sir Thomas Inskip, Dominions Secretary, who has just come from a meeting of ministers. The appointment of this genial old buffer as Minister of Defence in 1936, when some thought Churchill should be given the job, had convinced many that we were not taking Hitler seriously. Inskip had recently been transferred to the less challenging territory of the Dominions.

Because of my lobby days, we know each other. "How goes it?" I say. "It all depends on one man," he replies solemnly. This expression is becoming a cliché.

As we walk back to a flat near Caxton Street where we are billeted, I remark on the speed with which London has got itself on a war footing at night. Lights are low, windows are blacked out. With surprising speed we are learning to grope about in the dark.

WE SEEM TO HAVE STARTED
—IT'S ALL SO SILLY

Britain declared war on Germany 60 years ago today. W. F. Deedes organised his platoon of actors to guard Staines railway bridge

A letter to my mother written this afternoon begins: "We seem to have started the war, and it is all so sad and silly I really don't feel like bothering to comment on it." We had heard Neville Chamberlain at 11.15 that morning broadcasting from No 10 to the nation. I wish I had been in the House of Commons an hour later. Wireless is very disembodied.

The Commons at midday, by all accounts, presented one of its great tableaux. All the passion of the previous evening when the Government's intentions were in doubt was spent. A sympathetic House heard Chamberlain remark that while it was a sad day for all, to none was it sadder than to himself, for he saw all he hoped and worked for and believed in during his public life in ruins.

I disagreed with some of what he had done, but it would have taken a heart of stone to reject that. Our experienced Colonel, perceiving it to be a day on which emotions would run deep, sensibly resorts to action. My happy days in London, uselessly striving to make our battalion headquarters bombproof, are at an end. I cease to be an officer about town, and am given notice to pick up my platoon in C Company at Staines. We have now had two abortive air raid alarms in London, and I am not altogether sorry to go.

"Down here," I explain in a letter to my mother written from Staines, "I have a platoon of 26 men, all the actors' brigade. We are guarding a railway bridge which is taking most of the stuff direct from the North of England to the Western Front."

More specifically, I was given to understand, Staines railway bridge carried a lot of naval stuff between Scapa Flow in the North and Portsmouth. Scapa Flow! The Grand Fleet! What could be more romantic—and what a way to start the war!

Reality was more prosaic. "The men," I reported to my mother, "have been here since Friday [Sept 1]. I relieved an officer who was so tired he could hardly explain what I had to do. It's pretty tough duty."

It was in fact the routine duty of every guard, with two hours on and four hours off, but it was hard work for the inexperienced officer in charge. "I have to run the show all day," I explain to my mother, "and keep the sentries moving four of the 12 shifts: 6am–8am, noon–2pm, 6pm–8pm and midnight–2am. Which rather breaks up the night." I have two NCOs under me and three of us divide the 24 hours between us.

"The bridge is fearful, specially at night, as there are live rails all over it and two sentries are within three feet of the metals. Going round the posts, which are about a hundred yards apart in pitch darkness and interminable goods and munition trains on one side and live wires on the other, is no joke!"

Our billet, however, is an improvement on Buckingham Gate, being a British Legion hall on the river's edge. I sniff the air and there creeps into me a feeling to be experienced often in the war—what a blessing to be a safe distance from battalion headquarters!

Having been on the job 48 hours already, the riflemen are tired but happy, and are being well fed by a man and his wife who run the Legion hall. I think I am lucky with my first command. "The men are exceptionally good," I report to my mother. "All the actors ought to have commissions, of course; actually they've all applied for them and they are capable and helpful."

We have minor contretemps, mercifully unseen by the Colonel. There is one post for a rifleman on the pavement under the bridge. There, on a round of inspection, I find Guy Middleton, rifle tucked between his legs, signing autographs for giggling girls. He gives me a tremendous wink. What is there left to say? Middleton has taken to military life like a duck to water. Tam Williams has not. He is a melancholy figure. He has taken his first week's pay (amounting, after deductions, to a few shillings) and planted it on the railway line. So the coins are twice their natural size and useless. He displays this small experiment to me with a sad smile.

"I find," I tell my mother, "one has slipped into war routine very easily." In an earlier letter I claim that experience in Abyssinia, where I had spent five months in 1935 as the *Morning Post* war correspondent, had eased the transition. There is a grain of truth in that. Daily life in Abyssinia was rougher than life now; one lacked the supportive system which the Army extends to its soldiers.

"I hate having to wear the same uniform every day. You know, I always liked to wear a different suit different days"—buying suits in pre-war days was one of my extravagances—"and we are in steel helmets and respirators which are damned uncomfortable."

"The men rely on one so much one really feels compelled to do all one can. They are so pleased when one expresses a wish to set up the camp bed in their quarters and to eat with them. I really felt the solitary glory of an officers' mess for one, which I was pressed to accept, was too much."

My Army pay of about 45s a week seems ample and is, for the time being, supplemented by half pay from *The Daily Telegraph*, which intends to review the position after three months. None of us sees that far ahead.

"I fancy we shall be in these parts for another few weeks before training begins," I report home. "Maybe it will be all over by then."

What might I have written then had I known that it would not be all over for the best part of five years . . . if I had known that one or two of the riflemen with me at Staines would get their commissions in time to join the Queen Victoria Rifles, take part in the epic defence of Calais in May 1940 and become prisoners of war . . . if I had foreseen the hill that all of us had to climb. Most mercifully, it is not granted to any of us to see what tomorrow brings.

CHAMBERLAIN'S MOMENT OF TRUTH

How drama slowly unfolded

Neville Chamberlain's downfall was foreshadowed by a small item in the newspaper of May 3, 1940, which few noticed. It announced that there would be a debate in the House of Commons in the following week about the general conduct of the war.

I certainly failed to spot it, because at that stage in my life I barely read the newspapers. There wasn't time. Commissioned just before the war but without officer training, I was struggling to keep my end up as a platoon commander.

In early May that year our Territorial Army battalion of riflemen, 2nd Queen's Westminsters, arrived at Shrapnel Barracks at Woolwich. There, our colonel vainly supposed, we might catch up with our training. The first eight months of our war had been spent in six different locations around London guarding "vulnerable points"—railway bridges, wireless masts, anything thought worth the attention of enemy agents.

Our interest in "the general conduct of the war" was limited to these unexciting duties. Some still talked darkly of a settlement with Germany—talk that was anathema to our colonel.

A year or two earlier, I had been a political correspondent in the House of Commons. Much later in the war, this led to requests to lecture soldiers on what the army called *Current Affairs*. In May 1940, my small degree of political awareness rendered me faintly suspect in the colonel's eyes. But those of us who were at battalion headquarters in the evenings gathered to hear the BBC's radio news, and that was our main link with the outside world.

A few of us, bored with our guard duties, were looking round for something more militarily exciting. As for Norway, where our forces had been engaged in shadowy conflict with the Germans since April, we felt slightly envious of those involved. Highly sanguine communiqués led us to suppose that it was a bit of a lark. Those airy communiqués were about to form a main charge against Chamberlain's Government.

So, to set the scene, our actions in Norway call for explanation. Because Germany was drawing essential iron ore supplies from Norway and Sweden, who were neutrals, Allied naval forces laid minefields in territorial waters at three points along the Norwegian coast.

This compelled ships carrying iron ore from Narvik to Germany to leave territorial waters and so come within the grasp of Allied contraband control. Germany's immediate response was to send troopships and warships which occupied Oslo, Bergen, Christiansund, Stavangar, Trondheim and Narvik.

Our Cabinet and Supreme War Council, resolved that Norway should not be abandoned without a struggle, then set out to command the sea approaches to Norway. On April 9, near Narvik, the battle cruiser Renown encountered Germany's battleship Scharnhorst and inflicted damage. Next day we sank a German cruiser in Bergen harbour.

Reporting this to the House of Commons on April 11, Winston Churchill (still First Lord of the Admiralty) declared that the German fleet had been damaged in important respects and spoke of Hitler's invasion of Norway as a mistake and of advantage to the Allies.

Public spirits rose and remained high through most of April. Our naval and military forces landed in Norway in mid-April. For a while all seemed to go well, and while this was so the Government was happy to keep the public well-informed about the course of operations.

As the tide in Norway began to turn against us, official communications became less illuminating. An order to withdraw on April 28 naturally had to be kept secret, but the public uneasiness grew. Chamberlain was urged by parliamentarians to make a statement on April 29. He put this off until May 2.

Even then, desiring to make the best of a bad job, his statement was unduly sanguine. Yet we had been forced into retreat. Neither the House of Commons nor the public were mollified by Chamberlain's endeavour to put a gloss on it. Nor were those of us gathered at Shrapnel Barracks. The colonel, I remember, had to suspend his rule about gloomy war talk in the mess.

In the interests of men still in action, Clement Attlee, the leader of the Opposition, deferred cross-examination of the Prime Minister until the following week when the two-day debate that would transform the political scene and our chances of winning the war took place.

Like many great dramas, the two-day debate on the Government's conduct of the war which opened in the Commons on May 7, unfolded slowly. The first day was described as relatively dull. I cannot remember whether I took any interest in it, but I doubt it.

It is hard to convey at this distance how completely involvement in war changes the habits of a lifetime. For countless folk in this country life had undergone a metamorphosis. The Commons, which had never made much impact on their lives, became more remote than ever.

There was no inkling of the storm about to break over Europe, which would have sharpened our interest. Main news in *The Daily Telegraph* on May 7 was still about Norway. British and French troops involved there had landed in Scotland. We reported on our front page a startling declaration by Col Frank Knox, the proprietor of the *Chicago Daily News*, entitled "Time to Face the Truth." It outlined the possible consequences for America of Germany conquering Britain and France. In this hour of decision it declared: "No more dangerous enemy of American peace and security may be found than the champion of blind isolation."

That did catch my eye. I wondered how far Col Knox had been influenced by my friend Helen Kirkpatrick, who worked for the *Chicago Daily News* in our Fleet Street office. She had long foreshadowed war and was author of a book called *This Terrible Peace*.

Hugh Carleton Greene, later the director-general of the BBC, then our Berlin correspondent, reported from the German–Belgian frontier how the Belgians had fortified their defences by felling trees. It was soon to prove an unavailing effort.

Monday's *Daily Telegraph* had outlined arrangements for the debate. Chamberlain would open. At the end of two days, Churchill would wind up. Had I still been a reporter and not a soldier, I would have noticed a significant change at that point in Churchill's political status.

Seeking to give his sagging government a stronger look, Chamberlain had asked Churchill, as First Lord of the Admiralty, to preside over the committee of Service ministers which, with the three chiefs of staff as advisers, supervised the general conduct of the war. He was also authorised by the Cabinet to give guidance and direction to the chiefs of staff committee. When it came to the debate,

Chamberlain was closely examined on this. Answering Lloyd George, Herbert Morrison and others, he stressed that it was a recent arrangement, made on April 11 and *after* the Norwegian operations. At the start of his speech, the Prime Minister had a rough time. He sought to make light of the Norwegian affair. Worse, he had on April 5 declared publicly that Hitler "had missed the bus"—a phrase used earlier in the war by Gen Sir Edmund Ironside, the Chief of the Imperial General Staff, whom many of us thought an ass.

Vainly, Chamberlain assured the House that he was alluding not to the ill-starred Norwegian affair but to Hitler's failure to follow up his advantage in weight of arms by attacking the Allies earlier. It was not an explanation to win ringing applause.

As an account of our actions in Norway, the Prime Minister's speech was passable. He answered difficult questions sensibly and was not seriously challenged on that front. But, although preoccupied with military duties, I had enough political sense left to realise that his troubles ran deeper.

They ran at this time deepest with Tory MPs serving with the Forces.

The current of debate that first day ran firmly against Chamberlain's government. Attlee criticised combining Churchill's duties as First Lord with that of mentor to the Chiefs of Staff.

The echo of Leo Amery's emotional speech with Cromwell's injunction to the Long Parliament to "in the name of God, Go" certainly reached Woolwich—and beyond.

WITH PIKES AND PITCHFORKS, THEY WAITED FOR HITLER

In July 1940, W. F. Deedes was a young Army officer who had every reason to be grateful to the Home Guard. Sixty years after their creation he explains the key role that the real Dad's Army played in the defence of Britain at its most critical hour

"If you've half an hour to spare," the man in Home Guard uniform said, "I'd like to show you something pretty startling." In the late summer of 1940 one of my duties as an officer in 12 King's Royal Rifle Corps (TA) was to spend Sunday mornings picking up useful information from the police and Home Guard in our neighbourhood.

So we drove out to a farm near our quarters in South Wales and entered a field where the corn had been cut and laid out in stooks. What my friend in the Home Guard wanted me to see was the way in which the stooks had been set out in the field.

They formed a rough arrow designed, he insisted, to guide German aircraft onto a local target. I was sceptical. "You ought to have a quiet word with the farmer," I suggested. "Can't do that," said the Home Guard man with immense satisfaction. "He's been nicked!"

I remained sceptical until later that year when we were stationed near Newcastle-under-Lyme. There I heard a similar story. Was there anything in it? During those fraught summer months of 1940 we never stayed anywhere long enough to make sure.

Yet the tale illustrates one virtue of the Home Guard and why they have a lasting place in this island's story. They were *local*. They knew their neighbourhoods. They would know the name of a farmer who laid out corn stooks in a peculiar way; and would have a pretty clear idea of whether he was a man likely to be helping the enemy.

Sixty years on from the formation of the Home Guard in July 1940, it is impossible to convey to those not then alive the mood in this island that sent thousands of men racing to defend it. The Low Countries had fallen with hardly a shot fired. The French seemed paralysed. With the Continent overrun by the Germans, there was a natural anxiety about what was likely to happen here combined with a fierce determination not to submit to the Nazis.

Until the early summer, I was stationed with our battalion in the Gunners' barracks at Woolwich. Our daily routine had been that of most soldiers during the phoney war. We had guard duties, did a bit of drilling. London was conveniently close for recreation. In the evenings, we gathered in the officers' mess after dinner to hear the BBC news.

The sun beat down day after day. A lovely English summer seemed to be going to waste. But it brought the only scintilla of good news. The British Expeditionary Force was being ferried back across the Channel in miraculously calm weather. Churchill later described it thus: "The sense of fear seemed entirely lacking in the people. Nothing moves an Englishman so much as the threat of invasion, the reality unknown for a thousand years. Vast numbers of people were resolved to conquer or die."

That conveys the spirit which led 250,000 men to join the Local Defence Volunteers, as they were at first called, within 24 hours of the War Secretary Anthony Eden broadcasting an appeal for them in June 1940.

It was Churchill who objected to their original name. On one of his visits round the country, he had spotted a party of middle-aged men in civilian clothes wearing armlets marked LDV. "I don't think much of the name 'Local Defence Volunteers' for your very large new force," he wrote to Eden on June 26, 1940. "The word 'local' is uninspiring. Mr Herbert Morrison suggested to me today the title 'Civil Guard' but I think 'Home Guard' would be better."

Nobody argued much with Churchill in those days, so Home Guard they became on July 24. By that time, 1.3 million men had joined the force and recruiting had been suspended.

"Local" might sound uninspiring but local ears and eyes were indispensable. Another Home Guard officer whom I encountered while in the Newcastle-under-Lyme region wrinkled his nose at the name of a local university don who was booked to give a lecture to our battalion. "Defeatist. He doesn't think we can win, and he talks like that in the officers' mess before the lecture."

A lot of people thought like the lecturer at that time, but as we were moving again—our battalion moved six times in seven months—I left a cautionary note for the regiment taking over from us. I thought no more about it until the end of the war when the lecturer in question turned up in the House of Commons as a Labour MP and ultimately became a fairly successful minister.

Nor would anyone who started the war in the Territorial Army, as I did, make light of the Home Guard's routine duties, for they eventually took over some of the chores that we had been doing, and that included holding watch over "vulnerable points".

My first "VP" early in September 1939 was Staines railway bridge, over which trains carrying naval supplies were said to run between Portsmouth and Scapa Flow. My second "VP" was an Admiralty radio mast at Northolt. It was autumn by then and cold at night, and the men had no greatcoats. Furthermore, it was a duty that ate up manpower.

Consider: a patrol of one man guarding for two hours with four hours off, requires a minimum of three men during daylight hours. When doubled at night, as patrols were, it needs six men, plus an NCO to move them round. I had to deploy four patrols at Staines and Northolt, which permanently occupied the whole of my platoon of 24, plus a corporal and a platoon sergeant.

After a week or so of this, the men got tired, but at least we were not doing anything else—and we got the King's shilling. Many of the Home Guard, who received no pay, had heavy civilian responsibilities on top of their guard duties.

My neighbour in our village of Aldington in Kent, Clive Boulden, was a farmer—a reserved occupation. "I joined the LDV early on," he says, "and our job was to guard the village telephone exchange. We shared a horse-drawn caravan, I seem to remember. I think I did one night in three. My day's work on the farm came on top of that."

After six months of guarding the telephone exchange, Clive was seconded to a special unit of the Home Guard and trained in the art of sabotage. Our village, looking across the Romney Marshes towards the English Channel, lies only a few miles from the stretch of coast on which the Germans were expected to land.

So Clive learned how to blast trees across a road and other ways of making life difficult for the Germans if they came. "When you look back on it," he said as we took an evening drink together a few days ago, "you know that if the worst had come to the worst, you could never have survived."

Did you know the risks? "Yes, I suppose we did, but you had to do something. And we were all so much younger . . ."

Jimmy Perry, who with David Croft wrote the scripts for the much-loved television series *Dad's Army*, joined up for the same reason as did Boulden. Perry had joined the Home Guard at 15. Why? I asked him. "I couldn't *wait*. People in this country have no idea of the feeling there was at that time. You did it!"

He speaks movingly of the bank managers and others in reserved occupations, or those too old for active service—the model for Corporal Jones was a genuine veteran of Omdurman—who *longed* to get into the war. So he joined up just under the statutory age—"all young boys of 16 love to be armed to the teeth"—and stayed with the Home Guard for three and a half years. Eventually he was called up, on January 1, 1944, joined the Royal Artillery, went to the Far East and attained the rank of sergeant.

At the age of 15, though, he dreamed of holding a Thompson machine gun with a 50-round drum—but as things were he had to wait until September 1940 to get a rifle. "Two shiploads had just come in. By Christmas we were well armed." A year later, he got his machine gun, a water-cooled Vickers from the First World War.

His *Dad's Army* manages to convey the extraordinary spirit of those 1940 days, when thousands of men and boys *without* weapons rushed forward to fight the prospective German invaders. Our loss of arms and equipment at Dunkirk had been crippling. For a while it was difficult to find enough for our beleaguered Army, let alone the Dad's Army.

"The plight to which we were reduced . . . may be measured by the following incident," Churchill wrote. "I visited our beaches at St Margaret's Bay, near Dover. The Brigadier informed me that he had only three anti-tank guns in his brigade, covering four or five miles of this highly menaced coastline. He declared he had only six rounds of ammunition for each gun."

So in those long summer days of 1940, as we braced ourselves for invasion and the Home Guard scanned the skies for German parachutists, Dad's Army had to improvise its own weapons. Pikes and pitchforks, old shotguns and carving knives lashed onto poles were pressed into service.

There were strange encounters. *The Daily Telegraph* reported a

Local Defence Volunteer in a lonely spot who cried "Halt!" to a man in a car. The driver halted. "Halt!" said the man again.

"I have halted," said the motorist. "What do you want me to do next?" "I don't know," said the LDV. "My orders are to say 'Halt!' three times then shoot."

Though indelibly stamped by *Dad's Army* as comic characters, the Home Guard shared many of the soldier's hazards and all the risks of civilian life from bombing. Their gallantry earned two George Crosses, 13 George Medals, one OBE, 11 MBEs, six British Empire medals and 58 commendations.

The Home Guard caught a singular mood in this country, when so many men were prepared to step forward to repel the invader or die. But I have always seen more to it than that. In the closing months of 1940, a new resolve slowly ran through this country. We had more to do than defend ourselves against invasion: one day, we came to realise, we would have to fight our way back into Europe, for there was no other way to win the war.

From that point on, I saw the Home Guard as a gigantic shield, behind which we could safely leave our vulnerable points and other defensive duties and turn to training to attack.

The so-called phoney war was behind us. The Battle of Britain had held off the Luftwaffe and made us more secure. If German parachutists arrived, they would be accounted for by the Home Guard, by then organised into functioning military formations with proper weapons.

With the Home Guard on the defensive, our battalion moved to the moors of the North Riding. There, very slowly, an armoured division began to take shape that would eventually storm the beaches of Normandy.

Some of us were sent to battle schools, where we scaled cliffs, swam rivers in full equipment, and learned how to crawl under live machine gun fire. But it was a slow process: it was to be more than three years before the British Army crossed the Channel again.

So, in my book, Captain Mainwaring and his friends carry two battle honours. First, they constituted a crucial distinction between us and the Low Countries, where the invading Germans had encountered no civilian resistance. The swift fate of Holland stayed in all our minds.

Later, they relieved the Army of countless tasks in defence of this island, leaving us free to train for battle. Formed in a hurry while we were being pitched neck and crop out of Europe, Dad's Army gradually took over holding the fort and so helped to pave the way back.

WAS THIS BOMBING REALLY NECESSARY?

*As a young soldier entering Bremen, W. F. Deedes saw the terrible effect
of Allied air raids. He says that while German historian Jörg Friedrich is
wrong to dismiss Churchill as a war criminal, his book raises questions of
lasting relevance*

Most people old enough to remember the German blitz on London
and the V1s and V2s that followed will dismiss as absurd the charge
of the German historian, Jörg Friedrich, that Winston Churchill was
a war criminal.

"Give it back to 'em, Winny!" they called in east London when
the prime minister did the rounds of destruction. Later on, with the
help of Bomber Command, he did just that.

Yet as one who as a soldier saw the consequences in German
cities of our remorseless saturation bombing, I do not think we can
wave aside Friedrich's request to look our past in the face. Ever since
the day I entered the city of Bremen with leading elements of
General Horrocks's 30 Corps, very close to the end of the war, and
saw the consequences of our fire-bombing, my mind has been torn
by what we did there.

We set the city alight with fire bombs and incinerated much of
the population in a single night. We gave Hamburg much the same
treatment, the results of which I saw later. One was by then pretty
hardened to the consequences of total war. I accepted the need to
destroy Hitler's Germany by every means at our disposal.

But the tiny corpses I saw unburied in Bremen, shrivelled by the
tremendous heat that the fire bombs had engendered did enter
doubts in my mind. Later, within weeks of the war ending, when I
took a long drive south to visit a battalion of our regiment in
Klagenfurt and saw valleys of destruction in some of Germany's main
cities, my doubts took root. Even though this was the most desperate
of wars, we had in most departments sought to uphold certain rules.

We did not shoot prisoners—not even after some of the Hitler

Jugend, boys of 14 and 15 conscripted late in the war, began to play foul; nor, under orders from the corps commander, did we loot or needlessly defile property.

But it is unnecessary to bring one's personal doubts into this argument. The way in which our establishment came to view the consequences of saturation bombing, after the war had ended, is evidence enough that Jörg Friedrich's case cannot be swept aside. He wants us to face up to what happened on the ground, after the bombs had left the plane, then to make up our minds how far we moved in the closing months of the war from warfare to the indiscriminate massacre of civilians.

There can be no argument that, as soon as the war ended, we had second thoughts about the bombers' part in it. As Max Hastings has expressed it in his book *Bomber Command*: "The men of the Army of Occupation were first awed, then increasingly dismayed, by the total devastation of Germany." That encompasses my own feelings.

Consider also our post-war treatment of Sir Arthur Harris, who had directed Bomber Command. He was offered no further employment in the RAF and left for South Africa at the end of 1945. His request for recognition of his command with a campaign medal was refused.

Churchill's proposal for an honour for Harris was rejected by his successor, Clem Attlee. Not until 1953 did Harris receive a baronetcy, a lower award than any other service leader received. How far had we ourselves become ashamed of what Sir Arthur Harris had done on our behalf?

There is no denying, as Hastings concedes, that in the final months of 1944 and the early months of 1945 the Allied strategic bomber forces played a dominant part in bringing the German economy to the point of collapse. But there was disagreement at the top as to how this was best brought about.

Sir Charles Portal, the chief of the air staff, saw Germany's oil production as the main target, while Bomber Harris, his insubordinate commander, sought the destruction of 60 of Germany's main cities.

Then we have to take into the reckoning the extent to which Stalin was pressing Churchill for everything it took to enfeeble Germany and its capacity to defy the Russian advance.

Why is the thinking Friedrich enjoins on us important now? I see enough conflict in different parts of the world to realise that the question of how far the means can be held to justify the end is with us still.

.   Are methods of war acceptable which inflict death and injury on civilians, disproportionate to their military value? That is an argument some of us address to the use of landmines.

We are entitled totally to disagree with Friedrich, but I do not think we can dismiss his book as a German whine. As long as nations go to war, it has lasting relevance.

NATURE'S BOUNTY HAS HEALED
THE WOUNDS

Today, only the war cemeteries in Normandy remind you that this was once a battlefield. Nature's bounty in this region of France has healed the wounds. Villages ravaged by fighting in the Normandy bridgehead have risen again. A beautiful summer day, lilac, wisteria, red and white chestnut in flower, cattle grazing peacefully and such stillness everywhere make it harder to remember how it was.

We took the road south-west from Courseulles-sur-Mer, where Canada's Winnipeg Rifles had landed on D-Day, 10 days before our battalion came in there, and stopped at a field outside a village I faintly remembered. An echo of my old company sergeant-major's voice early one morning broke in on my thoughts. "The men, sir, complain they can't get their sleep, sir."

"Oh, why not?" "Stink of the dead cattle, sir . . . it's terrible."

Until the recent sight of fat cattle knee deep in pasture jogged my memory, I had forgotten this ridiculous exchange soon after our arrival in the bridgehead. The bloated bodies of cattle, which when alive were the source of delicious cheeses, was a depressing feature of early days in Normandy.

So like the riflemen to grumble about the smell of rotting cattle but to make silly jokes about the German six-barrelled Nebelwerfer or "moaning Minnie" which if it caught you unawares in an open field was a very nasty weapon indeed. The familiar cry after such an episode lingers on: "Stretcher-bearers . . .!"

There is one clue to where fighting in Normandy was fiercest. I noticed it as we went through Tilly-sur-Seulles and Fontenay-le-Pesnel of unhappy memory, a few kilometres west of Caen. Almost every dwelling is post-war. There are not many ancient stone walls left standing in the villages.

We had a light time of it for 10 days after our arrival. The three tank regiments of 8th Armoured Brigade to which our motor battalion was attached were scattered through the bridgehead working with infantry divisions. By a closely guarded war secret their tanks had been able to swim in on D-Day to the surprise of the Germans and train their guns on the narrow slits from which German machineguns were firing. "Posting a letter," they called it, and it saved many lives. When we came in there was enough sniping and shelling to teach us to dig trenches and sleep underground; but it was a gentle inoculation.

Then on June 25 came the battle of Tessel wood. Our colonel delivered his orders in the middle of the night. There followed a long approach march in the dark through narrow lanes.

The first thing that struck me when light came was the amount of foliage knocked off the trees that lay in the roads. There must have been a big wind in the night, I thought, without it entering my head that German shells had done the damage. Then I passed the body of a German on the bank of a sunken road. It brought the mind sharply to attention.

Staring again at Tessel wood 60 years later in this silent quarter of the countryside, it was not easy to retrieve memories of the battle scene. We were in support of 49 Infantry Division which had been ordered to capture the village of Rauray. Our main resistance came from half-a-dozen Tiger tanks with an attendant party of German infantry well dug in.

My colonel seemed to think it was a moment to lead from the front. Emerging from a corner of this vast impenetrable wood, he strolled through a meadow, thrashing the hedges with his stick as if he were flushing game. "We'll show them, Bill," he said fiercely.

We were on a forward slope below the wood in view of an enemy not far away, some of whom were sensible enough to fire at us. "Colonel," I said breathlessly and only slightly shamefacedly, "if you get hit we shall all be in trouble." He was persuaded to let off steam under cover of the wood.

It was not a great day for our 12th King's Royal Rifle Corps. The attack by 49 Division we were protecting petered out and we were ordered to withdraw under cover of smoke laid by our gunners, the Essex Yeomanry. Our tenuous wireless communications had been picked off by enemy fire, so there was no way of telling where everyone was.

Until the smoke came down I lay flat in a field with half a dozen riflemen, with a feeling that German snipers were awaiting our first move and wondering how the hell we had landed ourselves in such a mess. It was raining. I had yet to learn what a large part of any battle is unprofitable. All things considered, our casualties were light. A company commander, five other officers and 19 NCOs and riflemen were wounded. One platoon commander had been killed. Of the 13 other ranks who were missing, nine were subsequently known to have died.

Nor was it a great day for our colonel who returned to England. "It was a valuable experience," we said to each other doubtfully and spent a quiet few days at Conde-sur-Seulles nearby, a village unscarred by war. But I had learned a lesson for the benefit of young officers and riflemen who joined us later to replenish the ranks.

The first battle is often the most dangerous, because you have not acquired the art of sensible self-preservation, of learning the difference between getting the job done and being foolhardy.

Why was Rauray so important to them, I mused, as we stopped the car and took a look at this innocent hamlet. War poses many questions like that to which 60 years later it is hard to find answers. But from the end of June and through July 1944 this relatively small area was very sensitive indeed. Because the Germans knew the Allied armies were getting ready to break out the fighting was heavy and continuous. The six British cemeteries which lie nearby testify to that. The sunken lanes and high hedges of Normandy made it unexpectedly difficult for all of us. It has opened up a lot since then, I observed, with more arable land being worked and fewer apple orchards. Ah, those orchards. They produced a strong brew of cider and an even stronger distillation called calvados. Denied their beer, the riflemen sought comfort from the cider when they could find it. "Keep them off the calvados, sergeant-major!" I said lightly. "Do my best, sir."

There seemed to have been a gap in higher command thinking, for none of us had expected to fight in the Normandy bocage. Tiny fields and narrow lanes seemed to favour the defenders. You could enter an orchard without knowing that a couple of Tiger tanks lay in waiting behind the hedge.

The German Tiger was a formidable machine. The biggest at 56 tons was twice the weight of the Sherman tank and carried 100 mm of frontal armour and an 88 mm gun. Living and working for the most part with a tank regiment, usually the 13/18 Royal Hussars, occasionally with the 4th/7th Royal Dragoon Guards, I came to admire the tank crews who fought from the lighter but slightly faster tank. Some had been "brewed up" more than once, but had escaped with their lives and gone back to battle with a new tank.

There were plenty of Shermans pouring out of American factories. "Tanks a million," as one of our newspapers expressed it. American citizens subscribed to fill the tanks with goodies before they left America—binoculars, sun glasses, candy, cigarettes, every comfort. It was not until a tank slipped through intact that we fathomed most of them were systematically robbed of their goodies in the London docks.

In mid-July we took over part of the American line east of Caumont and occupied well-dug positions around Fontenay-le-Pesnil. We occupied ourselves by sending out patrols because the Germans were in some strength opposite us. Walking cautiously through the wood one evening I met a German corporal. Oddly, it seemed like meeting any stranger in a wood and mercifully the corporal must have felt the same. We turned aside without a shot fired. "Not an adventure to say too much about," I decided.

"It seems unimaginable now," I said to our photographer, Abbie Trayler-Smith. We sat by the big Fontenay-le-Pesnil village pond on which ducks swam and two swans preened themselves.

"I think," I said to her glancing up at a cloudless sky and eyeing the colours everywhere, "it's the weather that is making it so hard to relate 'then' to 'now'." The weather in Normandy during June 1944 was wretched. Eisenhower had to postpone D-Day for 24 hours because of rough seas.

On June 19 there had sprung up the worst summer storm in the Channel for 40 years. For three days waves 8ft high lashed the artificial Mulberry harbours. Ships were sunk. Some 140,000 tons of supplies were lost. Although only whispers of this reached us, it was depressing.

But life with the 13/18 Hussars was exhilarating. They all seemed braver than I felt. The colonel they had landed with had been wounded and for the Normandy battles the Earl of Feversham was in charge. His calm in all conditions was encouraging. Only small things troubled him. He did not take kindly to the tank, mainly because a tank crew tends to live, rest and eat together. The thought of officers eating meals with their crew disturbed Sim Feversham's Edwardian mind. If the battle quietened down, he would call his officers in, order a few small items of regimental silver to be laid out and eat an evening meal with them.

"I do not like my officers living 'mucko-chummo'," he would say. That sounds alarmingly old-fashioned now, but it was not 60 years ago. It was seen as a way of maintaining regimental discipline. Sim in the field passed on one piece of advice that has influenced my life ever since. "Any fool can be uncomfortable," he was fond of saying.

As the British cemeteries in Normandy have just reminded me, we had it easier than the infantry divisions, such as 50 Division from Tees and Tyne which Montgomery used for his main assaults until there was almost nothing left of them, 49 Division with whom we fought in Normandy and, later, 43 Wessex Division.

Jerusalem cemetery on the road that runs south of Bayeux towards Chouain is the smallest of all the 18 Commonwealth war cemeteries in Normandy. We spent time there, looking at the 48 graves, all of them decked with flowers.

I gave our cemetery at Bayeux, which I have seen before, a miss this time. There are 3,843 graves there, and although Normandy's cemeteries are mercifully smaller than the great monuments of the First World War, Bayeux where some of the names stir memories is a bit overwhelming. When you reach old age it is disquieting to be reminded how many young men in their early 20s and on the threshold of life died in Normandy.

I sat down in the Jerusalem cemetery, looked at the summer sky and the flowers round the graves and set my mind on finding a consoling thought. Well, I reflected, their mothers will have missed them sadly at the time; but they mourn the loss no more, for they too have passed on. It was such a long time ago, you see.

BRITISH POLITICS

THE MAIN POLITICAL DRAMA when I began journalism on the *Morning Post* in 1931 was the future of India. Stanley Baldwin, who later succeeded Ramsay MacDonald as Prime Minister, was anxious to move ahead with a long-standing promise to India to grant independence. Winston Churchill, with a minority in the Conservative party, stoutly opposed such a move. This controversy ran through the early part of the 1930s and as a result I became closely acquainted with Winston Churchill and his son, Randolph, who fought a couple of disastrous by-elections on this issue.

In the end, Mr R. A. Butler, as number two to the Secretary for India, Sir Samuel Hoare, made his name by piloting through a bill of 350 clauses granting India independence. It was a major issue, not only for India, but for Churchill as well, because it led many people to question Churchill's judgement. It was important also because, once India was granted independence, the cornerstone of what was still the Empire disappeared and it had its bearing on the demands for independence which came from so many directions after the Second World War, partly explaining why we had to act more hastily than was sensible.

Perhaps the most interesting thing that has happened in my time in politics has been the development of the Labour Party. In 1931 Ramsay MacDonald's Labour cabinet was falling under the pressure of the world financial crisis. Through the 1930s until the war I reported the activities of the coalition government created at the behest of King George V, which, under different prime ministers, ran until 1945.

I was among those least surprised by the outcome of the 1945 election. I'd had the good fortune during the 1930s to see a lot of England – the collapse of our main industries and the growth of what we then called the distressed areas. I saw a lot of poverty. I was close by when King Edward VIII, in almost the last speech he made, declared from South Wales, "Something must be done." So I realised that in 1945 people would vote for something different.

I remember the Atlee government very well, and I doubt whether in any recent times a government has had a heavier load to bear. We were short of almost everything, and the Labour Party had a hard struggle to keep its head above the waters created by a country disappointed by the fruits of victory. Thereafter the Labour Party became a catalyst for change. I think that Clement Atlee's drive for the nationalisation of industry was a mistake and lent itself to lots of critical journalism.

The Labour party's line on reform was more interesting. During the 1960s, censorship was relaxed, homosexuality ceased to be a crime and we lightened up in a number of directions, and I doubt that we would have done this without the influence of the Labour Party. On the whole they made more exciting journalism than the Conservatives, until Mrs Thatcher arrived. She ended an era in which we were not quite sure how best to play our economy. I became editor of the *Daily Telegraph* just before she was appointed leader and I was there throughout her term of office. I see it now, through the eyes of a journalist, as a highly controversial, exciting and at times revealing period of politics. Since then, the Conservative Party has been in the doldrums and the Labour Party the ascendant. That may be about to change.

I've come to value the arts of a parliamentary democracy and to see the value of changing the sort of government you have without turbulence and without bloodshed. I've visited so many countries in which democracy does not exist, and I remain doubtful whether it will become universally acceptable. What I am sure of at the end of a career spent largely in politics is that democracy is always worth striving for. There should be no giving up – not even in Iraq.

May 1933

YOUTH AND THE "YES-MEN"

India White Paper Condemned

A SHOCK FOR OFFICIALDOM

"Revolt" Carries Day After Big Battle

The Government's supporters of abdication in India received a shock on Saturday when the Junior Imperial League denounced the Government's White Paper after a spirited debate.

Meanwhile the revolt against the Government's policy is growing in the country. At Canterbury, on Saturday, reference was made to the manner in which Bombay Municipalities are boycotting British goods in their contracts.

The Junior Imperial League, that youthful but hitherto reliable stronghold of official Conservatism, have renounced their leaders and condemned the Government's White Paper on India.

At a crowded session of their annual Conference held in London on Saturday after an hour's heated debate, they succeeded in passing a resolution of revolt against the abdicationists by an overwhelming majority.

One uses the word "succeeded" advisedly. They were met with the eloquent—in one case, almost passionate—appeals from such staunch and distinguished supporters of the Government as Lord Castle Stewart and Lord Dufferin and Ava; they were thwarted (almost) by an official "amendment" calculated to obscure the clear issue of the debate; solemnly warned of the awful results of their contemplated folly; and they defied these factors in the presence of two Government private secretaries (Mr Geoffrey Lloyd and Lord Hinchingbrooke) and their leader, Lord Stonehaven.

Possibly it was as well that—as announced earlier in the day—the Junior Imperial League are now more or less financially independent. At least they could no longer be accused of having bitten the hand that feeds them.

The Test

Mr. Randolph Churchill, who moved the resolution: "That this Conference believes that no attempt should be made to set up a Federal Responsible Government for all India until, or unless, the experiment of provincial Home Rule has been proved to be a success in actual practice over a number of years," made first move in the campaign of revolt.

And if the applause which first greeted him was taken by his opponents as a personal tribute rather than sympathy for the cause which he was about to plead, the cheers which followed his speech can have left no doubt as to the temper of the Conference.

"We are told," he said, "that in passing this resolution we should embarrass the Government, but it is my firm conviction that it is more important to save our Indian Empire for the Crown than it is to save the National Government."

Only after he had taken his seat did officialdom endeavour to assert itself. With the air of one who has made a sudden and important discovery, the Chairman (Lord Burghley) offered the meeting an "alternative" in the shape of an "amendment."

Sprung on Meeting

Mr. Churchill rose to a point of order. He questioned the legality of such a proceeding. "Why," he demanded, "has this amendment been sprung upon the meeting in this fashion?" How was it that it had failed to appear on the agenda?

Apologies were made. Mr. Churchill was quietened, and with the uneasy feeling among Mr. Churchill's supporters that they were being systematically muddled, the meeting settled down to hear the opposition. They were treated, by the earlier opponents of the resolution, at any rate, to an irrelevant and highly entertaining (but not particularly original) comparison between personal qualities of their respective leaders.

"Was it not Mr. Baldwin who had recently said that it was much easier, much less hard work to go about the country trying to split the Conservative Party?"

". . . Mr. Churchill—a better destroyer than constructor."

"Mr. Baldwin—a Conservative born and bred and . . . not a man who was content to flirt with almost every political party in the country." (Cheers.)

Lord Castle Stewart, who confined himself to the question of India itself, tried new tactics. "Will those members of the audience who have been to India hold up their hands," he asked. Four embarrassed hands were raised. "Half a dozen at the most," said Lord Castle Stewart magnanimously.

And would those who had read the four important reports on India from end to end do likewise? Satisifed with the abysmal ignorance of his opponents, he continued in triumph. His five minutes of impassioned, yet fair appeal, received a good hearing from a conference beginning to weary of personal animosities. Lord Dufferin and Ava, calmer, but no less convincing, followed him.

As mover of the original resolution, Mr. Randolph Churchill had the last word.

"I do not propose," he began, "to deal with the remarks concerning my father." He might, he felt, do better by reading to the meeting the "long and complicated" amendment, of which they had heard so little.

The Amendment

"That this Conference" (read Mr. Churchill scornfully), "recognising the paramount importance of the Indian Constitutional problem and the need of a constructive policy which will provide the necessary safeguards for our Imperial interests, and at the same time fulfil our pledges to the Indian people, welcomes the appointment of a Joint Select Committee representing both Houses of Parliament, whose function it will be to frame a considered plan of reform as the basis of a Bill to be subsequently presented to Parliament."

Mr. Churchill dwelt on the amendment. Had it, he mused, any connection with the appearance at the meeting of Lord Stonehaven, who, he had noticed, arrived round the time of its "discovery." Could it be in any way connected with the Conservative Central Office?

Too late did Lord Burghley assure the meeting that the amendment had not arrived with Lord Stonehaven; that it had been received "late the night before." The meeting, worked on to a pitch of excitement, scented danger, and in a subsequent vote the amendment was summarily dealt with.

It was impossible to judge the precise result of the vote on the resolution. Suffice that it satisfied the most cantankerous of the Government supporters that they had suffered so obvious a defeat that no division or count of hands need be called for to emphasise it.

February 1935

WAVERTREE BY-ELECTION: MR. CHURCHILL ON HIS PROGRAMME

Square Deal for Lancashire

NATIONAL CREDIT: FREER USE

"Live Conservative Party"

THE CANDIDATES

Mr. Randolph Churchill (Con).
Mr. James Platt (Nat. Con).
Mr. T. Artro Morris (Lib).
Mr. J. J. Cleary (Soc).

The voting at the General Election in October, 1931 was:

R. Nall Cain (C) 33,476
G. G. Clark (Lab) 9,503
Con. majority 23,973

Polling—February 6.

LIVERPOOL, TUESDAY

Mr. Randolph Churchill to-day issued his election address to Wavertree.

Emphasising his opposition to the Government of India Bill, he set before the electors the five constructive aims for which he is fighting this campaign.

(1) A square deal for the cotton industry of Lancashire and the shipping of Merseyside.
(2) An Air Force strong enough to restore safety from invasion.
(3) A more vigorous programme of slum clearance and rehousing that will really grapple with the problem of overcrowding and also safeguard the property owner from confiscation.
(4) A freer use of our National Credit on public works to relieve

97

unemployment at home and to develop our possessions beyond the seas.

(5) A live Conservative Party appealing to youth, and served by youth, and free from the taint of Socialism, and independent of caucus influence.

Referring to his candidature, Mr Randolph Churchill writes:

"I come before you as the Conservative candidate for the Wavertree Division and as the opponent of Socialism in all its insidious forms. I will gladly support a Government upholding Conservative doctrines which welcomes men of good will from all parties, and opens high office to proved ability and patriotism. I am opposed to any pretence of National Government, which really means a whittling down of Conservative principles. These are not the times for compromise upon essentials or when statesmen should melt down their convictions to produce a sham unity. Such a National Government would not be above party, but beneath it. It would become a fraud upon the public; and a fraud which, when perceived, will produce an electoral disaster."

India Bill and Lancashire

On the subject of India and Lancashire, Mr Churchill continues:

"The worst feature in the present National Government is its intention to force through Parliament the present India Constitution Bill. It is the height of folly to set up a responsible Home Rule Parliament for all India before even provincial Home Rule has been proved to work. If I am returned your member, I shall vote against any irrevocable transference of British Sovereignty over that vast continent, which British genius during the last two centuries has rescued from war and anarchy.

No one would claim that Lancashire interests should predominate over national or Imperial interests; but what Lancashire suffers to-day Britain and the Empire will suffer to-morrow. By caucus methods, by wire pulling, by all sorts of subtle influences, some, no doubt, quite innocent, others less so, this great County Palatine and its interests have been reduced to a cipher in national affairs."

On Britain's peril from the air Mr. Churchill writes:

"We are the highest taxed people in the world and bear greater responsibilities than any other nation. If we are to sleep soundly in our beds we must possess the largest and finest air force in the world."

The address concludes:

"I come to you with an offer of service, which if you so decide, shall be lifelong. Never will I press your interests beyond the bounds of what is just and what is fair to the nation and Empire. Never will I agree to those rights and interests being neglected, ignored, discounted or otherwise shamefully cast away."

CONSERVATIVE SUPPORT

Mr. Churchill today received more offers of support from prominent Conservatives. Sir William Wayland, Conservative member for Canterbury, has written asking the India Defence League publicly to announce that he associates himself with those members supporting Mr. Churchill. In this letter he declares:

'I look upon this election as a test fight for Lancashire on the India policy of the Government. If there should be a dearth of speakers I should be pleased to come to Liverpool to speak on Mr. Randolph Churchill's behalf.'

Letters of support have also been received from Sir Michael O'Dwyer and Mr. J. R. Remer, Conservative M.P. for Macclesfield. Mr. C. E. G. Emmott, Conservative M.P. for Springburn, Mr. John Slater, Conservative M.P. for Eastbourne, and Mr. J. H. L. Cowin, the youngest member of the Manx House of Keys, have all offered to speak for Mr. Churchill.

Mr. Platt, the National Conservative candidate, is still, apparently, confident that Mr. Churchill will not seriously affect his position. "Our canvass shows," he said today, "that Mr. Churchill's influence is very superficial."

Mr. Churchill, for his part, intends to ignore Mr. Platt, and to concentrate upon the Socialist.

Mr. Cleary, however, would like to concentrate upon Mr. Platt. "The National Government is in the dock," he declares. "Labour will again be justified, and its policy vindicated by a great victory on February 6."

The Socialist candidate has received a message of good wishes from Mr. George Lansbury, who asserts "The National Government stands condemned in the eyes of all decent people for its inhuman treatment of the unemployed."

Mr. Morris, the Liberal candidate, without greatly disturbing any of the other three candidates, is finding little issues with which to interest himself in a quiet way. He asserts that, to those in the know, Mr. Cleary's election address is "the scream of the contest," and boldly added, "give me a pint of the honest to goodness (although foolish) policy of Mr. Randolph Churchill, rather than a gallon of Labour's political jugglery." People are asking Mr. Morris to state his reactions to Mr. Lloyd George's New Deal. Mr. Morris is an ardent Free Trader.

POLITICAL WARFARE IN THE EAST END

Fascist, Communist and Jew—How the Dangerous "Line-up"
Came About

The events of Sunday afternoon in Whitechapel, Stepney, and Bethnal Green again offered a disturbing glimpse of the bitterness and hatred which six months of active political and racial strife have generated in the East End of London.

Whatever the outside world has hitherto believed to be the significance of recent disorders in the East End, Sunday afternoon must finally remove all doubt as to the perils, and yet more perilous possibilities, of the present situation.

East London to-day is threatened by open social warfare. Political passions have reached a pitch when ordinary, apparently decent citizens, are ready to vilify, spit upon, and injure their neighbours. Social existence is being disrupted. Political and racial differences have swollen out of all proportion to their importance. Simultaneously an element of hooliganism, supposed to have died in the East End since the War, has been resurrected and let loose; and that is an element capable of adding death to injury. The East End is in danger of suffering far more than a few smashed windows and broken heads which in themselves may appear to be of small significance.

Until now the most important party in the dispute has remained strangely quiescent. To their credit, the Jews have suffered humiliation and insult without retaliation. But they cannot be expected much longer to remain unmoved to definite action. Their patience is exhausted, and there are signs that they are preparing to strike back. Only the patience of their leaders restrains them; if and when they join battle, open warfare in the East End of London will be declared.

The position at present may be simply stated. It is some months since the Fascist organisation of Great Britain decided that the East End of London offered particularly good ground on which to stage opposition at the Municipal Elections next March. With extraordinary efficiency a strong political campaign in the East End of London

was organised. Four headquarters were established, embracing
Whitechapel, Bethnal Green, Limehouse and Stepney.

It would be foolish to deny that the Fascists have made great
headway in their campaign. In an astonishingly short space of time a
corps of well-trained speakers—whose histrionic abilities exceed
those of seven out of ten members of Parliament—backed by several
hundred voluntary, subscribing workers, and aided by a small fleet of
motor-vans equipped with microphones and loudspeakers, have
spread the doctrine of Fascism far and wide through the East End.
These speakers and their helpers have not lacked courage in penetrating the heart of opposition.

On the grounds that it is inseparable from their policy, this
exposition of their policy has been accompanied by the fiercest and
bitterest platform attacks against the Jewish race. Anti-Semitism in
the East End of London is as old as East London itself. With so
great a volume of business in the hands of Jews, so much trade
conducted exclusively by Jews, so many shops, stores, and street stalls
in Jewish hands, it is inevitable that such feeling should exist in some
degrees. The Fascists have exploited and inflamed these feelings.
There are few better places than the East End of London for such
exploitation.

In addition to this natural "advantage" the Fascists have found
the political soil of Bethnal Green and elsewhere particularly suited
to their needs. Politics in Bethnal Green have changed like the wind
in recent years. The political weather-vane has swung in turn from
the reddest Communism to the palest brand of Liberalism; from
mild Conservatism back to Socialism. Whatever party is in power,
an unusually high proportion of malcontents can always be found to
oppose it.

From these two sources—Anti-Semitism and political malcon-
tentment—the Fascists have gained many of their recruits.

The Communist Party is never slow to exploit a political situation. It used the hunger-marchers and unemployed three years
ago to intimidate the National Government; and upon the Jewish–
Fascist differences in the East End, it seeks again to grind a new and
powerful axe. Lacking the militant organisation to unite against the
Fascist attack, the less responsible members of the Jewish community
have fallen easy prey to the clutches of the Communist Party. One
of the more disquieting features of the present situation is the way in
which the Jews are swelling the ranks of the Communist Party in

East London. The Communists can supply the organisation and driving power; the Jews may supply the money and manpower for an Anti-Fascist drive.

Thus the political line-up is complete. Out of the political turmoil which results from these unhealthy combinations has sprung the worst element of all. In the shadows of political differences, the hooligan has seized his opportunity to run amok.

The men who smash the Jewish shop windows in Mile End-road, who terrorise the streets of Stepney, who cast stones at policemen are not genuine members of the Fascist Party, any more than the hoodlums—who laid low Blackshirts with barbed bludgeons and iron tubing in Royal Mint-street—are passionate defenders of the Jewish faith or the Communist cause.

Few uniformed or active Fascists would dare openly to strike a Jew. They would receive as harsh treatment from their own organisation for so doing as from the hands of justice. The average practising Jew would not dream of assaulting a Fascist. The real Communists know well just how far disorder may be carried with impunity, and they stop short of physical violence.

Over and above the material and physical damage which they inflict, these hooligans, who have no political or racial allegiance, greatly aggravate the general situation. Each faction, anxious to disown them, attributes their activities to the other side.

The authorities now have a hard task before them to quell this accumulated turmoil of recent months. To ban the Fascists would almost certainly aggravate strife, for by now the Fascists have enough supporters in East London to fight bitterly for their existence. Yet further to increase police protection will prove an expensive undertaking, and would fail to approach the roots of the problem.

Assuredly, however, whatever is to be done must be done soon. Every day now unchecked insult and disorder inflict some damage on the life of East London. Each day this damage becomes harder to repair.

May 1937

MR. BALDWIN'S LAST FIVE DAYS
AS PREMIER

MR. CHAMBERLAIN'S CABINET RECONSTRUCTION TASK

A MEMORABLE WEEK IN PARLIAMENT

To-day's reassembly of Parliament, followed by publication of the eagerly-awaited Finance Bill, containing an amended version of Mr. Neville Chamberlain's National Defence Tax, will open a week in Westminster of outstanding political interest and importance.

Only five days remain of Mr. Baldwin's career as Prime Minister, Leader of the House of Commons and of the Conservative Party. His departure on Friday from active political life, accompanied by Mr. Ramsay MacDonald, with whom he has shared the last fourteen years of Premiership, and the Ministerial changes which must follow, will overshadow all else in Parliament until the beginning of June.

A CROWDED DIARY

The course of events, from to-day onwards, will be as follows:

TO-DAY—Reassembly of Parliament at 3 o'clock; publication of Finance Bill.

The Civil List, containing allowances for the King and Members of the Royal Family, will be debated in the Commons.

TO-MORROW—The Prime Minister will probably announce the Government's decision in regard to the raising of M.P.s' salaries.

Debate on the Civil List continued.

The King and Queen dine with Mr. and Mrs. Baldwin at No. 10, Downing Street.

THURSDAY—Mr. Baldwin's last full day in the House of Commons.

FRIDAY—The Prime Minister will go to the King at Buckingham Palace, resign, and formally recommend his successor; Mr. Neville Chamberlain will follow him.

The new Government will be formed.

104

Next Monday a Conservative Party meeting, attended by M.P.s, Peers, and candidates, will be held during the morning, to pay formal tribute to Mr. Baldwin, and to appoint Mr. Neville Chamberlain as Leader of the Conservative Party.

A change of Leadership, involving substantial alterations in the Government, would in any event be preceded by a week of exceptional activity and excitement in the House of Commons.

NATIONAL ENTHUSIASM

In this instance, there is a curious combination of circumstances:

The fact that there has been long notice of Mr. Baldwin's retirement, and the knowledge that he has given of his best in the last few months; the well-timed delivery of two brilliant valedictory speeches; and, not least, his own particular qualities and record, will arouse very deep emotion throughout the House of Commons.

As he promised, Mr. Baldwin is leaving in his own time, in his own way; the time and manner of his departure will be memorable.

MR. CHAMBERLAIN

Mr. Neville Chamberlain enters the fullest week of his career. To-morrow and Wednesday will cover a period of considerable anxiety for him when industry and the House of Commons will be reflecting on and reacting to his amended National Defence Contribution scheme.

There is little doubt that substantial alterations in the original plans made known on Budget Day have been effected.

Some were publicly hinted at by Mr. Chamberlain before the House adjourned; others have been worked out since in consultation with leading industrialists, Treasury officials and Government advisers.

While it will be found that the Chancellor has kept the principle of his plan intact, he has also removed or amended many of the objections to which prominent economists and industrialists were expressing opposition.

To-day and to-morrow, moreover, Mr. Chamberlain will be in charge of the Civil List resolutions. Throughout the week, the Imperial Conference will be meeting regularly; and since there is a general desire to press rapidly ahead with discussions, after an interrupted opening week, both the Prime Minister and the Chancellor of the Exchequer will be compelled to devote some hours at meetings of the principal delegates.

Mr. Chamberlain will have little time to spare, therefore, between now and the end of the week, when he succeeds Mr. Baldwin and announces the formation of his new Ministry.

THE NEW CHANCELLOR

Even as Mr. Chamberlain's succession to Mr. Baldwin has, during recent months, been taken for granted, so, it is now generally assumed Sir John Simon, Home Secretary and Liberal National, will become Chancellor of the Exchequer. This news leaked out, by accident or design, some weeks ago; and since little opposition to the idea has been shown by Conservative members, the appointment now appears to be a certainty.

Mr. Chamberlain will have at least three major Cabinet posts to fill. Mr. Ramsay MacDonald is leaving the Cabinet as Lord President of the Council; whatever else may happen to Mr. Walter Runciman, he will not remain at the Board of Trade; a new Home Secretary has to be found. Contrary to earlier expectations, I learn, Lord Hailsham will not resign from the Woolsack. His health is now much improved.

Ever since Sir John Simon's promotion has been known, Sir Kingsley Wood has been most confidently suggested as his successor. But many believe that Mr. Chamberlain will be unwilling to interrupt his unquestionable success at the Ministry of Health. In well-informed quarters there is a strong suggestion that Sir Thomas Inskip will end his association with Defence to become Home Secretary. In this event it is probable that Sir Samuel Hoare would leave the Admiralty to become Minister for Co-Ordination of Defence, and that Earl De La Warr, National Labour, will become First Lord.

DEFENCE MINISTRIES

The view is held by some, however, that Mr. Chamberlain might be prepared to drop the position of Minister for Co-Ordination of Defence, which, it is held, fulfilled a useful purpose during the initial stages of the rearmament programme. Such a decision, however, is scarcely credible, but in any case it will cause no surprise if all three Defence Ministers—Sir Samuel Hoare, Lord Swinton (Air Minister), and Mr. Duff Cooper (War Minister)—remain in their present positions.

Mr. Runciman's position is held to be one of the principal factors in the reconstruction. It is possible that he will go to the House of Lords, but this would not necessarily entail his departure from the Cabinet. If he went, Mr. Chamberlain would find it extremely hard to maintain the National Liberal representation in the Cabinet. If he remains, it will most likely be, I understand, as Lord President of the Council, in succession to Mr. MacDonald. This post would give him the freedom from active departmental politics for which he has expressed a desire, and would not be affected by his absence from the House of Commons.

It is strongly felt that if Mr. Chamberlain appoints a liberal (Sir John Simon) to be Chancellor of the Exchequer, he will require a Conservative at the Board of Trade. Sir Samuel Hoare has been put forward as a likely candidate—there was a suggestion that he and Mr. Runciman might exchange positions—but the strongest body of opinion is in favour of Lt.-Col. Colville. He is now Financial Secretary to the Treasury, an acknowledged stepping stone to Cabinet rank, and a position previously held by Mr. Morrison, Minister of Agriculture.

Minor Posts Surprises

There will be a number of minor posts to be filled, and it is here that the biggest surprises of the new Ministry may come. It has been decided, I learn, that Captain David Margesson shall continue as the Government's Chief Whip. He has held this position since November, 1931, and those who know the amount of work he has done behind the scenes during the last five years appreciate Mr. Chamberlain's difficulty in finding a comparable successor.

Captain Euan Wallace is most likely to follow Sir George Penny, created a peer in the Honours List, as the Government's second Whip. A Liberal National Whip will also have to be found to replace the late Sir James Blindell.

There is reason to believe that Sir Philip Sassoon will leave the House of Commons at the time of the reconstruction, when he will be offered a seat in the House of Lords; Captain Harold Balfour is being wildly mentioned for the vacancy, which would then fall for an Under-Secretary of State for Air. Mr. A. Lennox Boyd

(Conservative), Mr. Harold Nicolson (National Labour), and Captain Dugdale (Conservative), who has been Parliamentary Private Secretary to Mr. Baldwin since 1935, are the three members now outside the Government who are thought to be the most likely candidates for promotion.

WHITEHALL REBUILDING PLAN STOPPED

"TOO GREAT A TARGET FOR AIR ATTACK"

CIVIL SERVICE REHOUSING DILEMMA

All work in connection with the Government's £2,250,000 scheme for building a great block of offices on the site of Montagu House, in Whitehall, has been stopped.

It will be announced very shortly that plans for the new building have been "postponed." It is not expected that work will be resumed.

This surprising decision, it is understood, has been taken in the interests of London's defence from possible air attack, the problem of which is now under constant and anxious consideration.

The new building, when completed, would have formed one of Whitehall's greatest landmarks from the air, as well as from the ground. It is not thought expedient at the present time to spend £2,250,000 in constructing a building which would inevitably attract and guide aerial attack to the very heart of the Government of the Empire.

Rooms for 5,400

How great a target the new block of buildings would be may be judged from the description of its form published a year ago. The building was to be 550 feet long, with a breadth of 300 feet at Horse Guards-avenue end, tapering to 209 feet at the Richmond-terrace end.

It would have been faced with Portland stone, and built to the height of 128 feet. This compares with the Home Office, 89 feet high; the War Office, 82 feet; New Scotland Yard, 108 feet; and Shell-Mex House, 152 feet in height.

It was proposed, moreover, to house in the new block four vital Departments of the Government—the Air Ministry, the Board of Trade, the Ministry of Transport and the Ministry of Labour. About

5,400 Civil Servants would have been accommodated under the one roof.

The future housing of the personnel of these Departments is now being carefully reconsidered. In deciding this matter certain obvious difficulties arise. It is clearly undesirable that such important offices should be far from Westminster and the centre of public affairs. At the same time, the present accommodation is woefully inadequate.

FAR-FLUNG OFFICES

In the permanent buildings in Whitehall there is seating space for 10,000 Civil Servants out of 21,000 who should be there. The remaining 11,000 are spread over an area of about three-quarters of a mile.

One of the greatest advantages of the new block would have been that the Air Ministry, at present as far away as Kingsway, would have been brought nearer the Admiralty and the War Office, thus greatly assisting co-operation between the three defence departments.

It will be recalled that the old Metropole Hotel in Northumber-land-avenue was to have been used as temporary accommodation for the Ministries of Transport and Labour during the period of demolition and rebuilding.

A few small departments have already found their way there. The Ministry of Transport was to have moved at the end of last year. The change-over has not taken place, and at the moment there is no prospect of an early move.

24 YEARS PLANNING

The new Government offices would have taken 10 years to complete. The building itself was to cost £1,750,000, to which £1,500,000 was added by the cost of land and other contingencies. The annual cost would have been £100,000 compared with the £125,000 now spent on the rents of buildings which were to be vacated.

The scheme was contemplated as long ago as 1912, when an Act was passed authorising the erection of new Government offices in Whitehall. In 1931 the Royal Fine Arts Commission approved a scheme which was to cost £2,215,000 and provide accommodation for 7,500 persons.

Two years later the Office of Works invited the Royal Institute of British Architects to prepare a list of ten architects from which a final selection could be made.

Plans for the present scheme were eventually drawn up at the end of 1934 by Mr. E. Vincent Harris.

Not until March of last year, 25 years after the scheme was first conceived, were the final proposals approved and published.

WHITEHALL AMENITIES

The plans had been carefully thought out with a view to preserving the dignity and amenities of the neighbourhood. The Embankment front of the offices was to be parallel with the Embankment wall, and the ground between the building and the Embankment road would have been laid out as gardens. In Whitehall the block was to be laid well back from the thoroughfare, so that the Banqueting Hall, the Royal United Service Institution and Gwydyr House were not affected.

It was planned to erect the building in two sections. The first half would have been completed by 1941, and the whole structure ready by 1946.

Provision was made for the whole of the proposed site, part of which forms a section of the Crown Estate, to be vested in the Office of Works. Payment was to be made to the Commissioners of Crown Lands by annuities spreading over a period of 30 years.

STATE'S GRIP ON OVER EIGHT MILLION ACRES

When the Socialists faced the future in 1945 nationalisation of the land appeared to receive only a sidelong glance.

"Labour," we were told, "believes in land nationalisation and will work towards it, but as a first step the State and the local authorities must have wider and speedier powers to acquire land for public purposes wherever the public interest so requires."

That was the election pledge. Some of the Left Wing were dissatisfied by it. They felt that this blueprint for land lacked the bolder, sweeping lines drawn round the basic industries. They feared land might escape the treatment promised for coal, transport, steel, and so on.

From the Right Wing—among those who thought about it seriously—it looked as though land nationalisation, if it came at all, must be a matter for a problematical second term of Socialist office.

Left and Right were wrong. Socialism has fulfilled, indeed exceeded, this particular election promise, and to a degree hardly yet appreciated by supporters or opponents. Today, as figures here will show, about one-sixth of the countryside has come, or is about to come, under State control. More is under the hand of local authorities.

The "first step" promised in 1945 has been taken so effectively that central and local government can today speedily and legally acquire what they want of the remaining five-sixths.

A fair analogy would be a bath, linked by taps and pipes to a main water tank. The tank's contents represent the 50m. open acres of Great Britain. The bath's contents represent nationalised land.

Many of the connecting pipes were laid piecemeal by the wartime Coalition. The Socialist Government has built some more of wider bore and added a pair of highly efficient taps. One is marked "State" and the other "Local authorities." Both are running in fast.

Let us first examine the bath, already one-sixth full. Measuring its contents exactly is difficult because they spring from so many hidden sources. We can, however, account in hard figures for between 8m. and 9m. acres.

Leading contributors are the Forestry Commission, created in 1919. Their recent annual report accounts for 1,440,580 acres in State hands.

To this may soon be added 436,000 acres (15.5 per cent. of all private woodlands). That is the area that 821 private owners have promised to consider offering under the dedication scheme. These 436,000 acres are not, of course, State property, but an owner who has dedicated his woods and fails to fulfil his obligations can be dispossessed.

In the three years 1948–51 the Commission aim to acquire another 626,000 acres. Their possessions, interests and expectations, therefore, total 2,502,580 acres.

Then come the Services seeking, on the admission of their White Paper, a final settlement for 702,000 acres (compared with 252,000 before the war and 11.5m. during the war).

The lion's share of 648,000 acres goes to the War Office. More men under training, longer-range weapons and the use of live ammunition are three factors explaining this tremendous increase.

On top of this are 325,000 acres wanted for "other purposes." About 148,000 of them comprise R.A.F. airfields. Another 100,000 are needed for accommodation and stores held by the Ministry of Supply.

County Agricultural Committees on March 31 controlled or farmed 478,297 acres. Of these 354,609 acres were requisitioned. The rest was still requisitioned or owned by the Services and was being farmed by arrangements with the county committees.

Fourth on the list, surprisingly, are the National Coal Board. There is a touch of youthful pride in this observation, taken from their annual report:

> By the end of the year the listing of all the Board's assets could not be completed—it was a process like the making of the Domesday Book—but the Board had a reasonably good idea of the size and scope of their inheritance.

In addition to 1,400 collieries, 141,000 houses and 2,000 farmhouses and cottages—to say nothing of several country mansions—

this "inheritance" included 225,149 acres of land taken over by the Board, comprising 1,806 freehold, leased or tenanted farms.

The Coal Board also hold 31,600 acres of land for opencast mining. Between now and 1951 50,000 acres more are wanted for the same purpose.

It might seem ungracious to include in these figures the 142,000 acres held under the admirable stewardship of the National Trust. Mr. Dalton, however, linked the Trust to the State in 1946. He doubled the Jubilee appeal fund with taxpayers' money, and associated the Trust with the National Land Fund.

So far the fund, conceived in the Budget of 1946, contributes only a small total, but it promises well. About 40,000 acres have gone to the State from owners who chose, under Mr. Dalton's arrangements, to pay death duties in suitable land rather than by cheque.

Since the fund started with £50m., from which the Treasury is squared for the loss of death duty revenue, it must be regarded as a most promising child of an acquisitive State. Taxation, death duties and the bleak outlook for landowners suggest that it will wax fat.

Crown lands, totalling 250,000 acres, may be added without comment. The Duchies of Cornwall and Lancaster are excluded.

Now we come to the New Towns. Their prospective acreage has not been stated. From two sources of calculation, however, we may estimate 100,000 acres under this head. The original plan was to move 1,250,000 people. A figure of 12 persons to the acre was mentioned.

Again, there were to be 20 towns. Their average sizes—Welwyn Garden (4,260), Harlow (6,714), Hemel Hempstead (5,500)—indicate that 5,000 acres apiece would be a fair guess.

The total at present is 4,846,626 acres—far from exhaustive, but all attributable to official sources. It omits such obvious unknown quantities as the project for building 1,000 miles of double-track state highways, land incidentally acquired by other nationalised industries, and the airfields under the Ministry of Civil Aviation. There are more than 40 of these, demanding longer and longer runways for larger and larger aircraft. London Airport alone swallows 4,600 acres.

No report has yet been received from the Land Commission, established under the Agriculture Act of 1947. So far 49,000 acres of land have been placed at their disposal for management. Their first public action was to reconnoitre Romney Marsh (50,000 acres) with a view to State acquisition. It appears that their future possessions will be limited only by the difficulty of finding enough staff to manage them.

Clauses in the 1947 Agriculture Act—contested by Conservatives at the time—empower the Minister to acquire not only ill-farmed land, but any land which he considers needs more capital than the private owner has at his disposal.

One of the largest figures—that of land in the hands of local authorities—has also to be omitted because of insufficient data for calculating it.

One instance must suffice. In conjunction with seven Home County authorities the London County Council, under its Green Belt scheme, have acquired 23,118 acres and are negotiating for another 50,000—a total of 73,000 acres.

This second tap, marked "Local Authorities," had its washer removed by the Town and Country Planning Act. The beauty and strength of that Act, too complex to recapitulate now, is that few outside the legal profession have grasped its tremendous implications.

Compared with the potentialities of the Town and Country Planning Act, the acreage quoted here and the methods used to acquire it are modest.

Finally, we come, under a somewhat different head, to the National Parks, for which legislation will be introduced in the next session. It is true that this will not be land "acquired." But it will be land controlled—3,636,000 acres of it. For the Service departments, local authorities, private owners and the Ministry of Town and Country Planning, who have a hand in this pie, there opens a vista of limitless correspondence and negotiation. The last word will not rest with private owners.

So much for the bath. Let us look at the tank and the plumbing. What is the significance of all this machinery? The significance lies in a principle of land nationalisation which is not universally understood. The art of nationalising land is to acquire what is wanted and to leave what is not wanted where it is for the time being.

It is questionable whether the State, paying reasonable compensation, could afford to purchase outright all the land of England, Scotland

and Wales. It is even more questionable whether it could properly administer it. The Socialists have perceived that difficulty.

These eight or nine million acres represent the first stage of land nationalisation in a moderate but most practical form. Legislation safely on the Statute Book means that the Government can have as much as they want as soon as they want it. It is a planner's paradise. No other industry offers such a convenient approach.

As the day of the large private landowner draws to a close—and some saw the first shadows fall in the Lloyd George Budget of 1909—so the State prepares for its role as executor and residuary legatee. Some may deplore it, others delight in it. The fact remains that it will be a difficult, if not impossible, process to reverse.

Many landowners and farmers believe there is a battle to come over land nationalisation, if Socialism returns for a second term of office. If the time ever came for them to take up their shot guns they would find them unloaded. Their cartridge bags have been stealthily emptied. They have been disarmed.

"SOCIALISM HAS PASSED 'THE POINT OF NO RETURN'"

The Socialist Tragedy
By Ivor Thomas, M.P. (Latimer House)

Nearly everyone seems to agree that the issues at this next General Election are going to be momentous. Yet, curiously, few find it easy to say in simple terms just what these issues will be.

"My boy," a learned acquaintance (of Liberal inclinations) said to me recently, "there is no difficulty about the next election. It must be put straight to the people in these terms; 'Do you or do you not want a Socialist State?'"

He sketched in his theme with a few bold strokes, the last of which was Lysenko. "And how would you present that," I asked, "to a public meeting in Aylesbury, Aston, Aberdeen or Aberystwyth?" He shrugged his shoulders. "That is the Conservative party's problem."

THE FINAL ARGUMENT

It is a problem. How far the case for Conservatism against Socialism should be fought in the traditional, simple, superficial but juicy terms of rival party policies and performances; how far it is feasible to enlarge on the complex, deeper, long-term implications of a Socialist society.

If you think about it, the most cogent reason for voting anti-Socialist next time is not that Mr. Strachey in peace has produced less bacon than Lord Woolton did in war; nor that Mr. Bevan has proved a less capable housing administrator than, say, Mr. Neville Chamberlain; nor because the groundnuts scheme is a flop.

Nor is it nationalisation; nor because we stand a better chance of surviving in a hard, competitive world under free enterprise than under Socialism; nor even that beer might be better and cheaper.

It is none of those things. Probably the most cogent reason for voting anti-Socialist, is that by all history and experience the development of Socialism along the lines we now follow will lead, as dawn follows dusk, to a Socialist State, more disagreeable, more oppressive than the average elector likes to contemplate.

A state of society, incidentally, which most of our present rulers would cut off their right hands, if not their careers, to avoid.

A Prophetic Word

But when it comes to the point it is so much easier to woo electors on such topics as bacon, beer, housing, groundnuts and nationalisation (judiciously leavened with jolly jokes about Messrs. Shinwell and Strachey) than it is to inform them on the more sombre and significant theme of where we are going. No one likes to be told he does not know where he is going.

Mr. Churchill saw this problem in 1945. He summarised and dramatised the issue in one explosive, prophetic word: "Gestapo." Perhaps he over-estimated the perception of the average elector. Five years later there are not, in terms of 20m. voters, many who yet fully comprehend what he was driving at.

So it is not without significance that Mr. Ivor Thomas, M.P., and his book, which appears to-day, within a year of his crossing the floor of the House, should concern himself mainly with this darker theme. Where will Socialism end, and where shall we end up with it?

Nor is it a coincidence, that Mr. Alfred Edwards, the other M.P. to cross the floor from left to right, was clearly moved by the same misgivings. Ostensibly, Mr. Edwards left because he disagreed about steel. So did Mr. Thomas. Both saw in that measure something more significant and frightening than the nationalisation of one more industry.

"There is a point in every long flight by aeroplane" (writes Mr. Thomas) "known as 'the point of no return.' In drawing up his flight plan before leaving the ground the pilot is required to calculate it. When he has reached 'the point of no return' he knows that there can be no going back, as his reserves of fuel would be insufficient. He must press on remorselessly to his destination, whatever the consequences may be.

"In its acceptance of the Marxist outlook and programme the Labour party has passed 'the point of no return.'"

Tragedy of Socialism

Mr. Thomas wastes few words on the superficial failings and follies of Socialism. What obsesses him is the spectacle of Labour's leaders being pushed relentlessly down the road which Professor Hayek called, "The Road to Serfdom." He thinks that is the tragedy of Socialism. His aim is to prevent it becoming a tragedy for everyone else.

It is one thing to feel convinced, as Mr. Thomas puts it, "that although Socialism may differ from Communism in its methods and tempo, the final state of society will be the same."

Many sense that now. It is another thing to show the majority of electors just why it may well be so. Prof. Hayek argued the case with logic but not in terms calculated to catch the imagination of the million. Mr. Thomas relies less on logic than lucidity.

Loss of Independence

From the experience of Europe and Great Britain in recent years he concludes that Socialism and Communism alike have three main characteristics:

The communal ownership of means of production, distribution and exchange;
The abolition of personal incomes drawn from rent, profit and investment;
The central planning of production.

In all these respects Mr. Thomas thinks that Socialism has passed "the point of no return." Moreover, the stage has been reached when he can draw evidence not merely from the reckless utterances of Socialists seeking power, but from the consequences of their achievements in office.

He examines the progressive elimination of private property and the disappearing of independence which goes with it. This was once an academic argument. Now it is reality.

"In a fully socialised State it is more than probable, as we have seen, that all lawyers, like doctors, would be put on a salary, and the salary could be cut off if they became troublesome."

Sir Stafford Cripps himself illustrates the point. For, says Mr. Thomas, if Sir Stafford's policies prevail, there can never again be another Sir Stafford Cripps.

"It is well known that Sir Stafford Cripps has been able to pursue his rather independent line in politics because he has been in possession of private means, or in receipt of professional fees paid in the last resort by people who have private means . . .

"Not only could there not be another Sir Stafford Cripps—this consummation might rouse different feelings in different people—but there could be no substantial independence of thought, writing or action in science, religion or politics when we are all wage-earners in the Socialist commonwealth."

We might say that if Mr. Thomas himself were dependent upon politics for his bread he would never have written this book.

DIRECTION OF LABOUR

There are plenty of cosy arguments against central planning and we have lately been kept familiar with most of them. Now central planning is here and the problems which some foresaw would follow have thundered up and are galloping past political thinkers.

Can there be planning without compulsion? Labour, face to face with the question, is wobbling. Will planned economy work without direction of labour? What happens if labour declines to be directed?

Then the consumer. Cheese provides the most homely example of where the planner stands on the issue of consumers' choice versus planned consumption. Mr. Thomas quotes Dr. Edith Summerskill:

"The function of the Ministry of Food is not to pander to an acquired taste, but to ensure that the people who have never had time to acquire these tastes are suitably fed."

And from Labour's "Feet on the Ground":

"Many of the dollars now spent on American cheese would be saved if Europe concentrated on producing cheap cheeses for mass consumption instead of luxury cheese like camembert and gorgonzola."

Here, says Mr. Thomas, is the whole frightful doctrine of the planners put in a sentence.

ONLY ONE EMPLOYER

He catches up with current events when he discusses the outlook for trade unions. Can they exist in a Socialist State?

"In a Socialist society there will be only one employer, the State, though the fact may be disguised by the use of local authorities and public boards."

A demand for a shorter working week or higher wages becomes a demand on the State. To strike for them is to strike against the State. How is a strike to be distinguished from mutiny or rebellion?

It is a pity that many Socialists must approach this book unsympathetically. A man who changes his party is bound to repel rather than attract his former associates. Many of them will read this book with inward anger and outward contempt.

Yet I say that is a pity, because Mr. Thomas crystallises misgivings which must, if truth were known, be preying on a good many who took off with high intentions in 1945 and who know now, in their hearts, that they have passed "the point of no return."

CRIME AND THE CONSERVATIVES

The lesson of serious studies is that if next week's Tory Conference argues about juvenile delinquency exclusively in terms of the birch and detention centres it will be shirking the central challenge

It was predictable that crime and punishment would claim a big slice of the agenda for the Conservatives' annual conference at Brighton; and it is predictable that there will be a testing session for the Home Secretary.

Among all domestic issues this year crime has come nearest to running the Conservative party into trouble. Feeling goes deep for more than one reason.

Partly it reflects alarm at violence and a sensation that rising lawlessness has been feebly met by authority. There is a particular grievance that while more crime—and more beastly kinds of crime— have seemed to demand draconic measures, the Home Secretary, and his advisers, have pursued penal policies of quite another kind.

More subtly there is awareness that upholding law and order is a first charge on government, and failure to do so reflects grievously on a Conservative Government which has ruled for 10 years.

Looking back over four years, Mr. Butler's dilemma is apparent. He came to the Home Office to find prison building, penal reform, research and the police overdue for advance, and with a predisposition to tackle the job humanely.

By all the portents the climate was propitious. More education, more welfare, less poverty promised a better society. Barely had the course been set when gusts of lawlessness, whence blown and whither blowing we still do not know, confounded social expectation and embarrassed the reformers.

PEOPLE V. POLITICIANS

An issue within the Conservative party today is whether or not the Home Secretary has been right to hold to his original course without deviation. It is more than an issue within the party. Ostensibly on such subjects as corporal punishment, hanging and the treatment of psychopaths the Labour party in Parliament backs Mr. Butler.

That is no reflection of the national mood. A straight referendum would bring more than half of all parties in the country out in favour of the birch—and the rope. A Gallup Poll in April showed that 73 per cent. wanted corporal punishment back, and 70 per cent., more than ever before, favoured capital punishment.

In matters so closely affecting personal security, if the people of a democracy demand drastic measures, what is the proper response of authority? One reaction has been to maintain—but not to explain—that a dispassionate view of the criminal situation provides neither the evidence nor the conclusions on which popular demands are based.

As Mr. Leon Radzinowicz, Director of Cambridge's Institute of Criminology, has put it:

> There is a tendency to exaggerate the incidence and gravity of crime ... It is to be regretted that those who voice public uneasiness about the increase in crime, and who try to mobilise it, not to say exploit it, in order to bring about certain changes in our penal legislation and practice, so frequently indulge in colourful descriptions of a state of lawlessness which bears no resemblance to the actual incidence and distribution of offences.

All this makes good Brighton rock, but the Conservative party will falter if it fails to get the level of its discussion above the familiar arguments which have been rehearsed *ad nauseam* in all its recent councils.

Increasingly crime is becoming the object of serious studies by sociologists as well as criminologists. A glance at a dozen recent books supports the authoritative view that we are up against something more than stiff sentences and a return to the birch will resolve.

To read, for example, Mr. Merfyn Jones's account* of his experiments at Norman House with selected ex-prisoners is to know that we are still groping to discover how to restore prisoners to public life. To dwell on the importance of after-care raises popular suspicion of softness. To ignore it is to foster recidivism.

Most of the prisoners among whom Mr. Jones pioneered were so weak in character, though not necessarily vicious, that they turned

---

* "Safe Lodging." (Hutchinson, 25s.)

from the prison gate to fresh crime in an unbroken movement. Such men are a standing menace to society's security.

The retort "Well, keep them in," reflecting the common mood, is no solution in a free society. But how much is it prepared to spend and to support more Norman homes, to meet not the familiar problem of where the ex-prisoner is to work but where, homeless, he is to sleep?

Mr. T. R. Fyvel* has surveyed a bigger, darker part of the scene—the young offender. It is one of several recent essays on this subject, and possibly the best. Here is presented not merely the teddy boy, whose antics flutter the smug, but also the society of which we are members—which is less flattering.

Provocative Indictment

Here is a study on a scale which earns comparison with Galbraith's "Affluent Society" from which Mr. Fyvel draws heavily. It comes nearest to the line of thought Conservatives should be pondering if they want to get on terms with authority—and juvenile crime.

In general there is a strong inclination to treat youthful lawlessness as an isolated problem; a product of war's aftermath, of broken families, working mothers, Mr. Butler's intransigence—something right outside our orbit and open to remedy if only authority would throw the right levers. *We're* all right, Jack.

Are we? After a piercing look at the teddy's sub-culture, Mr. Fyvel gives the last half of his book to that question.

> Adding it all up, it seemed hard to doubt that there was something afoot, that there were some aspects of our materialistic, mechanised twentieth-century society ... which encouraged widespread youthful cynicism in general and rather violent delinquency in particular.

The crack-up of bourgeois society, new wealth and the mass attack by advertisers on its possessors, unbalance between private and public spending (pace Galbraith), the strain imposed on also-rans by an affluent society, the American example, ubiquitous television, an absence of national purpose—these are not fresh clues. But they have not yet been woven into a more provocative indictment than Mr. Fyvel's.

* "The Insecure Offenders." (Chatto & Windus, 25s.)

There are crumbs of consolation in the experience of other countries. As we have known for some time, all Western countries enjoying rapid industrial development are suffering comparable storms of delinquency among the young.

The author recalls chillingly some recent outbreaks of futile, inexplicable violence which flashed across European towns and cities. Less consolingly, no one's record is worse than our own.

The conclusions are not less convincing because they are obvious to some:

> The material advance of British working-class youth should be accompanied by an equivalent cultural advance. Just as in the mid-fifties there was a break-through in material consumption, so there has now to be a break-through in education, because it is evident that the present secondary modern school system is not adequate preparation for the new society.

No Short Cut

It is irresistible to wonder why such ideas have not fired livelier imaginations in the Labour party. After half a century's battle against poverty of pocket, what more obvious inspiration for a crusade than poverty of mind?

There is food left over for Conservative thought. A dozen plans have been drafted, for example, to make pay-TV possible, after Pilkington reports. Is it beyond the wits of the public sector to conceive ideas on these lines for a long-overdue advance in part-time education for adolescents?

Manifestly, if the Conservative party is going to argue about juvenile delinquency at Brighton exclusively in terms of the birch and detention centres it will shirk the central challenge and defy opportunity. Mr. Fyvel's reflections were put another way by Leon Radzinowicz:

> There is no short-cut or ready-made solution; no swift and cheap remedy, no penal tranquilliser or drug which will make crime recede. It is an obdurate problem deeply embedded in the very texture of our existence, calling for the imaginative and patient mobilisation of a great variety of means and resources.

In the United States these sombre reflections on the consequences of affluence have already taken hold. Thoughtful Americans are going on one of their rare pilgrimages through the vale of introspection. The dance-band has gone to supper, and someone is playing Chopin on the piano.

If this mood could prevail for a few hours at Brighton the Conservative party's encounter with the Home Secretary—and with one or two other Ministers—could bring light.

ELECTORAL REFORM AND THE LESSONS OF PAST DEBATES

Alternative vote, second ballot or proportional representation—the old choices are coming up again for judgment. The arguments of the past century or so take on new relevance in the conditions of today

Electoral reform is in the wind again. By all the portents we are due to resume the debate which has rolled inconclusively through Parliament and the nation since the 1832 Reform Act.

It revives, a study of the past century suggests, whenever the two-party system manifestly gets into difficulties or disrepute. This last happened in 1950, when Labour got back by a whisker and the Liberals scored nine M.P.s with 2,600,000 votes.

Sir Winston Churchill, to his party's mild alarm, at once proposed a Select Committee on Electoral Reform. Mr. Morrison declared that reform must have an electors' mandate.

Labour's view in 1930–31 was different. After governing uneasily on a minority vote for a year, they actually got a Bill incorporating the Alternative Vote through the Commons. Its remaining stages were killed by the "crisis" General Election of that autumn.

So it is 27 years since the nation heard a major debate on the subject. It is also, by no coincidence, 27 years since a third party counted for much.

22 BILLS REJECTED

According to my researches, Parliament since 1854 has rejected 22 Bills, mostly from private Members, and has debated electoral reform on 21 occasions. There have been one Royal Commission, in 1910, and three Electoral Reform Conferences, presided over by the Speaker of the day, in 1917, 1929–30 and in 1943–44.

Much of this, particularly the 19th-century debates involving John Stuart Mill (a strong protagonist of reform), Gladstone and Disraeli, is rewarding stuff for the student. But to get a sense of the

main arguments, the Royal Commission and the debates of 1917,
1930 and 1944 fulfil our needs.

Lord Richard Cavendish's Royal Commission did thorough
work. Its background was the birth of the Labour party and the
1906 General Election. That "landslide," which gave the Liberals
a majority of 200, warranted, in ratio to votes, a majority of 55.
The Royal Commission said:

> We recommend the adopting of the Alternative Vote when
> more than two candidates stand for one seat.

Here we must pause to refresh memory. The Alternative Vote,
sometimes called the contingent vote, is a self-contained system with
an attractively simple look. We could work it without radical constitutional reform.

The voter is asked to arrange the candidates in the order of his
choice by placing the figures 1, 2, 3, and so on, against their names,
instead of an X against one. If any candidate gets an absolute majority
of first votes, he is home. If not, the candidate with fewest votes is
eliminated and his voting papers are distributed among the rest
according to the names marked 2.

Papers with no second choice marked on them are withdrawn.
With only three candidates one round is enough. If there are more
than three, and still no absolute majority, the process is repeated.

There is another version of the absolute majority system—the
Second Ballot. Again, the candidate with more votes than all the rest
is at once elected. Otherwise there is a second election, in which
only the two top candidates stand. It requires the elector to vote
twice.

Proportional Representation, which the Royal Commission
examined with scientific exactitude, is a bigger proposition. Its claim
is to effect the return of parties in proportion to their strength at the
polls. To find the best way of doing this has occupied mathematicians
and constitutional reformers for two centuries.

There are said to be 300 separate systems in existence, many, of
course, like Indian dialects, with insignificant variations.

I have studied Prof. S. J. Nanson's appendix to the Royal
Commission's report. It leaves me at one with Mr. Gladstone, who
confessed in 1885 his total inability to grasp the mathematics and
essentials of the proposal.

What is relevant is that all the P.R. systems require multimember constituencies for their operation. To get the best results there should be eight to 10 candidates for each party in a constituency of 500,000 or more—a major departure from the ratio and relationship of one M.P. to 50,000 to which our people have grown accustomed.

All Private Members' Bills, seeking to give the Royal Commission's plans effect, failed. Not until 1917–18 did Parliament again give the subject serious scrutiny.

MODIFIED SCHEME

Early in 1917 Mr. Asquith moved to accept the main recommendations of the first Speaker's Conference. These were the single transferable vote in University seats; the transferable vote (under P.R.) in constituencies returning three to five members; and the Alternative Vote in single-member constituencies with more than two candidates.

The Commons struck out—by eight votes—the principle of P.R. The Lords restored it. In 1918 the Commons threw out the Lords amendment.

Then the peers proposed a modified scheme whereby about 100 M.P.s would be elected on the P.R. principle. To this the Commons agreed. Commissioners were appointed to draw up the 100 divisions. But in May, 1918, when the Government came to propose their scheme, the House declined to proceed. It was to be the final word for more than a decade.

In every year of the 1920s—when, mark, the three-party system was going strong—the House had Bills for electoral reform before it. None prevailed. During 1929–31 the familiar process was repeated. In 1929, 308 Members had been returned on a minority vote.

A second Speaker's Conference proposed P.R. The Labour party thought this too steep, but under Liberal pressure brought forward the Alternative Vote.

In these debates of 1931 we find the main arguments for and against. Moreover, they bring us in touch with contemporary opinion.

Capt. Anthony Eden declared the Alternative Vote was ideal for the political wangler. There emerges from several other speeches, including Mr. Butler's, the root objection to it. In the words of (as he then was) Mr. Winston Churchill, "The decision of 100 or more constituencies, perhaps 200, is to be determined by the most worth-less votes given for the most worthless candidates."

This is a stiff hurdle. First and second candidates cannot use their second vote. It is the second vote of the weakest candidate which decides. "'Devil take the hindmost' will acquire a new significance," observed Mr. Churchill.

That is not the only difficulty. Let us assume an election in which the Socialist wants nationalisation and the Tory protection. The Liberal wants neither and is bottom. His second votes, cast by people against Tory and Socialist policy—but possibly with a strong preference for one or the other as a man—will prove decisive.

CHURCHILLIAN FORESIGHT

Of all the views expressed then, or earlier, Mr. Churchill's were by far the longest-sighted. He did not reject P.R., seeing in it a chance to give our great cities a "civic entity"—Mr. Gladstone's phrase—which they now lack.

Under P.R., he thought, Birmingham, Manchester, Leeds and Glasgow would regain their collective personalities, their "collective intellectual force." Failing this, Mr. Churchill plumped for the Second Ballot. No disadvantage, he thought, to have 100 to 150 second ballot elections a few days after the General Election.

There was a real advantage in enabling electors to correct, if they wished, a landslide. General Elections in the old days spread over five or six weeks. Far more closely reasoned decisions, Mr. Churchill thought, were then reached. Now the nation goes to bed after voting and wakes up to find an irrevocable decision taken.

Mr. Churchill was speaking, with that gift of unconscious prophecy, 14 years before television, whereby electors can watch the irrevocable decision being unfolded, nightmare fashion, by Mr. David Butler.

Mr. Churchill's view was that second ballots were a powerful insurance against too violent a lurch in either direction. He accounted the stability and continuity offered by this system well worth the extra trouble of a second vote. Would the elector? Not on current form.

None can study these debates of past years without perceiving that they possess one inestimable advantage, denied to us. These matters were decided at a much more leisurely pace than the press of modern affairs now permits.

Parliamentary debates on many subjects turn quickly to dust. Electoral reform is not, I think, among them. Some of the fundamental arguments, springing from the loins of our Parliamentary system, are ageless. They remain today to refresh, to counsel—and to warn.

TO FLOG OR NOT TO FLOG?

W. F. Deedes, M.P., looks at the evidence in the controversy over corporal punishment for brutal offences, which is being revived as the Government prepares its new penal measures

A close observer of the General Election told me afterwards he believed that the simplest and most decisive stroke to improve Labour's fortunes would have been a firm promise by Mr. Gaitskell to restore corporal punishment for brutal offences.

Few candidates who encountered public feeling at the time will dismiss that as altogether nonsense. Such an undertaking would not have changed the result; but it would have weighed heavily with many women who now worry much less about the cost of living than the risk of living.

So the issue is potent. It will arise more acutely soon when the Government presents its new penal measures.

For 100 years our inclination has been progressively to discard ferocious punishments. We ceased to whip women in 1820, drastically curtailed flogging in 1847, discontinued public whipping a little later and almost abolished it in 1862. But the journey has not been unbroken.

Thus the apparent attempt on Queen Victoria's life in 1842 led by popular demand to retention of flogging for treason. An outbreak of garrotting in London in 1862 inspired a private member's Garrotter's Act whereby offenders could be "once, twice or thrice privately whipped." Widespread alarm about the white slave traffic in 1912 led to supplementary provisions for the whipping of procurers and ponces.

In 1948 the main tide swept away by statute birching and flogging for all crimes except serious offences against prison discipline. Increasing violence in the decade since then has produced a strong current in favour of its restoration for brutal crimes.

The Choice

When under fire on this subject during the election I resorted to saying: "What *kind* of corporal punishment do you want?" Nearly everyone was shy of the cat, but thought the birch would meet the need. Let us look at the exhibits.

The birch, for boys of 10–16, was a bundle of birch twigs, shaped like a besom, but without a handle. It was 40 inches long, with a central circumference of 6 inches and a weight of 9oz. The maximum penalty was 25 strokes on the buttocks.

For youths above 16 a heavier type was used, weighing 12oz. For adult men either that birch or the cat-o'-nine-tails was used. This is composed of nine lengths of fine whipcord, whipped to prevent fraying at the ends but not knotted, 33 inches in length and weighing 9oz. The maximum penalty was 24 strokes across the shoulders.

Though considered a much more awful prospect, the cat is barely less painful than the birch. Some say there is nothing between them. Both were administered under strict supervision and privately by officers who received 2s 6d for the job—5s in Scotland.

If we are to have controversy about corporal punishment at least the Government will be spared the need to set up another inquiry. The subject was exhaustively, some think classically, reviewed by a Departmental Committee under Mr. Edward Cadogan in 1938. This committee was fortunate to have as secretary Mr. (now Sir) Norman Brook, today joint head of the Treasury and Secretary to the Cabinet.

Its report led to those sections of the Criminal Justice Act, 1948, which abolished corporal punishment outside prisons. One can hardly do better at this point than look over the evidence and considerations which led this body of seven men and three women to such conclusions.

They dealt first with young offenders and the birch. They found that birchings had dropped in England and Wales from around 3,000 a year at the turn of the century—with one exceptional burst during World War I which reached 5,000 in 1917—to 166 in 1936.

Juvenile courts had discontinued the use of birching not on *a priori* grounds, but simply because they found it less effective than other methods. The Committee, setting all emotional considerations on one side, found other objections.

The birched boy tends to become a hero among his companions and a martyr to his parents—thus nullifying the effects. Birching ought not to be inflicted without reasonable inquiries into temperament and psychology—thus adding intolerable delay, sometimes six to eight weeks, between offence and punishment.

This vital question of delay was one of three distinctions the Committee saw between birching ordered by a court and a caning at home or in school, which they endorsed. Both in the home and at school there are bonds, at least of respect if not affection, between the child and the person who punishes him. Moreover the relation is a continuing one.

> After a judicial birching, on the other hand, there is no supervision or aftercare. The boy is birched by a police officer who has no direct interest in his future behaviour.... It is nobody's business to see how he reacts to the punishment."

For Juveniles

To this summary one must add a footnote. The committee saw the need for fresh measures to deal with juvenile delinquents. They outlined ideas for a new kind of detention centre where offenders could be kept under punitive conditions for a short period; where discipline would be strict and the work hard.

This seed blossomed in the Criminal Justice Act of 1948, which provided for such detention centres. After 12 years we have, I think, four detention centres established out of a modest programme of 12 and the courts are crying out for more. Despite the centres' proved success, their installation is resisted by nervous citizens all over the country. The delay has been politically inexcusable and socially lamentable.

In considering the cat the committee squarely faced the crucial question: does it in reality afford society the protection society seeks? It can satisfy a taste for vengeance. It can deter, as all punishments to some extent deter. Is it the most effective deterrent?

A list of 440 persons, convicted of robbery with violence during the period 1921–30, 142 of them flogged and 298 not flogged, was scrupulously analysed. The findings suggest that the cat had no better results than imprisonment or penal servitude. Indeed by subsequent offences the record of men flogged was found to be worse than that of those who were not flogged. Corporal punishment, said the committee, must be justified by the deterrent, not the retributive principle.

It is fallacious to assume that a man who has committed a violent offence is necessarily more susceptible than others to the deterrent effect of corporal punishment. As to the theory that "violence must be met by violence," Lord Oxford 60 years ago found this "at once fallacious and barbarous."

This committee was reviewing statutes which carried the penalty of flogging for a wide miscellany of crimes. Witnesses before them had many suggestions—as they might today—for supplementing the list:

Rape: defilement of girls under 13 years of age: incest committed by a father with a daughter under 16 tears of age: sodomy or gross indecency committed by older men on young boys: demanding money with menaces: sending or throwing explosive substances and throwing corrosive fluid: serious assaults with razors, bayonets, broken bottles, etc.: serious assaults on wives and children: gross cruelty to animals.

The difficulty is apparent—to find any common principle which can be accepted as a basis for distinguishing between offences for which corporal punishment is considered appropriate and those for which it is not.

More Effective

One exception was found. At the express recommendation of the committee prisoners are today liable to corporal punishment for mutiny, incitement to mutiny or gross personal violence to prison staff.

It is not difficult to see why corporal punishment is a more effective deterrent in prison than out of it. Freedom is no longer the biggest stake. Prolongation of sentence, loss of remission marks, less pleasant conditions—these considerations will not deter a violent man already in gaol from planning to assault a warder.

It will be said by advocates of corporal punishment that a decade without the cat or birch has led to more violent crime. To prove that to the satisfaction of the intellect as well as the emotions is not easy.

Since the rest of Europe has abandoned corporal punishment it is much harder to explain what singular strain our criminals possess which renders the cat a "must" for the British. When all strains of vengeance, fear and sadism are washed out of the argument, as the

Cadogan Committee tried to do, the residue leaves slender grounds for cat or birch.

Moreover, since Cadogan there has been some shift in the weight on punishment's three foundations, retribution, deterrence and reform, from the first pillar to the second and third.

Corporal punishment, admittedly an instrument of retribution, of doubtful value as a deterrent, is certainly inimical to reform. So it is harder now to fit the cat into the pattern than it was in 1842, 1862 or 1912.

To ask rhetorically: "Revenge or Reform?" will not cut much ice. But in which, ultimately, lies greater safety for the defenceless citizen? That bears thinking about.

HOW TO BE A CANDIDATE . . .

In spite of television and opinion polls, elections are still won by hard work on the ground. The 1,500 or so would-be M.P.s will find plenty to do in the next month

Rapid developments in the arts of electoral prediction and political television since 1955 make the course of the next General Election look delusively simple.

Given the requisite dates by the Prime Minister, a running forecast of the results by public opinion polls and full coverage by the BBC and ITV, democracy seems to have all it needs for an enjoyable campaign.

Beside these major distractions, however, upwards of 1,500 Parliamentary candidates will have a modest rôle; and most of them are now sitting round tables with their officers and agents discussing how it will best be played.

They face an upheaval in politics comparable with the Reform Act of 1832. When patronage and pocket boroughs came to an end seats became contests, not gifts.

Now television has developed a form of patronage, controlled, equitable, subject to law, but pervasive and perhaps decisive. This time it will have 9m. subjects compared with 2m. in 1955. None of the old Dukes had, in terms of power, anything to touch a peak five minutes on ITV.

But for purposes of a cosy talk with the agent these fancies must be put to flight. We shall all have about £800 to spend—nearer £1,000 in country districts—and the practical question is how best to spend it on the conventional weapons.

THE PAPER WAR

First, the election address: an expensive but indispensable item and, except for men like Sir Alan Herbert, a painfully difficult composition. Shall it be all words, and if so how many—30, 300, or 3,000? A photograph of the family? A homely message from the wife?

We settle for 750 words ("nobody reads it . . .") and this goes well until the paragraph on Foreign Affairs is found to leave 25 words for Agriculture, Housing, Education, Pensions, Colonies and the wife's homely touch.

That resolved, what about window cards? In a world still suscep- tible to visual influences they remain effective. A judicious arrange- ment, if Foreign Affairs can be brought under control, is to give all the back page of a quarto-sized election address to SNOOKS in monumental blue—or red—which, with a touch of gum, goes well in the window.

Posters? Before the campaign opens bill posters will expunge current offerings such as "Life's Better Under The Conservatives. Don't Let Labour Ruin It." Something else, presumably even less generous, will shoot up.

Printing and stationery will account for roughly half the £800– £1,000 and their cost has risen by about 10 p.c. since 1955. As few candidates spent their limits then there will not be noticeably less paper this time.

We shall not to-day get far past the next item on the agenda: Public Meetings. It will be well to assume a wearisome discussion and sum up.

For urban candidates who can satisfy the needs of wards with a dozen meetings in the campaign it is not worth arguing about. In country districts, where perhaps 70 villages will entail three or four meetings every night, the existence of 9m. television sets raises doubt.

But you can't ask television questions. Nor will any of the televised gladiators be touching the subjects which enrich meetings for most of us—and it is well to illustrate why.

Here in Upper Wedgehole the candidate has spoken competently about India, China, the Summit, the H-bomb and Leisure for the Millions. He has squashed the local Communist and evaded two questions on post-war credits.

"Our candidate," booms the chairman, "revels in questions. Now is your chance." At which an insignificant man rises and asks: "Can the candidate tell us why drivers with L plates are allowed to carry passengers?"

It is at once apparent that the man has struck oil. All knitting stops.

The chairman, a practised hand, looks first at the agent, then at his watch and then at the candidate's driver. But he knows well enough that it's a gusher.

Seventeen minutes later he is saying: "Well, ladies and gentlemen, we've had a very full discussion on this question; but the candidate has to get on . . ." And the candidate, pink, damp, late but undaunted is declaring: "I shall make it my first charge, if returned to Parliament, to ask the Minister of Transport . . ."

There remains one factor, out of the camera's range and beyond calculation by any public opinion poll: the local constituency organisation. By far the most important factor in all the conventional weapons a wise candidate will deploy is the army of voluntary workers who will use them.

From D-20 until D-Day itself they will distribute hundreds of tons of literature, address millions of envelopes, knock on a million doors, and endure a thousand hard words.

Assiduously by film and other media the parties have sought to persuade supporters of the charms and efficacy of door-to-door canvassing. There are two degrees of it.

The first, essential one, is a door-to-door canvass by volunteers which establishes whether the householder can be marked up blue, red, green or doubtful and so marked down for chasing up on the day.

Opening Moves

The second, optional exercise is a similar but limited operation by the candidate. As in chess there are established opening moves. One goes:

"Good morning. I am Snooks, the Conservative candidate . . ."

"And I'm telling you the ballot is secret. Good morning."

The second, perversely, goes:

"Good morning. Now I am not going to ask you how you're going to vote . . ."

"Well, we're all Labour here—and I don't care who knows it . . ."

It is a sacred article in every party's political creed that these intrusions are loved by electors and carry the real stuff of victory.

We may agree that a synthetised, televised, predictable election would deny electors, voluntary workers, candidates and innocent bystanders many joys. Perhaps the threat of such a thing will induce a reaction in which candidates' personalities, village meetings and questions about L drivers will become valued as a blessed relief from the screen.

Fireside or fun? The choice may matter a lot to democracy.

December 1959

A SHOT IN THE ARM OF THE LAW

The coming inquiry into the police will find no lack of subject matter. Pay, duties and organisation are not the whole story of what needs attention if the police are to be kept abreast of changing social conditions

Some future historian of these times may well record that towards the end of 1959 the Government of the day decided to appoint a Royal Commission on the Police.

Two events earlier in the year, he may add, precipitated this decision. One was the interference by a police authority at Nottingham with its Chief Constable. The other was the refusal of the police authority in London, the Home Secretary, to interfere with his Commissioner of Police in the case of Garratt v P.C. Eastmond.

For its action the Nottingham Corporation incurred widespread displeasure. For his inaction the Home Secretary was subjected to a censure motion in the House of Commons.

This odd conjunction of events illustrates the difficulties we have got into with police organisation. A risk for solid, well-established institutions like the police is that they tend to get marooned when the social tide is moving fast.

Not long ago the three Services were threatened by the isolation. We have by a series of inquiries and reforms brought them along. The soldier's shillin' a day and what he does for it now approximates to the demands of 1959. The policeman's lot does not.

Some think the threat of lawlessness against civilised standards is now such that we ought to see the police as a fourth arm of defence. As it happens, we have a fourth arm in Civil Defence.

This does not, as a foreign observer might suppose, relate to law and order at home, but to hopeful ways of defending ourselves against nuclear attack. To keep this work abreast of the times we have a large department in the Home Office—much bigger than the police division—staff an impressive College at Sunningdale for training leaders and three Civil Defence schools.

Four-Point Review

In Civil Defence the public takes practically no interest whatever. For combating crime, in which the public is profoundly interested, our arrangements are more haphazard.

They are not in the plight Sir Robert Peel discovered and remedied, but a thoroughgoing inquiry offers a chance for radical review such as does not occur more than once or twice in a century. Whatever the terms of reference four major aspects should get scrutiny:

Police recruiting, pay, promotion, duties, methods and training;
Local organisation;
Defeat of crime;
Relations with the public.

If we get the first three right, the fourth, which is getting out of perspective, might, with a single reform, right itself. The reform would be the establishment of an independent body to investigate complaints by members of the public against the police.

We have several working models—the General Medical Council, the Press Council and the Bar Council. Such a body would not destroy any cherished traditions and would please policemen as much as the public. Good policemen, who outnumber bad policemen, get as angry about incidents which damage their reputation as the innocent subjects.

If we are to have such a body let it above all be as simple in form and function as can be combined with justice.

Scandinavia has already established the "grievance man." That may be too elementary for our tastes which for so many quasi-judicial courts, tribunals and inquiries incline to the baroque.

When a citizen and a policeman have a tiff it ought not to require counsel for both sides, administration of the oath and statements of evidence taken by solicitors as preliminaries to settlement.

When it comes to pay and promotion, the inquiry could do worse than start with a look at what the Services have done. For a long time we counted on the Army as a calling. We had to supplement this with conscription. We are now trying to make it a career.

It is arguable whether more recruits would be drawn to the police by prospects of higher pay or by an outside but open chance of becoming Chief Constable at 48. There can be little argument on which prospect would bring in the best material.

As to duties, police authorities will declare they have cut down "the beat" as rapidly as the Army has reduced "square-bashing." We now face the residual question of whether or not policemen ought to remain responsible for motoring offences, or whether all or part of this responsibility needs a new force.

Bad motoring, which is pervasive, is a crime and there is no convincing evidence that a civilian force could handle it. The right step might be a gradual transfer. We could begin with a separate corps in charge of parking meters and proceed, in the light of experience, to expand its duties.

Outside Politics

Control is by far the most difficult subject because politics supervene, and local politics at that. On nearly every score the system of country control by Joint Standing Committees of councillors and magistrates is safer than the county borough system of Watch Committees, manned by councillors only.

We repose such faith in committees that the powers of a strong Chief Constable are made to seem more dangerous than the powers of a strong Watch Committee. But the reverse is more often true.

Chief Constables ought to be outside the pressure of local power politics. They take their oath of allegiance—like all policemen—to the Queen and are answerable to the law. They should never be answerable to Town Clerks—or even Lord Mayors. If we cannot find men fit to be entrusted with that degree of power the system of selection is at fault.

Some say the day of small, autonomous police units is over. They do not want to see control by central government but contemplate two or more national regions which would govern the promotion of senior officers, including Chief Constables.

Another safeguard would be to augment Her Majesty's Inspectors of Constabulary at the Home Office. They keep an eye on all police forces, acting as stewards for the 50 per cent. of police expenditure found by the Treasury. They are very thin on the ground.

It should never be possible for a Government to direct local police forces. But it has a right—indeed a duty to the taxpayer—to supervise local administration effectively.

What Parliament would like and ought to be denied is the right to raise questions about all the police with the Home Secretary. He can answer for the Metropolitan Police, for which he is the police authority, but not for the rest.

If control of the police outside London is to be independent of the central executive, it must also be outside the orbit of the House of Commons which is supposed to control the executive.

Given an independent body for public grievances and a strong Inspectorate of Constabulary at the Home Office to watch administration, for which the Home Secretary would be answerable to Parliament, there would remain no need for political interference. The law, not the legislators, should remain the policeman's master.

BEST USE OF BRAINS

There remains the defeat of crime. When this is discussed in Parliament much is always said about technical progress. It is characteristic of the times that people find it comforting to be told that we have now a thousand more police wireless sets, a hundred faster cars and forensic laboratories in every county.

What matters more but is harder to assess is the quality of manpower in charge of this equipment. Is the best use made of the ability we have got?

We do not, we think, want a Royal Military Academy, Sandhurst, for training police officers. Do we not want something more comparable to the Staff College, Camberley, than the present police college at Ryton-on-Dunsmore, Warwickshire? Or, better still, an Imperial Defence College which would embrace Commonwealth needs and experience? That would, among other things, assist promotion by means other than strict seniority. A likely man, sent to such a college, could count "p.s.c." a stepping stone to his career.

There is one final reflection for the future. There ought to be a channel through which responsible and senior policemen can contribute their knowledge and opinions to the shaping of policy on penology. Sociologists will be disturbed by such a suggestion, but they ought not to be.

A hidden source of police resentment is a feeling that as crime gets tougher and more violent society becomes more sympathetic to crooks. Between those who deal with crooks at large and those who deal with them as social studies there must be differences. It is not a question of who is right, but of admitting that both policeman and sociologist have something to contribute and both are entitled to have influence in police making.

A good test of the standing of any force, service or profession is to ask a man: "Would you choose it now as a career for your son?" Getting the right answer to that question is a strong but neglected fount of recruits. It will not be included among the inquiry's terms of reference. But it ought to overshadow a good many of their conclusions.

CROSSROADS FOR THE YOUNG OFFENDER

What goes on in a detention centre? It has a central place in our plans for dealing with young delinquents. But changes in its scope may produce some complications

An emergency parish meeting has been called and fills the local hall. "We're here, ladies and gentlemen," says the chairman, "to discuss this plan for a detention centre in the village."

Most of his audience have a wary look. "Can someone tell us," asks a lady who has taken the precaution of bringing plenty of knitting, "what happens inside a detention centre?"

No one is precise about this, but speculation inflames doubt and a resolution of solid disapprobation hums through without dissent to the local district council.

Such proceedings are some way removed from the earnest tones of lecturers to the United Nations Congress on Crime which recently sat in London. But they are part of the same process—that of reshaping our penal institutions to the needs of the young offender.

Two years from now, if present plans hold good, we shall have a dozen detention centres in this country and they will receive all youths of 16 to 21 serving sentences of six months or less.

That gives the detention centre a central role in the most anxious and perplexing of crime problems. And for 70 per cent. of these delinquents, which is the proportion of first offenders, it means that the detention centre will be the first big crossroads.

So it is difficult to exaggerate their importance. Politically, too, they carry weight, because, if the Home Secretary and the Government are to resist a return of the birch, the detention centre will have to be—and be seen to be—an effective alternative.

ODD HISTORY

Detention centres have an odd history. The idea was promoted in a pre-war report by the Cadogan Committee, which came down against corporal punishment. It got a place in the 1948 Act and two started fairly quickly at Kidlington, Oxfordshire (for boys of 14 to 16), at Goudhurst, Kent (for boys of 17 to 20). To-day there are still only four; three more are expected to open this year; there are five in stages between reconnaissance and angry parish meetings.

I first saw Blantyre House, Goudhurst, eight years ago during moves to mollify a local opinion appalled by the prospect of such a place entering a district favoured by private schools. Lately, I returned for a second visit. Goudhurst, incidentally, received last year 388 inmates and 1,100 inspecting visitors.

There has been a noticeable change since 1952. The original conception was a "short sharp shock." Boys moved at the double, silence was ordained except during 30 minutes of recreation at the close of day, and it seemed unlikely that anyone would seek a second dose. The first 65 first offenders to go to Goudhurst have not troubled the Prison Commission since.

The effect on visitors in those days was mixed. Ardent reformers found the proceedings distasteful. To those with memories of the battle school, or even an O.C.T.U., they seemed temperate enough.

Magistrates, who preponderate among the visitors, were impressed. Blantyre House has been refusing an average of 50 applications a week from the courts, which makes it more exclusive than Eton.

WALKING WILL DO

Today the régime is no less exacting. Walking will do and talking is allowed. But the work is hard, well laced with P.T., and sheer physical exertion has been steered towards a limited but positive form of training.

A youth starts in Grade I and should, after a month, enter Grade II. That depends on progress and conduct, and it demands endeavour. If he fails to make the grade after a chance or two he loses remission. Star performers can obtain Grade III, but there are not usually more than two or three in a batch of 80.

Good features remain common to both régimes. The boys put on an average of 20lb in three months. They have to stop smoking (upwards of 40 cigarettes a day), get four excellent square meals a day (which the staff pay to eat), and go through the kind of physical routine for which the affluent and obese gladly pay a clinic 40 guineas a week.

On arrival the youth is diverted from the cheerful approach of flower beds and a bright hall and ascends a back staircase. He finds himself in the solitary block, facing an hygienic but chilling cell with a table, chair and chamber pot.

He is told to go in and write a letter to his mother. After this meditative exercise he joins the community, sleeps first in a cubicle and then in one of two spotless dormitories. He enjoys offices which seem enviable to the middle-aged men with memories of their public schools' sanitation. A high standard of tidiness, dress and hygiene is upheld and, between rising for 30 minutes of P.T. and bed at 9 p.m., he will change his clothes perhaps 10 times.

It remains impossible to amble through Goudhurst as most will amble through prison. The demands are not immoderate and the physical tests are reasonable, but they have to be met, and there is a whiff of the orderly room as well as of good cooking. I arrived on my second visit in time for what soldiers would call Company Office.

The chief officer acts as C.S.M. "Parsons! Quick march, left-right, left-right, halt, face the Warden, stand to attention, hands to your side. Parsons, sir."

"Parsons, it is reported that when the P.T. instructor told you to lift your knees you said: What do you think I am—a ruddy horse?"

"Yes, sir."

"Did you say that?"

"No, sir. Not to him, sir."

Parsons had been driving a car, without papers. He had also changed his job 11 times in 12 months. He has now lost a day's remission.

This sort of régime makes high demands on the staff, from the Warden down. A full house of 80 requires a staff of 27, including 12 disciplinary officers, two P.T. instructors and five technical instructors.

PERSONAL INFLUENCE

Originally, all officers were volunteers from the prison service, a most desirable arrangement. It is vocational work, for which there is no special training, but it seems improbable that 12 detention centres, demanding perhaps 200 officers, will find enough volunteers.

An officer must know and be able to influence his small family of eight.

So far, so good. But this régime has heavy obligations ahead. If Parliament endorses the report of the Advisory Committee on the Treatment of Offenders, all sentences to a detention centre will comprise three or six months.

The mixture, in one establishment, must present problems. A youth can be geared to an ascending régime lasting 10 weeks—with remission, the full sentence. For a minority, serving double that time, the second half of the programme tends to become unproductive.

Again, detention has ceased to be the salutary shock for first offenders it was. Youths now go to detention with previous convictions—sometimes a string of them. They will be sent there increasingly, one suspects, not because it specially meets their needs but because the particular offence rates six months or less.

There is some danger of the detention centre becoming an anteroom to the main hall of disfame for youth. This hall, also yet to be approved by Parliament, will receive all young offenders with indeterminate sentences of six months or two years. These will be served preferably in Borstals and, exceptionally, in prison.

It is proposed that youths can be sentenced more than once to detention, but not to detention after an indeterminate sentence. Even so, the detention centre will have a mixed bag. There will be boys who know all the ropes.

A possible alternative would be to offer two kinds of centre. One would take those guilty of a first offence for three months, and efforts could be concentrated on ensuring, humanely, that it would be the last. The second centre would provide a six months' course for those with previous convictions and, in exceptional cases, first offenders guilty of grosser crimes.

MINOR RACKET

In one detention centre recently a small, experienced gang ran a "protection racket." The boys earn 1s 6d a week (at Goudhurst 6d is compulsorily saved), and invariably buy a brand of boiled sweets at 2d a package. The racket demanded that three such packets be paid as insurance against violence from the gang. It is difficult to see how such minor troubles can be avoided if the twin streams are to go through all 12 establishments.

It remains a gloomy reflection that 12 years after the relevant Act we should still be at this exploratory stage. That must be attributed mainly to the role of Cinderella that penology has played in the Welfare State until recently. It is also due to long local sieges against the arrival of detention centres.

Many who are ready to deplore the failure of authority to grapple with juvenile crime will be in the front row of the village hall's protest meeting. It is not yet appreciated that a concomitant of ending the long régime of prison fortresses for the herd is the spreading of special institutions through a small island.

"Anywhere but here" is part of the inscription on the young delinquent's tablet. It is tolerable when it happens in the next county, but the devil when it arrives on your doorstep. Well do I know it. A detention centre will open shortly a stone's throw from my home.

January 1961

MAKING THE CRIMINAL PAY HIS DEBT

A private Member's Bill to compensate victims of violent crimes is due for Second Reading to-day. But the first object of penology is not compensation, nor that prisoners should earn wages. It is that there shall be fewer victims

Last year it cost us an average of £399 19s 7d to keep a man in prison. Adults cost a shade over £368 each. A youth at Borstal worked out at £574—or £124 more than Eton's fees.

In round figures, our prison service cost £17 million and returned about £885,000 by sales of work done and £75,000 through hire of labour.

What crime cost the nation cannot be so exactly calculated. Robberies, thefts and damage can be roughly totalled. But there is no way of calculating the sum of human injury and deprivation.

It is not surprising, perhaps, that this rough balance-sheet, with its gigantic overdraft on society, should be increasingly exercising many minds. Not only in England but in many countries, and through the United Nations.

The quest has been well expressed by the present Home Secretary, soon after he took his present office:

> I believe that we might one day come to think of our prisons
> ... as places where an offender can work out his or her own
> personal redemption by paying his or her debt not only to the
> society whose order he has disturbed, but to the fellow members
> of that society whom he has wronged ...

ACTS OF REDEMPTION

The idea was not new in 1957 when Mr. Butler said this. Miss Margery Fry had worked on it. She has been succeeded by others. There is now an impressive body of advisers in the Home Office, the Prison Commission and among outside organisations following the thread.

Moreover, the idea has gained some popular hold. Only a few weeks ago a Conservative women's conference in London—generally associated with rather stiff proposals about the birch—discussed a resolution calling for:

> ... the early introduction of a scheme to provide compensation for the victims of crimes of violence, financed, as far as possible, from the earnings, in and out of prison, of persons convicted of such crimes.

This is seen by some to be the second cycle of our drive to bring crime and punishment into closer conformity with the needs of society. On the first we have nourished the police; started a big prison building programme; reorganised punishment for young offenders; and found a channel for dealing with lesser motoring offences, the sum of which amounted to three-quarters of the million cases before the courts each year.

The next step is going to be harder. Like many simple thoughts, the conception of compensation through acts of redemption is proving exceedingly difficult to work out in practice.

There are two separate requirements and they are inter-dependent. The first is that prisoners shall be allowed to work and to earn "the economic rate for the job."

At present a prisoner can earn something under 3s a week. The value of such a sum to him exceeds its intrinsic worth. It is remarkable how much of this is spent on gifts or on children who visit them.

But an economic wage enters a new sphere. Would it contribute to the prisoner's training, seeing that he would have little discretion over its disposal? How should such an income be divided between the upkeep of the prisoner (at least £7 a week), of his family and compensation to the victim?

At present, such questions, which no country has got far towards answering, are academic. Until prison industry can compete on level terms with industry outside the "economic rate" is unattainable. To approach it the attitude of trade unions must be changed and a very big programme of prison workshops put in hand.

Even then there are many other complicating factors. Not all prisoners are manual workers or skilled men. Many are capable of only simple tasks and those on short sentences cannot be properly trained in skilled jobs.

Transition to Freedom

It is difficult to gear requirements from industry outside to profitable work in prisons. Prison industries are expanding all the time, but their efficiency and productivity are low; and it would take heavy capital investment to make them competitive.

Perhaps the most hopeful experiment has been the establishment of hostels from which men who have served long sentences can acclimatise themselves to freedom by working in civilian jobs during the last six months of their sentences. This certainly raises the individual's output, but it is limited to a fraction of the prison population.

These obstacles to earnings at the "economic rate" are modest compared to the difficulties of finding a satisfactory system of compensation. Who is to be compensated? If we are thinking in terms of all victims of crime, some form of insurance is unavoidable.

Conclusions so far suggest a State insurance scheme, with some small addition to the weekly stamp in order to finance it. This will be more surprising than welcome.

Should compensation be limited to injury or extended to property? If it is given for injury to property, where do bank robberies and wage snatches fit into the balance? If compensation is given for these robberies, ordinary insurance would be unnecessary; and the moderately well-off would be subscribing, through their stamp, to protect property-owners.

Consider a film star who has left £25,000 worth of her jewellery in the back of a taxi cab. What should be her share of compensation?

Burden of Proof

So we fall back on compensation for injury. Here other difficulties arise. Should a conviction be a condition of compensation? The criminal courts often acquit on the burden of proof where a civil claim might have succeeded.

Only about half the crimes committed are solved. It must be reckoned that if claimants could obtain money from the State scheme without prosecution the number of undetected crimes would tend to increase.

Yet to withhold compensation unless there were a conviction would be manifestly unjust. Half the victims would get nothing, and it is not inconceivable that juries would convict wrongly in order to give the victim compensation.

Indeed, there is some danger that the whole balance of justice might be tilted. Rape, for example, raises particular difficulties. If compensation were given for victims of this crime, the number of charges would certainly multiply.

These are not departmental quibbles. They argue for themselves and they suggest how unwise it would be to rush enthusiastically into a half-cooked scheme. No doubt some kind of formula will be struck, but it will fall short of many current ideals and its arrival ought to be measured not in months but in years.

Meanwhile those who hanker after such an arrangement would do well to take fresh perspective. It is possible to become too ingenious in penology and until quite lately a good deal of hopeful thinking seemed to be straying in that direction.

A Government's first charge is a state of society where the citizen can walk without fear. Earnings, compensation and the rest are useful refinements, but they remain refinements.

It is sensible to bring the long-term prisoner into close contact with outside conditions before his release, because on release he will be less prone to falter at work and offend society again. It may well be less sensible to reduce the sharp, painful contrast between prison and freedom by the partial substitution of modern factory units for prisons.

Anyone who considers the course we have lately been striking in this deep sea will perceive how difficult it is to keep a balance: a line between order for society and oppression for the prisoner; between revenge and redemption; between punishment and psychiatry. Strongly divergent views are held on all this and in one sense such extremes offer a safeguard.

Police, prison officers, prison commissioners, probation officers, advisory committees, judges and magistrates—all exercise different influences on penal policies. It is this consideration which makes it doubtful whether we are wise in current proposals to terminate the separate existence of the Prison Commission and bring them wholly within the orbit of the Home Office. The outlook of Prison Commission and Home Office may, as Mr. Butler says, have become one. That is not necessarily a good thing.

DISCIPLINE FIRST

This collection of separate and differing influences ought not to be co-ordinated. Apart, they offer an automatic pilot to a craft which is particularly susceptible to sudden gusts and storms of public opinion.

It is instructive to see how, in quite recent months, they have, collectively, given the wheel a slight turn towards sternness. We are moving, imperceptibly but unmistakably, from reform and punishment to punishment and reform.

It seems possible that authority and discipline are returning to fashion. That would have repercussions outside prison. It would also make it easier to restore that perspective whereby discipline is seen to constitute the main body of order; and interesting ideas and experiments useful appendages to it—not the other way round.

May 1961

SEGREGATING CLUBLAND'S SHEEP AND GOATS

The Government's Licensing Bill is to be published to-day. The complexity of some of the issues involved promises intricate debating ahead

"A man's house is his castle," said Edward Coke. In the 16th century perhaps it was. In this age of television, the telephone and tyranny at the sink it is not a man's house but his club that has the portcullis.

And this is as true of the million who like their beer and billiards in the local Working Men's Club as of the clubmen of St. James's or of those who occupy the leathery Constitutional fortresses of our Midland cities.

Clubs are strongholds, which is why Governments have been careful in this century to ignore much good advice and to avoid molesting them. Clubs, it can be foreseen, will prove a tougher arena than pubs in the forthcoming legislation about licensing.

Why molest them now? To explain this satisfactorily it must be said that the word "club," like "democracy" and "colonialism," suffers from a Humpty Dumpty disease. "'When I use a word,' Humpty Dumpty said in a rather scornful tone, 'it means just what I choose it to mean—neither more nor less.'"

It used to mean an association of men and women, of like mind or tastes, for social, sporting or professional purposes. It has come to include places where conditions for drinking are less restrictive—but often less attractive—than the public house. "Unlicensed drinking shops" is not an unjust description. More latterly it has come to include a place where stripteasing can be performed without fuss from the Lord Chamberlain.

UNFAIR TO PUBS

Out of this jumble, the Government must aim at a state in which honest clubmen and women can still enjoy modest privileges without irksome restraint; in which premises, run primarily to defeat the liquor laws, are made to toe the line with pubs; and where places in which the law is broken are shut down.

"A distinction can be drawn," the Home Secretary has said, "between members' clubs and proprietary clubs." It is an important distinction, but sometimes a fine one. A members' club is run for the benefit of members, and what it makes by way of profit belongs to them.

A proprietary club is run for profit. Many reputable clubs—including one or two with the aura of St. James's—are run like this. A high proportion of proprietary clubs are every bit as law-abiding as members' clubs.

For both categories registration today is a formality. Members' and proprietary clubs are simply registered with the clerk to the justices, who has no choice in the matter. Here is the principal source of mischief—and, as the publican sees it, of gross injustice.

A public house must go to the magistrates' court for a licence and accept exacting conditions. What the publican resents is not the privileges of the *bona fide* club but the misuse of these privileges by club proprietors who are simply commerical rivals to him in the sale of drink.

What does the mischief amount to? The figures give an indication. At the turn of the century, when this business last received serious notice in Parliament, there were 6,000 registered clubs or about one to every 16 on-licences.

To-day there are 23,500 registered clubs—one to every three on-licences. It has been said that the proportion of drink consumed in them has risen from one per cent. in 1900 to 11 per cent. today.

That, in itself, is not conclusively incriminating, but the Principality of Wales gives the game away. A survey was made recently of clubs in Wales and Monmouthshire, where there is Sunday closing.

It showed that a fifth of the whole population—a quarter of the drinking population—belong to clubs. Their recent expansion, unquestionably designed to mitigate the effects of Sunday closing, has been much more rapid than in England.

Broadly, where licensing laws seem locally restrictive the club flourishes, and that is true not only of Wales. Apart from hours, which are more flexible, in clubs, the club enjoys many advantages over the pub.

The police can enter a club only with a warrant. They can enter any licensed premises to prevent or detect a breach of law. There is no age restriction on entry to a club and no redress by aggrieved neighbours at the Brewster sessions.

Structural conditions are strict for pubs and may easily lead to refusal of an on-licence. They are clearly not applied to many clubs. Moreover, whereas the brewer and magistrate put a prospective licensee through a severe test of suitability, club proprietors select themselves—and a minority are not discriminating.

This is perhaps the biggest scandal—because a prosecuted publican is finished, but when police proceedings are taken against a club its promoter can disappear and start again round the corner without hindrance. This is the cult of the mushroom club.

In seeking greater equity there is obviously more than one course open. One is to give the pubs such freedom that no club could score an advantage. There may be arguments in favour of this, but the Home Office—and the licensed trade—reject them.

There is not the smallest prospect of returning to conditions of a century ago when public houses remained open for 166 hours a week, closing only during Sunday morning service.

Striptease in Soho

The solution may be to leave the members' and reputable proprietary clubs, which can prove objects other than drinking, their modest advantages; and to compel the rest—places which simply sell drink for the profit of promoters, to conform to all the conditions imposed on pubs.

This segration of clubland's sheep and goats is fair in principle, but it will involve both herds in sharper scrutiny than hitherto. And there are signs that some of the white sheep will resent it.

For example, all clubs, white, grey or black, would probably have to go through the court, and not the clerk's office, for approval, and this may become an annual obligation. But that is not the main difficulty.

An obvious weakness in the plan is that the proprietary club will devise means of converting itself into a members' club. The best way to check that is to stiffen the rules and objects of members' clubs. That will not be cheerfully accepted by all committees.

There remains a third, and new, category of premises, where the lure is not drink without limits but ladies with suggestive limits. The Americans have more expressive terms for these establishments than we do. Humpty Dumptywise, we call them clubs.

The recent growth in popularity of striptease clubs is beyond dispute. So many ardent sociologists have crowded into the Soho area to study this social development at close quarters and described their experiences publicly, that a portrait here would be superfluous.

But they have features which are noteworthy. Rarely, for example, do they sell alcohol. A total abstainer can visit one of these establishments with a clear conscience. He will pay £1, more or less, for a soft-ish drink and this buys a look at the act.

So striptease clubs will not, I foreshadow, be caught up in licensing reform. If we deem them to be immoral some other restraint will have to be found.

CONTROL OF ADVERTISING

Are they immoral? Parliament will have a duty to debate that. According to some evidence many of them are disconcertingly well-conducted and few in reality justify the conclusion that prostitution, driven off the street, has found a fresh market-place.

Most are not "vice" clubs. If they were the police could jump on them. There seem to be two possible approaches and both, as one might expect in England, are oblique.

The first is to take a tough line about suitable premises and to doom any club for any purpose which can be shown to be ill-designed for its objects.

The second course—and this is truly English—might be to clip their wings under the advertisement regulations of the Town and Country Planning Acts.

If we have anything like the control over street advertisements we think we have, then some of the enticing pictures which now bejewel Soho are out of order. There is a certain consistency in this line of approach because if, as we decided over prostitution, we care less what is done than what is publicly seen to be done, the girls might be allowed to continue stripping—in suitable premises—but not to announce the performance by public advertisement.

No doubt great moral issues are bound up in all these clubs, for members, proprietors and for strippers. I hope, however, that it is not all going to be debated with unrelieved solemnity.

There are light reflections to be gleaned from club life. One of them may bring cheer to those clubmen who believe the politicians are about to rush their drawbridge.

Sir Reginald Manningham-Buller, the Attorney-General, is the principal law officer advising the Government on this forthcoming legislation. He is also a member of Pratt's, in St. James's Street. Pratt's, the Cabinet heard with some alarm, is a proprietary club.

March 1962

A MATTER OF DEATH OR LIFE

W. F. Deedes on the need for careful scrutiny of an alternative to hanging

With the fifth anniversary of the Homicide Act 1957, which fell last week, comes more than one sign of changing mood towards the death penalty. It could be described as the growth of anxious doubt, with which I find it increasingly hard not to sympathise.

Lord Parker has lately given his view that the law cannot long remain as it is. Both Archbishops are now abolitionists, with palpable effect on the Church Assembly. The Homicide Act, which the Government no longer tries very hard to defend, has few friends. I believe it fair to assert that more and more influential opinion at the Bar would now be willing to exchange what seems bad law for another Act, even if it omitted the death penalty.

That is not the same thing at all as public opinion, of which probably a majority wants to keep hanging and some to extend it. But the decisive body of opinion now lies neither with them nor with the abolitionists. It is to be found among those willing to treat with a strong alternative to hanging.

Thus the so-called life sentence, which Mr. Butler is reviewing, is becoming a central issue. Given a good formula, he could tip the balance against capital punishment. The right formula will be elusive.

Outside Broadmoor there is no imprisonment for life. Non-capital murderers are so sentenced, but the term is reviewed annually by the Home Secretary and it can, on advice, be terminated at his discretion. To say it averages nine years misleads. It may be as little as two or three years; it rarely exceeds 15.

Should the court be able to impose a minimum term—say 10 years—during which there can be no question of release? There would certainly be a strong demand for such a safeguard if hanging went. Would a distinction be kept between murder which is now capital crime and murder for which life imprisonment is already given?

A central question is how long a man can survive in prison. In the last half of the 19th century when prisons were harder than now a life sentence was 20 years. In some countries it still is.

Some Could Endure

Notwithstanding the doubts of the Royal Commission on Capital Punishment a decade ago, there is no reason to doubt that physically some men could stand up to 20 years in prison. Evidence suggests that hope, not health, is often the key. Extinguish in a man the spark of hope of being able to resume an active life outside prison, and he may disintegrate more quickly. The age of a man sentenced to life is relevant.

Not many want to substitute for sudden death by hanging slow death in gaol. As no two prisons are the same an element of discretion should be granted—to someone.

Ought it to remain with the Home Secretary? That seems to me among the biggest questions. His responsibility for advising on the Royal Prerogative is recognised to be an awful one. Yet responsibility for granting release from life imprisonment could be hardly less awful.

Even with strong-minded Home Secretaries there lurks a danger that the policy of release might change with Ministries. There is a stronger danger that particular cases would lead to public agitation and political pressure.

Power of Review

Protests which sometimes precede the execution of a man are mercifully limited; controversy over a life sentence could be prolonged. Parliament does not debate the Home Secretary's decision on reprieve. It would be hard to preclude discussion on controversial life sentences.

Some would like the periodical review of the life sentence to go to something like a judicial standing advisory committee. The idea of such a panel has attractions—but it raises less obvious difficulties. Would its advice be binding on a Home Secretary? If so, he would surrender important executive powers.

As long as the Home Secretary reviews life sentences for murder, these remain in a category of their own. If a judicial panel is to enter into it, why, in logic, should it consider only murderers and not other exceptionally long-term prisoners?

The more one sounds public opinion on this subject, the clearer it becomes how many are concerned primarily not with principle but protection. They cling to hanging because it is the most emphatic penalty for the crime most feared.

They will demand, to a degree which seems to me impracticable, that such emphasis be translated to the life sentence. What we need is a temporary truce on the death penalty so that these issues can get to the forefront of the debate. Without a breathing space we shall be in peril of exchanging one unworkable Act for another.

November 1966

ADAPTING PARLIAMENT TO TV

For some reason the House of Commons always believes that decisions it makes on a free vote are vested with particular virtue. Thus when it approves, as it will tomorrow evening, the first (and in my view decisive) step towards allowing proceedings to be televised it will do so more than usually confident that it is acting wisely.

Well, it may be so. As a renegade on this issue I can recite most of the reasons why admitting television to the Commons seems a good idea.

For one thing it would discourage television's recourse to extra-mural (and sometimes extraordinary) debates. More positively, it would boost Parliament's diminishing share of public attention.

It would revive interest—and so improve attendance—in the Chamber. It would provide the public with insight into Parliament's workings. It would stimulate "a participating democracy." It would simply represent a logical extension of the decision taken many years ago to permit publication of proceedings. It might even speed certain reforms.

These arguments, and refinements of them, will be crowded into tomorrow's debate and they will prevail. These will be strengthened by the proposal to start with an experiment.

Superficially, this is attractive. It appears to offer a safeguard. If the results of a close-circuit experiment are distasteful to M.P.s then, we shall be told, it will be possible to draw back.

KEEPING ABREAST

If, as now seems likely, the experiment has to be deferred until next year for financial reasons, no matter. The House will have shown willingness to keep abreast of the times. The prospect is not a quick plunge into these uncharted waters but a gentle dip.

Of course there will be counter-arguments. Editing will be difficult. Exhibitionism will be encouraged. There will be a premium on polished performances.

The peculiar brand of inarticulate sincerity to which the House has always responded will be at a discount. Viewers will have a

163

different set of values from those to which M.P.s subscribe. The peculiar atmosphere of the Chamber, which M.P.s cherish and which has shaped debate and decision, will be lost to viewers.

The root of this matter, I believe, goes a little deeper than any of this. It lies in the fact that television has become an immensely powerful technique—not yet at its zenith; so powerful that it no longer simply reflects what it sees, but influences the shape and functions of what it seeks to reflect.

This influence was more than ever marked at the party conferences of this autumn. There were two obvious manifestations of it.

At Brighton it induced Mr. Wilson to compose and deliver a speech, not to the Labour conference assembled in front of him, but to the nation watching television. Without being wholly aware of what had happened to them, delegates reacted unfavourably to this. They suffered a sense of deprivation.

And this was odd, because the Prime Minister is one of the few who comprehends what this argument is about. As David Butler's book on the General Election of 1966 very aptly observes on Mr. Wilson's quarrel with the BBC: "At the core of Mr. Wilson's complaint lay a plausible fear that the pressure of media coverage could distort campaigning patterns for the worse."

At Blackpool the influence of television had even wider effects on the Tories. These have been building up since Conservatives decided—before Labour—to admit television to their conferences.

It has passed through several phases. I recall one anxious discussion at Conservative Central Office after a conference, at which the distracting effect of women's hats behind the Leader while he was speaking was discussed with professional zeal.

A sound conclusion was reached, I think, that rather than attempt to dictate to women what hats they should wear it might be easier to reorganise the whole platform in the interests of television.

We have, subconsciously, moved a long way since then. At Blackpool there was every sign of awareness that if the conference must take place in a goldfish bowl, the goldfish had better conform.

So standing ovations became not spontaneous but obligatory. What might have been a constructively critical gathering became a compulsive demonstration of solidarity. Laughably, the predictable nature of the conference itself now requires television to juice up proceedings with additional interviews, to sustain interest in its programmes.

Now there is the world of difference between allowing the public to see democracy in action through a popular and pervasive medium, and presenting to the public a version of proceedings adapted to suit that medium.

Powerful Technique

This is not stage-management, which is usually transparent. It is something more serious, for the audience as well as the actors are dissembling. It is an innocent form of conspiracy. It is submission to a very powerful technique.

At party conferences, where decisions taken are not fundamentally important, this does not matter very much. In Parliament, where decisions of some importance have still to be taken, such a metamorphosis matters a great deal.

It is no part of this argument to imply that television has any sinister intent. Some will always argue from this standpoint, and they will always be wrong. As well for a man who tosses a 4.2 Jaguar through a hedge to declare that Sir William Lyons has designs on him.

Outside a very small circle, few professionals in television see the power of their culture in broad perspective. For most the limits are what is technically possible, and these are still steadily widening. We have not yet evolved any acceptable ethos to impose any other limit. Without it, all talk of limits is confused with censorship.

We have been reminded of this, twice, at Aberfan. The important example is not the interviewing to which Lord Robens took exception, but the sudden discovery by government that television could interfere with a quasi-judicial process. Television's technique of interviewing could materially alter the evidence given to a tribunal and so, possibly, the findings of that tribunal.

Without properly assessing their discovery the Government issued a clumsy ukase which, justifiably, infuriated the Press. What I find disquieting is not the threat to freedom (which in this instance was unintentional) but the palpable unpreparedness of authority. No one has thought this through.

Yet without such thought the Government will soon blandly propose that Parliament submits itself to another process of the same technique.

The safeguard for Parliament, the experimental period, seems to

me quite valueless. The trial period will prove nothing of importance. Whether the lights are too bright or M.P.s' faces shine or
the programme is ill-edited matters very little. The crucial point
is the extent to which Parliament will change in order to conform
to the demands of its new technical master. Three months or so
will prove nothing one way or the other.

CREDITABLE RESULTS

It will certainly be argued that if television induces reform of
proceedings, then that is to the credit of television. That is dangerous nonsense because the changes thus induced will not be
primarily designed to improve Parliament's performance. They will
be designed to improve television's performance, and may well be
inimical to Parliamentary practice itself.

To define this line, which both television and M.P.s will tend to
blur, will not be easy. M.P.s will be sensitive to adverse public
reactions. Television will obligingly offer suggestions for improving
these reactions. Both parties will desire to produce results which
present Parliament on television in a creditable light.

In pursuit of these, people in television who know what they
want will almost certainly dominate M.P.s who will disagree on what
they don't want.

Moreover, what some people in television want is not limited to
technical perfection. As they see it—as perhaps Rediffusion has seen
it in Rhodesia—TV has now the power to influence, not simply
report events.

Come to think of it, the Rediffusion team could, less provoca-
tively, have recorded an interview with Mr. Smith in Salisbury. The
decision to invite him here, the implicit desire to get involved, is a
sample of the new approach.

These arguments, alas, will not prevail. Television will lay its
cuckoo's egg in Westminister, ostensibly because M.P.s have taken
a bold decision; in reality because the television culture just now is a
stronger force than the Parliamentary institution.

M.P.s will vote it in, believing that this pervasive, popular,
influential technique will carry them along. And that is just what it
will do.

The bill was defeated by 131 votes to 130.

WOULD THE ROPE STOP TERROR?

What a contrast we see between the passionate campaign a few years back to end hanging and the dispassionate way news is now received of terrorism's toll. Hanging was obscene, some contended, because it meant deliberately taking human life, albeit from a murderer.

The capricious and usually brutal taking of innocent life by terrorists seems to arouse less emotion in that quarter. Indeed, we are all in danger of becoming, as have the people of Northern Ireland, conditioned to it.

That is not to say that those who are now calling, as President Nixon has done, for at least a partial restoration of capital punishment can be sure that, if they are successful, innocent lives will be saved. Restoration would be a signal of determination to do something, and, as I suspect President Nixon perceives, to that extent it would be publicly reassuring.

But those of us who were and remain retentionists have to pause and ask ourselves whether we see this new style of war which has fallen upon us as a pretext for returning to the death penalty; or whether we are genuinely convinced that it would be an effective weapon in our defence against it.

If Northern Ireland is any guide, hanging terrorists might well not reduce the death toll. Life would be taken for life, pieces exchanged as in some ghastly chess game.

Nor should it be too readily assumed that what President Nixon thinks is good for America holds good for us. The background to his dilemma is different from our own. Since 1967 there have been no executions in America. Last June the Supreme Court ruled by five to four that the death penalty as usually enforced in America was a violation of a constitutional amendment prohibiting "cruel and unusual punishment."

Thus the death sentences passed since 1967 on some 600 now held in death rows for capital crimes have been practically commuted. Nixon's new edict will not be retroactive.

Most of the 15,000 murders committed every year in America are of one citizen by another, which is not a Federal crime but a

State responsibility, and will so remain. What Nixon is proposing is to make a restricted category of murders, such as killing prison guards and policemen, hijacking, kidnapping and bomb throwing, a Federal matter. So there are fundamental differences between us. The dilemma we share is whether it is possible to impose and implement the death penalty for particular categories of murder.

We took this road in 1957. The Homicide Act attempted to single out heinous gangster types of murder which constituted a principal threat to society and to make them capital murders. It was not a success, not least because the pattern of murder which can be held to threaten a society is never constant.

The necessary degree of flexibility for the death penalty, I am now persuaded, can be achieved only if *all* murder is subject to capital punishment; and that sanction is administered sparingly through the judiciary and the Royal Prerogative exercised by the Home Secretary in the light of each particular case and the interests of society at the time.

We found, or perhaps I should say a minority found, that approach intolerable, partly because of the medieval ritual with which we invested all murder trials. The black cap for distracted lovers, mothers and social flotsam, who constituted small threat to society and whose sentences were invariably commuted became obnoxious and self-defeating.

This drove us to experiment with the selective approach, which survived less than a decade. The fact remains that if today we took a referendum, public opinion might well vote about three to one to restore hanging. I base that figure on tests of public opinion in the 1950s and the 1960s. The United Nations has just noted a similar majority for capital punishment among its member-States.

But the House of Commons has, since 1964, consistently, though by different margins, voted hanging out. In my political judgment it would do so again tomorrow. Such verdicts have at least in recent years been left to the individual conscience of Members. The verdict could be reversed only if the Government elected to make it an issue of policy, demanded and got the support of its payroll votes.

So the wide disparity between public and parliamentary feeling on this issue, if this style of war is going to intensify, poses a serious but apparently insoluble problem.

There are one or two problems for the public too, which have to be thought through. Do they recall, for instance, the Craig and

Bentley case, which played its part in abolition? Craig shot and killed a policeman. Because he was 16 he did not hang. Bentley who accompanied him but did not shoot was 19. He was hanged.

The case is relevant to recent experience in Northern Ireland. It is safe to assert that at least a proportion of killing has been done by minors under 18. Indeed, boys of 14 and less have learned to kill. At what age now would we set the limit to capital punishment? Wherever we put it, how many gunmen and bomb planters below that limit are going to be trained and used?

Again, are we right to assume that the considerations which weigh with the professional bank robber, for whom a gun is an insurance policy, weigh equally with a Black September terrorist?

There is, further, the factor of conviction. Though a retentionist I have always thought weighty the argument of abolitionists that juries are more likely to acquit on a scintilla of doubt the man who will hang than the man facing a life sentence. As some recent trials have shown, the evidence before juries on terrorist conspiracies may well be more confusing, leaving more room for doubt, than that in trials for simple murder. The case for providing heavy safeguards for the accused, which the Criminal Law Revision Committee would now have us prune, was founded on the death penalty because that sanction is final and irrevocable.

It can be strongly argued, nonetheless, that servants of the Crown who face the sharp end of all crime, including terrorism, have a right to the protection of the death penalty. This limited category came closest to winning acceptance from the Commons.

It failed to do so partly because not all could in logic exclude the same protection from the civilian coming to the aid of the policeman or prison officer. As soon as the Crown category is widened, its strength as a special case diminishes.

There remains treason, for which the death penalty was not abolished. It covers a surprisingly wide category of offences, including the firing of naval dockyards. Had a High Court judge been killed in the Old Bailey explosion, the act would have amounted to treason. It certainly embraces acts of violence amounting to constructive levying of war against the State.

We have chosen, however, to treat such acts in Northern Ireland as lesser offences. We need not have done so. Treason can be committed only by persons owing allegiance—which Ulstermen certainly do. But it can also be committed by aliens if they are resident within the realm or, if quitting the realm, they leave family and property within it and therefore subject to the Sovereign's protection.

That, had we so determined, would have brought a good many members of the I.R.A. into the net. But we chose in the context of Ulster a different course. Do we reverse it now? And if we do not, can we treat such violence in Great Britain as treason and a capital offence?

SUNSET GLOW FROM SUPERMAC

At the End of the Day
By *Harold Macmillan (Macmillan)*

I suppose that most people if asked what particular political crisis clouded the last year of Harold Macmillan at Downing Street would instinctively reply: "Oh, the Profumo affair, and all that."

How wrong they would be, and how satisfying it must be for one who possesses, outstandingly, a sense of political perspective, to be able now to present his own balanced account of those times. It will be no less satisfying to have it said, as I think it will be, that this final volume of six, the work of eight years, is in many ways the best since the first.

At the End of the Day, embracing the years 1961–63, brings his labour to a close and calls perhaps for a marginal note or two before we come to the volume itself.

It seems to me nonsense to assert, as some do, that political memoirs of these dimensions are out of our time and compare unfavourably with, say, Rab Butler's admirably succinct account of affairs which covers roughly the same period in much less space.

Some men sprint best and others prefer the mile—or even, to go metric, the 10,000 metres. Lloyd George and Winston Churchill, like Macmillan, preferred the longer distance. It would be absurd to attempt comparisons, but my own feeling is that a distinguishing mark of Macmillan's work is that self-justification, so irresistible to past Premiers, is marvellously subdued.

Take this excerpt from an account Macmillan sent his Sovereign at the close of the Profumo affair:

> Looking back upon all this tragic affair I can see, as one always can with hindsight, moments when one might have acted differently and perhaps thus avoided so many troubles.

It is not an isolated example of the style. He makes an even stronger admission of error about the great Cabinet upheaval of July, 1962. Part of the grand manner, some will say; but it also betokens a

171

degree of humility, rare in politicians, less rare in statesmen. It may also increase the confidence of the sceptical reader.

This final volume is some 540 pages long, and of these the subject of security and scandal occupies exactly 30. Something like three-quarters of the book relates to world affairs, Europe, Africa, the nuclear challenge, Cuba, the Commonwealth and the Far East.

Not all of it is exciting, but none of it is hard to read. Most of his life Macmillan kept the kind of personal journal which we should all like to keep, were we less slothful. This helps to recapture, as private papers and memoranda cannot—the private secretaries see to that—the mood of elation or despair on the day, and the day after.

Given this and the gift of writing prose which accompanies wide and continuous reading we have, as the author intended, not an apologia or even a slab of original history, but an attractive story of those times.

Some of it, as this last volume reminds us, is also the story of these times because bad situations have a way of recurring. It is difficult to read, for example, Macmillan's chapter on the pay pause of 1962, a decade ago, without a sense of profound depression. Here it all was—the Pay Board, a prices and incomes policy, and a much lower rate of inflation, and here we all are again.

Strange and ironical, too, to recall how closely at that time the pay pause coincided with a revival in Liberal fortunes. In March 1962, in order to clear his mind, Macmillan put some thoughts on paper. They could have inspired one of tomorrow's editorials:

> But we have been swept off our feet by a *Liberal* revival [which] seems to indicate a real movement, representing or expressing real grievances or emotions.... Then there is fashion. It is getting dull to be a young Conservative. It is not at all smart to go Labour. Liberal is not in the Establishment; it has the flavour of "something different."

Yet plainly these domestic distractions, which now dominate our political thinking, were not the dominant themes in Macmillan's mind during those years.

He was attracted by world events, preferably on the most challenging scale and the personal reserve of this account does not conceal that in such events principal actors like John Kennedy and even the Olympian de Gaulle welcomed and enjoyed close association with such a mind.

There is a capital chapter on the Cuba crisis, including verbatim extracts from the long telephone exchanges with Kennedy—and for narrative how could one better the opening of this chapter:

> I did not have to wait long; before the leaves had fully turned and the oaks and beeches at my Sussex home taken on their autumn glory, my dire forebodings were dramatically fulfilled. I was working quietly in my room in London on Sunday evening, 21st October, when about 10 p.m. I was handed by the duty clerk an urgent message from President Kennedy. . . .

Even more moving is the concluding passage about Kennedy's last visit when he and his entourage were accommodated—not, one supposes, without enormous domestic upheaval—at Birch Grove.

> I can see the helicopter now, sailing down the valley above the heavily laden, lush foliage of oaks and beech at the end of June. He was gone. Alas, I was never to see my friend again. Before those leaves had turned and fallen he was snatched by an assassin's bullet from the service of his own country and the whole world.

Even in grave moments, however, Macmillan had his own sense of fun, particularly with Americans. He offers a nice example of it during a dinner party in Carlton Gardens at which Dean Rusk was present. The President had called Makarios a "famous fighter for Freedom," a remark, as Macmillan observes, wounding to many English people. So he said he proposed to call Castro "that famous fighter for Freedom." "Rusk (who took it quite seriously) begged me not to do so."

So we wind up with what Macmillan calls the stroke of fate which swept him overnight from a major decision about his own future into a serious operation and a sick bed from which, courageously, he had to take major decisions about his successor's future.

He decided, during a long convalescence, to accept, as he himself put it, that inevitably *E finita la commedia*; to avoid involvement in affairs, and to devote his time to writing this story. For the second part of that decision, at any rate, a lot of us have reason to be glad.

MRS THATCHER'S JIGSAW

In the political gale which blew Mr WHITLAM out of office it is doubtful if Australians were much moved by the weight of talent of Mr FRASER's "shadows" as we call them. Voters the world over get fed up with Governments rather than enraptured by Oppositions. When Mrs THATCHER reshuffles her pack, if she wants, as she says she does, to take office this year, she has to assemble not an opposition shop window but the makings of an administration. In building such administrations, even in "shadow" form, leaders depend a lot on their predecessors. Broadly, the MACMILLAN era was a more fruitful period in this sense than were the CHURCHILL or HEATH eras. MACMILLAN was a better coach of young and middle rank talent than CHURCHILL or HEATH. So the difficulties facing Mrs THATCHER are not, as some would make out, simply attributable to her own methods. She is, in terms of a future administration, thin on the ground. This cannot all be made good by whisking talent (sometimes supposed to lie thick and latent on the Tory back benches) from obscurity to high responsibility. Men and women in both the main parties, even those of proved political ability, develop at different speeds. No sound administration can be founded on young "discoveries," at least at the top. Experience counts.

On that account in many eyes still Mr HEATH could give Mrs THATCHER's administration a boost. He is seen—rightly so—as a figure carrying prestige in other lands, a more commanding figure abroad than, say, Mr MAUDLING. But that is not where he might prefer to carry weight in a future Tory administration. His choice, we guess, would be nearer the economic than the overseas sphere. That would not work. There are political as well as temperamental differences between him and the present régime. The party must accept that he is not in the reckoning.

There then remains for Mrs THATCHER an urgent need to find someone to present more starkly and sternly than Tories are doing now our duty in the Western world, which means in effect the subjects of relations overseas and defence. They are always closely interwoven. At this point for us they are more than ever one. Mrs THATCHER needs someone to illuminate the joint challenge. Lord CARRINGTON has the experience and, when he pleases, the cutting edge. The urgency of the task, for the time being, overcomes the drawback of having a leading figure in the Upper House.

Nearer home Mrs THATCHER suffers palpably from having no senior henchman with working experience of the *industrial* economy. That is not to write down the qualities of Sir GEOFFREY HOWE, a barrister, who is her "shadow" Chancellor, or Mr MICHAEL HESELTINE, whose recent progress illustrates the point already made about the indispensability of experience. The Tories who should be fighting for the hard-pressed private sector of our economy have sore need of one or two whose working knowledge of what is actually happening in industry can set a Chancellor of the Exchequer on his heels.

Mr PETER WALKER? He is at present, as the actors say, "resting." At least it could—and would by some—be argued that as an administrator he has got, perhaps unfairly, a much worse Press for his part in local government reform than Sir KEITH JOSEPH got for bureaucratising the National Health Service. Both Mr WALKER (out) and Sir KEITH (in) present a Tory leader with difficult choices. Both men in very different ways are gifted. Both have experience of large Departments. Mr WALKER suffered in his early days from being too much the politician. Sir KEITH, latterly, has suffered (at least in some eyes) from precisely the opposite. His grasp of fundamental social and economic issues and his sense of public service are unequalled and indispensable but not easy to harness.

Not every saddle for that matter will fit Mr WILLIAM WHITELAW, who is effectively Mrs THATCHER's second-in-command. He carries political weight and experience but—as he would be the first to agree—on a restricted front. There will always be a place for him with more duties than he carries now, but he has not the Ministerial mobility of, say, a MACMILLAN, a BUTLER or a CALLAGHAN who (with most diverse results) could at least essay both Treasury and Foreign Office. Among others near the top Mr IAN GILMOUR (Home Affairs) was known at least at the outset of Mrs THATCHER's reign to be a reluctant soldier. His independent turn of mind could well settle his future and then Mrs THATCHER would have to find a different prospective Home Secretary. Ireland is near the top, or should be, and Mrs THATCHER has to make up her mind whether Mr AIREY NEAVE measures up to it or is more valued as a close parliamentary adviser, which every leader needs. He cannot do both and Ireland looms larger.

These are among, though not exclusively, the crucial appointments for a leader who wants power in 1976. Of course a lot of other names come into it. There is Mr JOHN BIFFEN, who could jump several stages from the back without the risk of promotion beyond maturity. Neither he nor Mr ANGUS MAUDE (who cannot forever remain the party's deputy chairman), nor for that matter Mr NICHOLAS RIDLEY and Mr EDWARD TAYLOR failed to win laurels in the last Tory régime through inability. Personal and political differences rendered them indigestible. Here—and it goes for many more—Mrs THATCHER enjoys some advantages. Her rating of ability is not too much influenced by thoughts on past fealty. She has a natural preference for loyalty but does not confuse it with conformity. She showed that in her first appointments. They had to reconcile pressures which bear on an inexperienced leader who has come up fast from the back of the field. The next choices will be more difficult. They will show under which colours she runs. More seriously, some of these choices may have to govern, sooner than we thought a year ago.

SECRETS

All Governments have secrets and a duty to protect them. As the functions of Government multiply, so do the secrets. But these functions impinge more and more on the lives of citizens; and they in turn demand quite naturally more openness in Government. This conflict, inherent in modern administrations, was turned over to a departmental committee under Lord FRANKS to resolve nearly seven years ago. They found Part II of the Official Secrets Act, which governs disclosure of secret information, unsatisfactory. They described it as a catch all. In this it resembles laws in Soviet Russia which, because they are broken by everyone, make everyone a criminal and thus exposed to selective (and political) prosecution. FRANKS proposed a new Act, with narrower provisions. In effect criminal sanctions would bite only where it could be shown that a breach of secrecy would seriously damage national interests. Defence and internal security, foreign relations, currency and reserves, and Cabinet papers were entered in this category.

While Government hummed and hawed over this for six years— Ministers hummed, Civil Servants hawed—an altogether more exciting idea blew in from across the Atlantic. This was a Freedom of Information Act, under which penalties would fall not so much on those who disclosed secrets, but on public servants who unlawfully withheld information which the Acts deemed the public had a right to possess. More humming and much louder hawing.

It will be said of the Government's final conclusion, published as a White Paper, that the mandarins of Whitehall have won a handsome victory. The FRANKS recommendations with some reasonable amendments have been broadly endorsed. A Freedom of Information Act (which might go down rather well during a General Election) has been put firmly on the shelf. Indeed, Labour's manifesto promise of 1974 of "a measure to put the burden on public authorities to justify withholding information" becomes just one more broken election pledge. This is not a White or a Green Paper, but a true blue paper which any Conservative administration would cheerfully endorse. Whoever said that Labour's special advisers in Whitehall would suborn the corridors of power!

The new and narrower perimeters of secrecy are sensible. Criminal sanctions, questionably proposed by FRANKS for the disclosure of information about currency and reserves, are withdrawn altogether from all spheres of economic information. The test of criminality, dwelling a degree less than FRANKS on precise categories of documents, latches on to *any* disclosure which will seriously damage national interests. That may sometimes be hard to define; and not everyone will like the idea of that criterion of damage to the national interest having to be, in effect, certificated by the Minister primarily responsible before prosecution. Overall it is an improvement on the FRANKS formula.

Possibly the hilarious example of Washington, where a Freedom of Information Act has made it difficult for public men to keep their tax returns private, difficult even for newspapers to keep their own secrets, has concentrated Ministerial minds. More tactfully (and rather challengingly) the White Paper dwells instead on its cost and the distinction between the American context and our own context "where the policies and decisions of the executive are under constant and vigilant scrutiny by Parliament and Ministers are directly answerable in Parliament. . . ." True or false? Discuss.

Most uncharacteristically, a Labour Government has reached the conclusion that to tell the people all the people are told they have a right to know is not conducive to good Government. As the late Lord BEAVERBROOK might have exclaimed: "Hallelujah!"

WHEN A MINISTER LOSES HER WIG . . .

The Castle Diaries, 1974–76
(Weidenfeld)

"You know," said the Rotherham Labour party chairman in the Mayor's parlour to Barbara Castle (after an "excellent" dinner with "excellent" wine), "if you hadn't been a politician, you would have made a great actress." Or journalist, I would soberly add.

Not that it will cut much ice with Mrs Castle, whose Diaries are sown with lamentations about her treatment by this and other beastly newspapers. "Why do the Press hate me so?"

Some time I must explain to Mrs Castle that medical treatment afforded to a senior Socialist Minister who is taking the political knife to private medicine and paybeds is of legitimate public interest. But not now. Dog doesn't eat—well, dog.

By any reckoning these Diaries are superlative journalism. They are also singular. Most political diaries lower the author's stature in inverse ratio to their sales. These will sell like hot cakes. They will also raise Mrs Castle's stock. There is more to her than she ever let on in public life.

As to how it all got put together, I remain perplexed. She tells us she typed a million words of diary in this two-year period. She writes shorthand and, though living perpetually on the brink of her tough constitution, typed her notes regularly. But how did she remember what they'd all said? We journalists, ma'am, are careful where we put in the quotation marks.

It will not be the quotes, however, so much as the asides, which will titillate former colleagues. A random selection.

Roy Hattersley: He is an able, tough, unscrupulous little tyke.

Roy Mason: He is a competent little right-wing so-and-so . . . that india-rubber little man.

Harold Lever: The trouble with Harold Lever is that he plays too much bridge with too many representatives of the establishment . . . (He is terrified of every socialist bit of our policy.) . . . I often wonder why that lad is in the Labour party.

Michael Foot: But as I listen to Mike these days the more conscious I am that, as they grow older, these Foot brothers all merge into one collective Foot type: rational, radical and eminently reasonable . . . they are natural Liberals.

Tony Benn: His ambition grows by the hour. I believe it is so dominating that it could be his undoing.

The juicy passages, however, are not the essence. These diaries have a quality which Dick Crossman's lacked: they are highly perceptive, yet capture the mood of the moment; they are innocent of *post hoc* self-justifying overtones; they are sharp but not bitter.

Slowly read, they explain a lot which up to now has remained opaque about Harold Wilson's final phase. They tell us more clearly than anyone else has done how the Labour party travelled towards its present tragic pass.

There were those remarkable Husbands and Wives dinners, held weekly and usually at Lockets. Their core was four Left-wing members of the Cabinet—Foot, Benn, Shore and Castle. Others sharing the table included Mrs Hart, John Silkin and Lord Balogh. By embracing wives (and husbands) the conspirators avoided alarming their Private Offices—or the Prime Minister.

Allied to this *ménage* were "dissenting" Ministers, Cabinet nucleus of the anti-Market campaign. It led to trouble:

Blissfully I managed to pair at 9 p.m. and had just got home, cooked myself some food and was watching the 10 p.m. news when the phone rang. It was Harold, angrier than I have ever heard him in my whole life. He was almost beside himself. The venom poured out of him. He had generously allowed us to disagree publicly on the Common Market and what had we done? "Made a fool of me," he declared.

As emerges from some of these passages, Mrs Castle was no medicine for a tiring Prime Minister, who at one point switched to meet a weight problem from brandy to five pints of beer a day. They had been close. Now (June, 1975) he is on the night shift of a Cabinet shuffle.

"You are a good girl," he replied. "I could never get you to be a bad girl even in the days when you and I were younger." (I am always amused by this myth he perpetuates between us. As I remember those days, he never even tried to make a pass at me.)

Be that as it may, the stars are out of both their eyes. Now, we suspect, he finds her rather a handful. Conceivably, these Diaries will also raise Harold Wilson's stock. One marvels as one reads how he maintained any *semblance* of Cabinet unity or coherent Government.

Mrs Castle told him more than once that she was the best Minister he had. Perhaps she was. It is possible, nay sensible, to disagree with every political objective she had, yet to admire her astonishing tenacity, her capacity for getting her own way in Cabinet and nearly everywhere else, for defending her political friends to the last ditch and her knack of ironing her party frocks at the last moment and frying egg and bacon suppers in between.

In moments of great stress in Cabinet she distributed Polo mints to her neighbours—whether they were on her side or not. (I wonder if anyone does that at NEC nowadays.) At times of personal stress she went to the hairdresser—"a dash to Xavier's for a hair comb-out"—took her two dogs for a walk in the country or dug her garden.

> A great peace always descends on me as I stroll through the orchard or vegetable garden, picking up fallen apples and gathering french beans for the deep freeze. There is no doubt that, like Nye Bevan, I am a peasant at heart and—what is worse—a *kulak*! There is nothing like the ownership of one's own four acres for making one feel rooted in the earth.

And she a Socialist! But Mrs Castle makes no bones about her liking for the good things of life, a good dinner, high company, a little pomp and circumstance—all right, she says, as long as you don't inhale!

On her own front, through most of these Diaries, she is in pitched battles with consultants, with junior doctors and defenders of paybeds. Of course one should argue that she misdirected prodigious energy on wrong and damaging objectives. Yet, after reading it all and taking a political holiday, I would argue something different.

These Diaries are, as perhaps she intended, more a portrait of Mrs Castle than of anyone else. They are, overall, the portrait of a parliamentary democrat.

With the advent of the new and nasty Left, one reads Mrs Castle's Diaries with something like nostalgia. Again, one can argue, and some will, that it was precisely the likes of her that paved the way to the new and nasty Left; that from just such political wombs the monster sprang.

But one thing that distinguishes the old Left from the new Left is the capacity occasionally to laugh at yourself. In these times I warm to a Socialist woman of over 60 and great personal vanity who can tell a story entertainingly about the day she lost Lucy while inspecting the ghastly ruins of a burned-out old people's home. Lucy, she explains, was her *nom-de-guerre* for a wig she occasionally wore when "I had to be on show without the benefit of a hairdresser."

> Cameras peeped at me through every aperture as I went through the ruined home, watching my feet in case I tripped. Alas, I did not watch my head and suddenly, to my horror, I felt "Lucy" snatched from it by a piece of wire trailing from the roof. The officer said: "Oh!" I snatched "Lucy" back and somehow pulled her on my head again, askew—and carried on. It was one of those nightmares one dreams about and I froze inside with embarrassment ... But some inner grimness of will always comes to my rescue in these crises and I walked on, looking, questioning and *willing* my entourage to believe they had imagined it.

Not at all Dick Crossman's style. But even with a wig awry I think she would (as he did not) pass some of Clem Attlee's acid tests.

Probably the Rotherham chairman was right. Mrs Castle is a born actress and she jauntily went through her political career as if her Ministry, the Commons, the Cabinet, her constituency were all part of a gigantic stage.

So wherein lies the appeal of these Diaries? Partly it's her gift for narrative and humour; more I suppose, it is one's astonishment at finding a human being on the Left. Mrs Castle has in her veins blood the new Labour Left will never have; and guts the Labour Right never had.

1931—THAT WAS A CRISIS

W. F. Deedes recalls 24 days in which the Government fell, the pound's collapse seemed likely and the Navy's loyalty was doubted

We talk, or were talking before the wedding gave us a better topic, as if Warrington might change the map of British politics. Fifty years ago today events began to unfold which in the space of 24 days did change the map, with consequences which have influenced our course ever since.

The chasm which opened before the Labour Government in July 1931 led directly to a National Government, which prevailed in one form or another through the 1930s until 1945.

It had lasting effects on the Labour party, in whose aetiology Ramsay MacDonald is forever branded traitor. It destroyed the Liberal party, eventually split between "Simonites" and "Samuelites" over Protection.

It thrust the Throne into a role which, erroneously, has been suspect by the Left ever since. It provoked a "mutiny" in the Royal Navy. It put a dye into our politics which has never quite washed out.

In mid-June the Credit Anstalt of Vienna had closed its doors. Panic spread to Berlin. France delayed for 14 fatal days President Hoover's proposed moratorium on war debts and reparations. The Bank of England came under pressure. Gold poured out.

A world economic crisis quickly became a political crisis for Ramsay MacDonald's Labour Government because it had an alarming Budget deficit—of about £120m.

On July 31 Sir George May's committee, which since March had been working out possible reductions in national expenditure, reported. That was the trigger.

To meet the deficit the committee urged new taxes of about £35m and economies of £96m. The latter were to include—imagine it now!—lower pay for Ministers, Judges, civil servants; for teachers (by 20 per cent.), for police (12½ per cent.) and in unemployment benefits (by 20 per cent.) from 30s to 24s a week.

Absurd? So it now seems; but consider. To save the pound the Bank of England had to raise large credits in New York and Paris. To make this possible the Budget had to be balanced. To convince world creditors of an earnest to live within our means, economies had to include social services and unemployed benefits (which had risen fivefold in an earlier decade).

Overall loomed the spectre of the pound crashing, and inflation for us on the post-war German scale when mark notes had to be moved in wheelbarrows.

On July 31 Snowdon, Chancellor of the Exchequer, told the Commons of May's report, to be published at once, and warned of shocks ahead. On the same day the Prime Minister set up a Cabinet Economy Committee of five under himself to formulate proposals. All then dispersed.

The House rose, MacDonald went to Lossiemouth, Baldwin towards Aix-Les-Bains, Neville Chamberlain to Scotland. King George V was at Balmoral. Lloyd George was ill. Winston Churchill was in Biarritz. (His published correspondence at this time relates only to his literary activities and their remuneration.) Montagu Norman, Governor of the Bank of England, was on a long sea voyage ordered by his doctors.

For his deputy, Sir Ernest Harvey, the sky darkened early in August. The May report had alarmed foreign depositors. There was a renewed and severe run on British funds.

On August 10 MacDonald raced back on the Scottish express from Lossiemouth. Baldwin, who had travelled in leisurely style via Cherbourg, Caen and Falaise, was summoned from Angers. Sir Herbert Samuel, the Liberal leader, came in from Sheringham.

After a meeting of the Cabinet's Economy Committee on August 17 and 18, the full Labour Cabinet sat for 12 hours on August 19. A majority reluctantly accepted economies—short of touching Transitional Benefits. A minority dug in against any cuts in the dole.

Next day MacDonald met the TUC and got the bird. It stiffened his back. During the next desperate 48 hours the issue essentially lay between two economy figures: £56m which the Labour Cabinet could just wear; and £76m which was anxiously tendered to the New York consortium of bankers under J. P. Morgan after the Cabinet on Saturday, August 22.

At 8 a.m. on Sunday, August 23, the King reached Euston from Balmoral. At 10 a.m. he saw MacDonald, who warned him that the figure referred to New York might well break his Cabinet and compel his resignation.

On MacDonald's advice—a point which many versions omit—the King sent for the Conservative and Liberal leaders, Baldwin and Samuel. He was acting with total propriety.

Baldwin could not be found—he was wandering the streets with Geoffrey Dawson, editor of *The Times*. So at noon the King saw Samuel first. Later he said that he found him the clearest-minded of the three. Samuel proposed a National Government under MacDonald.

Baldwin saw the King at 3 p.m. Up to then he had expressed a view privately that having smashed one coalition (Lloyd George's in 1922), he had no wish to form another. But he offered all support. The King was well pleased.

The Labour Cabinet met at dinner time that evening, then adjourned to the garden to await the fateful reply from New York. It was brought to No. 10 by Sir Ernest Harvey. MacDonald snatched it from him, tore it open and blurted the contents to his Cabinet. It was ill-phrased, and appeared to pass the buck by asking: "Does your package have enough support from the Bank of England and the City to restore confidence?" Pandemonium broke out among Ministers.

By 10.20 p.m. MacDonald was bustling back to the Palace. He looked, it was later said, "scared and unbalanced." He tendered the resignation of his Cabinet. The King strongly urged him to stay at the helm.

Next morning, Monday, August 24, the King saw all three Leaders together. The outline of a National Government emerged.

MacDonald had then to face his Cabinet. He told them it had been decided to form a "Cabinet of Individuals" to deal with the emergency. An astonished hush was broken by Herbert Morrison, a lowly Minister at that time, exclaiming: "Well, Prime Minister, it is very easy to get into such a combination and you will find it very difficult to get out of it. And I for one am not coming."

Within 15 minutes MacDonald had been deserted by all save Jimmy Thomas, Lord Sankey and a most reluctant Snowdon. On August 26 the new Cabinet of 10 Ministers was sworn in. Four were Labour, four were Conservative and two were Liberal. MacDonald was thrown out of the Hampstead Labour party, Thomas out of the NUR. Arthur Henderson led the Opposition.

Low point of a bitter and confused autumn came in September when, after a misunderstanding, naval ratings at Invergordon refused to obey orders. The episode flashed round the world as a mutiny in the Royal Navy, heralding a British revolution.

Gold flowed out again—£30m was gone in three days. On September 21 the Gold Standard was suspended—to this day.

The October General Election returned 558 supporters of the Government (471 of them Conservative!), giving the National Government a majority of 502 over Labour—although Labour actually polled 6,650,000 votes against 8,390,000 in 1929.

That was August 1931, that was; in which Downing Street and not a Royal Wedding became the focal point for tourists. It was never going to be quite the same again.

THE ARCHER AFFAIR: AN ARROW PIERCING MRS THATCHER'S SHIELD

W. F. Deedes assesses the political costs of another Tory scandal

Other things being equal, our recent history of political sex scandals, which is colourful, suggests that they cause governments less damage in the public eye than supporters immediately fear or opponents privately hope.

The public have their own way of assessing sinners and saints. They do not invariably put exposed politicians among the saints. Sympathies in matters of this kind today are fairly broad church.

Alas, however, in respect of Mr Jeffrey Archer, other things are not quite equal, and for several particular reasons. Taking first things first, a man is not appointed as deputy chairman of the Conservative party by the Whips. He is not drawn out of a hat. He is put there, bluntly, because the Prime Minister has reposed confidence in him. He becomes a trustee of his or her judgment, only a degree less so than the Chairman of the party himself.

After a smash like this, it is wise to look first at the most serious wound. It will be said by many—members of the Conservative party among them—that this appointment was a misjudgment of character. Too harsh? I think not. Among their many impossible duties leaders of parties and Prime Ministers are expected to be readers of character.

Of course this is a pretence. They cannot always be so. In the post-war years Clem Attlee was thought to be an exceptionally good reader of character. "Don't measure up to the job," he muttered tersely to a Minister he dismissed. His gift did not preserve him from the Belcher scandal of the 1940s.

It is well, however, to take the bull by the horns. The Archer affair will inevitably be linked to the Parkinson affair. Two is a lot, as Winston Churchill once exclaimed after a couple of German battleships had slipped our clutches in the war. Any minute now, we shall hear the question asked on some popular panel game: "Are women, and in particular women Prime Ministers, sound judges of men appointed to positions of trust?"

To which I think the proper answer, on reading the political scandal-sheet of recent years, is that males and in particular male Prime Ministers have shown no marked superiority in this department.

So we come to the second and more delicate aspect of the Archer case. It was not it seems a simple matter of jumping into bed with a woman and reporting next morning. Mr Archer himself denies such goings-on. When Mr Murdoch's News of the World was last notoriously engaged in an operation of this kind, it contrived to photograph the Viscount Lambton, then an Under-Secretary of State, in bed with two women—one black and one white, if memory serves.

In this instance, they missed the bedroom scene, but claim to have been in at the party. Notes changed hands, through an intermediary at Victoria Station.

"A set up," said Mr Archer and this must indisputably be partly true. Yet it leaves an uneasy feeling. Furthermore, it is damaging to the Conservative party for a special reason. All party officers here, in America and in Europe are vulnerable to a charge of "dirty tricks". They once destroyed an American president. Irrespective of this episode we were going to hear a lot about party-political dirty tricks between now and the election.

Taking the bull by the horns again: when the second-in-command of a political party is caught, fairly or otherwise, in a transaction of this kind, he has exposed his office to a danger it should avoid like the plague.

Some of the mud will stick. It will call for strenuous efforts by the luckless chairman of the Tory party, Norman Tebbitt, if Conservative Central Office is not to appear a spavined horse between now and the forthcoming election. This episode, though in due proportion small, ludicrous and pathetic, presents Opposition parties with a hostage which some will most readily exploit.

Without dragging a lot of worthy names through it all over again, it is to be observed that the most notorious of our political sex scandals in recent years have a factor in common. The damage has been done not by the act of fornication but by vain and misguided efforts to prevent the lapse from becoming public knowledge.

Reactions to the Archer affair will be diverse. In the more

sophisticated circles of Paris, irritatingly, it is likely to cause bewil-
derment. At a most serious point in the last war, France's Prime
Minister, M. Paul Reynaud, was found in bed with his mistress.
Naturellement, there was no fuss. Though never much drawn by
French culture I incline to think they have a point in associating
English attitudes to sex with dirty mackintoshes and needless
subterfuge.

Which brings us finally to the subject of dirty mackintoshes in
general. Mr Murdoch's News of the World has now established a
fair track record for unhorsing politicians who have dealings with
women of the night. The contacts in that department must be very
good; and perhaps awareness of this ought now to enter the Notes
for Guidance offered to men taking on responsible positions.

After the hot fit, the cold. After excitement about the Lambton
affair had subsided a certain amount of public attention was turned
to the methods of a newspaper which apparently ran its own dirty-
tricks department. There was also a powerful public reaction when
the same newspaper years after the scandal sought to publish the
memoirs of Christine Keeler.

The best friend the Prime Minister, the Tory party and the Tory
party Chairman have at this moment, is the odd sense of fair play
which runs through this country. It takes a certain amount of winding
up to get it moving. It may well be that the News of the World and
its methods will achieve this feat yet again.

The jury are out on the Archer case. We must await their verdict.
But meanwhile a friendly word of caution to Opposition parties may
be in order. Were the public finally to declare that they found less to
condemn in Mr Archer's performance than that of the News of the
World, then the political bullet would be spent. And politicians who
tried to fire it would find themselves firing blanks—which might well
blacken their hands. One supposes that it is enthusiasm for soccer
which gives this nation a quite extraordinary sense of what is and
what is not off-side.

THE NEARLY MAN WHO DID GREAT SERVICE TO THE STATE

Rab: The Life of R. A. Butler
By Anthony Howard (Jonathan Cape)

On the publication of a new biography of R. A. Butler, W. F. Deedes reassesses the career of a political colossus

A man who just fails to become Prime Minister, as Rab Butler did, will experience a double misfortune. He will suffer the immediate blow, the hurt to pride, the disappointed eyes of friends. He will then find that the failure colours his whole history.

No matter what other good he did, judgments will focus on those defects of character and performance which led to this fall at the last fence. His detractors, anxious to defend their positions, will be very noisy about this. They will be eloquent about his weaknesses.

Rab Butler has had more than his share of this second misfortune. Perhaps it is because the door of No 10 was denied to him not once but twice, in 1957 and again in 1963. The Tory party might admit that it was wrong once; but never twice. So there must have been something badly wrong with Butler.

What nonsense all this is. It is thinking thinly borrowed from authoritarian states, where only Number One counts. I lunched alone with Rab Butler a day or two after he had lost to Macmillan in 1957. He was downcast. "The great thing, however," he said, "is to remain part of the political process."

That is what he was for more than 30 years. And it is arguable that during that period he exercised more lasting influence over the political process than any other contemporary.

In the 1930s, when I first knew Rab, he was doing most of the work on piloting through the Commons the Government of India Bill. He was Under Secretary at India to Sam Hoare. When I ended political association with him in the 1960s he was engaged in the complex task of unscrambling the Central African Federation.

Somewhere between these two posts came his Education Act of 1944; his revival of the Tory party's ability to think, after defeat in 1945. He was at other times Chancellor of the Exchequer; briefly and unmemorably, Foreign Secretary, and a Home Secretary whose influence on penal policy, for better or worse, is felt to this day.

These attainments, half of them forgotten by today's politicians, add up to a great sum of service to the state. So to see Rab, as many do, as a fascinating study in political failure, is cock-eyed. The virtue of Anthony Howard's portrait of him is that he gets the proportions right.

How wise—and typical—of Rab to choose as his biographer, and turn his papers over to, someone who has never been a member of the Tory party. The only way he felt sure of getting his due? This shrewd choice leads us towards one sound conclusion about Rab which no Tory without a strong sense of humour could have guessed. Was it perhaps, Howard asks, Rab's *irreverence* that barred his way to the highest place?

For a man with such a professional approach to politics, whether in his own constituency, in Cabinet or when working through his boxes, Rab's moods of skittishness were deeply puzzling. Howard has rightly gathered up some of the more extraordinary—and damaging—gems.

I particularly like one, new to me, delivered when Master of Trinity: "Mollie and I are so glad to have got here in time to see you leave." Mischief? Again, ". . . the best Prime Minister we have." Calculated? Hard to be sure.

But such ambiguities left some of Rab's colleagues uneasily aware that he found it impossible to take them seriously. Indeed, in private, with that low gurgle of mirth, he would produce mercilessly comic one-liners about most of them. No way to make friends and influence people.

Another point Howard brings home is that Rab was extraordinarily casual about furthering self-interest. Macmillan, of course, was not. He used departmental achievements to build his political reputation. After Suez and Eden, when the Tory party had to make a choice, Macmillan dressed his shop window in a fashion which simply drew more customers than Rab's.

But this related to another factor in Rab's career. Lurking inside him were deep and rather quixotic ideas about service. He once caused a mild sensation by solemnly quoting a piece of doggerel which ran: "Nations earn their right to rise, by service and by sacrifice." Odd though it seems, that came very close to his private philosophy.

Rab Butler is said to have demonstrated his unfitness for the highest office by his failure to put up a fight for it. In reality, his view of public service made such a fight alien to him.

Howard is very rough on Macmillan in several passages and finally quotes Lord Blake as saying that by blocking Rab's claim to be Prime Minister, Macmillan did a lasting disservice to the party. That strikes me as letting the Tory party off a degree too lightly. They made the final choice, after all. If Rab was the right man but unfairly thwarted, it lay with Tory MPs and grandees to sort it out; they were at Westminster to exercise that sort of judgment.

No, I think it is nearer the truth and consistent with Howard's admirably clear narrative to suggest this. Throughout his career Rab's many different political chores included a few too many which rubbed the Tory party up the wrong way.

Self-government for India, for example, left the diehards deeply disenchanted with Rab. Being in the Foreign Office under Halifax at the time of Munich was no help. Nor was his persistent stonewalling in the Commons on non-intervention in the Spanish Civil War, which Howard does not mention.

Not all his post-war architecture on the Tory party, monumental though it was, got warm approval. His Industrial Charter was deeply suspect in some quarters. Later on, "Butskellism" was a damaging phrase. And then, to mention only one more of several examples, before his second chance of No 10 in 1963, Rab had proved himself to be an enlightened, but in some eyes too liberal, Home Secretary.

I know of no instance, and Howard makes no mention of one, when Rab trimmed policy for which he was responsible to make the light shine more brightly on himself. That should count for something at the last judgment. Nor should it be taken to mean that his best qualities were negative.

In the light of today's catastrophe in our schools, it seems to me extraordinary that Butler, with his 1944 Act, should be regarded as a man who failed; and Tony Crosland, who sowed many of the seeds of today's jungle, is seen as a brave and brilliant politician. That is standing history on its head.

Seeking perspective again, Macmillan is credited with the bold design of our modern Commonwealth. The door to that was opened by the India Act. Butler's strongest adversary on that was Churchill. Butler's instinct was right, Churchill's wrong.

For all his funny ways, R. A. Butler was a political colossus, overdue for fresh measurement. Anthony Howard has been working on this book for six years, so that its appearance just after golden eulogies have been heaped upon the memory of Macmillan is purely coincidental.

But, come to think of it, it is a rather neat bit of timing. Rab would have noticed it; and, I feel sure, it would have inspired one of his sly, memorable—and wholly self-defeating—digs.

A WHIFF OF MR BENN'S PIPE-DREAM

Out of the Wilderness: Diaries 1963–67
By Tony Benn (Hutchinson)

Publication of the first volume of Tony Benn's diaries presents an intriguing insight into the mind of Labour's most singular Left-winger

By a stroke of irony which Tony Benn may not perceive, the first volume of his political diaries appears in the week after Labour's inquest at Brighton. It is hard to think of any figure in the Labour party more symbolic than Benn of what Labour has been seeking to distance itself from. Not personally, of course, but politically.

In writing about Tony Benn one must try—though most Tories find the feat beyond them—to separate the individual from his politics. In private Benn is an engaging companion, has been a model son, husband and father and is, with an old-fashioned courtesy that went out with Edward VII, capable of exercising enormous charm. Indeed, as we learn from these diaries, he once charmed the Queen into a decision about the Post Office that had later to be adjusted.

When we turn to politics, however, this amiable figure becomes red in tooth and claw. Benn has the artistry of the bullfighter, knowing precisely where the political banderillas will cause greatest aggravation to the adversary. People find all this hard to explain, so they tap the sides of their heads knowingly and fall back on words like "bananas".

It is with the earnest hope of learning more about such a strange man that one turns to this large volume—only the first instalment, mark you—because diaries are often revealing self-portraits. This one does not disappoint. Between passages of stupefying banality there are scattered many clues to Tony Benn's character.

What they cannot explain, because this volume ends in 1967, is why Benn has changed in 20 years from a figure one could have some sympathy with to a figure for whom it is increasingly difficult to arouse sympathy in any quarter. We can only examine in any detail the clues to character available here. Of these, by far the most revealing is the clue of the postage stamps, which is worth reciting at some length.

The greater part of this volume's 500 pages relates to the months when Tony Benn was Postmaster-General (October 1964–June 1966). Throughout this period he set his heart on getting into circulation larger postage stamps with contemporary designs but omitting the Queen's head. According to David Gentleman, the stamp designer Benn was in league with, "it was impossible to get a decent quality of stamps in this country until the Queen's head was removed".

Were someone to write a novel about Tony Benn on those lines, it would be dismissed as fanciful and in poor taste. The stamps were to become an obsession, embracing the Palace, No 10 and the Cabinet Office and Benn's own senior officials. In audience with the Queen he got down on the carpet to spread the proposed designs before her. He left believing that the Queen had agreed to what he wanted. Then obstacles reappeared. Benn's darkest suspicions were fulfilled. He was being thwarted by the detested Establishment.

At one point even the Prime Minister was moved to make a joke about Benn's stamps. "This was more than Caroline (Benn) could bear: that Harold has dropped into the habit of making slighting references to me instead of referring to the serious work that we're doing." The fur flew. Benn quailed.

On the last day of that year (1965) Benn enters reflectively in his diary that he may be giving stamps too much time and should concentrate on the essentials of the job. The resolution was short-lived.

Marcia Falkender took Benn's side, declaring it to be a scandal that in modern England the Queen should have any say about anything at all. Harold Wilson was more urbane. "She is a nice woman . . . and you absolutely charmed her into saying yes when she didn't really mean it." Benn then claimed that the Queen had expressed delight at his proposals. "Ah," said Harold, "but the Queen was quite unable to resist your youth, enthusiasm and charm. You were clearly a working man's Lord Melbourne."

It is not the portrait of a well-balanced man. Many suffer from political aberrations in youth, but mellow with age. Benn seems to have reversed this process. Back in 1951 I broadcast some discussions with him on the BBC Light (sic) programme called "Argument"— for which we got the then generous fee of 15 guineas. I cannot remember what we argued about, only that it was a most enjoyable political encounter, which it would not be today.

I suspect, and close reading of the diaries supports this, that the long personal struggle Benn engaged in to escape his hereditary title added a certain amount of bile to his politics. He remembers very clearly who supported him and who did not and this crops up in several diary entries.

The diaries contain a great many references to his wife Caroline and her opinions—"my sternest critic"—so it is fair to add this. A woman married to someone like Tony Benn may well assist him by acting occasionally as a political sedative rather than a political stimulant. One gets the impression that Caroline Benn has not seen this as part of her wifely duties.

Far more central, however, to Tony Benn's failure to become the sort of political figure in the Labour party he aspired to be—oh yes, he had his personal ambitions in politics like everyone else—has been a failure to *observe*. Tony Benn, though a highly sensitive man, is not sensitive to what is going on around him if it is not what he wishes to see. He lacks political feel because his mind is dominated by the kind of society he desires to bring about.

He is not, as most Tories suppose, a Marxist. He is a very old-fashioned socialist, a Fabian Colonel Blimp, with the same sort of fixed ideas about our society that Sidney and Beatrice Webb indulged. It is a long time since I read Beatrice Webb's diaries but Benn's arouse echoes of them.

His diaries tell us of his disenchantment, first with Gaitskell and then after a time with Wilson, not least because both men, though socialists, deviated at some point from Benn's ideals and came to see, as Rab Butler saw, that politics has to be the art of the possible.

Again and again we observe his anger with civil servants, "royal flunkeys", the Private office at No 10 and the hierarchy of the BBC. They not only failed to share his visions but sometimes took active steps to preserve the nation from their fulfilment. As a member of Wilson's kitchen cabinet, he was valued for his ideas. As a departmental minister he found his civil servants altogether less receptive. It was a natural contradiction, but one Benn found intolerable.

Benn has more than the human share of personal vanity. It has not been so much the frustrating departmental experiences suffered by most ministers that have soured him as the failure of his peers to put his own valuation on his qualities. There has been a marked

petulance about his behaviour in recent years, when his main achievement has been to raise a standard for a wild miscellany of extremists
who have done the public life of this country no good at all.

In 1982, in the struggle for the deputy leadership against Denis
Healey, he missed getting greater power to exercise this influence by
only a whisker. Bluntly, for reasons one can only speculate about,
Benn in recent years has set out to foster a small political minority
which is not merely extreme but in some of its methods evil. Has he
done this wittingly or unwittingly? We shall have to wait to find
out . . .

While he was still a Minister, I went to have lunch with Tony
Benn in his office. With grave courtesy he hunted round for the
remains of a bottle of spirits—he does not drink alcohol—before our
plastic trays arrived on his desk. Then, banqueting over, we settled
down and he unfolded his political map. There would, he thought,
be a spell of what he termed "Thatcher plus North Sea oil" but not
for long. The longer future beckoned Labour for whom, it seemed
to him, the opportunities were comparable to those of 1945.

Now, with hindsight, these observations were wide of the mark
because they took no account of what was actually happening in the
country. If what Tony Benn observes runs contrary to his fixed
beliefs, he discounts it, falls back on his conspiracy theories. He
graphically illustrates one horn of Labour's present dilemma.

There is a telling entry for May 29, 1965, after a lunch with
Cecil King and Hugh Cudlipp at the Daily Mirror. They were
interested commercially in a fourth TV channel. Benn disappointed
them—and they showed it. "This highlights in my mind one of the
great difficulties of being a socialist in the sort of society in which we
live. The real drive for improvement comes from those concerned to
make private profit." There we have it all.

April 1989

SCOTLAND: PROSPEROUS, CONFIDENT, EAGER FOR A TASTE OF FREEDOM

A revived momentum north of the border for the Scots to have more control over their own affairs is being resisted by the Government. But it is not only the Tories for whom such devolutionary aspirations pose a problem. Even nationalists are divided about what they really want

Much of Scotland prospers. The new mood of self-confidence among its people is strong. The streets are clean, the windows shine. People in Glasgow walk with a lighter step. It is not difficult in Edinburgh to find places where dinner for two will cost £80; and along that rather dreary stretch of road between the two cities, the lights gleam a degree brighter than they have since the war.

Yet the politics are in total disarray. Roughly six out of every ten Scots, according to the latest survey, believe they would be better off as an independent state within the European Community; but barely a fifth think that this is likely to come about. Only three out of ten wish to remain under the Government at Westminster.

The tone and temper of the debate now going on among Scots about their future takes the mind back to the closing days of British colonial rule in Africa. "Free-dom! Free-dom," they chant. "Tell me," I felt moved to ask the Lord Provost of Edinburgh, "do you have any sense of groaning under the British yoke?" Cautious laughter. Eleanor McLaughlin, the first woman to hold the office of Lord Provost of Edinburgh, said that the idea had not occurred to her.

She went on wisely to recall that a hot fit of nationalism tends to seize Scotland roughly every ten years. In the 1960s it was wholly in keeping with the spirit of the times—"Bliss it was to be alive in that dawn . . ." In the 1970s it was North Sea oil. Now it is Europe. "The fashionable slogan of the moment," says Donald Dewar, Labour's Shadow Secretary for Scotland, "is Independent in Europe . . . It was invented to give a touch of respectability to the break up of Britain and has little to do with any genuine belief in European progress." Indeed, as he points out, the Scottish National Party has long been opposed to EEC membership. "There is a touch of desperation about their conversion."

For voicing such opinions, Dewar has been publicly assailed by Jim Sillars, Scottish National Party victor in the recent Govan by-election. A few days ago Sillars described Dewar as a "Scottish Uncle Tom . . . a subservient colonial towards his masters, deliberately denigrating the quality and ability of his own people."

In his forthcoming inaugural address to Dundee University, the new Rector will put the question: "Are we then to despair because we are prisoners of a Government which the people of Scotland have repeatedly rejected at the polls, and which is so alien to our instincts and our aspirations?" If this is to be the language of the forthcoming European elections in Scotland and the Glasgow Central by-election, then tempers will rise. Scotland will find it harder to keep the sense of proportion expressed by Edinburgh's Lord Provost.

Politics in Scotland today are upside down and need interpretation. At one extreme stands the SNP calling for an independent Scotland within Europe. At the other stands a Conservative Prime Minister who has made clear that she will have no truck with separatism. The United Kingdom, she has pointed out, is not the only country in Europe facing similar nationalist pressures. Were such movements to succeed, she insists, Europe would be fragmented and weakened.

Surprisingly, midway between the Nationalists and the Tories, we find the Scottish Labour party in an emollient role. "The Scottish Nationalists and the Tories have uncompromise in common. Labour is uniquely in the centre," they told me rather smugly at Keir Hardie House in Glasgow. Labour seeks not separatism but devolution. "It is something Lord Home has said he supports," they claim. "Most of Scotland would settle for the German pattern of Lander." (German Lander have their own parliaments.) "If you get it right at that level, you strengthen the unity of the Kingdom."

Surprisingly, the Scottish Liberal Democrats are to be found in the same camp. Over a supper in Glasgow, Jim Bannerman, SLD chairman, and his director, Ron Waddell, admit to being on a tightrope. "We are seeking to establish a new identity, yet we are with Labour on the issue of a Scottish convention. We are not seeking total independence. But if a moderate compromise is rejected, then there will be an explosion."

An undeniable weakness in this balance of political forces is the

Conservatives' strength at Westminster. Out of 72 Scottish parliamentary seats, they hold 10, one more than the Democrats, against
Labour's 49. Through Scottish eyes therefore the party of Government holds only one in every seven seats in Scotland. It can well be
argued that the Tory party in the past has been even less representative in Wales. And Labour has governed while holding barely a seat
in the South-East. There is no valid constitutional point to be made
against the Government's weak position in Scotland; but it enormously strengthens the cry of the moderates: "Give us more say . . ."

The Conservative Government in Scotland today finds itself a
minority amid a majority of Scots, who themselves are (within the
United Kingdom) a minority. History warns us that this is an
explosive formula. The Unionist party in Ireland is a comparable
example of it.

So, I am persuaded, the arguments of men like Campbell Christie, General Secretary of the Scottish TUC, simply cannot be
dismissed as of no account. "Europe is not a main factor," he says.
"The trigger has been the Government's expression of its own
priorities—which differ from Scotland's. Something different from
the *status quo* and less than independence is what is really wanted."

But, I put to Mr Christie, would a step in the direction you want
to take end the matter? Would not Scottish Nationalists then declare
it to be a useful move in the right direction; and feel encouraged to
demand more? A Government which perceives the likelihood of that
happening is not being obtuse, only prudent.

"Given a Scottish Assembly," replies Mr Christie, "we would lose
the ability to blame the English any more!" He cites the poll tax in
Scotland as an example of what exasperates him and his friends. "The
poll tax for Scotland, which was a symbol of something imposed
from without, virtually went through on the nod. But when it came
to England and Wales and *their* Members showed signs of restive-
ness, changes were conceded—but not on Scotland's behalf. Why
not? Because, there being fewer Tories in Scotland, they were
unconcerned."

Now even taking certain of these statements with a pinch of salt,
they help to illustrate what Mrs McLaughlin in Edinburgh tactfully
called "the sense of frustration." Is it necessarily more than that?
In political terms, Campbell Christie poses two possible scenarios. In
the next General Election, he concedes, an upsurge in the Nationalist
vote could well be at Labour's cost and would modify Tory losses.

In other words, the anti-Conservative majority would be split. "But the real losers," he insists, "would be the constitutional parties." It will be easier to measure prospective losses after the European and local elections. "If there were a pronounced swing to SNP," says Christie, "SNP might go for broke and tackle the Labour heartland in Scotland."

It is impossible to make a political assessment of Scotland today without considering the impact on Scotland of the Prime Minister herself. "She is a woman. We are very chauvinist," politely explains John Davidson, Director of the CBI in Scotland. "We are not chauvinist," says the Labour party in Glasgow. "We have many women in local government."

The Rev Roderick Campbell, founder of the pro-Tory Group within the Church of Scotland, offers another line of thought. "The Scot," he tells me, "is lord in his own manor. Mrs Thatcher calls that in question. He does not like it. She also loses the female vote because Scottish woman will not allow her man to be dominated by another woman. The Scottish woman is also feminist; she does not approve of Mrs Thatcher's goings on."

In his biography of Mrs Thatcher, One of Us, Hugo Young devotes a long passage to the Prime Minister in Scotland—gleefully reproduced by the Scotsman (with a horrid cartoon) during my visit under a heading: "She who won't be obeyed." Young declares she is stubbornly bewildered by Scotland, which represents much the more striking failure of her decade as Prime Minister.

If this is correct, it is also tragic. For the Prime Minister possesses personal qualities which the Scots retain and admire. Other things being equal, they ought to feel closer to her in spirit than many in the South. But they are not equal. The Moderator of the General Assembly of the Church of Scotland, the Rt Rev James Whyte, says there is "no dialogue".

A talk with the Moderator is instructive, if only for his dry account of what has become known in Scotland as Mrs Thatcher's Sermon on the Mound last May. "Prime Ministers," he says, "usually address the General Assembly at some time during their term of office. Macmillan, Callaghan, Harold Wilson all did. They usually thank the Church for its contribution to the life of the nation, that sort of thing. All very formal." He was unprepared for her controversial address defending the morality of wealth creation. Subsequently, he observed that her thinking had "a great hole".

There are however more profound reasons for Scottish discontent. Sir Thomas Risk, Governor of the Bank of Scotland, talks thoughtfully about Scotland's long industrial tradition. It is a radical tradition, which sprang naturally from what were Scotland's staple industries—coal, iron and steel, shipbuilding. The nature of the work has changed, but the national character has not. It still retains that strong element of collectivism and egalitarianism which, as more than one person reminded me, has characterised the Scots.

At a recent speech to the Adam Smith Institute, Malcolm Rifkind, Scottish Secretary, made the point himself. He accepted that Scottish society had retained the collectivist ideas forged in the first industrial revolution, even though economic life had radically changed. "The realities of the restructuring and recasting of Scottish industry did not . . . in themselves lead to attitudinal changes on the part of the individuals affected . . . the values of the old industrial era continued to exert a strong influence."

Sir Thomas entered another thought. The Scots played a great part in Empire. That remark of an American Secretary of State about our losing an empire and not yet finding a role applies with particular force to the Scots. The Empire gave them a sense of fulfilment, something which is lacking today; and Europe is not going to replace it.

Now it is readily understandable that sympathetic insights of this kind do not instantly commend themselves to Conservative Government supporters. Some of them feel even more frustrated than the Scots themselves. Ten years under Mrs Thatcher has unquestionably quickened the pace of Scotland's transformation from the old world to the new, and nobody seriously doubts it. "There is a lot of Government in Scotland," says Professor Bill Miller of Glasgow University's Department of Politics. "But this Government cannot get credit for it, because they don't believe in it!"

Governments are not normally slow to claim credit for initiatives taken in places like Scotland. There is something droll about a Government which gracefully takes less than its due for the contribution it has made to the Scottish economy. "Scotland benefits from a big public output," say Brian Ashcroft and Jim Love of the Fraser of Allander Institute at Strathclyde University, "but it is not fashionable to stress it."

This apparent reluctance to claim credit where credit is due is

BRITISH POLITICS   *203*

not the only trial for Mrs Thatcher's supporters in Scotland—whose numbers incidentally have probably not fallen as dramatically as the seats at Westminster suggest. Lord Ancram, who has been chairman of the party in Scotland and a junior Minister in the Scottish Office, rightly points out to me that even in 1987 the Tories got almost a quarter of the vote. "But the anti-Tory coalition got their act together in 1987." (It follows that under PR, which they oppose, the Tories could improve their position at Westminster.)

Most Tory leaders in Scotland believe they are up against a permanently hostile news media. There is a degree more truth in the claim than there usually is. Were I the circulation manager of the Glasgow Herald, I would warmly endorse its editorial policy of Scotland for the Scots. In the prevailing political climate, neither the Scotsman nor the Glasgow Herald would attract even the public support they get now if they were sympathetic to Mrs Thatcher.

Lord Ancram entered a thought in my mind which I have been pondering since. Do we get the worst of all worlds by maintaining a substantial presence in Scotland through the Scottish Office in Edinburgh? How far is the Secretary of State seen by Scots to be a Governor-General, and thus to be dealing with a subordinate people? If we governed Scotland from London and thus identified their interests wholly with our own (while respecting differences) might things improve? "I think," said a leading public figure in Scotland, with whom I raised the point, "that the downside of that proposal might prove to be heavier than the upside."

However that may be, I am left in no doubt that for those who follow the SNP's will o' the wisp notion of an independent Scotland in Europe, the downside would be infinitely heavier. Along with the latest System Three poll on Scotland in Europe, run by the Glasgow Herald and the BBC, is a study commissioned from the Fraser and Allander Institute for Research at Strathclyde University. The poll declares, as I have reported, that six out of ten Scots think they would be better off in Europe. Had the study been published before the poll was taken, I fancy the results might have been different.

The study assumes that Scotland would have access to about 70 per cent of North Sea oil receipts, a yield of £2.7 billion. This bonanza, it is conceded, would bring many problems. For one thing, the Scottish economy would be at the mercy of the oil market. And since oil is priced in dollars, it would be further dependent on the fortunes of the dollar. "The Scottish economy," say Clare Monaghan and Professor Iain McNicoll, who compiled the study, "is likely to be surrounded by uncertainty and volatility."

Whether or not an independent Scotland joined the European Monetary System is left open; but if it did, it would probably have to enter the system at an exchange rate which oil would make too high. Thus output would become uncompetitive. After independence, the study adds, there might well be demands for higher public expenditure—and for cuts in personal taxation. "The danger of rampant inflation would be considerable."

So the economic case for an independent Scotland in Europe is transparent. In his penetrating attack on the Nationalists' platform, Donald Dewar has more to add. "The SNP vision of a seat at the top table," he says, "is a fiction." He goes on: "It is power that counts in Brussels. France, West Germany and the United Kingdom have an effective vote because they have political clout. Denmark or Ireland do not have that kind of power and it is with these countries that Scotland would be grouped."

I asked a number of people how Scotland will fare in Europe if she remains part of the kingdom. Many Scots believe that they attract more sympathy from Brussels than from Westminster. In common with others, Sir David Nickson stresses the need to keep a strong independent business and industrial sector in Scotland—"so that Scots can get to the top of a company without going to the UK."

About 48 per cent of Scottish companies are independent, John Davidson of the CBI tells me. If Europe made Scotland less industrially independent, Scotland would be more vulnerable. "We have a large number of companies," says Davidson bluntly, "who think that Europe is a long way away; that Europe is not for them. Awareness of 1992 is high; preparations are not. We are better at manufacturing than marketing."

I doubt if any of this makes Scotland singular or particularly vulnerable to Europe. It could be heard elsewhere in the UK. But there are two other factors which may well have a bearing on Scotland after 1992. The first, a plus, is well expressed by Professor Jack Shaw of Scottish Financial Enterprise. Scotland's financial community is now looking after something like £100 billion. It has been the area of fastest employment growth since 1983. One Scottish job in 12 is now in financial services.

Scots perpetually remind you that they are on the periphery of Europe; but for Scotland's financial sector modern technology, as

Shaw points out, has swept away the disadvantages of geography. Shaw agrees that the transformation of Scotland from the old world of heavy manufacture to the new world of modern industry and finance means that more decisions are taken outside the country. "Capital markets are very centralist in their operations. Europe will want a lot of access points, capital to capital." But, he added, Europe's regional centres will also want access points and they are happier dealing with off-centre centres—such as Glasgow and Edinburgh.

Scotland's minus quantity *vis-à-vis* Europe, which Shaw and every other person I saw dwelt on, is the poverty of its international air links. "There are five airports, four of them international, all of which go somewhere; but there is nowhere in particular you can go!" At the root of this, as all Scotland is aware, is the tenacious political defence of Prestwick as the gateway to Scotland.

A compact between Mr Younger, Defence Secretary (whose constituency embraces Prestwick), and half a dozen Labour MPs named "The Gang of Six" has kept Prestwick alive against repeated attacks for a decade or more. The airlines want to use Glasgow, and Scotland's air links would be vastly improved if they did—but politics is politics.

Yet the dominant feature of Scotland today is the renaissance of self-confidence. It is not everywhere prosperous. In districts like Easterhouse, Blackhill and Castlemilk, levels of expectation remain very low indeed. As I discovered on Tyneside not long ago, regions in the North are now sharply divided between a majority of comfortably off and a minority poor in pocket and in prospects. The contrast we loosely—and falsely—apply to North and South is to be found within the regions.

Subject, however, to factors on which everyone is dependent—inflation and interest rates—the signs are bright. This is a far different country from the one I remember visiting on political occasions through the 1950s and 1960s. Yet Scotland is moving away from us. I am left in no doubt of that. It is not the shrill voices of the SNP which persuade me, but the moderate voice of Scottish leaders in many spheres. No blame for this, I must add, lies with Malcolm Rifkind and his Ministers. Rifkind, by all accounts, has done as good a job as Peter Walker in Wales, but in more thankless circumstances.

There is a new nation to be dealt with here, and we have not yet got the full measure of it. I say "we" because it applies to so many people in England as well as to members of the Government. "The values of this Government are not our values," a Scottish dignitary said to me. What I think you mean, I replied, is that the values of London and the South are no longer your values. Indeed they are not. A great many Scottish characteristics have survived what we in the South complacently believe has been a universal social revolution.

"The Scots never go to Blackpool; they go to Spain. So they do not compare the North to themselves," said Douglas Mason of the Adam Smith Institute in Edinburgh. The English also go to Spain, not Scotland, so they do not compare the Scots at home to themselves. So the Scots are old-fashioned? Yes, in a sense they are.

Let me put it this way. The characters of Dornford Yates, Berry and Jonah and Daphne and Jill, have long departed the English scene. But the characters of John Buchan, Sandy Arbuthnot, Dickson McCunn, Lord Lamancha—and I dare say Hannay himself, though I did not meet him—live on in Scotland. Take a look round Edinburgh, and see what they have managed to keep out of the clutches of housebreakers and developers. A lot of Scots character has been similarly preserved.

So what do we do? We cannot go on as we are now. For one thing, accelerating political confusion in Scotland will injure its long-term prospects, an issue we discussed seriously over lunch at the Royal Bank of Scotland. Investors do not like political uncertainty.

"Heart-searching should not be mistaken for belly-aching," Jack Shaw says to me. We too should do some heart-searching, and then recognise that in Scotland today there are principles which we have temporarily mislaid in the South. A small sign to the Scots now from Mrs Thatcher's Government, acknowledging their new place in the scheme of things, a modest grant of stewardship in certain of their affairs, a nod towards that empty Assembly, would catch the Scottish Nationalists like the first breath of frost catches dahlias.

At least we should listen to what the Scottish Constitutional Convention is trying to say. It is not extreme, it is not unrepresentative and it is not in a tearing hurry. It is prepared to take a year or more working out a scheme for an Assembly for Scotland. "We are conscious of the difficulties," says Canon Kenyon Wright, of the Scottish Constitutional Convention and Campaign for Scottish Assembly. The argument that such an assembly could challenge the sovereignty of Parliament at Westminster would be stronger if Westminster's sovereignty were not increasingly being shared with Europe. Scotland does not seek the Government's patronage any more. It wants this Government's trust.

HONG KONG: TREADING THE NARROW PATH OF HONOUR

The risk of civil war in China presents Britain with acutely difficult decisions over the future of the colony. Here, W. F. Deedes analyses Mrs Thatcher's options

Hong Kong, where the stock market yesterday suffered its worst fall since the global crash of 1987, now confronts the British Government with harder decisions than any that were taken during the dissolution of the British Empire.

Our agreement with China in 1984 on the territory's future after 1997 was always controversial, because this was the first British colony in history to be handed over *not* to its own people and to independence, but to another sovereign power. Worse, to a totalitarian Communist power. To justify a decision of that order everything between 1984 and 1997 had to go right. In Peking, this last week or so, everything has gone wrong.

When we signed the agreement with Peking, China seemed to be on the road to stable development. Not long before, it had been rediscovered by the West. By the early 1970s we were establishing an Anglo-China Society in this country. The late Malcolm MacDonald, Ramsay's son, was made president. Jeremy Thorpe (Lib), Michael Stewart (Lab) and myself (Con) became vice-presidents.

When, in this heady atmosphere, the future of Hong Kong after 1997 came to be negotiated with the Chinese Government, we were playing the most difficult of all international combinations: a weak hand, coupled with an earnest desire not to take the smile off the face of the tiger.

Our hand is *still* weak. The Foreign Office has a difficult and, as we shall see, an increasingly unpopular role to play, but it is not, as some would now have it, an altogether contemptible one. As countless Foreign Secretaries have learnt, foreign policy is dictated by the power available to their government. To those ready to declare, as many people are, that after the bloodbath in Peking we should immediately abrogate our agreement with China, it is necessary to bring forward certain uncomfortable facts.

Supposing we abrogate the agreement. Supposing even that we were now to propose, in the light of events, that after 1997 Hong Kong should neither remain a British colony nor be handed over to China, but should for a period of time be protected by a United Nations mandate. In the prevailing climate that might even attract a degree of international support. And if Peking then marched in— what then? An uncomfortable fact about Hong Kong is that it is militarily indefensible against a determined aggressor. We are not in a position to defy China.

Yet, as the British Government must by now have recognised, events in Peking must signal a fundamental change in our arrangements with Hong Kong. Already, work on the post-1997 constitution has had to be suspended. In any event, the so-called second draft of Basic Law could no longer stand. As at present drafted, it would allow Peking to declare a state of emergency in Hong Kong and to impose national laws when it considered there was "turmoil" in the colony or when China was herself at war. By imposing martial law in Peking without the prior consent of the National People's Congress, Li Peng has rendered such language meaningless. He has destroyed the last vestige of confidence in Hong Kong that an agreement with Peking is anything but a scrap of paper.

By the same token he has destroyed any understanding that may have existed—and at best it was pretty slender—on the future government of Hong Kong. We have been accused of showing weakness here, of agreeing, with a nod towards Peking, to a postponement of full democracy. The Basic Law's second draft delays the introduction of democracy until at least 2012. Such dates and agreements have been reduced to dust by this latest turn of events. Nothing to which any Chinese ruler puts his name will be acceptable to Hong Kong.

The only course now open to us is to explore by one means or another a refuge for those in Hong Kong who are now convinced that after 1997 their futures and their lives will be at risk.

Pressure to leave the colony was building up before Tiananmen Square. Hong Kong had already become the crossroads of desperate human movements. At one door the boat people, seeking escape from China's former friends in Vietnam, have been hammering for entry. By another, the people of Hong Kong have been voting on their future by leaving the territory—45,000 of them last year. That second movement will be greatly accelerated from now on.

In April the House of Commons Select Committee on Foreign Affairs listened in Hong Kong to heart-rending pleas for the right of abode in Britain for the 3.25 million people who enjoyed it until our Nationality Acts removed that right. Members of the committee were firm in insisting that restoration of that right was a non-starter. It would, they stressed, prove politically impossible to persuade Parliament to pass a law giving so many a right of abode here.

Now, of course, it will be said that Tiananmen Square alters that. Failing an international agreement, the British Government, which holds moral, though no longer statutory, responsibility for over three million members of a British colony, will have no option but to persuade Parliament to think again. But Tiananmen Square *also* dramatically alters the numbers we might have to expect.

Hong Kong's reasoning in evidence before the Select Committee was that if China's promises of independence for the colony were kept, few would wish to leave. To offer right of abode, therefore, might cost us very little. But if China interfered in the colony, and rendered life intolerable for former members of it, then we would be under a moral obligation to rescue them from tyranny. That persuasive argument has now been turned upside down. It has been made abundantly clear to us that were we minded, as Portugal as done for ethnic Chinese in Macao, to grant passports to those born in the colony or resident there for more than eight years, the floodgates would be opened.

Granted our military impotence, we are not called upon as a matter of honour to scrap our agreement on Hong Kong and then vainly to defy China. Our obligations to those in Hong Kong who formerly had rights in this country are another matter. Almost invariably in the winding-down of our colonial empire, those from whom we parted became citizens of independent states. Hong Kong is an exception to this, and up to now we have been able to persuade ourselves that to make such an exception is not incompatible with honour.

We have now had brought to our notice the sort of future which may await the people of Hong Kong as a result of our agreement with China. On past form, I think it unlikely that we can count very heavily on international rescue operations. We are going to be required to help by opening our gates here more widely, perhaps on a scale hitherto unthinkable.

There will be a strong public reaction to this; and much of it, notwithstanding today's feeling of outrage and pity, will be hostile. Somewhere between that cry and its inescapable moral obligations, Mrs Thatcher's Government will have to tread the narrow path of honour.

WHAT PRICE A SEAT IN THE HOUSE?

If we looked at a dozen established professional careers and compared their respective salary levels today with what they were 50 years ago in real terms, we would obviously get some surprising results. Accountants up? Doctors down? None, however, has changed more than the salary of a Member of Parliament. Until not much more than half a century ago, most MPs actually paid for the privilege of doing a job which today offers a salary of £26,000 and upwards of as much again in secretarial and other allowances.

Until 1912, MPs received no pay at all. Such Labour MPs as there then were counted mainly on the support of trade unions. Almost all Tory and most Liberal MPs paid the full cost of their elections—and subscribed to their local constituency organisations as well.

Duff Cooper, later the Earl of Norwich, described in his memoirs his experiences at Stroud in Gloucestershire, where he sought to be the Tory candidate in 1924. "I undertook to contribute £300 a year (roughly £9,000 today) to the local association, which I hoped I should be able to do out of my parliamentary salary."

The parliamentary salary at that time was still what it was when established in 1912, namely £400 a year. So Duff Cooper, never a wealthy man but one who had to count on the stage earnings of his wife Diana to assist his political career, was ready to part with three-quarters of his prospective salary to the Stroud Conservative Association. It was not enough. "Two days later I learnt that an old, possibly wiser and certainly much richer candidate had been selected."

In the financial crisis of 1931, the modest salary was actually reduced to £360 as an economy measure, and was not restored until 1934. It was still £400 in 1937, when I was a political correspondent at Westminster—on roughly twice that amount. Politicians in all parties assured me that some Labour MPs without private means were suffering serious privation. They had, most of them, to sustain two homes; and they were simply not getting enough to eat.

In those days there were two teahouses across the road from the

House. One immensely wealthy Tory MP—Labour's Ellen Wilkinson once described him as a "keep the change man"—urged me to join the campaign for higher parliamentary salaries and to watch how some Labour MPs took their "high teas" at Lyons or the ABC. For about sevenpence, it was possible to buy a pot of tea and a poached egg on two slices of toast.

If the two slices of toast were arranged in a step formation, and the poached egg was perched on the top step before incision, both slices of toast were made tasty. As a result of what became established in my mind as the "poached egg campaign" the pay was raised to the noble sum of £600 in 1937—where it stayed until after the Second World War.

After 1946, when the salary was raised to £1,000, increases in pay and allowances came pretty regularly, although it was not until 1965 that the Members' Pensions Act was introduced, since when all MPs and their dependants have enjoyed a comprehensive pension scheme. From 1983, MPs' pay has been linked to Civil Service rates.

The major changes in a parliamentary career which began in 1946 were due less to Mr Attlee's Labour Government than to the fact that this country was going through its second post-war social revolution. The parliamentary career and salary from, say, 1912, charts those revolutions better than most other indicators. It became obvious after 1945 that a selection system which could find room only for wealthy Tory candidates, and virtually ruled out poor ones, had had its day.

Nor was it simply a matter of money. Oliver Lyttelton, later Lord Chandos, who joined Churchill's Government early in the war, has given a graphic account in his memoirs of his own approach to a Tory seat. He was called to appear before Lord Windlesham, then vice-chairman of the Conservative party.

> It was a warm, cloudless day, and I put on a pair of flannel trousers, a short blue coat, an IZingari tie and brown and white shoes, sometimes described as Monte Carlo strollers. As it turned out, I could not have been worse dressed for the occasion, because I arrived in the middle of an air raid . . . The conversation went something like this. Lord Windlesham: 'I understand your candidature is backed by Winston?' 'Yes.' 'A great mistake, but it can't be helped. Have you been through the

Divorce Court lately?' 'No.' 'Well, that's something, quite a lot of candidates have, you know. Not lately bankrupt? No? Forgive my asking, did you marry a lady?' I thought I had. With a smile, 'Great help, great help in the constituency'.

From the late Forties, whether or not he had married a lady, a Tory candidate was relieved of his election expenses, and his subscription to the local party organisation was tightly regulated under rules drawn up for the party by Sir David Maxwell-Fyfe, QC, later Lord Kilmuir. A candidate's election expenses had in any case been restricted in the Corrupt Practices Act of 1883, by a formula based on the number of electors. A candidate could no longer buy electors in relation to the length of his purse. But even in the election of 1945 the average expenditure per candidate amounted to £638—say, £16,000 in today's money—which was a sizeable sum for a private purse.

So, in effect, from being a patron of his own parliamentary career, the Tory MP became a charge on subscribers to his local party organisation. No other profession has gone through such a metamorphosis. Today's Member of Parliament is required to "keep his constituency warm". About half Labour's MPs traditionally look to trade unions for support, but they, too, are expected by their constituents (who are also tax payers) to "earn their keep".

Before the war I was faintly acquainted with an immensely grand Tory MP, representing an East Anglian constituency, which (he declared) he visited only once a year. This was on the occasion of the local Tory party's annual summer fete. "And I only go if it's a big one," he would explain.

During my time in the House of Commons, by way of contrast, I had a colleague in the Tory party who visited the House as seldom as possible, in order to spend time with his constituents in what was a marginal seat. He claimed to visit every house in the constituency once a year.

Between these extremes, the majority of MPs today strive to keep a demanding House of Commons in balance with constituencies, which vary widely in what they expect of their incumbent. For some that amounts to a seven-day week; and, if they represent Scotland or the North, one or two nights in a train as well. From being an honour for which you were expected to fork out, the parliamentary seat has become a career from which you appear to cash in.

Naturally, therefore, the selection process—to which has now been added the deselection process—has become more searching (some would say, downright intrusive). There are, however, consolations. In no constituency, Tory, Liberal Democrat, Green or Labour, is a candidate likely to be asked whether or not he has married a lady.

HOME TRUTHS ABOUT THAT THATCHER TAPE

"Thatcher shattered by her speedy exit" was our front page headline on May 9 above the summary of an interview she had given in Washington to Vanity Fair magazine. It was fair comment, but not a phrase to linger long in people's minds. The phrase that lingered and was much discussed came in our second headline, taken from the interview, "Home is where you come to when you have nothing better to do."

Reactions were swift. Letters appeared in many newspapers (including this one) pointing out that upwards of two million unemployed had nowhere else to go but home, and criticising Mrs Thatcher for snivelling about it. The phrase made a field day for those who cordially dislike her. Mrs Thatcher, though deeply hurt, made no public comment.

There existed, however, an independent tape of the interview and a second version of Mrs Thatcher's fateful words appeared in The Times of May 24. At this point in the interview she was discussing her family. The sentence as spoken ran on these lines: "And sometimes if something happens and we don't see the family as often as we would wish, and they go off I say: 'Well, look, home is where you come to when you haven't anything better to do. We are always there.'"

Paul Johnson took it up in The Spectator June 1, concluding that Vanity Fair "was guilty of an infamous piece of journalistic misconduct". Love of home and family, he rightly pointed out, is one of Mrs Thatcher's strongest emotions. The disputed passage in the Vanity Fair interview conveyed precisely the opposite impression. I commented in my column: "Accidental, I suppose, but are we sure?"

The effect of all this was to draw the badger. On June 4 a lengthy letter appeared in The Times from Tina Brown, editor-in-chief of Vanity Fair, defending the interview. To call the letter disingenuous would be charitable.

"Whoever released the transcript of her interview with Vanity Fair," she wrote, "has chosen to punctuate these words and those surrounding them in such a way that they read as an exhortation to her children. But the tricky business of punctuating spoken remarks without the nuances of voice and expression should not be allowed to obscure the main issue."

The "tricky business' has now been taken up by the editor of The Times, Simon Jenkins, in a reply of his own.

It is established beyond doubt that Mrs Thatcher, in her interview with Vanity Fair, entered a long passage about her family life and that what she said about home related to the way in which she addressed her children.

The remark was not in any way extraordinary. On the contrary, it was commonplace, being what many parents are moved lightly but lovingly to say to children who grow older and move away: Your home is always here, and when you have nothing better to do come back to it, because we are always here to welcome you.

That was what Mrs Thatcher said, and what people who know her would expect her to say. What she was made to say by Vanity Fair—which highlighted the sentence in its promotional material— was a travesty, though not one which a great many people have noticed. People are careless about injustices towards those they have no liking for, and the reaction of many of Mrs Thatcher's detractors will be to shrug and say that she was foolish to give the interview in the first place. But I think that we must be more particular than that. "Modern communications corrupt good manners," Anthony Eden once observed when he was Foreign Secretary, and that is truer now than it was when he said it.

I believe strongly in the value of antagonism between politicians and the media. It gives the discerning citizen caught between these powerful groups a chance to use common sense and to spot the truth of a matter.

In any sound democracy these relationships ought to be abrasive. The chief feature of almost any dictatorship is the *demand* of the politician that the media should submit to political requirements.

But this valuable abrasiveness is destroyed if one side cheats; if, on the one hand, the media resort to untruths about the politician— or, on the other, the politician (who has the last word) responds by throwing legislation against the media. To make this arrangement work, both sides must play fair.

Oddly, I think this is something Mr Tony Benn, with whom I seldom agree, understands. Rarely without a tape recorder, he is vigilant against cheating. In this respect, he seems to me eminently sane.

In this instance one side did cheat, and the rest of us were misled into doing Mrs Thatcher a serious injustice. We looked at what appeared to be an unusual interview with Mrs Thatcher and (naturally) reported the most controversial parts of it. One part was wrong.

No matter whether Mrs Thatcher is universally loved or loathed. That has no relevance. Mrs Thatcher was distressed by what appeared, though she made no complaint. We were wrong, and we are sorry.

THE UNSPEAKABLE IN PURSUIT OF A HANDFUL OF CHEAP VOTES

Labour's declared intent to ban fox hunting is based on discrimination, not principle, and points the way towards out-and-out authoritarianism, argues W. F. Deedes

As the recent troubles of the Quorn and the National Trust reminded us, most arguments about fox hunting have become tediously familiar. Turning up my records of what has been written and said on the subject during the past 40 years, and recalling debates in which I have taken part, I observe that the line of country taken by both those who love hunting and those who loathe it has changed remarkably little over the years.

The argument is given a new dimension by a recent pledge from the Labour party that, if returned to office, it will legislate against the hunting with hounds of foxes, deer and other mammals. A further undertaking that the Commons would be given a free vote is valueless. No vote on Government business is free—as long as the whips are there.

What Labour's declaration amounts to is that a pursuit rooted in the countryside for a long time, and harmless—in the sense that it inflicts no harm on other people—is to be put down by a government on grounds that those of a different, mainly urban, culture find it objectionable. That opens a new and alarmingly wide political door. At a stroke, the Labour party has shifted the debate from animal welfare to civil liberties.

We can all think of cultures which are lawful but which some find objectionable. Since she founded her television clean-up campaign in 1964, Mrs Mary Whitehouse and her friends have campaigned unceasingly against screen violence, obscenity and bad language—because in their view they *do* inflict harm on others. It remains, however, a tenet of Liberal and Socialist faith that Mrs Whitehouse and her fellow travellers must be resisted at all costs. The Whitehouses of this world are portrayed in modish circles as prigs seeking to restrict a popular culture—that is conveyed to us as intolerable, and successive governments have submitted to that view.

So what principle lies behind Labour's proposal to ban hunting? It surely has no moral content. Those who care passionately about animals and who are genuinely distressed by cruelty to them may well seek to argue that hunting animals with hounds is not a conflict between cultures but a moral issue, on which a Labour government must act.

The Labour party has demolished that argument. Fishermen, more numerous than fox hunters, will be left alone. So will those who shoot game and vermin. So will the man who goes rabbiting with nets, a ferret and a terrier. All these sports involve cruelty to animals. Taken together, they also involve too many votes for the Labour party's comfort. On social grounds, the fox hunters are recognised as by far the best political target. Labour's policy on field sports is nakedly selective. To pretend to see any *moral* purpose in the proposal is laughable.

In reality, once fox hunting goes, the fishermen are doomed. So are those who shoot game birds for pleasure. Heartened by success, the anti-blood lobbies very swiftly will turn their forces on to remaining field sports—and they wil have every logical right to do so. If one goes, all must go. For that reason Labour's tactical move against fox hunting is not only transparent but too illogical to stand for long.

What other pretext can they find?

It might be argued that so many people have decided to take the law into their own hands that official action is imperative. Hunt saboteurs are at large, and a minority among that *galère* is not above inflicting damage on humans as well as animals; there have been scenes of public disorder and animal rights activists are waging a campaign of direct action against butchers, involving criminal damage. The threat to the countryside today is not the huntsman but the rural terrorist. In the interests of keeping the Queen's Peace, the most provocative—and vulnerable—source of these disturbances must be proscribed.

If that thinking has contributed towards the Labour party's decision to ban fox hunting, then indeed we are on a slippery slope. To ban a hitherto lawful activity because those opposed to it are threatening disorder is one road to anarchy. This argument came up, I recall, at the time of the Grosvenor Square march in protest against the Vietnam War in the 1960s. Mr Callaghan, then Labour's Home Secretary, rightly decided that the march was lawful and should take place—notwithstanding advice that it would provoke serious public disorder. He proved to be right and was applauded for his decision.

In short, there is not a vestige of principle behind this Labour proposal: the basis of calculation is electoral advantage. The countryside has lost a lot of electoral weight in recent years. The farm worker, who numbered about two million just after the war, has dwindled and the farmer himself is at a discount. As one writer put it recently, country dwellers themselves now feel part of an endangered species.

The Labour party's own position in the countryside has changed. One or two earlier attempts to legislate against coursing of hares and stag hunting by way of Private Members' Bills were laughed out of court by members of the Labour party themselves—one or two of whom hunted, and some of whom were still beholden to the rural vote.

The urban culture, which now rules, has also undergone changes. Its population is keener on golf courses and theme parks than on field sports. It is a culture cocooned against the crudities of rural life. It no longer sees bloody carcases hanging in the butcher's shop and dead game on the fishmongers' slab. The supermarkets' shelves are innocent of these horrors. They present meaty items with discretion and exquisite packaging.

By this relatively small measure, today's Labour party unknowingly tells us a great deal about itself. Such a measure puts its stamp on a party. Mr Kinnock's claims to be moderate, purged of its old fevers. No party which legislates arbitrarily on a matter best left to an individual's conscience is moderate. No party which outlaws a culture, not because it is socially evil, but in order to appease those of a different culture, is moderate. That is a mark of authoritarian governments everywhere.

Thus we are entitled to see in this a warning of what the next Labour government might do. And the citizen who is not interested in field sports, and is heartily sick of hearing arguments about them, should pay heed. Unprincipled, tactical discrimination, which is what we witness here, puts all citizens at risk.

WHY THIS ELECTION AND 1950'S ARE POLLS APART

Those who attended the Ashford Theatre for my eve-of-poll rally in the General Election of 1950 got full value for their money. After the chairman's opening remarks at 8 pm came a 12-minute address by the son of a former Liberal MP and a 10-minute address by the late chairman of the local Liberal Party. There followed a sorbet in this feast, a Mrs Webster with 15 minutes on "The Housewife's Problem".

After her came 20 minutes from someone who had been for 31 years a member of the Labour Party. My agent had produced these renegades like rabbits out of a hat, believing that public figures ratting on their former party were political trump cards. I was too inexperienced to know that he was wrong. England, Disraeli said, does not love coalitions; it is even less enthusiastic about political turncoats.

After more than an hour of these proceedings, the audience reached the high point of the evening with the arrival of the prospective Conservative candidate. I had prepared, on advice, an address of some 30 minutes. Then the audience was invited to put questions—too many for my taste. Another platform speaker got up to propose a vote of thanks, with one or two things to say on his own account. It was well after 10 o'clock before we closed proceedings with God Save the King.

Such a meeting in this General Election is unimaginable—which illustrates how far removed electioneering in 1992 is from that of 40 years ago. A big shift came about the time of the 1966 election, when Harold Wilson sought and won an improvement on Labour's narrow majority of 1964. Television was in the ascendant. The shrewd political agent calculated that in order to draw them in to the local eve-of-poll rally, there had to be in the hall a television screen showing the party leader's final broadcast. We were moving stealthily towards what we have today, a cellular society of totally self-contained units, not much interested in offerings outside the living room.

In this sense the General Election of 1959 was *fin de siècle*. That was the year of Macmillan's triumph. My agent was sanguine. "If I were you," he said, "I'd take it easy, first half of the day, and come up looking good for the evening meetings." In a rural division there had to be three of these every night of the campaign—sometimes four.

"*Mens sana in corpore sano*," I reasoned, taking him at his word, and played a round of golf every morning of that campaign. It was my last joyride. By 1964 we were up against it, cycling into the wind, swimming against the current. My wife rang a friend and said, "Please give him a game of golf on Sunday, or he'll sink into the ground." I was late for a meeting with religious leaders about gambling, but it was worth it.

By 1970, campaigning had shifted decisively. My then agent put it tactfully. Evening meetings would continue, because I was not too bad a speaker and they had grown accustomed to my face. But the key to winning had become the house-to-house canvass. I went on the streets. There is indeed a certain affinity between ladies saying "Hello, darling!"—thereby opening up a train of thought—and the candidate on the doorstep seeking favours. That is what gives canvassing its edge. It has replaced oratory as the harlot of the arts.

For the first of the two elections in 1974, my last, most talented agent issued a guide to canvassers. It began: "Knock on the door politely, avoid taking short cuts across gardens, close the gate behind you, be pleasant—smile!" His script went on: "I am calling on behalf of the Conservative candidate, Bill Deedes. Can we rely on your support? (The answer 'Yes' with the door closed in your face does not identify a Conservative voter—it indicates that the elector has no interest in you, or your party.)"

With so many women now working outside their homes, the golden hours for canvassing lie between seven and 10 pm, when couples are most likely to be at home. Why occupy such time addressing thin meetings of a dozen or so, when brisk canvassing will bring you face to face with upwards of 100?

Electioneering has become more efficient and a lot less fun. In retrospect, what good sport it was to see the hard-pressed candidate rise to some barbed question from the back of the hall, declaring with a ghastly smile: "I'm so very glad you've asked that question."

The *pons asinorum* in my day was a small, beautiful village where the election meeting attracted people of dangerous intelligence—a former ambassador, a director of The Times, a Companion of Honour. Their examination was invariably severe.

"How did it play?" I would say anxiously to my agent as we scrambled into the car, already late for the next meeting. And he—reflecting that this poor devil of a candidate had another week of it ahead—would answer unblushingly: "You did fine! Just fine!"

TRADITION TAMES—OR DOES IT?

The House of Lords has a reputation for quenching firebrands. Can it keep it up? W. F. Deedes, himself a Tory peer, looks forward to finding out

There is—as the peers' bemused reception of Lady Thatcher's maiden speech illustrated—a marked distinction between parliamentary styles in the Commons and the Lords. I sometimes wonder what on earth will happen when Mr Dennis Skinner, the assiduous Labour MP for Bolsover, is translated to the Lords. His friends and admirers may declare that he would jump off a cliff before accepting a peerage. It is my fancy that he might find the prospect of doing to the Lords what he does in the Commons irresistible.

Traditions in the Lords has it that chaps like Dennis Skinner are quickly tamed; that firebrands are quenched—and indeed there is some evidence of this. Mr Shinwell, for example, was a turbulent character in the Commons when roused to anger; his anguish there was barely within rules of order. In the Lords, he became the Old Home's favourite figure.

But in the case of Manny Shinwell—and some others I can remember—the burden of years was mounting and the blood was cooling by the time they took to ermine. A man of 80 is less excitable than a man of 40, or even 60—which is Mr Skinner's age. Furthermore, these men could usually be tamed one by one.

With Mr Major's dissolution honours, promoting 21 parliamentarians at a gulp, to say nothing of 10 new working peers and three more in the Birthday Honours, the Lords face a new challenge. I doubt if the burden of years has yet altogether cooled the blood of Nicholas Ridley, Ian Gilmour, Peter Walker, Nigel Lawson, Norman Tebbit, David Owen and Denis Healey—to name but a handful of those in this Trojan horse. Then there is Jeffrey Archer to reckon with.

It is some time since I heard him in the House of Commons, but I have doorstepped with him in recent by-elections. He is a specialist in smart repartee. What on earth is he going to do with smart repartee in the Lords? In the Commons it establishes reputations. In the Lords, it destroys them.

Other things being equal I would back the Lords eventually to tame even as many as 30 thrusters from the other place. But they are not equal. We are engaged in a strongly felt, if not always articulately expressed, argument about our future in Europe. I take the view that it is a topic on which people are entitled to speak their minds freely and with passion, no matter how much it embarrasses government. Soon we shall be engaged in another, no less passionate argument. What can be done to mitigate the recession which is engulfing us? To which the truthful answer is, given our commitments to Europe and its monetary system, not as much as we would like.

Here surely is the stuff of vigorous debate. And when such debate arises, do we expect two dozen experienced hands from the Commons to lower their voices and join the mellow tones which distinguish the Lords' debates? I think it unlikely.

What, after all, causes turmoil in the Lords? It is not individual members. It is not uncouth manners. It is great issues. Home Rule and Lloyd George's budget come to mind. Now today we have a great issue combined with an exceptionally strong intake from the Commons, and I think the combination will be formidable. Certainly it is going to test the government's front bench in the House of Lords.

It is simply not possible for a government to give the Lords front bench the sort of guns it deploys in the Commons. In Cabinet, Commoners outnumber peers by something like 10–1—and what a row there would be were it otherwise.

Thus opposition benches in the Lords are accustomed to conscientious but sometimes pedestrian replies from the government side. Manners in the Upper House forgive a young minister who reads every word of his department's brief. The question is whether these shabby tigers flooding in from the Commons will be as generous.

I think much may turn on Lady Thatcher herself. On arrival in office, she proceeded to bust up the Tory establishment. It is on the cards that, given the kind of debates that lie ahead, she will do some busting up in the Lords as well. I do not share the view that Lady Thatcher's stridency will prove self-defeating. I think that, for some of the new intake from the Commons, it may be infectious. In which case, I venture to suggest to your Lordships, that we may be about to live in interesting times.

A PENANCE THAT HAS LIFTED
THE HUMAN SPIRIT

If the Profumo Affair has to be dredged up all over again, then let it be as a hymn to redemption, argues W. F. Deedes who, as a minister in 1963, played a part in the saga

Making public the Cabinet papers of 1963 under the 30-year rule had one certain consequence. It provided yet another pretext for raking over the embers of the Profumo affair, which occurred in the early part of that year.

Knowing what Jack Profumo has done with his life since then, I have become increasingly, perhaps unreasonably irritated by this perpetual itch among petty authors, second-rate TV producers and people like Rupert Murdoch to squeeze the last drop of profit from this affair.

For the tale worth telling is no longer what happened then. It is what has happened since. It is about the way Jack Profumo set about his own redemption in a way which, to the best of my knowledge, has no precedent in public life.

Toynbee Hall in East London—named after the social reformer Arnold Toynbee, and where Jack has worked since 1963, has been chairman and of which he is now President—emerged from what might loosely be called the Christian social reform movement, which took shape in the last quarter of the 19th century. Clem Attlee, who has a memorial there, spent a formative part of his early life working at Toynbee.

I knew about it in the early 1930s because for a while, as a drone not a worker, I was a resident at the Oxford House in Bethnal Green, a companion of Toynbee Hall.

It might be supposed that in these more egalitarian times these settlements have outgrown their usefulness. On the contrary, as I was reminded a few weeks back, when at Jack Profumo's suggestion I attended a lunchtime meeting at Toynbee, they have a bigger part than ever in easing the human tragedy.

Though we were contemporaries at both private and public schools, I heard nothing from Jack Profumo after 1963 until the early 1970s. Then he called me from Toynbee Hall and asked if I would agree to meet Mary Dynes of the Joint Council for the Welfare of Immigrants, who seemed under his wing. We met and achieved a most improbable understanding. I began to wonder about Jack Profumo's new dimension.

When the Toynbee Hall centenary came up in 1984, I persuaded him to mark it with an article for *The Daily Telegraph*, the first thing he had written under his own name since leaving public life. It struck me then how much more cheerful he seemed to be than many of our contemporaries; and I began to reflect that this chosen course of his had become a deeper affair than any of us realised.

If we must go over all this again, I pray for the last time, I must record that I have long felt deep uneasiness about the way some of us handled this business in 1963, and contributed to the disaster. Was it really sensible to convene a meeting of Ministers at 2am in the Chief Whip's room at the House of Commons, and summon Jack Profumo from his home to this Star Chamber, instantly to answer "yes" or "no" to charges which Labour MPs had been bandying in the House earlier in the night?

Because the news media had laid siege to his house, Profumo had taken a sleeping draught not long before being woken and summoned. He reached the House in a mildly bemused state. As one present at this extraordinary gathering (because I had been sitting on the Government's front bench when Labour was laying the charges), I have often wondered whether in these bizarre circumstances I would instantly have owned up to the truth, the whole truth and nothing but the truth. I doubt it.

Later, we were accused of being hoodwinked; but I think the charge against us is graver than that. We created circumstances which made the truth extremely hard to tell. If it emerged in court that policemen had been guilty of such procedures, I think it likely that a judge would order the accused to be discharged.

We were moreover, in a desperate hurry. This was the early morning of Friday, when the House would meet again at 11am. Questions would be asked. A quick answer had to be found. So much so that at the end of this clumsy inquisition, I withdrew to my room with one of the Government's Law Officers to type out the hastily composed statement.

I set out the circumstances in full for the first time, so that others may consult their consciences and declare confidently, if they can, that in those circumstances they would unhesitatingly have owned up. It is a difficult test, but a crucial one; because for three decades the chattering classes, adulterers among them, have been pleased to say that it was not the infidelity that mattered but a lie to the House of Commons.

Whether circumstances that led to this lie constitute mitigation or not, I leave others to judge. It matters not what they decide, for Jack Profumo has elected to serve the full sentence he appointed for himself. In the course of this, he has done more in the service of other people's lives than anyone I know. As well as that, he has transformed his own life.

On further reflection, it may be a good time for this sorry tale to be revived. For politicians stand in low regard just now. I take a more liberal view than most of ministers who fall by the wayside, because I know something of the unseen pressures and temptations of public life. But, unquestionably, the majority of citizens are disappointed by prevailing standards in public life which fall short of their ideals.

Well, let them turn their minds to Jack Profumo, who has silently submitted to 30 years of seeing his name perpetually dragged through the mud, and who, ultimately, has set us all an example.

He is a reminder of an important part of the human story, which many seem to have forgotten. Man may fall; and yet, by seeking his own redemption, rise again. What more hopeful message could there be for us on entering 1994?

LANDMINES: DIANA IS RIGHT, THE TORIES WRONG

W. F. Deedes, who has helped lead the move to ban landmines, rides to the defence of Diana, Princess of Wales

Finding fault with Diana, Princess of Wales is becoming a habit among some Tory backbenchers. They may have caught her on the wrong foot at the cinema last week, but they should know better than to bully her for her crusade against anti-personnel mines.

Some of them declared themselves shocked because she was to attend a meeting in the House of Commons on the subject. Thus, they reasoned, she laid herself open to the charge of dabbling in politics. In reality, the meeting she has now felt compelled to abandon was staged by an all-party group of peers and MPs who concern themselves with the subject of anti-personnel mines. It convenes meetings occasionally, but they are usually sparsely attended. Mines have not been high on the agenda of most MPs.

That this particular gathering had promised to attract a much larger number underlines the value of the Princess in this realm. She has focused attention on an enormous human tragedy, in which precious few politicians showed much interest until her expedition to Angola this year.

That venture, which appeared to those of us travelling with her to be faultlessly carried out, drew public criticism from Earl Howe, then a Tory defence minister. His complaint boiled down to the fact that the Princess was highlighting the scandalous loss of life, limbs and land caused by mines in much of the developing world.

Naturally this caused embarrassment to a Conservative government which up to that point had found itself unable to support a total ban on the making, selling or use of anti-personnel mines.

Her cause has fared a degree better under the Labour Government, which has recently taken a more decisive move against the use of anti-personnel mines. There perhaps we detect grounds for the Tory backbenchers' grievances. Yet I do not find them reasonable.

MPs of all parties must bring themselves to accept that mines and their destruction of innocent people are now a humanitarian rather than a political issue. As the Princess exclaimed in Angola when she stood accused by a Tory minister of political interference and of being a loose cannon: "I am a humanitarian. I always have been and I always will be." That is her cause here, and it is a wholly legitimate one.

What has caught her emotions is the scale of human suffering which these anti-personnel mines cause. There are known to be well over 100 million scattered around some 60 countries, but most heavily in war-torn countries such as Somalia, Angola, Cambodia and Afghanistan.

In these countries something like one in every 350 persons is an amputee. Though the death and casualty roll remains high it is not much noticed by the world at large—for all the fatalities occur singly. When an old woman foraging for firewood in Cambodia dies on a mine, when a child carrying water for the family in Bosnia suffers fearful injury from a mine, the news does not carry far. What the eye fails to see and what the ear fails to hear the heart does not grieve unduly. My conversion to the cause came after visiting hospitals in Cambodia and seeing what a Chinese mine costing a few dollars could do to a child's body.

The Princess underwent the same experience in Angola. Part of the Tory defence mechanism on mines relates legitimately to the needs of our Armed Forces. I am sensitive on that score. There is a duty to think twice before campaigning against a weapon which may help to defend our Armed Forces. This aspect was addressed last year by the International Committee of the Red Cross. It undertook an inquiry in conjunction with the military of many countries into the use of anti-personnel mines in recent conflicts.

It turned out that these mines had played no decisive part in a score or more of recent conflicts. A report, *Friend or Foe*, was published by ICRC, under whose auspices the Princess travelled to Angola, and she has studied it. What the Red Cross underlines is a long-standing principle of war. Weapons must not be used which cause human suffering out of all proportion to their military value.

In Bosnia, where Diana may elect to go next, many more mines have been laid in recent times than the total raised elsewhere in the world. As she pointed out this month in a speech for the Mines

Advisory Group, detecting and lifting mines is a slow and dangerous occupation.

There is a need for both non-government organisations and private enterprise. Depending on the terrain, there is a role for commercial mechanised methods as well as for the men who are trained to prod their way painfully forward.

Above all, as the Princess emphasised, a huge demand for artificial limbs has somehow to be met. Those who lose limbs in such places as Angola will not find openings for the disabled as they might in the West. They live off the land and if they cannot cultivate it, they are as good as dead.

International Red Cross leads the field in orthopaedics and prosthetics, but demand far exceeds supply. Artificial limbs are expensive. A young child who loses a leg may require half a dozen separate casts before reaching maturity.

What Diana, Princess of Wales has done is to quicken attention to these needs. To quibble about the way she pursues this cause is sad and rather silly. The refugee struggling home and crippled by a mine will not be unduly troubled about who convened a meeting in the House of Commons on behalf of him and his kind.

FOR LANDMINES, TIME IS
RUNNING OUT

W. F. Deedes sees the shade of Diana, with whom he travelled to Angola, behind the Government's haste to help ban mines

Political minds have been wonderfully changed on the subject of landmines since that day in London in January last year, when a Tory minister met two political correspondents for lunch. The mission of Diana, Princess of Wales to the minefields of Angola, he confided to them, was unwelcome. He accused her of "meddling".

News of this encounter swiftly leaked out. Diana, toiling round the minefields of Angola, was distressed. Her mission, she declared emotionally, was not political but humanitarian.

Eighteen months on, we find a government being driven to find parliamentary time to ratify an international treaty banning land-mines before the first anniversary of her death.

This is not to make a point against the last Tory administration. Before Diana came on the scene, pretty well every government in the world was dragging its feet on this issue. What has happened simply illustrates the way in which she changed the world's attitude to a nasty situation.

She had only eight months in which to do it. In January 1997, she went to Angola. Last June, she made a speech about landmines in London, which outlined her objectives. Last August, she spent three days in Bosnia, visiting the afflicted. That was all she had time to do.

Had she lived, she would probably have accepted an invitation to visit Oslo last September, where an international gathering was moving towards the ban. When she died, her personal crusade ended. But it had gathered an extraordinary momentum, and that was what the Cabinet had to reckon with.

We can set aside what the Foreign Secretary had to say to the Royal Institute of International Affairs yesterday. Of course, he had to declare that the Government had been in the front rank of those working for a ban. Of course, he had to insist that the Government's record in this matter was one of which it could be proud.

The fact remains that, earlier this week, ministers felt sure that parliamentary time could not be found to ratify the Ottawa treaty before the first anniversary of Diana's death. Later this week, they changed their minds and decided that, at all costs, such time must be found.

In fairness, the ratification of this treaty is not a simple matter. There are contingencies that have to be weighed. What happens if our soldiers find themselves alongside allies who have not signed the ban? We have destroyed half our stockpile of mines. What is to be done about Nato's stockpiles?

For what seem to me good and sufficient reasons, America has felt unable to sign. Many are critical of this attitude. One reason for it is the frontier between North and South Korea, where mines are considered to be indispensable. There is also reluctance in the Pentagon to deny American forces a weapon that might, in certain circumstances, save the lives of American servicemen and women. As things stand, America will implement the ban in 2006, behind the rest of the world.

Of greater importance is the future attitude of countries such as Russia, China, India and Pakistan, which still manufacture the anti-personnel mines. International pressure is being brought to bear. If the vast majority of nations sign the ban, then those who persist in manufacturing mines will come under increasing pressure. China is not wholly insensitive to world opinion on a matter of this kind.

Then it remains to be seen how many nations will be willing to follow Britain's example and destroy even part of their stockpile of mines. The continent of Africa has many such stockpiles; and many of them will remain.

What matters most is that nations should not regard signing the ban as a full discharge of their obligations. The number of mines still lurking in areas of former conflict has been exaggerated. It is to be reckoned in tens of thousands, rather than millions. But there remain enough in the earth to produce a constant toll of killed and wounded, most of it among innocent citizens. It is children fetching water and women foraging for firewood who are at risk.

This was an area of special concern to Diana. She expressed her feelings on the subject during her final mission to Bosnia, in the month of her death. The ban, she perceived, would do nothing to reduce the number of mines already in the ground.

Nor would it ease the plight of those who had lost a limb and found it difficult to procure an artificial replacement. A child who loses a leg at the age of, say, six is probably going to require four or five replacements before he reaches maturity. Orthopaedic work in this field has expanded, but it is still far short of demand.

Signing the treaty does impose on governments obligations in the field of mine clearance. How far will they meet such obligations? It is pressure from those determined that Diana's crusade shall not be allowed to peter out that brought the Government to this point. That pressure needs to be maintained if her wishes are to be fulfilled.

CHURCHILL: FORTUNES OF WAR

If he had done nothing else in his life, Winston Churchill would have won fame and fortune as a war correspondent. He spent half a century at it—if we add to his early ventures in Cuba, India, Sudan and South Africa, his reporting of both world wars. Soon after the First World War, Lord Birkenhead observed that "Winston is writing an enormous book about himself, and calling it *The World Crisis*." It ran to six volumes. During the Second World War Churchill kept copies of all his papers, then wrote, by arrangement with *The Daily Telegraph*, another six volumes called *The Second World War*.

The two handsome volumes of *The River War*, his account, published in 1899, of Lord Kitchener's reconquest of the Sudan, well illustrate Churchill's art of putting any war in which he was involved profitably between hard covers. But it was in pursuit of danger, rather than profit, that he embarked on his first war in Cuba in 1895. As he saw it at the time, "In the closing decade of the Victorian era, the Empire had enjoyed so long a spell of almost unbroken peace, that medals and all they represented in experience and adventure were becoming extremely scarce in the British Army."

But at least the military year was divided between a seven-month summer season of training and five winter months of leave. So off he went to Cuba, where the Spaniards were fighting a long-drawn guerilla war with Cuban rebels. It was, as he saw it, one of the bright spots of the world. On his 21st birthday, he recalled, "for the first time I heard shots fired in anger, and heard bullets strike flesh or whistle through the air".

The *Daily Graphic* paid five guineas for each of the letters he sent, which eventually appeared in five parts entitled *Insurrection in Cuba*. It was not riches, but it was a start, and it attracted notice. The *Newcastle Leader* observed sourly: "Spending a holiday fighting other people's battles is rather an extraordinary proceeding, even for a Churchill."

He next toyed with the idea of joining the war between Greece and Turkey in 1897, but before that plan could materialise, the Greeks were defeated.

All through this early period, Churchill was an officer in one regiment or another. His constant pursuit of action led him to serve altogether in eight regiments—4th Hussars, 31st Punjab Infantry, 21st Lancers, South African Light Horse, the Oxfordshire Yeomanry, the Grenadier Guards, the Royal Scots Fusiliers and the Oxfordshire Artillery.

It was this zest for battle that made Winston Churchill an extraordinary war correspondent—and his survival even more extraordinary. Most of those who practise the trade put safety first. As H A Gwynne, editor of the *Morning Post*, remarked on dispatching me to Abyssinia in 1935, a dead correspondent is useless to his newspaper. One bore it in mind. Churchill, by contrast, relished the smack of bullets passing over his head. His account of the 21st Lancers cavalry charge at Omdurman, a murderous battle in which he took part, rings with the enthusiasm of a man thrilled by his experience.

But that was a year away when, in the summer of 1897, he stood on the lawns of Goodwood and learnt of a rebellion among the Pathan tribesmen in the North-West Frontier of India. Abandoning his leave, he took the next boat to India, cabling an offer of his services to the general in command of the British expedition, Sir Bindon Blood.

Joining the Malakand Field Force was Churchill's first serious undertaking as a war correspondent. An Allahabad newspaper, *The Pioneer*, commissioned him as its correspondent, and *The Daily Telegraph* paid £5 a column for his letters from the front.

During this campaign, incidentally, he discovered for the first time the pleasures of a whisky and soda. Up to then, it had been white wine or red wine, "or better still Champagne", and, very occasionally, brandy and soda. Then, while with the Malakand Field Force, he found himself for five whole days with "nothing to drink, apart from tea, except either tepid water or tepid water with lime juice, or tepid water with whisky." Faced with these alternatives, "I grasped the larger hope."

This long and complicated expedition established Churchill's reputation. The letters he wrote anonymously "From a Young Officer" for *The Daily Telegraph* attracted close attention. They formed the substance of his book, written in five weeks, *The Malakand Field Force*, which secured notices from the critics, a letter of praise from the Prince of Wales, later King Edward VII, and, at a critical moment, an interview with the Prime Minister, Lord Salisbury.

Critical because, after India, Churchill scented adventure in Sudan, where the British Government was aiming to march on Khartoum and crush the Dervish power. "I was deeply anxious to share in this," he wrote.

Unfortunately, Sir Herbert Kitchener, sirdar [commander-in-chief] of the Egyptian Army, was not among Churchill's admirers. Always endowed with influential family friends, whom he did not hesitate to use, Churchill persuaded the Prime Minister (on the strength of his earlier interview) to wire Kitchener on his behalf.

Back came the crushing reply: "Sir Herbert Kitchener had already all the officers he required, and if vacancies occurred, there were others whom he would be bound to prefer before the young officer in question."

Undeterred, Churchill turned to other influential sources and got himself attached as supernumerary to the 21st Lancers. The terms were that he should travel at his own expense, and that in the event of death or injury, the Army bore no responsibility for him.

Happily, yet another friend stepped in. Oliver Borthwick, son of the proprietor of the *Morning Post*, offered £15 a column for another series of letters. Borthwick got a bargain with a first-hand account of the battle of Omdurman.

"This kind of war," Churchill thought at the time, "was full of fascinating thrills." It proved to be a turning point in his life. Lord Randolph, his father, had not left much money. Churchill had an allowance of £500 a year, which came nowhere near meeting the cost of polo and the Hussars. The Army was paying him 14 shillings a day.

"To go on soldiering . . ." he reasoned, "would plainly land me and all connected with me in increasing difficulties . . . On the other hand the two books I had already written and my war correspondence with *The Daily Telegraph* had already brought in about five times as much as the Queen had paid me for three years of assiduous and sometimes dangerous work."

If the Army was paying him £250 a year, I calculate that income from journalism and two books had earned him over the three years something like £3,750. He got about £300 from the *Morning Post*. He also got £3 for a weekly letter to the Allahabad *Pioneer*.

From that time until 1919, when he unexpectedly came into an inheritance, Churchill earned his own living with his pen—"without ever lacking anything necessary to health or enjoyment".

My early edition of *The River War* is a lavish work. The two volumes, replete with maps and illustrations, weigh 8lb. While working on it, he encountered one of the *Daily Mail*'s star turns, G W Steevens, who became a valued critic: "The only criticism I should make is that your philosophic reflections, which while generally well expressed, often acute and sometimes true, are too devilish frequent. If I were you, I should cut out the philosopher about January 1898, giving him perhaps a short innings at the very end."

The River War was to be published in November 1899. Churchill counted the days until "the two massive volumes, my magnum opus (up to date) upon which I had lavished a whole year of my life, should be launched upon an expectant public".

But October brought other surprises. From South Africa came news of the Boer rebellion, and from the *Morning Post* an offer to make Churchill that newspaper's principal war correspondent in return for £1,000 for four months, thereafter £200 a month, all expenses paid, total freedom as to movements and opinions.

These terms, making Churchill the highest-paid war correspondent in South Africa, owed something to an earlier offer from Alfred Harmsworth of the *Daily Mail*—which Churchill took care to bring to the notice of Oliver Borthwick. I cannot but ruefully reflect that when, 35 years later, the same newspaper sent me to Abyssinia, the rate was a mere £60 a month, all expenses paid.

Before he sailed, Churchill saw Joe Chamberlain at the Colonial Office. They discussed the prospects. "Of course," said Chamberlain, "I have to base myself on the War Office opinion . . ."

On which Churchill, in his philosophical vein, comments: "The British War Office of those days was the product of two generations of consistent House of Commons parsimony, unbroken by any serious call." He added, more appositely: "Never, never, never believe any war will be smooth and easy, or that anyone who embarks on that strange voyage can measure the tides and hurricanes he will encounter."

Churchill travelled to South Africa on the Dunnotar Castle. His luggage included 18 bottles of St Emilion at 24 shillings a dozen; 18 bottles of Scotch—10 years old—at 48 shillings a dozen; 6 bottles of very old brandy at 160 shillings a dozen. Such were his finances that the bill was not paid until more than a year later.

His first idea was to get into Ladysmith, where a friend, General Ian Hamilton, was in command. He was too late for that. The door was shut. He then found company with another friend, Captain Aylmer Haldane, who had been placed in charge of a company of Dublin Fusiliers and a company of Durham Light Infantry.

This force was to travel in an armoured train of six trucks along 16 miles of unbroken railway track to assist the outlying cavalry. Haldane invited Churchill to join him—"because I was eager for trouble, I accepted this invitation without demur". Fourteen miles out, the train was attacked by Boers. Retreating rapidly at about 40 miles an hour, it struck an obstacle and was derailed.

There followed a desperate struggle under heavy fire, in which Churchill took the lead, to clear the line. He then encountered two Boers whom he mistook for plate-layers and finding himself without his Mauser pistol, had no option but to surrender. "When one is alone and unarmed," he quotes Napoleon as saying, "a surrender may be pardoned." All this happened on November 15, 1899.

In captivity, he at first despaired, seemingly of everything, including his *Morning Post* contract. He spent November 30, his 25th birthday, miserably in captivity. His capture, of course, created the sort of stir that even rival newspapers had to acknowledge.

Despite his performance when the armoured train came under fire, he claimed to be a non-combatant, and so entitled to release. On that, the Boers took time to make up their mind. While they were doing so, Churchill escaped on December 13.

A price of £25 was put on his head. But his stars—perhaps we should say our stars—held their course. After further vicissitudes, he arrived off Durban on December 23. It was the only bright spot in what became known as the Black Week of the Boer War, with the British Army defeated at Magersfontein, Stromberg and Colenso.

But for Churchill, the hour had struck. He was a hero. A hero, at least, to most eyes. The *Daily Nation* of December 16 dissented. "Mr Churchill's escape is not regarded in military circles as either a brilliant or honourable exploit. He was captured as a combatant and of course placed under the same parole as officers taken prisoners. He has, however, chosen to disregard an honourable undertaking."

There was other comment on those lines. Finding himself, in the main, a national hero, Churchill then filed some trenchant comment on the conduct of the war. Though reluctant to have him as correspondent on this account, Lord Roberts eventually gave way— "for your father's sake".

Churchill proceeded to get the best of both worlds. He had

imparted a certain amount of useful information to Sir Redfers Buller, who had been replaced as commander-in-chief by Roberts, but still commanded British forces in Natal.

Buller asked in return what he could do for Churchill, who plumped for a commission in an irregular corps, while making it clear he must continue work for the *Morning Post*. After the Nile expedition, however, the War Office had firmly decided that soldiers could not be correspondents and correspondents could not be soldiers.

This put Buller in a fix. He eventually granted Churchill a commission in "Bungo's" regiment—"Bungo" was Colonel Byng, later Lord Byng of Vimy—and told him that he could do both jobs but would get no pay from the Army. Thus Churchill joined his fourth regiment, the South African Light Horse, took part in the battles of Spioenkop and Ladysmith, saw the rest of the Boer War out and kept the *Morning Post* happy.

With the relief of Ladysmith, the tide of war began to turn. In March, 1900, Churchill cabled the *Morning Post* urging a generous and forgiving policy. It was ill-received in England. The *Morning Post*, "while printing my messages sorrowfully disagreed with my views".

"I always get into trouble," Churchill wrote later, "because so few people take this line." Invited to devise an inscription for a monument in France, he once wrote: "In war, Resolution. In defeat, Defiance. In victory, Magnanimity. In peace, Goodwill." The inscription was rejected.

Returning home to a wave of popular feeling, he was narrowly elected to Parliament for Oldham. Furthermore, he found himself comfortably off. The *Morning Post* paid him 10 months' salary. His profits on *The River War* brought this to £4,000. He took to lecturing at £100 a night—it was £300 in Liverpool. In the month of November 1900 he banked the then enormous sum of £4,500.

By the time he entered the House of Commons, he was able to invest some £10,000, which today would be worth 50 times more. It is agreeable to point out that these foundations for his political career came largely from two newspapers, the *Morning Post* and *The Daily Telegraph*—the only two newspapers I have worked for throughout my life.

Based on a lecture to the International Churchill Society at Bath, July 23.

August 2000

BLAIR'S BABES ARE STILL
ON THE WARPATH

W. F. Deedes predicts that Labour's men will let the women do the fighting on Commons conditions—and then join in the victory

They want to breastfeed their babies in the House of Commons chamber. They demand that parliamentary hours be changed to suit their family. They unblushingly ask parliamentary questions planted on them by the whips. They're sycophants. They're wet!

Some hard things have been said about the so-called "Blair Babes" who won parliamentary seats in the 1997 General Election, when 101 newly-elected women entered the Commons.

Equally hard things have been said by the Babes about certain male MPs, whom they accuse of male chauvinism, sexism and downright rudeness.

Tess Kingham, MP for Gloucester, who is not standing again, has called it "a 19th century gentleman's debating society".

Maria Eagle, MP for Liverpool Garston, accuses Tory MPs of "public school antics". Some of them have "a juvenile, stunted approach to women," she declares.

Jane Griffiths, MP for Reading East, has described MPs as "putting their hands out in front of them as if they are weighing melons" when women speak in the chamber. "They have a breast obsession," says Miss Eagle.

"It's real schoolboy stuff," says Miss Griffiths but, adds Jackie Ballard, Liberal Democrat MP for Taunton, the offenders are careful to avoid their behaviour being picked up by the Westminster television cameras.

Some of this antagonism runs deep. The Commons has lost something of its collegiate feeling since the advent of New Labour.

Clem Attlee, a keen follower of cricket, remembered Tory and Labour MPs sitting round the same dinner table and choosing from their fellow MPs what they called the "Shits XI".

"It was always pretty even pegging between the Labour and Tory

242

side of the House," Attlee once told me. That game would find fewer players now.

Critics of Blair's Babes—a description attributed to an early group photograph with Tony Blair and which they abhor—claim that collectively they have been a parliamentary disappointment.

Yet six of them, new to Parliament in 1997, have won jobs in the Government and there are others tipped for Government posts in the next reshuffle.

By my calculation, 42 of them are still under the age of 50 and 19 of those have relatively young children. One of them, Ruth Kelly, 30, MP for Bolton West, has had two children since the General Election and is expecting a third. She is widely perceived to be among the ablest of the new intake.

A former Bank of England economist, she was a valued member of the Treasury Commons Select Committee before being appointed PPS to Nick Brown, the Agriculture Minister.

She was one of only three of Labour's 320 backbenchers to be invited to a brain-storming Downing Street think-in. A hard worker, Miss Kelly is not among those crying loudest for creches, but she joins those who are critical of parliamentary hours. "The very late hours are ridiculous—and unpredictable," she says.

Ideally, she would like to see the Commons start work on Tuesdays, Wednesdays and Thursdays at 11.30 am and close at 7.30 pm.

Where does that leave an Opposition which, outnumbered in the lobby, finds the use of Government time a valuable weapon against objectionable proposals?

Miss Kelly sees that as an outdated concept. The news media and public opinion, she thinks, now carry more weight with the Government.

She wants to see a cross-party business committee in charge of Commons business. That would ensure fair play for the Opposition.

Above all, she seeks more flexibility in her working hours. Before this session ends, she anticipates a debate about parliamentary hours on a free vote.

A rough survey of parliamentary opinion suggests that things are moving her way. Much may depend on who is chosen as Speaker in succession to Betty Boothroyd.

She vetoed breast feeding in the Commons and in committees and was seen by Blair Babes as a hard-liner. Parliament's business, she insisted, came before domestic convenience. At the same time, she yielded to the mothers' baked beans, fish fingers and jelly in the Parliamentary dining rooms. Toys, children's videos, bottle-warming facilities and microwaves to heat baby food have been granted for the Commons family rooms.

Margaret Hodge, the employment minister, says: "Hours are difficult for everyone, not simply women. A change would be for everyone's advantage and would encourage more to enter Parliament.

"Talking about Section 28 at 2 am defeats accountability. So the hours ought to be more compatible."

She thinks Thursday's working hours of 9.30 am until 7 pm work well.

But what of those with work outside Parliament? "Being an MP used to be part-time," she says. "It is not so any more. People can combine it with other interests but their main job is being an MP."

Eight out of 10 women now work. "Every employer has to face up to that and support women who work for them," she adds. "Mum can find facilities to change nappies at a petrol station but not in the House of Commons."

So, she argues, there are three considerations: the long parliamentary hours; the arrival of women in the chamber, and the need to provide facilities for the young children of members.

In due course, the Conservative Opposition will argue that conditions in Parliament are not kept secret: prospective MPs know in advance what life will be like.

It is a point made by Gillian Shephard, the former Tory minister. "If such conditions are unacceptable, and they may be to parents of young children, then it is better to wait to get elected until it is an easier proposition," she points out.

"Other professional women—lawyers, accountants and teachers —do not demand the right to breastfeed while in court, with clients or in front of class."

Women MPs lamenting conditions in the Commons, Mrs Shephard says, give their profession a bad name by demanding privileges not available to other women.

So how will it end? I predict that Labour's male MPs, most of whom favour a change of hours, will let the young mothers make most of the running and take the flak.

When it comes to a vote, they will move smartly in behind them. Blair's Babes have a genuine grievance there.

WE SHALL ALL MISS THE VOICE THAT PROVOKED DEBATE

W. F. Deedes recalls the dynamic style that dominated politics

All Prime Ministers, when they leave the bridge, are free to choose where next to go in the ship of state. Some prefer to retire to their cabin and lie down. Others feel so driven by concern over the course their country is taking that they cannot bring themselves to do that. They go on watching the path of the ship and, now and again, can be heard shouting impetuously at the man at the wheel.

Lady Thatcher is one of the second category. Not for her the philosophy of Arthur Balfour, a former leader of her party, who towards the end of his days had come to the conclusion that "nothing matters very much, and very little matters at all".

Balfour's aphorism is the antithesis of the Thatcher philosophy. The passion that brought Margaret Thatcher into politics, drove her to the House of Commons, then on to No 10, and kept her working there furiously for 12 years was never spent. "Freedom under the law," she could be heard saying at supper parties, when everyone else was talking about Wimbledon or Ascot. "That is the key . . ."

Throughout her working life and in what passed for her as retirement, she has been a constant reader in search of self-improvement, of knowledge to buttress political beliefs, of wider horizons.

In truth, Margaret Thatcher from her earliest days had always to work extremely hard to follow her star, and this has become a habit.

In many encounters with her, I have rarely observed her to relax, engage in small talk, or put her feet up and say, "well, it's been a good day". This eventually takes its toll. At the end of a long dinner at No 10, while she was Prime Minister, an aide might come and say: "Do you mind staying on a bit; she'd like a word?"

She might then kick her slippers off, but the word would be rigorous and unhurried. When at last you left her to go home, reckoning it had been a long day, she would be off to deal with the half dozen red boxes, which were then the Prime Minister's nightly portion. Cumulatively, that routine also takes its toll.

When she first became leader of the Tory party in 1975, the leader writers of this newspaper gave her a supper party. It lasted four hours. Watching her, and leaving the cross-examination to keener intellects, I never once saw her attention flag. Such phenomenal ability to concentrate on what other people are saying is rare.

So, notwithstanding her critics—many of them in the Tory party—who thought that Margaret Thatcher should belt up and allow her successors to get on with it, I have come to recognise and to respect the force that, up to now, has driven her on.

If her spouse, Denis, the calmest man I know, could not quieten the endless concerns that rampage through her mind, who else can be expected to do it? He's calm, that is, as long as the bacon at breakfast is to his taste.

Years ago, when Margaret Thatcher was at the Department of Education (which I always reckoned was an exceptionally hard stint), the Permanent Secretary caught her leaving the office early one evening. She was going, she explained, to buy the bacon for Denis's breakfast.

The Permanent Secretary pointed out that someone could readily be found to buy the bacon. The offer was firmly declined. Who could know better than her that Denis prefers lean bacon and likes it cooked to a cinder?

But such light interruptions to the serious business of politics have played less part in her life than any other senior political figure I can think of.

It would be wrong to call it patriotism, because the word is so given to misunderstanding.

It is better expressed as concern for your country that runs so deep, you find it physically impossible to switch off and cultivate the garden.

There is also another, less personal and perhaps stronger defence for Margaret Thatcher's refusal to stay quiet.

Our politics have become very bland. Everything No 10 can do to give a smooth face to events, failure, scandal, is done.

We are in effect being discouraged from looking into anything too deeply. "Carry on shopping! Eventually, we'll sort it out."

So these are times when an authoritative voice, however unwelcome it may be to some people, is useful. That is what we are now going to miss.

The party Margaret Thatcher led is now a young party. It may well be full of promise and I think it is, but it lacks the voice of experience, the voice of someone who has had to navigate this world and knows something about the shoals it holds for the unwary.

It is possible to disagree with her last utterances about Europe —which some will now quietly seek to dismiss as a symptom of ill-health—and at the same time see virtue in making people think harder about Europe and where it is taking us.

In several conversations with Margaret Thatcher, I have silently disagreed with something which she has been trying to persuade me; but, later, have found myself thinking more about it, still disagreeing, but perceiving that she had a point everyone else seemed to have missed.

That, it seems, is now something all of us are going to miss.

November 2003

WHY THE TORIES CAN'T PICK A LEADER THEY CAN LIVE WITH

W. F. Deedes says it is the calibre of person who becomes an MP that is to blame, not the voting system

Small wonder, looking at the past, that the Conservatives decided to take a short cut last night when it came to choosing a leader. The way they have set about doing this has changed a lot, though not necessarily for the better, since it set about finding a successor to Eden in 1957 after Suez.

It was pretty simple in those days. Macmillan and Butler appeared before the 1922 Committee, comprising every Tory MP and any Unionist peer interested enough to attend. Harold talked of leaving the stage and retiring to the Lords. We liked the tone of that. Rab Butler was more Delphic. Some were uncertain in their minds just how solid Rab had been during the Suez crisis. That swung the balance. Macmillan took the prize.

When, in 1963, a flare-up of his prostate gland led to Macmillan's sudden retirement, it was altogether more difficult. The choice of a successor lay not with two, but five or six. I was at the Blackpool conference with a heavy cold when news of Macmillan's decision to go came through.

There followed heavy meetings in the bedrooms of Tory heavy-weights. I remember thinking what hard luck it was on the wives. There they were, putting on pretty gowns for evening parties, tying up their hair, while we sprawled about the room planning and telephoning.

That conference programme has since been seen by political pundits as a gigantic conspiracy—and that is not entirely wide of the mark. Just before he addressed a big Tory gathering one evening, word reached us that Quentin Hailsham would, responding to a vote of thanks, declare that his hat was in the ring.

The Tory chief whip, Martin Redmayne, and I, as minister without portfolio, were due to take our seats on the platform.

Redmayne warned me of Hailsham's intentions. "There will be cheering and applause from the audience," he said to me. "You and I, facing the audience, will take no part in this. We will sit silent and un-applauding."

It is an interesting example of how the mind of a chief whip works. "Martin," I said, "if everyone is standing and applauding, and you and I sit silent and still, shall we not look rather conspicuous?" He took my point. "We will stand," he said, "but not clap."

Much then depended on how the major figures competing for laurels performed at the conference. Rab Butler had caught my cold and failed to shine. Alec Home was more to taste, saying no more than was necessary, but tidily and modestly. Back in London, a day or two later, Redmayne summoned me and showed me the figures. The count from cabinet, Commons and Lords made Home the decisive winner, at least in our eyes.

Those who preferred Butler then staged a mini-rebellion, condemning our system of selection, so paving the way to a more elaborate way of picking a leader that has also displayed flaws and led to the present mess.

For Alec Home determined to bequeath the party a method that, to all appearances, was more democratic than the old "magic circle". It got a trial run when, in his first year of opposition, 1965, Home realised he was not up to it and handed the reins over to Ted Heath. The midwife of that delivery was Willie Whitelaw; he drew up figures from within the parliamentary party and showed them to Home, who unhesitatingly stood down.

The deposing of Ted Heath and the shift to Margaret Thatcher in 1975 was stormier. Lord Curzon's bitter cry when Stanley Baldwin was preferred to him after Bonar Law's resignation—"A man of the utmost insignificance!"—paled beside Heath's fulminations.

This newspaper had a degree of influence in that transition. My predecessor in the editor's chair, Maurice Green, had become increasingly critical of Ted Heath's economic policy. Not long before I succeeded Green in 1974, I lunched alone with Ted Heath in the Commons. I had just forked a portion of veal and ham pie into my mouth, when Ted leant across the table and remarked angrily: "Why can't you get some sense into the heads of your people!"

At first I took this to refer to my blameless constituents in Ashford, and protested mildly. This made Ted more cross. "No, no! I mean *The Daily Telegraph*." Maurice Green was showing himself to be better disposed to what emerged as Mrs Thatcher's economic ideas than he felt towards Heath's. I found it a valuable inheritance.

Margaret Thatcher's downfall is too recent to require rehearsing. So is John Major's. But that involved an interesting succession, which I spotted early on. Mrs Thatcher threw a lunch party at Chequers to mark her 10th anniversary at Number 10. Only personal friends joined the company of about 60 that gathered for lunch. John Major, who sat one place away from me, was the only minister present.

As we travelled home, I said to my wife: "I believe I have seen the heir apparent." Then I had to explain to her who John Major was.

So do we conclude that the Tory party is a bed of snakes, chronically disloyal to its leaders, and that this incontinence has now cost it yet another leader? Or do we say that the old magic circle system, to which it can never return, proved soundest, and that its increasingly elaborate successors have simply produced chaos?

Not that that takes us to the root of Tory weakness, which, in my judgment, springs from its failure in recent times to attract enough outstandingly able men and women to enter Parliament. I know at least a dozen people I would like to see as Tory MPs who would not touch it with a bargepole. The economic risks to a family man are high. The media make Parliament a far rougher life than it was. Modern business does not readily yield its stars to the public service.

All the more credit to those who have taken the plunge and given up more profitable occupations to enter Parliament.

But from a much smaller field than half a century ago, it has become harder to pick a leader the party can live with for long.

DENIS: A SOUND JUDGE OF MEN WHO CHOSE A GREAT WOMAN

W. F. Deedes—"Dear Bill"—pays tribute to his friend Denis Thatcher who died yesterday

Those who remember the letters in *Private Eye* that Denis Thatcher wrote his pal Bill during Margaret Thatcher's tenancy of 10 Downing Street may well have thought they knew just what sort of man he was: a genial fellow with one or two slightly disreputable pals, in awe of his wife, fond of golf and even fonder of a glass of gin.

The caricature was politically useful. It made it difficult for journalists seriously to infer that Denis had the smallest influence on his wife's politics. But it was a caricature, not the portrait of a man who, all through his wife's career, chose a self-effacing role, revealing relatively little of himself even to friends, let alone the news media.

In a world in which so many figures in the public eye strive to make themselves bigger than they are, Denis Thatcher set about doing the reverse, which made him a difficult character to read.

Some of us will remember him not as a man who stood in awe of his wife, but who so admired her that much of his own life became dedicated to her best interests. When we were on golfing holidays and slightly boring people asked for his autograph, he smiled upon them and signed their books—always with a fountain pen, never a ballpoint—because it was furthering the interests of "the blessed Margaret", as he sometimes called her.

This, I came to see, was a closer partnership than the world ever guessed. To the casual acquaintance, Denis Thatcher's principal talent lay in his ability to read a balance sheet upside down and then pronounce on what was wrong with each of the directors. It came naturally to him. He had been brought up in a family business, a company that traded in paint and other products founded by his grandfather.

But as his wife must have known from their earliest days together, his value as a friend, philosopher and guide lay in deep-rooted common sense. Most of us think we are blessed with common sense—until we put our foot in it. Denis Thatcher had more opportunities than any man alive to put his foot in it during his wife's 12-year occupation of 10 Downing Street. Furthermore he was under the constant scrutiny of the "vipers"—as he described journalists. Yet he rarely attracted a headline.

He was a sound judge of men, helped as some of us were by experience in the wartime Army, but also by his principal recreation, which was refereeing rugby matches—a field in which he almost qualified at international level. He put me right on such judgments about mutual acquaintances once or twice, but I cannot remember faulting him. "I said to my woman"—as the blessed Margaret sometimes became—"I said, that chap's a wrong 'un." His ability to sum up people who crossed the political scene was one of the gifts he brought to the marriage partnership.

All prime ministers need a trustworthy friend with whom, when the day has quietened down, they can privately discuss their innermost feelings and look for sensible advice. Often for Mrs Thatcher the day never quietened down. But she found time to consult.

Part of his value to her can be traced from a short sentence in Carol Thatcher's biography of her father, describing the earliest years in her mother's political career. "Denis says: 'She stood for Dartford twice and lost twice and the second time she cried on my shoulder I married her.'" In later years there were other occasions when there were tears to dry.

Stanley Baldwin spoke of the loneliness of Number 10, where prime ministers may be called on to take decisions alone, and accept sole responsibility for them. Margaret Thatcher had her share of those, particularly when Denis was overseas on business, as he was when she made her maiden speech in the Commons. But he was there to share some of the burdens. This was a marriage strengthened by the rare degree of trust that one partner felt able to repose in the other.

For Denis Thatcher, the loneliness of Number 10 was hardly less acute than it was for his wife, though in a different sense. There would be international gatherings in London or at Chequers where his presence was simply not wanted. It does not add to the happiness of a man to be told that his wife is engaged in business in which he can play no useful part at all. I visited him once or twice at Downing Street during such weekends and felt the isolation.

When required to play a part on missions abroad, he earned his keep. At one state banquet where he sat next to the president's wife and found that neither of them spoke a word of the other's language, they conversed happily by drawing little pictures on the table cloth.

Three of us sought to leaven life at Number 10 for Denis with regular overseas golfing trips. He suffered from a painful back, made worse by continuing to referee rugby matches too late in life. But it never stopped his golf for long. In the early years, there were 18 holes in the morning and, after a pint of beer and a light lunch, another 18 holes in the afternoon. Later, we settled for nine after lunch.

More than once we spent our week at La Manga, where Seve Ballesteros was the visiting professional. He took a liking to Denis and once challenged him to a round in which Ballesteros would drive off one leg. At the last moment, reckoning there would be cameras photographing this exhibition and never one for the limelight, Denis modestly declared himself to be an unworthy opponent and handed the baton over to the rest of us, but consented to walk round.

I look back gratefully on those golfing holidays, which were always fun and sometimes produced unexpected laughs. We reached our hotel one evening later than expected because of a delayed flight, to find a balloon dance in progress. Couples tied balloons round their middle and the object of the dance was to burst other people's balloons by backing into them. We all took part. Denis's policy always was to do what redounded to the credit of his wife. On balance, going into a balloon dance looked more matey than staying out and going to the bar for a gin. So, into the balloon dance.

He could be seen as he really was, cheerful, approachable and considerate of others, at the receptions the Thatchers often gave at Number 10. On such occasions Denis would wheel round the room, gathering under his wing anyone who looked solitary. "You must meet the archbishop," he would say to some unescorted woman guest. "Chancellor, have you met Mr Briggs from Exeter?" He was an excellent host.

All meals with Denis were entertaining, not least because he was so particular about the way his food was cooked. "Waiter," he would say affably, handing him a plate of steak only faintly pink, "will you very kindly take this back to the kitchen and ask them to cook it, because it is practically raw."

Which explains why, when she was Secretary for Education,

Margaret was seen one evening by the Permanent Secretary leaving the office early. She was going out, she explained, to buy bacon for Denis's breakfast. There were, the Permanent Secretary assured her, plenty of people in the department who would be glad to do that for her. No, the bacon had to be just as he liked it, and only she knew what he liked.

That helps us to understand why this was a successful marriage, proof against the fierce light that shines perpetually on the occupants of 10 Downing Street, protective against the disappointments of life at the top, assured of breakfasts at which Denis could eat his bacon without complaint. This was a partnership to remind the world what matchless gifts marriage can bring.

THE WORLD WAS WEAK IN 1935—AND MUSSOLINI HAD HIS WAY

W. F. Deedes, who covered the 1935 Abyssinian war as a young reporter, agrees with Tony Blair that the current stage of the Iraqi crisis is "an Abyssinia moment"

If we're seeking lessons from the past to help us deal with Saddam Hussein, then the way we dealt with Mussolini's conquest of Abyssinia in 1935 is—as the Prime Minister understands—the place to look. I was particularly reminded of my own Abyssinia moment when I read about Saturday's anti-war march—hauntingly matched by the Peace Ballot of 1935, the national referendum in which millions voted for peace at almost any price, thus unwittingly persuading Hitler and Mussolini that bold predators had not much to fear.

Then, as now, the authority of what was then the League of Nations and is now the United Nations was at stake. Then, as now, many felt reluctant to take action against a dangerous dictator, even with the authority of a body like the League or the UN, lest it lead to war. Then, as now, our difficulties were compounded by the duplicitous behaviour of the French.

In 1935, after many brave words and much wriggling, we fudged it. So Mussolini took all he wanted in Abyssinia, without hindrance. He and others drew conclusions from this display of impotence. In 1936, the same year as Mussolini's conquest of Abyssinia was completed, the Spanish Civil War began. Germany and Italy felt free to play a military role in that affair, without reprisals. Then, it has always seemed to me, our slide towards the Second World War became unstoppable.

Oddly, seeing how it turned out, the behaviour of the government (then a coalition) won widespread approval in Britain at the time. This was partly because ministers kept repeating that Britain would stand firm by all its obligations to the League.

Both Sir Samuel Hoare, the foreign secretary, and Anthony Eden, the minister without portfolio for League of Nations affairs, first sought to reason with Mussolini and dissuade him from his African adventure. We even offered him a strip of British territory in Somaliland if he would waive his demands on Abyssinia.

When that was rebuffed, we declared that we had gone to the limit of concessions to Italy and, if these were rejected, we would not hestitate to call upon the League to take action. Relations between the League and Mussolini were much as they are now between the United Nations and Saddam Hussein.

On September 11, 1935, three weeks before Mussolini plunged into Abyssinia, Sam Hoare delivered a resounding speech at Geneva, declaring our unswerving support for the League but making it clear that our undertaking was conditional on other members of the League doing their share. Acclaimed by the assembly, praised by the British press, and music to the ears of the Liberal and Labour parties, this speech was questioned only by those with the wit to perceive that, if we were to take the lead in sanctions against Italy, then we must be prepared for war.

We did, in fact, as a precautionary measure move British warships into the Mediterranean, and we reinforced British garrisons, rather as we have been doing in the Gulf.

But reckoning this build-up might provoke a sudden Italian attack on the British fleet, our naval authorities insisted they must withdraw part of the fleet unless better provision were made for its security. The French were asked whether, in the event of an Italian attack, we could use their ports. They agreed in return for reciprocal treatment.

The crisis in 1935 came closest to where we are now after October 4, when Mussolini launched his attack on Abyssinia. Britain's eagerness to set in motion the machinery of the League against Italy ran into immediate difficulties with France. Pierre Laval, the French foreign minister, was unwilling to antagonise Mussolini. The sticking point was the likelihood of action by the League, involving sanctions strong enough to thwart Mussolini, precipitating war. Though never a strong believer in the principle of sanctions, Eden believed that on this occasion they would be effective.

He wanted the League to apply sanctions—including oil sanctions—to bring Mussolini to the negotiating table. Without the co-operation of France, this became a farce. When I passed through the Suez Canal in 1935 en route for Abyssinia, Mussolini's ships were drawing all the oil they wanted. Financial backing for Italy,

I was told, came from the Banque de France. When I came back a few months later, the same conditions prevailed.

In Britain, we had a section of the Labour Party protesting against endorsing a policy—namely effective sanctions against Italy—which might ultimately lead to a "capitalist" war. The leader of the party, George Lansbury, declared that he could not support the use of armed force either by the League of Nations or by individual nations and resigned, giving way to Clem Attlee. Labour's leader in the Lords, Lord Ponsonby, resigned on the same point.

By contrast, the Trades Union Congress, driven by detestation for fascism, was more robust. Sir Walter Citrine, TUC secretary, declared there was a price to pay for peace, and it might entail taking deliberate action against a breaker of the peace. It might mean war, but that was one of the things they had to face. There was no alternative left except to take the risk of applying sanctions involving the possibility of war.

The Tory leader, Stanley Baldwin, told his party's conference that it was useless for Britain to accept obligations under the covenant of the League until it had at its command adequate forces with which to carry them out. He promised to repair deficiencies in military equipment—another relevant echo from the past.

The Abyssinian affair ended shamefully, after Hoare and Pierre Laval, with the broad assent of our Cabinet, cooked up a plan in December 1935 to reach a compromise with Mussolini whereby he stopped fighting in return for a slab of Abyssinia. When that became public knowlege, there was uproar. Hoare had to resign. Eden succeeded him.

The whole affair was an object lesson in what happens when nations seek to deter an aggressor by proposing a course of action against him with two conditions: one being that everyone binds themselves to the same course of action; the other, that nothing they do will provoke the aggressor into striking back.

There is, of course, one big difference between now and then. America wasn't a player in 1935. Europe handled it. Now America is the lead player, which may be just as well.

TERROR IS ON THE WANE, BUT BIGOTRY IS NEVER FAR BELOW THE SURFACE

W. F. Deedes returns to Belfast after two decades to find a city at peace, but still as divided as ever

Belfast's smiling face misleads you. Walk down Main Street in the city centre and you look on one of the most handsome and outwardly most prosperous capitals in western Europe. That is not altogether surprising: Europe's interest in Northern Ireland, together with the millions we have pumped in there, have smartened the place up a lot since I used to make regular visits between 1969 and 1980.

What a wonderful setting, too. From so many points in the city, the green hills just outside seem within walking distance. Turn out of Belfast on the Holywood side and you instantly pass through green fields. I know no city that suffers less from urban sprawl.

We turned into the Europa Hotel for a mid-morning cup of coffee. In past years, when I sought that hotel's hospitality, there were nearly always broken windows because the Unionist HQ in nearby Glengall Street were a target for the bombers. Now the UUP has moved elsewhere and the Europa is just like a thousand other good hotels in Europe.

The great overhead cranes above the silent and empty Harland and Wolff shipyard cast a shadow; but the shipyards on Tyneside and Clydeside lie under the same shadow. The great liners that came out of the Thompson graving dock at Harland and Wolff are no longer in demand.

There is a charm about Belfast, too, and it comes sadly home to you that most Ulstermen and women mind their manners better than some citizens of our cosmopolitan cities. Ask your way in Belfast and you will get a civil response. Everyone, whatever their religion, speaks the same language. Asylum seekers and economic refugees seem not to be drawn towards Ulster's capital.

So hurrah for the peace agreement that our Prime Minister has painfully negotiated and kept alive? Give him his due. To all appearances, it has paid off. The bombs have stopped going off in Main Street—and in other main streets across Britain. So we move towards more peaceful times? The lion is preparing to lie down with the lamb? That is the illusion that the smiling face of Belfast invites you to accept.

For, by one of those paradoxical strokes that occur sometimes, as what we interpret as terrorism appears to be receding, so sectarianism (which in the autumn of 1969 gave rise to terrorism and turned Belfast into a battleground) seems to be taking deeper root than ever.

"The children here are growing up as bigoted as their parents," said my experienced guide, as we travelled down the long Falls Road. How could it be otherwise? Given that the children of Belfast's Roman Catholics live in their own quarters and go to their own schools, and the Protestants' children do likewise, why should they grow wiser than their parents? They will be 17 or 18 years of age before they have a chance of meeting across the divide.

One looks at the great walls that have been put up at sensitive points between a Catholic majority and a Protestant minority—or the other way about. They have had yards of wire netting added to their height, so that it takes an athletic figure to lob across a petrol bomb.

One observes that the offensive messages in chalk or paint that were flung up during the really rough years of 1969–75 have become permanent fixtures. They have been painted with the artist's brush in the Protestant zones. Take this for a sample: "If the Provos or the pan-nationalists press the British or Irish governments to keep trying to succeed in United Ireland, then they may spare themselves for another 30 bloody years, for the battle will have just begun."

There are some vivid images as well, designed to remind you of the Easter rebellion of 1916, and of the martyrs who died with it; but most of the pugnacious orders of the day are to be found in Protestant territory. There is a defensive note in most of them that bodes ill.

What chills the blood in Belfast today is the way in which a tiny lawless minority seeks to impose the law. You have a wayward son who is a social nuisance? They'll come to you, these enforcers, and require you to hand him in for punishment. He's less likely to be knee-capped these days, but he will be shot through the calf, in a style calculated to inflict the maximum damage. Another little job for the surgeons of the Royal Victoria Hospital.

Alternatively, he will be savagely beaten up.

Our vigilant and patient Army records two or three such "executions" most nights of the week. Who rules, eh? Terror of this order is a powerful instrument—and totally alien to what the Unionists never allow us to forget is British territory. That is the dark side of Belfast; but, as often happens, where it's darkest, candles shed their strongest light, and you find that light among the soldiers we employ there.

Such a thankless task. Both sides are jealous of their rights and swift to complain of other people's wrongs. After all, the peace agreement depends on our soldiers holding to a line that, as some see it, is being too often renegotiated in ways that strap their hands behind their backs. There is no other army in the world that could so skilfully combine the martial arts with diplomacy.

Talking to senior NCOs, you get a sense of what sustains them, and so of a great source of strength to our Army. The old hands know well enough what they are up against. On our rounds, we went past the Red Devils bar. "Now that's a pub where Protestant and Catholic feel able to meet together," said my guide, "drawn by their devotion to Manchester United Football Club."

I found that depressing. Is that really the only thing that can unite them? But it is the sort of thing that our Army has learnt to understand. In days when I saw more of the soldiers in Northern Ireland than I do now, it helped if they felt there was recognition in this country of the duties they were being called on to fulfil. They have grown in stature since then. They know Ulster's nature and they know our nature, too.

They know there's no gratitude in politics.

WE HAD A PISTOL TO OUR HEADS:
WE NEEDED TO REACT

W. F. Deedes, a lifelong friend of Profumo, was the minister who wrote his Commons statement. Here he questions the wisdom of his own actions

It has long lingered in my mind how far what became the Profumo scandal was compounded by the way that some of us parliamentarians handled it.

Jack Profumo might just have survived, even as a minister, the affair with Christine Keeler. It was misleading the House of Commons about it that proved his undoing.

There had been rumours of Profumo's misconduct for some time. Newspapers had caught wind of it. Then, late one Thursday night, while the Commons was engaged in harmless business with the Home Secretary, Henry Brooke, Labour MPs on the benches opposite began to throw knives.

What was the truth about the Secretary of State for War, which Jack Profumo then was? Leading the quest for truth was Col Wigg, who had a famous nose for scandal. Barbara Castle joined the inquisition.

When the House adjourned, I went over to the Chief Whip's room and gave him a brief account of what had gone on. Then I went home to my bed in London.

At 2am I was awoken by a call from the Chief Whip, Martin Redmayne. "We're calling a meeting about this," he said. "Come along." On my way back to the House, it occurred to me why we were up against it. In those days, the House of Commons met at 11am on Fridays. Labour would resume where we had left off the previous night—and from its front bench. Some reply had to be prepared.

So half a dozen of us met in the Chief Whip's room at 2.30am. Jack Profumo, his house surrounded by reporters, had taken a sleeping draught and arrived looking sleepy before 3am.

"Jack," we said, "we need a statement for the House in seven hours' time." Then we set about drafting it with his agreement. I typed it out on a typewriter I kept in my room at the House for old times' sake.

Was it a sensible way of going about it? I have constantly wondered about that. It was the imminent meeting of the House that held a pistol to our heads.

Lord Denning conducted an inquest into the scandal that in that summer of 1963 engulfed the whole Cabinet.

As he observed, our task at the meeting with Profumo was not to draw the truth from him—we assumed that ground had been covered earlier by other people—but to prepare something that might meet the Government's urgent needs when the Commons met. Was it a fair way to deal with Profumo? I leave that to the judgment of others.

Eventually the truth emerged. I do not know how Jack came to his decision to own up to the Lord Chancellor of that time, Lord Dilhorne, or how he decided thereafter to order his life. I have a feeling that his wife, Valerie Hobson, was a decisive factor.

Would she have stayed with him had he decided to take shelter overseas? He adored her. But Jack, good-looking and popular with women, was a philanderer. I feel pretty sure he's had a wifely warning on that account. Did he lie to save not his job but his marriage? We shall never know.

His departure had consequences. If a bomb had gone off in the Cabinet room, it could hardly have inflicted more damage. Chief Whip on the telephone again. Enoch Powell was threatening to resign from the Cabinet because of the hash we had made. "Please handle it." Thanks to Enoch's eminently sensible wife, Pam Powell, it was handled.

I did not follow closely the work Jack Profumo did at Toynbee Hall, the east London charity, until a year or two ago, when this newspaper included it among the charities in its Christmas Appeal. But I heard something about it from his beneficiaries. There was no task too menial for Jack to take on. He won a high reputation among some of the poor of east London.

And for more than 40 years he stuck to it and kept his mouth shut. He gave no interviews, offered no defence. I had the greatest difficulty in persuading him to write a piece for this newspaper on a Toynbee Hall anniversary.

We enjoyed one memorable experience together. In 1954, Winston Churchill, then Prime Minister, went for the last time to the

Speech Room of his old school, Harrow, as he had done throughout the war, to hear them sing the Harrow Songs.

Profumo and I had been at Harrow at the same time. "I think we should support him," he said to me. So we went together, not only to Songs, but also to join Churchill in the headmaster's study where, in accordance with his practice throughout the war, he talked in confidence to the prefects of his old school—and was never let down.

I remained on close terms with Jack Profumo, and not only because we were at school together. Most people forgave him, though as he grew frailer it became difficult to keep authors and film-makers off his back.

"It's a great story," they would say, when I declined to take part, and so it was.

I never wanted to see him knighted, because I sensed it would draw him back into controversy. On Mrs Thatcher's 70th birthday party at Claridges, the Queen, Prince Philip, Denis and Margaret and Jack Profumo sat at the same table. That was sufficient.

There were those who thought the whole episode was grossly over-dramatised. I met some of them at his old parliamentary seat, Stratford-upon-Avon.

Not long after Jack had gone to make his peace at Toynbee, I was invited down to make a speech at the annual Conservative women's summer lunch at some stately home in a park. Afterwards, I took a refreshing drink and started to feel pleased with myself.

Then I became aware that a number of women were moving towards me and looking deeply unhappy. "Why did you let Jack go?" they demanded. "You wimps! We'd have got him back to Parliament. We loved him. So did everyone in his constituency. There wouldn't have been a problem—but for your lot!"

I left with my tail between my legs, but I treasure a memory of those women.

INTERNATIONAL AFFAIRS

INTERNATIONAL AFFAIRS in my time have really been dominated by two major considerations. Before the Second World War, it was the extent to which the European dictators, Hitler and Mussolini, threatened the peace of Europe. After that war, the question was whether the Soviet Union posed yet another threat, and this produced the Cold War. It was resolved by many things, partly the strength of America, but more by the spread of communications.

I saw enough of Russia at different times to realize the consequences of allowing its people to see how other countries lived. Once the news barrier broke down, and Communism no longer remained an island immune to the rest of the world, it was effectively doomed. I was lucky enough that one visit to Russia coincided with the downfall of Gorbachev, and I found myself able to talk, for the first time since the revolution in 1917, to Russians willing to speak openly. It made a good piece.

Since the end of the Cold War, we have suffered a series of conflicts, many of them springing from the end of Communist rule. I think particularly of the Balkans and the upheaval in Yugoslavia where I spent several weeks reporting.

My particular interest in the conflicts which occurred in Africa and in Europe lay in the deadly consequences of the anti-personnel mines which were laid so freely. I was struck by the cruelty wrought on those who lived off the land when struck down by a mine, which cost them an arm or a leg. It virtually ended their life.

The International Red Cross encouraged me to take an interest in this. At one point Diana, Princess of Wales, became struck by the same sense of hardship inflicted on the very poor of the world. I joined her on a trip to Angola and later we paid a visit to Bosnia and talked to the afflicted only a few days before Diana's death in Paris. Had she lived on, I often think the campaign against landmines would have grown stronger and many more lives and limbs might have been saved. All war involves cruelty, but no department of it, in my judgement, inflicts more cruelty on innocent lives than the spreading of anti-personnel mines.

SALE OF BRITISH LINERS TO JAPAN

NOT RAW MATERIAL OF ARMAMENTS

Solely for Scrap

40 VESSELS WAITING TO BE BROKEN UP

Alarming reports to the effect that seven old British liners have left for Japan, where they may be broken up and used to make guns and shells or converted into troopships, were circulated in London yesterday.

The "Morning Post" is able to state that there is no foundation for the belief that the ships, which, in the usual way have been sold to Japan as scrap, will be used for purposes other than those laid down in the contract between the British and Japanese authorities.

"There is no chance whatever of the ships being used to manu-facture guns or shells," an authority stated yesterday. The metal of these ships is useless for such purposes.

"Forty other ships are at present laid up in Japan, all of which have been sold in the same way, and not one of them has yet been adapted as a troopship or broken up to manufacture armaments. None of the liners which have just left this country will reach Japan before May, and even then the depth of water which they require—in the case of the Baltic it is between 30ft. and 40ft.—will make it practically impossible for them to navigate Japanese ports.

"We have dealt with Japan for many years, and they have never broken a contract with us yet."

ITALY AND ABYSSINIA AT WAR

Menelik's Drum Sounds

CHIEFS RALLY TO THE EMPEROR

Addis Ababa Calm

BOMBARDMENT EXPECTED AT ANY MOMENT

ADDIS ABABA, OCT. 3

This morning, from the Royal Palace of Addis Ababa, Menelik's war-drum thundered out the order for general mobilisation.

The order followed receipt in the capital of news that Adowa and Adigrat had been bombed by Italian aircraft, and that fighting had taken place in the province of Agame.

In brilliant sunshine, against a background of green hills, chiefs, ready for war, had assembled in the Palace yard. The Grand Chamberlain of the Court ascending the steps and standing between fluttering Ethiopian flags before the great drum, began to read the proclamation.

Even while he was reading, with a motionless sea of dark faces below him, the news from Adowa was heard in whispers on all sides.

A few minutes later, as the proclamation ended, the chiefs, shouting, yelling, and waving their sabres, poured up the steps towards the Palace.

An official, rising above the seething mass, struggled to obtain silence. At the top of his voice he tried to make the dread telegram audible among the clamour, and here and there a phrase penetrated the mad enthusiasm of the warriors.

It was stated that the Italians had bombed Adowa and that women and children had suffered in the fighting.

The bombardment of Addis Ababa itself is expected at any moment.

Little news, however, is filtering through to Addis Ababa.

Unconcerned

This afternoon men and women are still going unconcernedly about their business. The streets are crowded, and no one would guess from the general calm that fighting had begun and that the Italians had already crossed the Abyssinian frontier.

The Government, however, is keeping in close touch with its armies. Officials at the Palace are in a state of extreme tension, and the Emperor is informed immediately of every development, however minute.

An official telegram states that the Italian attack began at sunrise to-day. In the dawn enemy aircraft circled over Adigrat, 50 miles to the north-east of Adowa, and a hail of bombs fell on the town, wrecking at least 100 houses and causing a general stampede.

Nor did Adowa escape. The town—famous in Abyssinian history as the scene of the battle of March 1, 1896, when an Italian force was heavily defeated—was bombed at the same time as Adigrat, but here the damage proved to be less severe.

Heavy Losses

Fifteen houses were wrecked, and although at present it is not possible to state the exact number of casualties, it is known that many women and children have been killed.

Another message reports firing from Dessie. Yet another which, at the moment, is unconfirmed, states that the Italians had advanced seven kilometres from Wal Wal when they were repulsed. The victory was not won without heavy losses. It is believed that many hundreds of Ethiopian troops were killed and wounded.

At 1.30 this afternoon, although fighting had proceeded since early morning, the British Legation in Addis Ababa remained—like the rest of the city—entirely unaware of the developments on the frontier.

About one o'clock an Ethiopian official whom I knew to be in full possession of the facts visited the British Minister.

Strangely enough, he left without mentioning the news from Adowa and Adigrat, and when I saw Sir Sidney Barton immediately afterwards I was able to inform him of the situation and to give him the first news of the Italian advance which he had received from any source.

Pouring Over Frontier

The Italians are reported to be pouring over the frontier into Agame. It is stated officially here that the first attacking force has advanced 20 kilometres into Abyssinian territory.

The advance is almost certainly an encircling movement westwards towards Adowa, otherwise Adigrat would have already fallen.

The Ethiopians are making a sturdy resistance. Heavy fighting is proceeding in this sector, but up to the present no authentic casualty figures are available.

The Government has kept in touch with Ras Seyum, the Governor of Tigre Province, and communications are still being maintained. Addis Ababa remains calm, although troops are guarding various parts of the town.

The Emperor is in constant conference with his Ministers and advisers at the Old Palace.

Legation Precautions

The Italian Legation is in a state of siege. No one is allowed in or out.

A member of the Legation motored through the town this evening with a mounted armed guard.

It is officially stated that Adowa was bombarded by four aeroplanes, the first bombs hitting a hospital marked with the Red Cross. The second raid took place at ten o'clock this morning. Seventy-three projectiles have been counted.

Many Europeans are planning to sleep out during the night.

Anti-aircraft guns have been mounted in St. George's Square.

May 1936

THE BRITISH STRONGHOLD IN ADDIS ABABA

Legation Becomes a Fort Sheltering European Lives

From the tiny fort recently built on the hill which rises almost sheer behind the British Legation in Addis Ababa an anxious guard must have watched the Imperial Road from Dessie yesterday. Doubtless it was from this post, five hundred feet above the capital, and commanding a vast panorama of the northern approaches to the city, that the first glimpse of the advancing Italian army was obtained.

As the leading Italian transport column dipped into the last valley, some ten miles distant, its approach must have at once been known in the British Legation; and two thousand British and European subjects have heard with relief that the Italian advance on Addis had entered its last phase, and that within a few hours they would be secure from far greater perils within the capital.

Those crowded into the Legation compound would be the first to hear and see the Italians' entry into Addis Ababa. The British Legation is the first building of importance on the road from Dessie, and at this moment the earliest Italian columns must inevitably sweep towards or past its gates.

From the other side of the advance, the Legation's well-kept garden—now ablaze with English and Abyssinian summer flowers— the tennis court and smooth green lawns, and the solid, dignified residences of the Legation staff, would provide the Italians with the first sight of real civilisation for many months.

As their leading mechanical column grumbles along the rough, boulder-strewn highway—inches thick in white dust or black mud, according to the previling weather—curious glances would be turned towards this northernmost outpost of the capital. Perhaps by now the emergency encampment of two thousand Europeans, which is spread, locust-like, over the green slopes of the Legation compound, may have somewhat obscured this refreshing view from the Dessie road; and the garden, usually under the supervision of Lady Barton, lost a little of its traditionally immaculate appearance; the flowers may have wilted a trifle, and the grass, trampled beneath many feet, lost its lush green complexion.

Even so, the Italians cannot fail to notice the imposing entrance of stone and wrought iron, typical of the entrance to any English country house; they are bound to see something of the well-trimmed, weedless paths which wind through the compound, under the shady eucalyptus trees, toward the individual residences of the Minister and his staff; they must surely observe the neat, newly thatched roofs and clean whitewashed walls of the Secretary's house and the Consul's bungalow and, further back, the grey facades of the Legation building itself.

Those Europeans who have been able to find refuge in this sanctuary during the weekend—and no less, their respective Governments—have reason to offer devout thanks for the foresight and skill of the British Minister, in taking what have proved to be such vital precautions. It is said that the British Legation was ideally situated for such defence, and for that reason was selected by the Diplomatic Corps as an emergency centre. That is only in part the truth. All the Legations (except America's) by reason of their situation in the hills some miles from Addis itself, are fairly placed for purposes of defence. It is only because the British Minister has from the first feared the dangers which have become so real in the last few days, and has taken adequate and early precautions, that a terrible situation has been averted, and several hundred white people, including British and Americans, have been saved from massacre by drunken Abyssinian bandits.

Many now sheltering in the cool oasis of the Legation compound will recall the amusement, amounting almost to light contempt, with which certain individuals in other Legations received the news that the British Minister was about to instal armed British troops in the Legation. The Minister's intentions became known last September, and the arrival by night a few weeks later of the Sikh troops, with a certain and justifiable amount of secrecy, was considered by some to be the best Diplomatic joke Addis had heard for a long time. The ancient fable of the "Three little Pigs" has been told again in Addis Ababa.

For many months Sir Sidney Barton, acting in part co-operation with the rest of the Diplomatic Corps, has exerted himself, in addition to all his other onerous duties, to consider and to take every conceivable precaution against the grave situation which has now arisen. Under the command of British officers, the Sikhs and Punjabis have been trained since their arrival for these particular conditions; and for seven months they have been busy making the Legation compound safe and snug for the present occupation. Their collective ability to undertake work of any description, from first-aid to excellent cooking; their magnificent physique and training; their ability with the rifle; and their appearance of complete dependability in any conceivable circumstances, must indeed be a comfort and relief to the British Minister and his fellow sufferers.

Last year precautions were taken to ensure an independent and unassailable water supply for the Legation, which I believe comes from a spring or well on the hillside at the back of the Legation. Food was purchased in abundance, without which the siege could not have lasted twenty-four hours. It was reported during the week-end that the big stores of Mohammed Ali, the Indian merchants, were assaulted by the mob. Had they but known, most of the food and drink usually stored there has almost certainly been in possession of the British Legation for some time. The Legation electricity supply is, of course, independent, so that the private radio transmitter and receiver, the searchlight, and interior lighting cannot be endangered. Big supplies of oil and gasoline have been in store for a long time.

The Americans in Addis should indeed be particularly thankful to Sir Sidney and his staff, for without the shelter of the British Legation walls, which they were forced to accept on Sunday, few of them would have survived death or serious injury. The American Legation, structurally and strategically, is one of the worst buildings in Addis, and it is not surprising that it fell early prey to the rabble. Unlike all the others, it is not in the sanctuary of the hills, but entirely isolated in the crowded western quarter of the town. Its defences were always poor, its approaches open to attack; its guards, other than native police, non-existent.

The strain of the present situation upon the Minister and his tiny staff, consisting of no more than a Secretary, Consul, two Military Attachés, and four or five assistants, is tremendous. It is a year now since Sir Sidney Barton was asked to postpone his much-needed leave by an apprehensive Foreign Office in London. For seven months he has shouldered great responsibilities; he has been faced by difficulties, unknown and happily unguessed by the British public at home. At the end of it all he has had two thousand British and European subjects thrust upon his hands. Beyond all his other difficulties and problems he has in his care the lives of two thousand men, women and children—lives preserved from the hands of a drunken armed Abyssinian rabble by barbed wire fences and one hundred and fifty Indian rifles.

THE EMPEROR INTERVIEWED

"We Never Desired War"

RULE OF FORCE OVER RIGHT

With grave
Aspect he rose, and in his rising seem'd
A pillar of state; deep on his front engraven
Deliberation sat; and public care
And princely counsel in his face yet shone
Majestic, though in ruin . . .

Milton's *Paradise Lost*

The anguish of recent months, crushing defeat, and exile have not yet broken the spirit of Emperor Haile Selassie, nor altered his proud bearing, nor robbed him of his Imperial dignity and calm, writes a "Morning Post" representative recently in Abyssinia.

The small figure which stood upright, silent and motionless before a sofa in a gold and white reception-room at No. 6, Prince's-gate yesterday, received representatives of the British and foreign Press with that same majestic serenity which he had showed months ago on similar occasions in the Imperial palace at Addis Ababa.

Trappings and finery of state were absent, yet his presence was not less impressive. His face is now pinched and sharper; his hair has thinned a little, and his remarkable eyes, though still strong and steady, at moments betray the great weariness which must be afflicting him.

But his bearing is unchanged, his shoulders are still square and held high, his features, always expressionless on public occasions, are still able to mask all emotion he may feel. The military cloak, well-polished riding boots and spurs have gone. A dark cloak covered the neat navy blue suit and chamma.

A Changed Scene

As the Emperor received his guests in the bright, finely decorated suite of his temporary London home yesterday, it seemed inevitable that his memory should recall him to those same occasions, not long ago, when in like circumstances the world's Press had stood about him in his own Palace.

As we filed through the doorway to stand grouped in the familiar semi-circle around him, it was clear that the irony of the situation was not lost to him. To a few of us he gave the slightest nod and faintest smile of recognition.

He remained still and silent, while beside him an official began to read a statement:

"We have never desired war. It was imposed upon us. . . ." The Emperor rested absolutely motionless, his eyes staring straight before him.

"Devastated fields and ruined villages . . . the bodies of the aged and of the women and children. . . ." The Emperor's unblinking eyes slowly swept the assembly before him. He was still erect, his hands folded before him in the sleeves of his loose, black cape.

". . . Cannot in silence and indifference be destroyed without subjecting humanity to the triumph and rule of force over right. . . ." At these words, the conclusion, he bowed to us stiffly and still with rigid features, to signify that the interview was terminated.

Again memories must have caused him pangs of suffering when the photographers pressed forward with requests for photographs, and the familiar scenes followed soon after in the spacious garden attached to the house. So, a little time back, it had been in Addis Ababa.

Photographs

With his daughter, Princess Tshai, shy and unused to such occasions, and his sons, who seemed honestly bored, he consented to pose on the balcony and then to walk about the garden paths. In daylight, the weariness and strain in his face were more clearly visible, yet he chatted quietly and cheerfully to Dr. Martin, the Abyssinian Minister in London, and members of his retinue.

He dislikes intensely being photographed, yet no trace of displeasure showed in his face as he stood before the whirring and clicking cameras. His movements were slow and unhurried, his features expressionless whenever facing those not personally known to him. As ever, he remained until all were satisfied.

It is obvious, from his demeanour and from the comments of his staff—a poor, pathetic remnant of the staff which once served him—that Haile Selassie is genuinely surprised with the gentleness and enthusiasm of his welcome here. He is faintly mystified, and not unpleased that as many journalists are prepared to welcome him to London as were present to report the war in Abyssinia.

About his future plans he himself is uncertain and his staff diplomatically vague. They speak smoothly and suggestively of Geneva.

The reaction from earlier months of furious activity and anxiety has not yet attacked him, though it is certain that a personality and brain such as his cannot long remain wholly inactive. It is safe to assert, however, that his natural pride and dignity will stand between him and any step which might cause embarrassment to the Government which is his host.

PALESTINE COMMISSION'S PROPOSALS

"TERMINATION OF BRITISH MANDATE"

SEPARATE SOVEREIGN STATES FOR JEWS AND ARABS

Termination of the British Mandate for Palestine, the substitution of two Treaties with independent sovereign Arab and Jewish States, and a permanent mandate to Britain for governing Jerusalem, Bethlehem, and Nazareth are recommended by the Palestine Royal Commission, whose Report was issued last night.

The Commission, after an exhaustive survey of Palestine's history, Constitution, and administration, which occupies 400 pages of the Report, state that they can find no other way of achieving settlement and lasting peace.

Their unanimous Report, which has been eleven months in preparation and must rank among the greatest State documents of post-War history, is accompanied by a Statement of Policy by H.M. Government.

Government in Agreement

The Government find themselves in general agreement with the arguments and conclusions of the Commission. They state:

"In the light of experience and of the arguments adduced by the Commission, they are driven to the conclusion that there is an irreconcilable conflict between the aspirations of Arabs and Jews in Palestine, that these aspirations cannot be satisfied under the terms of the present Mandate, and that a scheme of partition on the general lines recommended by the Commission represents the best and most hopeful solution of the deadlock. His Majesty's Government propose to advise his Majesty accordingly."

The Commission's plan of partition may be replaced by a Treaty System in accordance with the precedent set in Iraq and Syria.

Treaties of alliance should be negotiated by the Mandatory with the Government of Trans-Jordan and representatives of the Arabs of

Palestine on the one hand and with the Zionist Organisation on the other.

These Treaties would declare that within as short a period as may be convenient, two sovereign independent States would be established—the one an Arab State, consisting of Trans-Jordan united with about two-thirds of Palestine; the other a Jewish State consisting of that part of Palestine which lies to the north and west.

The Mandatory would undertake to support any requests for admission to the League of Nations which the Governments of the Arab and the Jewish States might make.

The Holy Places

A new and permanent British mandate designed to keep the sanctity of the Holy Places inviolate should be framed. An enclave should be demarcated extending from a point north of Jerusalem to a point south of Bethlehem, and access to the sea should be provided by a corridor from Jerusalem to the sea. The policy of the Balfour Declaration would not apply to this Mandate.

It would accord with Christian sentiment in the world at large if Nazareth and the Sea of Galilee (Lake Tiberias) were also covered by this Mandate, which should similarly protect religious endowments and such buildings, monuments and places in the Arab and Jewish States as are sacred to the Jews and the Arabs respectively.

The Frontier, dividing the two States, starts from Ras an Naqura, following the existing northern and eastern frontier of Palestine to Lake Tiberias and crossing the Lake to the outflow of Jordan, whence it continues down the river to a point a little north of Beisan. It then cuts across the Beisan Plain and runs along the southern edge of the Valley of Jezreel and across the Plain of Esdraelon to a point near Megiddo, whence it crosses the Carmel ridge near the Megiddo road. Then the line runs southwards down the eastern edge of the Maritime Plain, curving to avoid Tulkarm, until it reaches the Jerusalem–Jaffa corridor near Lydda. South of the corridor it continues down the edge of the Plain to a point about 10 miles south of Rehovet, when it turns west to the sea.

The Treaties would include strict guarantees for the protection of minorities in each State.

Military Conventions

Military conventions would be attached to the Treaties, dealing with the maintenance of naval, military, and air forces, the upkeep and use of ports, roads, and railways, the security of the oil pipe-line, and so forth.

The Jewish State should pay a subvention to the Arab State. In view of the backwardness of Trans-Jordan, Parliament should make a grant of £2,000,000 to the Arab State.

The Commission's plans will have to receive the approval of the League of Nations. A special meeting of the Permanent Mandates Commission has been called at Geneva for July 30. Mr. Ormsby Gore, Colonial Secretary, and the Palestine Commission's Secretary, Mr. J. M. Martin, will undertake negotiations on behalf of Great Britain. Later, a report will be made to the League Council, without whose consent no step can be taken.

During the week after next both Houses of Parliament will debate the Royal Commission's Report.

It is clear that some time must elapse before the Commission's proposals can be put into operation, always assuming they are accepted by the Jews and Arabs.

In the immediate future, while the form of a scheme of partition is being worked out, the Government propose that, as an interim measure, steps should be taken to prohibit any land transactions which might prejudice the scheme.

The Commission regard the two-fold problem of exchange of land and population as the most important and most difficult of all the questions involved.

The problem partly centres on the present distribution of population. It is estimated that 225,000 Arabs now occupy the area allocated to the Jewish State. In the proposed Arab State there are only about 1,250 Jews, but there are about 125,000 Jews as against 85,000 Arabs in Jerusalem and Haifa.

In Palestine, it is pointed out, there is no cultivable surplus land available for the settlement of Arabs evacuated from the Jewish area.

It is urged that Trans-Jordan, Beersheba and the Jordan Valley be surveyed and an estimate made of the practical possibilities of irrigation and development as quickly as possible. If it is shown that much of the land would be available for the resettlement of Arabs living in the Jewish area, the most strenuous efforts should be made to obtain an agreement for the transfer of land and population.

The Commission discuss the alternative possibility of Cantonisation, that is, division of Palestine into watertight provinces or cantons, but the area is rejected as impracticable.

The Commission think it improbable that either party will be satisifed at first sight with the proposals submitted for the adjustment of their rival claims. For Partition, they add, means that neither will get all it wants. "It means that the Arabs must acquiesce in the exclusion from their sovereignty of a piece of territory, long occupied and once ruled by them. It means that the Jews must be content with less than the Land of Israel they once ruled and have hoped to rule again. But it seems possible that on reflection both parties will come to realise that the drawbacks of Partition are outweighed by its advantages. For, if it offers neither party all it wants, it offers each what it wants most, namely, freedom and security."

Centre of Problem

Elsewhere in the Report the Commission sum up their analysis of the character and sentiment of the "two national groups whose opposition constitutes the problem of Palestine."

The establishment of the Jewish National Home has so far been to the economic advantage of the Arabs as a whole;

Jewish nationalism is as intense and self-centred as Arab nationalism. Both are growing forces, and the gulf between them is widening;

What the Arabs most desire is national independence. What they most fear is Jewish domination.

What the Jews most desire is freedom to develop fully the ideas inherent in the National Home and, in particular, to admit to it as many immigrants as they themselves think can be "absorbed." What they most fear is a crystallisation of the National Home as it is, leaving the Jews in a permanent minority in Palestine, exposed to the possibility of Arab domination, or even, in certain not inconceivable circumstances, of suffering the fate that befell the Greeks at Smyrna or the Assyrians in Iraq.

The Commission, though insisting that no permanent solution or peace can be achieved under the present administration, suggest temporary measures, designed to prevent a recurrence of open rebellion.

FRONTIER PATROL

They involve an efficient patrol force along the frontier, with probably heavy expenditure on wiring parts of it; a large increase in the British police; the rapid construction of barracks and married quarters; an extension of wireless telegraphy; and the retention of a strong British garrison. The entire cost could not be met from Palestine revenues, and the grants-in-aid from the British Government would, it is pointed out, have to be on a generous scale. "The immediate effect would be to widen the gulf that separates Arab from Jew, with repercussions spreading far beyond the borders of Palestine."

The Commission are severely critical of the British Administration in Palestine. "To-day it is evident that the elementary duty of providing public security has not been discharged."

SEARCH FOR SOLUTION OF PALESTINE PROBLEM

COMMISSION UNABLE TO AGREE ON PARTITION PLAN

Three separate schemes for the partition of Palestine are outlined, examined in close detail but rejected by the Palestine Partition Commission, whose report, the outcome of nine months' intensive labour, is published to-day.

The Commission was appointed last March to examine in further detail the proposals of Earl Peel's Royal Commission, which reported in July, 1937, in favour of a scheme of partition for Palestine. This scheme involved establishment of independent Arab and Jewish States, and the retention of certain other areas under British mandate.

Members of this Partition Commission, which spent three months in Palestine investigating the economic, administrative and political aspects of the Peel plan, were: Sir John Woodhead (chairman), Sir Alison Russell, Mr. A. P. Waterfield, and Mr. T. Reid.

They unanimously advise against the original scheme of partition outlined by the Peel Commission, described as Plan A. Two variants of this proposal, plans B and C, which were drawn up by the Partition Commission as possible alternatives, are closely examined.

Scheme Impracticable

Accompanying their report is a statement of Government policy endorsing the Commission's opinion that the creation of independent Arab and Jewish States in Palestine is impracticable.

The question whether partition is practicable, states the Commission, involves considerations of two kinds: practical and political.

"The former concern chiefly finance and economics; the administrative difficulties are great, but they cannot be called insuperable, if the will to find a solution is present. But the financial and economic difficulties, as described in this chapter, are of such a nature that we can find no possible way to overcome them within our terms of reference.

"Rather than report that we have failed to devise any practicable plan, we have proposed a modification of partition which, while it withholds fiscal autonomy from the Arab and Jewish States, seems to us, subject to certain reservations, to form a satisfactory basis of settlement, if his Majesty's Government are prepared to accept the very considerable financial liability involved."

ECONOMIC FEDERALISM

This modification of partition is described by the Commission as economic federalism.

"Under this both states would be required, as a condition of the surrender of the Mandate, to enter a customs union with the Mandated Territories in which the fiscal polity would be determined by the Mandatory after consulting both states. The customs revenue would be collected by the Mandatory, and the net surplus after meeting certain common charges would be distributed between the three areas according to an agreed formula, subject to periodic review.

"The Commission suggest that initially each area's share should be one-third. To enable the Arab State to balance its budget without subjecting it to external financial control, it should receive a supplementary share out of the share of the Mandated Territories, under conditions which will entitle it to share in any expansion of customs revenue resulting from an increase of prosperity in the rest of Palestine. This arrangement could be extended, if desired, to cover internal communications—railways, posts and telegraphs—thus removing certain obvious administrative difficulties consequent on partition."

Even this tentative modification of partition is, however, rejected, as indicated by the Government's statement of policy.

HIGH BIRTH-RATE AMONG ARABS

Migration Off-Set

At the outset of their report the Commission comments on the abnormally high birth-rate of the Arab population. If no change takes place, it discloses, the Arab population in Palestine will have increased by 250,000 in 10 years' time.

"It is probably not generally realised," adds the Commission, "that in the 15 years between 1922 and 1937 the increase of Jewish population by migration was less than the natural increase of the Moslem population, and that the total increase of the Jewish population is still less than the total increase of Arab, including Christian Arab, population."

In plan A, the Royal Commission's scheme for partition, with the boundaries adjusted for purposes of defence, the figures of population are shown to be:

	Arab State (Including Beersheba sub-district)	*Jewish State*	*Jerusalem and Nazareth Enclaves*
Arabs	485,200	294,700	221,400
Jews	7,200	304,900	80,200
Total population	492,400	599,600	301,600

Strictly in accordance with its terms of reference, the Partition Commission proceeeds to examine the boundaries which would have to be adopted to implement the Peel plan. It describes the modifications necessary in the boundary of the Jerusalem Enclave, and the boundary of a fresh enclave proposed for Nazareth.

DIVIDED ROAD

It agrees with the Royal Commission that Jaffa should be part of an Arab State, but rejects the idea of dividing the towns of Jaffa and Tel Aviv by a belt of mandated territory. Instead it is suggested that a new road shall be made between the towns, ·20 metres wide, with a high iron railing down the middle. The total cost would be £115,000.

In the Committee's task laid down in its terms of reference of devising boundaries which will necessitate the inclusion of the fewest possible Arabs and Arab enterprises in the Jewish State and vice versa, the Commission examines at considerable length the possibility of exchanges and transfer of population. It discloses that the number of Jews and the amount of Jewish land in the Arab State under plan A are:

Jews—

Urban	5,600
Rural	1,600
	7,200

Jewish land—

Citrus land	1,300 *dunums*
Other cultivable land	28,300
Uncultivable land	7,400
	37,000 *dunums*

* A dunum is about a quarter of an acre.

The figures for the Arab population and the Arab land in the Jewish State under plan A are:

Arabs—

Urban	77,500
Rural	217,200
	294,700

Arab land—

Citrus land	78,600 *dunums*
Other cultivable land	2,153,000
Uncultivable land	1,623,100
	3,854,700 *dunums*

From these figures, the Commission points out, it is clear that there is little scope for the voluntary exchange of land between the Arabs in the Jewish State and the Jews in the Arab State, and little possibility of voluntary exchange of rural population between the two States.

TRANSFERENCE OF POPULATION

Avoiding Minorities

Concerning the possibility of transferring the population, the Commission reviews exhaustively the resources of Beersheba sub-district, the Jordan Valley south of Lake Tiberias, the southern part of the Beisan Plain, Trans-Jordan hill country, and Gaza subdistrict. In every case prospects are disapponting, and it is concluded:

"There is practically no scope for the exchange of land and population between the Arab and Jewish States or between the Jerusalem Enclave and the Jewish State."

The results of well-boring experiments in Beersheba are stated to have been most disappointing. In the Jordan Valley no substantial increase in the irrigated areas can be expected either from wells or from the better utilisation of the water of the perennial streams.

It is thought unlikely that the Beisan Plain could support more than 4,000 persons. Trans-Jordan offers small scope for intensive settlement.

GALILEE PROBLEM

The hill country in the Arab State cannot be regarded as holding out any considerable opportunities for additional settlement. In the Gaza sub-district intensive cultivation could be increased over a considerable area, but the change would at best be a slow one, and great caution would have to be exercised.

Next, the Commission considers the possibility of excluding Galilee from the Jewish State, with a view to reducing the huge Arab "minority" which must inevitably be found in the Jewish State proposed by the Peel Commission. It is pointed out that the population of Galilee is 88,200 Arabs and 2,900 Jews. Of the total land, 1,321,100 dunums are owned by Arabs, only 35,900 by Jews.

Reasons which finally convince the Partition Commission that the Peel Royal Commission's plan of partition is unacceptable are summarised as follows:

(i) The number of Arabs in the proposed Jewish State under plan A is almost equal to the number of Jews, the figures being 295,000 Arabs as compared with 305,000 Jews. Further, the Arabs hold four-fifths of the land in the proposed State, 3,855,000 dunums out of a total area of 4,995,000 dunums.
(ii) The problem created by the large number of Arabs in the Jewish State cannot be solved by means of either an exchange or a transfer of population.
(iii) An area, predominantly Arab, at the southern extremity of the Jewish State should not be included in that state.
(iv) Galilee should not be included in the Jewish State, for three reasons: First, the population is almost entirely Arab and the land is almost entirely Arab owned. Secondly, the Arabs in Galilee are vehemently opposed to the inclusion of that area in the Jewish State; they will resist such inclusion by force, and there appears to be no justification for using force to

compel this large body of Arabs, in what is a purely Arab area, to accept Jewish rule. Thirdly, its inclusion would create a minority problem which would endanger, not only the stability of the Jewish State, but the prospect of securing in the future friendly relations between Arabs and Jews in the Middle East.

(v) Galilee does not offer scope for the settlement of large numbers of Jews on the land. At best, there is room for only a moderate increase (say 15,000 persons) in the agricultural population, and even this is dependent upon a change in land utilisation, which must inevitably be slow.

MODIFIED PLAN "A"

Secondly, the Commission examines the possibilities of Plan B. This is described as Plan A, with the southern section of that portion of the Jewish State lying south of the Jerusalem Enclave excluded from it.

If Galilee is excluded from the Jewish State, it is pointed out, the possible alternatives are (a) Arab control, and (b) Mandatory control.

SECURITY AGAINST AGGRESSION

Fatal Weaknesses

Regarding the first alternative, the Commission concludes that, if the Jewish State is to be assured of adequate security against aggression, it would not be possible to allow Galilee to pass under Arab control. The retention of Galilee under Mandatory control is open to the strong objection that it means that all, or at best the majority, of the Arabs of Galilee would have to be denied their independence in order to ensure the security of the Jewish State.

Even with the exclusion of Galilee and the area in the south from the Jewish State, the number of Arabs in that State would still be very large, 188,000 Arabs as compared with 300,000 Jews. The problems created by Galilee are considered fatal to Plan B.

But it is pointed out that Haifa, the only deep water harbour on the coast of Palestine, is not by any means an entirely Jewish town and that the Arabs have considerable interests therein. The conclusion is reached that Haifa could not be included in the Jewish State without serious detriment to Arab interests and that, similarly, it could not be included in the Arab State without serious detriment to Jewish interests. It is suggested that the best course, if that should prove to be possible, would be to retain it under Mandatory control so that it can be developed for the benefit of both.

Having rejected Plans A and B, the Commission proceeds to examine Plan C, "which although certainly not perfect (for it is impossible, if for no other reason than the geographical distribution of the two races, to produce a perfect scheme), is the best which the majority of us have been able to devise."

IN THREE PARTS

Plan C is summarised as follows:

(a) The Arab State as proposed in plan B subject to the following modifications:
  (i) A slight alteration in the north-west corner along the Carmel Ridge; and
  (ii) The exclusion of the Beersheba sub-district (except for a small area on the west) and the village lands of Rafah.
(b) The boundary of the Jerusalem Enclave as proposed under plan B.
(c) The Jewish State to consist of the coastal area between Tel Aviv and the Carmel Ridge, and of the portion south of the Jerusalem Enclave as proposed in plan B. The boundary to be as proposed in plan B throughout, except on the north, where it will be cut off from Haifa about 24 kilometres (15 miles) south of that town.
(d) The whole of the territory, including Haifa itself, north of this line and of the northern boundary of the Arab State to be retained under Mandate.
(e) The Beersheba sub-district (except for a small area on the west) and the village lands of Rafah also to be retained under Mandate under conditions to be described later (in the same chapters).

For the purpose of this plan Palestine may be considered as falling into three parts, as the map shows: A northern part, to be retained under Mandate, and known as the Northern Mandated Territory; a southern part, also to be retained under Mandate, and known as the Southern Mandated Territory; and a central part, consisting of all the territory between the other two, which will be made the subject of partition.

Arguments in Favour

The arguments in favour of Plan C are set forth as follows:

(i) It is impossible, without injustice to either Arabs or Jews, to partition the northern territory. Nor can this territory be handed over intact to either side.

(ii) It is also impossible to hand over the Negeb to the Jews without a violation of our terms of reference, while it would be unfair to the Jews to hand it over to the Arabs so long as there remains any reasonable prospect of Jewish settlement taking place therein without prejudice to the rights of the existing inhabitants.

(iii) Both the northern and the southern territories must therefore be retained under Mandate for an indefinite period.

(v) The only part of Palestine which can be partitioned is therefore the central portion, within which the boundaries of the proposed Arab and Jewish States and of the Jerusalem Enclave will be as on the map.

Under this plan the Commission calculates that the figures of land (in dunums) and population for the whole of Palestine would be:

ARAB STATE	*Arabs*	*Jews*	*Total*
Population	444,100	8,900	53,000
Land	7,329,000	63,800	7,393,500*
JEWISH STATE	*Arabs*	*Jews*	*Total*
Population	54,400	226,000	280,400
Land	821,700	436,100	1,257,800*
MANDATED TERRITORY			
(i) Jerusalem Enclave	*Arabs*	*Jews*	*Total*
Population	211,400	80,100	291,500
Land	1,485,200	78,700	1,563,900*

(ii) Northern Territory	*Arabs*	*Jews*	*Total*
Population	231,400	77,300	308,700
Land	2,730,500	677,300	3,407,800*

(iii) Southern Territory	*Arabs*	*Jews*	*Total*
Population	60,000	—	60,000
Land	1,944,500(?)	55,000	2,000,000(?)*†

Total Mandated Territories	*Arabs*	*Jews*	*Total*
Population	502,800	157,400	660,200
Land	6,160,200	811,500	6,971,700*†

* Excluding roads, railways, lakes and rivers.
† Excluding 10,577,000 dunums of desert in the Beersheba sub-district.

CONTROL OF LAND OWNERSHIP

Mandatory's Powers

The Commission devotes more than half its report, or 130 pages, to examination of Plan C. Its principal recommendations are as follows:

1. Northern Mandated Territory

(i) The Mandatory should be empowered to prohibit the transfer of land to any person in any part of the Mandated Territories, and in Galilee should immediately prohibit the transfer of land by a non-Jew to a Jew, but not Jewish residence.

(ii) After 10 years this prohibition should be reviewed but not withdrawn or relaxed unless Arab opinion favours such action.

(iii) Haifa and Tiberias and any other urban area approved by Government should be declared "free areas" in which the transfer of land to Jews should not be prohibited.

(iv) Elsewhere the transfer of land to Jews should be prohibited except—

    (a) Transfers with Government approval for the consolidation of existing Jewish holdings, &c.

SHARING SURPLUS LAND

   (b) Any other transfers respecting which Government are
       satisfied that—
       (1) There are possibilities of closer settlement on the land;
       (2) Adequate provision has been made for the resettlement
           of the cultivators;
       (3) Save where Government are satisfied that conditions
           make it impracticable, any surplus land resulting from
           closer settlement will be shared equitably between Jews
           and Arabs.
  (v) Government should be prepared to spend additional sums on
      agricultural development and agricultural research, experiment
      and education. While this expenditure, funds for which it is
      proposed should be provided by His Majesty's Government,
      would benefit both Arabs and Jews, its primary object would
      be to facilitate Jewish settlement.
 (vi) Surplus agricultural land which may be made available as the
      direct result of such development schemes should be shared
      equitably between Arabs and Jews.

2. The Jerusalem Enclave

All the above recommendations apply to the Jerusalem enclave
except that it is not thought that the Government will find it
necessary to declare any of this territory a prescribed area, in which
the transfer of land to Jews shall be prohibited. The urban area of
Jerusalem should be declared to be a free area from the outset.

3. The Southern Mandated Territory

For the purpose of facilitating Jewish settlement therein, we
recommend that the Negeb be regarded as divisible into two parts,
an Unoccupied and an Occupied area, which should be dealt with
separately. The Occupied area would be that portion of the
Beersheba sub-district which the Bedouin tribes are accustomed to
cultivate and over which they claim tribal or hereditary rights of
occupancy. The Unoccupied area would be the rest of the sub-
district.

   The dividing line between the two might be roughly a line
corresponding with the 5in rainfall contour and the change in the
character of the country which we have described in paragraph 110;
it has been suggested to us that it would run more or less from Al
Auja to Asluj and Kurnub.

Regulating Immigration

Immigration into the Mandated Territories would be regulated thus:

1. The Balfour Declaration should no longer apply.
2. The rate of immigration should be decided upon political, social and psychological, besides economic considerations.
3. Among intending immigrants from outside Palestine and Trans-Jordan preference should be given to Jewish immigrants.
4. Persons of whatever race habitually residing in the rest of Palestine and Trans-Jordan should be free to enter the Mandated Territories for short or casual visits but not to reside habitually therein without Government permission.
5. Before fixing the immigrant quota the Mandatory should consult with representatives of both Arabs and Jews and with experienced opinion independent of Government and both races.

SAFEUARDING SEA OF GALILEE

Preserving Sanctity

In subsequent chapters of its report the Commission examines in detail demographical, economic and political consequences of Plan C.

It explains in detail administration of the Nazareth Enclave, and puts forward proposals for safeguarding the sanctity of the waters and the shores of the Sea of Galilee. It suggests means of providing effective safeguards for the rights of religious and racial minorities in the areas to be allocated to Arabs and Jews, including protection of religious rights and properties.

The problems of internal communications—railways, broadcasting, ports, postal, telegraph and telephone services—are examined in close detail. Finally, finance and budgetary prospects are surveyed at length.

It was proposed by the Royal Commission that the Jewish State should make a subvention to the Arab State, and that the British Government should contribute £2,000,000 as a capital payment towards the cost. The Partition Commission rejects both these proposals.

FINANCIAL EFFECT

But on the existing standards of public administration, and without
making any provision for defence, the Commission estimates the
financial effect of Partition Plan "C" as follows:

(i)   For the Jewish State a surplus of about £P.600,000;
(ii) For the Arab State (including Trans-Jordan) a deficit of about
      £P.610,000;
(iii) For the Mandated Territories a deficit of £P.460,000.

These figures, the Commission admits, are extremely disquieting.
The financial position of the Arab State, they point out, will be no
better under any conceivable plan of partition. It is only the Jewish
contributions to tax-revenue that have enabled Palestine to balance
its Budgets.

The Commission understands that the total cost in 1938 to the
United Kingdom taxpayer of the emergency in Palestine is likely to
be in the neighbourhood of £2,500,000.

"The Commission cannot," it is stated, "recommend boundaries
which will afford a reasonable prospect of the eventual establishment
of a self-supporting Arab State. If partition is carried out Parliament
must be asked to provide the necessary financial assistance from
United Kingdom funds.

"If assistance takes the form of a direct subsidy, financial control
will be necessary, and the Arab State could not then be called self-
supporting. The United Kingdom must also provide the means of
balancing the Mandated Territories' budget, including the proposed
cost of development.

"Altogether partition would cost the United Kingdom say
£1,250,000 annually, whereas the Jewish State would have an annual
surplus of say £600,000, excluding the cost of defence in either case.
The result would be much the same under any conceivable plan of
partition."

Possibilities of a customs union between the Mandated Territories and the Arab and Jewish States are examined at length.

"The object of this union would be two fold. First, it seemed to
us that without the assured market for their produce which the
Mandated Territories would afford, the economic situation of the
Arab State, and the prospect of economic expansion in the Jewish
State, would be precarious; and, secondly, we felt that the financial

effects of partition were so unsatisfactory that we ought to take advantage of any proposal which seemed to offer a prospect of improving the financial position of the Arab State, and therewith of reducing the liability of the British Treasury."

After due consideration, however, the Commission find themselves unable to recommend such a union which will leave unimpaired the sovereign rights of those States in the matter of fiscal policy.

"If partition is carried out, a customs union in some form between the Arab and Jewish States and the Mandated Territories would seem to be necessary to preserve the economic stability of the former and to provide the latter with scope for economic expansion; but the form of union would have to be one in which the will of the Mandatory was enabled to prevail on questions of fiscal policy; and that would not be consistent with the proposed grant of independence to the two States."

At the conclusion of this prolonged survey the Commission reaches the final conclusions on the general subject of partition outlined above.

As already stated, all four members of the Commission reject Plan A of the Royal Commission. In a note of reservations Sir Alison Russell considers that Plan B is preferable to Plan C. In a similiar note, Mr. Reid, while agreeing that Plan C is the best that can be devised under the terms of reference, considers that both Plans B and C are impracticable. He classifies his reasons under the following heads: 1, Absence of consent; 2, Absence of equity; 3, Absence of security; 4, Dismemberment of Palestine; and 5, Absence of solvency.

A LOCAL LOOK AT EUROPE

*W. F. Deedes, MP, on his experience of holding public meetings on the
Common Market*

Politics being the art of persuasion as well as the possible, we are
putting together our autumn programme of meetings, aimed at
improving the local outlook on Europe and upholding democratic
principles before Parliament votes.

We took a preliminary canter at this in late July. It is an
unfamiliar course, even for seasoned horses, and those coming up
from grass at the end of August may welcome a marginal note or
two on some of the jumps.

The unexpected thing about a public meeting on the Common
Market is the eagerness of people to hear what you have to say. This
will take Members of Parliament by surprise.

Television conditions our captive audiences to observe closely
style, mannerisms, dress and sympathies, seldom what is actually
said—unless it is obscene. To address a public audience which is
actually listening to you is a disconcerting experience. It calls for
readjustment.

First of course they must be gathered in. My agent drafted the
handbills. "Britain and the Common Market—a momentous
decision." No doubting that. "Your Member of Parliament will
address a Public Meeting on —— at ——. Your views and questions
invited." Democratic indeed, but suggesting the need for certain
precautions. A hand-picked chairman, for a start.

He must grasp the fact, and so must you, that a public meeting
on the Common Market is an open-ended commitment. If he thinks
he is going to get to the vote of thanks with that well-tried gambit—
"Well, ladies and gentlemen, they will be closing over the road
shortly . . ."—he can think again.

Nor will he get away with the General Election formula. "Time,
I think, for one more question before our candidate, who has an
exceptionally heavy programme this evening, must move on." Our

first four meetings ran for between one hour and 50 minutes and two hours and 20 minutes. Not more than 35 minutes was spent on the opening speech.

For the speech itself, as with Hamlet's soliloquy in Act III, it is well not to vary the words too much from one night to the next. Among a refreshingly *unfamiliar* set of faces there are some which will reappear. They are not for Europe. Their ear is tuned to variations of the theme, and their method is that of prosecuting counsel. "I heard you say a week ago that the dynamic effect of our entry can be exaggerated. May I ask why you have deliberately left that out tonight?"

There was a time when Scots MPs would rent a Burns night speech to the Immortal Memory for a guinea or two, and very useful it was. A speech on Europe is somewhat less specialised, and most of us can make one up on our own. Questions are an altogether sharper examination.

It is possible to be tolerably well-grounded on the history of the Community, negotiations, the White Paper and a lot of European Movement literature, yet not to have absolutely at the fingertips what the Commission has in mind for harmonising qualifications in the nursing profession.

"You've raised a most interesting question here, madam, but one which I incline to think lies very much in the future." Small wonder, poor dear, she shows every sign of enlisting with the "doubtfuls"— and so, one fears, will some of her geriatric patients.

"What about Japan?" What indeed. "They're an island. They're industrialised. They don't need a damned great market, do they?" "Perhaps I could answer that important question in my own way." Japan is much in favour among those sceptical of our chances in Europe.

So are Sweden and Switzerland. "And why did Gen. de Gaulle leave Nato? He was in the Community, wasn't he? I wouldn't trust the French an inch." Sympathetic murmurs, which seem widespread.

A MOVING QUESTION

Certain exchanges produce surprising reactions. "What's to stop foreign workers flooding in here?" A nice opening for candour here, perhaps. "I think there has been rather less of this sort of movement within the Community than was expected. I am bound to add, that some of our workers may flood over to them." This appears to be received with intense satisfaction.

Lest the point has been missed: "A drain of our skilled workers could be serious." Deeply contented faces. There is, perhaps not surprisingly, a touch of claustrophobia as well as xenophobia in this crowded island. Britain for the British is good; Britain with fewer Britons, even better.

Public interest in Europe is strong enough, or was in July, to attract those who rate themselves much too intelligent normally to attend political meetings. "I listened very closely to what the speaker had to say about the balance of payments," says a voice unmistakably from Lombard Street. A clearly phrased but unanswerable question follows involving Eurodollars.

"We are all very grateful to you for that intervention"—the first palpable falsehood of the evening. "But I wonder if you are altogether right in believing . . ." With one faint movement of the head, the distinguished stranger signifies resignedly that he has not underrated his man. But he is a sportsman, and says no more. After a few moments, he gathers up a wonderfully well-behaved spaniel and his good-looking wife, scans the audience compassionately, and steals out. These are dark moments.

At the other end of the scale, a knot of warriors—National Front?—are pressing as often as the chairman will allow the case for regarding the whole venture as a Communist-inspired conspiracy. Broadly, the poltroons who pass for politicians in this country have delivered Britain, trussed like a table fowl, over to her enemies for roasting. This view seems not to attract many adherents.

"Shall we be able to keep Sunday like it is?" Supporters of the Lord's Day Observance Society are present. Their anxious question springs from the conviction planted by this earnest movement that links with Europe would transform our dark-suited, church-going, devout people into the sort of Rabelaisian mob which so disfigures Sunday in the Continental cities. "I think—I hope I may say that my religious views are now tolerably well known in this constituency."

The general run of questions, more heartfelt than what is heard at a General Election, are spontaneous, searching and (in retrospect) moving. A lot of people seem to care very much what happens to this country, as well as themselves. Of course they are worried about the cost to their purses. Why not? It is surely arrogant to assume that the housewife has no right to be.

Inflation at the pace we are running it, whoever is to blame, leaves many feeling that one more straw, however small, will break the camel's back. The Member of Parliament who fails to get that message at his Common Market meetings is tone deaf.

Only once, in 76 questions, did anyone mention the culture we share with Europe. Painting? Literature? Music? Alas, no takers; nothing stirring in the depths.

"Well," says the chairman truthfully, "we've had a splendid run." A faithful supporter sidles up and murmurs disturbingly: "I thought you were *much* better tonight."

Back home and close to midnight, the treasure is taking the dried remains of supper from the oven. "I suppose you all went on to the pub afterwards." "No, no,"—with a hint of pride—"our meeting ran until after half-past 10." "What *were* you all talking about?" Good question.

July 1980

REPUBLICAN MOMENT OF TRUTH

Reagan's crisis choice of Bush against background of economic gloom

In the end it was Walter Cronkite, the veteran CBS anchorman, and not Ronald Reagan who made the only unexpected news of the week at the Republican convention in Detroit.

Mr Cronkite, once very nearly a vice-presidential candidate himself, cannot exactly claim to have brokered George Bush as vice-president, but he was instrumental in shaping the manner in which it was done.

He threw a spanner into the smooth-running Republican machine and he caused Mr Reagan to break all precedent by appearing suddenly before the convention at midnight on Wednesday to announce his choice.

In a convention dominated by the television networks, which had 2,000 men and women on the job, it was appropriate enough.

Mr Cronkite's stroke had been to catch former President Gerald Ford for a television interview late on Wednesday evening. Everyone knew that Mr Ford and Mr Reagan, both occupying suites on the 69th and 70th floor of the Detroit Plaza, had been in touch and were getting closer.

In previous interviews that day, however, Mr Ford had reiterated his unwillingness to accept the vice-presidential nomination. Personal feelings between him and Mr Reagan apart, he had a little local difficulty.

He is a resident of California, so is Mr Reagan. Under the 12th Amendment California's 45 electoral votes would have been forfeited because both resided in the same state. There were even stronger personal considerations.

"Betty would divorce him if he took the job," said Mr Stuart Spencer, a long-time Ford aide. The possible alliance was rumoured and discussed through the day, described by some as the dream ticket but thought likely by outsiders to remain—a dream.

Suddenly, Mr Ford changed his tune. Caught late in the evening, he told Mr Cronkite: "I would not go to Washington to be a figurehead Vice-President. If I go to Washington I have to go there in the belief that I would play a meaningful role on substantial decisions across the board."

The change of mood may have owed something to a Republican delegation of weight which had visited Mr Ford in mid-afternoon, urging him to take second place.

A spokesman for Mr Ford said that the former President was not sure if members of the delegation represented just themselves, or had the blessing of Mr Reagan.

They spoke together for 30 minutes. Mr Ford promised to weigh what they had said. There were a good many other meetings on these lines.

About the same time as the delegation met Mr Ford two reporters bumped into Mr Reagan. They asked him about Mr Ford. "Oh, sure," Mr Reagan is reported to have said, "that would be best."

Exactly who said what to whom after that is not yet firm history, but as the night wore on, Mr Ford seemed more and more the man most likely to.

For one thing the networks had taken things to a point where anyone but Mr Ford began to look like being condemned as an also ran. Mr Cronkite began to unfold "from an excellent source" the sort of terms Mr Ford was held to be holding out for.

"A sort of co-president," was one phrase which Mr Cronkite floated out on to the air.

Somewhere, we are also led to believe that Dr Henry Kissinger was in there—as indeed he was—masterminding Mr Ford's conditions for acceptance.

There is a long and gloomy tradition about vice-presidential nominations. Always when offered the ticket they are assured that their role will be different from all that has gone before, that the work will be meaningful and the Second Lady will sit at high table.

It seldom works out that way. Indeed it cannot, because the Constitution, which defines the respective roles, requires it to remain the way it is. That seems not to have been much discussed on Wednesday night.

Mr Ford was warned that as a former President he would be made a laughing stock in the role as it has always been. Hence the attempt to exact a higher price.

Mr Ford wanted several things—control of the National Security Council and the Office of Management and Budget, and in effect to become the White House chief of staff. He also wanted to be chief liaison with Congress.

In effect the White House would take on the complexion of a large corporation with one man as chairman and another as chief executive. Constitutional difficulties aside, in satisfying Mr Ford, Mr Reagan would have thrown up sharp questions about his own standing and role as President.

It must have been around this point that the red light came on. Both parties began to have doubts about the workability of the proposed partnership.

At 9 pm it had looked and sounded like a deal. At 11 pm, a now exhausted Gerald Ford was back in Mr Reagan's suite to turn down the job. "You know," he is reported to have said: "I just don't think we can put this thing together."

Dr Kissinger has said since that another 24 hours might have done the trick. He could be wrong.

So at 11.37 Mr Bush got the call. He had had a thin day, trailed everywhere by newsmen and camera crews. The chances looked increasingly forlorn. He went out jogging.

After Mr Ford had turned the job down he told Mr Reagan he would campaign his heart out for him. At least the extraordinary episode seems to have brought relations between the two men closer than they were.

Arguably Mr Reagan came out of it with considerably more dignity than Mr Ford. There is something not totally dignified about a former President fishing in these waters and using television interviews as rod and line.

Around the time Mr Bush got his call the networks, which had been having a wonderful time, began to sweat. Lesley Stahl was on the convention floor for CBS. At 11.52 she frantically called Don Hewitt, director of CBS convention floor correspondents.

"Don, they're yelling Bush, Bush, all around me," she cried. "Tell the anchor booth that something strange has happened. The Bush people are as excited as hell. They say the Ford deal has come unstuck." The biter had been bit.

But Mr Reagan was still left with a problem. He had, between negotiatons with Mr Ford, spent the evening in his suite, surrounded by family and watching television. Everyone close to Mr Ford and Mr Reagan was grabbed for interviews and proceeded to tell all they knew or surmised.

It was as if all serious figures and aides in the Republican party had received a massive injection of the truth drug. As the *Wall Street Journal* observed tartly: "the whole business was becoming ludicrous."

Mr Reagan had to act. At 12.15 am on Thursday, less than an hour after he had himself been nominated—and accompanied by his wife Nancy, he was on the podium, breaking all recent tradition, to announce that it was to be Mr Bush.

Somebody slipped a comforting arm around Nancy Reagan's shoulders. Consummate actress though she is, her face, usually fixed adoringly on her husband's, could not conceal her awareness that this line was not on cue.

Mr Reagan in his time has looked a lot happier and will again. Indeed he did 24 hours later, on the same podium delivering his impressive acceptance speech.

When he rose to make it, he was addressing a wildly excited carnival. By the close of his speech he had a sober audience attending to serious business. In a dark grey suit, he was the most sombrely dressed man in the stadium.

There was very little rhetoric. The style recalled not John Kennedy on a similar occasion but the fireside chats of FDR. Events of the preceding evening receded a little but they will not be forgotten, they will linger on.

Out of what the *Detroit News* aptly called the network-cultivated speculative jungle, a Vice-President had emerged. In fairness, it was the manifest willingness of all principal parties involved to talk their heads off when confronted with a microphone which made this possible.

Jeff Greenfield the CBS analyst declared that "CBS was one medium through which this deal was attempted." He called Ford's talk with Cronkite "a public negotiating session." Daniel Henninger in the *Wall Street Journal* has put it another way: "It reminded one of that eerie and famous scene from the movie '2001: a Space Odyssey'" in which the spaceship's friendly, talking computer, HAL, tells the pilot that he has taken over complete control of the ship. "Who whom?" as Stalin once asked, that question is going to echo from this convention for a long time to come.

HOW REAGAN'S RIGHT-HAND WOMAN SEES THE WEST

The special relationship between Britain and the United States has at times shown signs of strain. In an interview with W. F. Deedes, editor of the DAILY TELEGRAPH, Mrs Jeane Kirkpatrick, United States ambassador to the United Nations, discusses the issues which have caused friction between America and Western Europe.

This protest which we've now entered about mining in Nicaraguan waters—does that seem to you one more example of a failure by Europe to appreciate your anxieties in that region? Can we start there?

OK, we'll start there. In a word, yes. I think that I feel, and a good many other members of my Government feel—Americans who support the Government too—that our European friends, including Britain, though I belong to a generation that was never accustomed to considering Britain as part of Europe . . .

So do I!

. . . are not as concerned about threats to our national security in Central America and the Caribbean as we very much wish they were, both for our sakes and for theirs. We feel they're not as concerned about those threats to our national security in that region as is prudent from their point of view, as well as ours, and that disappoints us a lot.

We feel as a consequence, *perhaps* of not being as concerned about our security as we would wish, they are very tempted to apply to that region standards inappropriate to situations like the one that exists in the region which is one really of a very high level of conflict and guerrilla war; and also tempted to apply standards to that region that are different from those that are regularly applied in other areas, for example Africa or the Middle East and so forth.

What has been your experience of getting support from Europe at the United Nations?

Well, you know, it depends on the issue: let's emphasise the positive, "accentuate the positive" as the old American song said. We look at UN votes, which I have done, and the US mission now does by law. One finds that the United States and the Western democracies, particularly the United Kingdom and Federal Republic, far more often than not vote together, about 85 per cent. of the time. In the last General Assembly, for example, on contested votes the United States and Britain stood together. So that's quite good. And if you look at the issues which we identify as the most important to us, generally speaking our closest European friends, certainly including the UK at the top of that list, are more often than not standing on the same side. Now, that said, I would have to say that support on a number of issues of great concern to us is not what we wish it were, by any means. Let me give you a specific example.

Earlier this week in the United Nations we dealt with a complaint of Nicaragua against the United States on the mining question. I won't go into details of that but I would simply say that France played a role in the negotiation of that resolution which, I guess, we regarded as very unfortunate, a negative role, and France and the Netherlands ended up voting for the resolution which we vetoed. The UK, I'm happy to report, abstained on the resolution which was a very great deal more welcome than the French and the Dutch positions.

One of the things that disturbed us most, and always disturbs us most, is that a bad resolution—expressing outrage about mining in Nicaraguan waters—expressed no outrage at all about the violent disruption of El Salvador's elections. Violent efforts at disruption of those elections were directed from Nicaragua.

It expressed great concern about the devastation of Nicaragua's economy because of mines, but it expressed no concern about the devastation of El Salvador's economy which has been deliberately targeted by those Nicaraguan-based guerrillas for the past three years.

And on Central America where most of our European friends take an even-handed approach, (mainly they don't), they take an uneven-handed approach on the other side, and favour our adversaries; not just favour our adversaries, but favour those countries and people who are destroying peace in the region, undermining democratic institutions in the region, imposing repression at home and aggression abroad. So obviously we feel badly about that.

Historically there has been a shift, certainly since 1945. Lawrence Eagleburger for example is quoted as saying, he thinks your centre of gravity is shifting from the Transatlantic relationship towards the Pacific basin. In historical terms, do you think that is such a shift?

No, I addressed that question in a speech yesterday in Paris. I believe that, first of all, the United States has always been interested in the Pacific. We have a life-long movement towards the Pacific. You remember that phrase so famous in our history "Go West, young man." We went West, all the way to the Pacific. We got there and even when we got there we didn't stop. We went on going West, to Alaska and to Hawaii and in fact to the Philippines. We've always been interested in the Pacific just as we've always been interested in Latin America. I would remind you of the Monroe doctrine which in 1823 defined our deep concern with the security of the hemisphere as a primary concern.

That said, our concern with the Pacific has been enhanced by the growing importance of trade in the northern Pacific nations. In 1980 for the first time the US trade with Pacific nations was higher than with Europe. One of the marks of the level of our involvement with the Pacific has been the very bloody wars which we have fought: the Pacific section of World War II, Vietnam, Korea.

Primarily, however, I conclude that, from our point of view, there is no likelihood or danger, depending on how you view it, of the United States abandoning its concern with Europe or its identification with Europe in favour of some more intensive identification with the Pacific nations. The most basic reason for that is that we are part of the same civilisation. We are all part of Western civilisation, we are part of that Greco-Roman, Judeo-Christian civilisation which really defines us, and in which our identity is founded, and that I think is not going to change.

It still means Europe has got to pull some weight of its own?

We cannot, we the United States, cannot accept the responsibility for the defence of the whole world. I have said that Europe, whose population was larger than the Soviet Union, whose technology was more developed than the Soviet Union's, its industrial capacity much larger than all of the Soviet Union, had all the requisites for being itself a super-power except perhaps the will. But you know, I'm not sure *we* have the will to be a super-power; I don't think we ever decided, suddenly, either take those burdens, or assume those risks or any of this.

No, but Europe counts on certain things from the United States; can the United States count on reciprocity from Europe?

That's a *very* important question I think. I think that's really what bothers a lot of people a lot about the whole configuration of

European attitudes and behaviour vis-a-vis Central America. It confronts us with the question of reciprocity. Can we, who make a very large commitment to the security of Europe, count on some sort of reciprocal concern by Europe on our security? Without reciprocity . . . under conditions that the countries of Europe are strong economically, technologically . . . reciprocity becomes the only basis really for a meaningful relationship.

Do you think that any damage that happened over Grenada has been ironed out now?

Yes. And I want to say this: I don't believe in frictionless marriages. They don't exist. I don't believe in perfectly orderly households, perfectly behaved children. I'm speaking now as a housewife and mother. I don't believe in the frictionless alliance. I think it is absolutely inevitable that there will be differences among countries who are in fact closely related in basic points of view, values and views. I think they happen from time to time and it's inevitable that they should happen. It's awfully important when they happen that we don't exaggerate them and imagine that we don't have the most important things in common.

Do the media help?

I think that disagreements are better news than harmony.

Do rifts get exaggerated?

Oh, I think so. I think they get exaggerated and that it takes a real act of will to continue.

One way and another it seems that the Soviet Union has not had a very good year or two, do you see any perils in that?

In what sense?

That from past experience when they are down they tend sometimes to behave unaccountably.

I don't know what you mean, they haven't had a very good year or two—you mean the death of Andropov, a lot of sickness, the necessity of replacing the head of State twice within a two year period? They've had some problems economically; they weren't able, for example, to build the gas pipeline in the period that they anticipated, apparently, which we never thought they could. They haven't made much progress in the agricultural domain, but they they never do. They had a set-back over Grenada, one for which the Grenadan people are deeply grateful along with all their neighbours.

I suppose you could call it a set-back that Europeans decided to defend themselves by deploying missiles. I don't know whether that's another way of saying that if the countries of the West stand up, declining to accept the sort of unilateral vulnerability the Soviets created by deploying the SS 20s threatening European cities, that if the Europeans don't accept that then that's an affront to the Soviets. I think that's the kind of affront the Soviets have to accept, or that Europe has to risk imposing for its own safety, for its basic security.

We in the US Government would like very much to have better relations with the Soviet Union. We would like to see the arms control talks resumed. We would not like to see them resumed so much that we would be willing to withdraw the missiles after the Nato countries had decided by their own decision processes that they should be stationed there. We want to maintain parity in the vital fields, fields vital for our own security and that of our allies and we are not prepared to abandon that. But we are prepared to do whatever we can to be very open in ameliorating relations with the Soviets. We are not going to try in any way to humiliate the Soviets.

One of the many things we don't know about the Soviet Union is the extent to which its current, very intransigent positions are dictated by the desire to influence the American election, or an outgrowth of internal Soviet politics. We don't know really whether there is a struggle for power going on within the Politburo. We don't know who's calling the shots in foreign affairs. But no matter what they do, we are going to continue to try to make clear our desire for better relations, resumption of the arms talks and as broad and constructive a relationship as is possible.

Is it still the concern of the administration that the pull of the Soviet Union economically has dangers for the transatlantic relationship? The natural pull, that goes back to the pipeline.

I personally have some concerns. You know Lenin's dictum about the hangman and the rope. It has occurred to me, it never occurred to Lenin, that the West may provide the credit on highly paid-up terms on which to buy it. I think it's a mistake for Western countries to subsidise the Soviet economy because I think that frees Soviet resources for concentration on military production and, as I have said, I think we end up by having to pay for it twice, we in the West. We pay for it once through the subsidy, and again when we have to spend money on armaments to meet the new level of armaments which they have produced. I don't think that's a prudent policy for us to transfer to the Soviets sophisticated technology which they can use in the development of armaments. That's dangerous.

Do you include grain?

I frankly believe there's a difference with grain. As long as the Soviet Union has to pay for its grain, then I do not think that constitutes a subsidy. You will notice here I have emphasised the subsidisation of the Soviet economy. I think if we lent them the money or we gave them the grain, it would be comparable to trade on subsidised terms. I think, for example, the French subsidisation of the gas pipeline in which the Government provided credit on terms that have not been available in France to Frenchmen for many many years, is an example of subsidisation that's very different from the sale of grain. I think transfer technology is also different because grain can't be converted into rockets. But I think that it's very important that we Americans take care not to become dependent on the sale of grain in that market. That's a danger always—a danger for us.

AS REAGAN STARS IN THE WEST, SOMEONE'S SUN ALSO RISES

Dallas, our city of tomorrow—and, my hat, what a tomorrow—was an odd choice by the Republicans for a convention to thank, honour and re-nominate their 73-year-old President. Amid these futuristic, gleaming towers in the Texas plain, at a gathering lacking the excitement of conventions long past, how natural that the thoughts of good Republicans should drift a little to the future, away from President Reagan and the November election, towards 1988.

This indeed has been the week's main drift. As one commentator put it in exquisitely bad taste: "When Reagan rides off into the sunset some day, this convention will have been the sunrise for someone."

So this is a party already surreptitiously in search of a successor, a process in which some of the aspirants are being conspicuously less surreptitious than others.

It cannot all be blamed on Dallas and the lure of tomorrow; America's politics run that way. This jumping of the gun does not shock or surprise. We have been watching the start of the 1988 campaign.

In making such judgments we have to bear in mind that in Britain we only read of Reagan and sometimes glimpse him on the screen which is not at all the same as living under his Presidency. None of the platform rhetoric here about him—and there has been plenty of it, especially from those who would like his job—has come near to conveying why Reagan has such a strong hold over so many hearts and minds, not all of them lifelong Republicans.

His nonchalance, his gaffes (so eagerly recited in the newspapers), his alleged indolence (so deeply refreshing after the indefatigable Carter) disguise from many outside America what an accomplished politician he is—but not from grateful Republicans assembled in Dallas. In their eyes he has restored not only America's strength in the world but America's pride in herself.

We may beg to differ, but it is their view that counts. They are looking back on a generation of unsettling political crises in America, starting if you like with that terrible warehouse in Dallas from which the fatal shots were fired in 1963.

Against that background they are thankful for these last four years. They are comfortable with their President. If they seem to be speculating in unseemly haste on what is to come after him, that is largely because they have come to see more than we have how great the gap will be.

Before going on about the future, one cautionary word has to be entered on behalf of the present incumbent of the White House. Like every great party, the Republicans are a coalition. Reagan's gift is the manner in which he has united the party's interests.

As long as he is there the arguments which, for want of anything better, have been rehearsed all this week on whether the conservatives or the moderates hold the edge, do not amount to much. (In fact there is at present no argument. The conservatives comfortably hold the edge.) After Reagan, these arguments will come into the open and will matter tremendously. They will determine the outcome of the 1988 election.

Come to think of it, a second cautionary word has to be entered. Not every thinking Republican in Dallas this week is positive that this November election will be the pushover it looks now. Due to *l'affaire* Ferraro, the Democrats have had a terrible 10 days, which have given some observers and many Republicans a false compass bearing.

At the time of writing it is hard to predict whether the burning at the stake of Gerry Ferraro will recoil on Democrats or Republicans. Short of being told what Mr and Mrs Zaccaro say to each other in bed, there seem no other details open to discovery.

But not all Americans think like the news media. The only certainty is that public life for an American couple with a joint income is going to become a bigger nightmare than it is already. Heaven defend the Republican caught henceforth with undisclosed assets.

Mrs Ferraro, incidentally, has emerged from her burning looking quite different from the humble Queens district of New York housewife in legal practice, to whom we were introduced in San Francisco. She is as tough as they come. Ironically her two hours TV ordeal on Tuesday resolves a lot of doubts about her. If, as some Republicans thought, she was an unexpected bonus to the Democrats' ticket in July, she could be even more so in November.

Such reservations entered, we return to the longer future and those who could seek the Reagan mantle. It is not easy for an observer of Westminster politics to assess these fairly—and since their names would ring few bells with readers who have missed seeing this week's parade, it might be unwelcome. The man on the Clapham omnibus is not discussing with his wife over supper why the hungry representative Jack Kemp of New York (who appeared at 22 separate engagements in Dallas yesterday) may have the edge over Howard Baker, who has surrendered his Senate seat to give full time to his 1988 aspirations.

Nor will he be wondering whether handsome Senator Robert Dole, a war veteran, is a better presidential prospect than his younger wife, Elizabeth, who is already in Reagan's Administration as Secretary of Transportation. He is in no position to compare the Hispanic charm of Katherine Ortega, who, as United States Treasurer, signs the banknotes, with the ever younger Anne Armstrong, once American Ambassador in London. Nor will he necessarily see Governor Pierre du Pont of Delaware as a dark horse.

He might well take the view, as 50 per cent of the Republicans in Dallas this week have done, that Vice-President Bush, a moderate in politics, would be a better successor than any of these beautiful people.

Then there is the intriguing figure of Jeane Kirkpatrick, still a Democrat but as Reagan's ambassador at the United Nations with more experience of responsibility under her belt than any of them except Bush. Before making her impressive speech to the Convention on foreign affairs on Monday night, she murmured: "You know, they think I'm going to turn Republican tonight. I'm not, but I'll make them wish I were."

Down on the floor they did their best to woo her with a forest of messages on cardboard, some of which, however painfully, must be recited in order to bring out the flavour of these proceedings. "I dream of Jeane." "Jeane we love you." "Texas loves Jeane." "Cream for Jeane." "Kirkpatrick is fantastic."

Notwithstanding these blandishments, Mrs Kirkpatrick declares she wants only to return to "her husband and her sons and her cats and her university" (in that order). On the contrary, if Republicans win and Reagan gives her a bigger job, she will be at the front of the pack.

*

For sure, the American Dream cannot come true for all these aspirants. It could well be that in the days ahead the cards will fall in quite a different way. Suppose that three years hence at 76 President Reagan decided of his own volition to call it a day. He must surely turn to his faithful Vice-President Bush, who has served him well and the mantle would fall.

Would that not settle the 1988 nomination? Oh no, it wouldn't, because under the rules of the game President Bush could be challenged at the 1988 Republican Convention—and that is precisely what Reagan did to President Ford (who had succeeded Nixon in 1976). Reagan lost to Ford then, but he dominated the platform.

There's the charm and the endless adventure of American politics. As the early morning sun rises, promising yet another day in the low 100s, and flushes the glass panels of Dallas's amazing skyscrapers, that's what they lie in bed dreaming about.

COLONEL NORTH AND THE BATTLE OF CAPITOL HILL

W. F. Deedes witnesses a tour de force in Congress

As the testimony of Lt-Col Oliver North on Capitol Hill was exploding across America this week, we were witnessing a fascinating double game. Congress inquisitors thought they had the Colonel, and through him his superiors, in the dock. The Colonel knew that he had a vast American audience—around 55 million. Most adroitly he made an ordeal his opportunity.

One way of viewing Colonel North's 24 hours of testimony, every word of it carried on the television networks, is to see it as the longest address on foreign policy ever delivered to the English-speaking peoples.

At the heart of this week's contest has lain the issue of how America's foreign policy should be formulated and carried out. Congress in the name of the American people sought to show that the conduct of North and his White House associates had been covert, unlawful and undemocratic. The Colonel set out to persuade the American people that today's dangerous world offers no other way.

We were listening to a moving version of Sinatra's song "I Did It My Way." A lot of his answers have been 10-minute speeches, an indulgence protected by his admirable counsel, Brendan Sullivan. At the close of Wednesday's proceedings he told us that since he was fired eight months ago he had received about 50,000 letters. All but 50 supported him as a guy who tried.

With a catch in his voice he thanked America. Again, his personal statement delivered first thing on Thursday morning was aimed smack at the heart of American mothers everywhere. For this occasion Betsy, his long-suffering wife and mother of four, appeared for the first time in a blue frock with white collar and cuffs. As she sat quiet as a nun, hands in her lap, much of her recent life with him could be read in her eyes.

It is early days to say which side in this extraordinary struggle has won the American heartland. I will, however, predict that although the totally independent special prosecutor sits watchful as a hawk throughout these proceedings, he will find it very unpopular to prosecute Col North. The Colonel has been fired from the White House. Against expectations, this week he has re-established himself as a force in American politics.

Congressmen like their proceedings televised because it gets to the voters back home. Two can play that game. At the last count, more Americans (58 per cent), believe North than believe the President he is striving to defend.

He had bad moments when cornered by counsel, particularly by Arthur Liman, Chief Senate Counsel, whose quarry was not North but the President himself. A central weakness of North's case is that while insisting that he and his colleagues sought to act within the law throughout, he busied himself destroying incriminating evidence immediately the balloon went up last November and, as he puts it, the unravelling began. He is up against the best lawyers in the land, who know how to make their questions drip like water torture. But marines learn how to break out of tight corners. North's longest speeches came when counsel rapped out after a question, "Yes or No."

This assessment of him will make no sense to those led to suppose that North is a Rambo-like figure, a dim-witted marine who was absurdly out of place on the National Security Council. On the contrary, North's tragedy has been that his extraordinary qualities rendered him an indispensable vessel in combat against what torments America most in these times, international terrorism.

North is not a lightweight. Watching him this week warily thread his way through the maze of five intensely active years, defending his President, his beliefs, his shredding, his family and his honour, I concluded that Winston Churchill could well have sent a directive: "Pray ensure the services of this brave and resourceful officer are fully employed."

What the Colonel shredded in his office has been a main area of examination. There is a deep irony here. For what has landed North and the American administration in this unholy mess was not the shredder but the duplicator. The joint Congress committees conducting this inquiry are awash with paper. Piled on end, the documents in the case rise several inches higher than the upstanding Colonel.

These secretive fellows on the National Security Council appear to have suffered a compulsion to commit their every waking thought to paper. It has required a back-up staff of some 200 to sort it all out. "I must have generated thousands and thousands of memoranda while I was at the White House," declared the Colonel proudly. Nooses, every one of them.

Much of this, however, is peripheral to what this conflict is really all about. It is part of the unending battle between a president and Congress, but in a new form.

America, says North, can no longer fight her enemies with sword and cannon. He had learned that bitterly in Vietnam. Against the insurrectionist, the terrorist, he says, America can only win by cunning, deception, superb intelligence and the covert—he pronounces it with a long "o"—operation. Only thus can the foreign policy of the President be fulfilled. Such operations by their nature cannot be discussed with the American people or their representatives in Congress. Secrecy is of the essence. Lives may depend on it. It may even be necessary to deceive a close friend. That is Col. Olly's world, not altogether balanced, easily mocked, but not entirely without substance.

To Congress, and in particular Senator Inouye of Hawaii, who is presiding over this inquiry, such implications are infuriating. North is telling them that if secrets have to be kept, Congress is not to be trusted. At Wednesday's close, Senator Inouye angrily rebutted it, emotionally citing the awards he had received for probity in handling sensitive matters. "We can be trusted."

Here are tomorrow's battle lines between the White House and Capitol Hill. In this wild world, operations against the principal enemy, international terrorists, must always be clandestine. How does a democracy like America's, founded on government of the people, set about that? As Chief Senate Counsel Arthur Liman put it to North on Thursday afternoon, "To promote democracy abroad we must never sacrifice our democratic values here." North is a victim of the eternal dichotomy between America's executive in the White House and its legislature on the Hill.

With intelligence above his rank, North has shown moving awareness of this through the hours of examination. Not even his blue eyes and ready smile, however, can save the President of the United States from losing this round of the historic struggle with Congress. The White House botched it and everybody knows it.

Whatever comes out of this interminable inquiry, the balance of power has shifted decisively towards Congress. That shift will be recognised in next year's presidential election campaign.

"We won every battle and we lost the war," said Col. North bitterly of Vietnam during his testimony on Thursday. Sadly, I think he has won the battle with Congress for himself but lost it for the President. Being the sort of man he clearly is, that is the last thing in the world he would wish to have done.

REAL LIFE DRAMA NOW CZECHS HAVE STOPPED PLAY-ACTING

Freshly returned from Prague, W. F. Deedes assesses Britain's debt to the country it "shopped" in 1938 and which needs every help in its uphill struggle towards a free society

For the Czechs, history will say, the high point of this century was that tumultuous night in Prague's Wenceslas Square, where tens of thousands greeted the arrival of 1990. Virtually half a century of tyranny, Nazi or communist, had ended. A new President, symbol of a free people, had just been installed. No wonder the corks popped, the rockets soared and the tears ran.

I think the mixture of drinks, which elderly strangers offered from their bottles, had disagreed with me; or perhaps because I helped to report Munich for this newspaper in September 1938, I had difficulty in looking so many of these happy citizens fully in the eye. Perversely, Christina Rossetti's lines kept running through my mind: "Does the road wind uphill all the way? Yes to the very end."

So it does, for Czechoslovakia has reached only, in Churchill's old phrase, the end of the beginning. After half this century in the wilderness the long march back to a free society, a market economy and democratic institutions begins. It will be uphill all the way; and the central question in my mind is—how far can we atone for our past by lending them a hand now?

Bluntly, we "shopped" the Czechoslovaks in 1938 to save our skins. Because of past neglect, we were not ready for war. We and the French sold the Czechs for time. Churchill again, in September 1938, said: "We seem to be very near the bleak choice between war and shame. My feeling is that we shall choose shame, and then have war."

We need not be too much troubled about the Czech spirit now. I saw a country which has lain under a blanket of snow for many years. As the snow melts, so there returns what was there in the last spring—and in many springs before that. The head is unbowed, the spirit unbroken; though for people of my generation the lost years and opportunities have gone and can never return.

"We are at an end of play-acting," an ambassador said to me. "Adults had spoken openly within the bosom of their family. When they put on hats and coats and went to work, they paraded loyalty to the state, through the working day, then returned to normal in the evening." The students, he added thoughtfully, did not play-act. They spoke as they felt.

President Havel dwelt in his first broadcast to the Czech people on the moral pollution which communism had spread among his countrymen; "The worker's state has humiliated the workers . . . we are living in a debased moral environment." True, and many Czechs, including their President, are suffering pangs of guilt because they did not rise up against oppression sooner. But that will pass. Most of the trouble ahead for Czechoslovakia springs not from spiritual but from material degradation. "Our industrialists," President Havel said in the same broadcast, "produce what we don't need and what we need they don't produce."

Between the stifling state economy of the past and the market economy towards which the new order has to grope its way, there is an unimaginable gulf. A lot of people are going to be hurt. Imagine a country of 15 million people in which there are not only 100,000 secret police but two million unproductive bureaucrats.

While in Prague, I procured the copy of a surprisingly honest official document from Hungary, a country which began the shift to the free market economy in the late 1980s. Although there are differences between the two economies, several passages apply. "Hungary—as well as the rest of Eastern Europe—has not known a trade in stocks and bonds for many decades," it says. "Two generations of talented economists, lawyers and bankers have grown up since; they all lack even the most elementary knowledge about securities. To overcome this crippling ignorance, Hungary has secured Western help; in 1988, a management school for future bankers was established in Budapest."

Again: "Under the old system, everybody had a right to a job and it was very difficult if not impossible to dismiss anybody. A new, private owner may well decide to get rid of redundant employees. People will have to resume much more responsibility for their own lives than they were used to."

I foresee clearly that, when it has recreated a competitive market economy, Czechoslovakia will have, like the rest of us, to create and finance social services for those who fall in need. Meanwhile, much that has to be done will cause hard feelings. Even before June's free elections, voices will be saying: "It was better under the Communists."

Nobody knows the value of anything. What, on today's open market, is the value of a state company which has been churning out redundant tractors at fixed prices for the Soviet Union? The Manager—a party man or he would not be in the job—has had simply to fulfil a quota. The state took it off his hands. Small wonder the Czechs have called for the dissolution of the Soviet-inspired Comecon trading group. Trading conditions between Czechoslovakia and the Soviet Union are chaotic.

Commercially, there is now a crying need for bankers, brokers, accountants, managers, dealers. These and many other disciplines have had no scope since the end of the 1939–45 War. The professional mind has been starved. There are no young professionals. The Central Bank is to lose its stifling monopoly. Merchant banks and savings banks are being set up, but nobody knows how to work them. That is an area where our own banks and business houses can extend a helping hand.

Czech industry has to learn to become competitive and accountable. It has also to clean itself up. It is the dirtiest in Europe. In the prevailing climate we can be confident that the environmentalists will reach Prague a lap or two ahead of the entrepreneurs. So, as Czech industry restores its long tradition of high quality in the unfamiliar market economy, the cost of anti-pollution measures will be piled on to it.

Communism has not only smothered free institutions and the economy but also ethnic differences. With borders on six different countries and a turbulent history the Czechs are vulnerable to what we now call racial tensions. Some of them will revive. Among older people the Germans are unpopular but that will not, in my judgment, stop Germany from playing a major role henceforth in Czechoslovakia. There is a huge potential there for a close neighbour.

And where do we stand in all this? Is Czechoslovakia still to us, in that immortal phrase, a faraway country with people of whom we know nothing? I walked slowly down Narodni Street in Prague, where on November 17 the police (for reasons now being investigated) went mad and beat hell out of the students. Candles have been lit and flowers laid close to the bloodstains. It was a decisive night. Barely a week later the entire Communist Government had resigned.

The students, 120 of whom are in hospital, proved braver than some of us in 1938. Now they urgently need help. They seek people who can teach languages, specialists who can teach marketing, management, international law. They want to know how students in the West study and how they organise their student unions—which were forbidden in Czechoslovakia. They lack photocopiers, facsimile machines, computers, printers and money.

Lucy, who was in the thick of the battle of Narodni Street and is now part-time interpreter for Francis Harris, the Telegraph correspondent in Prague, drafted in English on behalf of her student friends a little shopping list of needs, which she asked me to read through. It concluded: "We are sorry if it appears that we are asking for a lot, but we are starting from scratch. Remember it is for a country trying to come in from the cold."

"Is it too much, you think?" she asked anxiously. No, Lucy, all things considered, it is not too much.

June 1990

THE VISION ON THE WALL

"I know of no more moving spectacle than of a people, after persistent failures, clutching at fresh straws of hope." As Peruvians prepare for tomorrow's presidential election, W. F. Deedes sees glimmers of light emerging in Latin America

A new wind blows today down the Amazon and across the Andes. There are moments when you can even catch a breath of hope. Most of the people in Latin America, like those of Eastern Europe, have had a rough time of it since the last war. Military leaders have tortured them. Popular leaders have ruined their currencies. (On my arrival at Lima airport in Peru, the inca was 30,000 to the US dollar, but it deteriorated so quickly that on departure my hotel bill was more than 25 million incas).

Unlike the people of Eastern Europe, however, Latin Americans in their struggle for life in shanty towns have not much engaged our sympathies. The United States is preoccupied with Central America's convulsions. Most of our historic ties with Argentina, Brazil, Chile and Peru have languished. Europe is our goal. The old European colonies of South America sense the world's lack of interest in their special problems.

And special they are. "We have had a democracy for 10 years, and are poorer than when it started," said Mario Vargas Llosa as he discussed his chances of becoming Peru's next president. Vargas Llosa is striving to become Peru's Vaclav Havel. "Three years of electioneering!" he exclaimed, when I suggested he seemed buoyant. "I *am* tired." Later he says: "We have a social democracy, but not an economic democracy"—and that is part of the ticket on which he is campaigning.

If he succeeds in the second ballot tomorrow, he will inherit a country on the brink of catastrophe, with inflation raging, terrorism widespread, and every day an explosive protest march by public sector workers through the streets of Lima.

Peru has become a dangerous place in which to live. Poverty on the greatest scale I have seen has turned the murderous Sendero Luminoso (Shining Path) into a popular movement, though in five

324

years it has assassinated 30 judges, 37 mayors and 350 politicians, and cost the country about $10 billion.

In Chile, by contrast, the military dictatorship of General Pinochet, who bowed out after last year's election, left a bloody record of human rights violations (an inquiry into which is rocking Chile's politics), but a relatively stable economy. Inflation under the new president, Patricio Aylwin, runs at 20–24 per cent, low in these parts.

Aylwin is a good man, a Christian, they tell me; the right man at the right time, ready like Lincoln to heal wounds. But his Commission for Truth and Reconciliation, probing atrocities of the Pinochet years, has strained relations between the president and the military. In theory, the commission's proceedings and report to the president will be private. In practice, a free press will spot who goes in and out and blazon the incriminating facts.

In Brazil, after years of daft economic politics, unmanageable inflation, pervasive corruption, but, until recently, not much torture, President Fernando Collor, aged 40, and his young team of academics from the University of Sao Paulo have stunned many by throwing the economy into a freeze. Without question, Brazil has an extraordinary president, with a taste for stunts in hang gliders and motor cycles to illustrate (I suspect) that he has strong nerves.

He will need them. There is in Brazil today a whiff of John Kennedy's New Frontier of 30 years ago. "The old ways will not do any more . . ." The words may be political old hat, but men still thrill to them.

"There is no other way," the head of a large company in Brazil told me at a party in Rio de Janeiro to welcome our new Consul-General, Miss Patricia Kelly. Win or lose, he believes, Collor will change the mentality of this country. Foreign Minister Rezek had echoed that belief. "Above all, we have to change public perceptions, our entire way of thinking," he said.

I know of no more moving spectacle than a people, after persistent failures, clutching at fresh straws of hope. In Brazil, Chile and Peru, the human spirit stirs again. They are—to recall a phrase once used about us—at "last chance saloon".

I went to Latin America to find out how they squared democracy with the sort of thing Collor has to do in Brazil. "He does things a dictator would not *dare* to do," said the Mayor of Rio de Janeiro. He is of another political persuasion. "People have accepted a bunch of young academics with a plan!"

Latin America persuades me that democracy is a Humpty Dumpty word. It means what you say it means. There is no guarantee that people will not starve and freedom to starve, as one military spokesman reminded me, is no big deal. In Santiago, Chile, I came across people whose diet of tea or bread sometimes left them too weak to stand.

Nor has every military regime led to torture and oppression. Since 1920, said Hector Cornejo Chavez, a retired politician in Peru, they had 14 administrations in Lima, nine of them democratic and five military. "In four out of those five, the army established order and then handed over to the civilians. The only one that did not was the last . . ."

Brazil's Minister of Justice spoke of the conflict between what his president was trying to do and constitutional propriety. Of course, he said, there are grey areas. He was talking about the struggle with the lawyers of business houses in Sao Paulo who are furiously challenging Collor's economic freeze. The grey areas pervade these countries. Democracy good, military bad—to paraphrase Orwell's "1984". But it is less simple than that.

Hernando de Soto, director of Peru's Institute for Liberty and Democracy, comes close to it when he declares that what countries in Latin America call democracy is nothing of the kind. The lights of Liberty and Democracy burn late in Lima. It was long past 8pm when I found de Soto still at work in his office. "We have the trappings of democracy," he says, "but we are 200 years behind the times."

He declares, truthfully, that 90 per cent of the rules which govern Peru—and much of Latin America—come from the executive branch; and, by contrast with the United States, they are simply not open to inspection, discussion or challenge. I had talked about this lack of control over the executive in Brasilia with Marcia Kubitschek, handsome daughter of the former president, who created that extraordinary and extravagant capital. She is now an influential member of Congress, and chairman of its foreign affairs committee.

"We had a long period of the military, who treated Congress as a façade," she said. (The military also deposed her father in 1964.) "Now the new constitution gives Congress stronger powers, which it is still shy about using." That is the nub of it. In none of these countries does Congress remotely resemble Parliament or the Congress of the United States. Nowhere can Congress much alter the chosen course of a determined president.

Brazil's congressional elections in October will tell us something about the state of public confidence in President Collor and his plans; but for the time being, the political complexion of Brazil's Congress is no great impediment to what the president wants to do. This may change in 1993, when under the new and rather exotic constitution, Brazilians will decide by referendum whether they want a shift of power from president to parliament. In Chile also there is serious talk of getting closer to the French system. Vargas Llosa did not rule it out in Peru, but thought that it might be a long time coming.

So Hernando de Soto in Lima has a point when he declares: "Our governments are elected, but then totally dissociate themselves from the law." He stresses the privilege of those who have access to the executive machine. "No company would dream of operating in Latin America without obtaining a special private understanding with the government." We are talking about "crony capitalism" or, as he prefers to call it, mercantilism.

The public knows perfectly well that the privileged and the politicians "fix it at the top". There is pervasive public contempt for all politicians. One of the main holds President Collor now has over his congressmen is the amount of patronage available to them. Patronage flourishes in a country where there are 1.7 million jobs at the federal level—of which Collor now promises to chop 400,000—and about six million public servants in all. President Sarney, Collor's predecessor, unwisely filled all the posts which are within the gift of congressmen, and then asked for their support. Collor, shrewdly, is withholding 40,000 jobs—until he gets support.

In such surroundings, the citizen has to look to himself. When Vargas Llosa told me that more than 60 per cent of Peru's economy was "informal", I was incredulous. "Perhaps more," he asserted confidently. I found it to be true. The streets of Lima teem with small traders, money changers, people living off their wits—and paying no tax. They stand, selling something or other, at every traffic light. "Peruvians are resilient," said General Luis Cisneros, a man of the Right, now retired. "Perhaps too resilient," he added sharply, clipped moustache bristling. "Politicians," he said through our interpreter, "have given the vote to illiterates. The thinking minority has very little influence." He thought military government made a shaky system more viable.

The general's room was a model of its kind. There were framed photographs of meetings elsewhere in Latin America with national leaders—invariably in uniform. There were scale models of tanks and helicopters on a shelf behind him. There were swords of honour, scrolls, medals galore, commemorative plates and shields, and two small standards set on either side of his desk.

So the informal sector prevails in Peru; yet, insists de Soto, it is the informal sector which keeps to its own rules. Its practitioners are more ethical than the crony capitalists. To make it even more confusing, some of the informal sector's activities are sanctioned by the government. In Lima's Ocona Street, which runs a huge money market, it is perfectly safe to change dollars under the noses of the police. Ocona Street struck me as far more orderly than the Tokyo stock market in a panic.

It is tempting to conclude that this remains a monstrously ill-governed continent. It would be fairer to say that it has missed the social tides which have swept over Western shores in this century. Over and over again on this journey I was reminded of the extremes of wealth and poverty in much of this country when I was young. Lloyd George, Ramsay MacDonald, Clem Attlee, and the conscience of the rich, to give them all their due—and their counterparts in Europe—did help to reduce extremes, and so preserve us from the near-anarchy which lurks today in countries like Peru.

The behaviour of the rich in much of Latin America today, their dollars stashed away in overseas banks, defies the lessons of modern history. They smack of Louis XVI. Radical leaders—and there have been plenty of them—have managed to destroy their nations' economies, without disturbing the rich. "I doubt," said my neighbour at a lunch in Lima, "if there are 100,000 people here who pay their taxes." I found this incredible; but the proportion of taxpayers is certainly amazingly low. "When the first guerrillas appeared in 1965," said General Cisneros, when we discussed this gap between rich and poor, "the military warned the government that something had to be done, or violence would spread upwards—as it has done."

Therein lies much of President Collor's appeal to Brazilians. He and his 36-year-old Economics Minister, Zelia Cordoso de Melo, have produced a plan to perplex the Left and enrage the Right and the rich. They have tickled the nerve of envy. Life may be tougher when your hard-earned savings are frozen; but just hark to the rich squealing! "It's time." Collor did a lot of market research before his election. It seems to have borne fruit.

The Brazilian banks, which had a nice little earner when inflation was at its height and the overnight rate was 2 per cent, are now losing money and are distraught. "The banks are powerful, they are heavy losers, and they will destroy the plan," confided an elegant stranger at the Consul-General's party in Rio. An industrialist who overheard us turned and shook his head. "Everyone wants it to succeed," he said.

Collor's government declares that inflation in April was zero, which is doubtful; but it is certainly well down. He has now to relax his freeze sufficiently to avoid pushing Brazil into a depression, but slowly enough to keep inflation at bay. With their balances blocked, many companies are desperate, borrowing money to pay wages and putting their staff on half-time or unpaid leave. Some manufacturers have lost an indispensable source of revenue, because they recovered losses on their products by manipulating money on the market—which is what every other citizen tried to do. President Collor is on a high wire, and the waters below him are boiling.

He and Zelia—"She is not brilliant, but she is tough and brave," said an old hand gallantly—have now to begin fine tuning. It will be difficult in a state-dominated economy. One guess is that Collor will unfreeze the savings of those willing to invest their money in the state industries. Since many believe they will never see their money again, it might work. But most of Brazil's vast and inefficient cartels are simply not fit for the market in their present state.

On top of them is a huge burden of debt, internal and external; and at federal, state and municipal levels pork-barrel politics on a staggering scale. What can you do about a mayor who, after only five days in office, awards himself a pension for life of £300 a month?

Happily, the press is now free to interest itself in this sort of nonsense—as it is in Chile and Peru. I called on editors or proprietors in all three countries. Come on, I said, how much arm-twisting goes on? I take their word for it. There is none. So in Brazil today newspapers rejoice to publish day by day juicy disclosures about gross misuses of public money.

While I was raking over clues to explain Latin America's predicament, the Sunday Telegraph published extracts from Peggy Noonan's book, in which she describes the core of George Bush's acceptance speech—which I heard at the time in New Orleans. The significant passages which Noonan and others drafted are these:

"For we are a nation of communities, of thousands and tens of

thousands of ethnic, religious, social, business, labour union, neighbourhood, regional and other organisations, all of them varied,
voluntary and unique.

"This is America: the Knights of Columbus, the Grange Hadas-
sah, the Disabled American Veterans, the Order of Ahepa, the
Business and Professional Women of America, the union hall, the
Bible and study group—a brilliant diversity spread like stars, like a
thousand points of light in a broad and peaceful sky. Does government have a place? Yes. Government is part of the nation of
communities—not a whole, just a part."

All of us in the West belong to such communities, though we no
longer comprehend their value. Indeed, we have prime-time entertainment programmes devoted to mocking them. "What does the
fish know about the water in which it swims?"—to quote Hernando
de Soto in Lima again. Latin America, I perceive, enjoys no such
inheritance. This social fabric of ours has been built up over 200
years or more. It will be a long, long time before a thousand points
of light appear in the skies above Chile, Peru, Brazil, Argentina.

But there has to be a beginning. We may be seeing it now.

THEY WERE BAD JOKES AND NOT VILLAINS, SAY THE VOICES IN THE STREET

What are the ordinary Russians saying now?

The two young girls strolling slowly down Moscow's Prospekt Marxa in the morning sun look as if they have not slept for days. I nudge my interpreter. She is helping me to fathom the thoughts of Moscow's unimportant people who, for 70 years or so, have not been consulted by anyone about anything.

So the girls sidle up and I put one of my stock questions: "If you could, would you leave this country?" "Yes!" they chorus, jumping out of their sleepwalk. They look to America. Friends have described it. Any job in mind? Youthful shrugs. Each wants a career "to make money".

Then I think back to what, earlier on this same spot, a truck driver had said: "I think a lot of young people want to get out. But not half of them want to work hard. They just want to live well." (Truck drivers in Moscow, incidentally, live considerably better than the doctors.) So I look knowingly at the girls and say: "What do you do now?"

They are students from Krasnoyarsk in Siberia. Two months' work being obligatory, they have chosen to be attendants on the Trans-Siberian Railway. Six days each way and 400 roubles (perhaps £8) for the round trip of 12 days. This for two months. They blink with exhaustion. Which illustrates the danger of jumping to conclusions in Russia.

But after hours of such talk on the streets, I have reached one conclusion. Women have borne the brunt of Russia's pain: while their men were in armies or Stalin's prisons, they have coped alone; have learned not to depend on men. Women speak from the heart, men from the head.

Here at a bus-stop in Zagorsk, 40 miles out of Moscow, is a veteran with his four rows of plastic medals. Nicolas was a pilot in the Soviet Air Force (1941–1945) and wounded badly enough to double his pension.

"Bandits against the people!" he exclaims. "They are against the people. Nothing for the people. People do not trust anyone in the upper management. What can management say when there is nothing in the shops?" He offers me a Russian cigarette from an old-fashioned case. "We need a man who gives food to the people," he ends sagely.

Here, by way of comparison, is Lena, sitting on a bench in the sun outside the monastery walls of Zagorsk, rocking her baby's pram. "A fine pram," I say, with grandfatherly intuition. Sad smile. "Yes, but I can get no shoes for my baby. I can sew, I can knit, but I cannot make shoes!"—a cry heard from every mother in the land.

We talk of her husband, a computer engineer in a fruit depot. She laughs. "That is why you find me eating this apple." Her mother-in-law in the next village has two cows. "So twice a week we get milk." But her mother-in-law has to fetch water and is growing old. "So I am not typical. We exchange milk for food." She took higher education, is a specialist in haematology. We discuss communism. "My mother understood it. Said it was just a game." And the young. "Our young people are not bad, many good."

Then suddenly her heart bursts out. "We must influence our system so that people are not afraid to show high feelings like patriotism, generosity. To write a love letter I need feelings. People do have feelings. The system tries to crush feelings." She turns her face away. "Communism goes with other 'isms', but the human spirit does not. Oh, it is so easy to command people when they are poor and depressed."

Then rocking her pram, she looks at me. "You see, we do not have stockings for men here. So I queued for 7½ hours, and I was pregnant, for my husband's stockings, to get them. And when I got them, I was so happy. That is our system."

A lot of the young—more than you would find in London—are academically well qualified, but with no wish to leave Russia. "I cannot say for everyone," says Myzhny, a woman of 30, "but I shall not go. I have many friends here. I feel it is my motherland."

"I might go for a time," a young computer engineer tells me, adding as an afterthought: "To give my mind a bath."

I expected to find a few young minds unbalanced by upbringing in the Soviet Union. On the contrary, they speak with robust common-sense. They see their past rules as stupid rather than wicked, as bad jokes, not villains. A dozen to whom I spoke separately, ranging from 14 to 21, claimed immunity from communist indoctrination, which in any case was abandoned in about 1985.

This is the testimony of Olga, an intelligent woman of 35: "I was brought up in the Young Communist League system. I was very active, though I never took a leading position. I was critical, because of my mother's influence. She was not for or against the party. She was non-political. The moral quality with which she brought me up conflicted with the party."

"You changed?"

"Later. At 18, I met someone older. He changed my mind, but my mind was ready for it." And now? "I have a daughter of five. She does not know the name of Lenin, but I am reading her the Bible."

They have suffered the vileness of Stalin and his apostles—fear, endless lies, a denial of almost all earthly joys—yet none speaks to me of revenge. "We have had a catharsis," says Lolita, who works in a trading association. "We should punish only the ringleaders. Extremism will not lead to good, as we saw in 1918." Some men speak differently, but women have had enough. They have supped with horrors, lived with violence all their lives. Let the past lie.

The KGB? "I think it should be dissolved," says Peter who is strolling along with two companions in jeans. He wears a tie. "Intelligence should be kept. We need it. But radically changed. Democracy will move on now. I thought the tanks were the end of everything. But those three days may be equal to 30 years in our history."

Olga is a white-haired grandmother whose grandsons are now studying architecture and engineering. She excuses herself. "I am not well educated," she says simply. But she thinks the worst is over—thanks to Yeltsin—and only good will come, eventually. Is she a pensioner? "Yes, I worked for 40 years in a factory. It was not easy work." Her pension is 103 roubles (say, £6) a month, plus 60 per cent for inflation, and lately another 40 per cent. Not much for 40 years' work? "It is very little, but I am grateful."

If people do not know, I say to my interpreter, they say so. In London, the less people know, the more they talk. "Democracy," she says tartly.

My second conclusion is that the young will take command in this country sooner than anyone expects.

Eugenia is a woman of about 50 with heavy make-up round her eyes. Happier? "Yes, the threat for 70 years has gone, and the young will be free. That is so important. The most active part after the coup was taken by the young. It was a revelation to see them in action. We women thought it was always up to us. It was so heartening to see the young men in action. The women were crying and bringing them food. Everyone was involved. The common people understood quickly. Common people get the point quicker than those on top."

The common people! Nowhere in the West is there a capitalist society with a wider gap between privilege and poverty than I have seen in Moscow. This is the sort of society which in Britain 70 years ago persuaded honest men to become socialists.

Now the poor face winter, dire shortages and a collapsing currency. Maria, aged 12, goes to secondary school in Zagorsk and studies Russian, German, biology, chemistry, drawing, from 8 am until 1 pm with two hours' prep. She looks and sounds to me like a flier. What does she hope to be? "A saleswoman." Why? "Easier to get food."

GHOSTS OF WAR

Twenty years after the Vietnam war Americans are using the issue of troops "missing in action" as a pretext for failing to come to terms with defeat

"We call it the Ranch," said the American colonel wistfully, glancing round the severe corridors of his headquarters in Hanoi. His earnest face reminded one a little of battle-weary colonels encountered in the Second World War. The hair was of strict military cut, but he wore the shirt and blue slacks of a civilian.

So did the major, built like an all-American half-back, who joins us in the colonel's office. An American flag occupies half of one wall. On the desk is a photograph of the colonel's wife and two children. "I am without my family," he says, when we discuss his compulsory isolation.

Lt-Col John Cray leads America's Missing in Action (MIA) task force, part of whose macabre mission is to trace and analyse every bone and button from graves of American soldiers still unaccounted for in the Vietnam war.

Only thus can he establish proof that Airman Jones, last seen on a parachute after his plane had been shot down over Hanoi, is dead, not held captive. He has to exorcise a ghost which has been haunting Americans for 20 years or more—the spectre of Americans still held captive and under duress somewhere in Vietnam.

There are hidden depths to this. This is a tale of pain felt when a long war has been lost; it is also about a sense of guilt. With the end of the Cold War, America's war in Vietnam, at the cost of 58,000 Americans dead—and millions of Vietnamese—will come to be seen by the world, even more than it is already, as an appalling aberration. It is a history trap, easily fallen into.

"How could Americans bomb and napalm folk like this?" I exclaimed to a companion, as we walked among gentle, friendly people in the markets of Hanoi. They did it in days we have mostly forgotten, when it looked odds-on that much of South-East Asia would fall behind the Iron Curtain. The Vietnam war left wounds, as all wars do, but also hindsight and blame and an inner desire for revenge, which helps to explain the depths of the MIA issue.

There were 2,248 Americans unaccounted for in South-East Asia, 1,648 of them in Vietnam. Every one of them has to be accounted for. The MIA issue has made itself a lead factor in America's future relations with South-East Asia.

Washington's long-standing embargo on all trade with Vietnam has been slightly eased in recent months; but it seems likely to stay in place until Cray reports fulfilment of his mission.

Part of his force comprises teams of a dozen specialists, chasing shadows in 14 of Vietnam's provinces, seven in the North and seven in the South. With a telescopic pointer the colonel indicates the little white tags which mark their whereabouts on his large-scale map.

One senses he has had this pointer out many times, not for the likes of us, but for American citizens who still dream that the missing loved one is out there somewhere, and alive. Other detachments of the MIA command check rumour, pursue every village legend, investigate every "last seen alive . . ." report. "Seen alive but likely to be captured . . ." reports have led to 100 separate investigations since 1992.

Cray fetches off his desk a well-thumbed paperback copy of *Kiss the Boys Good-bye* by Monica Jensen-Stevenson and William Stevenson. The book implies both that American servicemen are being held captive in Indochina, and that there is a conspiracy within US-government ranks to cover that up. It has had a solemn effect on the colonel.

A whole generation has been brought up on such books, and on films like *The Deer Hunter* and *Apocalypse Now*, which have made Americans ashamed of a brutal war which they failed to win.

To meet the President's requirements, other military units are working in Bangkok (Thailand), Vientiane (Laos) and Phnom Penh (Cambodia). Findings go back to a laboratory in Hawaii. Commander of the Joint Task Force-Full Accounting (JFA-FA) and based in Honolulu is Maj-Gen Thomas Needham. He reports to the Admiral who heads CINCPAC—Commander-in-Chief Pacific.

During the past two years, the whole process has been deliberately opened up—in the circumstances, a sensible policy. "The family has a right to entry in the examination system," says Cray solemnly.

Because the system is more open, the colonel can offer me grisly details about his excavation teams. Each team consists of the commander, a non-commissioned officer, an anthropologist, a photographer, two linguists, four people to deal with grave registrations, one for ordnance explosive disposal, and a life-support medic. All such men are drawn from the active or retired list of the three services. Many of them have had to become proficient in the Vietnamese language. In every war until this one, nations have sadly accepted the unknown warrior: in the two World Wars, the Korean war and the American Civil War, the ratio of "unaccounted for" was far higher than in Vietnam.

Are we discussing reality or illusion? "I do not believe there is any American alive," said the colonel. An ambassador in Hanoi, better nameless, was more brutal. "We are dealing with the inability of America to come to terms with the fact they lost . . ."

Yet, at a total cost so far of around $100 million, the colonel must plough on. They established the fate of 39 hitherto "unaccounted for" in 1992, and did the same for 58 more this year. One year from now, Cray reckons, and his mission might be coming to a close.

A bizarre twist in the tale is that on their side the Vietnamese seem no longer to bear America ill-will. For one thing, half the population has been born since the war ended. There are other reasons for the apparent lack of bitterness.

"So many wars," sighs Mrs Hao, a writer in Hanoi. "And then again," she adds, "the first day of the New Year in Vietnam represents a fresh beginning. We try to expunge memory of what has happened in the previous year."

Third and strangest of all, relatively few Vietnamese saw their assailants. "Whole valleys," exclaimed Mrs Hao, "were killed by the bombing. In many villages there were not enough coffins to bury the dead. There were villages without men, only mothers left to bring up families. But 80 per cent of the population did not fully understand what was happening. The Americans were disembodied invaders. The only American boys most people saw were either dying or dead."

From several sources there comes the same tale. The Vietnamese do not bear grudges. Theirs is a tradition of forgiving their enemies. Washington imposed a trade embargo on North Vietnam in 1964, a year before American combat troops were sent to South Vietnam. It extended the embargo to the South in 1975, when Hanoi toppled the Saigon government.

"Henry Kissinger lost face," said a European diplomat in Hanoi. "From then on, America could not act objectively. Emotion took over." He paused. "Put diplomatically, the US government is not strong enough just now to defy the pressure groups, and people gulled by tales of hidden prisoners. Undiplomatically, they lack the guts to take the right decision."

There is a second twist to the tale. "The Vietnamese, North and South, had 300,000 missing in action," cried Mrs Hao. "They offer Americans good co-operation,"—a fact Cray would not deny—"but America is only interested in Americans, not the missing Vietnamese.

"And then we have the American relatives," she adds, pouring tea into tiny cups, hallmark of Vietnamese hospitality. "They come to Vietnam looking for what is not there. Of course, they hear tales— from people to whom a dollar is a lot of money. They go out with the excavation teams, rent helicopters for $1,000 an hour, stay in luxury hotels—what is the poor Vietnamese peasant to make of that?"

Searches can be very difficult, she admits. "A plane was shot down in one place, the pilot landed in another. It is Catch 22. It is 99.9 per cent sure that there are no live Americans here. If you come to see, all is plain. If you do not, you disbelieve. It is a mysterious area."

We dropped in on the solitary representative of one of America's biggest corporations. His newly decorated office was bare. His total staff comprised a woman receptionist and a boy on the doorway. He is feeling his way forward cautiously, awaiting a green light from Washington which never comes.

He threads his way through a labyrinth of regulations the US government has devised, short of lifting the embargo. US companies are now permitted to compete for projects which are being funded by international bodies, such as the World Bank and the IMF. "How do you define international funding? You do it and see what happens."

The MIA issue is central, he goes on. "The argument goes that if they lift the embargo, there is no incentive here to co-operate. On the contrary, it would be easier to get at the truth if we had good relations. It is not only a matter of lifting the trade embargo, but of diversifying our relationships . . ." In the US decision process, he adds, China is more important than Vietnam. "It is important because it is a threat. But if China saw that we had friendly relations with Vietnam, it would be less of a threat."

As he stops for breath, I take a look round this stark, empty office, belonging to a corporation which might be doing millions of dollars worth of welcome business in Vietnam, and I wonder if I am living in a real world. A world of make-believe, a realm of fantasy now stands between America and serious decisions in this region.

It is to dissolve this world, to bring America back to realities, that Cray works in his austere office, cut off from the outside world. He and his mission must not fraternise with the local population in a land still defined in American law as an enemy country.

We discussed some of the hardships imposed on the mission. Among them are no diplomatic relations, heat and humidity, strict and model behaviour at all times, malaria-ridden areas, substantial pressure, ragged terrain, no medical support, unexploded munitions.

He wears his uniform only when he attends the small, solemn US military ceremonies held at Noi Bai airport in Hanoi when sets of US remains depart. It is an emotional occasion, done with full honours. Remains go to the US army's Central Identification Laboratory in Hawaii (CILHI). If their identification is accepted by the family, they are flown back to the family. Some are buried at Arlington National Cemetery, others in their home town.

Finally the colonel shows me a piece of paper on which his task has been officially described. It is "to co-ordinate all US Department of Defense efforts to achieve the fullest accounting for Americans still unaccounted for".

In reality, as Cray knows full well, his task is harder than that. It is to strip away, bone by bone, button by button, ghost by ghost, America's last pretext for refusing to forgive a smaller nation which defeated her.

DON'T LET THIS GO ON

This week, the Red Cross has pressed for a ban on land mines which each year kill and maim many thousands. W. F. Deedes urges Britain to change its policy

Roughly every 15 minutes a human being is blown up by one of the 84–100 million land or anti-personnel mines scattered indiscriminately round the world. It is a conservative estimate, UN mines expert Brigadier Paddy Blagden explained to me in New York, because at least a third of the victims never get to hospital. Caught in remote places, they die unaided and alone.

Worldwide, 800 people, most of them innocent folk in the developing world, are being killed outright by mines every month. If slaughter on this scale were caused by nuclear or chemical weapons, the media would be ablaze, the world horrified and demanding action.

As it is, none of these single casualties is reported. Who knows if an old woman and her grandchild, gathering firewood in Cambodia, die on a mine? When one gets abreast of what is happening to people, it is the unawareness that shocks, as well as the scale of human suffering. Virtually none of us in the West are at risk. Why worry? "I wish to God," said a senior official at UN, with savage humour, "there were mines on Third Avenue."

Mines are present in 62 countries, the worst of them being Afghanistan, Mozambique, Cambodia, Somalia and Angola. All five countries have scarce medical resources for dealing with the dreadful injuries caused by mines. It was seeing the injured in Angola last August, where 20,000 of the amputees are women and children, that set me on this trail. In that country, 20 million mines have been laid over a third of the country, much of it fertile; so starvation is aggravated.

In Cambodia's 12-year civil war, more people were killed by mines than by any other weapon, and today the country claims the world's highest percentage of the disabled. One in every 236 Cambodians is an amputee, compared with 1 per 22,000 in the United

States. Against this carnage, manufacturers determined to make them, governments determined to export them, and military determined to use them, the world seems powerless. Humanity is losing ground. More than a million mines have been laid, and are still being laid in former Yugoslavia. They will claim a host of innocents.

In theory, there is a convention, concluded by the UN in 1980, imposing conditions on the use of mines, which came into force a decade ago. These instruments have been brushed aside. At the last count, just 39 countries have ratified them, while 60 companies and government agencies in 35 countries continue to manufacture these weapons.

In Washington, as this newspaper reported before Christmas, the Clinton administration seeks a blanket ban on the export of anti-personnel mines. In London, the Ministry of Defence says we have not exported such mines—insofar as they can be identified—for five years.

But the Foreign Office opposes a blanket ban, declaring it would be unworkable, and on grounds that we want to develop the technology for manufacturing mines with a limited life, which self-destruct. That will take time. "Self-neutralising and self-destructive mines," says Ariane Sand-Trigo of the International Committee of the Red Cross in New York, "have a 15 per cent failure rate."

In truth, the British Army has not used mines since the Korean war more than 40 years ago, though they were used against us in the Falklands. This week the International Committee of the Red Cross, appositely, convened a seminar in Geneva to examine the military on why "anti-personnel mines are seen as indispensable to defence". So, once, was poisonous gas.

In his UN office, Paddy Blagden keeps a black museum of mines, ranging from the most sophisticated—fitted with a £1,750 electronic "brain"—to crude anti-personnel devices which can be made in a small workshop for a dollar or two. An international ban on the export of mines would be a giant step forward, but it would still take a long time to make much of the world habitable again.

At the present rate, and with the means at our disposal, it will take at least a generation, probably much longer. Funds are short. Those who manufacture or lay mines assume no responsibility for clearance, nor help care for those disabled by mines.

No one has yet come up with a method that would meet the

UN's standard of 99.9 per cent clearance. Lifting a single mine by present methods costs between £200 and £750 per mine. In Cambodia, where there are nine million people, 4.5 million mines and an income of about £90 a head, it would cost several times the GNP to clear the country of mines.

In Afghanistan, the UN has trained a force of about 2,000 to lift mines—training instructors, team leaders and managers from the local population. Only a handful of expatriates stay on to handle political pressures and monitor new technology.

South Africa, lifting mines laid along the border with Zimbabwe, heads the field in mine-lifting technique with a mixture of dogs and their trainers and mechanical methods. Dogs can smell chemicals even in mines designed to be undetectable, but they tire easily and fail in certain climates. Mercifully, said a UN source, the embargo on South African mine-lifting equipment has been lifted. To illustrate the task ahead, it took from 1945 until 1977 to clear 15 million mines laid in Poland, yet during that period 4,000 were killed by mines and 9,000 injured.

So the slaughter and maiming will continue for a long time yet—longer still if the export of mines continues unchecked. "What appals," said Ariane Sand-Trigo, "is the psychological terror aroused in people returning to their homes after a war. At least 80 per cent go back to the farm. And that is where mines may be."

Kathy Bremer of America's CARE organisation in Atlanta, Georgia, expanded the point. Imagine yourself a displaced person, locked outside your country by a long civil war. At last you can go home—to what? Ariane Sand-Trigo's figures offer a guide. A quarter of all war casualties are victims of mines. Of these, 22 per cent are women and children. In Kabul, Afghanistan, that figure is not 22 but 50 per cent.

She reminded me of two of the International Red Cross's fixed principles, which we shrug off. You cannot use a weapon which strikes indiscriminately. You cannot use weapons disproportionate to military achievement. The military are unlikely to concede either point. But what of nations, not at war, which profit from this trade?

My firm conclusion is that the efforts of UN, IRC and others will not prevail without more public awareness of what is going on, and consequent revulsion. As I looked at photographs with the UN and IRC of women and children maimed by mines, it struck me that this affront to humanity is not far removed from certain of the last war's crimes which horrified us.

We must be horrified again. "Do not show people too much," murmured Sand-Trigo. "They cannot stand it. They turn away." No one has to look at the pictures. Facts are enough. These mines are not legitimate defence weapons, but vicious devices aimed at harming civilians. It is for *us* to say, "Enough." We will no longer tolerate this being done in our name.

A TRIUMPH AMONG THE DANGERS OF DIPLOMACY

The Princess has played it by the book in Angola, says W. F. Deedes

Seen from the war-ruined cities of Kuito and Huambo, where Diana, Princess of Wales ended her Red Cross mission in Angola yesterday, any quarrel that British ministers may have with her looks petty.

There has been a vast amount of human suffering in both places—30,000, or a third of its population, perished in Kuito. Now there is simply privation and anti-personnel mines everywhere.

They threaten life and limb. They strangle local endeavours by the population to get going again. Only the grass, green and lush after recent rain, flourishes.

On the outskirts of what is left of Huambo, the Princess donned mine-clearing kit and went off to look at a belt of territory where the Halo Trust is at work detecting and lifting mines. Last week their harvest there was 50 mines.

Asked about reported differences with ministers, she did well to say: "It is a distraction we don't need." Having followed most of her movements out here, I can testify that the way she has set about her mission of support for the Red Cross campaign against mines has been irreproachable.

The whole scene in this ravaged country is calculated to catch her heart. She has been absorbed by some of her encounters with victims of mines.

Her first call in Huambo yesterday was to the local hospital where she met Rosaline Domingo, 16. A mine had destroyed her right leg and her baby. In this region that is a commonplace tale.

She was also absorbed by what the smart ex-soldiers of Halo Trust told her about their work. They had gathered a pile of unexploded ordnance for inspection. Later she detonated another pile.

A pity, some thought, that Lt Col Colin Mitchell—"Mad Mitch" of the Argyll and Sutherland Highlanders—had not lived to see this recognition of Halo Trust's work on mines in the world. He founded it.

What makes the mine clearers' work so difficult in this region are the fragments of war that litter the surrounding fields. For every 20 pieces of metal that set the mine detectors humming, only one may be a mine.

Like the Princess, the Red Cross leaders who are out here with her can see no valid reason for government anger. As one of the world's leading humanitarian organisations, International Red Cross believes that A/P mines transgress a convention of war in that they cause human suffering wholly disproportionate to their military value.

So they are calling for an immediate global ban on them by all countries. By undertaking this position on behalf of such a powerful international organisation, the Princess has unmistakably signalled her support for this.

The British Government, on the other hand, opposes an immediate ban.

It does not think it would be workable. So it seeks to reach foggy compromises by which, some think, it simply compromises itself. So there are important differences that cannot be glossed over but, made aware of the Government's position before she came out to Angola, the Princess has played it by the book.

Accompanied most of the time by our ambassador in Angola, she has said and done nothing to trouble him or the Foreign Office. Her visit, inevitably, attracted enormous attention from the news media; but it was not seriously controversial until someone in London made it so. In the light of how the Princess has handled this serious humanitarian issue, those of us who have been with her reckon she deserved better.

PRINCESS SUFFERS THE EMOTIONS OF SARAJEVO

As a campaign in the land-mine war closes, W. F. Deedes weighs up the demands of a punishing schedule

Diana, Princess of Wales's visit to Bosnia came to a close yesterday with a crowded and often emotional morning in Sarajevo, a city with wounds calculated to grieve any heart.

She looked at the ruins of homes, she saw the massive cemeteries, she spoke to the damaged children. She was told of the mass graves of those buried alive and the graves of women and children who had died with hands tied behind their back.

After two hours of this emotional turmoil she spent another two with the UN Mine Action Centre and Norwegian People's Aid on their de-mining work in Bosnia and the forthcoming treaty negotiations on a mines ban.

She began with the ruins of Sarajevo. "Keep off the grass," cautionary voices urged us. It was an instruction to command earnest attention.

What she saw among the ruins was a reminder that years, perhaps decades, will elapse and billions will be spent before this city looses the shackles of war.

Then she visited one of the vast cemeteries that cast shadows all over Sarajevo and spent a little time walking among the graves.

Tending one of the graves was the mother of Tadic Dragan, who was killed three years ago. The Princess spoke to her for a moment then broke the language barrier by laying her hands on the mother's shoulders. It was an encounter that needed no interpreter.

Then on one of the numerous slopes above Sarajevo she visited the tiny and impoverished home of Gabelig Mirzeta, a 15-year-old girl who stepped on a land-mine in the past year. The girl was quieting her nerves with chewing gum as she told her stories through Robert Maryks, of the Jesuit refugee service, who has been working with 30 child survivors in the Sarajevo area.

Gabelig's mother, a widow who remarried, was not present. The child seemed alone. On a bed in the same house was a much younger child with chronic muscular disability and almost non-existent eyesight.

On impulse the Princess took the child in her arms and stroked the stricken limbs. Whence came care for this child, she wondered. We were left to speculate.

After such experiences it seemed remarkable that the Princesss felt able to sit and listen attentively to a long briefing on mines from the UN Mine Accident Centre and Norwegian People's Aid.

She learned why mines in Bosnia are more intractable that in most other parts. "This land has not drawn together yet," a UN official told her. Consequently there has not been the co-operation among authorities that might be expected.

The army, she learned, became experts at planting mines with cunning, so that the traps they set were particularly dangerous. "These mines," they told her, "reflect the political situation of this country."

The de-mining effort so far has uncovered 12,400 devices at the cost of six soldiers killed and five seriously wounded. At a conservative estimate a million remain.

At least nobody of any persuasion could call the Princess's expedition to Bosnia political. From start to finish it was confined to the human suffering caused by mines, not the desirability or otherwise of banning them.

This was ground of her own choosing, as it embodied what she feels most deeply about—the consequences rather than the causes of man's inhumanity to man.

She has spent hours listening to mine victims, who talk of their ordeal. In doing so she discovered how many people in this war-torn country long to pour out their feelings to someone. The wells of bitterness run deep.

We agreed over supper on Saturday that the most moving interview of the day had been with a young Muslim widow whose husband had been killed on a mine last May while he was engaged in his favourite sport of fishing.

The man's mother and widow sat either side of the Princess. The widow spoke of their short but happy married life. The mother told of his last hours and of her dream in which he told her that he was happy where he was. Both were in tears. As the Princess grasped their hands in hers, they went on with their story.

Both her principal guides on this tour from Mines Survivors' Network, its co-founders Jerry White and Ken Rutherford, were mines casualties. They could tell her whom she was going to meet, but not what she would hear. Some victims' accounts of what they saw and felt almost turned the stomach.

Having seen the proposed programme before we set out, I reckoned we would be lucky to get through two thirds of it. Enthusiastic organisations tend on these expeditions to extract the last drop of energy from someone like the Princess.

In the event, notwithstanding rough roads and a long detour for reasons of safety, we accomplished the lot, without cutting anyone short. There were one or two stops for picnics which provided blessed relief.

Somewhere is a snapshot taken by the Princess with my camera of me using her satellite telephone to communicate with this office.

Her critics might say this slightly risky journey was part of her quest for recognition. They would be wrong. Victims of land-mines are the world's Cinderellas when it comes to support for them through the costly business of prosthetics and rehabilitation. The Princess was aware of this before this journey.

Her visit to Angola earlier this year unquestionably put land-mines higher on the agenda and indirectly quickened the movement towards a universal ban. She hopes that this mission to Bosnia will serve to stir consciences on the plight of the victims.

It was not a matter of her showing compassion towards people who have been crippled. Most of the mine victims we met showed pride in what they did to keep their minds and the rest of their body in good shape.

They knew that the lion's share of their rehabilitation rested with themselves. In this sense the Princess's appearance in their homes offered welcome encouragement in their task.

One reason the Princess can take such a punishing programme as this one was lies in her capacity to relax for very short intervals on extremely uncomfortable road journeys. She is an exponent of the very short but refreshing cat nap. On Saturday, after 14 hours at a stretch, she was still able to enjoy a joke at 10 pm.

Smoking by others is always a trial to her, and smoking the tobacco they seem to prefer in Bosnia must have been a double trial, but at no point would any smoker have suspected.

This mission, as I can testify, has been a feat of physical endurance by the Princess. The long day ended with the presentation to the Princess in a popular Sarajevo restaurant, the Belle View, where she was snatching a late lunch.

They then begged her to come to Oslo, where the next major conference on international banning of mines will take place in the first half of next month. Who knows?

YES, DIANA DID MAKE A DIFFERENCE

As our aircraft taxied across Luanda's airport, I caught a glimpse of the shabby little pavilion from which just 18 months ago Diana, Princess of Wales opened her crusade against landmines.

"I hope," she then said to assembled journalists, "that by working together in the next few days we shall focus world attention on this vital but until now largely neglected issue. So let's get on."

For a day or two, she did catch the attention of the world. Landmines became news. People found out where Angola was on the map. But what difference did she make? Flying around the country for a week, you get an unexpected answer.

Set aside Angola itself, where the thin veil of peace between the government and Unita is trembling again. Set aside the capital, Luanda, into which war drove three million people—one third of the entire population—to occupy a city designed for nearer 500,000.

Most of them are now destitute—in a city that ranks as the second-most expensive in the world. Oil is booming at 750,000 barrels a day, and rising. Meanwhile, the government is broke. Corruption is rife. The police are out of control. Diana's trip to Angola in January 1997, however, was not designed to cope with these afflictions. "I think she hastened help to those who had no help at all," said Clare Crawford, of the Mines Advisory Group, who knew Diana and travelled with me; and that's about it.

We went to the Swedish Orthopaedic Centre in Luanda, where they fit the legless with artificial limbs and where Diana had spent a morning in 1997. There we spotted a young amputee in a T-shirt with her face on it. Unaccountably, she is wearing spectacles, but it is the thought that counts.

Oh yes, they remembered her. Yes, the centre was expanding. They were fitting about 78 limbless patients a month and this was rising to 150 a month. The waiting list? "Not too many now."

To get a broader picture of just what has happened in this war-torn country during the last 18 months, we flew east to Luena, a town that war endowed with 166 landmines. Clare and I had been there before, six months before Diana's visit. Then, the refugees were pouring back. We saw one of them blown up on a mine and took him to hospital.

Thousands of them were crammed into the derelict railway station and the museum and the theatre in conditions of squalor that turned our stomachs. Some of them are still there; but a lot have re-settled.

What caught my attention this time round was the rate at which mines are being traced and lifted. The Mines Advisory Group, to which this newspaper's readers generously subscribed through the Diana (Mines) Memorial Fund, are working around Luena across something like 18,000 square kilometres.

Some 76 minefields have been cleared, another 21 have been surveyed and marked. Surveying minefields, as Diana came to see, is the most dangerous job of all. The locals tell you what they can remember of where the mines were laid. After that, those who have to mark off the minefield take their chance.

People talk of 10 million mines in Angola, which is nonsense. In truth, nobody has any idea of how many mines have been laid there, or anywhere else. In my judgment, we are talking in terms of tens of thousands rather than millions.

And to pick up Diana's turn of phrase, they *have* got on. There remains a lot to do, and there are always setbacks. Local military commanders, who seem ready on the drop of a hat to return to war, refuse to allow certain minefields to be cleared.

One particularly nasty mine was found recently that was set off by light or the detector. It killed the operator. Its origins have been traced back to South Africa and its provenance is being investigated. Meanwhile, all work on that particular road has been temporarily suspended.

But these are hazards implicit in all mine-lifting operations. It will certainly not, as some suggest, take a century to clear the land in Angola. The task, this visit persuaded me, is now well within our compass.

Along with the mine-lifting, there has been an expansion in the realm of prosthetics for the limbless. We visited a new centre in Luena, which the Mines Advisory Group persuaded the Vietnam Veterans of America Foundation to set up.

Opened in March of this year, it is already producing 50–60 limbs a month, and this will expand. A dormitory will open in August, where 10 patients can stay for the three weeks needed for treatment. When fitted with an artificial leg, the amputee takes at least that time while learning to live with it.

There are about 700 limbless on the Luena waiting list, but the centre has been endowed by America's Veterans with three million dollars spread over four years.

All this is wholly in line with what Diana hoped to see. So is the spread of Mines Awareness, which has become an important wing of MAG's work. It is difficult to keep people constantly alert to the danger of mines. It calls for a special technique, and the wider this can be spread among school teachers and others, the lower the casualties.

We stood on a little hill near Luena looking across former minefields where today 4,000 people have resettled. "These were people who had become dependent on feeding programmes," said Dave Turner of the MAG team. "They have broken out of that dependency into self-sufficiency."

Soon, another 4,000 will follow them. That is a true indicator of the progress that is being made.

"She put Angola on the map," said a senior source in our embassy there, where we discussed her influence. But the difference she made went beyond that. For Angola has a government that appears not to give a damn for its people. Conditions in Luanda and elsewhere proclaim it. I have never encountered such urban poverty anywhere in Africa. And this is in a country that some reckon to be potentially richer than South Africa.

"If we all packed up and went away tomorrow," said one aid worker, striving to ease the lot of deserted children, "the government would not turn a hair. They wouldn't miss us." She expressed the inner feelings of many non-government organisations.

Into such a country, Diana, Princess of Wales briefly entered a wholly different spirit. It caught the air, and it has endured.

As we were finishing up in Luena, Clare suggested a visit to the market. Guarded by a suitable escort, we went. There, on a tatty clothing stall, were T-shirts with Diana's face on the front. This time, she was wearing, not spectacles, but a tiara.

"They remember her," said Clare as we walked away. "Yes," I said, "they remember her." For a few days early in 1997, a light wind from a fresh quarter blew across this shattered, heartless land, so careless of its people. And it is blowing still.

FACING DEATH IN FIELDS OF SQUALOR

W. F. Deedes in Blace on the Kosovo-Macedonia border

Not even during the Second World War did I witness a scene of human anguish comparable to what I saw yesterday at Blace on the Kosovo-Macedonian border.

There are still more than 50,000 refugees waiting in chaos and without shelter in a field by the River Scubi, and some of them have been in this condition for seven days. There is no priority, no order, no precedence for the most vulnerable; the very old or young.

Across the road from this inferno, stretcher-bearers were ferrying in casualties. "They are coming in at the rate of one a minute," a French doctor standing outside an improvised first-aid post told me.

Some, of course, will die. The daily death rate of around 20 is sure to rise. "They are throwing the dead bodies in the river," cried one man and, although I disbelieved him, the scene at Blace is calculated to make it seem probable.

On Sunday night, at a meeting I attended, Clare Short, the International Development Secretary, demanded that 10,000 refugees be cleared from the field that night. In the event, 1,700 were moved. Another train from Kosovo with 5,000 on board also arrived; this pile of human agony is growing larger rather than smaller.

"Never have I seen such disorganisation," said an experienced aid worker who had also been in Afghanistan.

It is necessary to stress that this is not because the United Nations agencies or aid organisations have fallen down on the job.

It is because they are not being allowed to function as they desire by a government profoundly anxious lest this influx of Albanians upsets Macedonia's delicate ethnic balance.

Even the UN agencies are finding it uphill work against official obstruction.

The scene of human anguish is surrounded by police and military, all armed. The priority is to ensure that the refugees are admitted cautiously and conditionally—and sooner or later are persuaded to go elsewhere.

So the batons are out against old women who stumble on the wrong end of the line. Any charge of brutality is misplaced. These men are doing what they have been told to do—contain this potentially explosive invasion.

The weeping figure of Lumnije Azemi, 21, was an illustration of the chaos that prevailed. After four days in the field, her mother had collapsed with a panic attack. Accompanied by two children, the mother was borne to rough first aid.

The father, grandmother and two sisters who were sick were stopped from accompanying her. So the family was separated and kept apart by the Macedonian police.

Lumnije declared that the police were pushing and striking people in the field. When children fell down, they stepped on them. Mothers were shouting: "Don't beat our children." Such tales of woe were legion.

We were able at least to do something for Fatmira, 20, who came up to ask me if I carried a mobile telephone. She had escaped from Kosovo with her mother and father but had become separated. She had an uncle in neighbouring Skopje who she called on my telephone. We hoped for a happy ending.

On leaving Kosovo, Fatmira insisted she had seen soldiers trying to hide tanks and bodies of murdered people on the streets of Bablo. Some of the bodies were being eaten by dogs. Death no longer commands respect in this region of Europe. She had not eaten for four days and was laughing loudly. She was badly traumatised.

As the slow process of registering these people is completed, they are released to form another disorganised crowd awaiting buses. First come, first served.

The buses take 50 at a time to one of five improvised transit camps organised by Nato and UNHCR. Most of these are still under construction. There the refugees are fed and await transfer to a host family or asylum overseas.

According to the government, more than 50,000 have already been admitted through this process. A proportion of these is under local roofs, but in a country of only two million it will not be long before the capacity of host families is exhausted. Macedonia is a poor country.

The next scourge at Blace is likely to be an epidemic. Already, there are reports of meningitis and polio. Appalling sanitation among so many poses a huge health risk.

It is such a squalid scene. Human distress is always painful to witness; when surrounded by filth it is almost unbearable.

The bodies of the exhausted lie awaiting help from the first-aid posts amid broken loaves of bread, lost belongings, empty tins and all the detritus of a vast human panic.

I looked towards the hills that surround this awful scene. There were all the signs of spring. Just above this squalor, the hillside was bursting out in new green and some of the trees were wearing white for Eastertide.

Then I looked down again at an old woman stumbling past me, crying and in the last stages of exhaustion. I thought: what have we got to flatter ourselves about at this new millennium? Man's inhumanity to man has lost none of its venom.

NATO'S DEADLY LEGACY WILL CAUSE YEARS OF SUFFERING

W. F. Deedes in Pristina, reports on the Allied threat to refugees in Kosovo

A tour round some of Kosovo's ubiquitous minefields makes painfully clear that many of the casualties suffered by civilians are being caused by cluster bombs dropped by Nato from the air rather than mines sown by the Serbs or Kosovo Liberation Army.

Since the refugees returned to Kosovo in June there have been 232 casualties attributed to mines, or around 80 a month. It is officially admitted that at least a third of these have been victims of the cluster bomb; and some estimates put it higher.

Nato is known to have dropped a total of 1,300 containers of cluster bombs over Kosovo. Each container carried 208 of these bomblets. So something like 270,000 of these deadly weapons were scattered over the country.

It is not precisely known how many of these failed to explode on impact, but it is accepted that the failure rate was not less than 5 per cent. That would leave around 14,000 bomblets scattered over Kosovo of which some 3,500 have been traced and cleared.

But experienced professionals engaged in mine clearance in Kosovo are positive that the failure rate was a good deal higher, partly because the cluster bombs were dropped from 15,000 feet rather than the optimum height of 9,000. So the chances are that there are considerably more than 11,000 still to be traced and destroyed.

Unlike the countless cluster bombs dropped over Vietnam and Laos by the Americans in the Vietnam war, which are about the size and shape of a cricket ball, the cluster bomb in Kosovo looks more like a long thin beer can. They are yellow, innocent in appearance and, fatally, almost bound to arouse curiosity in the passer-by. They are also highly volatile, and have to be exploded on the spot.

Touring the minefields with two leading British groups, Halo Trust and the Mines Advisory Group, I watched one of these bomblets being expertly detonated. It produced a bigger bang than most anti-personnel mines. Because of its power, it probably causes a higher death rate. The death rate from mines is in the region of one death to three injuries.

Two main types of cluster bombs were dropped, the anti-tank bomblet and the anti-personnel bomblet. The anti-tank bomblet is constructed to pierce armour on impact.

Walking along a road where both types had fallen, one observed that the anti-tank bomblets had drilled holes to a considerable depth. The anti-personnel bomblet had burst like a mortar bomb on impact with a wider lethal range than most a/p mines.

We looked at a Serb tank struck by an anti-tank bomblet which must have scored a direct hit on the ammunition locker. The turret of the tank had been blown 50 feet away. It is going to take the combined efforts of Kfor engineers and some 16 mines clearance organisations now working in Kosovo some time to clear Serb mines and Nato's cluster bombs.

The Kfor map of minefields shows the western side of Kosovo to be worst affected, but cluster bombs have been found in most of the country, making a great deal of land too dangerous to cultivate. In consequence much of rural Kosovo will remain dependent on humanitarian feeding for a long time to come.

While these conditions prevail, a number of organisations such as United Nations Children's Fund and Save the Children are making mines awareness propaganda a priority. Save the Children has organised a course of instruction which will eventually cover 200 villages.

As winter sets in and the search for wood intensifies, the expectation is that casualties from mines and cluster bombs will rise.

When all the facts become known, the cluster bomb, manufactured in this country as well as America, is likely to arouse controversy. It can be argued that legally it is a weapon exempt from the land mine ban to which Britain is a signatory. Given the high failure rate, the question of whether it is ethically defensible is harder to answer.

THE END OF STRIFE IN THIS REGION IS STILL JUST A DREAM

The flight of Kosovo refugees into Macedonia became a humanitarian disaster. W. F. Deedes returned to Blace, the scene of their suffering

There were traces of white on hills around Blace where snow had fallen when I passed through that frontier post between Kosovo and Macedonia yesterday.

There were, I remembered, traces of white there last Easter when the trees were in blossom and in the valley below 65,000 desperate refugees from Kosovo were locked in a muddy water meadow guarded at gunpoint by Macedonian police.

In neither peace nor war had I ever witnessed such a sea of human degradation. The field, a few yards short of the frontier post, is empty now. But everything else on a grey winter morning looked very much the same.

The Macedonian frontier police examined our passports for a while. Then they asked the driver of our United Nations Children's Fund vehicle for its engine number. As if he knew.

This leopard hasn't changed its spots, I thought, as eventually we moved on. It clicked a shutter in my mind on the scene there at Easter 1999. The Nato bombing had begun on March 24, refugees streamed out of Kosovo towards Macedonia through Holy Week. By Easter Sunday the field at Blace was crammed.

I had arrived just in time to join an ominous meeting that night of top brass in the Hotel Continental, where I am staying now. They met to discuss the crisis at Blace.

Clare Short had flown in from Britain. Lt Gen Sir Mike Jackson, the Nato ground force commander, was there. One or two deeply unhappy Macedonian ministers were also present.

"I want 10,000 out of that place tonight," Clare Short demanded. The ministers looked even more deeply unhappy and went to work on their mobile telephones.

It became apparent to all present that tens of thousands of

starving refugees in a muddy hell hole were grievously compromising our Government's declared humanitarian intentions. Hence, the presence of Clare Short.

A European official sitting next to me scribbled a note which informed me that 17 of the refugees had died on Saturday, including seven children. The figure for Sunday was 20, including six children. Next morning, Easter Monday, we went to Blace, 20 minutes' drive out of Skopje. A local Red Cross aid post had been set up to deal with the worst cases of exhaustion and panic. That was all.

The grim scene was made grimmer by the Macedonian authorities refusal to allow aid agencies near the place. The only relief afforded to this despairing mass of human beings were loaves, bottles of water and thin plastic sheets.

It presented a vast picture of human misery that television cameras, dodging the police, sent out to the world.

Astonished and ashamed that their police had been made to look like brutes, the Macedonian government pressed every available bus into service and began rapidly to clear the field.

There is still bitterness felt in government circles at the way in which Nato, whose bombing of Serbia had precipitated the exodus, appeared in knight's armour while the Macedonian police were made to look brutal.

Some of the 5,000 refugees in Blace were moved to Struga on the Albanian frontier to which I returned this week for a heart-warming reunion with Mother Teresa Association workers. We went there in April searching for MTA, which had provided an invaluable medical alternative for those who mistrusted Serbs.

In response to our Christmas Appeal of 1998 *Daily Telegraph* readers had given around £130,000 for this organisation which was then torn apart and scattered by the Kosovo crisis. By some happy chance I reached Struga a day or two after the refugees had arrived. The town had greeted them and had individually volunteered to offer homes for every one. But where was the food for poor hosts to give their guests? I handed over enough of our readers' money to take care of that.

This week, the same faces from the MTA greeted me—and produced a copy of their accounts explaining how the readers' money had been spent in the crisis of last spring. The refugees have gone home, but the medical problems locally are huge. So the work goes on. That was the up side of my visit to Struga. The down side was the collective centre where Roma refugees from Kosovo reminded us that for a lot of people the war is not over yet. The Roma refugees occupy what was once a children's holiday home. Ohrid was a popular tourist centre for Europeans. It offers a gorgeous outlook across a lake and towards the snow-capped mountains, but a most doubtful future for the Romas who now have nowhere to go.

They exist in the state of semi-detention in Struga. Only 25 are allowed out at a time. The World Food Programme gives them food, but they have no money to speak of and some are living seven to a room. This is part of the detritus of our humanitarian war—and, alas, only a small part of it. A school for Roma children, fostered by Unicef, opened two days ago. Demili Ramadan, a Roma schoolteacher, had 45 children between the ages of seven and 14 in his care. He had attended a secondary school in Gnjilade in Kosovo which he will never see again. No Roma has a future there. The seed of hope for the many left with "no hope" by the Kosovo war may lie somewhere here.

Watching a class of these children, I saw the force of Unicef's approach to the Millennium. To invest in education is a way to end strife. That is their dream, to put a sort of firebreak down against man's inhumanity to man, and help the young to find a better way. The Unicef programme in Macedonia is impressive. By the end of 2001, with luck, 50 per cent of the children will be attending pre-school.

Well, one finds at the end of this return journey there is a desperate need for some such contribution. For the end of strife in this region is nowhere in sight. Refugees are unpopular in every country. If they are Serbs or Roma and return to Kosovo, their lives are instantly at risk.

All my experience of civil wars in places such as Afghanistan, Sudan and Liberia supports that warning. Ethnic cleansing poisons its practitioners and they turn against each other. Besides the Romas and the Serbs there are hosts of refugees from Kosovo still in no man's land.

Tens of thousands, purged by the Serbs a decade ago, are still sheltering in Switzerland and Germany. There are reckoned to be around 100,000 in those parts. Now that Kosovo has been liberated, the Germans and the Swiss would like these "refugees" to move on. But *has* Kosovo been liberated? The country is in no man's land and will remain so until the international community can make up its mind what is best done with the place.

And then there are some 250,000 Serbs taking refuge from Kosovo in Serbia. Where does their future lie? The component parts of what was once communist Yugoslavia are suffering from a thrombosis. There is a blockage of the arteries.

In Macedonia the unemployment rate is nudging 40 per cent. Social services have been cut. None of this region is going to revive let alone flourish, as things are.

Some tell me the region is crying out for another Marshall plan. I differ. What is lacking is the will of those in the West who, coming up to a year ago, decided to fight a humanitarian war and who indirectly piled up all those refugees at Blace, to see the business through.

SAPPERS SEEK THE DEADLY HARVEST OF NATO'S KOSOVO CLUSTER BOMBS

As snow melts slowly on Kosovo's lower slopes, the largest international army of de-miners ever deployed in one country resumes clearing the quantities of Serb mines, unexploded ordnance and, most treacherous of all, hundreds of cluster bombs dropped by Nato.

It will be for future military historians, appraising the war of 1999 in Kosovo, to decide whether in retrospect the cluster bombs the alliance dropped represented a spectacular own goal.

Some 1,400 containers, each carrying between 147 and 202 armour-piercing or anti-personnel bomblets, were dropped by aircraft from the prescribed height of 15,000 feet. They did relatively little damage to the Yugoslav army, but they suffered a failure rate of between 10 and 15 per cent and so remain live and dangerous on the ground.

About 8,000 of these highly volatile bomblets have so far been traced and blown up *in situ*. I watched a couple being dealt with from a safe distance. Something between 14,000 and 20,000 more remain to haunt Kosovo. The longer they remain in the ground, the harder they become to trace.

Watching Royal Engineers from Kfor demonstrate how they tackle these objects, always a risky business, I wondered how I might feel when called upon to chance my arm with one of these bomblets—they have a lethal range of 60 feet—which had been dropped by an allied airman from his safe height.

So, some 20 international organisations, 17 of them established de-mining practitioners, and our own Royal Engineers have their work cut out. Two British organisations, Halo Trust and Mines Advisory Group, have kept going through the worst weather of the winter.

Most of their work has been surveying and marking off dangerous areas.

Casualties have been sharply reduced, mainly by winter, partly by massive mine awareness campaigns in schools and villages. As spring returns and cultivation starts again, casualties caused by mines, which so far number 92 dead and 332 crippled, seem likely to increase.

In their gathering of intelligence about minefields in Kosovo, the de-mining organisations have received all the guidance Nato can offer. They have been given the 333 strike areas over which cluster bombs were dropped.

This is essentially of limited value. After release from the aircraft, the bomblet container falls, breaks open and from the British pattern discharges 147 bomblets. The American version carries 202 bomblets.

One container is designed to scatter with bomblets an area of roughly 300 × 100 yards. Even granted precision bombing from 15,000 feet, the value of subsequent guidance from Nato on where the bomblets may have fallen is plainly limited.

Tracing mines, bomblets and unexploded ordnance after this particular war is exceptionally difficult because most of the population had flown. They were not there to see what happened. This has prolonged the business of gathering local intelligence and marking off minefields. More than 600 minefields have been mapped so far; but nothing under 20 mines qualifies as a minefield.

Mine-laying for defensive purposes can often be claimed by the military as a legitimate weapon, particularly when manpower is in short supply. That is why America's refusal to sign the international ban on mines, mainly because of the tense border between North and South Korea, has extenuating circumstances.

The cluster bombs dropped by Nato, however, were not related to our defensive positions. We had none. They were designed to damage the Yugoslav army and plainly failed to do so. That army, it is now agreed by our military in Kosovo, retired in good order.

Now the unexpectedly high failure rate of these bomblets poses a threat to the life and limb of our own soldiers and civilians, together with hundreds of Kosovar de-miners, who are called upon to snuff them out.

A country which signs an international ban on land mines with a flourish, as Britain has done, but then permits cluster bombs manufactured in Britain to be flung around a country we have subsequently to administer, seems to me called upon to re-examine its military priorities.

FINAL RESTING PLACE FOR THE LION OF JUDAH

As Ethiopia prepares to give Haile Selassie a dignified burial, W. F. Deedes reflects on the Emperor's coronation and courage in the war with Italy

Many ghosts are walking in Addis Ababa this weekend, as the capital prepares for the reburial of Emperor Haile Selassie in St Trinity Cathedral tomorrow, a day or two after the 70th anniversary of his coronation in November 1930.

The Emperor himself has haunted this capital since his overthrow by Marxist military officers in 1974 and his death in dark circumstances a year later. His remains had been buried—allegedly under a lavatory—in the Imperial Palace.

Now they are to be translated to a tomb long in readiness for him, close to his family's private burial ground in the cathedral.

A few of the ghosts walk for me too, because although I cannot claim to have attended the coronation, some of those who did were companions in Addis Ababa five years later for the war with Italy.

One of them was Sir Percival Phillips, a famous correspondent, who had reported the coronation for the *Daily Mail* but covered the war in 1935 for *The Daily Telegraph*. Another was Evelyn Waugh, who represented *The Times* at the coronation, but the *Daily Mail* during the war.

Waugh and I then occupied the same small German pension in Addis, the Imperial Hotel being already overcrowded with war correspondents sleeping four to a room. Phillips, at 58, found the 8,000ft altitude of Addis Ababa uncomfortable, retired to Djibouti on the coast and became the fictitious Sir Jocelyn Hitchcock in Waugh's novel about the war, *Scoop*.

By contrast with the coronation in 1930, tomorrow's reburial will be relatively subdued, though it is clearly going to attract big crowds, both for the procession between the old palace and the cathedral and in the cathedral itself.

It has been organised unofficially by the Emperor Haile Selassie I

Memorial Foundation, which has raised enough money for the ceremony and other modest memorials to the Emperor.

Walking round the cathedral and looking at the open tomb awaiting his remains, I reflected on the extraordinary history of this man. He had had to fight within his country for the throne in 1930. Five years later he was fighting Mussolini, who took eight months to defeat him.

That was when I first met him at a dinner he gave in the palace to the war correspondents. He was a quiet, reserved figure indulgent with the journalists, who drank far too much *tejd*, a powerful drink with a honey base.

After losing the war he came to England in May 1936. There I met him again and wrote of "the small figure which stood upright, silent and motionless before a sofa in a gold and white reception room at 6 Prince's Gate, to receive the press with the same majestic serenity he had shown months ago in the Imperial Palace of Addis Ababa".

His aides intoned: "We have never desired war. It was imposed upon us . . . devastated fields and ruined villages . . . the bodies of the aged and of the women and children."

Oh God, I thought recalling those words—how often have we all heard them intoned since? But the Lion of Judah, as he was called, fell early in what we now recognise as an overture to the Second World War.

Cabling from Addis Ababa in 1930—and in 1935—was a hazardous undertaking. In 1930, by some appalling mischance, the cable office was shut for the day.

Nearly every dispatch appeared a day late in newspapers. Waugh, punctual in *The Times*, was said to have transmitted his copy from the Italian embassy. That is possible. Waugh was always friendly with the Italians, very much so five years later when he wrote of Mussolini as civilising a savage country.

Sitting in front of my laptop linked to London, and with my fingers crossed, I recognised that communications have improved since the 1930s.

Addis Ababa itself is transformed. It has become an untidy and slightly incoherent international capital. I took a look at the old Hotel Imperial, where the war correspondents were in 1935. Now called the Itegue Taitu Hotel, it has kept all its dark brown paint and the old piano at which we sometimes sang. And the old railway,

Chemin de Fer: Djibouti—Ethiopien, a miracle of French engineering in 1897, still runs. Every visitor to the coronation in 1930 had to come that way. So did we all in 1935.

Emperor Haile Selassie was the only African to become Knight of the Garter. That is why Sir Conrad Swan, Garter King of Arms, is here. We have always been close to the late Emperor.

But our closest association, I reflected as I left the cathedral, is to be found on a memorial plaque, on which is inscribed: Dedicated by His Imperial Majesty Haile Selassie I Emperor of Ethiopia in memory of those British officers and other ranks who together with Ethiopian patriots sacrificed their lives for the liberation of Ethiopia 1940–1942.

As they move the Emperor's remains tomorrow to his last resting place, we should remember them.

AFTERSHOCK

When W. F. Deedes suffered a stroke in the earthquake zone of Gujarat, it cut short his reporting assignment but gave him time to reflect on the tragedy. Now, restored to health, he reports on the devastation of a region and how its people are putting their lives back together

'Earthquakes have a place all their own in the human tragedy,' I wrote in my notebook as my helicopter, which had been flying round devastated Gujarat, finally turned towards its base in Ahmadabad. Unfortunately, before I could enter any more reflections, my colleagues on board pointed out that my left hand was having trouble in turning the pages of my notebook and that I was dragging a left foot. So, after our return to Ahmadabad, I was packed off to hospital for tests, following which an Indian specialist at once pronounced reassuringly on a minor stroke: 'You're fortunate,' he said. It follows that the further reflections have been delayed, and are probably all the better for it, because one leaves the sort of earthquake India suffered at 0846 on January 26 in a state of shock.

It is the random violence of an earthquake—this one measured 7.9 on the Richter scale—that makes you wince. In the old and once beautiful city of Bhuj, our last port of call, solid fortifications had been kicked about like toys. Yet some of the frailer buildings stood intact. Bhuj, 20km south-west of the earthquake's epicentre, seemed to have been in the hands of a giant, blind and enraged.

Our helicopter pilot tipped expertly over two of the worst-hit towns, Bhachau and Anjar, and flew low enough to get pictures. I entered in my notebook, 'Not even after the worst bombing or shelling have I seen anything like Anjar, for it seems to have crumbled to pieces.' Both towns had become shapeless places. Groups of people stood around the ruins. An entry in my notebook ran, 'There are flashes of United Nations blue plastic everywhere, which always betokens homelessness.'

On the main roads running towards these towns, we could see convoys of vehicles moving in with supplies. What real relief could they offer? Tents, yes, and food and water, blankets and family survival kits so that at last some cooking could take place. But the citizens would be living under canvas for months to come, and then a decision might well be taken to rebuild both towns elsewhere.

The irony was that this region of Gujarat looked from the air like prosperous farmland. There was a lot of green, lush, market-garden stuff below us. Now many owners of these fields were dead. You got that sense of loss even more strongly in the shattered villages, where cattle would be nosing their way through the streets, as if searching for their missing owners.

After an earthquake on this scale—the first I've seen—there follows a remorseless cycle of action. First call is to get the bodies of those still alive out of the rubble. That takes four to five days. Our own teams of rescue workers that were rushed over from Britain, whom I met returning home from Ahmadabad, had been toiling in Bhuj for just under a week. Then the most seriously injured have to be transported to hospitals—some by air, but most by road—and in the remoter villages that can take a painfully long time. At the civil hospital in Ahmadabad, they had performed 300 operations inside a week, mostly for head and spinal injuries.

An earthquake smashes water pipes, drains and power lines, so that survivors lose the bare essentials of life and the seeds of an epidemic are sown. Worse, the poorest lose their homes and all shelter. This earthquake occurred during the Indian winter. In Gujarat the days offered early English summer temperatures, but the nights were cold. People left with nothing except the clothes they stood up in had to sleep in the open without cover until blankets and plastic sheeting arrived. In one village I visited they had waited a week for two blankets.

Then in this cruel sequence there follows a melancholy search through the ruins for dead bodies. There is a smell of death, and those clearing the rubble use face-masks. Post-mortems are waived to hasten burials. Even in the smallest villages, nobody could be quite sure how many had died and in the larger towns it was incalculable. No death count was reliable until there had been a house-to-house census.

What I found eerie was the unnatural calm of so many Indians who had been caught up in this tragedy. As we left the stricken village of Bakutra, where no home had been left standing, we met a small group of women bearing cans of water on their heads. They turned serene faces towards us and smiled faintly, as if to say, 'We're perfectly happy in our work, thank you.' Yet almost all of them, we had been told, were needlewomen and earned their living by embroidering cotton—an industry for which Gujarat is famous. Under the ruins of their homes lay their work and all their tools.

There was talk, of course, of post-traumatic stress. A doctor working for the United Nations Children's Fund advised me that those who remained calmest at the time were most likely to suffer after-effects. Children were especially vulnerable. Yet he agreed that the prevailing atmosphere was one of grief, but no hysteria. 'Truly,' I exclaimed at one point, 'I feel more distressed than these people seem to be.' Shock accounted for some of this calm, but by no means all of it. Whence came this gift of looking upon calamity with such serenity?

The last phase in this grim sequence that I witnessed was the hopeless search through piles of rubble for possessions; and in some respects this was the saddest sight of all. In Ahmadabad, where some tower-blocks were toppled, people moved about in crumbling ruins at the risk of their lives, hoping to lay their hands on some treasured object. As the bulldozers crashed about, they stood under trembling walls looking about them. I could hardly bear to watch.

In conflicts I have seen in various parts of the world, most people have fled their homes and are in refugee camps. They do not return until later. But in an earthquake there is no enemy to fear, except Nature. So people stay by their ruined homes, forlornly shifting stone by stone, and searching in hope. To see small children doing this is heart-rending.

In Bhuj, motor-scooters and small cars were humming around such streets as were open. 'There are too many sightseers about,' I said to my companions. Then I observed how many were not sightseers at all—they were there to collect what they could of their belongings. A man and his wife on a scooter passed me. Sitting pillion, she was clutching their radio which had somehow survived. Where would they go? To a camp, an open field, the home of a friend or relative? My eye then lighted on a child flying a kite in the sun. It is such distractions that catch the heart. In the village of Bakutra, I looked at the school where the roof had caved in. The children had been about to celebrate Republic Day with a play when the earthquake started. Through the wreckage, I could glimpse the bunting they had put up for that day, and that seemed most moving of all.

In nearly all human tragedies there is a silver lining. In Gujarat, it was the readiness of the world to throw in a helping hand. Pakistan flew in tents and blankets. China sent experts in seismography, which was as well, for the tremors continued for quite a while. One night, the hospital I was in got shaken. Unknown to me, the staff and some of the patients left the premises. Next morning they told me I had slept soundly through 4.5 on the Richter scale.

India received what the world could offer more gladly than sometimes in the past and by my reckoning, the Indian government responded well to an emergency for which no nation could hope to be fully prepared. Of course, the flood of aid did tend to be concentrated in places where freight planes could land but the UN agencies were starting to shunt some of the traffic directly to the worst-hit villages.

Everywhere, it seemed to me, a strong feeling of community prevailed. India has countless little societies that offer a healing hand. The sense of close neighbourliness that helped us through the worst of the Blitz was much in evidence. I went to Gujarat thinking to find Mother India weeping for her lost children. Nothing of the kind. It was the calm and the courage shown by so many in such dreadful circumstances that stirred one's emotions.

Yet, come to think of it, there was nothing unusual about what happened in India. Every natural or man-made calamity I have witnessed in recent years has left me marvelling at the tenacity of human beings, when everything except life has been taken from them. From where is it drawn? Ah, there's the mystery.

WEEKLY NOTEBOOK

When I was a young man, an international disgrace of our times was the failure of the League of Nations to stop Mussolini from assaulting the people of Abyssinia, in a then remote and little-known corner of Africa. In my old age, the prolonged agony of Darfur in another remote corner of Africa and our inability to stop it is a worse disgrace.

When I visited Darfur in 2004, I had a sense of entering a huge graveyard, of which I could see only the fringes. It is indeed the graveyard of many Africans, and it makes our political posturing over Africa look ridiculous. This persecution in Darfur has been going on for a long time, creating human suffering beyond telling, while the world has stood by, occasionally wagging a finger, but apparently unable to intervene. Khartoum has had it all its own way in Darfur. Why?

Darfur is a long way off, inaccessible and therefore even harder than Iraq to police internationally; but there is more to it than that. Khartoum, once an outcast, has made many friends in the world since it discovered oil. China is increasingly influential.

A few years back, when I visited Sudan's oil fields, and saw the burning of African villages in that region to safeguard work in the fields which are in southern Sudan, it struck me what a great solvent of international morality oil has become in this oil-thirsty world. You don't make enemies of a country that has oil to sell these days. That is one reason why the persecution of Darfur's people in western Sudan by the Janjaweed militia will go on for a while yet and the regime of President Omar el-Bashir in Khartoum can breathe just as easily as Mussolini did as, assisted by mustard gas, he dragged Abyssinia into his empire all those years ago.

Like most of these who have served in the Army and are proud to have done so, dismay was my first reaction to the videos blazoned by the *News of the World*, illustrating gross misconduct by British forces in Iraq two years ago. "Oh, here we go again," I thought. "A few stupid soldiers, soiling our Army's reputation in the world and then cashing in by selling pictures of it. Not the Army of my time . . ."

Like many other "veterans," as Gordon Brown wants to call us, I fumed about this for a couple of days before an altogether different train of thought entered my mind. Sorting out Iraq against a cunning and treacherous minority is simply not comparable with what some of us had to do – those of us at any rate who ended the war in Germany.

True, we were warned that it might be. We got chilling advice about what Germans could do to us when the guns ceased firing. It proved misleading. Settling Germany down, mainly due to the preparations Winston Churchill's government had made in advance, proved a cushy job. Worn out and hungry, a lot of Germans stayed in bed to conserve their energies. I was in a battered Hanover. Not a shot was fired.

I won't make too much of it, but bluntly the comparable preparations made by Blair and Bush for post-war Iraq were not of the same order. We've lost a hundred soldiers on the job, America many more. More trouble lies ahead. But I'm not writing a polemic, only a few lines to cheer up old soldiers who mistakenly feel their successors in Iraq have let them down.

They haven't. They are as good as ever, but caught up in a situation, not of their own making, which, thank God, none of us "veterans" ever had to face.

ROYAL FAMILY

I CARRY MANY SNAPSHOTS of the royal family in my mind.

I remember the look on the face of King George V as he travelled down the Mall on the occasion of his silver jubilee. He was astonished at the reception he was receiving from the crowd. He had never thought overmuch of himself, though he carried us through the First World War and got on famously with the first Labour cabinet to be elected. His death was widely mourned.

I've another portrait of the Prince of Wales, as he still was – later Edward VIII – going round the clubs of East London in the early 1930s. I remember him entering the house occupied by my uncle, who did social work down there, and kicking the butt of his after-dinner cigar into my uncle's grate. I accompanied the Prince on the tour and I was struck by a personality which seemed hard to handle.

I have another snapshot, after the abdication of King Edward VIII, of King George VI and Queen Elizabeth, leaving their home in Piccadilly and departing for Buckingham Palace where they assumed the role of monarchy. One of the remarkable partnerships in the Second World War lay between George VI and Winston Churchill. Churchill had supported King Edward VIII during the abdication crisis, and at first King George VI wondered very much how they would get on. As it turned out, they worked ever more closely together, supporting each other through the intolerable weight of the Second World War.

I have another happy snapshot of a dinner party, given by the Speaker of the House of Commons, to which Princess Elizabeth was invited. Winston Churchill was present and he looked towards the young Princess and future Queen with something which stays in the memory in the same way as the lying-in-state of King George V in Westminster Hall, and the funeral of the Queen Mother.

There were the moments in the life of Princess Diana when she won hearts by her sympathy with those who suffered. I am one of those who, travelling with her in the last month of her life, formed the conclusion that she had set upon a new course because she had discovered her gift for bringing comfort to those in suffering or sorrow.

If you look through the history books, you will not find a period in which we have been better served than by King George V, his son, George VI, and his granddaughter, Queen Elizabeth. And yet, today, people are critical of the monarchy and I find myself asking, why should this be? Regretfully, I come to the conclusion that my own profession has a great deal to do with this. Of course, one must allow for social change, but having done that, I am still left wondering how far we the news media – and here I include television – have been responsible for a decline in public support for the monarchy.

April 1932

THE PRINCE IN THE EAST END

TOUR OF CLUBS AT BETHNAL GREEN

COMEDY OF GAME OF DARTS

PACKET OF "WOODBINES" AS PRIZE

The Prince of Wales and Prince George paid a surprise visit to Bethnal Green last night, where they spent nearly two hours visiting the principal boys' and men's clubs in the borough.

The Princes first went to the local branch of the British Legion, where a concert was in progress. There they were met by the President, Sir Wyndham Deedes, the chairman, Mr E. R. Trott, and the secretary. The Prince of Wales went on the stage and made a short speech.

"As it is a concert," he said, "I am glad you have not asked me to sing a song." The Prince then spent half an hour with the men. He was told that 80 per cent of the members were unemployed, and he asked several men what they were doing.

The Prince next visited the University Club for Boys next door, which has a membership of 500, and spent 35 minutes there. The Prince was particularly interested in a game of miniature bagatelle.

"It is one of the best games of its sort," he said, "but two boards make a better game than one. I shall send you two boards."

Woodbine Wager

Next he came to a dart board. "Now that is a game I never could play," he remarked. When the game in progress was finished, he said, "Give me three darts." In three shots the Prince scored 35. Then turning to the manager of the club, Mr. Riley, he said: "You have a shot."

The manager took the darts. "Is there anything on this?" he asked.

"No," said the Prince, smiling. "A packet of Woodbines?" begged Mr. Riley.

"All right," said the Prince. Then, seeing the manager had failed to equal his score, he said, "let us have the best out of three."

In the last round the Prince was left to score 45. He did so, and won his Woodbines.

"Well, have one yourself," he said to the manager, as he was given the packet, and then smoked one himself.

The Prince next saw the club's gymnasium. "That's a good punch ball," he commented. "I have one myself, and punch it when I feel annoyed with anyone—he turned to his equerry—like yourself, for instance."

Afterwards the Prince visited the Webb Club and joined his brother, who had been to the Repton Boys' Club and the Oxford House Bookshop at the Oxford House Settlement for Students.

September 1936

"£150 TO KILL THE KING"

McMahon Sentenced: Story of a Plot

George Andrew McMahon was sentenced to twelve months' hard labour at the Old Bailey yesterday on the charge of "unlawfully and wilfully producing near the person of the King a pistol with intent to harm his Majesty."

The jury, which included three women, were absent only ten minutes before returning their verdict of "Guilty."

Earlier in the day, on the direction of the Judge, McMahon was found not guilty on two other counts in the indictment—"unlawfully possessing a fire-arm and ammunition with intent to endanger life" and "Presenting at or near the person of the King a pistol with intent to break the peace."

During his examination in the witness-box by Mr. St. John Hutchinson, K.C., his counsel, McMahon told the Court a remarkable story of a plot instigated by a foreign Power, by which he was to shoot the King for £150.

He alleged that at the end of October, 1935, he was in touch with this Power, and was asked to do spy work. He said that he informed the War Office; that he had been put in touch with this Power by an Englishman belonging to a political body in England with the same objects as the foreign Power; that he had met at the Embassy of this foreign Government a certain "baron," and that representatives of this Power then tried to inflame him, as an Irishman, against Britain.

Attack Suggested

Mr. St. John Hutchinson asked McMahon: After a time before the Trooping the Colour did they make any suggestion—direct suggestion—to you to do anything?—Yes.

What was the suggestion?—An arrangement was made that the King should be attacked at the Trooping the Colour.

Did they give you any reason why he should be attacked?—They told me that it would benefit this country.

379

Why should it benefit this country for the King to be shot?—
They talked about it at length, and one of the reasons was that
certain parts of the Empire would be handed over to other countries.

And some of the colonies?—Yes.

McMahon said the idea was that if there was turmoil going on in
this country, Britain would be less likely to interfere in foreign
affairs.

He said that nine men were to accompany him, and arrangements
had been made for his escape.

A man from M.I.5 Department of the War Office, to whom
McMahon alleged he had reported these arrangements on the
Monday preceding the Constitution Hill incident, was said by Mr.
St. John Hutchinson to have been subpoenaed for the case and to be
present in court. He did not give evidence, however.

McMahon said that the letter he wrote to Sir John Simon,
referring to certain private grievances, had been dictated by two of
the men in order that suspicion would be thrown on him alone.
McMahon said he had no intention of shooting.

"Did you hear from them," asked Mr. St. John Hutchinson, "that
if this plot failed the King was to be shot in France?"

"Yes," was the reply.

McMahon, who was neatly dressed in striped trousers, white shirt
and collar, dark tie and black jacket, remained calm and unmoved
throughout the greater part of the day. He refused an offer to be
seated in the witness stand (due to his foot injury) and stood
throughout his examination of an hour and ten minutes.

His voice rose sharply on occasions during his cross-examination
by the Attorney-General (Sir Donald Somervell).

The Attorney-General suggested that the story of the plot was a
product of McMahon's imagination.

"I wish to God it were," was the reply.

Later McMahon cried, "I want to go to prison. I want you to
give me the heaviest sentence possible. It is only by doing that that
you can save my life from the people I have given away."

The court was crowded all day, and there was not a vacant seat
when the Attorney-General began his last speech. He suggested to
the jury that a large number of McMahon's statements were wholly
inconsistent with what he said in the police court, and he asked them
to accept the police court story.

FANTASTIC

Mr. St. John Hutchinson, in his final speech for the defence, said that McMahon's story might sound like "Oppenheim at his best or even Edgar Wallace at his worst," but because it was fantastic it did not follow that it was untrue.

When the jury had given their verdict, Mr. Justice Greaves-Lord, addressing McMahon, said: "I can well understand the jury not being misled by the story you told today. I do not want, and I am not going to make you into a sort of fancy hero. No description would be further from truth, and therefore I am not going to pass sentence which would have any tendency to do that."

McMahon stood still and expressioness while the Judge spoke to him. He turned away as the Judge pronounced sentence of . . . "Twelve months," and was brought round by his warders to face the court as Mr. Justice Greaves-Lord concluded . . . "with hard labour."

January 1936

110,000 MOURNERS AT THE LYING-IN-STATE

VISIT LAST NIGHT BY THE KING AND QUEEN MARY

QUEEN MAUD'S TRIBUTE

When the doors of Westminster Hall closed to the public at 10.30 last night—half an hour later than the time fixed—110,004 people had passed before the bier of King George.

By 6 o'clock in the evening, the numbers exceeded 80,000, and up to the closing hour the rate of passing was 9,000 an hour. At times the queue stretched as far as Lambeth Bridge—a mile away.

Because of the press of people, indeed, Westminster Hall was kept open for half an hour after the appointed hour for closing.

The King and Queen Mary, with members of the Royal Family, paid an unexpcted visit last night to Westminster Hall. During their stay—about a quarter of an hour—the admission of the public was interrupted.

The Royal visit was not realised by the waiting throng.

At the Palace Yard entrance, two Royal cars had drawn up, and the King and Queen Mary, the Duke and Duchess of York, the Duke of Gloucester, and the King and Queen of Norway, who had arrived in London in the afternoon, alighted.

They walked quickly through the members' entrance, and entered Westminster Hall under the archway. The Guard of Honour around the coffin alone were with the Royal party, who, after remaining for nearly ten minutes, drove back to Buckingham Palace.

Endless, Silent Throng in Slow Procession

By Our Special Representative

The vast and unceasing pilgrimage to Westminster Hall began yesterday many hours before the dawn, and lasted, through six hours of darkness, into the night.

Where, in the darkest hours of Thursday, there had been hundreds, there came thousands in the early morning of yesterday; and when darkness fell again tens of thousands were waiting.

The shape of the multitude, marshalled and controlled by police, which were strengthened throughout the day, spread in line, ten deep, from the narrow entrance of the Hall, where King George was lying, for a mile to the west along the riverside. So great was the press that those who arrived in the late afternoon were standing opposite the Tate Gallery.

Since so many were aged, weak, and infirm; and others, young children who could scarcely walk, the reverence and devotion of the people were not more remarkable than their great fortitude.

PATIENT WAITING

It seemed not to matter whether the last mourners reached to Lambeth Bridge, where their destination was scarcely in view; or to the Tate Gallery, where it was out of sight.

None was discouraged to join the queue because it was a mile long. None shrank from enduring the restless weary hours of waiting and discomfort.

Yet these were rewarded. For when their pilgrimage ended (after one, or two, or three hours), upon the steps of Westminster Hall, they were able not only to pay homage, but also to see the temporary resting place of their late King in circumstances of beauty, simplicity and tranquillity, which can never fade from memory.

When the first stroke of eight sounded, the morning was still so grey and heavy that it was not possible from the Hall's entrance to perceive where the crowd began. The sombre dress of nearly every man and woman was lost and shaded against the grey walls to which they had been shepherded.

It was a solemn crowd; very silent, very still and reverent.

Some were dressed entirely in black. Others had been able to find only a single token of their grief to wear.

TRAVELLERS FROM AFAR

At first they were ushered across the Hall five and six abreast, so that by ten o'clock the crowd had dwindled, and there was practically no queue waiting. But it increased when great numbers of cars began to arrive, some of which had travelled many miles through the early morning.

With them came classes of school children, mostly very young; and though the older ones of the crowd showed little physical distress when they left the Hall, nearly every child was brought to tears.

At eleven o'clock, the end of the waiting crowd had reached the parapet of Lambeth Bridge. It so covered the pavement that the great and incessant stream of people approaching from Westminster in search of the queue's end were pressed into the roadway.

At this hour about 20,000 mourners had already passed the doors of Westminster Hall. All traffic moving west along Millbank was stopped, and sudden arrangements had to be made to clear the entrances to the bridge.

Eventually, later in the afternoon, the bridge also was closed to all traffic, which crossed instead Westminster and Vauxhall bridges.

At noon it was apparent that neither the swollen, congested traffic stream, nor the rapidly lengthening line of people, would in any way check the great human flow which poured from the direction of Westminster and Victoria.

Far Stretching Line

It was difficult to tell whether those walking along the roadway to the end of the queue were in greater numbers than those moving toward Westminster Hall.

With anxiety as well as wonder, the mounted policemen saw the crowd fall further and further behind, until newcomers stood level with the pillars of the Tate Gallery.

When the afternoon faded into evening this crowd was still growing. Still very silently, but insistently, they pressed further westward along the River. It was evident that many would have to be turned back if the Hall was to be closed at ten o'clock.

Sixty thousand had been through Westminster Hall at five o'clock, and it seemed that at least 12,000 more were waiting. Police began to warn those at the end of the queue that they might have to wait two hours and a half. Yet none left, and always they were joined by others. Hundreds of mothers were carrying children in their arms; and as many more had children by their side.

Just before six o'clock the flow of people at Palace Yard was interrupted to allow space for two closed cars.

Time Limit Fixed

Early in the evening it had become clear to the authorities that steps to cut short the procession would have to be taken if the door at St. Stephen's end of Westminster Hall was to be closed at the prearranged hour.

The police decided to intimate to the crowd that anyone who arrived at Lambeth Bridge after 9.30 p.m. would not be admitted to join the queue. Their cars patrolled Millbank vicinity issuing orders to the constables who were marshalling the queues.

A large body of police was kept in reserve at Lambeth Bridge to guard against the possibility of a last minute rush, but up to 10 o'clock the file was moving slowly and in an orderly manner towards the doorway.

Last night King George's robe was brought to the Hall by his valet, as the final touch to the sombre magnificence of the scene.

By 10.30 p.m. the last of the queue had reached the doorway at St. Stephen's. It was not necessary for the police to enforce extraordinary measures to discontinue the file.

The remaining hundreds passed into Westminster Hall. When the last had entered, the door was closed and barred. Parliament-square by 11 p.m. was a normal London thoroughfare.

January 1937

OFFICIAL DETAILS OF THE CORONATION

ELEVEN FULL WEEKS OF CELEBRATIONS

THE KING'S BROADCAST TO THE EMPIRE

Details of Coronation arrangements and celebrations, approved by the King, are announced to-day. From early May—a week before the Coronation in Westminster Abbey on May 12—until the end of July there will be a round of more than thirty important events.

These include Royal Courts, State Banquets, Garden Parties and Court Balls at Buckingham Palace, a week's visit of the Court to Scotland during July, and a Review of ex-Service Men by the King.

For eleven weeks of the three months of May, June and July, the events as outlined in this programme will provide the most magnificent summer of celebration which London has known for a quarter of a century.

Coronation events will open on May 5 and 6, when Courts will be held. They will not end until July 22, on which date the last Royal Garden Party will take place.

The King will broadcast to the Empire on the evening of Coronation Day. His Review of ex-Service Men will take place on Sunday, June 27. The visit of their Majesties to Scotland will last from July 5 until July 11.

The first State Banquet will be on May 10 after the arrival of Envoys and Deputations on the same day. On the day before the Coronation, May 11, there will be a Presentation of Addresses and Loyal Greetings by Prime Ministers of the Dominions and by representatives of India and of the Colonial Empire. The King and Queen will give a Luncheon Party at Buckingham Palace for British Commonwealth representatives, and the evening Dinner Party will be given by the Duke of Gloucester.

Foreign Office Dinner

There will be a Dinner to the King and Queen by the Secretary of State for Foreign Affairs at the Foreign Office on May 14, and this will be followed by the first Court Ball at Buckingham Palace.

On May 19 the King and Queen will drive through London to lunch at the Guildhall. They will pass through the Strand, Fleet-street, and Cheapside, and will return by way of Queen Victoria-street and the Embankment.

The Naval Review by the King will take place the following day.

On Empire Day, Monday, May 24, the King and Queen attend a Service at St. Paul's Cathedral. The Prime Minister will give a Dinner for the King and Queen at No. 10, Downing-street on May 25. There will be a Court Ball at Buckingham Palace on the evening of Queen Mary's birthday, May 26. On the following evening the King and Queen will be present at an evening Reception by the London County Council.

Trooping The Colour

The first event in June will be celebration of the King's Birthday and Trooping the Colour. There will be Investitures on June 10 and 11, and a Levee and Garden Party on June 22.

On their return from Scotland, the King and Queen will visit Wales on July 14 and 15.

If the weather permits, street decorations will remain in place until midnight on Thursday, May 27. Selected buildings in London will be floodlit on the evening of Wednesday, May 12, and on subsequent evenings up to Whit Monday, May 17, inclusive.

It is announced by the Coronation Committee that every effort is being made to provide seating accommodation along the route of the Coronation procession without encroaching upon ground to which the public can claim right of access without payment.

Seats For 85,000

Seats are being, or will be, erected along the East side of the East Carriage Drive in Hyde Park and in Hamilton Gardens, on both sides of Constitution Hill, in the Queen Victoria Memorial Gardens, on both sides of the Mall, within the precincts of the Palace of

Westminster and in Parliament Square, and in Whitehall Gardens along the Embankment.

From these seats about 85,000 persons will be able to view the procession without obstruction from trees, &c. Standing space for an additional 30,000 will be reserved in Constitution Hill and at the Queen Victoria Memorial, and on the pavements round Parliament Square.

After provision has been made for visitors from the Dominions, India and the Colonies, the seats on the stands, for which charge will be made, and the free standing space will be allocated to representatives of public life. This selection is being given careful consideration.

QUEEN AND COMMONWEALTH

Early in July Mr John Turner, who had lately succeeded Mr Trudeau as Liberal Prime Minister of Canada, whistled into London by jet and travelled to Windsor.

He came for a hurried audience with the Queen of Canada to discuss the awkward conjunction of her forthcoming visit to three Canadian provinces and his own ill-starred impulse to stage an early General Election.

Without fuss, the Queen clearly intimated to her Prime Minister that if that was how he wanted it, so be it; that her firm policy was not to visit a country during an election campaign; but she could postpone the visit.

Her grateful Prime Minister returned to Canada, fought and lost his elections on Sept. 4 by an enormous margin and plays no further useful part in this story.

It is worth recalling only because it tells us something about the Crown which is so taken for granted that nearly everyone over-looks it.

There is no one else in the world today (which we commonly regard as dominated by two super-Powers) who enjoys this particular relationship with other large countries. It is hardly news but as the Queen starts the 22nd visit of her reign to Canada, to mark bicentennials in Ontario and New Brunswick, it is worthy of remark.

The Commonwealth itself, which is news when its sometimes quarrelsome Prime Ministers meet for their conference, gets rather a bad Press nowadays. It is fashionable and sometimes justifiable to observe (as this newspaper does) that its ethnic, political and ideological differences are hard to reconcile and it might be wiser to recognise that fact.

This was in fact first recognised by Lord Balfour in 1926 (the year the Queen was born). He drafted a formula which recognised in effect that Rudyard Kipling's empire had reached its close; and which left allegiance to the Crown as the only common bond. Round that was built the Statute of Westminster a year or two later.

So this week's tour is entirely a matter between the Queen and the Government of Canada. British Ministers will be aware that they have no part in it. So will British High Commissioners.

How, if you come to think of it, could they expect to play a useful part? For they also represent HMG, not the Crown, and the jewel in the Crown, here or in the Commonwealth, is immunity from politics or political controversy. Even the Governor-General, who represents the Queen, not her Government, takes a back seat.

The Governor-General will join Canada's Prime Minister to greet the Queen on arrival. Then he can return home. He does not join the tour, throughout which the Queen is exclusively in Canada's hands.

Some guidance has been offered by her own staff in London but Canada has been left free to make the arrangements they want. The Queen has a Canadian secretary permanently in Ottawa, who regularly supplies the briefs which she has to study. Nothing comes from our Foreign and Commonwealth Office. Transport throughout the tour is handled by the Canadian Forces—except when she is in a train.

Up to a dozen members of the Palace staff here travel with her. They have formed over the years bonds of their own with the Commonwealth people. At any point on the tour the British or Canadian entourages could change hats with each other. This rather special sort of private kinship aids harmony—and getting to the right place at the right time—but the operation is planned, staffed and executed by Canadians. When, after an earlier visit to Canada, the Queen visited Seattle in the United States, Canada provided her escort on the grounds that they were closer neighbours to Seattle than we are.

No differences can arise between the British Government and the Canadian Government about where the Queen shall go, what she shall do or say, because the British Government is not consulted.

One root of Canada's constitutional crisis in 1982 lay in the fact that advice tendered by British Ministers and Canadian Ministers differed. Nothing of this kind can arise during the next fortnight; so the Crown is protected from controversy.

Within Canada there are of course differences, most marked in relationships between Quebec and the rest. Canadians outside Quebec regard Queen Elizabeth as their Queen. French-Canadians see her in much the same light as they do in Paris: head of a famous family which does a good job, and is entitled to warm respect.

There is no hostility even from this quarter and remarkably little republicanism. There is a republican movement in Western Canada, but it has not yet managed to return an elected candidate. All the Queen's speeches in Canada carry passages in the French language, which present no problem to her because, like New Brunswick, she is bilingual.

The days of the grand tour, coast-to-coast, are over. When those visits were made by ship and train they were long-drawn and elaborate and sometimes lasted three exhausting months. The jet enables the Queen to set about it much as she would a tour of Lancashire or Cornwall. A number of events in two or three provinces not recently visited are pulled out and made the focus of the tour.

Because this visit has been postponed the itinerary remains the same but the main events have had to be changed; so presumably there is subdued disappointment for some.

These limited expeditions to particular parts of Canada, by contrast with the grand tour, are much closer to the spirit of the thing, with the Queen doing much what she might be doing here. She was in Canada last year, twice in 1982.

Moreover the Queen will be in territory visited so often by members of her own family that the match is far closer than it was when there really was a British Empire. Within days of her conversation with Mr John Turner, the Duke of Edinburgh was in Canada for a regimental occasion. In her own private circle the Queen will speak familiarly of personalities in the Commonwealth—"Oh, he was a friend of my father"—who are unknown to her own staff.

This familiarity seems to arouse rather than diminish popular interest. Canada is a relatively thinly populated country, but the turn-out will be comparable with crowd scenes here; and in places there will be flag-waving, out of which (except at the Proms) we have been indoctrinated here.

It might be argued that Canada is a special case. The magnetic pull of America, economically, culturally, industrially, is powerful. It is something most Canadians consciously resist. The link to the Crown helps. It is a counterweight.

Australia, much farther away, has no corresponding anxiety. The Commonwealth cord may have become less binding there, but not the Crown.

Mr Hawke, the Labour Premier there, shows signs of recognising this. Though not royalist by nature, like the citizens of Quebec, he respects the family.

In a world which has remorselessly politicised so much, the Crown has a fresh appeal for many. Jamaica also has a Labour Government. It does not diminish the Queen's welcome there.

The most modern communications run on a hair-thin line called fibre optic. It is not altogether fanciful to see the Crown's thin purple line as comparable. One is modern; the other is ancient. It is rather comforting—and no small tribute to the House of Windsor—to think that they can co-exist in the same world and at the same time.

ROYAL WEDDING: LET US REJOICE

*WILLIAM DEEDES CELEBRATES "A FAMILY AFFAIR"
THAT IS ALSO A JOYOUS EVENT FOR THE NATION*

As the wedding bells ring out, this is the moment to dwell not only on the young couple whose day it truly is, but also on the family which is at the centre of the marriage being solemnized in Westminster Abbey. Millions will be watching the ceremony from afar, but it is essentially a family affair—a family which is drawn together today, as families are at all weddings.

It is a joyous event which causes us to think and to voice thoughts which at other times we are often too reticent or too unthinking to express.

Those who witnessed the Silver Jubilee of King George V more than half a century ago, are entitled to remark that this generation is richly endowed by its royals. If we were able to gather all their diaries together and mark up the entries for this year or next, we would discover that collectively they are the most ubiquitously active family on the throne in English history. Air travel can speed them to duties all over the globe. Three-quarters of these duties pass unnoticed here yet precious few parts of the Commonwealth, old or new, are out of touch with a member of the royal family for long. The same can be said of our own cities.

It is also a diverse and attractive family with a cast of strong and colourful characters. They do not all lead uneventful lives: how dull that would be. In the past Prince Andrew attracted more media attention than might be considered desirable. But it must be entered that some of his activities were greatly entertaining! Princess Anne also went through a difficult phase as far as her image was concerned—mainly because journalists ignored a wise axiom, "Never bandy words with a woman on a horse." We might suppose the Queen Mother to be above criticism. But no, when the Duchess of Windsor died there were stories that bad blood lay between them.

These stories are important because they illustrate a significant fact of contemporary life. Our royal family is more exposed today than ever before. Tennyson's lines were written long ago: *wearing the white flower of a blameless life/before a thousand peering littlenesses in that fierce light which beats upon a throne/and blackens every blot.* The light today is fiercer, and unceasing.

Amid all the joys of this very public wedding, hardly a slip or a gesture or smile or kiss will go uncommented upon or uncaptured on film and tape. What should astonish us is not the occasional, inevitable mishap but that under that remorseless scrutiny we spot so little that is wrong.

Over the years, our Royals have proved themselves to be adaptable to an extraordinary degree. More sensitively perhaps than many of us, they take stock of the times in which they serve and with infinite care adjust their bearings.

In this as in much else the main influence within the royal family circle comes from the Queen herself. She more than any other has changed the role of the monarch in relation to her people. When she is in foreign countries she does not always travel in closed carriages nor sit on a remote dais. She enjoys walk-abouts. She is on far easier terms with the modern Commonwealth, which has some awkward corners these days, than some of her ministers.

In Australia where there was talk of royalty being "old hat" the Queen won hearts wherever she went. The Prime Minister, Mr Robert Hawke, who had previously shown distinctly Republican tendencies, sent Prince Andrew and Sarah Ferguson warm greetings on their engagement and begged them to come to Australia soon.

As we watch and listen to today's wedding service it would surely not be inappropriate to allow such happy reflections to cross our minds and, thus reflecting, rejoice at the happiness we feel on their behalf.

For me personally there is this to add. The first royal wedding within my experience was that of the Duke and Duchess of Kent, George and Marina, who married in 1934. My portion was to travel on their train from London to Birmingham because they were starting their honeymoon at Himley Hall. It seemed an odd mission and I inquired what precisely was required of me. "You are to report rejoicing along the way," they said. And indeed there was rejoicing. From every station we passed, cheers rang out.

The recollection is relevant. On this day when Andrew weds Sarah, and so adds another member to this remarkable family, let there be rejoicing all along the way.

THIS WILL ONLY MAKE IT WORSE

By authorising his biography, the Prince of Wales has told his side of the story of the break-up of his marriage. But, argues W. F. Deedes, it will only further damage the Royal Family, and call into question the Prince's suitability to take the throne

How is the world now expected to judge a man who, in seeking to justify himself, explains to his authorised biographer how he came to marry the wrong woman, and who blames his father for urging him into the mismatch? It is not the behaviour of princes. So judgments where they matter most will be unfavourable to the confessions of the Prince of Wales, and fears for the throne heightened.

It reminds me of the last scene in *Hamlet*, I said yesterday to a friend who asked what I thought of the Dimbleby story. "O God! Horatio, what a wounded name . . ." No, came the reply; it is a Greek tragedy. But even the writer of Greek tragedies would be stretched to convey this wretched scene in which an heir to the throne and his estranged wife are found in full public view throwing the book at each other.

What a feast for the publishers. What a disappointment to those who share some of the Prince of Wales's ideals, and wish a bright future for them. What a blow to privacy. What a wrench for the throne.

Broken marriages draw sympathy. But to seek sympathy by, in effect, calling public attention to failures of the marriage bed is a bewildering misjudgment.

Broken marriages disturb children too. Does either parent reckon what this perpetual public parade of private grievances inflicts upon their sons? The throne and those next to it are mainly about example. They are the first victims of these petty revelations.

The second victim is our concept of a family on the throne. Unwittingly perhaps, contemplating only his own woes, the Prince of Wales speaks of an ultimatum from his father, of remoteness from his mother. In what comes sadly close to dishonouring his father and his mother, it will appear at least to some that this future Head of the Faith has broken not one, but two commandments.

What purpose does the Prince of Wales suppose is served by this outpouring? The suggestion that it is a biography to mark his 25 years as Prince of Wales is a figleaf. This is a self-centred act, and altogether contrary to what we are entitled to expect from a future occupant of the throne. It is one thing for an unhappily married man to look for comfort elsewhere, to seek a confidante. To throw the doors of his unhappy private life open to public inspection will seem to many an extraordinary thing to do, an act of pure self-indulgence.

It is of no service to the crown. Nor, as the Prince seems to think, will it end his torment. He's scotch'd the snake, not killed it. A thousand clues in this so-called biography will be eagerly followed up, discussed, debated and disproved. There will be no end to it. A whole sheaf of material lies here for further exploration—and exploitation.

Though they are said to have worked closely together for two years, there has been a fundamental and fatal misunderstanding between the Prince of Wales and his biographer, Jonathan Dimbleby. It emerged after the television interview in June, when Dimbleby asked the Prince of Wales if he had ever been unfaithful to his wife. "If I had not asked that question," Dimbleby admitted later, "I would have been pilloried."

In other words I had, for my own good name and reputation, to take the Prince of Wales on to a more dangerous course than he would have wished to run. That professional egoism is reflected again in what we have seen of the book. It seems to have been overlooked when this foolish compact was made between Prince and journalist. If the Prince is now—as he hopes—to make a fresh start he must emphatically choose a fresh pack of advisers.

His advisers are said to regard this pact with Dimbleby as a gamble worth taking. What kind of advisers can tender such advice? This is a gamble with the future of the monarchy. Agreed, the Prince of Wales is partly a victim of a fresh balance which has been struck between public figures and the press. Newspapers are more intrusive than they were. They are crueller to private tragedies, and they constantly confuse the public interest with what excites the public.

But these are facts of life which royal advisers should recognise. There has been this fatal misapprehension in royal circles that adverse publicity from one branch of the news media can be reversed by resorting to another branch. This book is a prime example of it.

Now a second, subsidiary struggle will open up between those responsible for giving advice to the Queen and those who advise her Heir. It can, in my view, be resolved in only one way. Members of this family must draw closer together. They must become more aware than they are of each other's inner feelings, fears and hopes. Their respective households, their programmes of duty, the great entourage which Diana found so intimidating create an unnatural remoteness between members of this family. This whole unhappy affair is coloured by that remoteness.

It is not a new development. The late Duke of Windsor, when he was Prince of Wales, felt sadly distant from his father, sometimes complaining bitterly to friends of the lack of understanding he felt from that quarter. It seemed to me at the time that only after he had gone did his mother, Queen Mary, display in quiet ways the great love she had for him.

This present estrangement cannot be resolved by shunting advisers around. Fundamentally it is a family affair; and those who wish them well will join a prayer that they may feel able to draw closer together.

I hear chortling among the tabloid newspapers at this catastrophe. How can they well be accused hereafter of injuring the throne if the Prince of Wales chooses to shoot himself in the foot? This is hypocrisy.

It *is* abominable behaviour by sections of the press in this country that has driven the Prince of Wales into this sorry enterprise. Dimbleby's tale makes plain that the Prince of Wales was driven well nigh mad by it. Those of us who have had to talk to the couple about their private dreads know the reason why. Their phobia about pervasive reporters and photographers and damage that might be inflicted on their children by these incessant attentions was not at all misplaced. In so far as the Prince and Princess have plainly lost their balance in life, some of our newspapers have much to answer for.

Why was Diana a favourite in the first place? Why was the Prince of Wales pushed towards her? In part, at least, it was because of awareness that she was a girl without a significant past. Unlike the Duchess of York, she offered no opening to the prurient journalist. There was nobody to tell him or sell to him "my nights with Diana". To those influencing the Prince of Wales it enhanced the attractions of Diana.

From the betrothal onwards the uneven partnership was seen by journalists as a juicy target, a matcher for any soap opera running on the box. It began, if I remember rightly, with the story in a national newspaper about the couple spending a night together on the royal train. It was a foretaste of much to come. The Queen invited editors to the palace to discuss confidentially the difficulties in which the Princess found herself, and appealed quite vainly for more considerate treatment.

Secure in the belief that members of the Royal Family rarely sue for defamation, or complain to the Press Commission, the journalists gleefully converted the marriage into a soap opera, fact and fiction inextricably entwined.

When for other reasons the marriage began to crumble—oh, bliss! She looked like this. He looked like that. The paparazzi were in ecstasy and getting richer all the time. The papers sold. I have a collection of them; and glancing through it yesterday, I saw what a test it had been of stoicism. Diana is not a stoic. A deadly combination of private misery and tabloid torment broke her. Now, later and more damagingly, it has done the same to the Prince of Wales.

We are, though it is rarely acknowledged, a wonderfully stable parliamentary democracy. We were tested by the abdication of great uncle David nearly 60 years ago. This botch will test us again.

Standing back a little, flipping over my press cuttings, I am left with one thought uppermost. It is whether an absentee landlord like Rupert Murdoch of News International should have so much ordering of our estate.

WOULD WE ACCEPT THEIR MARRIAGE?

The divorce of Camilla Parker Bowles prompts speculation about her future relationship with Prince Charles. W. F. Deedes assesses the likely public reaction

We can hardly claim to have been taken by surprise. Everyone has heard the name of Mrs Parker Bowles, and knows why it is familiar. Since that famous exchange in the Dimbleby television interview last year, we have known how matters stood. So the sense of shock which struck the country almost 60 years ago, when King Edward VIII put love before the Throne, is lacking.

On the other hand, that crisis was resolved in 10 short days. On December 1, 1936, the Bishop of Bradford, Dr A. W. F. Blunt, broke the long silence that had more or less prevailed over the King's affair with Mrs Simpson. On December 10 the instrument of Abdication was signed. Unquestionably, the speed with which it occurred limited damage to the Crown.

Now we are confronted with what is bound to be an altogether more drawn-out and potentially damaging affair. It is something everyone can understand, on which strong personal views are held, on which arguments will go far into the night. It is an issue on which friendships may founder and even husbands and wives may quarrel.

Worse, there is no easy outcome to be seen on the most distant horizon. This is the stuff on which the popular press—well, let us say, all of us—thrive. Mrs Parker Bowles, for all we know, may elect to go alone to the furthest end of the earth. Would that quell speculation and invention in our world of newspapers? I can think of nothing more likely to stimulate it.

In any calculations we make about the consequences of this divorce, we must take into the reckoning the well-nigh unendurable pressures from the news media which will now surround the Prince of Wales and Mrs Parker Bowles. It could well be strong enough to influence the outcome. Few outside our world of newspapers can easily grasp the sort of pressure which has surrounded Mrs Parker Bowles in recent months.

In what many will regard, not unjustly, as a pretty squalid affair, she has emerged, as someone put it yesterday, as the only gentleman. No word of indiscretion has come from her. In the dirty market of royal revelations and lucrative publishing contracts, her hands are clean. I have long thought my friend Denis Thatcher came through his years of temptation at No 10 from different branches of the news media with distinction. Mrs Parker Bowles outclasses him.

Not that it will count in her favour with the public. People who strive to keep out of the limelight do not win public favour these days. Reticence irks the news media, which likes to get everything out in the open. Privacy smacks of privilege and elitism. People's curiosity is insatiable; they have come to expect it to be indulged. Sadly, the impeccable behaviour of Mrs Parker Bowles will win her no Brownie points.

People will declare that this affair has parallels with the Abdication crisis of 1936. There are some. There are also important differences. Mrs Simpson had an extremely hard side to her. As one shrewd judge put it at the time, she was fundamentally selfish. She thoroughly enjoyed the attentions of the Prince of Wales and relished his expensive gifts. There were moments during the crisis when she appeared willing to withdraw from the scene. I found them totally unconvincing.

The biggest difference of all is in ourselves; how we thought then, and how we think now. There was, in the first place, an Empire to reckon with, and Baldwin, Prime Minister, thought that opinion from that quarter had to be taken seriously. The Church had an influence which it lacks today. The Archbishop's role in the Abdication, somewhat exaggerated I thought at the time, aroused intense bitterness among the King's friends and admirers.

Gerald Bullett expressed it in these four pungent lines:

> My Lord Archbishop, what a scold you are!
> And when your man is down how bold you are!
> Of charity how oddly scant you are!
> How Lang, O Lord, how full of Cantuar!

Whatever turn this affair may take, one cannot imagine the present Archbishop of Canterbury bearing down on the Prince of Wales with bell, book and candle.

But the main shift comes from within ourselves. At a critical point in the Abdication crisis Baldwin privately made one of his appeals to Conservative MPs, among whom he detected dangerous differences about the King's position. He asked them to abandon fixed weekend engagements and to go into the pubs and the clubs to find out what ordinary people were thinking. When the party next met, its collective mind was resolved. On his own terms, the King had to go.

What might Members of Parliament from London, the Midlands, the West Country hear in the pubs and the clubs of today? The Crown does not occupy the high ground it did in the 1930s. The so-called Establishment holds nothing like the influence it did in that decade. Divorce is taken less seriously. Partnership without marriage is no longer a matter of remark at any level of society.

A considerable obstacle confronting the Prince of Wales, if he seeks public acceptance for a permanent relationship with Mrs Parker Bowles, is the support enjoyed by the Princess of Wales—not a factor in the 1936 crisis. Notwithstanding the mistakes she has made, Diana is widely regarded as the wronged wife. That view will persist for some time yet. Insofar as there has been a contest between them for public support, the Prince is the loser.

Furthermore among officers and gentlemen, or what is left of them, the Prince of Wales will stand in low regard. The position of Brigadier Parker Bowles, a wholly innocent figure in all this, leaves the Prince of Wales in a thoroughly bad light. There is a whiff of arrogance about the Windsor family's attitude towards other people's spouses. Edward VII's attitude was flagrant, though he found a certain safety in numbers. Edward VIII declared that life was intolerable without the woman he loved. The fact remains she was someone else's wife. Here we see it again.

Yet when all that is said, we need to look realistically at the present state of mind in this country. In matters of the heart it has become remarkably tolerant. Given a sufficient passage of time, I judge there to be no outcome to this affair which one can confidently assert would be *publicly* unacceptable.

Other factors may prevail. The constitutionalists will have a lot to tell us. There are the Queen's wishes to consider. There are the private intentions of Mrs Parker Bowles herself. There is the havoc which sections of the news media may wreak.

But we should not pretend to be other than what we are. We

have become more indulgent about private morality. We are inattentive to matters of high principle. The Church carries small influence outside its own flock. Values have become relative, not absolute. In our cosy homespun philosophy, morality which conflicts with happiness is unacceptable. Given this public tolerance, I judge there to be no outcome to this affair which can be confidently ruled out.

May 1995

QUEEN MOTHER STARS AGAIN IN THAT FAMOUS BALCONY SCENE

Half a century after the war W. F. Deedes reflects on the central figure in a touching Palace tableau

It was a moment that caught the heart and almost a hundred years of our history. Well into the next century some will be telling their children: "I was there at that famous moment. I was outside Buckingham Palace when Queen Elizabeth the Queen Mother stepped out on to the balcony."

"But why was she there, Granny?" "Because she embodied so much that some of us felt so deeply about at that time. It was 50 years after a long and terrible war; and as Queen in that war she had been steadfast in danger, a comfort to many who suffered—and her smile had kept hope alive when things looked pretty bad."

Some of us felt all that and more as this figure stepped on to the Buckingham Palace balcony yesterday, just after Vera Lynn had led us in A Nightingale Sang in Berkeley Square. The Queen Mother stood in the centre, a little way in front of her daughters, the Queen and the Princess Margaret.

In the same balcony scene 50 years earlier there were two other figures. Churchill and King George VI were there. Princess Elizabeth wore the uniform of the ATS. Now the three women stood alone. The cheering was fervent enough, especially when those saviours, the Hurricane, the Blenheim and the Lancaster, began to fly over us; but naturally it carried a different tone from the cheer they had raised in May 1945. The nation then was rendering heartfelt thanks for its deliverance. Yesterday it was celebrating the anniversary of a famous victory and many who remembered nothing of 1945 had come to share an exciting hour.

"Yes," said the woman next to me in a low voice, "I'm just celebrating. I shan't be here fifty years hence." She spoke for the majority.

What evokes memories is music. Soldiers' singing on the eve of battle carries an echo through the rest of your life. As we sang Bless 'em All and Vera Lynn's Bluebirds over the White Cliffs of Dover, I felt I had an inkling of what must be passing through the Queen Mother's mind.

Close to where I stood outside the Palace railings was a party of French school children, behaving fairly badly. They prompted me to look over their heads towards the multitude outside the Palace, stretching far back into the Green Park. I reflected on the experiences this central figure had undergone in her life and wondered how many of those now singing the songs and waving flags were aware of them.

She was "called suddenly to the most tremendous task on earth," as Prime Minister Baldwin had expressed it in 1936 when Queen Elizabeth and King George VI were summoned to fill a sudden gap on the throne.

Soon afterwards came this war, in the course of which she had expressed pride in the fact that Buckingham Palace had received its share of the bombs. There was enough there to exercise the emotions, without the singing, the flypast and the flags.

At the climax of it all the Red Arrows flew, as always, with wonderful precision and trailing lovely colours, reminding us that even after 50 years of European peace not everyone has taken off their uniform.

The fire crackers bursting over our heads were another matter. At my distance from the balcony I thought the royal ladies looked startled. Some of the old soldiers, I reckoned (simply out of a sense of discipline, mind you) would be looking round for slit trenches that were not there.

When it came to Rule Britannia and Land of Hope and Glory, the Queen Mother, with a wonderful sense of the appropriate, stood back a shade. Her hour had passed. Given all the circumstances, it seemed most unlikely that future generations would ever share such an hour again.

JOIN IN A ROYAL SALUTE

The Queen is 70 this year. W. F. Deedes gives thanks for a reign of selfless dedication

Whatever else this year has in store for us, it will bring into much sharper focus the qualities of our Queen. We treat the attainment of three score years and ten more seriously than most other anniversaries. So her 70th birthday in April will become a time of reckoning as well as rejoicing.

How welcome! I can think of nothing more likely to restore public esteem for the monarchy than reading more about the life of Queen Elizabeth and a lot less about the affairs of her offspring. There enters my mind that moving sentence in her broadcast from South Africa on the occasion of her 21st birthday: "I declare before you all that my whole life, whether it be long or short, shall be devoted to your service . . ." Happily for us all, it is already a long reign.

Yet, as this anniversary approaches, and even after rendering 44 years of pretty faultless service to this country, the Queen is not going to be accorded universal public acclaim. A certain perversity has entered into our affairs. There is a class of writer and television presenter who, while the rest of us gather laurels, hunt round for thistles. It will be instructive to see with what innovative brand of iconoclasm Channel 4 signals this event.

A new and appreciative biography is coming from Sarah Bradford, whose life of George VI I admired. There will be other tributes. And of course the bells will ring out. But, what will distract our attention and, given this perverse mood, receive most notice will be a small minority eager to advance their reputations as original artists by being critical of the Queen—and in some cases being downright cruel.

So clearly, loyal subjects ought to think more deeply of how much this nation owes to Elizabeth II. Much is hidden from our sight. I remember something Harold Macmillan said to me soon after she came to the throne. He expected her to have a long life ahead, and thought the day would come when she would have had longer experience of public affairs than any of her Prime Ministers.

We do not know what passes between the Queen and her Prime Minister at the weekly Tuesday evening meetings. But I can easily envisage some proposition being discussed on which the Queen feels moved to remark: "Well, go ahead, but I should remind you that Harold Wilson tried something of this kind, and it failed for these reasons . . ."

The portrait of the Queen as happier to discuss horse-breeding with her stud manager than to talk politics to her Prime Minister is false and lopsided. Because we see pictures of her looking elated over an Ascot winner, it does not follow that she looks bored when discussing parliamentary business with John Major. Which of us fails to look animated when following a favourite recreation?

As her often strained eyes reveal, the Queen attends closely to all official papers laid before her. I can think of no more conscientious figure in public life during the last half century. Many ministers, including Churchill, have come to regret failing to do their home-work on some political question as thoroughly as the Queen. Like her father, King George VI, and her grandfather, George V—but unlike Queen Victoria—she is blind to the colour of her ministers' politics.

It is open to the rest of us to disparage today's British Common-wealth, to talk or write cynically about some of its members and its foibles. Yet, as the Queen recognises, it is *still* a great part of our history. The way we dismantled our imperial role, from India onwards, in such a short space of time, and yet maintained kinship with former possessions, has no historical parallel. In this, the Queen remains the central pillar. She is on familiar terms with more Commonwealth figures than the entire Cabinet.

It cannot have been easy to fulfil such a strong sense of duty combined with the role of a loving and attentive mother. Tours of duty while the children were still young; constant preoccupation with affairs of state . . . Politicians can retire "to see more of their family". That option is not open to monarchy.

There is a stern, unbending side to this woman which extends even to personal risks to be faced in the line of duty. The only time I have known the Queen to be angry was when ministers became over-protective about a proposed visit to a Commonwealth nation.

She will agree to the requirements of the security services. Then, she insists, she will take a chance.

During her 44 years as Queen, our society and culture has changed out of recognition. This has left the Throne far more isolated than it was, and the Queen exposed to the criticism that she has not moved sufficiently with the times. Her high sense of duty combines with a deep and loving regard for her father, who in 1936 was summoned suddenly to an awesome task. There is a strong inner desire faithfully to follow the example that he set, to remain faithful to the traditions of his lifetime.

And as well as that there has been his widow, and her feelings, to consider. This matriarchal factor, conveyed to some of us who witnessed that memorable scene on the balcony of Buckingham Palace on VE Day, is very strong. Because of the Queen Mother, the sort of change people imagine they would like to have seen, a touch of homage to this more egalitarian age, would have been a degree more difficult.

But what kind of change, if any, do most of us expect from the Queen? To many in this country, change has become anathema— and that is not restricted to sexagenarians and above. However, the itch for change in other quarters has become feverish and destabilising. There seems to me a strong case for the titular head of our affairs to calm things down a bit. A social revolution like ours, which has no leader and no final destination, needs a steadying hand.

A salient fact about our parliamentary democracy is that it has been virtually the only one in Europe not to go down before or after either European war. (That fact weighs heavily on the subconscious of some Euro-sceptics.) Viewed in this light, Queen Elizabeth becomes an exceedingly reassuring figure.

She has a dry wit and in private conversation can be very funny indeed. But with the approach of her 70th birthday, I find Robert Louis Stevenson's line on an unfortunate peer the most appropriate. "On he went up the great stairway of his duty, uncheered and undepressed."

September 1996

ROYAL CRISIS THAT BROKE
THE SILENCE

W. F. Deedes, who covered the Abdication as a reporter, says it makes little sense to examine the media approach of 60 years ago from today's standpoint of full disclosure

Two or three months before King Edward VIII abdicated—60 years ago tomorrow—the editor of the *Morning Post*, H A Gwynne, sent me, as a young reporter, on an unusual errand.

Doubtful whether his friend the Prime Minister, Stanley Baldwin, was fully aware of what the world outside this country was saying about the King's association with Mrs Simpson, he instructed me to gather relevant cuttings from overseas newspapers and magazines.

With these he hoped to convince the Prime Minister that time was short. This country, outside a small circle at the top and journalists in touch with it, had little idea of what was going on. Some of the foreign press was buzzing, particularly in America and Canada.

Newspapers in this country remained silent about the King's affair—for reasons including fear of libel. This made my task more difficult. Publishers in self-defence were cutting or blacking out foreign stories about the King and Mrs Simpson.

Let us pause there, and try to imagine the editor of this newspaper feeling it to be his duty a year or so back to reveal to John Major, in the absence of press comment here, the attention being given overseas to gossip about the Prince of Wales and Camilla Parker Bowles.

An absurd idea, it will be said—which illustrates the difficulty of trying to present the drama of King Edward's surrender of the throne for love against a social background so totally different from that of today.

I am sometimes asked how far the conspiracy of silence about the King's affair with Mrs Simpson was contrived. Was it a plot between the newspaper proprietors?

408

Did Lord Beaverbrook, who wanted to keep Edward on the throne no matter whom he married, enjoin silence on them? There was no plot. Lord Beaverbrook, crossing the Atlantic, was urgently summoned by the King at a point in the crisis.

He took the first boat back and fussed about, partly because he disliked Baldwin intensely and was happy to oppose anything he was trying to do.

But neither *The Times* under Geoffrey Dawson and his deputy editor Barrington Ward nor this newspaper under its owner and editor-in-chief Lord Camrose, and its managing editor, Arthur Watson, were going to take their cue from Beaverbrook. Nor was the *Morning Post*. The truth—hard though it is to make credible in these days of "total disclosure"—is that newspapers 60 years ago treated the liaisons of public figures, including royalty, as private and unpublishable.

They had said nothing about Mrs Dudley Ward or Lady Furness, both of them well known to be Edward's mistresses. Having a nodding acquaintance with Edward when he was Prince of Wales, I knew about both relationships. It never entered my head to write about them. There were other women. So, at first, Mrs Simpson was simply the next favourite.

Wallis Simpson became a serious figure after King George V died and Edward came to the throne. The first time I might have set eyes on her, but failed to do so, was during Edward's proclamation as King. I was on duty as a reporter at St James's Palace. The King decided he would like to watch his own proclamation from that vantage point. He invited Mrs Simpson to join him. They were photographed together.

From my corner in the *Morning Post* office, I thought I could see the way things were going and argued that we, a small inoffensive Right-wing newspaper, were the best newspaper to bring matters to a head. This was conveyed to Gwynne who saw the Prime Minister regularly. Baldwin insisted, with every right, that he needed more time.

So this volatile atmosphere prevailed until, almost by accident, the Bishop of Bradford, Dr Blunt, blew it. "In a long period of drift," as Frances Donaldson puts it in her biography of King Edward VIII, "so much steam had been built up that almost any movement of air would blow the lid off".

Extraordinary though it may seem today, newspapers had virtually ignored the Ipswich Assizes on Oct 27 1936 at which Wallis Simpson was granted a decree nisi by a troubled Mr Justice Hawke on grounds of adultery by her husband, Ernest Simpson.

The act of adultery, according to the evidence, had been committed at the Hotel de Paris at Bray the previous July. The suit was undefended. Norman Birkett, KC, was in court on behalf of Mrs Simpson.

I took a professional interest in the alleged co-respondent, whose name was Marigold. She was, I supposed, the sort of figure A P Herbert had in mind when he wrote his book *Holy Deadlock*. When he became an Independent MP, he changed the divorce law.

Today there would have been a fierce auction among newspapers for Marigold's story. As it was, *The Times* carried 12 lines about the divorce at Ipswich and *The Daily Telegraph* gave it 22 on an unimportant page.

Just before the crisis broke, the King began on Nov 18 a visit to the valleys of South Wales. I did not report the tour but I was close to it because the King undertook it as Patron of the National Council of Social Service on which an uncle with whom I resided, Sir Wyndham Deedes, was a prominent figure. Lionel Ellis of the NCSS subsequently gave us a blow-by-blow account of the tour.

To quote Frances Donaldson again: "It was at the gate of the derelict steel works at Dowlais above Merthyr Tydfil that, less than a month before his departure from the country, the King delivered the most memorable sentence of his career."

The exact words he used were: "These steelworks brought these men here. Something must be done to see that they stay here—working."

"Something must be done . . ." That was the phrase later picked up by some of the King's supporters. Ministers want to rid themselves of a radical King who takes that line, they said—falsely.

The bishop made his pronouncement on Dec 1. The benefit of the King's coronation, Dr Blunt said, depended on two elements.

The first was the faith, prayer and self-dedication of the King. "On that it would be improper for me to say anything except to commend him and ask others to commend him to God's Grace, which he will so abundantly need. We hope he is aware of this need. Some of us wish that he gave more positive signs of such awareness."

The *Yorkshire Post* gave these remarks prominence. The London newspapers at first ignored them. We in the reporters' room of the *Morning Post* were more excited by a fire which on the night of Dec 1 destroyed the Crystal Palace. One of our reporters at the scene told me that the King and the Duke of Kent, both in dinner jackets, appeared to watch the fire.

Thereafter, the crisis moved quickly. Between Bradford's remarks and the instrument of abdication only 10 days elapsed.

During these days it became increasingly difficult from within a newspaper office to know how the crisis was turning. Within the Cabinet, Duff Cooper was the only figure to support the King's position.

The King worried about editorial comment in *The Times*. He feared it would deliver an attack on Mrs Simpson. According to Frances Donaldson's account, *The Daily Telegraph* emerged with most credit. It has since emerged that this newspaper's main source of information was Viscount Davidson, a former chairman of the Conservative Party, and closer to Baldwin than anyone else. "The crisis," he wrote subsequently, "was the making of *The Daily Telegraph* . . . I thought it essential that one respected newspaper should be properly informed. I saw to it that *The Daily Telegraph* was completely informed . . . it was striking how accurate was the information carried by the *Telegraph* and how out of date was that carried by *The Times*."

Walter Monckton, closest to the King in the final days, helped to draft the speech broadcast from Windsor. At a private dance I was attending we stopped the music to hear it.

Then we resumed dancing. In their different ways the people of this country did much the same. The river ran on with barely a ripple.

IF THE MOTHER OF OUR FUTURE KING IS DRAWN TO CHERISH THE AFFLICTED, WE SHOULD STOP CARPING AND BE GLAD

The journey to Angola has been a watershed for the Princess, reports W. F. Deedes

As she left Angola yesterday after her four-day visit, Diana, Princess of Wales made clear that she intends to continue as a Red Cross volunteer and play her part in the worldwide campaign against landmines.

It emerges as the sort of cause she has been seeking. She will pursue it in other countries on behalf of the Red Cross, with whom she intends to work exclusively.

"I'm not a political figure," she declared yesterday when asked about the political implications of her choice. "The fact is I'm a humanitarian figure. I always have been and I always will be." So this journey to Angola can be seen as a watershed for her.

It has also yielded fresh material about her and answered some of the questions being raised about her suitability for the role she most wants to play.

There was this health post, as they call it, in one of the less salubrious districts of Luanda, where they greeted the Princess with drums and dancing. There were also a lot of mothers with small naked babies. It was fearfully hot.

She walked round for a while, then saw a space, sat down and asked a mother what the problem was. Then she picked up the baby and looked at it carefully.

By now half a dozen cameras had engulfed her—"we've got our job to do, ma'am." But, unruffled, she continued in the style that comes naturally to her. This was the district nurse talking to a mother, not a VIP.

There was another scene later that morning that caught the eye.

We were at the Red Cross orthopaedic workshop, where they manufacture and fit artificial limbs to victims of mines.

The Princess sat down beside a man who had recently lost his leg and heard his story. Then she placed her hands on his upper arm and stroked it lightly a couple of times. He looked at the Princess blankly as if to say: "This has never happened to me before." Reporters on the trip, who travel regularly with the Princess, are apt to view such scenes as part of the act.

That is one way of looking at it. Another is to think back over the years and ask which member of the Royal Family could have performed the act as well as the Princess does.

Queen Alexandra, perhaps, but she takes us a long way back. Queen Mary had a warm heart, but she spent all her life concealing it—even from her eldest son. The Queen herself often looks happiest in poor corners of the Commonwealth.

But there is ample room—indeed, there is a call—in the world of today for someone with the Princess's qualities.

A lot of pictures appear of the Princess dressed to the nines at some New York charity ball. Yet this rough experience in Angola gives rise to other thoughts. It is among the poorest of the poor in the world that she shines most brightly. Yet not exclusively among the poor.

While she was with them, I watched the faces of the young British soldiers who, on behalf of the admirable HALO Trust, are engaged in finding and destroying the anti-personnel mines that infest the Huambo region.

These brave young men working dangerously far out of our sight and mind were greatly cheered by her. They rigged her up in their protective gear and marched with her down the track that led to the minefields. She made their young hearts flutter—and why not? In the God-forsaken Huambo region, smashed by bombs, they will talk about her for days.

Her principal mission on this trip was of course not simply to comfort Angola's suffering poor, nor to cheer young soldiers, but more testingly to support the work the Red Cross are doing to lift the curse of anti-personnel mines.

It was testing because Red Cross policy on mines does not square with our Government's policy on mines. By aligning herself with the Red Cross the Princess was making a political statement. Indeed—and it is well to bring all this into the open—her critics would put it more strongly. In the competitive search for a fresh direction in which both the Prince of Wales and the Princess are engaged, so the cynics would say, the Princess reckoned that Angola, its minefields and the Red Cross put three aces into her hands.

Those who want to see it that way are entitled to their view. But there is room for an altogether different interpretation of this trip. In a harsh world the International Committee of the Red Cross has become a bulwark against man's inhumanity to man.

In a country such as Rwanda, for example, now emerging from a nightmare, the ICRC carries more weight than the United Nations. Worldwide, it acts professionally on behalf of humanity in ways no single government can do. Thus it is sometimes bound to cross with governments, even with the British Government.

That, as any sensible government should be able to grasp, calls for breadth of mind and tolerance, certainly not for petulance.

What emerged clearly from this trip the Princess made with the Red Cross to a ruined country is how closely her instincts and their aims are related. That is why there are the makings of a match.

Of course there is a bit of the actress in it. How do you avoid acting when a hundred photographers are calling the shots? She used to hate the cameras. This time, in temperatures high enough to make some tempers snap, she bore with them serenely.

Seeking a role in the cause of humanity, the Princess passed some stiff tests in Angola. But she is not, as many people suppose, particularly complicated, or extraordinary.

She has this yearning so many of our younger people have today to take a hand in the world's woes, to tie up wounds, to cherish the afflicted.

Those of us who witness some of their work in the developing world believe this country is the richer for it. In so many ways it is a better world than the Empire that is behind us. In any case, it is today the real world.

If the mother of our future King feels drawn in that direction, no matter what form it takes, we should stop carping and doubting. We should be glad.

THE PRINCESS OF SORROWS

W. F. Deedes, who travelled to Bosnia with Diana, Princess of Wales, remembers a compassionate and vulnerable woman

They told us that the main road we wanted to take from Tuzla was dangerous. So we made a long detour. That was three weeks ago in Bosnia, where Diana, Princess of Wales and I were travelling together, talking to those who had been injured or bereaved by mines. The road hazard which ended her life in Paris was of another kind.

To have witnessed the way she brought comfort to these people, many in deep distress, some in tears, is to understand what we have lost, for ever.

It was not all sorrow. She was an engaging person to travel with because she had this penchant for simple jokes. When we stopped for a break, she would sometimes approach, one arm behind her back. "Would you like a gin and tonic?" She would wait to see my eyes light up at this prospect of the unexpected, then hand over a small bottle of Evian.

We had first discussed this Bosnia trip early this year before she made the expedition to Angola in January. It had been a subject of concern to me from the early 1990s. Travelling in Asia and Africa to write about famine, refugees and other crises, I saw what a deadly enemy mines had become to some of the poorest people on Earth. The Princess of Wales shared that concern. Furthermore, she emphasised to me, her concern about mines and their victims would continue. Angola was not, she insisted, to be seen as a one-off. Where next?

Well, I told her, they will certainly not allow you to go to Cambodia because you might be kidnapped. Nor will they let you go to Afghanistan because the Taliban are shelling Kabul. Her best bet, I suggested, would be Bosnia. So it came about, and on August 8 we took off from London in a private jet and flew into Sarajevo.

If you are going to concern yourself with the consequences of man's inhumanity to man as closely as the Princess of Wales desired to do, Sarajevo is a place to go. On this first day we had no time to stop there, because of engagements in Tuzla, which was a long drive away.

So we drove straight through the city, past its huge cemeteries, up what was called Sniper's Alley, through streets of shattered offices and homes. At one point I murmured to her something about the bridge on which the Archduke had been assassinated in 1914. Otherwise we sat in silence, as she looked around her, taking it in, saying nothing, betraying no emotion.

Part of her gift in bringing comfort to those in anguish lay in this sensitive awareness of when silence is best. She was not a voluble sympathiser, quite the reverse. At some point during an outpouring of grief, she would stretch out a hand or both hands and touch the person on the arm or face.

I found some of the tales we had to hear almost unendurable. Yet I never saw her lose this calm, which plainly had a most soothing effect. As I reported at the time, she saw dreadful wounds, heard horrifying stories while maintaining the demeanour of a professional but sympathetic nurse.

Nor in the course of those three days did I see her concentration flag; and this was remarkable because the distractions were intense. The cameramen and the reporters who met her at every stop had an interest in her encounters with victims of mines, but, unlike the Angolan expedition, it was not their main interest.

She had, as it later transpired, interrupted her holiday to visit Bosnia. Much of the holiday was spent with Dodi Fayed. The pictures were public. Therein lay the main press interest. It was a test of temper, of temperament, of character and of many other things.

She would utter a faint murmur of dismay at the sight of 40 cameramen lined up outside some humble home. Then self-discipline would assert itself. It afforded an opportunity to witness, at uncomfortably close range, the dichotomy of Diana's attitude to photographers.

Defending their profession, some of them claim she was hopelessly inconsistent in her attitude to the camera. She resented their presence, so the argument goes, yet depended upon their work for the standing it gave her and her causes.

Our expedition helped me to reach a conclusion about this. She accepted the value of photographers in her life, and acknowledged the inestimable value they held for her good causes. What she found harder to stomach was the intrusive lengths to which some, in such an intensely competitive game, were ready to go and sought to take her.

She was happy to work with our own photographer, Ian Jones. He made various requests of her, with which she complied professionally. One of them, as we returned through Sarajevo, was to take some pictures of her among the shattered buildings.

They told us to keep off the grass, which might be mined. I found the experience altogether more trying than she appeared to do.

It was the unknown and the unexpected which troubled her. It is hardly a human aberration to resent being spied upon. I had a camera of my own for taking snapshots. She was fairly happy with this, but liked me to tell her when pictures were being taken. If I failed to do this, a finger would wag lightly. "Now then . . . Lord Deedes . . ." It was one of her little jokes to persist in calling me Lord Deedes all the time. Not to be outdone, I peppered our conversations with "ma'am's". "What smart shoes, Lord Deedes!" she exclaimed one morning as we set off. "Entirely for your benefit, ma'am," I said, with heavy emphasis on the ma'am.

Because this newspaper wanted copy, I spent a lot of the time sitting beside her scribbling. "Sorry about this," I would say from time to time. Her response was generous. It might help, she thought, if I used her light satellite telephone to send stuff back. "Give me your camera," she said, "and I shall take a picture of you, Lord Deedes, on my telephone." For an amateur photographer, she made a good job of it.

These emotional encounters we had with victims and the bereaved left their mark on her. What often seemed a calm, soothing response to a tale of woe took more of a toll than one at first supposed. She made it hard for herself, insisting that every interview be granted at least 30 minutes. What made it even harder was the depths of bitterness sown by this civil war in former Yugoslavia. "So many people," I said to her, "long to find someone who will listen while they express their inner feelings about all this—and they've found you." Sad smile. No response.

Instead, she asked me which of the interviews during the day I felt had been the most emotional. We agreed on the answer. It had been a meeting with a young Muslim widow whose husband had been killed by a mine while he was fishing in May. The widow sat on one side of the Princess, the man's mother on the other.

The mother told us how she had been with her son in hospital, "as he died, smiling". The widow spoke of their short but happy marriage, and described him simply as a good man, an honest man, concluding: "And he was only 29 when he died."

Diana said very little. She caught up both their hands and held them. The mother explained her dream. In this, she told us, her son had returned to her, and explained that he was happy where he was. "That might well be so," Diana responded. It seemed at the time a perfect rejoinder. The mother's face was transformed.

There was a similar encounter in one of Sarajevo's largest cemeteries. The Princess of Wales went off alone to walk round it. As she did so, she encountered a mother tending her son's grave. There was no language barrier. The two women gently embraced. Watching this scene from a distance, I sought in my mind who else could have done this. Nobody.

Now, of course, there will be much bitter and profitless argument about the part played by photographers in all this. It has to be borne in mind that Diana has found photographers a trial from her earliest days in public life. A point was reached even before the marriage when the Queen felt it necessary to invite editors to Buckingham Palace to enlist their sympathy. As the then editor of this newspaper, I joined the company. "It comes hard on a girl," said the Queen to a small group of us at one point, "when she cannot walk down the village street to buy a bag of sweets without being followed by photographers."

After that, there was a brief lull for the Princess of Wales, but no lasting easement. How could it be otherwise? Then her deep-laid feelings about photographers extended towards her two sons. She passionately desired for William and Harry the freedom to live natural lives. She saw the camera as a direct obstacle to this.

This time round, it was thought best for her to approach the newspapers herself. The then editor of *The Sunday Telegraph*, John Thompson, and I lunched with the Prince and Princess of Wales at Kensington Palace.

The Princess was open about her fears. One of them, she told me, was that William, then three or four years old, would be out in the park with his nanny, would feel the call of nature and be photographed relieving himself behind a tree. It sounded a degree far-fetched at the time. We smiled over it. Some time later, what she most feared actually happened—and such a photograph was printed.

Of course photographers will protest, as one or two did to me in Bosnia, that the Princess wanted it both ways. For many of her appearances, particularly on behalf of good causes, photographers were welcome. The pictures they took of her in protective clothing, braving one of Angola's minefields, went round the world.

"She uses us, and we use her. Fair enough?" Not quite. It does not excuse the excesses, the subterfuges, the spying with long-range lenses. As individuals, all the professional photographers I know are friendly men. As a pack, they are unnerving. The competition, as we experienced in Bosnia, is savage.

It is savage because much of the modern news media will pay enormous prices for certain photographs. The man who took the pictures which plagued the Princess of Wales in Bosnia, pictures of a holiday spree with Dodi Fayed, is today a rich man.

In the dismal inquest on this affair which lies ahead, that is something the news media, not the paparazzi, will be called upon to re-examine. A volume of public wrath is about to overflow over this tragedy; and it will make a permanent mark on certain media methods.

There will be a strong temptation in some political quarters to avenge her. There will be talk of curbs on the invasion of private lives, a law on privacy and the rest. That would not be the right memorial for that free spirit.

"I am a humanitarian. I always have been, and I always will be," she declared within my hearing during the Angola expedition when they accused her of meddling in politics. In saying that, she wrote her own epitaph, for that, I came to learn, was what she really thought about herself. Yet nobody could write about Diana, as I sometimes had to do, without being made aware of the passions which swirled around her, and will go on swirling.

She had her critics, and even in death she will continue to have them. It does her memory no service to brush that aside. There were, as this newspaper observed in an editorial last week, two Dianas; and sometimes one of them appeared to conflict with the best interests of the other.

All that said, it is surely right to dwell just now on the supreme quality of one who sought above all to help the vulnerable people in society, and who did it so well. She was good at this because she herself was vulnerable. She knew the feeling. She did not set out to be a saint.

This was a human being, with all the faults of most of us, but also with a bigger heart than most of us. As I discovered on that last mission for humanity, there was an underlying humility which, at least to me, redeems it all.

She was not a grand person setting out to bestow favours on the poor. She knew herself too well for that. Recognising her own frailty, she was the better able to understand and to sympathise with the frailty of others. As I perceived in Bosnia, she saw herself as an equal with those she sought to comfort. That was part of her gift. As she told *Le Monde*: "To begin with we are on the same level, on the same wavelength." That is why she could sit in absolute silence, holding a hand, and transmit this feeling of "we're in this together".

A friend of long standing, Lady Barbara Bossom, called me yesterday. Her father, the Earl of Guilford, was killed on a mine in this country. "What a wonderful memorial to Diana it would be," she said, "if the world could bring itself to abandon mines."

Indeed it would, but the world, alas, does not work on those lines. More simply, Diana gave us an example, in this mechanistic world, which we should heed and try never to forget. Her instinct was so right: all those wounded people in Bosnia, crying aloud for someone to hear their tale, to hold their hand, to be able to communicate the uncommunicable.

We should tell our children and our grandchildren about her. We should say to them, the world you are about to enter remains in sore need of her gifts. Remember her.

THE FUNERAL OF DIANA, PRINCESS OF WALES

During the one-minute silence for Diana, Princess of Wales there entered my head a phrase used long ago by country folk after someone had died: "She has gone home." That restless, loving, homeless spirit had found somewhere to lay her head.

Absurd, you may say, to talk of someone who lived at Kensington Palace as being homeless. Yet in the essential meaning of the word, she was. And so, during that silence, it struck me that we were not only mourning her loss to us, we were also welcoming her home.

In truth, the arrangements made for her funeral in Westminster Abbey left us all free to interpret this event in any manner we chose. Never in its long history has the Abbey opened its arms to anyone in such a wide embrace. This sepulchre of kings and poets and statesmen set aside the rules and conventions associated with it. When this service was first mooted, most of us had our own unflattering ideas of what the Establishment would make of it. How entirely wrong we were.

There was a piano for Elton John. There was mention of other faiths. And in the opening prayer for her there was this striking sentence: "Although a Princess, she was someone for whom, from afar, we dared to feel affection, and by whom we were all *intrigued*." That is an unusual word to find in any form of Christian prayer.

And finally, to all our surprise, there was the clapping that rolled towards us from the world outside and ignited in the Abbey itself; something never heard there in modern times, and not likely ever to be heard again. We will come back to that.

Tribute is due to the reverent and loving hands which arranged the order of service for this funeral. It was not only all-embracing, it was appropriate. When I heard that Elton John would sing, strong doubts arose in my mind—as might be expected of someone of my generation. When it came to the moment, his rendering of *Candle in the Wind* seemed to me entirely fitting. More than that, it was a joy. It came so close to her. I fancy it moved many elderly and conservative hearts present in Westminster Abbey into totally unexpected trains of thought.

I watched the faces around me while Elton sang. All seemed content, and some found themselves caught up by it. Come to think of it, this was natural enough. For what they contrived so well to do was make this farewell to Diana from one of Christendom's greatest places of worship a close reflection of her life and spirit.

So often when the great and the good depart, the drums roll and the trumpet sounds. It is all very grand and eloquent and fitting, but it seldom draws us close to the spirit of the departed. Winston Churchill was one of the few to be aware of this. He took a close interest in his own state funeral and was anxious there should be hymns that people could sing and good melodies. He knew what a heavy hand solemnity can lay on memory of the dead.

This funeral was arranged on altogether different lines. There were many moments during that hour inside and outside Westminster Abbey when all who knew Diana and loved her must have felt drawn closer to her. A skilled and forgiving hand had gone towards the prayer we said for all who mourn, prefaced by these words: "Diana was not alone in losing her young life tragically. We remember too her friend, Dodi Fayed, and his family, Henri Paul, and all for whom today's service rekindles memories of grief untimely borne."

Perhaps we should pause there, and reflect gratefully how extraordinarily difficult it must have been to put together this form of service, itself without precedent, in a manner which would win approval from the Royal Family, the Spencer family, the custodians of Westminster Abbey's conventions—and from the nation itself.

And having it all composed, agreed and in print in the space of four or five days. We have lost many things that touched our pride in the last half century or so. But still, I reflected, as I watched the cortege leave Kensington Palace on a screen before entering the Abbey, we have this matchless touch for high ceremonies.

The police outriders were sitting to attention on their horses. There was the slow clop, clop of hooves. How good the horses were, how dependable they looked. That bright, early autumn sunshine around the Palace and the Park was so evocative. Setting eyes on something beautiful that a friend will never see again always brings pain.

What we all saw from the moment the gun carriage set out from

Kensington Palace was a revival of the old confidence we once had in our way of doing things, blended with something entirely of this age which caught the elusive spirit of Diana.

I remembered also that when Princes William and Harry were in London, she would sometimes emerge with them from Kensington Palace and, at their bidding, head for a hamburger. "My sons," I heard her say with motherly exasperation while we were working in Bosnia last month, "seem to be hooked on McDonald's."

Westminster Abbey is a place which makes prayer easier. The beauty of its stained glass and the soaring columns enter the spirit. How was it, though, for those outside? They had stood for hours, sleepless and with little food. At dawn they had felt the early chill of autumn. Their devotion, I thought at one moment in the Abbey, reaches further than our own, those of us who have slept in warm beds and made breakfast. Many of them who could follow the service from screen and relay responded reverentially to what took place in the Abbey. When we rose, they rose; when we prayed, they prayed.

And what, I wondered, was going through some of those minds. Many, I did not doubt, were grieving in the belief that Diana had gone for ever, and with the close of her earthly life, there remained nothing but dust.

When loved ones die, we draw about us such hopes as we can muster about a future life. Did some of the public grief we have been witnessing come from the absence of such hopes? Or was it the cruelty of a life so suddenly taken at what seemed a happy time in her life? It is a mistake to try to over-sanctify such an occasion. The love for Diana spoke for itself. As we walked across Parliament Square on our way to the Abbey, we saw flowers everywhere. Holding the people in, where they stood 10 to 12 deep on the pavement, hardly required a policeman's arm. They were hemmed in by flowers.

Yet, there was more to it than that. Many people today lead lonely lives. They feel outside the mainstream. Watching everything on television is no help; it adds to the sense of isolation. So many people long to play their part in momentous occasions. They want to feel they have taken a small share in a collective historic experience.

That was what supported so many during the long and inhospitable vigil, when you were lucky to get your hands on a plastic cup of tea and keep your place on the pavement. Diana's death was a tragedy. It was also a tremendous event. It will be remembered by this generation and the next. It will go in the history books.

Whatever inner thoughts were passing through people's minds, Westminster Abbey on Saturday morning seemed not to be a place of isolated worship, but more a focal point for the millions stretched across London and other places seeking to express inexpressible feelings.

On the motorways, they stood on the bridges and dropped flowers as the cortege passed. Flowers, I reflected during prayers in the Abbey, have had a central role in this week of love and grief; a tender reminder, perhaps, that all beauty is mortal.

As her coffin under the Royal Standard moved towards the Great West Door of Westminster Abbey towards her final resting place, I glanced at one of the pall bearers. He was moving along with his comrades of the Welsh Guards with all the style and grandeur we expect from the Brigade of Guards—the gleaming boots, the practised step. From the corner of his eye, and down his cheek, a tear ran. Contrary to good order and military discipline?

From within the Abbey walls, inexplicable sounds reached us from the outside world. At one point, some time before the service began, a tremendous cheer was heard. What could it mean? It came, we learnt later, as the Queen stood outside Buckingham Palace to watch the cortege pass. And as it passed, she bowed her head.

Watching each member of her family enter and leave Westminster Abbey offered a timely reminder that, whatever loss we may suppose that we have suffered, theirs is infinitely greater.

My eye dwelt on Queen Elizabeth the Queen Mother, walking firmly but just a shade anxiously up the aisle with the help of her stick. It *is* a long aisle. What a lot of sadness she has known in her life. And now? So often personal loss strikes hardest in old age.

Prince William walked by with his head bowed low. Understandably, we have become familiar with that look in recent days. Of all the partnerships that this sudden death has severed, that between him, his brother and their mother was infinitely the most precious. So the prayer was well chosen: "Lord, we thank you for the precious gift of family life, for all human relationships and for the strength we draw from each other. Have compassion on those for whom this parting brings particular pain and the deepest sense of loss."

The burden on Prince William's shoulders will now rapidly increase. Part of it, I reflected penitentially, comes from journalists.

He shared so closely his mother's apprehensions of the long lens. The cameras were there in the Abbey, of course, at every vantage point and all-seeing, but immobile—and so I hoped, to people like Prince William, less intimidating.

Which takes us to the substance of what Diana's brother sought to convey to the congregation in the Abbey, but even more to the world outside. Naturally one so close to her was able quickly to strike a chord. "For such was her extraordinary appeal that the tens of millions of people taking part in this service all over the world via television and radio, who never actually met her, felt that they, too, lost someone close to them in the early hours of Sunday morning." He was right also to dwell on Diana's God-given sensitivity, without which we would be immersed in greater ignorance about the anguish of Aids, the plight of the homeless, the isolation of lepers and the random destruction of landmines.

Right again about her sense of insecurity, which never left her. It was what her brother called this childlike sense of unworthiness, of rejection even, which gave such poignancy to the helping hand she sought to extend to others.

It would be happy if we could be left to dwell on these endearing qualities. Alas, no. They will be remembered, but not for too long. What will echo on, the world being what it is, are Earl Spencer's other words . . . "the most hunted person of the modern age . . ."

It is no good turning away from what he said. We have to weigh it. "She talked endlessly of getting away from England, mainly because of the treatment that she received at the hands of the newspapers. I don't think she ever understood why her genuinely good intentions were sneered at by the media, why there appeared to be a permanent quest on their behalf to bring her down. It is baffling."

Then he pledged himself to protect her beloved boys, William and Harry, from a similar fate. In all, it was a lovely panegyric; and who better to deliver it? In the long run, brothers and sisters who grow up together come to know each other better than anyone else on earth. It expressed better than anyone else could have the feeling in so many other hearts. Then there came to us in the Abbey this distant rustle, this ripple of sound. It travelled on its own wavelength into the Abbey itself. Suddenly people were clapping, it seemed to me with surprising confidence. There was none of that furtive looking round to see whether we should be kneeling, sitting or standing. The clapping took hold and it continued. And this was the

more surprising because it was a congregation in which I thought
the senior citizen was extraordinarily well represented.

What were we to make of it? Soon after leaving the Abbey, an
American television crew rushed up to me. What did *I* make of it?
Were the Earl's strictures against the media justified? Should he have
spoken thus in the presence of the Queen?

I felt in the wrong mood to deal with such questions seriously.
"He feels deep emotion on this subject," I said off the top of my
head. "And not without cause. He had an embittering experience of
his own with the press."

Then, perhaps influenced by the spirit of the preceding hour, I
found myself saying something like this. The tabloid newspapers
have their faults, but they do not have hearts of stone. Were this
entire tragedy to lead us towards—even a few degrees towards—
gentler methods, especially towards the two sons that Diana so
cherished, then there would be the makings of an appropriate
memorial to her. What so many of us shared on Saturday morning
was more than a farewell to someone we loved. There was also
promise of a fresh beginning. It was a service from which it was open
to all to draw strength as well as sadness.

After Lord Spencer had ended his homily to such unexpectedly
enthusiastic applause, we moved into the hymn "Make me a channel
of your peace" with its final verse:

> Make me a channel of your peace:
> where there is hatred let me bring your love,
> Where there is injury, your pardon, Lord,
> And where there's doubt, true faith in you.

It seems to me pointless to mourn for Diana without at the same
time taking serious account of the example she set in certain important ways. As one of the prayers reminded us, she showed compassion
towards people most of us do not have a lot of time for.

The Bidding prayer, read by Dr Wesley Carr, Dean of Westminster, gave the rest of us our marching orders. We were to
remember her life and enjoyment of it with thanksgiving. We were
to rededicate to God the work of the charities she supported. We
were to commit ourselves anew to caring for others.

That leaves it open to everyone, including the tabloid editors, to
decide, after all the tears have been shed, what influence she really
exercised on our lives in her own, all too brief life.

TRUE LEGACY OF PRINCESS WHO KNEW DESPAIR AND DELIGHT

On the first anniversary of her death, W. F. Deedes recalls Diana, the Royal who meant different things to different people

This is the day, flags at half-mast remind us, on which to be sad but also to try to see her as she really was, not as so many like to dream of her. For Diana, Princess of Wales meant so many different things to different people.

Mr Fayed sees her as a "martyr". Her brother, Earl Spencer, thinks she was "murdered by the press". Julie Burchill wrote of "a spirited, compassionate and beautiful Englishwoman". For Andrew Morton and—let us be honest about it—also for newspapers, she was and still is a source of revenue.

Did she leave something of lasting value? Yes, I think she did. At one point in her relatively short span, she reached the pit of human despair. Was ever the break-up of any marriage so cruelly advertised? How many could have endured such exposure and stayed in our right mind?

Yet she rose from those depths and, in the final days of her life, she was reaching the stars; so it seemed to those of us who were with her on that last mission to Bosnia. That is what made her death so sad, but there remains the solid legacy.

A lot of people in this world go through the sort of despair she suffered, feel their life is in pieces, their spirit irreparably broken— and are then often moved to behave unaccountably, as she certainly did. For them, it seems to me, she left a gift of gold. Yes, you can pick up the pieces again. Sooner or later, night ends and daybreak comes.

So when people, as they will, begin to strip away the hyperbole and judge Diana more critically than has seemed appropriate in the year after her death, that gift of hers needs to be weighed.

Oh yes, the revisionists will soon be along. It is the way of the world. Give her the wings of an angel and sooner or later there will be those who tear off the wings. The trouble with Diana was that she lent herself to superlatives and they provoke iconoclasts.

To resist them, those who loved her need to move away from the pantomime stuff: the Princess in the darkest of towers, trapped between a faithless husband and an inflexible mother-in-law with what a *Guardian* writer called "her obdurate courtiers".

We went through all that, and the bulimia, in the *Panorama* interview which I thought abysmal and so reported in this newspaper. As Cardinal Hume points out, she was not a saint. She was not within light years of being a saint. It was, as he said, a flawed character.

But that is partly why so many loved her. She caught the heart of those who believe in neither heaven nor hell and who see glamorous boyfriends and easy morals as no obstacle at all to living a decent life in love and charity with their neighbour.

She was an inspiration to people, and there are hosts of them, who do not believe in God but who do believe in helping those less fortunate than themselves.

Of course, the Church has a problem in reconciling some of her behaviour with her acts of Christian charity. The Church should keep tight hold of the words they entered in the Bidding Prayer at her funeral.

"Although a princess, she was someone for whom, from afar, we dared to feel affection and by whom we were all intrigued." Nobody can gainsay that.

And while we are about it, let us consign "The People's Princess" to the dustbin.

It was a crass observation by the Queen's First Minister, not least because it provoked so many to say that the Princess Royal has set a flawless, though less well advertised, example in the humanities with her work for Save the Children Fund. Furthermore, it triggered a degree of animosity against the Queen.

The Princess Royal and, indeed, the Queen herself illustrate where Diana's detractors will find something to work on. Is the value of charity or duty diminished because it remains largely unseen? Does it have constantly to be photographed and publicised to prove its worth? I think not, though many will disagree with me.

Ours has become very much a "first name" society. Diana, Princess of Wales invariably made people feel they could call her "Di". The Princess Royal, the Prince of Wales and the Queen herself are simply not in that mould.

"The People's Princess" was "one of us". The others are not. So what she did was special to us and what they do seems hardly relevant ... "doesn't relate like". The image in many eyes has become the substance.

In reality, the Queen showed much kindness towards her daughter-in-law. She was sometimes puzzled by her, occasionally exasperated, but she did what she could to ease the way.

When, at the time of her engagement to the Prince of Wales, Diana stepped from obscurity into the limelight and found the attentions of the press alarming, the Queen did not tell her to pull herself together. She called the editors to Buckingham Palace, gave them a drink and asked them to go easy.

It was then the Queen showed her true colours. "It's hard on a girl," she said, "if she can't walk down the street to buy a bag of sweets without a flock of photographers."

"Why can't she send a footman for the sweets?" asked an editor. "Never heard anything so pompous in my life," said the Queen.

Later on, when Diana formed even deeper fears about what modern journalism might inflict on William and Harry, the Queen encouraged her to set about enlisting the sympathy of editors in her own way. The stern unbending matriarch versus the cringing princess is simply not a runner.

Holding firmly to realities, it will be sad and unfair if what Diana did to bring to the notice of the world the cruelty of landmines is belittled, as Channel 4 (in the vanguard of the iconoclasts) appeared to do last week with a programme absurdly entitled *Diana, the Wrong Crusade?*

She supported a ban on landmines which is going to run into difficulties, so the message ran, whereas the right aim is to clear the mines already in the ground faster. Diana wanted a ban, as any sensible person would, but recognised its limitations.

In speeches here and in America, she stressed the urgency of clearing mines now in the ground, dwelt on the misery they created and called for more to be done for their victims. Had she lived, she would have gone to Oslo, while they were discussing the ban, and said just that.

It was tactless of her in a botched interview just before her death to declare that the Conservatives had been "hopeless" on the mines issue. The fact is that nobody in politics was much interested in the subject until Diana entered the field. She stirred things up and a good thing too.

Her choice of admirers after the divorce did not excite anyone's admiration but it struck me as following a familiar pattern. Before the war there was a popular song, *I get along without you very well, indeed I do* . . . It is often what people wish to convey after a hurtful marriage break-up.

For a long time to come, the true portrait of Diana will be difficult to read because there is so much else dotted about on the canvas. There is the Diana Memorial Fund and its earlier muddles, for which she holds no responsibility whatever.

People ask: why on earth did she go holidaying with Mr Fayed? Because he gave her and the boys a lovely holiday is the straight answer, and let them make what they can of it.

There is the apparently unending mystery of what happened in Paris, though there seems no mystery about it. Dodi Fayed was the boss. He took charge, gave the wrong instructions and paid for them with his life.

It does begin to look as if, most unexpectedly, she did the Royal Family a good turn. But the manner in which she set about doing this will seem to some less generous than the manner in which the Royal Family have bowed to it and responded. In this and other ways she was a catalyst, bringing back to life the ancient magic of days when the poor could bring their woes to the throne.

She was not the only woman of 30-something to rebuild her life, a life darkened by low self-esteem, early loss of her mother and finally a mistaken marriage. But she brought to their attention the way it can be done with the head high.

Adam Lindsay Gordon's lines from *Ye Wearie Wayfarer* sound right for today: *Life is mostly froth and bubble, Two things stand like stone, Kindness in another's trouble, Courage in your own.* There is no hype there.

When much else has been stripped away, that example will endure; and it leaves, as she would so much have desired, a shining path for her sons.

QUEEN ELIZABETH THE QUEEN MOTHER'S CENTURY

Courage and Wisdom; Behind the Smile Lies a Character of Steel

She is much loved and smarter than she looks. The legs are shaky, the eyes are weak but they don't miss much and the mind is sharp as ever. Behind that famous smile lies a racy disposition, a firm hand on the family helm, infinite courage and a flair for extravagant living.

My favourite portrait of Queen Elizabeth the Queen Mother is drawn from the scene at Buckingham Palace in May 1995, The VE-Day jubilee. She stepped out on the balcony, central figure between her daughters the Queen and Princess Margaret, a reminder to my generation of the star she had been when the enemy was at the gate.

What an artiste, I thought; and so she is, at 100 years of age. On the stage she would have wrung laughter and tears from her audiences; but mainly laughter, for she is a bit of wag and a good mimic. Part of the act is looking straight at you when she talks to you. She can make people feel, even in a crowd, that she is speaking to them and them only.

There was another and more poignant thought to be drawn from the balcony scene. It recalled the pain she suffered almost half a century ago when her sick husband King George VI died in his sleep, leaving her a widow at 51 without a throne, without a role and without a home.

She set about creating a life of her own and she has stuck to it. The world has changed a lot since then, but she has not. She clings to the routine of a past era, quite regardless of expense. Clarence House is staffed as it might have been during the reign of King Edward VII. She is, after all, an Edwardian. Everything around her is of the best.

There is also Birkhall on the 50,000-acre Balmoral estate, which is more bracing but no less well appointed. She owns a second home in Scotland, the Castle of Mey, which she bought as a ruin, restored and made snug soon after the King died and its isolation caught her mood. To keep Birkhall and Mey going costs a packet, and the Queen sighs, but the Queen Mother would probably say that Scotland, where she was born and spends the late summer and early autumn, is her spiritual home. It seems to be the rugged outdoor life that draws her still, the chilly mists, the driving rain. Diana, Princess of Wales loathed the Scottish life and was glad to escape from it. The Queen Mother cannot wait to get up there. She sees it also as a retreat from the disciplines of royal life. There is wisdom in seeking a place where you can be yourself for a while.

She hates to part from her personal staff. My old regimental mate, Lt Col Martin Gilliat of the King's Royal Rifle Corps, joined her as private secretary in 1956 and was coaxed into staying with the job until almost the final years of his life. The affection is entirely mutual. The staff are fond of her and enjoy indulging her little eccentricities.

When members of her family argued recently about GM crops, there appeared a headline: "Royals should be seen and not heard". Therein lies part of the Queen Mother's secret. She is rarely heard to speak, and so discloses very little of herself. Her circle is not one in which she "is overheard to say during a dinner party . . ." or in which "sources close to the Queen Mother say . . ." So nobody knows what she really thinks.

But she is the source of some good stories. My favourite relates to her visit to an old people's home. "Do you know who I am?" she asked one of them playfully. "If you don't know who you are, dear," came the reply, "go to the desk at the end of the corridor and they'll help you."

Towards the end of the Second World War, reading letters sent home by soldiers (as we had to do in those days) it struck me that when the boys came home many reunions would soon fail. I entered a plea through a third party for Queen Elizabeth to make a sympathetic broadcast about this, warning families of the difficulties ahead, urging patience. It didn't come off, because she didn't then and doesn't now like holding forth. But I sometimes wish it had. She would have made a good job of it, and in the post-war years the divorce rate among ex-service families soared.

There is, of course, a drawback to guarding your privacy as successfully as the Queen Mother does. It leaves critics free to tell tales about you which, for want of any other evidence, people tend to believe. Well-loved as she is, and though ardent republicans usually step carefully round her, the Queen Mother has not been immune from sniping. When Buckingham Palace was bombed during the war, for example, she was quoted as saying she was glad about it, for she could now look east London in the face.

On which Penelope Mortimer, a hostile witness, observed: "The East End, however, was not able to retreat to Windsor for the weekend to catch up on sleep, or to spend recuperative holidays in Norfolk and Scotland. Nor was the East End able to supplement its diet with pheasants and venison shot at the royal estates."

In reality, the King and Queen lived in huge discomfort at Buckingham Palace during the war. Rationing was observed. Eleanor Roosevelt, who stayed there in the autumn of 1941, found no heating, one electric bulb in each room and shallow bathwater.

There is light criticism of her enormous overdraft and her refusal to budge from an Edwardian style of life. A more persistent cloud hangs over the personal vendetta Queen Elizabeth is reputed to have conducted against the Duchess of Windsor. It runs so contrary to the public vision of the Queen Mother as a tender-hearted old thing.

As a reporter around the time of the abdication of Edward VIII, I have always thought it would be unnatural if the then Duchess of York had not heartily disliked and mistrusted the then Mrs Simpson. Bertie, the Duke of York, was closer to David, as the Prince of Wales was known within the family, than any other brother. Bertie and Elizabeth watched with anguish David's infatuation with an American divorcee.

It was a hole in the corner business because the British press (mainly from fear of defamation, but also with a sense of propriety that prevailed in those years) said nothing about it. Most of the gossip came from imported publications. So when the Bishop of Bradford unwittingly lit the touchpaper, the short-lived crisis exploded over a largely unsuspecting public. As a reporter, I was outside 145 Piccadilly, where the Yorks lived, to see their departure for the Palace. They looked strained with anxiety. "I don't think we could ever imagine a more incredible tragedy," the Queen wrote later, "and the agony of it was beyond words."

What few of us knew at the time was how much the Duke of Windsor, after his departure, preyed on his brother's peace of mind. We now know that Windsor could never have rallied support for his return, but it was not like that at the time. The King felt uneasy on the throne.

Edward then plagued his brother about money (after lying to him as to the extent of his own resources), about granting the Duchess the rank of HRH, and when war came what job he could do. Such was the pressure that at one point Queen Elizabeth feared it would cause her husband a breakdown.

She has been described as the sworn enemy of the Duchess of Windsor. It is nearer the mark to say that the King was driven almost batty by his brother and Elizabeth was fiercely protective of her troubled husband. How could it have been otherwise?

Ill-feeling between the two women was mutual. Wallis was contemptuous of Elizabeth: she and her husband referred to her as Cookie, an intended slight on her ample figure and her domestic inclinations, and called the young Princess Elizabeth "Shirley Temple". I met Edward as the Prince of Wales a couple of times. We once entertained him in Bethnal Green where my uncle, Wyndham Deedes, was engaged in social work. On short acquaintance, he struck me as fretful. I see him now pitching a half-finished cigar towards the fireplace of our sitting room—and missing it. But then and later he had countless admirers, among them (up to the war) Winston Churchill.

The waters ran deep. So deep that the King hoped Churchill would not be made Prime Minister in 1940. He and Elizabeth saw him as one of the old enemy. It was war that brought them together—war and the fact that Churchill came to see for himself the flaws in Edward's character. There is a good study to be made of how Churchill developed this thinking, how it communicated itself to the King and Queen, and slowly bound the three of them closer together.

As some have it, the Queen vetoed the title HRH for the Duchess of Windsor. As history has it, the King took the decision, cordially supported by his wife. In taking that decision, he had no precedent to guide him. Come to that, there was no precedent for the title of Queen Elizabeth the Queen Mother. It was a style she established for herself.

Before the Duchess of Windsor died, Elizabeth, while on an official visit to Paris, sought to make peace with her. The Duchess was too unwell to receive her, but flowers were left with a card: "In friendship. Elizabeth."

It is a plain statement of fact that the Queen played a heroic part in the war. The King told his wife virtually everything of importance and valued her opinions and advice. After wartime expeditions of her own, she would sometimes return with insight and fresh guidance. Between them, they travelled some 50,000 miles in this country alone. It was a close partnership, which made the pain of losing him so relatively early so acute.

Given the life she has led, it would be strange if the Queen Mother had not developed a strong will. She was a stronger character than her husband, who at first badly lacked self-confidence. When King George VI died, Churchill put on his wreath the VC's inscription "For valour." But the King was also a man of many moods, which Elizabeth understood better than any of his staff or his ministers.

We have forgotten how uncertain was the process of that war, and how many heavy blows it delivered before it was won. The strain of it wore him down. Without Elizabeth, it might have destroyed him.

Some reckon that the visit they made to Canada and America in the summer of 1939, and at the eve of war, was the most important voyage of their lives. The tour was a triumph. It altered the minds of some Americans who until then had inclined to side with the Duchess of Windsor as one of their own, and who saw Edward VIII as the rightful occupant of the throne.

The tour also had its bearing on American attitudes when war came. "It was," the President's roving ambassador Harry Hopkins later told Churchill, "the astounding success of the King and Queen's visit to the US which made America give up its partisanship of the Windsors."

If that was providential, so was the way they found each other. From the day Bertie first set eyes on Elizabeth at a London ball and fell in love with her, almost two and a half years elapsed before she accepted him. At the first time of asking, she turned him down. Not for her, she thought, the life of a servant to the country.

Blessed with other admirers, she seemed at one point more likely to marry the handsome James Stuart, a Scottish neighbour, MC and bar from the First World War, an MP at 26, Churchill's wartime Chief Whip and a serious philanderer. Bertie's luck seems to have turned on a false report in a London newspaper that Elizabeth was really destined for the Prince of Wales. In the flurry of embarrassment that caused, they went for a walk in the woods and Bertie won acceptance.

Talking at schools, I sometimes find the young have a better understanding of what the Queen Mother embodies by way of history than their elders. She was our last Empress of India, the last Queen to reign over the British Empire. A week before their coronation, Prime Minister Baldwin, appealing for peace in the coalfields and making the last speech of his life to the Commons, spoke of "our young King and Queen, who were called suddenly and unexpectedly to the most tremendous position on Earth". So it was, in May 1937.

Naturally, to some eyes in these times, the Queen Mother's level of living borders on the eccentric. She no longer has that talented snob Hartnell to dress her extravagantly well; but he more than anyone else established the regal style and her love of expensive clothes. In those days she never bothered to discuss prices and she doesn't now. The lure of milliners and hatters remains strong. Hence some of the overdraft.

The bank account joins other difficulties in life which the Queen Mother simply shrugs off. She has been described as an "emotional ostrich". The awkward things of life are gently pushed out of sight.

The same applies to little local difficulties within the family. She adores Charles, her favourite grandchild, and if she had had her way he would have gone to Eton, not Gordonstoun. But he won no support from her when he complained about school life.

Some of the bruising caused by his ill-starred marriage to Diana must have hurt her, mainly because she saw her as a threat to the stability of the Royal Family. But a remark she is said to have made to the Queen on one occasion—"different generation; let them get on with it . . ."—gives the flavour of her philosophy towards the young mismatches. When it came to the Townsend affair with her own daughter Margaret, she was described as "serenely detached". There is no knowing how she really felt about it. Perhaps she owes something of her longevity to this gift of shrugging off life's awkwardnesses.

No sensible person grudges the Queen Mother's style of life, her ample staff, stable of horses in Norfolk and love of racing over half a century, her talent with rod and line, her taste for a stiff gin and Dubonnet. One does wonder though how far that formidable will had discouraged changes in the Royal Family's ways of doing things.

There has, after all, been a conscious endeavour by the Queen and her family to adjust to the fact that we are no longer an imperial power; that she no longer occupies "the most tremendous position on Earth".

But we "mustn't upset granny". And granny, in common with many grannies, likes things as they were. If she strongly opposes an idea, the chances are she will get her way. Prince Philip exercises caution in that direction.

A devout Christian, she does not take divorce as lightly as some. A divorced acquaintance is liable to suffer banishment. Yet she is not a prude. In the old days, she relished an after-the-show supper at the Savoy Grill with Noel Coward, a discreet but notorious homosexual. She can thoroughly enjoy herself in pretty raffish company.

Then again, there are times when we see the stoic in her. She has always taken her physical mishaps lightly, and there have been quite a few. Yet, along with the cold Scottish mists, she loves the pampered life. A woman of attractive contradictions. Such a well-known figure to us all, and yet how little we know of her. Behind the smile, steel.

1952: THE WAY WE WERE

The year of the Queen's accession was marked by continuing shortages, colonial insurrection and disaster, both natural and man-made. Yet optimism about the new reign was undimmed. W. F. Deedes recalls a Britain that believed itself to be at the dawn of a new age

What caught people's hearts was a picture of the young Queen, dressed in black, descending the steps of the BOAC plane that had flown her back from Africa. It is difficult now to convey the depth of emotion aroused by the sudden death of King George VI in February 1952 and the accession of his elder daughter, the mother of two young children. It's difficult, because we have changed so much in the past half century.

Waiting to greet her as she stepped off the plane in the early dusk at London Airport was Winston Churchill, bare-headed, black-coated, Clem Attlee, the Leader of the Opposition, and other officers of state. On his way to the airport to welcome the Queen, Churchill, in tears, had been dictating the broadcast he was to deliver later that evening. He spoke of a King who had "walked with death, as if death were a companion, an acquaintance whom he recognised and did not fear".

Then, after reminding his audience that the second Queen Elizabeth now ascending the throne was the same age as the first Queen Elizabeth nearly 400 years before, Churchill concluded: "I, whose youth was passed in the august, unchallenged and tranquil glories of the Victorian era, may well feel a thrill in invoking once more the prayer and the anthem *God Save the Queen.*"

Churchill's words point to the confluence of two powerful currents of emotion that passed through the nation in those days. There was mourning for a well-loved King, who had unexpectedly been called upon to shoulder the burden of monarchy, who had led his people through a terrible war and whose life had ended at the relatively early age of 56.

Throughout the days and far into the nights of February 12, 13 and 14, tens of thousands waited in rain, sleet and snow to pay their last respects to the King at his lying-in-state in Westminster Hall. The queues at times were four miles long.

Equally, there were fervent hopes of a fresh beginning under this young Queen. The country had taken a long time not fully to recover from the toils and ravages of the Second World War. People had grown weary of shortages, second best and warnings about our dire circumstances. A younger generation had tired of its elders' lamentations.

There was a life to lead and here, in the person of a beautiful young Queen, was someone who would show the way.

These emotions ran deep. The Serpent had not yet entered the Garden. Cynicism about all things royal, later imported by Rupert Murdoch, was in abeyance. When, immediately after the death of the King, the Queen and Prince Philip left their lodge in Kenya for home, thus abandoning the long tour that had been planned for them, the world's press lined the road. Lord Charteris, Queen Elizabeth's Private Secretary, asked them not to take pictures. Not a single photograph was taken.

People were full of solicitude. Admiration and hopes for her were mingled with sympathy "and a feeling almost akin to pity", as someone expressed it at the time, "that this charming young woman should be set apart on an awful eminence and dedicated to a service that in the ordinary course could only end with death".

There was anxiety lest a Queen with two young children became overburdened by the cares of state. The National Federation of Women's Institutes passed a resolution urging the nation "not to overwork our beloved young Queen, remembering that she has her duties also as wife and mother".

The Queen's response to all this was sensible. "My father died much too young," she said later, "and so it was all very sudden . . . it was a matter of making the best job you can . . . and accepting the fact that it's your fate."

In the 16 months that lay before the Coronation, fate took a hand. In reality, although most people failed to appreciate it, our slow recovery from the aftermath of war was quickening. Churchill had taken office after the autumn general election of 1951, four months before the King's death.

The haemorrhaging of gold and dollars that threatened in the words of his Chancellor of the Exchequer, R A Butler, to leave

Britain "bankrupt, idle and hungry" had been checked. Churchill had gone with a small party to America at the start of 1952 to resolve certain mutual problems. The gap in power and wealth between the United States and Britain—and, indeed, post-war Europe—had grown disturbingly wide.

Shortages here were gradually easing. Controls were coming off. "Set the people free" was proving a useful slogan for the Tories.

> Far back through creeks and inlets making
> Comes silent, flooding in, the main . . .

That, however, was not at all as it appeared in the months immediately after the Queen's accession. True, the meat ration was up to 1s 7d a week, but in March 1952 the cheese ration had to be cut to 1oz a week. One household in three still lacked a bath. There was a chronic shortage of homes.

Overseas, a dangerous war was still running in Korea, to which Labour had thought it right for us to contribute our forces. There was insurrection in Kenya. The process of dismantling our empire had begun. Within a month of the Queen's accession, Kwame Nkrumah led the way by winning power in the Gold Coast, which became Ghana. Some Conservatives were unhappy at the gathering speed with which this dismantling was taking place.

Yet, as the Queen was aware, there was an historical inevitability about it. Once India had won independence in 1947, the cornerstone of empire had gone. America, upon whom we had become heavily dependent, was anything but supportive of colonialism. In any case, drained by war, we could not afford colonies.

The situation in Kenya was alarming. A violent underground movement dubbed Mau Mau had grown to a point where a state of emergency had to be declared and many arrests were made.

In April 1952, Jomo Kenyatta was convicted of having "managed" Mau Mau and sentenced to imprisonment with hard labour, where he became a symbol of Kenyan nationalism—and ultimately the country's first Prime Minister.

We tried to take one positive step in Africa by creating a Central African Federation. Comprising Northern and Southern Rhodesia (now Zambia and Zimbabwe) and Nyasaland (Malawi), it was presented as a viable unit. Electric power would come from the new Kariba dam, harnessing the waters of the Zambesi river. But the idea never really caught on. It aroused hostility among Africans in all three countries; and it ended in tears and Ian Smith's unilateral declaration of independence in Southern Rhodesia little more than a decade later.

Back in this country, nature took a violent turn. A flash flood at Lynmouth in Devon killed 31 people and left hundreds homeless. Early in 1953, the sea invaded East Anglia, killing 282 people. On the last day of January, a spring tide coincided with a sea surge of between 6ft and 8ft. Sea surges, produced by barometric pressure, are unpredictable, but do not normally exceed one foot in height. This, one combined with a strong north-easterly gale, led to catastrophe.

So the earliest days of the second Elizabethan Age we yearned for was marked by a litany of disasters. In the late summer of 1952, a jet fighter at Farnborough broke the sound barrier and crashed, leaving 26 people dead. In October, a railway smash at Harrow killed 112 people.

In May 1953, the crash of one of our new Comet airplanes killed 43 people. The stars were off their course for the Comet, which was running overnight flights from South Africa to this country. It was a beautiful machine. I remember seeing people gather on airport roofs in Nairobi to watch the London-bound Comet go through. More crashes led to its abandonment. Churchill was furious when he learnt that a dozen MPs had flown in a Comet. He counted the number of by-elections that might have threatened his slender majority.

The Queen's Prime Minister, nearing 80 years of age, was entering the last phase of his long public life. I had seen them together at a dinner given by the Speaker of the House of Commons in 1951. Churchill, sitting opposite her, was enchanted by the young Princess. She treated him with affectionate respect and an occasional twinkle of amusement. On her accession, Churchill told the House of Commons: "She comes to the throne at a time when tormented mankind stands uncertainly poised between catastrophe and a golden age. That it should be a golden age of art and letters we can only hope. Science and machinery have their other tales to tell.

"But it is certain that, if the nations will only let each other alone, an immense and undreamed of prosperity, with culture and leisure ever more widely spread, can come, perhaps even easily and swiftly, to the masses of people in every land.

"Let us hope and pray that the accession to our ancient throne of Queen Elizabeth II may be the signal for such a brightening salvation of the human scene."

Now, that voice was fading. In 1952, as his physician, Lord Moran, revealed in his memoirs, Churchill suffered a spasm of memory loss. Moran was reasonably reassuring. But within a month of the Queen's Coronation in June 1953, Churchill suffered a fairly severe stroke, which put him out of action for several weeks.

He recovered sufficiently to return to duty and reshape his administration in October 1954, before taking his final bow from No 10 in the spring of 1955. Anthony Eden succeeded him, but not for long.

Thus, within the first three years of her reign, the Queen had to acclimatise herself to three different Tory Prime Ministers.

But before Churchill went, she had persuaded him to accept the Garter, an honour he had declined at the close of the Second World War. "I took it because it was the Queen's wish," he wrote to a friend. "I think she is splendid."

Half a century ago, most people shared Churchill's view. Aware of it, newspapers and the BBC were cautious about comment that might be seen as unfriendly to the Queen or her family.

Malcolm Muggeridge wrote a couple of faintly irreverent pieces about the Royal Family for the *Saturday Evening Post* that today would have passsed unremarked. Two Sunday newspapers led an attack on him and Muggeridge found himself in the stocks being pelted with abuse. He became embittered by the experience.

Those gentler years are beyond recall. But in this Jubilee year, can we find nothing that distinguishes the second Elizabethan Age? We need to look beyond the end of our noses. I find it extraordinary that in a shaky world we stay on such relatively good terms with what was formerly the British Empire. Precious few empires of the past could claim as much and we owe it very largely to this Queen's determination.

Proclaimed on her accession Head of the Commonwealth, she had embroidered on her Coronation dress of white satin symbols of the Commonwealth countries. Australia's wattle, Ceylon's lotus flower and Pakistan's wheat and jute were added to the traditional English rose, Scottish thistle and Welsh leek.

This thread has run through her reign. That the British Commonwealth exists today owes more to the Queen than any of her 10

Prime Ministers. Harold Macmillan paid lip service to it, but his heart was in Europe. "The great majority," he told the Queen, "feel that our position in the Commonwealth, should we weaken industrially and economically, would ultimately fade away."

Ted Heath was even less enthusiastic about it. When we eventually got into Europe, the former Empire was elbowed aside and told to make its own way.

Differing quietly from her Prime Ministers, the Queen has seen her role as Head of the Commonwealth as a trust no less important than her position as Queen of Great Britain. After her Coronation in June 1953, she set off on a six-month tour of the Commonwealth and countless tours have followed. The Queen has established friendships not simply with Commonwealth leaders but also the people who work with them. She remembers their names, members of their family and past encounters.

People may ask: what has it gained us? It has contributed to peace in an ill-tempered world and, if you doubt it, look at the odd man out, Mugabe of Zimbabwe. The triumphs of the first Elizabethan Age, with its conquest and pillage, would not win much support in today's world. But in this second Elizabethan Age, we have pulled off an extraordinary trick.

We have dismantled an empire, imperfectly, but far less disastrously than earlier empires. Thanks to the Queen, we have reshaped it in a form acceptable to the 21st century; and with its members we remain friends. That's something to remember when we mark this Jubilee.

April 2002

SHE REMAINED A CHEERFUL FIGURE THROUGH YEARS OF TRIAL, SORROW AND ANXIETY

W. F. Deedes looks back at previous State funerals and considers how the Queen Mother's death will have a profoundly emotional effect on people of all ages

For people of all ages, but particularly older folk, the funeral of Queen Elizabeth the Queen Mother, like the funeral of Queen Victoria just over a century ago, will mark the passing of an age.

That is why, all personal feeling for her apart, it will be a profoundly emotional occasion.

This was a woman whose experience stretched back beyond the recollections of nearly all of us.

Some of her friends were killed in the First World War, when she was old enough to nurse the wounded. You would have to be over 80 years old to remember her marriage to Prince Albert, Duke of York, in April 1923.

When Queen Victoria died early in 1901, at the age of 81, people looked back thankfully on an epoch of marked British success. They had won most of their relatively small wars, occupied vast territories and, as a nation, were prosperous.

Rudyard Kipling had perceived the other side of this triumphalism with his Recessional, but the feeling among most people was that the old Queen had left us on top of the world.

Two world wars have helped to make the era of Queen Elizabeth more one of sacrifice than success. She was aware of that, which is why almost to the end of her life she would visit the Armistice Sunday crosses outside Westminster Abbey.

But what people will remember on the day of her funeral is what a cheerful figure she has steadfastly remained through years of trial, sorrow and anxiety.

In one respect, we should remember on taking farewell of the Queen Mother, the two Queens shared the same burden. Queen

Victoria had been a widow for 40 years when she died; this Queen suffered ten years more than that of widowhood.

Churchill's funeral in January 1965 in St Paul's Cathedral, which I attended, carried much of this profound sense of an epoch that was closing.

It was a magnificent event, which he had taken time and pains to prepare. There was a big military presence and an RAF flypast. Minute Guns were fired from St James's Park and the Tower of London.

"There will be lively tunes," Harold Macmillan promised us in Cabinet, after discussing Churchill's preparations with him a year or two before he died. Sure enough, we opened with the hymn *Who would true valour see, / Let him come hither . . .*, followed by *Mine eyes have seen the glory of the coming of the Lord . . .*

Then, after the Lesson from 1 Corinthians 15.20—"Now is Christ risen from the dead, and become the first fruits of them that slept . . ."—the organ and choir led us into *Fight the good fight with all thy might . . .*

As the coffin was carried out of the Cathedral, we sang *O God, our help in ages past . . .* Given the character we were mourning, it would be hard to better that selection.

When it came to *Last Post*, I remember glancing at one or two of Winston's old political adversaries, sharing to the full the sense of loss, all past differences out of mind.

On these occasions the emotion aroused by remembrance of the years that have slipped away is all-powerful, wiping away past grievances.

Yet, even in death, the greatest of statesmen cannot altogether convey that sense of history sweeping past us that comes to us when, after long reigns, crowned heads depart.

For all but a minority, which disapproves of monarchy anyway, feel uniquely drawn together by this message of the passing years.

Queen Victoria was accorded a military funeral. On Feb 1, 1901 the yacht Alberta, passing between long lines of warships firing a last salute, bore her coffin from Cowes to Gosport.

A day later it was moved to London. No British sovereign, it was said at the time, was more sincerely mourned. She had had her dark years after Albert's death, when she became reclusive to the point of arousing republican sentiments.

But, as the historian G. M. Trevelyan observed, though Victoria was possessed in a high degree of queenly instincts and dignity, they were softened and popularised by a mind and an emotional nature of great simplicity . . . "she was a simple wife and widow-woman, who would have been at home in any cottage parlour." That is not far removed from how many will remember this Queen.

We have retained a wonderful gift in this country for ceremonial which we shall display to the world when this Queen is buried; but strangely, it does not always depend on the prolonged thought and care which Churchill gave to his own departure.

The funeral of Diana, Princess of Wales in September 1997 in Westminster Abbey had to be drawn up very rapidly, well inside a week. Yet I remember thinking how well it managed to convey the right message.

One difference between all these state occasions, from Queen Victoria's funeral to Churchill's, from Diana's to this well-loved Queen's lies in changed attitudes to religion.

When Victoria was buried, poverty was much more widespread than it is today, and so also was religious belief.

Yet, as we shall see when this funeral takes place, the depth of public feeling aroused by the loss of a familiar and well-loved figure has not altered a great deal.

It still runs deep. Gratitude? Affection? Sentiment? This sense of an age that is passing? Or is it "a twitch on the thread?" Hard to tell.

NO CORNER OF THE QUEEN'S REALM CAN HAVE FELT EXCLUDED FROM THIS JOYOUS CELEBRATION

For two days we saw a page of our history unfurled and brilliantly illustrated by sketches of us as we truly are. Of all the royal pageants I have seen in the past 70 years this one came closer to the life of our nation than any before it. And never at the close has The Mall been so crammed.

There has certainly been no great state occasion with a wider embrace. No corner of the Queen's realm can have felt excluded. Certainly not elderly pop stars, the bikers, nor performers in the Notting Hill Carnival Parade, nor young children of the Commonwealth, nor the many who render service voluntarily.

Nor, bless its heart, was Slough, where the Queen and Prince Philip did a walkabout on Monday, finally expunging, we may hope, that mischievous line by Betjeman—"Come friendly bombs".

Slough, it is good to report, saw Prince Philip at his most benign, smiling and waving at the children. "Newspapers only notice me," one supposes he sometimes murmurs to the Queen, "when I've dropped a clanger."

Well, to mark this jubilee let us say something different. He can be salty, as some sailors are; but, one judges, when storms blew up and seas raged, as they have occasionally done during this reign, he could be trusted at the wheel.

Do we really suppose the Queen has never had dark hours during her time on the throne, has never felt the need for a supporting arm?

The Prince will never get his due for the part he's played in helping to keep things on an even keel; and to his credit he won't expect it.

Down in The Mall as Monday night's concert struck up and sent the Golden Jubilee into orbit, crowds streaming everywhere, you could see how skilfully they'd guarded against any feeling of exclusion. People wanted to see the stars as well as hear them—which you did all through St James's. High marks to whoever thought of screens in The Mall.

These were the foot soldiers, one felt, defying the weather forecasters, forsaking their cosy chairs and television at home, humping their young and their bedding—for some of them, I saw, slept out in the park.

For ever after they could say, "I was there—I saw Dame Edna Everage greet the Queen, saw Rod Stewart bow low to her, heard Paul McCartney sing to her."

"I don't think any of us will forget this evening," said the Prince of Wales as he stood among the performers delivering a tribute to his mother, the Queen. Yes, they'll remember it for a long time; an evening made memorable by its music and dazzling by the technicians to whom the Prince paid tribute. The critics will have their say about individual performances, but the evening didn't belong to them. To my untutored eye the whole show looked a triumphant success.

As the fireworks went off, I saw the Queen glance at the roof of her Palace and with that dry humour her face conveys so well, express the unspoken thought, "Well, if that doesn't set the place on fire, nothing on earth can."

How astounded Queen Victoria would have been to see 12,000 of her subjects chosen by lot and feasting off chicken and champagne on the lawns of Buckingham Palace. So for that matter would this Queen's grandfather, King George V. From what I saw of it, the Queen looked as if it happened every day.

But once or twice towards the end of Monday evening, as the cheers went up from a huge crowd, there crossed her face the touching look her grandfather wore at his Silver Jubilee, which said I hardly knew they cared so much.

Glancing through the ranks of young children brought to The Mall and close to the Palace to share the joys of recent days, one fell to wondering what in, say, fifty years' time they will remember of all this. What will they be telling their grandchildren about this Golden Jubilee?

Some of the boys, I suppose, will long retain in their mind's eye that final scene as Concorde and aircraft not on the drawing board at the start of her reign thundered over the Palace roof and those acrobats of the air, the Red Arrows sprayed out the national colours in the sky.

The girls will carry the music in their heads for a while. They led the field, I thought, in this festival of song because wherever they were they sang as if their hearts were in it. They did so much, those younger children, to spread the joy around. They'll remember these days and will be passing some of it on to their grandchildren half a century or so on.

Today's grandparents are more likely to remember that balcony scene itself—the Queen surrounded by her family—and yet in one sense alone there have been quite a few of those scenes in this half century, but none perhaps conveying so poignantly the lonely eminence of duty at the top.

Just suppose, I imagined, as she stood there waving at the million in The Mall, that she had learned during the day that war between India and Pakistan was now virtually unstoppable and that all her subjects still in India were menaced by nuclear war.

At the age of 76, with that on her mind, she must still acknowledge those cheering thousands round the Queen Victoria Memorial and look entirely happy at this, the climax of a tremendous show and fifty years on the throne. A lonely eminence indeed.

The music we heard at different times will echo on for a while in many heads. The Beatles, as Paul McCartney reminded us, have run through most of this reign; but they are exceptional. Modern songs tend to die young. Whatever happened to those hits at the start of this reign—*I Love Paris*, *Rock Around the Clock* and *Rosemarie*?

It is more likely, I think, that when the children who were there this week become grandparents they will still be singing, as the congregation sang in St Paul's Cathedral during yesterday morning's Service of Celebration and Thanksgiving, Ralph Vaughan Williams's timeless rendering of *Who would true valour see* or H F Lyte's *Praise my soul, the King of Heaven*.

For the Queen herself, one senses, the service in St Paul's of celebration and renewal was the climax of her jubilee. When she uses the expression, "and with God's help," she means it. Some of her subjects feel they can do without it, but this Queen emphatically does not. How else to bear all that responsibility for fifty years?

Yet an early footnote is called for at this point. In days past, before what is denounced as deference (but is no more than courtesy) became incorrect, newspapers' criticism of the monarch was camouflaged by phrases such as "it is felt that royal advisers were wrong to . . ."

Now it should go on record, I thought while listening to Chicken Shed Children's and Youth Theatre and the Golden Jubilee Gospel Choir, as they sang about the future in The Mall yesterday afternoon, that this time round, the royal advisers got it right. Maybe Prince William and Harry got a word in their ear.

This Golden Jubilee, I think I hear them agreeing round some paper-laden table months ago, must put its shirt on the future. If the Crown is to draw the respect and affection of those now in their teens and younger, then it must show them how far it is in tune with them and what they like the most. The path to their heart is music and that is the path this jubilee must take. The grand old men of music, my ear at the keyhole hears them saying, must have a place; but if we want the hearts of the young, then these are the stars who must play and these are the songs they must sing.

And let those of mature years, who have no taste for pop and harbour dark thoughts about Ozzy Osbourne, yet wish the future of the monarchy well, swallow their prejudices and agree that this was a very good idea.

And while in generous mood, let's give the BBC its due because it gave this grand theme reality. Of course, being famously neutral about the monarchy, it had occasionally to tip its hat to those who felt the whole thing was a waste of time; simply an opportunity, as one sourpuss put it, "for the Royal Family to engage in self-promotion".

The Corporation contrived to do this through what they called Interactive, a running commentary from those who wished to deliver bouquets or brickbats. But much may be forgiven the BBC for constantly keeping us in mind that this was a national and not a metropolitan festival. This was not simply London and its visitors rejoicing around the Palace and The Mall. There were, the BBC reminded us—especially in Monday's nationwide rendition of *All You Need is Love*—a lot of people rejoicing in less exciting places.

There was consolation for the traditionalists with that gold carriage commissioned by George III—and one in the eye for Civil List nitpickers with the Windsorian coach which conveyed the lesser lights to St Paul's so economically.

"But granny, did the Queen really approve of all those funny people they brought into her Golden Jubilee?" "Yes, dear, I've always understood she wanted them brought in."

It's never easy to read the truth in these great state occasions.

This one was more imaginative than any I have seen. Yesterday morning in St Paul's illustrated so well the wide embrace.

Different faiths, the unknown young, and members of the Commonwealth were drawn in, alongside church leaders. Come to think of it, the homespun words of the Archbishop of Canterbury fitted the occasion very well.

Of course, as we saw in The Mall yesterday, the girls have only eyes for Will. That's natural enough and anyway he's part of that family of which the Queen spoke with such feeling at the Lord Mayor's lunch.

And after she got her standing ovation—hey, what is this? None other than our Prime Minister! Swallow your prejudices again. I thought it came at a funny time, but it wasn't half bad. Prince Philip blinked a bit when Mr Blair paid him a compliment; but to do Mr Blair justice, he got close to the heart of it. She has adapted monarchy successfully to the modern world. Awareness of that drew a lot of cheers.

If you want to know what people really think about her, wake them up in the park, as I did early yesterday, after they've spent a damp night there, sleeping rough. For the time being, and let's say no more than that, this thing has sunk in. Deep.

And it does seem that the warm feeling she drew from so many owes something to the quality that Mr Blair spoke of, "commitment to the service of others".

What a day of contrasts it was. From the choir of St Paul's to the best that the Mansion House chefs can put on a plate, the City ascendant. Then back to The Mall again where the dress designers reminded us that the Empire has indeed got much smaller since Queen Victoria's Diamond Jubilee of 1897 but the Commonwealth, which this Queen more than anyone else has distilled from it, is far more colourful.

Good to think she hasn't travelled all those thousands of miles for fifty years to no end. We caught glimpses of what she has been looking at, over and over again, on the dusty plains of Africa and other distant lands. Multiracial? Obviously. One heart? Ah, harder to say; but nobody could have tried more than this Queen has done to make it so.

Then the young singers with their message to the youth of the world. Never in our history have so many baseball caps come within sight of the Palace windows. But this is how they wanted it to be:

young voices hailing the world that lies in wait for them, not older voices regretting the world that has gone past.

After Notting Hill and the river of gold, the Services parade seemed unremarkable; but service save in dire emergencies is usually unremarkable, which is why it goes unthanked. Then how did we live in the five decades of this reign? How did we dance, what did we drive—and why did we pour all that gravy and sauce over our food? Interesting, but not riveting. The Queen contrived for the most part, towards the end of a long two days, to look riveted.

Last and rather more colourful than our living habits, the Commonwealth. Well, I thought, as they rolled past, how many nations in history after their empires had gone could have put on a show like this? None of them could. As in those final moments she marched cheerfully along with those children, we witnessed her finest hour.

"But granny, didn't it cost an awful lot of money to give her that big party with all those fireworks?" "Yes, I expect it did. But it's a dull heart that never rejoices. We wanted to show that monarchy might have drawbacks, but we liked it best."

"And her as well?" "Yes, deep down we were and still are a fair-minded people. Most of us felt in our hearts that she'd done her duty well, had come through sad times composed and dignified, had shown, as the Archbishop said at the time, 'the steadfastness of a faithful servant'. She was old enough too, remember, to wear uniform in that war of long ago.

"She'd salvaged a Commonwealth out of a lost empire without much encouragement from any of the 10 Prime Ministers who'd kissed her hand.

"For fifty years she had walked on a swaying tightrope between tradition and the need for change. So all in all she deserved the fanfares, the pop stars, big bands and lots of fireworks."

"And after all that, she went on working, granny?" "Yes."

WHY BURRELL TURNED FROM
JEKYLL TO HYDE

The reason for his betrayal runs deeper than the money he received from the Mirror, writes W. F. Deedes

Most people will be moved by the protest from Prince William and Prince Henry at Paul Burrell's betrayal of their mother; but some will also be asking a leading question. What has led Burrell, who at one time was apparently the devoted servant of Diana, Princess of Wales and has shown discretion during the years since her death, into committing this gross abuse of trust; what turned him from Dr Jekyll into Mr Hyde?

As one who travelled overseas with both of them and came to know Burrell a bit, I have been pondering this. Was it simply, as it often is, betrayal in return for money? Was it the *Daily Mirror*'s £300,000 that persuaded him to inflict such hurt on the sons of a woman he served with devotion? I have an idea it runs deeper than that.

One must start I think with the extraordinary but genuine friendship which developed between the Princess and Burrell. It was formed some time before her marriage to the Prince of Wales broke down. One day, when we met at a charity lunch, she said lightly to me: "My butler is finding *The Daily Telegraph* crossword puzzle much more difficult. Have you changed the system?"

"Yes," I said. As editor at the time I had agreed to a fresh batch of compilers, so that solving the puzzles became less of a routine. Thereafter when we met, this subject of the crossword came up. "My butler still feels very strongly about it." I did not meet this crossword puzzle fanatic until August 1997, when Burrell came with us both to Bosnia, where we were meeting victims of landmines.

By then he was valet, butler, companion and confidant to her; and bodyguard as well. At one point on that tour, we spent the night in a small, newly opened hotel. As I left my room for breakfast, Burrell emerged from the room opposite after delivering her breakfast. "Join me for a meal downstairs," I suggested. He agreed, but never appeared. When I went back to my room Burrell was sitting in a chair with his back to Diana's door, looking fierce.

The hotel manager, he told me, had burst into her room eager to hear her opinion of his new hotel. "Very continental," I told him consolingly. "They think nothing of barging into women's bedrooms over here." He was not appeased and kept sentry duty at her door until she had dressed and was ready for the day's work.

This was a close and innocent companionship, consoling in those difficult days for Diana, who treated all class distinctions lightly, but as it turned out, highly dangerous for Burrell.

It left him with the invincible impression that he was her only friend in the world, and furthermore her personal trustee in life and death. "My rock," she called him. This sad delusion, I am convinced, is what persuaded Burrell after her death to form that extraordinary treasure trove of her possessions which led to his prosecution and such trouble for so many others as well.

It was selfish and wrong of her, some will say, to lead a valet into such a false position. But when in distress, human beings do sometimes find companionship and consolation in unexpected quarters; even Queen Victoria was not above seeking an escape from loneliness through the companionship of one of her servants.

And how could Diana tell that her life was about to end, as it did a week or so after our Bosnia trip? The fact remains that this relationship and its abrupt termination left Burrell hopelessly off balance.

He secretively stowed away Diana's property in that possessive mood with which she had endowed him—though not neglecting to make some mention of it to the Queen. When I heard they intended to prosecute him, I reckoned they were barmy, thought of putting in an oar, then thought better of it. What defence would it be to declare that psychologically I held some dim idea of why he had hidden away this strange treasure trove?

In the end that line of thinking prevailed at his trial, but not without leaving a trail of trouble for other people and, I have reason to think, throwing an unbalanced Burrell even further off his balance. That trial cost him dear, certainly morally and probably financially. Is that where we begin to see the features of Dr Jekyll altering terribly into those of Mr Hyde?

There are some of course who will take a totally different view of all this, who will declare that Diana was born to make trouble as the sparks fly upwards and, choosing her servants carelessly, entered a wholly false position with a rogue butler. That will satisfy her detractors, but it is false and not at all the right response to this agonised cry from the two Princes.

They are wholly innocent parties in this and should be offered the clearest explanation I can muster. Burrell in selling these revelations—some of which should never have seen the light of day—gives every appearance of being a thorough rogue. But I do not think he is that. He is in truth an extremely simple-minded fellow, wholly unequal to the moral responsibilities that Diana unwittingly imposed on him, tormented by a trial that should never have been allowed to take place, thus easily persuaded that he owed himself the proceeds from this book, in which he declares incongruously he takes great pride. That statement really tells us all we need to know about his state of mind.

This is not to brush aside the conduct of publishers and newspapers who exploit fools like Burrell, but that is a different story. We know enough about their state of mind. Burrell, once the apparently faithful servant to the mother of Prince William and Prince Henry, is the enigma.

He'll now get his chat shows on television, will be able to restore his depleted bank balance, but in most other respects will be cast into outer darkness, even deeper than the darkness that enveloped him during that silly trial. It would require the hand of Shakespeare to do justice to the sources and the consequences of such a tragedy.

February 2005

DIANA WOULD BE HAPPY
FOR HER SONS

Most people will take their cue from the Queen and be glad. Only those clinging to our well-deserved national reputation for taking pleasures sadly will ask impatiently: "Why has it taken so long?" Yes, it has been a long road; I think inevitably so. For that first unhappy marriage undertaken by the Prince of Wales divided this nation more sharply than we realise.

I think back to the moment in Westminster Abbey during the funeral of Diana, Princess of Wales when her brother, the Earl Spencer, delivered the address in words bound to cause distress to the Royal Family and embarrassment to the Prince of Wales; and through the doors of the Abbey, we heard the sound of clapping from the public stands outside. I scribbled in my notebook, "This will run deep." And so it has.

In a spasm of emotion that none of us quite understood, part of the nation—quite a large part, too—took upon itself to endow the late Princess with sainthood; and worse, to see her as a victim of other people's misconduct. Our own profession of journalism took on itself to reproach the Queen for not displaying in public sufficient sorrow over the death of her daughter-in-law.

A victim of this national mood, which the passage of time has been setting in proper proportion, was Camilla Parker Bowles. That she had behaved irreproachably throughout this feverish bout stood her in no stead at all. In the irrational mood that seized much of the nation after Diana's sudden death, and that some now look back on rather questioningly, Camilla Parker Bowles was out in the cold.

There were, let us remember, the "Camillagate" tapes as well as the "Squidgy" tapes, telephone conversations picked up by hams. They found their way into newspapers. Small wonder the Queen felt moved in her Christmas broadcast of 1992 to describe the passing year as *annus horribilis*.

Time would have to pass before memories of that epoch faded, and that is one answer to those now heard muttering, "and about time, too". Nor in what is coming up to be the decade since Diana's death have the efforts made by the Prince of Wales's entourage to speed matters up been altogether conducive to a happy ending.

Obstacles have been strewn along the way. One of them was the prosecution of the butler, Paul Burrell, an episode calculated to lay bare old wounds and revive nightmares.

In a piece I wrote about Diana in a recent book, I declared that the role of the news media in the trials of that first marriage had been seriously underrated. That remains true and in all honesty has to be repeated here. Since the affair of Edward VIII leading on to his abdication, so discreetly handled by the press of those days, newspapers have changed a good deal. The face of our tabloid brothers has sharper fangs and a more derisive smirk, as one writer has put it, and that remains true. It applies to their treatment of modern royalty.

Inevitably that abdication story will be dragged out again now, with particular reference to the future status of the woman the Prince of Wales intends to make his wife. So it is well to get clear now the facts of an event so long out of public memory.

Edward VIII forfeited the throne because the Cabinet of those days, in the light of feeling in the British Commonwealth and in this country, felt unable to support him. Sir Ivor Jennings, in his authoritative book on Cabinet government, has it right: "The Sovereign cannot act unconstitutionally so long as he acts on the advice of a minister supported by a majority in the House of Commons."

Stanley Baldwin, prime minister at the time of the Abdication, knew very well how the Commonwealth felt. Telegrams established that. He felt much less sure how the public felt. He found his own party in a wobbly state of mind, partly because of Churchill's attitude, which was friendly to the King.

After a cloudy meeting with the Conservative Party, which dominated the then so-called Coalition government, Baldwin gave sensible advice. "Cancel smart engagements you have have for the forthcoming week-end," he instructed Tory MPs. "Go into the pubs and working men's clubs, listen to what they are saying, and we will meet again on Monday." When they all met again, the issue was resolved. In a humiliating scene in the Commons, Churchill was shouted down.

Baldwin is credited or discredited with getting rid of the King. In fact, he played by the book. He acted with the authority of his Cabinet, which was swayed by opinion in the Commonwealth, and which knew it had the support of a majority in the House of Commons.

We may be sure that Mr Blair has been made privy to all these arrangements and has been able to give the necessary assurances. His Cabinet will not quibble over what is proposed and, in the House of Commons he has forged, he can be confident of ample support.

I recall the circumstances of the abdication and I also have a clear memory of Edward's temperament when he was Prince of Wales. He did not make life easy for ministers. He carried a grudge for not being allowed to fight in the front line of the First World War, seemingly unaware of the difficulties his country would experience were he taken prisoner and not simply killed. Royalty is entitled to a touch of arrogance, but not petulance.

Prince Charles takes this step under altogether happier auspices. There has been a vast change in the nation's attitude to marriage for one thing. It is open to question whether more liberal—or should we say, forgiving—attitudes to second marriages are to be approved or disapproved. But they exist in a way they did not 70 years ago. This fresh match should be put in the context of our times, not the Edwardian era.

Let those with doubts about it ponder one or two questions.

Will the lives of Prince William and Prince Harry be made easier or harder by this step? What a relief no longer to read endless speculation about their father's future intentions. This nation, or part of it, has turned to drawing entertainment from tormented feelings. The long struggle to decide whether this move was right and acceptable has drawn a huge audience, not all of it supportive of monarchy. That has ended. The two princes are beneficiaries. They will be happier. To that extent, it may be seen as fulfilling Diana's dearest wish—that her sons should be happy. "I take them to McDonald's," I once heard her explain to someone. "They consider it a treat."

Yes, let those who would greet this marriage with mawkish memories of Diana days reflect on the thoughts she had for those two sons and their future happiness. Yes, she worried incessantly about the shadow of Camilla Parker Bowles. It became something of an obsession and led to acts of folly. That is all behind us now. Let's give the imagination a chance. Yes, she'd be happy now for those two boys.

And let the vast majority of citizens who support the monarchy reflect on the weight that this announcement lifts from the Queen's mind. For she has had to ponder the issue more than anyone else, more indeed than the couple directly involved. Though thoroughly down to earth in many ways, the Queen takes with great seriousness how any action by her may rebound on the monarchy.

After living through so many prime ministers, she has unmatched experience and that in itself imposes great responsibility. She cannot, as other mothers are free to do, let the heart govern the head. This a woman who puts duty ahead of family joy. Through this long crisis, she has put first things first.

I can still feel the Queen's critical eye upon me when, as editor of this newspaper, I heard her make a plea to all editors to give Diana a bit of breathing space. This was right at the start of marriage to the Prince of Wales. Let every mother in the land ponder on what she has put up with since then. She gave Diana all the support she could, but, as it turned out, it was not enough. She will give this match her blessing, as indeed she has already done, with the consoling thought that Mrs Parker Bowles has borne with impeccable dignity in sharing what Tennyson called "that fierce light which beats upon a throne, and blackens every blot".

Though we are possessed by this itch to have a say in other people's affairs and relish forms on which we are invited to enter answers to "What do you think?", I think we can this time relax and leave it to a conscientious mother. If, after all the agonised thought that has gone into this decision, Queen Elizabeth II, with that volume of experience, thinks it is OK, then I think it is and we should accept it without too many quizzes or quibbling. It's safe for us to say: "Bless you both and all the best."

SOCIAL ISSUES

MANY PEOPLE BELIEVE that the greatest period of social change was the decade of the 1960s. This was a period in which we began to cast off Victorian restraints, but it was not of such significance as is often assumed.

War accelerates change, as we can see from the numerous advancements after both the First and Second World Wars. However, with this acceleration comes the risk that changes can occur too quickly, before society is ready.

The most influential change is something that is often overlooked – the growth in the use of the motor car. This has led to greater social mobility and has transformed the way we live. The English village was not designed to accommodate the motor car and the city was not constructed to give it parking. More than attitudes toward sex, or the impact of television, the motor car has altered the direction of our lives. Ernest Marples, when he was Minister of Transport, said to me, "Unless we get a grip on the motorist, and control him now, he will rule the roost." It seems that this, in many ways, has come to pass.

August 1931

BANK HOLIDAY AT WHIPSNADE

SMALL ATTENDANCE AT NEW ZOO

With unpleasant memories of Whit Monday, the Whipsnade Zoo officials made provision yesterday for a crowd of between 40,000 and 50,000. On Whit Monday, it will be remembered, 26,000 visitors caused a complete breakdown in the traffic and catering arrangements, and many hundreds were unable to gain admission.

Since then, however, several new roads have been brought into use, and the main routes to Whipsnade widened. A special one-way traffic system has been enforced, and the omnibus and railway officials have done their utmost to ensure speedy and smooth transport. A new car park for thousands of cars had been opened and numbers of extra police placed on duty.

In addition to the improvements to the traffic system, food was provided for 50,000 and an army of waiters and waitresses held in readiness.

The actual attendance yesterday was in the neighbourhood of 12,000.

A Whipsnade official said: "Would-be visitors have been frightened by the weather reports, and there has been a cold wind here all day. Most of the staff engaged for the occasion were idle, and the quantity of food that is uneaten will have to be put into cold storage."

"MOTOR-CAR POISONING"

CARBON MONOXIDE IN THE STREETS

Home Office Inquiry

A Departmental Committee of the Home Office is at present conducting an inquiry with a view to considering, among other things, the inclusion of carbon monoxide in the list of occupational diseases under the Workmen's Compensation Act.

The Home Office has in its possession, it is understood, statistics relating to carbon monoxide poisoning, which reveal the danger existing from this particular type of poison and the gastric ailments which are believed to result from it.

The danger of poisoning arising from engines running in garages with insufficient ventilation has long been realised, but the danger of air pollution in narrow streets from carbon monoxide has not yet, however, been fully recognised.

It is likely that the investigations which are being made by the Home Office Committee will include the question of fumes from omnibuses and lorries, as well as in factories and workshops.

A Subtle Poison

An authority, discussing the matter with a representative of the "Morning Post" yesterday, stated that carbon monoxide was the most subtle and dangerous poison in existence, because it could be neither smelt nor tasted.

"One part in 100,000 is deadly," he said. "The carbon monoxide is absorbed into the blood corpuscles, and renders them incapable of extracting oxygen from the air. Thus, the blood becomes an inert fluid.

"The poison is cumulative. A man may be gradually assimilating it in small quantities, and only after a considerable period begin to feel the effects.

"The fumes from motor-cars are naturally most dangerous in

narrow streets, where traffic is heavy and where high buildings prevent the gas from dispersing. An even greater danger lies in old motor omnibuses and closed cars, in which the fumes may percolate through the floorboards to the danger of the driver—particularly by making him sleepy.

"I am inclined to think that the present gastric ailments, which are attributed to monoxide poisoning, may be the result of the recent increase in motor transport and the corresponding increase in the pollution of the atmosphere in towns."

The Car Mixture

Our Motoring Correspondent writes: Other things being equal, the richer the mixture used in motor vehicles the larger the proportion of carbon monoxide in the exhaust. The proportion varies between about .5 per cent for a very weak to about 12 per cent for a very rich mixture.

It is generally accepted that the concentration of carbon monoxide is greater during acceleration, and that it falls to the lowest figure during medium speed running in top gear.

DICTIONARY RANK FOR "BLIGHTY"

JAZZ, WHIZZBANG AND WHOOPEE TOO

But Tote and Dora Left Out

MODERNITY AND THE "SHORTER OXFORD"

The astonishing growth of the English language during the past 30 years and the numerous changes which it has undergone are revealed today by the publication in two volumes of the Shorter Oxford English Dictionary (Oxford University Press, 63s).

The dictionary has been designed primarily to give in miniature all the features of the great Oxford English Dictionary, which was only recently completed. In the second place the new work has been designed to include all words in regular literary and colloquial use—including words which came into use with the Great War, scientific changes and importations, chiefly American.

In the first volume of the Oxford English Dictionary, which was published in 1888, "Airmanship," for example, was described as "skill in managing a balloon." An aeroplane was a "plane placed in the air for aerostatical experiment."

AUDIBLE MATTER

"Broadcasting" (unheard of in 1888) is now "to disseminate (audible matter) from a wire transmitting station," and 1921 is quoted as the year of its origin.

The Great War has led to many new words. "Blighty" (1951) is included in the dictionary, and "Whizzbang," which is described as a "shell of a small-calibre high velocity German gun (1915)."

"Bolshevik" and "Fascist" are included for the first time. The former is "a member of the extreme wing of the Russian Socialist Party (later, the Communist Party), which seized supreme power in Russia after the revolution of March, 1917; first applied to the party advocating the maximum Socialist Programme in 1903."

A Fascist, on the other hand, is "one of a body of Italian Nationalists organised in 1919 under Benito Mussolini to oppose Bolshevism. Hence Fascism."

Coming to American words, there is "Jazz" (American Negro), which is "a kind of music in syncopated 4-4 time, as played by negro bands in U.S.; a dance to this music characterised by a rolling step and zigzag procession."

PUTTING US WISE

"Wise" has been given a new and special meaning. "Wise (1919) —To wise up" (United States slang), "to get wise," "put wise." "Speakie" (or "Talkie") is attributed to the United States and dated 1928. "Speakeasy" is the United States slang "for an illicit liquor shop."

"Whoopee" (United States 1845 and pronounced "hoopi" with a short "i") can now be taken officially as being "an exclamation accompanying or inviting to hilarious enjoyment—to have a good time, go on the razzle-dazzle."

The much-abused "Hike" is given its origin in 1809, and means "to tramp (now especially for pleasure)." "Undergraduette" (1920) and "Nightclub" are included for the first time.

"Shavian' (1920) appears as "latinised from proper name Shaw. Of, pertaining to, or characteristic of George Bernard Shaw (1856–) or his plays or other writings."

"Gangster" (in its new sense), "Dora," "Tote," "Floodlighting," "Wisecrack," "Non-stop," and "Gasper" have not yet achieved dictionary rank.

LAST SCENE ON WATERLOO BRIDGE

Sunrise, Then Barriers

THE POLICEMAN'S GOOD-BYE

Sound of Market Carts Recorded

As the distant clocks of London were striking six yesterday morning, two men, simply clad in blue dungarees, stepped across the South side of Waterloo Bridge and with elaborate carelessness placed end to end two scaffold poles across the entrance.

An approaching pony cart drew up sharply at the barrier, and, after excited pleas by three Press photographers, was allowed by authority to pass; a small group of unemployed cheered lustily (to order); and the two B.B.C. engineers, squatting behind a single microphone, recorded for posterity the sound of the last vehicle crossing Waterloo Bridge.

Seventeen minutes later, as the last barrier was erected on the other side, I crossed to the northern end of the structure—and so became the last foot passenger to leave Waterloo Bridge as it is today; the last pedestrian to cross the River at this point for at least five years.

Thus the curtain has fallen upon a great London memorial, and it will not rise again. For better or worse, Waterloo Bridge as London has known it is dead.

SUNRISE

A few hours before this rather unsatisfying ceremony, in company with a London police constable and an unemployed steeplejack, I had watched for the last time the sunrise as it may be seen from the footway of the bridge.

Imperceptibly, magnificently, the dawn had crept over London from the east, until the dark stonework on which we stood grew lighter and its outline was reflected in fantastic shapes upon the sluggish waters of the River Thames. The bridge lamplighter passed for the last time down the footway, extinguishing the gas lights.

The policeman and the steeplejack, it must be confessed, were unmoved; the policeman, because he said frankly that he had watched the same spectacle many times before; the steeplejack, because he regarded a new bridge as a source of employment for many years to come.

Yet it was an impressive finale. The hand of man was mercifully absent. We watched in silence.

Market Carts

At half-past three the "regulars," as the policeman called them, who have driven over the bridge in cart and car at the same time every day on their way to Covent Garden and elsewhere, began to go by. I noticed that the relentless policeman thought it worth saying good-bye to them.

Here and there small groups of unemployed, with hope in their eyes and despair in their hearts, gathered beneath the shelter of the wooden awning on the western side to avoid the cold wind that swept across the River. A dozen times, Waterloo Bridge was pulled down, rebuilt, enlarged, improved—miraculous undertakings that would provide perpetual employment.

In friendly fashion they exchanged views with the policeman about the whole matter. The steeplejack put forward his own proposals.

By 4.30 a.m. the B.B.C. engineers had arrived, and their efforts to record (unaccompanied) the sounds of two horses and a dray, a pony cart, a milk van, "the last 'bus," and the Royal Mail provided a welcome diversion.

Microphone Troubles

It was unfortunate that the conspicuous microphone encouraged passing van drivers to provide vocal accompaniments of their own. Despite frantic signals from the man in charge, several perfect renderings of vehicles crossing Waterloo Bridge were ruined by the cheerful comments of passersby. Loud guffaws, raucous cries of "Wotcher, Charlie," and "Make me a star," had, unhappily, to be censored.

By six o'clock a crowd of perhaps 20 persons, which so far as I could see held not one single sentimentalist, had gathered at the southern end of the bridge.

The end, already described, was not long delayed, because by then it was nearly breakfast time.

The policeman observed, "It's a good job done." The steeplejack hurried off to seek his job.

July 1934

TWO BRIGHTON TRUNK MYSTERIES

SECOND VICTIM A DANCER

All-Night Police Activity

WANTED MAN

Escape After Police Interview

Our Special Correspondent at Brighton telephoning at 3 a.m. to-day stated that there was intense police activity there in regard to the two trunk mysteries.

Chief Inspector Donaldson and Detective Sergeant Sorrell, who only returned to their hotel about 2 a.m., were recalled to Brighton Police Station at 2.30. They were preceded by Chief Detective Inspector Pelling, head of the Brighton C.I.D.

The officers had been recalled as the result of an urgent telephone message which was received at the Brighton Police Station.

Immediately afterwards a fast motor-car was prepared for a long journey into the country, and left with officers on board.

Throughout yesterday the police search for a man they want to interview in connection with what they describe as "Brighton Trunk Crime No. 2" was carried on.

This man, known as Toni Mancini, was actually questioned by the Brighton police last Friday in connection with "Trunk Crime No. 1," and afterwards left the police station.

From Our Special Correspondent

Brighton, Monday

The extraordinary developments of the last twenty-four hours here have doubled, rather than in any way assisted, the work of the police in connection with the Brighton trunk murder, for it now appears probable that the discovery of a second woman's body in a black trunk which was made at a house in Kemp-street, Brighton, last night is in no way connected with the earlier crime—revealed by the finding of a torso at Brighton Railway Station on June 6.

This, I understand, is the conclusion which the police have reached after a day and night of ceaseless activity, and they will continue to work on this understanding until they have evidence leading them to believe otherwise.

Thus they are now in the remarkable position of having to investigate two crimes unconnected, yet in the same town and in certain characteristics almost identical.

These two crimes, moreover, may have to be solved separately.

What was at one time believed to be a connecting link between the two murders, namely, the reported discovery in the second trunk of the head and arms of the woman's torso found a month ago, has broken down. No head or arms were, in fact, discovered, it was officially stated to-day.

A PROFESSIONAL DANCER

Another report which at one time was thought to furnish a connecting link between the crimes—a statement to the effect that a canvas tray fitting the first trunk, which was discovered a month ago at Brighton Station, was found in the black trunk at Kemp-street—has also proved untrue. The second tray is similar, but not identical with the first.

It is in the case of the second crime, however, that investigations have proved most fruitful.

It is almost certain, though not officially admitted, that the woman whose body was found last night is Miss Violette Kaye, a professional dancer known as Mrs. Violette Saunders.

The police have, too, a very complete description of a man whom they wish to interview in connection with this crime.

To-day a search covering the whole country was made for this man, who is in the habit of using several names, but who is known here as Toni Mancini.

The proprietor of the café at which Mancini had been working in Brighton until recently was questioned at some length by the police to-day, and then sworn to secrecy. He has, it is understood, been able to give them valuable information regarding the man's habits.

Mancini was employed there as a chef or waiter, and it seems that he was a well-known frequenter of Brighton dance halls. He lodged at the house in Kemp-street.

As lately as Friday night, when he was questioned by the police in connection with the earlier crime, he was seen dancing in a big hall in the centre of Brighton. He was then in the company of another man and two women.

His movements from the time when he left Brighton on Saturday after the police questioning are a complete mystery.

POLICE THEORIES

It is believed that the autopsy carried out by Sir Bernard Spilsbury, the pathologist, proved that Miss Kaye met her death before the unknown victim of the first crime.

One thing is certain: she had been missing since the middle of May.

It is believed that her death, caused by a blow at the back of the head, occurred at another house in the locality and that the trunk containing the body was carried to the premises in Kemp-street, where it was found.

The police have obtained a statement from a man who, it is understood, states that he assisted to carry a heavy trunk to Kemp-street.

Miss Kaye was on the stage for some years, both with troupes of dancing girls and with a partner as a music hall "turn." It is understood that she married a man named Saunders several years ago.

She was 42 years of age, but looked considerably younger. She had lived at various addresses in Brighton. She was the daughter of Mrs. Watts, who lives at Palatinate Flats, New Kent-road, London.

Mrs. Watts has stated that from photographs shown her she has no doubt that the victim is her daughter, who has a son 19 years old.

To-day Scotland Yard detectives visited several empty houses in and around Brighton. These visits are believed to be connected with the second crime.

At a house in Park-crescent—not far from Kemp-street—Chief Detective Inspector Donaldson, of Scotland Yard, and other police officers in plain clothes made a thorough search of a basement flat which changed tenants some time in May. In the words of a resident in the house, "they went through the place with a comb."

It has been officially stated that the house to house search which has been going on for some days all over Brighton has not been, and will not be, abandoned until completed, and a large number of men are concentrating on this search in the hope of making some discovery regarding the first murder.

During the day a number of "clues," which may or may not ultimately prove to be of importance, were reported to the police by private individuals. A long knife, alleged to be stained, was picked up on the beach near the pier and handed to the police.

Marriage Recalled

A clue which may prove of considerable assistance to the police has, I am able to state, been placed in their hands by the Superintending Registrar of Brighton. The Superintendent, Mr. Horace Burfield, has noticed a remarkable similarity between the handwriting of the woman Kaye and that of a woman who signed the register on March 10 on giving notice of her marriage, which took place on April 2, and who addressed a letter to him concerning the nationality of her bridegroom. This marriage took place from the house in Kemp-street where the second body was found.

The police are anxious to trace the whereabouts of a Miss Lilian Millicent Pickett, a dancer, who is said to have gone to London in company with a certain Miss Johnson.

Her father, who is employed in Brighton, has since been unable to trace her.

He has stated that his daughter was friendly with Miss Kaye and that the girl Johnson was something like the description of the woman whose torso was found at the railway station.

GRESFORD EXPLORERS' SUCCESS

Workings Pierced at Foot of Shaft

GONG SIGNALS TO SURFACE

Seven Descents Without Mishap

WREXHAM, THURSDAY

The great wheel above the Martin shaft of Gresford Colliery has been turning all day. From early morning until late this afternoon I have watched it revolve—at times so slowly that one could count the spokes, and at other times so rapidly that all but the whirling outer rim became invisible.

To the long grey line of watchers standing outside the colliery gates this wheel has told the whole tale of the long-awaited descent of Gresford pit. The men have been down, and to-night they are back safe and unharmed by their ordeal.

Operations have been entirely successful, and a great deal of valuable information has been gained. It is now known that the bottom of the pit, in which 265 men met their death in the explosion of September, has suffered much less damage than was expected.

The last four men to descend the mine late this afternoon were able to penetrate about 250 yards along the road at the bottom of the Martin shaft. They reported that in general the condition of the Martin district was surprisingly good.

ESSENTIAL RISKS

No mishap of any kind marred to-day's success—a great tribute to the work of the experts. Essential risks were taken and justified, but nothing was left to chance.

Seven descents occupying about six hours were made by three of the five selected recovery parties. The Llay Main and the second of the three Gresford colliery teams went down twice.

The third team of men from Hafod Colliery descended three

times. Communications with those at the surface were made by means of hammers and gongs.

Llay Main was the first party to be called for duty. Just after 11 o'clock—two hours later than was expected—three of the team's six members entered the airlock and descended five hundred feet to the pump room inset, where examination was made of the dam constructed last Monday.

They returned to the surface and the second half of the team, with Mr. Collinson, Inspector of Mines, went down as far as "meetings"—that is where, in normal circumstances, the ascending and descending cages must pass. The shaft was carefully examined and found at this depth to be in good order.

After they returned at noon Parry Davies, the captain of the team, told me that very little water was now flowing down the shaft. "Conditions were most satisfactory," he said.

First Exploration

The Hafod team, second to be called up, left ten minutes later. They carried the descent a stage further and reached a depth of 600 yards. The last 200 yards were taken slowly to enable further examination of the shaft to be made.

The first half of the team came back to the surface, and the three remaining members, with Mr. Collinson, made the fourth descent of the day to the very bottom of the pit. There they remained in the cage for two minutes.

On their return the third and last team should have taken over, but some Hafod men went down for the third time, on this occasion leaving the cage to inspect thirty yards of the road at the bottom of the shaft.

By 1.40 p.m. they were back at the top of the pit. Their captain, Mr. Robert Ellis, who is a collier with a first-class certificate, and a member of the Denbighshire County Council, said that there was water to the level of the landing in the sump.

"The bottom part of the cage went into it," he added, "but it was quite safe. We came off the cage and went along the road for about thirty yards until we came to a cabin.

"The water had soaked well into the ground and there was a great deal of mud. We met no falls along the part we travelled; the only damage seemed to have been done by water."

Finally the Gresford team No. 2 made their two descents—the sixth and seventh of the day. By now the crowd along the lane nearest the pit head had grown considerably.

Men and women who had bicycled to Gresford from the surrounding districts watched silently, and with grave eyes, every movement of the shaft gear. The last team were able to explore 150 yards in one direction, and 90 yards in another, at the bottom of the mine.

In the first direction they almost reached the Dennis pit, which is the second Gresford shaft and the scene of the disaster. Soon after 4 o'clock they were back at the surface.

To-night Sir Henry Walker, Chief Inspector of Mines, who has been at Gresford all day, expressed to me the great satisfaction he felt at to-day's results.

"Thank Heaven everything has gone according to plan," he said. "We have had no accidents; not the smallest mishap. To-morrow we may be able to start a little tidying-up at the bottom of the shaft."

The men, Sir Henry added, would do no work on Saturday.

Soon it should be possible to erect air locks, which will expedite the work of exploration, although this will in the ordinary course of events occupy several months.

It will depend upon circumstances whether the 265 bodies will be brought to the surface for burial, or whether the workings in which they lie will be bricked in.

December 1936

CHRISTMAS HAPPINESS BROUGHT TO POOREST HOMES

GIFTS FOR OVER 264,000 CHILDREN: TOY FUND'S SUCCESS

Santa Claus visited the poorest homes in England and Wales during the weekend, bringing unexpected joy to thousands of children.

This was made possible by the generosity of readers of THE DAILY TELEGRAPH AND MORNING POST. Nearly 264,600 toys were distributed by means of our Christmas Toy Fund, to which there were 42,000 contributors.

Correspondents toured the black areas of the North and of South Wales, and in their messages, printed below, they describe how the toys were received.

Special efforts were made by postal staffs to complete the deliveries in time, and, despite the difficulties of transport in areas where roads were made treacherous by ice and snow, there were no last-minute disappointments.

Postmen were met by crowds of excited children, and, as if following the Pied Piper, they ran laughing through the streets. Unemployed fathers stammered their thanks, and mothers smiled again.

The unqualified success of the fund was made possible by the co-ordinated labour of shops, manufacturers, THE DAILY TELEGRAPH AND MORNING POST organisation and Post Office workers, who carried out the last phase of distribution without error.

SANTA CLAUS DID NOT FORGET

Joy in Stricken Homes

From Our Special Correspondent. Liverpool, Monday.

Among families of the unemployed in stricken areas of the North, Christmas has been rediscovered; a spirit dead for a long time has stirred again.

During a two-day journey across the Black Country, through 20 of the 30 towns to which readers of THE DAILY TELEGRAPH AND MORNING POST helped to send toys to poor children in Lancashire, Durham and Northumberland, I saw countless different ways in which this spirit had revived.

A tiny Christmas tree in Blackburn, bought specially to celebrate the opening of the children's parcels in a desperately poor home; a Post Office lorry besieged by children in Jarrow; tales of how parcels had been hidden from the children in a Durham village.

Such pictures made Christmas warm and real in places where it is usually cold and remote, and any one of these scenes would, I think, have repaid the most generous donor to our Christmas Toy Fund.

GLEAM OF HAPPINESS

Some, necessarily, one saw with mixed feelings. It was sad to walk down streets in Liverpool on Christmas Eve where every child in nearly every home had received toys—toys sent only to children of the unemployed or distressed.

Off Moon-street, Liverpool, one of the blackest patches in a dark area, there was a family to whom the arrival of a parcel had caused pitiful anxiety for two days. The address was right, but the name mis-spelt. Was the doll really for "our Elsie"?

Eagerly the wrapping was sought and presented as evidence. "Surely it's right, isn't it?" Elsie, nine years old, was speechless with shyness and delight, but her eyes betrayed the fear that someone had come all the way from London to reclaim the only parcel she had ever owned.

A happier scene in Miry-lane, Wigan, where three toys for Jean, Mary and John made Christmas into a family festival—the first for seven years. Where there would only have been a sixpenny box of chocolates for the children, there were chocolates and three parcels, their wrapping already frayed by constant handling.

So Christmas had seemed worth celebrating, and a tiny tree was bought from the corner shop to make it all more realistic.

On the icy doorstep of a broken cottage at Hindley, Lancashire, where six pits and four factories once employed thousands who are now workless, I heard of Ronny, 13 years old, the only son of an unemployed collier and his wife. Ronny, and his future, is all they live for now; a gift for him had restored the light in their eyes.

He knew nothing yet of the parcel, which his father and mother had hidden in their tiny room, for he had been out when the postman called. Gleefully, Ronny's mother brought it to show me, to tell me of the surprise they had planned.

So, on to the West Riding of Yorkshire, touching Barnsley, where children were included this year for the first time, and through Durham to Tyneside. Christmas morning on the Tyne was black and sullen, and in the back streets of Gateshead and Felling, before many were astir, Christmas seemed to be at the other end of the earth.

But I met a weary, unshaven postman slithering over freezing, greasy streets. It had been the hardest week he could remember in those parts; the children had tormented them all the time gifts were going out. Oh, they were happy enough, but who had thought of sending so much, anyway?

Presents Taken to Church

In some of the dreary back streets which run in hideous confusion along the southern bank of the Tyne parcels were going out all Christmas morning, and when everyone was astir the children were out and following the Post Office lorry like seagulls in the wake of a liner.

We stopped for a few moments outside St Bede's Church, in Jarrow, at noon on Christmas Day, just as the children came out from their service. Some had managed to bring their gifts to church; girls who clutched with unpractised fingers their tiny handbags. Nearly all were dressed in humble, but very tidy, Sunday clothes.

A few, even in the best they had, showed the desperate poverty of their homes, and one hoped fervently that they had found the shining new sixpences which had been sent with their purses.

After going through Sunderland, South Shields, over the ferry to North Shields and back through Wallsend, one began to wonder how many of the thousands of parcels sent out were left for any other part of the country.

So much happiness among the children, so much gratitude among poor parents; and something more. Astonishment that you, so far away, should remember and bring renewed faith in the Festival of Christmas among those whose faith had nearly died.

FROM KATIE TO THE TEDDY BOYS

The Shook-Up Generation
By Harrison E. Salisbury (Michael Joseph)

The "youth problem," it seems, has always been with us. One aspect of it was debated in the Commons yesterday. Most nostrums tend to assume that it springs from an "age of violence." In fact it may be an expression of something much more prosaic.

When I was young there was a bestseller called "What Katie Did." I can visualise the red back of this nursery classic on my sisters' shelves, and on the shelves of their friends.

Though I never read the book, Katie cast a long shadow. I understood she had been disobedient and had nearly broken her back falling from a swing. She tended to haunt acts of childish indiscipline. She came to represent—unjustly, I believe—the archetype of juvenile delinquent.

Katie came back to mind while I read a more recent book "The Shook-Up Generation' by Harrison E. Salisbury. Its heroines, drawn from New York's lower East Side, are more desperate characters than Katie. But they have one affinity. They both provide the image round which at any age we find it easiest to crystallise thought about social behaviour.

Over here our image of bad boys and bad girls is softer than Mr. Salisbury's. We have the flick knife but not yet, I think, marijuana or the "zip" gun. From the gallery of portraits of our young to-day, if you want a fair painting, the House of Lords debate last February comes nearest to seeing it steadily and seeing it whole. But after a round of the gallery we are left to conclude that the worst of our children now constitute a heavy charge on the social conscience.

RECURRENT THEMES

The last time this happened was about 25 years ago. Paradoxically, the world was then hauling itself out of an economic trough, instead of surf-riding breathlessly on the crests. At that extreme we had idleness at the street corner—at best, blind-alley employment—malnutrition, slums and Welsh miners out of work for 20 years.

Today we are spending over £600m. on national education. Our 5m. adolescents between 15 and 24, it has been estimated, have £900m. a year, after insurance and home charges, to spend. From which it appears that whether you have a Welfare State and high prosperity or a slump and 3m. unemployed, a degree of original sin remains to be reckoned with.

If you turn back to the social literature of the 1930s and compare it with the social reflections of to-day you will find recurring phrases: "Youth service," "club leaders," "home influence," and "the social needs of our young people."

Because it is difficult to get the right perspective the image of Katie is uppermost: Katie's brother with a flick knife; Katie's brother at Notting Hill; Katie's brother beating up coppers; Katie a teenage prostitute.

We have made up our minds without reading the book that Katie needs taking in hand. The Government has a committee working fast on it. The Labour party has a youth commission. Our far from negligible voluntary social services are being mobilised for a youth drive.

At least the most enlightened sociologists seem determined on one thing; the smaller the Government's hand in all this the better. That is a blessing. The man in Whitehall most certainly does not know what is best for Katie. It is well that the voluntary services should make the running.

I remain doubtful about the image which is stimulating this endeavour. "Look at the figures!" Certainly, more boys and girls are being convicted of crime. It is pointless to speculate whether boys and girls today are morally better or worse than 25 or 50 years ago. It is demonstrable that a fraction are showing a disposition to savage violence, which is startling; sexual behaviour, among a large fraction, is less restrained; and in modern industry, to quote Lord Feversham:

> More than ever before, large numbers of young people regard work merely as a means, a boring, irksome means, of providing income for leisure, which to them is the real business of living.

It is the natural reaction of a society whose social consciousness has developed in inverse ratio to its social conscientiousness to see here the stuff of a crusade. A fine opening for social workers, the Church, scouts, clubs, good sportsmen, school teachers and the Home Secretary. A crusade to be fought by most of the rest with cosy maxims and recollections of how much father believed in sound, old-fashioned methods.

It is a gratifying conclusion. It keeps the skeletons in the cupboard and offers a bone for society to get its teeth into. Moreover, since nearly every other country—East and West—has this problem of a disturbed minority we must be on the right track. That settles it. Good luck to the club leaders and Mr. R. A. Butler.

Other countries' trouble with their young is one of the obstacles to clear thought on this subject. It inspires another image:

> Tiny and afraid
> In a world he never made . . .

No Social Architects

What can you expect after two World Wars and this nuclear business? This is an age of violence. So was every age before it, and I note with satisfaction that Mr. Salisbury—and some other respectable witnesses here—give small weight to it.

> . . . the origin of the shook-upness of our generation lies not in the international situation nor in the headlines of the tabloids. Such feelings play no more than a secondary role. The source of the disturbance is more prosaic.

Much of it lies where we least want to search; not, ironically, in our failures but in some of our outstanding material successes.

Consider our splendid building record. Between the wars, I recall, new housing estates were a social worry. I recollect a day with a social worker exploring juvenile crime in Dagenham.

Such places have multiplied since the war, reproducing—with honourable exceptions—nearly every social drawback which caused anxiety between the wars. These contributions to "the social life of our young people" can be found not only in countless acres of new, spiritless suburbs but in a thousand English villages, where fat blocks of council houses have been run up "the wrong side of the tracks" and the inhabitants are "them" to the rest of the village.

We complain aesthetically because these places went up without landscape architects. They also went up without social architects.

Best and biggest of them all are the New Towns. We are so pleased with these that they are a "must" on the itinerary of every distinguished visitor. These are the figures for children of 15–19 in three towns:

Town	1956	1961	1968
A	750	2,000	4,000
B	221	347	1,620
C	1,011	2,091	4,741

In those towns, in terms of trouble with the young, to-morrow already walks.

If you do not fancy architecture try the Ministry of Labour Gazette. Our dynamic economy demands a shift system to make the best use of expensive plant (awkward for the "family unit," the shift system) and several million mothers are in work. We have thoughtfully provided from public funds places where the youngest can be safely penned while the mother works.

Which Is Master?

How can it be otherwise? Our economy demands it. Our livelihood hangs on it. In any case the place of women in national life to-day is one of our attainments. That is unanswerable. "The question is," said Humpty Dumpty, "which is to be master—that's all."

We are permeated with industrial welfare. Goodness knows what it costs the employers to-day. Can we assert that the demands of industry and the demands of the home are approximately in balance? Which gives way? To-morrow, all being well, the heads of industry will find that they have become the aristocracy of this age, and have inherited some of the responsibilities of the feudal system. But to-day we are dealing with yesterday's concepts.

Finally schools. I have read again the Government's recent paper on the progress of secondary education. It is a great success story and will so appear to everyone except those nearest to it. It also affords a glimpse of what poor fun it must be to-day to be a really stupid child.

Not the failure of our schools but their considerable achievements—technical education, rungs of the ladder, scholarships, exhibitions, a job with I.C.I. in every satchel—these bear hardest on the dimwit.

Were I a dimwit in school to-day I would certainly have a big pocket knife—not a flick knife, of course—but sharper and shinier than anyone else's. No childish emotion runs deeper than a sense of inferiority to all about you. Has anyone yet found a Teddy Boy in the Sixth Form?

Surveying the extent of our success in only three spheres—housing, industry and education—towards doubling our standard of life in 25 years' time one is left faintly in awe at the resilience of our young.

The surprising thing to me is not what Katie did but what Katie and her brother haven't yet done. By all means let us set the scout masters, street workers and club leaders to work. Let us also reflect on some adult activities in this century and then recall the old saying that each generation sees through its children a reflection of itself.

There, at least, is comfort for us. Katie isn't that bad.

WHERE AND WHEN TO DRINK

Our new licensing laws must take account of new social requirements.

Britain's drinking habits have changed considerably in the 30 years since any comprehensive legislation on the subject was passed. What should we seek in the reform now promised by the Government?

A good social history could be written of the British, during the past two centuries at least, in terms of their drinking habits.

To explain why we drink to-day half the quantity of spirits we drank in 1938; why we now drink two-fifths of our beer from bottles, compared with one-quarter before the war; or why we had 100,000 pubs in 1900 and 70,000 last year—this would involve more than a study of distilling, brewing or licensing.

Such relationship between changes in society and in our taste for drink needs to be borne in mind when we turn our thoughts, as we soon shall, to reform of the licensing laws. For in one singular respect the changes we make can differ radically from nearly all that have gone before.

Our approach will not be dominated, as it has been in the past, by fear of excessive drinking among the working population and the overriding need to curb it. We are still drinking plenty of alcohol and drunkenness accounts for well over 1,000 cases in the courts every week. But the trend towards sobriety, first noticeable in the early years of this century, has continued. Drink is no longer "the curse of the working classes."

CHANGED OUTLOOK

A glance at some of this century's surveys strongly suggests this conclusion: that a nation moving to prosperity by way of industrialisation will tend, in the primary stages, to drink more, even excessively. Thereafter, the higher standard of living and competing luxuries reduce consumption.

Thus in 1899 we were drinking nearly 37m. barrels of beer a

year, or 32.53 gallons a head. To-day, with a far higher standard of living, we consume about 25m. barrels or 18 gallons a head. Sixty years ago we were drinking 31m. proof gallons of spirit a year—just under a gallon a head. To-day (with a larger population) we are drinking about 12.5m. gallons, or a quart a head.

It will be said that our relative sobriety is due to fiscal, not social causes. If whisky were still 4s a bottle, as it was in 1914, or even 12s 6d as it was in 1939, instead of 37s 6d the figures might be different.

Yet successive Royal Commissions in 1896–99 and 1929–31 observed other influences: the spread of education, a "passion for games and athletics," cinemas, wireless, travel facilities, better housing—and a very appreciable change in the public attitude towards drunkenness.

"Drunkenness," said the last Royal Commission, of 1930, "has gone out of fashion and a drunken person is not tolerated as he used to be. The vital importance of this change of outlook hardly needs emphasis."

Despite this comforting discovery the same Royal Commission, which produced our last main survey on licensing—an undistinguished document—clearly believed that excessive drinking remained a real threat. Most of its proposals held or tightened the reins instead of loosening them.

That report, which ratified many of the special restrictions imposed during the First World War, largely governs our drinking today. There has been no comprehensive legislation since.

It perpetuated the sandwich which dogs the Englishman's later drinking, the embargo on all games for stakes in pubs and the present licensing hours. It expressed anxiety about "perpendicular" drinking and put "cocktails" in quotation marks. Its approach was well summarised by its response to pleas that travellers by air at airports might be allowed a therapeutic nip before or after flying:

> On principle, we are loth to introduce exemptions to the general application of the system of permitted hours.

Still governed by such principles 30 years later, no wonder many sense that our licensing laws are out of touch with our social requirements.

The Government now proposes to act without more guidance from Royal Commissions. What do we seek?

Ignoring those who think it simply a matter of freedom to drink round the clock "like they do in Paris," some obvious considerations arise:

Unfair relations between clubs and pubs:

Inflexible hours, particularly in hotels and restaurants;
Drunken motoring;
Admission of young people to licensed premises;
Off-licences;
Sundry anomalies which are redundant, irksome and unenforceable.

Socially the case for greater freedom is easily made out. It may be more difficult to administer in practice. The Englishman may have shown his fitness to drink freely until midnight if he wishes. Will he find publicans willing to oblige him?

TABLES TURNED

One popular notion is far wider discretion in permitted hours, so that drink can be bought for, say, 18 hours out of 24, but "staggered" public house hours to provide the service.

Would this lead to pub-crawling by motor-car late at night from early houses to later houses? The "Continental" school will dismiss the idea as nonsense. But the menace of drink on the road will not be lightly dismissed. It is going to overshadow reform.

Lord Amulree's Royal Commission of 1930 thought drink a danger to industry but dismissed the intoxicated motorist in a short paragraph. To-day we have these problems in reverse.

Less controversial is the future course most sensible people wish to see pursued for the public house. It has moved a long way from the squalid alehouse or boozing den of the 19th century which haunted the Royal Commissions and which have led to the thicket of licensing laws.

Fewer now enter a pub solely for alcoholic satisfaction. More go there for company or relaxation—and some drink no alcohol at all. A major development since 1930 has been the increased consumption of soft drinks, now 330m. gallons a year, nearly a third of the beer consumed, and thrice the pre-war total.

Even the Royal Commission of 1930 tremulously suggested the time had come when, subject to control by licensing justices, some space in pubs might be set aside for children. Yet the policy of making pubs a place for family refreshment instead of bolt-holes for male tipplers has not moved far from that day.

Against the discouraging background of counsel and legislation the brewers may be forgiven much. Yet it remains curious that so many of our public houses to-day are subdivided, not between soft and hard liquor: but socially, artificially and illogically between "public," "saloon" and "private" customers.

If we accept the fitness of public houses to-day to be more socially attractive, the problem of games and gaming falls into perspective. The last Royal Commission refused to relax the prohibition on games in pubs "even for trivial stakes such as the price of a drink." It quoted approvingly some words of Mr. Justice Wills— used in 1889!—implying that such liberties might lead to incitement to drink, disputes and assaults.

So to-day, within my own knowledge, a women's bridge club meets every Thursday in a room of the local inn and settles up afterwards outside, under the bus shelter.

John and Jack

In registered clubs other rules prevail. This raises the outstanding social anomaly. Our licensing laws rest on the assumption that what William, John and Ernest do in a club is one thing; but what Bill, Jack and Ernie do in a pub is another kettle of fish.

To-day it is not the conduct of the pubs but the conduct of a minority of clubs which excites concern. A set of outworn restrictions on one class of premises have led to abuses in another—a familiar paradox. Allowed a shade more social allure, public houses would quickly eclipse the charms of squalid clubs.

Reverting to the social theme, I think there may be a particular reason why, pleasure and sense apart, we should seek to increase the social attractions of our public houses.

An increasing and disquietingly large number of our people, for reasons too complex to discuss here, are becoming socially self-sufficient. The contented family circle round the telly is one thing. Quite another is the self-contained citizen, who shows a lessening desire to mix with his neighbours, to contribute to the human small change of social contact—let alone local life.

We are developing centres of population to which the word "community" does not apply. They suggest not the purposeful bustle of the anthill but the cellular isolation of a wasps' nest. It is early to suggest that the technocrat inclines to be a misanthrope, but we have here a social trend which some find disturbing.

Could it be that the public house, seen 30 years ago as threatening to put sand in the wheels of industry should now be welcomed as a partial lubricant to the dry wheels of technocracy? Perhaps that is going too far, but it should not be left out of our thoughts.

ONE FOR THE ROAD AND
HOW TO STOP IT

THE PROBLEM is to discourage drinking before driving without prohibiting it

THE ANSWER might lie in a combination of two rival criteria—the capability of the driver and his alcoholic content

A government needs to feel sure of itself before embarking gratuitously on a course of licensing reform, as this one intends to do in a few months' time.

Commercially and socially it is the steepest of political glaciers. Every pace has to be cut, and there are some frightful crevasses which have a way of trapping and then preserving indefinitely the consequences of a false step.

So in one sense it is gratifying that the Government feels strong enough to risk the journey, unprompted by any Royal Commission or by public uproar, but simply through a sense of social zeal.

What makes this venture peculiarly hazardous is the probability of a dual expedition. As the Home Secretary moves one way, bent on liberation, the Minister of Transport is likely to be marching from another direction, bent on wringing drink out of motoring.

No doubt these aims will be correlated by the autumn. But they are complicated because motoring is now as much of a national recreation as drinking—and perhaps the more dangerous of the two. Whatever courses are chosen we approach a classic version of the argument about liberty and licence.

STRIKING A BALANCE

The Government faces a paradoxical situation. Off the roads drink is not considered to be the social menace it once was. Freed of the belief, which haunted legislators for years, that drink is the curse of the working classes, the prospects of sensible social arrangements in keeping with modern tastes are bright.

On the other hand there is a deepening suspicion, strongly held by the Ministry of Transport, that drink is a much bigger factor in road accidents than we have been led to think. The circumstantial evidence, partly from other countries, is too strong to be set aside.

It appears, therefore, that a course has to be struck between more rational arrangements for public drinking and more rigorous arrangements to restrain drinking while motoring.

Anticipating this dilemma, the brewers have got under weigh with a campaign to caution motorists, and discreet slogans are now appearing in many public houses. They aim to induce a mood in which "one for the road" becomes not a jest but a gaffe. If motorists drank only in public houses their mission would be decisive, but this is not the case.

The longer one studies what little evidence there is, the clearer it becomes that what can be done through the licensing laws to reduce drinking on the road is severely limited.

It would be necessary to impose intolerable restrictions on the majority in order to achieve an appreciably higher margin of safety. The alternative is to fulfil intentions to give the majority a little more freedom and deal directly with the minority which offends.

That is the predictable course of Government policy and it brings us to the heart of the problem: how to apply justice to the driver who has impaired his ability to drive by drink.

That objective needs to be stressed. It is not to catch more drivers who have drunk too much, nor to deal more harshly with those who are caught, but to relate the law to realities.

According to the latest returns 3,721 motorists were convicted of driving under the influence of drink in 1959. Some competent judges declare that this figure misleads. At least as many again, they allege, were proceeded against on a lesser charge of careless driving and form part of the total of 55,268 convicted for that offence.

The truth of this, without more evidence, is impossible to establish and leads to futile argument. What is beyond argument is the shortcomings of the present law—from everyone's point of view.

It could be likened to the apocryphal story of the judge who, in his last days, reflected: "True, I have allowed some guilty men to go free; yet, some innocent men have been hanged. So on the whole, I think, justice has been done."

The law is inadequate because it is so difficult to enforce justly. The police often have a struggle to get their evidence and, having got it, are occasionally tempted to produce it in court with a collusive, foolproof formula.

Doctors sometimes disagree when examining the accused, and the interval between apprehension and examination varies a good deal.

When it comes to the courts magistrates are prone to convict and juries to acquit. In 1957 91 per cent of offences of driving under the influence dealt with summarily by magistrates resulted in conviction. At quarter sessions, to which an increasing proportion elect to go, 48 per cent were convicted.

WHAT KIND OF TEST?

If the law is to be changed, how is it best done? Simply to increase penalties, as some urge, does nothing to restore justice or meet realities. Steeper penalties could conceivably lead to more acquittals by juries, thus reducing the deterrent effect of the criminal sanction.

As the English law stands the offence lies in having drunk sufficient to impair driving ability, and that has been so since 1930. What has attracted attention are those countries in which the offence lies in having more than a certain proportion of alcohol in the system, irrespective of driving ability or whether an accident has been caused.

That standard presupposes that the intake of a fixed amount of alcohol must impair driving ability—among all alike—and automatically renders the driver guilty of an offence.

To change from our system to the other would involve a major principle. It would also raise some difficult questions. What should the fixed level be? In countries where it applies it varies.

There is also involved a switch from medical judgment to scientific tests. Should such tests be voluntary or compulsory? It is difficult to make blood tests or urine tests compulsory. Practically, though not politically, it is less difficult to make tests by something like the breathalyser compulsory.

If tests are accepted and the "content system" replaces the "ability system" how far should the ensuing punishment be automatic? How much discretion should remain with courts?

Finding the right answers to these questions will help, but it would still leave a big difficulty unresolved. What troubles so many jurists, doctors, policemen and motorists, irrationally but understandably, is the dire consequences of a conviction for driving under the influence. It is neck or nothing.

It is for this reason that some thought is being given to another possible change in the law. Given the scientific test which could establish, with reasonable accuracy, the amount of alcohol in the system, might there be created a second and lesser offence—that of "driving when drink has been taken," or words to that effect?

Three Whiskies

The limit, for the sake of argument, might be two fluid oz of whisky (just under three small whiskies). The test would establish whether the limit has been exceeded. The penalty would be a fine and, for the first offence, a light but tiresome suspension of one to three months. For the second offence the penalty would be somewhat higher. The graver charge of driving under the influence would remain.

Those who have considered this change put forward plausible arguments in its favour. First, it would discourage but not prohibit drinking while driving. It would meet the point that a high proportion of road accidents are caused not by drunken drivers but by drivers who have been drinking.

According to police records only .9 per cent of all casualties and 2.1 per cent fatalities in one recent year were due at least partly to drink. There is a disturbing gap between these figures and some unofficial estimates, one of which attributed 50 per cent of all accidents after 10 p.m. in one county to drink.

Again, it is said, the new offence would leave the motorist in no doubt where he stood. There would be no question of snooping or spot checks. But where the police had occasion to question a motorist involved in an offence or an accident and had grounds to suspect that "drink had been taken" the test could be applied. It might be compulsory or voluntary. If voluntary, and refused, that would be part of the evidence submitted to court.

There can, of course, be foreseen strenuous opposition to the move on social grounds, and some of the arguments which would be heard need no rehearsing. There are also counter-arguments.

If the authorities are right in believing that drink is a bigger factor in road accidents than the range of the law can control, it is not easy to assert that a statutory inducement to drink in strict moderation when driving would be a social outrage.

Perhaps the strongest counter-argument is also the simplest. All the evidence, such as it is, suggests that the pleasures of drinking and the pleasures of motoring will in future be enhanced by the distance they are kept apart.

CABHORSE COBWEBS AND TO-DAY'S TAXIS

About 500 "minicabs" will be unleashed on Monday in London's streets, hitherto the preserve of the Victorian-flavoured taxi service

A man who wants to drive a cab in London must, among other things, fill in an application form to the Public Carriage Office and answer four questions. The last time I saw them the third ran: "Horse or Motor Cab . . .?"

It nicely illustrates the Victorian flavour of the London cab service, governed still by Gladstone's Public Carriage Act, which will be celebrating its centenary in eight years' time.

For years half-hearted attempts have been made to wipe the cobwebs off the London taxi cab system. For several reasons, one or two of them quite mystifying, it has defied reform.

There are now signs of disturbance from other quarters. More than one enterprising business man has lately started new services of private hire cars of modern design and linked to the customer by radio control.

Any examination of this business must distinguish between London's taxi service, which has anomalous features, and London's taximen, who have admirable qualities. The ancient figure who wore six coats and kept small change in the pocket of his undervest has moved on, with the horse. The best of the present crew are the best in the world.

Leading Rein

There are to-day about 6,600 taxis licensed to ply for hire in London. That is about 1,500 below the pre-war figure, which reached a peak of 8,200 in 1935.

Numbers fell to their lowest point of 5,553 in 1953 and have risen steadily since by just over 1,000. But the present total can hardly represent the higher post-war demands of commerce, tourism and 500,000 more daily breadwinners in London.

Nearly half of the cabs belong to owner-drivers. Small proprietors own another quarter of the balance and the rest are in the hands of a few big firms.

Outside London most taxi services are controlled by local authorities—and usually on a loose rein. In the Metropolitan Police District they are run with a snaffle and leading rein by a Public Carriage Office, which comes under a Deputy Commissioner of Police—and through him, the Home Secretary, whose sanction is needed for any change in fares.

The standards demanded of men and machines in London are far higher than in any provincial city. Some, related to public safety and the demands of London traffic, have virtue. Others, more closely related to the hackney and the horses, are museum pieces.

The six-mile radius of action, for instance, beyond which prescribed fares do not apply and a driver may bargain with the hirer, relates to the capacity of a horse. Similarly, the habit of many drivers of returning to base between 5 p.m. and 6 p.m.—the evening "rush" hour—is an ancient custom founded on a horse's interior economy.

It has always seemed necessary to provide London with a taxi which the Army would call a light armoured fighting vehicle. Nothing like it is seen in any other city in the world. Its special steering gear gives it a 25ft turning circle. It must also be robust enough to run an average of 40,000 miles a year—and up to 60,000.

The present cost of such a vehicle is £1,250. Lord Runciman's committee in 1952 led to the dropping of purchase tax on top—but not to much else. Only this month, with 500 or more "minicabs" on the horizon, has the Deputy Commissioner decided to set up a small committee of independent inquiry to examine present conditions of fitness and the possibility of modifying them.

Like Guardsmen, the taxi must be faultless on parade; and it is noteworthy that 3,308, or just half the total, got "unfit" notices in 1960. A quarter of these "related to defects of a minor nature"—usually a scratch or a dent.

In equity, all taxi services in London ought to be governed by the same rules. It may well be that the Metropolitan standard is too rigid, and conditions for the rest are not strict enough. The injustice lies in compelling the Metropolitan driver to keep an accurate meter, to pass a strict test, to keep his cab clean, to possess an accurate knowledge of London and to insure his passengers—all obligations which the new rivals can escape.

One of the constant pleas of the taximen and their union spokesmen is for a "stable labour force." Runciman recommended that there should be no statutory limit on the number of cabs and, as it has turned out, there has been no need for it.

Economic conditions, which Runciman mistakenly thought would lead to a continuous decline, curb new entry. It amounted to 650 last year, more than usual, but in the last resort numbers can be controlled by stiffening the entrance examination. As it is, this may involve a man in a year's work, on a bicycle, learning his London.

What the Metropolitan system needs is an infusion of new ideas, which enterprising men, outside this close circle, are now introducing. One of them is the lighter, smaller cab.

Again, it ought to be possible to improve the communications system. Today a man can dial infallibly for the weather, time and the Test Match score, but rarely for a cab. Ranks can be called, but often fail to reply—particularly at early and late hours when cabs are most urgently wanted.

A strict central administration governs the appearance, maintenance and behaviour of cabs. It does little to relate them to the customers' needs. The system combines the worst features of private enterprise and public control.

Ten Years Ago

It is 10 years since the Working Party on Hackney Carriage Law observed, in 1951:

> ". . . a revision of the hackney carriage law . . . is overdue, and it
> is to be hoped that the time and opportunity may be found to
> introduce new legislation which will accord more with the
> present-day type of 'hackney carriage' and its use than does
> the existing law, much of which goes back to the first half
> of the 19th century."

Since then the Home Office has limited itself to stressing at intervals to the Tory M.P. who has shown most persistent interest in the subject, Mr. Rupert Speir, the great difficulties entailed in such legislation. The difficulties are indeed considerable, comparable perhaps with those of Covent Garden, where several conflicting interests were wedged behind old statutes.

Tourism is one reason for a new effort now. A stronger one is the possibility of trouble if new systems outside the jurisdiction of the Public Carriage Office are allowed to establish themselves and, as the cab drivers see it, nibble some of their bread and a lot of their jam.

For those who feel sentimental about horses there are established outlets in London, notably in Rotten Row, the Household Cavalry barracks and at Horse Guards. It should not be necessary to hang the cabhorse's memorial round the neck of London's taxi service.

WHY OUR PRISONS FAIL

Penology is in trouble. In their different ways the sentences of 30 years passed on Roberts and his associates and the escape of an aggressive psychopath in whom confidence had been "misplaced" cruelly expose the gap between our penal precepts and practice. They mock our pretensions.

Mitchell's escape is butcher's meat for those, a popular majority, who regard the Home Secretary as soft, our prison administrators as suspect and psychiatrists as a-social. Less obviously, the new interpretation of the life sentence, the declaration by Mr. Jenkins that "life" for some will mean *life* has caught us out. We have nowhere to keep killers that long. The solemn words of Mr. Justice Glyn-Jones cannot be met. They are beyond our present capacities.

These events have not precipitated a crisis, except in the temporary political sense. But they foreshadow where the crisis may soon break.

Penal ideals are outstripping means. We are moving too fast ahead of our resources. Penology is prolific of humane ideas just now. The Treasury is far less prodigal. Whether our penal ideals are too high or our allocation of resources to prisons too low is something we should be seriously arguing about. The gap is indisputable. While it persists there will be mistakes and scandals.

"A calculated risk," said Mr. Jenkins of the Mitchell affair. What he might have said was "a risk which we have not yet adequate means to evaluate or contain."

"Calculated risks," said Mr. Fred Castell for the prison officers, "are all right for those who make the calculations, but they are not so good for those who take the risks." The public will applaud him.

In truth, those who believe in prison reform, those who want to see something better than souped-up Victorian punishments, feel more anger, more dismay than the public. A mess like the Mitchell affair is a real, not just a psychological setback for penal reform. In the days ahead muted trumpets in the Prison Department of the Home Office will sound Retreat across the prisons of the land. Fresh precautions, new prohibitions will go out.

Many will be glad to hear it. Some will grieve. For the fact is the new concepts for penology, first outlined in Rab Butler's "Penal Practice in a Changing Society" eight years ago, are beginning to bear fruit.

Smaller, specialised prisons, which offer real hope for the future, are coming into action. There *are* some new bottles for the new wine. At Risley, our first remand centre for adults, opened last year, every man sentenced to 18 months or over is returned for observation and assessment. His reactions are tested, his background weighed, his special problems considered.

This must be right. It is fatuous to call it soft. It is, as the Prison Department declare, the beginning of an experiment in a more sophisticated form of observation, with a view to allocating prisoners to the right prison.

At Grendon, foreshadowed in "Penal Practice" in 1959, some 160 prisoners now occupy the first psychiatric prison hospital. Work formerly done at Wormwood Scrubs, Wakefield and Holloway is now concentrated there. It is work that urgently needs to be expanded and deepened. Risley illustrates the cardinal policy of choosing courses for horses; Grendon symbolises the new approach; smaller, purpose-built, specialised institutions, where some men can be repaired as well as punished.

Most of this augurs well. But staff, buildings and above all research to evaluate results are still far behind our needs. The temptation to over-stretch limited resources to keep pace with new ideas is too strong. We are not being realistic about our shortcomings. We are not calculating risks.

"You cannot train men for freedom in conditions of captivity." Alex Paterson's old cry is now the watchword of the prison service. It is also a principal cause of escapes.

Our Victorian prisons were founded on secure cells. The new doctrine, giving men more life outside their cells, imposes a severe strain on insecure perimeters, offers a standing invitation to rescue gangs. Either selection must be more scientific, more exact—and more costly—to segregate the violent, the escapologists, the aggressive psychopaths—or perimeters must be strengthened nearly everywhere, at even higher cost. Lord Mountbatten will tell us more about that.

Even when science has done all we can afford to let it do, we shall be left with a residue of imponderables, incurables and thoroughly dangerous men. There is a minority which will probably never respond to treatment. This cannot be burked or blurred. Realism about those below the line demands a degree of toughness which our administrators in their present mood show reluctance to apply. That is a weakness.

It is scandalous that, 20 months after it was promised, the maximum security block at Albany for murderers serving very long sentences is still on the drawing-board. "We are finalising the plans," said Mr. Jenkins last week. It would be a mistake to do so, he thought, before Mountbatten reported.

There has been a blunder here. We now know, whatever we may have hoped, that some men like Roberts will have to spend 30 years inside prison. Where—and how?

I have never accepted the professional view that 15 years in prison is the limit of a man's endurance. A very long sentence can be served, and is served in other countries, but it calls for very special environment. We have nothing approaching this in hand. Until last week we seem hopefully to have assumed that it might never be needed. At best, it was a low priority.

Here and in a dozen other directions we have got to envisage planning and spending on a scale to which this branch of our Social Services is unaccustomed. Cost will certainly prove the crux of the new Criminal Justice Bill, with its bold proposals to release on licence and probation.

These ideas demand staff we have not got, expertise we have not trained, research which is not available, hostels which have not even been planned. Are we prepared to find the means as well as will the ends? If we are not, the public will insist that the sights are lowered and they may prevail.

I think we cannot turn back now. We have embarked on a course of penal reform which is right, is enlightened and can be justified for society as a whole. If we continue to run it pretentiously, on political euphemisms, on high sentiments and low budgets, it will founder in a sorry mess of scandals and public recrimination.

DRUGS DILEMMA

Pending appeal, opinion about sentences passed on two of the Rolling Stones pop group and their companion, found guilty of drug charges, must be restrained. It can be more outspoken on mounting confusion in the public mind as to what our social, moral and legal attitudes ought to be towards the different drugs we now loosely lump together as "dangerous." Without more authoritative guidance, there is real danger that the Law will look ridiculous, and growing defiance, founded on ignorance, will aggravate what has become among the young not a cult but an epidemic.

We are heading for trouble unless we set about distinguishing more realistically in their minds between addictive drugs like heroin, which may eventually destroy; barbiturates and amphetamines and their compounds like Drinamyl, which circulate by the million; and non-addictive drugs like cannabis.

This is *not* to argue, as eminent doctors and sociologists as well as pop singers sometimes do, that cannabis should now be made as socially acceptable as alcohol and tobacco. It is to recognise that these advocates have a point when they claim that if the young are misled into regarding heroin and cannabis as equally noxious they may, after harmless adventures with cannabis, assume a fatal disregard for heroin. The case for fresh differentials lies not in the innocence of cannabis but in the deadliness of heroin.

Heroin and hard addictive drugs should be seen to be in a class alone. The penalties, at least for pushing them, could well be higher than they are now. Many doctors consider promiscuous use of barbiturates, which are addictive, and amphetamines, which in excess can damage health and personality, as more dangerous than cannabis. They will find it difficult to establish the right place for LSD, which can damage mental health. However we arrange these B and C categories, their place must be clearly established well below heroin in category A. Ideally, they should be subject to a separate statute. Eventually there will have to be forms of treatment, for those who have become dependent on "soft" drugs, which are distinguishable from punishments such as fines and prison.

What the young have a right to hear is convincing reasons why smoking cannabis is outside the pale. Homosexuality has shown the difficulty of enforcing laws against private behaviour. Mature judges as well as teenagers, who insist that smoking cannabis is also a personal matter, raise the same dilemma. If we decree otherwise, we must establish facts and clear categories. To slither about between condonation and condemnation, without establishing either, is to confuse ourselves and, more fatally, the young.

June 1971

WELFARE: ONE WOMAN'S WAY

W. F. Deedes, MP, on the achievements of the Women's Voluntary Service, and its founder

Stella Reading, who died last month, founded Women's Voluntary Service in 1938 with five names taken from her address book. That was the year of Munich, when many thought for the first time in their lives of what this country might want of them.

It was the year of "peace with honour." An MP with a like gift of fatuous intuition feared that WVS in the hands of a Marchioness and the widow of a Viceroy, would consist of "society women" and "young débutantes."

One year later WVS had 336,000 members, and by 1941 about a million.

From those years until her death Lady Reading set herself and others exacting standards, not all of them high on today's index of human equities. The best volunteer, she wrote at the end of her life, "is one whose name has never been known, who has neither had recognition nor been honoured in any way."

"Public relations," the *sine qua non* of the successful modern enterprise, were alien to her. Thus they had trouble to persuade her last year that WRVS (Royal since 1966) might go to the lengths of publishing an annual report. After 33 years the first appears today. A short foreword says:

> The chairman often said that WRVS was good at doing but bad at reporting, and she hoped that this report would repair the omissions of the past, and present an accurate and worthwhile picture of WRVS as it goes forward into the 'seventies.

So now we know that WRVS has 54,221 women trained and ready for action at "the drop of a hat"; that it issued 1,555,800 garments last year and served 12,393,799 meals—10 million of them on wheels; that its membership includes 2,000 men. A minor revolution was needed at WRVS headquarters before such facts could be ascertained, let alone presented to the public.

507

The very idea of a statistics department within the movement caused a flutter. Accepting, however, their own slogan—"Not why we can't, but how we can"—WRVS turned the job over to a former teacher in mathematics of undoubted probity, who has done her work in a style which Price Waterhouse & Co. would pass on the nod.

How refreshing to get a report wrung out of an organisation which has proved itself over 30 years or more. One's daily mail is lumbered with projects, appeals, manifestos and grandiose bits of publishing on aims which, if only we will lend a hand, may reach the stars or at least swiftly improve the human lot. WRVS has neatly reversed the usual process.

It is no bad moment for them to engage in a little public stocktaking. Our welfare services are being transformed. The magic word is Seebohm. Good riddance to "overlapping" and "duplication" in social welfare. Hail "co-ordination," the more "comprehensive" and "efficient." Though most of our social ideals and blueprints since the war have recklessly overdrawn our resources, we still cheerfully assume a capacity to recruit and train enough skilled professionals for this brave new task.

Yet, as we know quite well, there will be gaps. Domiciliary care, for example? WRVS are entitled to boast that they invented Home Helps. Though they have passed this over to the public sector, care in the home is still very much their business. "Meals on wheels," now their biggest activity, is a primary example of it.

A WRVS fleet of 700 vans and 25,000 private cars "on call"—for which mileage allowance is often waived—are large assets. "Today," as they put it, "WRVS stands in relation to local authorities as sub-contractors." So they are long likely to remain.

Voluntary bodies, as Lady Reading liked to point out, can do things which statutory bodies cannot. They can experiment. They can make mistakes. Home Helps apart, many fertile ideas tried out by WRVS have become part of our welfare's fabric.

Five-Year Argument

For five years there was argument in Whitehall on the wisdom or otherwise of instructing young children on dangerous drugs. Lady Reading argued with nobody. A year ago she simply arranged for suitable WRVS members to get up a talk, based on Home Office

notes, for parents of primary schoolchildren. Then she called a mixed
gathering to the House of Commons to hear one of the team deliver
her piece. There are now 80 WRVS lecturers in the field.

But there is, I think, more to it than that. WRVS began, they
say, as "handmaidens" to local authorities, because there was work to
be done. The ethos, like the annual report, came later. It evolved. In
the long series of encounters she waged in Whitehall, a memorable
love-hate relationship with officials, Lady Reading rarely brandished
her philosophy.

Only at the last moment was she persuaded by friends to set
down her innermost thoughts on voluntary service. She did this in a
paper which is not to be published but circulated to WRVS members.
It is a valuable companion to the annual report for anyone seeking
the key to this movement's inspiration.

Voluntary service, she well understood, needs organisation but
depends on individuals.

Lady Reading was clear about essentials—steadfastness of purpose, determination, a will to surmount obstacles. Before all these
things she put motive. Self-interest, personal aggrandisement, individual advancement—these she saw as pitfalls. Absurd? Or do they
lie very close to some of our present discontents?

The question perhaps is not simply what use the new professional
may make of volunteers—a delicate relationship of which WRVS
have varied experience. It is also how far these volunteers can leaven,
indeed enlighten, the work of statutory bodies, Directors of Social
Services and those with university education who know their books
better than their humanities.

WRVS have learned a lot about humanity. When they were
running the scheme, they never sent a pretty woman Home Help to
the home of a woman in hospital having a baby. They sent a much
older woman to look after the husband and children, and the pretty
one to an old lady needing help. Over-talkative Home Helps were
sent to deaf old men, and fat ones to flats, not homes with lots of
stairs.

Is it not in just such particulars that statutory bodies seem
sometimes to lack imagination?

It will, of course, be said that much of this sprang from a woman
of great ability, of genius even, and that it will now wither away. I
doubt if this is true and it would be a poor memorial to Lady
Reading if it were. Leadership, or "steersmanship," as she called it,

was not at the front of things, by her reckoning. The vast reserve of human beings, willing to help, to give time, to serve, given the method, given the call, in her mind came first.

Ideals, she might have said echoing ghosts of the past, are not enough. There must be efficiency, flexibility, method. Gaiety in the work, she was quick to add, does not come amiss.

Her special contribution to our times was to harness this, to bring the gift of well-ordered voluntary service to women who had not dreamed that it lay within their reach. The unwise MP who loosed his tongue in 1939 had yet a point. When WRVS began, voluntary service *was* linked, closely, to charitable patronage, to conscious giving by the "haves" to the "have-nots."

At the end of her time, the founder of WRVS could record: "The very finest volunteer I ever met was the widow of a riveter in Jarrow. She was a volunteer because she wanted to do things for people. She had very little to live on, but she gave unstintingly of herself." There Stella Reading found her answer to:

> Whither is fled the visionary gleam?
> Where is now the glory and the dream?

Not patronage by the few, but personal service by the many who wish to make "the generous gift of a thinking human being" of time, energy and skill—that is what today we call community service. That is service now.

Many besides the founder of WRVS have contributed to its making, but she did more than most to find and to foster the staggering sum of service which women of this country have in their hearts to give, and so make good her final claim: "We in the British Commonwealth of Nations can think of the ethical strength of true voluntary service as something of infinite value that we can show to the world."

Happily, many who helped to make that true are still with us.

RIGHT AND WRONG WAYS
TO MEET VIOLENCE

There is not the least likelihood of Parliament restoring the death penalty for any category of murder, whatever the police, in an excusable mood of frustration, may say. Nor will the Lord Chancellor tell magistrates to get tougher. Nor will the Home Secretary direct that prison regimes for ruthless criminals be made rougher. Nor will the Parole Board radically change its ways.

One asserts all this confidently, if reluctantly, aware that it will anger many, yet sensing it to be political reality. When a senior policeman, leading his men, is shot dead by a gang of jewel robbers, a climax to daily occurrences only a degree less disastrous, predictable demands are made as a catharsis.

The Home Office is adept at handling such over-reaction—from any quarter. "The impression at the Home Office," we heard last week, "is that sentences for violent crimes have become longer, not shorter." Just so. We finish up, as we so often do nowadays, with the arguments polarised. Right-wing M.P.s and law enforcement on one side, liberal thinkers on the other, and the Home Office playing pig-in-the-middle.

The tragedy is that our way out, our way to improve order in our society, lies not on the lines of these fixed and extreme attitudes, but in just the reverse. It lies in a willingness to rethink attitudes and policies, to admit that wherever each of us has taken our stand on law and order, conceivably we have been wrong. Apologising to the public for delays caused by his roadblocks round Blackpool, Lancashire's Chief Constable, William Palfrey, offered the best counsel of the week: "It will give them time to think what is wrong with our society."

Abolitionists, for a start, can search their own consciences. Did they weigh the need to find a sufficient deterrent in the mind of the armed robber, after the rope had gone? Did they face that or dodge it? We all dodged it, and to this extent, the police are right.

In the mind of the man who carries a gun or is ready to beat life out of a bank clerk or watchman to further his aim, there is now no "fail-safe" mechanism. If we did not fudge our rising homicide figures by methods which M. F. Harvey exposed in THE DAILY TELEGRAPH on Thursday, we would be more aware of this than we are.

Policemen and penal reformers could move closer to each other if each conceded a point. There *is* a category of offenders on whom rehabilitation is not wasted, whose reclamation is a gain for policemen as well as society at large. He justifies parole and profits by supervised liberty. There is also a category of villains, some alarmingly young, on whom the all-purpose remedies of the penal reformer will not work, on whom their endeavours are profitless.

Treating his sentence, less remission, probably less parole, as an occupational risk, he has "never had it so good." If reformers could bring themselves to acknowledge that, they would advance their wider cause and policemen would talk less offensively about "do-gooders."

Sir John Waldron, Commissioner of the Metropolitan Police, put it so exactly in his last annual report on the Metropolis, that his words are worth recording: "Sincere and deep-thinking police officers are anxious to see a potential criminal reformed, but . . . there is now a cadre of seasoned and top-class criminals who have a succession of convictions over a decade or more and who, when at liberty, have never made any endeavour to follow honest employment. These professional criminals have little fear of going to prison and build their future on the hopes of parole."

For the executive, for the legislator and administrator, there are sharper questions to assist self-examination. Why such intolerable delays between a man's arrest and trial? Why do so many on remand have to be packed into overcrowded gaols? One reflex answer is Treasury parsimony and bad administration. A second, which is arguable, is that we are mean about bail.

There is a third. It is Treasury bounty on legal aid, which turns an increasing number of straightforward cases into protracted contests thus choking the judicial process.

Justice for the defendant, as the threatened collapse of America's system proclaims, is finely balanced. It is not preserved—as some of our radical young lawyers seem to think—by an excess of zeal, by rules of evidence which impede true justice, which was once seen to be arriving at the truth of the matter.

As the misuse of suspended sentences, unwise pressure to extend parole too soon, gross overloading of the probation service all testify, penal policies aimed simply at cutting prison populations will not work. Our penal philosophy has been increasingly shaped by short-comings in our prisons, not by expertise but by expedience. Can we wonder that we fail and compound failure by reluctance quickly enough to acknowledge misjudgments. Not surprisingly, the viler our crammed prisons become the louder our voices, so insidious to the police, proclaiming that prison has become a causation not a cure of crime, and so could well be abolished.

We dwell on the upsurge of violence, yet display reluctance to dig among its possible roots. "The cure is in the hands of society," said William Palfrey, "particularly in the education of children." Who doubts it? Are we so positive that the persistent, simulated violence presented nightly for our entertainment assists this education? The onus lies on us, we are told, to prove otherwise. Is this really so?

More widely, we know well enough that our society today is not made up by a law-abiding majority, threatened by a small criminal population. In a vast grey hinterland, where the police lose heart, a deadly neutrality prevails. It ranges from downright indifference to shoplifting, fiddling, peculation, and "perks" on a staggering scale. It includes a great many motorists who have been at odds with the police.

It attracts some ready to turn to their own ends our innate reluctance to tolerate anything smacking of the police state. Slow to condemn violence, urban terrorists, vandalism, they move nimbly enough to discover and decry motes in the eye of the police force. A valuable function indeed; a society needs its National Council for Civil Liberties as well as its Police Federation—but can it really be that policemen are *always* wrong?

It embraces many who affect contempt of pseudo-intellectuals, yet absorbs some of their half-baked propositions: "'Grab' is part of the Conservative creed anyway." "Deviance is a form of social protest."

Back in May, when tempers were cooler, John McKay, Chief Inspector of Constabulary, put forward some reflections of his own. A community so eager to join the fray against pollution, he said, "might show more awareness that crime, violence, and anti-social behaviour also imperil a nation's standard of life." McKay, Palfrey and Sir John Waldron have all within recent months made the same point, their relative powerlessness without community support and action.

Can a community, losing a battle, submit itself to critical self-examination, to disciplines, dare one add, and show the will to apply them? It is easier to look elsewhere for scapegoats, to engage in ritual calls for simplistic solutions.

Such examinations are sharp tests for the modern sophisticated society. They call for an unfashionable degree of humility, for one thing. There are no prophets with honour among us here. That is partly why conflicting opinions cling so obstinately to positions now manifestly hard to defend. We do not need a Royal Commission to tell us what less stubborn consciences, more open minds, could yield.

January 1972

WHAT ABOUT MORAL POLLUTION?

Where will a Conservative Government stand on the quality of social life?

A future historian of these times will note a curious contrast between the deep concern we are showing for our environment and our unconcern about society's tone. We are all conservationists now but, it seems, selectively so.

Erosion of man's physical surroundings, dramatised by Europe's Conservation Year, has inspired something like a crusade, worldwide, sincere and in my judgment destined to be unexpectedly effective.

His manners and morals raise banners of another kind. Some insistently proclaim our right to make pigs of ourselves in private—in public, no less. The portrait of liberalism, which most of us carry around in a small locket, has assumed, as in some nightmare, a hideous mask.

Dirty rivers, sooty chimneys, pollution of the sea by oil are now taboo. The birds are our friends. Shame on the farmer who corrupts our fruit with chemicals. Grubby books, full frontal nudity on stage, copulation on the campus, "pot" galore—these liberate the spirit. There is something awry here.

Perhaps those conservationists are right who declare that man must now regard himself as the most threatened species on earth.

The word "unconcern" in my first sentence needs qualifying. A minority shows concern. It was borne in on me—and I think some of my colleagues—during the General Election campaign. There were many questions about abortion, pornography, narcotics, divorce reform and the more violent manifestations of our affectless society.

WILL OF THE PEOPLE?

Election platforms are poor places from which to argue moral values. One temporised by declaring a conviction that we must at any rate have done with social reform under the cover of Private Members' legislation. It has proved a pernicious system, seen at its worst with the botched Abortion Bill.

A Government, lacking the courage of conviction—or just conviction—can too easily misuse the Private Members as a stalking horse; then, wetting its finger to the wind, suddenly declare that the House, voting in its erratic way on Fridays, has proved the will of the people and justified Government time for the Bill. Hanging, homosexual and divorce reform, stage censorship, as well as abortion, all ran under Private Members' colours.

It is not too hard to declare and to intend that this practice should end. It is also begging the question: Where is a Conservative Government going to stand on the quality of social life? We shall have to improve on a daft plan for local commercial sound radio. What have we to say about the kind of society we want for ourselves and our children? Law and order, emulsified into freedom under the law, begs the question too.

Can we, for example, reconcile more individual choice in economic affairs with collective restraint on social conduct? Partly what confuses is the absence of a clearly defined principle.

Gambling, for example, which touches the exercise of free will, seems fair game for any system of control Ministers choose to devise. They can make up the rules as they go, without protest, except from the proprietors.

Pornography, on the other hand, is an intensely sensitive area. It is the ark of the covenant: Lennon, Hefner, Girodias, Ginsberg, Tynan have but to light faggots and men—some in lawn and cope— will scamper to get a hand in the flames. Good luck to the Minister who tries his hand at amending the Obscene Publications Act.

Yet there is a change. A little wind has come up and, were I in pornography for profit, I would do some finger-wetting and note the quarter from which it blows.

While I was facing social questions in my quarter of the election I noticed, rather jealously, that Dr Benjamin Spock, hero to the *avant garde* of American parenthood, was to speak (vainly, as it turned out) for Anne Kerr in a neighbouring constituency. I would like to have had the doctor as witness on my stand. This "uncompromising social libertarian"—his own phrase—has developed a reactionary view on obscenity and brutality. I take two quotations from his latest book "Decent and Indecent." On shock-obscenity he has this to say:

> The motivation, as I see it, of such authors and producers—in addition to making easy money—is the same particular pleasure

that pedlars of lurid gossip enjoy or that loosely-brought-up children gain from expounding crude "sex" information to pro-tectively-reared children. I think such works are unhealthy for society because they assault the carefully constructed inhibitions and sublimations of sexuality and violence that are normal for all human beings (except those raised without any morals at all) and that are essential in the foundations of civilisation.

And:

The abrupt and aggressive breaking down of inhibitions can be disturbing to a society as a whole and particularly to its children, even if sincere efforts are made to shield the children. This seems more risky when a society already has soaring rates of delinquency and crime, an insatiable appetite for brutality on television and what I consider an unprecedented loss of belief in man's worthiness.

Dr Spock is not the only social libertarian to have such second thoughts. Since her book on the Moors murders, Pamela Hansford Johnson has been dicing the face of pornography with an uncommonly sharp sword. The other day she sloshed a book (I shall not publicise) in the *New Statesman*. A joyful sequel was an angry letter of protest from the publisher, an uncompromising "No limits" man, denouncing the editor for printing such an attack as a book review. (Our views on the freedom of literature tend to be subjective.)

Miss Hansford Johnson made an important point, which conservatives as well as liberals ought to heed. "Among other human rights is the right to be appalled, and say so."

That will strike some as the nub of this awkward question, and it governs more than pornography. To hark back, what disturbs me about so many of our disagreeable fashions is not the act, but the unconcern, the failure to be appalled. War taught some of us that man can be conditioned to anything.

I reject, as many have come to do, the "drain off" or "catharsis" theory. I challenge the proposition that sado-masochism, which has some affinity with sex off the meat hook, exorcises evil spirits, and so might we all.

The persistent patter of some publishers and TV producers, claiming that research leaves us without clear evidence on this, is assuming the look of a guilty bluff. Prove, they cry indignantly, that anyone has been depraved by obscenity, screen violence or brutality.

Well, those like Dr Fredric Wertham of America who predicted quite some time back that we were raising a generation of violence-worshippers are creeping up on them. So are the predictions.

Set morals aside. Let us revert to this paradox of man's environment and man's behaviour. As Pamela Hansford Johnson exclaims:

> Yes, and raising ugliness all round us. No beauty, terrible or otherwise, is being born. Soho is a nightmare of ugliness, and so is the façade of many a cinema.

Why only on the polluted beaches and in filthy rivers is *laissez-faire* a dirty word? Let no one, by the way, delude themselves that this sweet crusade for more beautiful countryside is going to leave human liberties untouched. If we mean business, there will be dire restraints, costly standards to impose.

COMPLETE BREAK

Have we conditioned ourselves past the point of no return? There are reasons for thinking this might be so. I mistrust no less than the "catharsis" theory the popular supposition that moral fashions swing like a pendulum between extremes. De Tocqueville was closer to it in predicting 135 years ago that "a kind of virtuous materialism may ultimately be established in the world which would not corrupt but enervate the soul, and noiselessly unbend its springs of action."

In just such a world we shall be more appalled by smog than sadism; more concerned to protect hedgerows than the reading and viewing of our children; more angry about coursing hares than aborting unwanted babies.

In the reign of unconcern for man's spirit those who have to determine from day to day the regulation of human behaviour from the Home Office will face something of a quandary. As Lord Radcliffe pointed out more than a decade ago, they are confronted by a social revolution, singular in that it has no identifiable leader.

There is in this democracy no one to parley with, none to cry halt to their own followers. That led Lord Radcliffe to conclude that the English revolution might well lead in the end to a more complete break with the past than other more cataclysmic disturbances. We see more plainly now that a number are determined on just such a break.

It is going to require a main effort of will, an unexpected capacity in relatively few, to prove that Lord Radcliffe was wrong.

September 1974

NOT BY BREAD ALONE . . .

Sorting through 25 years' accumulation of political papers, I laid aside and marked one pile "Not for burning," though it gave rise to more melancholy than the rest. It was the earlier post-war Conservative manifestos and principal testaments of faith.

"The Right Road for Britain' (1949), for example, with a Foreword by Winston Churchill and its conclusion: "Man is a spiritual creature, advancing on an immortal destiny, and science, politics and economics are good or bad as far as they help or hinder the individual soul on its eternal journey."

What in the world would the Days and Dimblebys make of that now? And from that august group of Tories, Macleod, Carr, Heath, Powell et al in "One Nation' (1950): "The existence of a nation depends on the steady and indeed instinctive acceptance of those who comprise it of a scheme of duties."

Quintin Hogg again, in his "Case for Conservatism" (1947): "Political liberty is nothing but the diffusion of power." Finally, R. A. Butler (1959): "Prosperity politics is not enough. Without an equal growth in the character and moral stature of man, his material benefits will neither add lastingly to his happiness nor bring comfort to his soul."

This and much else in the same vein is not the thinking of our times, and no blame to the talented young men who stitch together the modern-style Tory manifesto for steering clear of souls and duties.

It is vain to lament that this should be so. The Conservative philosophy incorporates a touch of fatalism. We have, at least for the time being, hung our ideals on pegs in the cloakroom and chosen to make our public appearances in other clothes. So be it.

Rab Butler also predicted in 1954 that we would double our standard of living in the next 25 years, and we seem to have done that comfortably. Yet while we have been doing this, it would be true to say that we have moved steadily away from the conditions for a good society postulated by Tory philosophers and drawn steadily closer to the collectivist idea, the stronger State.

Private rights have been eroded. The individual has lost standing. His duties, if not at a discount, are certainly not in the forefront. The "responsible society" has not arrived.

Labour, in passing, would indignantly repudiate this and shout that our society has in reality moved closer to "social justice," a phrase no less ridiculous than "social conduct," as Euripides told us in one of his plays, "The Phoenician Women":

> Eteocles:
> *If all men shared one judgment of what's noble and wise,*
> *All wordy quarrelling would vanish from the earth.*
> *But as it is, there's no such thing as "equal right,"*
> *Or "justice." These are words; in fact they don't exist.*

If one thing more than another has impressed itself on me in politics it is the force of the prevailing idea, and its capacity to render irrelevant which party is actually chosen to govern. Once a party banks its philosophy with its silver, it loses all influence on the prevailing idea.

Thus for most of this time the prevailing idea has been, not quite Marxism, but one owing much more to the Marxist concept of society than to the Tory creed of the early 1950s. We are all collectivists now.

Those who declare sorrowfully that blame for this lies with the Tories who abandoned their principles in 1951 or 1959 or in 1970, or whenever it was, have only half a point. They assume accusingly that it was done deliberately, invariably discounting the strength of the tide against the swimmer.

Now, looking ahead a little, it seems that materially we may be undergoing a sea change. I take the word of our political leaders who declare, in rare unison, that great difficulties lie ahead, and probably a downturn in our living standards—after a generation of turning up.

WHAT EXPECTATIONS?

The question which then occurs to me is this: if during these 25 relatively prosperous years we have moved so far from the concepts which thinking Tories apparently at the outset thought desirable and attainable, and have moved so much closer to the all-powerful State, where are we likely to move in a period not of rising but falling expectations?

It is a question which in one form or another has arisen in other minds. They perceive that a shift from a generation of what Rab Butler disparagingly called "prosperity politics" to something less agreeable may well render at least some sections of our society less amiable.

They suspect that we might soon not be arguing and bargaining about our share of an expanding product, but fighting for a share of diminishing returns. At least, it is not difficult to see how new stresses could arise very sharply in our society.

A product of this line of thought of course, is Gen. Walker and his friends. They scent storms ahead, and think citizens would do well to get ready to bail water and trim sails. I readily see why this disturbs the Left and infuriates the Marxists.

I wish I felt, however, that these worthy endeavours would deflect by even one degree the Marxist-minded, who are also sniffing the air, from their aims and further intentions in industry and elsewhere.

As observation of the Northern Ireland scene, alas, makes plain, all the King's horses and all the King's men cannot themselves stop ideologues from working to get their way, from disrupting and even destroying legitimate régimes. Security forces, regular or voluntary, may reduce bloodshed and help to get the milk delivered. But upwards of 21,000 soldiers in Ulster could not stop a Civil Rights movement from being permeated by Marxists and then contributing abundantly to havoc. Doubling the police does not help. Would that it were otherwise, but it is not.

To come nearer home, our own intelligence services have a good idea of what Communists, International Socialists and the like are about. (The Communists are infinitely better organised, disciplined and more efficient than any of the other fringe groups.) In our free society it stops there. A good thing, too, most will say.

What Mr Heath said the other day to Mrs Sarah Hogg on television about the limitations of Government has peculiar relevance here. The hopeful feeling of some that, if new stresses arise in our society and the worst comes to the worst, Government will cope is wholly misconceived. History suggests that Government is much more likely to fall.

Might adversity, even in mild form, persuade us, as prosperity has not, that the individual *has* still a role to play? What answer is there to creeping collectivism and the sort of State it engenders, as Solzhenitsyn and others have shown us, but the individual's independent word or deed? "But what can we *do*?" they cried in my platform days.

They can note for a start, as the Communists have always done and as some of our social democrats are starting to do, that in this society still we are at liberty, each one of us, to speak out of turn, to dissent from the prevailing idea. That is a colossal gift.

There are no penalties for trying, as there are for Solzhenitsyn. If we have failed, in the term of prosperity, to determine clearly enough the kind of society we want, at least before a possible term of adversity we should think more urgently about the society we do not want.

For such an adventure there are no fairy godmothers in White-hall, the Conservative Central Office, trade unions or in any form of organisation whatsoever. Government is of no avail—an unfamiliar feeling after all these years.

This has to be an adventure by the thinking man, alone, who entered this world alone, will leave it alone and is alone now; and who may, deep in the recesses of instinct, sense, as it seems Winston Churchill sensed in 1949, that "man is not made for the State . . . Man is a spiritual creature adventuring on an immortal destiny."

Only he now, this lone man, summoning resources so long discounted and disused that he no longer knows he has them, only he can prevail against the prevailing idea.

DEALING WITH MURDER

Writing on this page about hanging in 1973 Mr Enoch Powell, an abolitionist, declared that a settled and preponderant public demand ought to be taken into account and at a certain point prevail. He did not, he concluded, think that point had then been reached; "but it would be disingenuous to deny that it could exist." Many would declare that it exists now. A calculated policy of smashing innocent people to death to further political aims imports a fresh bearing into a well-worn argument. The killing of Ross McWhirter was an appalling act which stirs deep public anger. If such murder goes on, as it probably will, a public demand for the death penalty will certainly preponderate and will be hard to resist. Would hanging deter terrorists? Would it create martyrs? Would it provoke reprisals? People will tend to argue round such questions as these subjectively, that is to say according to whether they accept or reject the death penalty. There are also wider considerations.

Western society is being tested by a savagery that has moved beyond the old frontiers. It has to decide whether this savagery can be countered by sanctions which omit the strongest sanction available in former times. A society which appears to lack the will and temper to defend itself against those taking war to it stimulates obvious dangers. And, where it seems that many citizens possess that will but their rulers do not, other dangers arise. It would be disastrous but not impossible, for example, to reach a point when a minority of the public determined on reprisals of their own; or when policemen, always nearest the danger zone, came quietly to conclude that it was mistaken to take terrorists alive. Home Office figures on murder and manslaughter give us no reliable comparisons with a decade ago. But, by any reading of them, what we once called murder has increased significantly since abolition. To implement the death sentence here might indeed be very difficult. Minorities opposed to it would themselves go to extremes. But to capitulate to that threat is to abnegate authority.

Those for the death penalty have also to think through certain questions. Is the death penalty to be available for all murder, leaving it wholly to the discretion of judges to determine the small minority of murders where a death sentence shall apply? Most who want the death penalty now would probably prefer to see it restricted to certain classes of murder, perhaps only to terrorism. This course demands definitions and, as experience with the ill-starred Homicide Act of 1956 taught us, defining capital offences is fraught with difficulties.

It is hard to make any single category of murder exclusive. Let us, said some in the debate of a decade ago, limit the death penalty to those found guilty of murdering a policeman on duty. They carried strong support until others asked whether it was just to exclude the citizen who went voluntarily to the aid of a policeman and, in saving the policeman's life, suffered fatal injuries.

Supporters of the death penalty have also to satisfy themselves—and others—that it might not actually increase the rate of acquittals for vile offences. We will assume—and it is not a small assumption—that juries could be selected so as to avoid the risk of perverse verdicts arising from the conscientious objection of some jurors to hanging. There will still arise in many trials—for terrorists—that scintilla of doubt which will weigh on a jury's mind far more heavily when a man is to be hanged than when he is to receive a long sentence.

In many such trials, moreover, there will be a conflict of evidence, possibly of a scientific nature. The scintilla of doubt will be activated. Justice is not served if, for every terrorist hanged, two are thus wrongly acquitted and put back on the streets. It is this consideration, there is reason to suppose, which weighs on the minds of some senior policemen—not all of whom favour capital punishment as warmly as might be supposed. Much of English criminal law procedure was shaped in earlier days by the cardinal need to ensure that no innocent man should hang, even if on that account some guilty men went free. The weight still lies on that side though, since abolition, many have urged (vainly) that it should be shifted slightly the other way.

Many such trials will be dealing with a conspiracy in which six or more plotted the crime and two executed it. It is not impossible, taking into account examples from Northern Ireland, that the two executioners will be below the age of criminal responsibility. Who shall be hanged? In circumstances analogous to this, the hanging of

BENTLEY for the shooting of a policeman by CRAIG raised public outcry a generation ago and paved the way to abolition.

In principle those who now call for a return to the death penalty have a far stronger case than they had. By Mr POWELL's careful criteria it should prevail. But the debate that lies ahead will not be confined to principles. The practical questions will be posed and pressed; and the onus will be put on those seeking to change the law to explain how they would answer the questions.

THE LURE OF THE LINKS BETWEEN OLD AND NEW

W. F. Deedes reports from the British Open at Muirfield on how golf has been influenced by the commercial drive

On the road from Edinburgh one morning this week there could be seen two or three helicopters glinting over Muirfield like dragonflies in the sun. For a second or two it looked as if one was approaching Houston or Dallas where the local millionaires use helicopters as taxis. The vision was not wholly illusory.

It goes without saying that the 116th Open Golf championship at Muirfield is the richest of its long history. The prize money is £650,000, of which tomorrow's winner will collect £75,000. That is his starting point. It is reported that Greg Norman who won the first prize of £70,000 last year has since signed contracts worth £10 million.

Part of the lure of the Open is to watch the best players in the world take an exacting examination for increasingly high stakes. To stage an Open costs the Royal and Ancient about £1 million, which is covered by receipts. Most of the profit is made up by selling upwards of 20 hours of television to the BBC. The days are far behind when Walter Hagen of America (who won his second Open at Muirfield in 1929) contemptuously handed his prize winning cheque to his caddy.

Remorselessly, the show gets bigger every year; the tents get bulkier, and the golfers stay the same size. The canvas that goes up around the British Open used to be called "the tented village." They have more than a village at Muirfield this year, they have a tented city. The hospitality pavilions for something like 100 customers cover a larger acreage than Muirfield's ample practice ground. The first hole at Muirfield stretches 447 yards and this year the tents stretch beyond its full length down the right hand side.

The last of them is tastefully described as the "R & A Exhibition tent." It is in reality a huge neighbourhood shopping centre for golfers. I paced out its length at 150 yards, which is two yards shorter than the 13th hole at Muirfield. There on offer at a price is everything a golfer could ever dream of possessing and much else that he never knew existed. On Thursday afternoon, as a drizzle set in, it was doing a roaring trade.

The famous 17th, 550 yards, where Trevino dished Jacklin in 1972, has canvas down two thirds of its length. Curiously we are some way ahead of the Americans in all of this. They stage nothing on these lines at even their biggest tournaments. We are even ahead of the Japanese who have commercialised golf, and whose corporations buy scarce golf club memberships for colossal prices as part of their investment portfolio and where again a round of golf will cost £100.

Even more curiously, this great commercial bonanza is being staged on the property of one of the most exclusive clubs on earth. Many tales of Muirfield's exclusiveness are apocryphal but some are not. The Royal Company of Edinburgh Golfers, founded in 1744, and claiming to be the oldest golf club in the world, does not in the ordinary way entertain casual visitors. After St. Andrew's it is the Open venue which excites Americans most, and with every reason.

The Honourable Company's clubhouse is crammed with the riches from another age and of another kind. No visitor should enter the smoke room without studying the portraits on the wall. Glance for example at the painting of William St. Clair of Roslin (1700–1778), last of the line said to have come to Britain with William the Conqueror. He was captain there in 1761, 1766, and 1770–71. His picture bears a handsome tribute from Sir Walter Scott. Next to it is the painting of Robert Maxwell, captain in 1912 and 1913, the only man to win the Amateur Championship on his own course. He sits with a club athwart his knee and brooding eyes, as if with some inkling (I always think) that the world in which he has been champion is soon coming to an end.

These are the sorts of treasures which draw Americans—and increasingly Europeans as well. In 1980 one Spanish journalist came to the Open—this year there are 26. Sweden, which sent one journalist in 1980, has sent 11. The Hon. Company cannot open the doors of its club—still the size of a small country house—to all of them, still less to the 100,000 or so visitors who are flocking to Muirfield even in the rain; but for many it is enough to know that the treasures and the history are there.

How is this extraordinary mixture of ancient and modern to be kept in balance? The R & A championship committee under Alistair Low has a more difficult choice to make than its opposites at Wimbledon and Lord's. There are physical limits at both Wimbledon and Lord's to future expansion and commerce that could be transacted there.

At Muirfield, where the R & A has just purchased another 40 acres or so, there are virtually no limits. Why should there be any limit to what in reality is a huge financial success—most of it sensibly used by the R & A for the good of golf elsewhere? The administration of this event has shown itself to be not only competent but also wise. There is a small professional staff under the direction of Michael Bonallack, secretary of the R & A, but much of the organisation is local talent. Professional players win the prizes; unpaid gentlemen make the arrangements.

The R & A is not given to calling in people like Saatchi and Saatchi for assistance. It follows that there are probably enough sound heads in this business to know when enough is enough.

In my judgment, there are two clubs in this otherwise blue sky which have to be watched. Muirfield with its grand prospects across the Firth of Forth is one of the loveliest as well as one of the most testing golf courses on earth. The first quality has been sadly diminished this year by the mountains of canvas and I would say a limit has been reached there. Secondly, with a glance at experience in the US, I would not be altogether confident that television in future will use 20 hours or so of Open coverage and be ready to pay a lot for it. There also the high point may have been reached.

Next year the Open will be at Royal Lytham on the Lancashire coast. That might be an opportunity to show that a small Open is not less beautiful—nor necessarily less profitable. They do not come from the ends of the earth to our Open because it is so big. They come because it is haunted—by men like William St. Clair of Roslin.

PLASTIC CAN BE SO INFLEXIBLE

As the latest building society figures are published, W. F. Deedes considers the perils of a system where growing numbers of people are lured into hopeless debt

Like gin in the last century, credit cards have come under attack from social workers. It was gin—"Drunk for a penny, dead drunk for tuppence"—that once threatened to break up marriages and destroy family life. By some accounts the seamy side of consumer credit today is having the same effect, although, in fairness, today's building society figures suggest that borrowings on that front hold steady.

I find it possible to approach the subject coolly, having never possessed a credit or banker's card of any description. The credit card was launched on an unsuspecting public in this country in the Sixties, when my children were of impressionable age. Dismayed by the direct appeals to them to "take the waiting out of wanting", I sacked my bank, one of the big five, and have lived happily with someone else ever since. It cut junk mail at a stroke.

Difficulties arise when visiting America; hotels regard any form of direct payment as fraudulent, because it confuses the computer. But, given advance warning of my singularity, even the most progressive American hotels will usually admit me. As Churchill once sagely observed, we shape our institutions and after that we are shaped by them. No question, credit cards shape our ways.

It has also appeared to the sceptic since the dawn of this carefree shopping era that, since banks are not by nature charitable foundations, the credit card is designed to profit them at our expense. This minority view seems to be shared by Sir Gordon Borrie, Director-General of Fair Trading. His decision to refer the credit card market to the Monopolies and Mergers Commission last May created a flutter. Prisoners, it seemed were reluctant to lose their chains.

What caught Sir Gordon's eye, among other things, was the annual rate of interest accruing to banks from plastic. Around two per cent a month looks one thing; 23 per cent a year (compared with a base rate of less than half that) looks another. As Sir Gordon put

it, there was a prima facie case that banks which were earning 50 per
cent on capital invested in credit cards were making Monopoly type
profits.

Sir Gordon's enquiry was launched at the time of another
controversy, raised by Barclays' plan to introduce the Connect card
and to charge retailers for the privilege. Connect replaces cheques,
automatically debiting the customer's bank account for the cost of
the purchase. Retailers jibbed at Barclays' proposed terms. The City
comment was that the bank was being greedy.

Other things being equal, I see everything in favour of a policy of
caveat emptor. In other words, consumer protection, which is a thriving
industry of its own, can be overdone. They are not equal, however,
in so far as companies dispensing credit cards justify charges to
retailers on grounds that the card induces customers to spend more
than they would if they were using cash. Drivers buying petrol,
housewives filling trolleys in the supermarket, men buying books are
all higher spending customers on credit than those who are putting
down cheques or cash. In short, credit cards are a stimulus to spending.
A third of all clothes, shoes, furniture and cars are bought on credit.

According to the Chancellor of the Exchequer not long ago, four
out of 10 credit card customers pay off their bills almost immediately.
Unquestionably, a minority are drawn into debt and despair. They
then plague estimable bodies like the Citizens' Advice Bureaux and,
if they can reach one, the social worker. It is probably fair to say that
at least some of this *galère* a couple of generations ago would just as
readily have run up debt on tick.

What few seem to have grasped is that the credit card revolution
has been superimposed on our rapid social revolution. Today's
mothers of 45, who may themselves have got their first taste of
honey in the Seventies, are not invariably equal to guiding their
newlywed daughters in good housekeeping. When it comes to credit
cards, the blind are sometimes leading the blind. Now, we are told,
they have been joined by clergymen.

In fairness again to the plastic card purveyors with their 25
million followers, the extent to which they are held responsible for
the growth of credit is widely misrepresented. As today's building
society figures remind us, people use far less credit for shopping than
for buying their houses—a main plank in this Government's platform. Any analysis of consumer borrowing shows that housing
mortgages account for the lion's share of it.

Furthermore, the price of housing today is far more distorted than the cost of goods in any store. It is a startling fact that before the war most people could buy a house appropriate to their needs from their annual income. In the mid-1930s a schoolteacher, say, could buy a new house for £375; a bank manager on £1,000 could run to a three-bedroom, semi-detached with a garage and a patch of grass.

We are not discussing the purchasing value of the pound here, but an industry which has got so far out of hand as to defy the economy of scale which applies to cars, computers, most electronic goods and the general run of household commodities. There are books to be written on why our post-war housebuilders have come to put a ball and chain round the ankles of most married—and unmarried—couples. The short point to be made here is that anarchy in the housing market should not be confused with looseness in consumer credit.

Holding to this dispassionate line, however, I am still left wondering in which direction these great banks wish to travel. Our institutions may shape us, but it is the chairmen who are supposed to shape institutions like the joint stock banks.

As a Tory who believes that self-regulation is invariably preferable to state regulation, I am puzzled by these banks. In pursuit of profits from credit cards and other forms of loan, without regard for the social consequences of their action, they have courted intervention.

To incur such intervention under a Labour government would be a misfortune; to invite it under a government led by Mrs Thatcher of all people is carelessness. It suggests to me that priorities in the board rooms are not quite right. They appear to need fresh guidelines. They are unlikely to get them from the Chancellor of the Exchequer, who has ruled out action to curb the growth of consumer credit. Others must oblige.

In determining their competitive policies for drawing consumers into the credit system, so augmenting their profits, the banks should stop short of methods which may bring into discredit the system under which they flourish. How do they tell when that point is reached? It is precisely for that sort of judgment that chairmen of the joint stock banks are chosen from what we are led to believe are the great and the good.

THE FALL OF A FAMILY TRADITION

Holiday Commentary

I once asked Fred Coleridge, a legendary figure at Eton—this was when we were together during the war—how a national schoolboy might expect to fare there. Eton presented no difficulties, he said; but the difficult question would be: "Where did you spend your summer holiday?" That consideration would give much less rise to difficulty today. If the English revolution has achieved nothing else, it has eliminated class distinctive summer holidays.

In reality, before the 1939–45 War, the well-to-do did not take summer holidays. The South of France and Mediterranean resorts were too hot. They kept out of London during August when the clubs were shut for holidays and the streets were up; but unless someone offered to take them to sea, the chances were they lay fallow until early autumn when Scotland or Ireland beckoned those with a pair of guns or a bag of golf clubs. Arthur Balfour, an Olympian figure, always spent September at North Berwick.

Lesser folk are supposed to have headed for the seaside, where landladies awaited them, made high tea a feature of their day and provided jokes for Punch. I live close to one of the small but then fashionable resorts, Dymchurch on the South-East coast. It was only recently that I discovered the source of its popularity for summer holidays. The rainfall on that bit of coast is well below the national average. The rainfall was important if you had saved up to take a family of four to a seaside boarding-house for a week.

In the Fifties I was in Blackpool during a wakes week with Richard Crossman, for some forgotten reason. Very early one morning we watched the mill workers pour off the trains from the cotton towns and immediately run the gauntlet of stallholders on the seafront.

"They will spend all they have before they go," said Crossman and rather uncharacteristically talked about "exploitation of the workers." It was about the only time we saw eye to eye on a social issue. I wonder what he would make now of Gatwick on a summer Saturday.

Moving from the extremes towards the centre, our own conservative family did the same thing every summer for 26 years. We rented a house in the village of Thorpeness, near Aldeburgh, in Suffolk, and occupied a fortnight with tennis, golf, the sea and a country club, where one wore a black tie for the Saturday night dance.

The owners of this private estate, the Ogilvie family, sought to make Thorpeness an attraction for families with young children but not a great deal of money to spend. High rollers were discouraged.

This being before the dawn of Equal Opportunities, we saw nothing strange in pursuing our sport and leaving our wives to clean the house, prepare meals and keep the children in order. Taking a furnished house—cosier than a hotel and roomier than a caravan or canal boat—is ideal in many respects, but it is hard on mother.

It was of course partly this consideration that inspired Billy Butlin to create his camps. The mother of a family is willing to put up with a lot of "Wakey! Wakey!" in return for a respite from the daily chores. Which brings us to the question which every family must answer before embarking on a summer holiday. Do we seek solitude or company?

There are self-contained families for whom the essence of a summer holiday is freedom from the company of others. They are, I suspect, in a minority.

For many urban families such solitude is an affliction. Bliss is collective activity, dances with competitions and an incessant master of ceremonies, with housey-housey on the quieter nights—the more we are together, the happier we shall be.

I have a feeling that family summer holidays are on the wane. My older grandchildren seem to spend a great part of their holiday staying with different friends. The British summer holiday has had a lot to do with fulfilling childhood dreams. But the span of childhood has sadly grown much shorter. And tastes are more sophisticated. "Daphne and I have decided to go ski-ing with friends this year. Okay, Mum?"

DIVIDED WE STAND

Half a century ago, as a young reporter, W. F. Deedes found himself in charge of The Daily Telegraph's Christmas appeal for the children of the unemployed. He became a frequent visitor to the so-called Distressed Areas of a divided Britain. Recently he went back to Tyneside, West Cumbria and south Wales to judge for himself whether, 50 years on, there has been any real improvement.

If you can dine from time to time in Newcastle's excellent Chinese Palace Garden restaurant, can take the family regularly to the MetroCentre, can occasionally visit the Theatre Royal, with its marvellous staircase of Italian white marble—why then, you will have a better life than millions who live in and around London. If you live on the vast Scotswood estate, which frowns at the MetroCentre half a mile across the river, or on the Ridges (renamed Meadow Well to make it prettier), then you will not be all that much better off than most of the people I saw on Tyneside half a century ago, when visiting what were known in those days as the Distressed Areas.

On my recent visit we were discussing poverty in Scotswood. There was this boy, they said. The marriage had broken up. The boy's Christmas present from his father was an orange. 'They are not dying on the streets,' they said at Meadow Well, 'but they are poor in hope.'

The striking fact about Tyneside in 1989 is that it contains all the extreme social contrasts that we have been led to believe mark the great divide between north and south. The north-south divide is not altogether a myth, but it widely misrepresents the true state of England now.

This is not to undervalue the astonishing transformation that has been wrought on Tyneside in recent years. Here is something I wrote, quoting social workers, back in 1937, when this newspaper was appealing—successfully—for enough money from readers to send every child of unemployed parents in the Distressed Areas a Christmas present by post. 'There are so many cases that wring the heart. There are so many families that just rub along from day to day. They really cannot get anything except bread and potatoes, and not enough of those. Fathers and mothers, however much they want to, simply cannot spare one halfpenny towards a present that would change their child's outlook on Christmas Day.'

The river Tyne stank. Decaying wreckage from its past lay everywhere. Jarrow had marched on London. Tyneside had the worst-housed population in England and Wales. The amount of tuberculosis was alarming. In South Shields they were living 180 to the acre.

A lot has changed since then. It is easy now to grumble about the MetroCentre, as Mr T. Dan Smith does—in my view wrongly—claiming that a pharmaceutical centre would be better; to smile at the moderns who call the building 'significant', because it reveals nothing at all. 'I am sometimes told,' the industrial chaplain there said to me, 'that it is an obscenity to send a chaplain to this place which flaunts riches in front of the poor.'

'We are promoting a quality of life,' said the marketing manager. In support of this statement, no sign of litter, vandalism or graffiti can be found along the three and a half miles of splendid shops. Even the security people are quaintly described as 'user-friendly'.

One of the north's secrets is that the proportion of disposable income left to the average family is higher than it is in the south. Because house prices are 65 per cent lower than in the south, the mortgage represents nearer 20 than 30 per cent of income. So it is not surprising that families spend on average £52 a visit to the MetroCentre. We dined in the Palace Garden Chinese restaurant (£85 for five) on a Monday, which tends to be a quiet night in the south. Every table was full, many of them with young people.

People in work on Tyneside are not rich, but a number are a great deal better off than they were even five years ago. So there is a gap between them and people out of work (about one in seven, against one in 12 for the country as a whole). The gap is wider still between them and the long-term unemployed (four out of ten of the unemployed have not worked for a year), and this gap continues to grow remorselessly wider.

That is one reason why, confusingly, Tyneside talks with two voices. 'We are not a depressed area,' John Hall told me. He is an extrovert, the miner's son who has made himself a multi-millionaire with the MetroCentre and now occupies the former seat of the Marquesses of Londonderry. 'You are not going to change the past overnight, but the north-east has turned the corner.' He thinks, as many others do, that Labour politicians have a habit of talking the north-east down too much. He also sees profound changes coming in that party. 'The new Labour man,' he says, 'has a car telephone and a Filofax.' He welcomes him.

The many who speak and the few who work for the poor see it otherwise. They are angered by the inertia that grips places like Scotswood. Because debt is a problem there, and loan sharks follow debt, Scotswood has a Credit Union, formed by volunteers in 1983 as a savings club. It now has £50,000 available to help its 200 members. I spent two hours with them, discussing the finances of the very poor, the difficulty of replacing things like cookers, the impossibility of shopping in bulk, and Christmas, which had led me to Tyneside in the first place.

'The difference between then and now,' they said, 'is that children expect to get what they see. The pressures are so great. Families get the catalogues . . . credit is so free.' When this leads to debt, the downward spiral is alarmingly fast.

'What I did,' said a mother working in the Credit Union offices, 'was to make three separate Christmas presents of a pencil, a sharpener and an india-rubber. They love opening parcels.' I mentioned the community spirit that I remembered from the late 1930s on Tyneside, the sense of solidarity with neighbours. 'Communities in the 1930s,' they said, 'were like extended families. The spirit of comradeship among men born in the great Tyneside industries was strong. It has got fragmented. If you are in crisis in 1989, you're on your own.'

One visible economic indicator on these vast council estates is the number of cars parked outside houses. There are very few at Meadow Well, built in the 1930s in response to chronic overcrowding. Nine out of ten people there are on housing benefit. There are plenty of houses where no one has ever worked. 'Many of them do not notice any more the differences between working days and weekends, day or night.' I think that is new since the 1930s.

The curse of such estates, by no means confined to the north, where they feel, as someone put it, 'that they have run out of their future', is that they become repositories for desperation, for the chronically indigent, and now a high proportion of one-person families. To repair the devastation caused on the Tyne by the collapse of its staples, coal and shipbuilding, must clearly take a long time. But what is to happen meanwhile to this generation of children who, on Meadow Well and Scotswood and many more places like that, find themselves at the bottom of the pack, while the grindingly slow process of regeneration takes place?

The obvious conclusion to draw may not be the right one. About six years after my final pre-war visit to a destitute Tyneside, some of us found ourselves in battle alongside 50 Division, drawn from the Tees and Tyne, which Montgomery used as the spearhead for some of his hardest battles, including D-Day. Indeed, he used them up. 'They were simply the best,' he said to me after the war. Human beings, particularly those in adversity, have a way of wrongfooting sociologists, economists, journalists and even politicians.

The Credit Union at Meadow Well, however, which assists those who can save £1 a week, did not share all my anxieties about the children. Their evidence was that the children are cared for, but the parents undernourished. Their worries—which I found elsewhere—related to the children's future expectations. 'We are in a new generation of kids,' they said, 'who know what is going on. If they know there is no job when they leave school, they become less interested in what they learn at school.'

I went to Jarrow on a lovely winter's afternoon which seemed to lift all the shadows off its recent history. Down at the bottom of what was once Palmer's Yard, there stands a statue to Sir Charles Mark Palmer, Bt. They are making a small park round it, which gets vandalised, where the traveller can sit down, look over the river and reflect. A lot of history is written here.

I ran my eye over the inscription on the statue. 'Founder of the Palmer works,' it reads, 'and of the town of Jarrow.' He was the town's first mayor in 1875, designer of the first steam screw collier, MP for Durham in 1874 and then Jarrow. On his 80th birthday in 1903, the workers of Palmer's Yard erected the statue, 'commemorating a life devoted to the social advance of the working class, the prosperity of Jarrow and the industrial progress of Tyneside'. One of the four copper plaques on the statue is missing. There, as I say, the visitor may sit and contemplate the empty river and the past, perchance to shed a tear.

As the tiny but enchanting Bede museum and art gallery in Jarrow reminds you with some of its old pictures, Jarrow built a lot of what some of us grew up to believe was an invincible navy. It stirred a faint echo in my mind, and I recalled being told on one of my visits in the 1930s that Tyneside lacked enthusiasm for the peaceful persuasions of the League of Nations Union.

While I was there this time, I spoke with a schoolmaster. We talked about the children's motivations. Half of his top three bands, he reckoned, counted on having a skill. The other half and most of the three middle bands will not apply themselves to acquiring special skills. Not even the parental urge, if it exists, will move them. They know, or they think they know, their future. They lose the desire to push themselves academically.

The schoolmaster was troubled by children who came from social pockets where family life and care had virtually collapsed. Many of them had horrifying family backgrounds. There was a 'no-home-work' girl. On enquiry, she was found to come from a home with no heating and no electric light. She could only see to do her work if she lit a coal fire.

In Haltwhistle, on our way to West Cumbria, a headmaster talked about this. He called it the factory ethic. Mothers, he said, were traditionally a strong presence in northern homes. When the mothers were out and the children lacked supervision, things went downhill. He was not the only person during my travels to put the John Kenneth Galbraith thesis back to front and to speak of private squalor amid public affluence.

When I had visited Haltwhistle in the 1930s, one of many devastated mining villages, the schoolmaster had spoken only of food or the lack of it. So this time I looked at the day's lunch menu. The 'Champion Dinner' offer for 65p included soup and bread, sweet and sour pork, sausage rolls, 'surfburgers', scotch eggs and sandwiches. There was also a 'rich dessert'. 'Not all our needs are physical,' said the headmaster.

I crossed the hills to West Cumbria with one or two thoughts about Tyneside uppermost in my mind. It is a mistake to dismiss the laborious work of cleaning up and renovating the landscape as merely cosmetic. It is imperative work, if people here or from overseas are to be persuaded to invest in the north, and if their senior managements (and families) are to be persuaded to live there. Not a penny spent on making Tyneside look a decent place in which to live, which it is, has been wasted. All of the £10 million spent renovating the Theatre Royal with its alabaster stairway, was bread on the waters. Alas, there, as almost everywhere else I travelled, the most

urgent task of rehabilitation has become to tear down the warehouses
we built for human beings in the 1960s. What on earth did we think
we were doing then? One of Tyneside's greatest housing disasters,
more horrifying than the slums I saw in the 1930s, is Gateshead's St
Cuthbert's Village, flats built in the grey slab block style favoured by
prize-winning architects in the 1960s. Having helped to dehumanise
the Gateshead population, some of the flats have been ripped out—
after 20 years.

By contrast, the Byker Wall of the 1970s, where blocks of
strikingly designed flats surround well-landscaped low-rise housing,
is Newcastle's most attractive contribution to housing architecture.
The Swedish architect has produced colour and variety for about
2,000 dwellings and contrived to make the density look far lower
than 126 to the acre. He has banished monotony. The doctor in
South Shields with whom I talked laid great emphasis on housing. 'It
is one of the most important factors in health,' he said, 'and it has
improved no end.' Top of his list of social problems was early
marriages followed by chronic unemployment.

Back in 1938, I thought West Cumbria was the Cinderella of all the
Distressed Areas. Its geographical isolation, bad communications and
relatively small population had hidden its miseries away. An excellent
commission of enquiry for the Labour Party, chaired by Hugh
Dalton in 1937, showed that 37 per cent of west Cumberland's
35,400 workers were jobless; nearly half had been unemployed for
over a year, a third for over two years, an eighth for over five years.

Most dismal of all was Cleator Moor. 'The distress is dreadful,'
wrote Dalton. So I found it to be. In Cragg Road now, Mr John
Mann manages Cleator Moor Workspace, run since 1984 to assist
and encourage small business ideas. He had worked in the Haig pit,
which straddles the high ridge like a spectre between Whitehaven
and the sea. It was the last in Cumbria and closed in 1986, having
opened in 1916. There were daffodils in the corner of his office and
a pair of wrought-iron gates from one of his customers. There is
promise.

On our way out of Cleator Moor I spotted the long façade of a
cotton mill. The Dalton report on Cleator Moor had written of
'a thread mill which employed about 300, mainly women and girls,
and closed in 1925'. This indeed was the old Cleator Linen Thread
Mills, the oldest flax-spinning mill in the country. Now it is in the

hands of Kangol (3,000 different hats) which employs 650 hands there. The old mill of the early 19th century, driven by a mill-race from the river Ehen that runs alongside, has gone. Work goes on in what was built in 1900.

As mill owners did in the early 19th century, the founder, Henry Birley, lived in a property near by, curiously named The Flosh—now the Flosh Hotel. And not far away is Ehen Hall, once the property of the Burns-Lindow family (motto: *Vi et Virtute*), mine-owners, and now occupied by the granddaughter of the Lindow estate manager. More of the old—good and bad—is left in West Cumbria than on Tyneside, perhaps because less money is available to change things quickly.

There is a wide gap, I found, between the glossy brochures that tells us how Maryport and such places will look tomorrow, and what it looks like today. The Maryport Harbour brochure—'Your First Port of Call'—where a joint development is in the hands of Allerdale District Council, Cumbria County Council and English Estates North, has all the allure of a marina in the Caribbean. I took a look at the harbour. Progress has been slow, but perhaps that is not a bad thing.

Down the coast at Workington a lot of clearing up has been done. Indeed, they knocked down about 600 houses and half of eight pubs until they ran into the superb bond storage building, which is listed, and left the rest of that street standing—with only four pubs. 'What did they get out of the place they knocked the houses down in?' excitement a wag in the George IV, where I went for enlightenment. 'Why nothing, but they are beautifying the area!'

At the centre of West Cumbria's economy today is British Nuclear Fuels plc, or as I prefer to call it, the Duke of Sellafield. Here is the richest duke of them all, with countless millions at his disposal, 15,000 estate workers and some thousands of acres of land. 'We are becoming good farmers,' they said to me. This remote region of West Cumbria is heavily dependent on the Duke, whose staff includes 6,500 site workers, who will not be wanted for ever. Nearby Whitehaven, destitute when I saw it in 1938, is now what a local editor calls 'a canny little town'. It prospers. There are traffic jams and there are some lovely shops, including Michael Moon's antiquarian bookshop.

Yet, as history reminds one, most of West Cumbria's suffering has sprung from dependence on one or two industries. So the Duke,

for all his good intentions and his undeniable sense of social responsibility, leaves a faint question mark in one's mind.

But they are very unusual people, these West Cumbrians.
Inward-looking, perhaps, but their roots are deep, and they have kept
a feeling for their land which we are losing in the amorphous south.
Material wealth is not their only standard of life. So, as I took the
road back to Newcastle, I glanced again at some lines which Patrick
Gordon-Duff-Pennington, Cumbrian landowner, farmer, poet and
goodness knows what else, had rather shyly placed in my hands over
dinner the night before. They end like this:

> So the land declined and the old industries died,
> But the lakes and the hills
> And the timeless surge of the sea
> Survived, as year after year,
> A few of the native people returned
> To their roots.
> Just as the silver salmon,
> Just as the seeds of the birch
> In the autumn wind,
> Returning to the holy places of their birth,
> Man, too, returns
> In praise of his God, and Cumberland,
> Seeking tomorrow.

I did not recognise the scene at Dowlais in south Wales, where the
great steelworks had once stood. It was there that Edward VIII, less
than a month before his abdication in December 1936, had stood,
looked up at the huge derelict works and, turning to the unemployed
steel workers around him, declared, 'Something must be done.'

A week or two after that speech, I visited the place. It had once
produced the finest steel in the world. Then it was a symbol of the
Great Depression. Dowlais Steel Works, property of Guest, Keen,
Nettlefold, lay at the top of the long steep hill that winds out of
Merthyr Tydfil. To the right of the road there stretched an almost
unbroken line of terribly bad houses.

Today, the works have been swept away, and so have the houses.
The vast slag-heaps from the steelworks have been contoured and
are green. All that remains is the handsome GKN power-house,
towering proudly over the modern OP chocolate factory which
occupies some of the old steelworks territory. Several interests

combined to preserve and restore the power-house. A tiny park near by is in the making. It seems to be standard practice now to create these small shrines—as they have done at Palmer's Yard in Jarrow—to memorialise a chapter of our industrial history.

Curiously, the King had not originally intended to visit Dowlais on his two-day tour of November 20 and 21. He was persuaded to make a special detour there, I learned the other day, by John Denithorn, a Quaker in Merthyr, who died only a year or two ago. Nor did the King say quite what history has handed down to us. His words were, 'These steelworks brought the men here. Something must be done to see that they stay here—working.'

It was in Merthyr one winter evening just before Christmas in 1938 that I saw a girl of about seven, clutching the hand of her small brother, with her nose against the window of a dingy toy shop. Her face was grubby enough to mark the course of a tear. Good copy for fundraising, I thought, and so it was. Merthyr Tydfil today is still relatively poor, but it no longer has an unemployment rate of 47 per cent (it is nearer 14 per cent).

In 1938, I remember, hopes were centred on a projected button factory. Imagine the joy, 50 years later, of meeting the man whose father founded it and who is now expanding it. His father, Rudolf Adler, ran a family business in Czechoslovakia. After Munich, he decided to move on. A friendly British consul pointed him towards Cardiff. The MP, S. O. Davies, and the Town Clerk of Merthyr gave him a hand. By August 1939, Adler was indenting for more space and employing 90 people. When Rudolf Adler began, his son explained to me, there were 300 button factories in this country. Today there are only 15, and Merthyr employs some quarter of the work-force in buttons.

One of the men with fresh ideas in Merthyr Tydfil today is Canon Bill Morgan, BSc Econ, the vicar of Pen-y-darren, whose church stands near the top of the hill leading to Dowlais. Canon Morgan has strong views on what the Church should do about inner-city problems. Too many, he says, are theologising about them. 'When they have said something, they think that they have done something.' So he has set up a business—several businesses, in fact—to provide work and to make money. 'Others in the Church could do it,' he insists. I demur. 'Not many names in Crockford carry BSc Econ after them,' I remark. 'A matter of training and self-confidence,' says Canon Morgan briskly. He appears to lack neither.

Archbishop Tutu of Cape Town, a freeman of Merthyr Tydfil, has just been to preach in his church and open one of his enterprises. 'We had just 14 days' notice of that,' says the Canon, 'and it all worked.' His version of Christian capitalism—'There is a need to be hard-headed about profits'—has been built up in two years to provide about 2,500 people with jobs.

He has restored his church, which he inherited as a ruin. The insurance company offered him £20,000 to knock it down. It is now worth, he says, £250,000. Most of the business seems to be done from an office in his own vicarage next door. St John's Industries is a private company, chaired by the Canon, with a lawyer and an accountant on the board. It is into bricks, concrete, timber and furniture, makes its own doors and staircases and will soon be into forestry and leisure. There is also a 70-acre farm a mile or two away, where young men with little to do can learn farmwork under supervision. Attached to it is a £500,000 riding school, built by the company for the use of the disabled. Christian privatisation, Canon Morgan calls it.

The world being what it is, I do not doubt the Canon has his critics, for he is forthright in his opinions; but in his eyes this is the right pastoral work in a place like Merthyr. He believes in the parable of the talents. 'Let the Christian church identify itself with the poor,' he says, 'but let it also do something practical for the poor.' Unlike Adler's pre-war button factory, St John's is not Merthyr's only bright star. The biggest in Merthyr's constellation is Hoover, which once employed 5,000. Modern methods reduced this to 2,000, and the impact of high mortgages on the purchase of household goods elsewhere may reduce it yet again.

'Of course,' said the senior official at the local Department of Employment office, 'the old industries were more labour-intensive than modern industry.' That is profoundly true. Moreover, they offered something of deeper social significance, which cropped up in a talk with Canon Morgan and his friends. 'If we constantly denigrate ourselves,' he began, 'investors are put off.' 'That must be the right philosophy,' replied another, 'but if you attract new industry, do you cater for the bread-winner in our tradition?' He put his finger on one of the deepest changes in all those areas. They were founded around heavy industries. The bread-winners were almost exclusively male. They are not any more. There has been a profound human change there.

A call on Eric Baker and his friends was followed by what he called a 'leisurely lunch' (which ended at six o'clock). He and his cousin run one of the most successful motor businesses in these parts, with branches elsewhere. Baker emphasises communications. 'Merthyr Tydfil to Heathrow in two hours!' he exclaims. He admits that in Surrey the car market still sells three times as many cars, and that the car is a social barometer. But because communications are shrinking the United Kingdom, he sees most of the old obstacles created by geographical isolation breaking down.

The retired probation officer with us shared only part of Baker's optimism. 'This is a "hard town",' he said. When I was there in the 1930s, the crime rate was negligible. There was, after all, not a great deal to steal. It is high in Merthyr now. Chapel attendances in the valleys have fallen heavily. The old faiths that sustained a good many people in the 1930s have dwindled.

Which led us, once again, to the soulless stuff we built for homes in the 1960s. Merthyr's share of it is the Gurnos estate. Plastic drainpipes for economy, broken and swinging in the breeze; grisly walkways and graffiti everywhere. 'We have a special style of humour in the valleys,' says someone grimly. 'We say it should be "twinned with Beirut"!' Yet it is by no means the worst in Wales.

'Take a look at Penrhys,' they said in a friendly way at Labour's by-election headquarters in Pontypridd. So I travelled up the Rhondda Valley to see it. 'It won an award,' said my driver in a hollow voice. Isolated and a thousand chilly feet up, the Penrhys housing estate contains 951 properties of appalling aspect, its accessible walls smeared with graffiti, grey slabs on a windy hill. If I lived there, I would unhesitatingly join the Militant Tendency and work to make it more extreme. The 1960s stuff is haunting.

Travelling through Maerdy, to see one of the last Welsh pits at work, I crossed the heights into Cynon Valley, which in my days there we called the Aberdare Valley. I think that some of Eric Baker's ideas may take time to reach this valley. One of its ironies is the gigantic smokeless fuel plant that belches and fumes like everyone's idea of a satanic mill. In this valley, reputedly the poorest in Wales, 60 per cent of households live on less than £4,000 a year (£77 a week). These Welsh valleys in the 1920s had 270,000 men at work in 600 pits, producing 46 million tons of coal a year. Now Japan's factories in Wales employ more than the hand-ful of remaining pits. Of all the places I have just visited, I think

Mountain Ash in this valley comes closest to what I remember from the 1930s.

A lot of places have been left behind, I reflect after this journey through the north and the Welsh valleys. Yet that is true today of many parts of more prosperous Britain, not least of London. We have in fact had an unbridgeable chasm to fill in these old Distressed Areas. There stands out in my mind a remark by Chris Tighe, *The Daily Telegraph*'s perceptive correspondent in the north. 'These places grew up,' she said as we travelled back from Cumbria, 'because the industrialists had a reason to be here. Much of what has replaced those industries, which were founded on natural wealth, has an arbitrary look because it has no reason to be here.'

In all that has been done to rescue the old Distressed Areas from decay and human despair; in saluting the host of people, past and present, whose faith and zeal have made this possible; in acknowledging all the changes I have just seen, it is well to bear in mind that in terms of recent history, the remedies represent second best. We must respond to change or perish—the keynote of Mrs Thatcher's Government—and that is right. But what we need also to remember is that those people who have worked in the industries—coal, ships, cotton, heavy engineering—that founded the country's fortunes in the 19th century have been called upon to change far more than most of us.

There was a comradeship that pulled men together in places like Palmer's Yard at Jarrow and Dowlais Steel Works. Later, in the south, we came to see these places as dark satanic mills. Yet it came home to me as we travelled along that bleak Cumbrian coastline between Workington and Whitehaven that there was a lot more human warmth in some of those old places, ghastly though they looked, than is now to be found in the modern factory unit.

This Government, and future Governments, will not come up with easy answers to this widening gulf between a majority that has most of what it needs and an under-class that has virtually nothing at all. There are no obvious answers, I concluded, while traipsing around the ghettos of the 1960s in which, for reasons I have been striving unsuccessfully to analyse, the under-class gets dumped.

But this problem of the poor getting poorer is not exclusively part of the north-versus-south rhetoric that has become a familiar political signature tune. It is grossly unfair to the reviving north to pretend that it is. The brightest clue to the future lies in the remark of a PR man in Newcastle, which I heard echoed in other places. 'You have to be pretty good to survive up here,' he said. In the north-east, in West Cumbria, in south Wales, there are abundant signs of a new, vigorous and healthier grass-roots capitalism. The thought first occurred to me in the Cleator Moor Workspace office. The new capitalists of the north work with people more than with other people's money.

How strange to think that, in parts of England which half a century ago I found dying, there is now to be found the start of a fresh cycle of capitalism. Capitalism, John Hall had said to me in Newcastle, has to be related to people as well as to money. He sees that as one of the hills that the Conservative party has to climb. It would, of course, be over-fanciful to see some aspects of modern capitalism as practised today—the speculative takeovers, the junk bonds—as the future spoil heaps that represent the north's past today.

But there is a cycle in human affairs. There has to be a fresh beginning and it is not altogether fanciful to see the old Distressed Areas, their slag-heaps greening over, starting a new cycle for us in the south, reminding us what capitalism in the service of humanity ought to be about.

HAS ENGLAND LOST ITS
DAYS OF GRACE?

ENGLISH CRICKET, INSIGHTS INTO VALUES
OF OUR TIME

W. F. Deedes wonders whether our cricket captain's feelings live up to great occasions like a Lord's Test

A sunny day at Lord's, Australians in the field, comfortable chairs in the President's box, a small refreshment in the right hand—a good moment to muse on the condition of English cricket. My instinct tells me that it is going to be a heart-in-mouth day.

This is not only because England is fighting a rearguard action, and their captain is out here with his back to the wall. It is because the method of today's English batsmen, even the best of them, keeps the heart perpetually near the mouth.

There is a certain lack of solidity. We see flashes of brilliance, especially from David Gower, but also unaccountable streaks of folly from people who are supposed to be at the very top of our game.

I glance across to the Mound stand and think of a Saturday in 1930 when I watched Bill Ponsford and Sir Donald Bradman bat most of the day and help Australia eventually reach 729 for 6 wickets. No lack of solidity there, I recollect.

I was too young to see Warwick Armstrong's renowned side in the 1921 Ashes, though it is right to recall that the triumphant progress of those Australians left us very much in the mood we are in now.

England's cricket was widely perceived to be at rock bottom, but then we were only two years out of an exhausting war. Many of shining promise in 1914 had not returned to the cricket field.

We were also, as to some extent we are today, moving through a period of rapid social change. Some of the certainties and old sureties had gone. A game like cricket is susceptible to this sort of thing. Change is not always its ally.

On the other hand, I reflect, looking round the capacity crowd at

Lord's, this scene could well be drawn from the 1930s or earlier. A Test against the Australians at Lord's (though we find it very hard to win one) carries a certain aura. The crowd's behaviour is irreproachable. There seems to be plenty to drink, but no louts.

It is traditionally a very special occasion, the pinnacle of international cricket; but this starts another train of thought. Does David Gower out there, does Mike Gatting or Graham Gooch have this sense of a very special event? Or is it just another big cricket match?

Here am I, a septuagenarian who has watched cricket all his life and this to me is an historic match. But is it to them?

I very much doubt if it is, but why is it not? Two answers occur to me. The first and obvious one is that we play far more international cricket than is good for our cricketers. By some freak, when we gave up our Empire and the white man's burden, we passed much of the load over to our cricketers.

Today's Commonwealth teems with independent nations panting to appear in a Test match at Lord's. It is an important symbol to them, the badge of equality. We are usually happy to oblige them.

It keeps the turnstiles clicking, and cricket needs the money. We could not maintain the traditional shape of first-class cricket in this country without the cash raised in international matches, much of which the Test and County Cricket Board recycles to the counties.

Cricket is working harder at earning its living than it has ever done before, and perhaps this is beginning to show. Was Lord's last Monday a day to remember for David Gower—or was it just another day at the office?

Last Saturday, it had been a very bad day at the office. By custom and practice, the journalists meet the English skipper on the Saturday of a Test match. Certain sections of the Press are tremendously unkind to skippers they deem to have failed Queen and country.

My impression of David Gower's short-lived meeting with the Press was that it resembled the sort of encounter Alan Bond might have expected last week with some of his shareholders.

I very much doubt if Dr. W. G. Grace had to engage in such encounters, nor even the Hon. Lionel Tennyson, who was suddenly thrown into the front line as captain against Armstrong's men in the last three Tests of 1921.

Cricket, we need to remember, is there to be enjoyed by those who play it as well as by those who watch it. If through too much of it, it becomes a treadmill; and if through the critical attentions of the news media, it becomes a torment, then much joy will go out of the game, and we on the stands will be the first to notice it.

"Our batsmen show a marked reluctance to follow orthodoxy," someone murmured to me over the rim of his glass as one of our bats returned to the pavilion. "And not only our batsmen . . ." I replied, and then began to consider what I had said.

Orthodoxy, if we think about it, is not enjoying a tremendously good innings just now in any main department of our lives. Within the Church it is sharply questioned. Modern architects condemn it. More relevantly, in education it has been under persistent challenge.

Between those who believe that a grasp of English syntax and grammar is indispensable to clear self-expression, and those who insist that it is old hat, battle lines have been drawn. There is widespread disbelief in the classical method, and I do not think that cricket can expect to be altogether immune from such tendencies.

If our schoolchildren are taught that Shakespeare does not repay study, being irrelevant to the needs of these times, why should a young English cricketer feel impelled to model himself on Trumper or Hobbs or Rhodes or Bradman?

The answer ought to be: because it is the only way to reach the stars. If we look back on the masters of this game, particularly the batsmen, we find that with few exceptions their method was sound. It was the foundation of their success.

If you desired to reach the top, indeed if you sought to earn a living from the game, the method had to be right. To some it may have come instinctively, from most it called for a capacity to take infinite pains, or as we put it less elegantly today, to take sweat.

There is a satisfactory living to be made today without going through all that. The game has been wholly professionalised. The bad old days of two gates at Lord's for the Gentlemen and the Players, of professionals left out of county sides to make way for schoolmasters on holiday are behind us.

If we are in cricket, we are in business. If it is riches you desire, then the publisher you choose may well count for more than a classical defence with the bat.

On reflection, that is not an honest statement. It should be amended to read that, if as a former first-class cricketer you are invited by a newspaper to write outspokenly about your former colleagues during the Test match season, you will earn more in one year than the captain of England in three.

Perhaps one should not be too cynical or despairing about the state of our game. If we examine the cycle of English cricket in this century—or Australia's for that matter—we shall find peaks and troughs at fairly regular intervals. Where we could account for the troughs, we re-examined ourselves, pulled ourselves together and came up again.

It might not happen quite like that this time. For one thing, we are less ready to take a hint than we were. We suffer more from hubris than we did. The correction of mistakes calls for a higher degree of humility than we seem able to muster.

In the spirit of these times, our cricketers are more interested in winning tactics than in techniques. For another, there has been a sea-change in the upbringing of our young.

Furthermore, fostering high talent is for the time being out of fashion. Our schools resemble the convoy system; the pace of all is governed by the slower boats. That makes it at least a degree harder for the child of that rare clay from which great cricketers are drawn to reach his potential.

We shall have to care more than we do now about team games for our children, particularly cricket, before much serious rebuilding can be done. There is nothing intrinsically wrong with this beautiful game, but it has an awkward way of reflecting what is wrong with us. It is the mirror on the wall.

The fault, dear Brutus, lies not with David Gower or Ted Dexter, but in ourselves.

DRINK AND BE MERRY

The health education industry is threatening to make drinking as socially unacceptable as smoking, much to the chagrin of W. F. Deedes. Here he reflects on the joys and benefits of "moderate and regular" alcohol consumption

When, soon after the First World War, one of my great aunts was taken ill, I overheard a conversation between my father and the family doctor. "She's a bit pulled down by this," the doctor said. "Half a bottle of champagne a day is what she needs, if you can run to it." My father, at that time responsible for the upkeep of four maiden aunts, thought this a bit steep but complied with the doctor's prescription. The old lady lived to a great age.

A doctor making such a recommendation today would probably be struck off. It is true that the episode occurred in the reckless 1920s, when jazz, nightclubs and cocktails were all the rage, and almost anything went. Yet, as late as the 1950s, I received not dissimilar advice from my own doctor. "Try to relax a bit before dinner," he said. "A stiff gin will do you no lasting harm, nor even a second gin."

He would hardly dare tender such advice today. Alcohol is in the dock. Hardly a day passes but fresh charges are pressed against it. Those who drink find themselves in the same tumbrel as those who smoke. Dr Stuart, of Ware in Hertfordshire, declared earlier this year that drinkers are more likely to catch Aids. Alcohol, he says, weakens the immune system. We are back to the days when gin was a mother's ruin. "Drunk for a penny, dead drunk for tuppence."

In respect of all self-indulgences, most of us carry in our heads little homilies which we find forgiving and therefore comforting. I have long drawn solace, for example, from some words Winston Churchill wrote in the 1930s. He was describing his experiences with the Guards Division in France, where he joined the Grenadiers after the Dardanelles disaster and after ceasing to be a Minister. Here is the relevant passage:

I said that I thought I should learn of the conditions in the trenches better if I lived with the Companies actually in the line instead of at Battalion Headquarters. The Colonel considered this a praiseworthy suggestion, and made arrangements accordingly. I must confess to the reader that I was prompted by what many will think a somewhat inadequate motive. Battalion Headquarters when in the line was strictly "dry". Nothing but strong tea with the condensed milk, a very unpleasant beverage, ever appeared there. The Companies' messes in the trenches were, however, allowed more latitude. And as I have always believed in the moderate and regular use of alcohol, especially under conditions of winter war, I gladly moved my handful of belongings from Ebenezer Farm to the Company in the line.

As we know, Winston Churchill did not restrict his use of alcohol to the conditions of winter war. I once had to call on him at No 10 to receive a small appointment at about 4.30 in the afternoon. A weak whisky and soda sat on the Cabinet table within reach of his right hand, with a little white card over the top of it. The card was there to protect the contents because the glass might well sit there for a couple of hours, untasted. He just liked to feel that it was close at hand.

But his phrase "moderate and regular" merits discussion. "Regular" in this context is a Humpty Dumpty word; it can mean what you want it to mean. What it means to me is that alcohol is only enjoyable if it is drunk at certain times of day. A whisky and soda just after half-past six in the evening—there is a beguiling sense of virtue in being a few minutes behind time with it—is one thing; I find it delightful.

On the other hand, I do not share the pleasures derived by golfers at very good clubs for a glass of Bucks Fizz—or black velvet in winter—before a morning round. Winston occasionally enjoyed a glass of hock with his breakfast. An old gentleman I knew on the Morning Post, who had been a lobby correspondent in Gladstone's time, took a pint of porter at breakfast time. He lived to be well past 80, but breakfast drinking is not for me.

A few years ago I was in Northern Ireland for an Orange Day march. My host called me with a cup of tea, which I drank, and a triple whisky which, shamefully, I poured down his sink. A whisky which smells inviting at sundown smells disgusting at sunrise. So "regular" is the word, with very few exceptions. If courtesy positively demands it, I find it not impossible to take a glass of dry sherry, champagne or chilled white port after 11 in the morning. Champagne in the middle of the afternoon at wedding receptions makes no appeal, and there is much to be said for the modern habit of holding wedding receptions later in the day.

What the host is pleased to call "a little surprise" or "my own invention" makes no appeal to me either. I dread evening parties where a steaming wine punch of unknown ingredients is being poured into glasses. It virtually rules out any orthodox drinking for the rest of that day, for nothing else mixes cheerfully with mulling. It disrupts the rhythm of the "moderate and regular" drinker.

Because of the Wall Street crash of 1929, I did not go to Oxford, but my early life on a London newspaper was spent close to colleagues who had been either there or at Cambridge. To some extent, therefore, one's drinking habits were influenced by those who had been at university in the late 1920s. Evelyn Waugh thought his generation at Oxford, 1921–24, was the last to preserve more or less intact the social habits of the 19th century.

For undergraduates of average means, he said, beer was the staple. "Luncheon was served in our rooms with jugs of beer. Beer was always drunk in Hall. At one time I used to drink a tankard of beer for breakfast, but I was alone in that. It was drawn and served without demur." Waugh declares that he and most of his friends were drunk three or four times a week. "We were never pugnacious or seriously destructive. It took very little to inebriate at that age . . . Not many of us became drunkards."

For young men who had developed this taste for beer, Fleet Street in my early days offered a broad horizon. So my friends and I also drank a great deal of beer in preference to anything else, but the requirements of our newspaper discouraged drunkenness, even once a week; and we were certainly not pugnacious. The habit formed, I have since dismayed many generous hosts at lunch and even dinner by preferring draught beer to wine. A pint, mind you, and preferably in a decent tankard—and essentially draught, not bottled.

The habit was reinforced through early reading of John Buchan's novels. Richard Hannay struck me as a man who would always prefer a tankard of ale to a château-bottled wine. Indeed, at a critical point for Hannay in "The Three Hostages", we find him saying to Barnard, butler to his wife's aunts, "Get me a drink like a good fellow. A tankard of beer, if you have it, for I've a throat like a grindstone."

So I do not change but, alas, the beer does. The specific gravity is of course lower than it was before the war, and seems destined to go even lower. The chairman of a well-known brewery told me confidently at lunch recently that he reckoned to be on a winner with the company's new low-alcohol beer. I felt drawn to point out to him that people who had reached a certain age liked their drink to carry *authority*. This remark fell on stony ground.

A certain policy seems to be taking shape on which we are not being consulted, though it may eventually transform the lives of moderate and regular drinkers. The consumption of alcohol is on the road to being regarded as no less socially opprobrious than smoking cigarettes. This mood has, I think, come about for several reasons.

There *is* excessive drinking among a minority of the young and even among the very young, some of whom, according to the recent survey "Young People in 1988" start drinking before they are 11. The so-called lager lout probably drinks no more than Waugh and his friends at Oxford, but there are many more of him and he is not gracefully veiled by college walls.

Furthermore, unlike Waugh and his friends, he does become "pugnacious and seriously destructive", particularly when watching football. Vain to deny there is a social problem here—though the combination of watering the beer by brewers on the one hand and extending licensing hours by the Government on the other strikes me as a rum way to go about it.

The truth is that the people of this northern climate have always been fairly hard drinkers. The Romans developed a great taste for the stuff during their stay. Drink in the last century created enormous social problems. During the first World War it became so bad among factory workers, particularly those in the munitions industry who were earning good wages, that Lloyd George declared at one point: "Drink is doing more damage in this war than all the German submarines put together." So the Pledge was introduced, whereby people foreswore alcohol for the duration of the war.

The problem today has something in common with that of the wartime munitions workers. It arises, not because the young people of this country are depraved, but because (like Waugh's contemporaries at Oxford) they have more money to spend than they have ever had before. Because they have money to spend, they will probably also run a car. In the days of my youth there were many fewer cars and it was quite a feat to get run in for drunken driving.

A friend and I, disgracefully, left a London nightclub early one summer morning, discovered that our golf clubs were in the dicky of his car, and drove unsteadily in tails and white tie to a golf club near London, where we played in boiled shirts, wing collars and evening shoes. I have been trying ever since to identify the club we honoured in this way. It was a salutary as well as unique experience. I call it to mind when tempted to condemn the irresponsibility of the young in 1989.

Excessive drinking by the young and very young and some of its consequences are indeed matters of legitimate social concern. I would not make light of them. I am a degree less willing to accept the new doctrine of certain medicos that my enjoyment of moderate and regular drinking puts me in the same category as drug addicts.

"After alcohol," wrote Dr Colin Brewer in a newspaper article not long ago, "heroin is our main drug problem." He quoted another GP as saying, "When someone asks for a double gin, it takes a special kind of barmaid to say 'Never mind the gin. Let's sit down and talk about why you need it.'" I have never turned up my nose at anything a barmaid wanted to say to me; but if one of them pursued that argument, I would hesitate to patronise the place again.

I am, however, not unfamiliar with this line of country, for at one time I was politically involved in dangerous drugs. Those who desire to see drugs like cannabis legalised lay stress on the fact that *all* who resort to artificial stimulants, whether sherry or cocaine, are in the same boat. There is no simple rejoinder to that. But what the dear old Fleet Street printers, before making some outrageous claim, used to call "custom and practice" renders my large pink gin, when the sun is well down, a degree less perilous than injecting drugs of unknown origin.

Not long ago, the Health Education Authority entered a full-page advertisement in the newspapers which bore a heading in large type, "The Strike that cost 50 million Working Days last year". According to the Royal College of Physicians, it went on, smoking has become a major industrial disease. I mistrust mega-guesstimates of this order, but no matter. Similar figures can—and soon will—be laid against those who drink. It will become more difficult to take a modest prophylactic at sunset without that immortal cry from Peter Simple creeping into the mind, "We are *all* guilty."

The main charge against both smokers and drinkers is fundamentally the same, that their wanton self-indulgence occupies too many beds in the National Health Service which would otherwise be available to more deserving customers. Thus they are bad citizens, whose dirty habits squander national resources. George Orwell might have been able to explain the thinking behind this better than I can. When human beings cease to believe in immortality, mortality can be presented as something very terrible indeed.

The defence of the moderate and regular drinker lies in the established fact that a sensible intake of alcohol may prove no less beneficial than it was in the case of my great aunt. I was discussing this with a doctor before a game of golf recently. He asked if I knew about the J-curve. Then he took out a piece of paper and drew a vertical line marked mortality and a horizontal line at right angles to it marked alcohol. In the angle formed by the two lines, he scrawled a large letter J, with the right-hand side of the letter sloping to the right.

As long as the consumption of alcohol remains in line with the short side of the J, the mortality rate goes down. When it reaches the long side of the J, it starts to rise. Rather a jolly man to have as your doctor, I thought.

I do not doubt that the worthy Health Education Authority will condemn such theories as dangerous talk; but never mind, the time has come when the moderate and regular man is sorely in need of cheering up. Brief life is here our portion, as the old hymn says. But if he can run to half a bottle of champagne a day—or, if he cannot, the equivalent in some other tipple—then he may succeed in making it less brief. On that I rest my case, and await an ominous knock on my front door, which heralds the men from the H.E.A.

WHY ACID HOUSE SHOULD NOT STOP THE PARTYING

Graham Bright, Conservative MP, yesterday proposed a Bill that would restrict Acid House parties—but, argues W. F. Deedes, legislation that attempts to deal with new social phenomena is invariably unwise

Almost everything we read about Acid House parties is calculated to arouse the governess who lurks in every legislator. For one thing, the parties take place at unsocial hours, roughly between midnight and dawn. For another, they provoke heroic efforts by local police forces to head them off. They are linked to drug-taking and promiscuous behaviour. Some of the tabloids, which like to mix a bit of nanny with Page 3 girls, have condemned them as dens of vice.

It was a moral certainty, therefore, that sooner rather than later the statutory wheels would start to grind. Yesterday, Graham Bright's Bill, aimed at raising to six months' imprisonment and a £20,000 fine the maximum penalties against those organising entertainments without the proper local authority licences, unsurprisingly got an unopposed second reading in the House. In earlier times our legislators sometimes invited outside bodies, Royal Commissions and the like, to examine social nuisances and to offer recommendations before bursting into law; but not now. Action this day is the call, even if it means sometimes putting the cart before the horse. The most notable example of this was the rapid decision to introduce the football supporter's identity card, subsequently made to look distinctly shaky by Lord Justice Taylor's report on the Hillsborough disaster.

The answer will be that we know all we need to know about these parties, more accurately described by the police as pay parties. The word Acid, incidentally, according to Mr Tony Colston-Hayter, a leading party tycoon, has nothing to do with the hallucinogenic drug, lysergic acid, but comes from the streets of Chicago. It means to steal—and, insofar as the music played at these parties is made up from recordings, it is in a sense stolen.

There seems to me, however, a good deal more to be discovered about these parties than known facts. We dwell, perhaps too much, on the deprived young people of this country. These party goers do not strike me as deprived. As the promoters (who may take upwards of £100,000 from a big party) have grasped, there is a lot of money jingling in the pockets of many young today. To say that the whole attraction is the illegality of these affairs strikes me as a superficial as well as stuffy judgment.

Let me go on to say to police officers, who understandably have lost patience with these people, that if we do not analyse more sympathetically the attraction of these events, putting them down with a heavy hand will do more harm than good. Chasing out nature with a pitchfork is notoriously difficult. I do not doubt that the money involved attracts criminal elements to some of this pay party business. If it is clumsily put down, the criminal element will be attracted to all of it, and the police will be busier than ever.

Insofar as these parties interfere with other people's sleep, safety or privacy, Mr Graham Bright, his supporters and the police have an unassailable case for action. What troubles me about this Bill is the smell of moral outrage attached to it. A politician is safer when he is slightly tipsy and accompanied by a prostitute than when he is under the influence of moral outrage. Some terribly bad legislation has sprung from moral outrage.

In dealing legislatively with social nuisances which arouse moral outrage, precision is imperative. Many years ago I learned at a desk in the Home Office that a law which is going to work properly must be enforceable. Laws provoked by moral outrage frequently are not: the police have a hard time and the lawyers have an innings. If the wording of the proposed law is to be precise, those who direct the drafting must know their subject.

There was an instructive parallel to Mr Bright's Bill on pay parties some years ago when the Government of the day was persuaded that gambling in this county had become a national menace. Crooks were moving in. A government Bill was produced. It drew profitably from Lord Rothschild's Royal Commission on Gambling, but it was still not a good Bill. It was unworkable. A few of us involved in its committee stage decided to tour the gambling houses of London to find out what really happened. There was a pretty rum club in Finchley, I recall, with bullet holes in the front door.

One or two of our number made enough out of blackjack at the

Playboy club to see the bright side of the business. Purged of moral outrage and *informed*, we put forward some practical amendments, which were passed and improved the Act. As Mr Bright shows signs of recognising, the basis for gaming might be the right basis for pay parties. I remember enjoying before the war hunting for the party of the night in London, but the scale was smaller. I accept, if only for reasons of road safety, that people should not be encouraged to race around motorways hunting for raves on unnotified sites.

Some sort of licensing system may be desirable, but it need not be designed as if we were licensing houses of prostitution. As Lord Devlin observed 40 years ago, in a lecture on the enforcement of morals, there must be toleration of the maximum of individual freedom that is consistent with the integrity of society. Nothing, he added, should be punished by law that does not lie beyond the limits of tolerance. It is not nearly enough to say that a majority dislike a practice; there must be a real feeling of reprobation.

That is a learned way of saying that we should not legislate against activities simply because we dislike them. Much stress in our society today springs, not from families broken up by parents separating from each other, but from children who separate themselves from both parents. I accept all the arguments about rival mentors. The parent, the school master and school mistress often feel helpless against the rival teaching of some modern journalism and the little screen.

This is all the more reason for legislators to strive to narrow, not to widen, the cultural gulf. I suspect that many adolescents of this world, far from supposing that they inherit liberties founded in the hedonistic 1960s, have it in their heads that they are living at a time of severe interventionist politics. Journalists often complain of it. Why should the young not feel the same?

To be careful about this is not to be charged with the behaviour of Peter Simple's go-ahead Bishop of Bevindon. There is a line to be drawn between tolerance and permissiveness, though it is often hard to find. As long ago as 1959, Lord Devlin was moved to declare: "Statutory additions to the criminal law are too often made on the simple principle that 'there ought to be a law against it'." Forty years on, there is even more of that about.

HOW WE CAN HELP 300 MILLION WOMEN TO HELP THEMSELVES

As John Major prepares to address the Rio Earth Summit on birth control tomorrow, W. F. Deedes says that what's needed in the Third World is not sterilisation but education

Neither in the heady atmosphere of the Earth Summit, nor down in the Dog and Duck, is there a subject more likely to stir wrathful discussion than population control in the Third World. The figures are big, alarming and not hard to remember. It is a subject made for Alf Garnett himself. "Stands to reason, dunnit? Breedin' like rabbits they are. An' we have to give all these people money, out of our own pockets. Why? 'Cos the Pope doesn't hold with condoms, that's why . . ."

As Paul Harrison, an authority on population and environment, has observed: "Population, like politics or religion, is not a subject for polite conversation. Debates spark fury, fuelled by underlying attitudes on religion, politics and gender."

Indeed, until Baroness Chalker, Minister for Overseas Development, plunged into the subject at a fringe meeting in Rio this week, population control was in danger of becoming too controversial a subject for public discussion. That conclusion had been tacitly reached before the Earth Summit, and it is not hard to see why. For one thing, it implies that guilt for outstripping the world's resources lies with the Third World, simply because it is producing more children. The Third World, on the other hand, insists that blame for squandering the earth's resources lies squarely with the so-called North. Furthermore, the subject digs into the most controversial question of the day: how far is it right to bring the creation of human life under artificial controls?

In reality, as Baroness Chalker and the Prime Minister recognise, neither the Third World's susceptibilities nor the Vatican's doctrine are going to halt the main thrust of prevailing policies, which are designed, putting it mildly, to impart to as much of the Third World as possible what we in the industrialised nations have learnt about eugenics. The temperature around this subject of fertility would be lowered if we saw it in better proportion. As our own Overseas Development Administration has lately pointed out, population pressures are only one factor in environmental degradation. They are not, it says, the ultimate cause, the only cause or necessarily the most important cause. Far from being what looks to most of us a simple matter, links between population and environment are complex, short of sustained research and largely unresolved. It needs also to be stressed that reducing the fertility rate can be no more than a long-term contribution to easing Third World poverty.

Ahead of us lie four decades of the fastest human growth in all history. The rate of increase will average 97 million a year until the end of the century, then 90 million until 2025. Some 97 per cent of the increase will be in today's developing countries, a third of it in Africa. At 10 billion, the world's population in 2050 will be almost double that now. Half the global population today is below reproductive age—up to 45 per cent of it is under 15. The medium projection for 2000 is 6.26 billion people in the world, with a variation between high and low of only about 160,000 million. But by 2050, there is a difference of 4 billion between high and low projections—which is about the total size of the world's population in 1975. By contrast, in most developed countries, and in six developing countries, fertility has already fallen to replacement level, and even below it. Nobody knows whether this trend will continue. There is no historical precedent. If low fertility persists, the world's population will reach a peak in 2050, and start to fall thereafter.

What we know for certain is that the factor most likely to influence these projections is the status and education of women. Those who regard Vatican doctrine as a block to family planning in the Third World betray ignorance of what is going on. It is not so much of a block as a brake on family planning. The expression "population control" is drawn from Alf Garnett's vocabulary. It conjures visions of compulsory sterilisation, such as India disastrously attempted in 1975–76, and condoms issued off the back of trucks delivering food relief from overseas.

When some of the world's international relief organisations are asked by donors if they support family planning programmes, as they sometimes are, they can only truthfully reply: "Yes". If they were asked *why* they supported family planning programmes, the answer would be more enlightening.

A thousand women die every day from problems related to childbearing. A third of all infant deaths worldwide are associated with motherhood at too early an age and with inadequately spaced births. Thus the emphasis is on health, the health of the mother, the health of the child. Too frequent pregnancies contribute to low birth weights, poor child growth rates, early weaning and malnutrition. Anyone working on the ground sees the consequences of bearing child after child. Those helping the world's poor to help themselves cannot turn a blind eye to this.

Access to guidance and means of deciding the size and spacing of the family has been accepted as a human right for a generation. Yet, as lately as 1990, this was denied to some 300 million women in developing countries. Those developing countries which have had most success in reducing fertility rates have laid emphasis on education and health care, especially for women. In this contentious field, nobody disputes that the status of women is the key.

Thailand's experience illustrates this. The average number of children per woman there has fallen from 6.14 in 1965–70 to 2.2 in 1987—primarily the outcome of increasing use of contraceptives. Thailand's economic growth has averaged 4.2 per cent a year over 25 years to 1989, the seventh fastest in the world. There have been similar population falls in China, Cuba, Korea, Indonesia and Tunisia.

There can be no development for anyone, the United Nations Population Fund has just declared, without development for women. "Economic growth has been fastest in countries where women have higher status, and slowest where they face disadvantages." That seems unexceptionable, but I suspect my friends at Care (who occasionally give me access to the underworld) are right publicly to express their awareness that involvement in population planning provokes sensitive cultural and moral questions, and inevitable difficulties. But, as do most of the world's non-government organisations, they see it as an issue too urgent, too big and too important for humanity to be sidestepped.

THE ENGLISH GENTLEMAN—AH YES, I REMEMBER HIM WELL

Flanders, Lloyd George, the Sixties obsession with equality ... W. F. Deedes charts the forces that killed off the man whose word was his bond— to the benefit only of the lawyers

There used to be a figure, so familiar as to need no definition, called the English gentleman. The term still exists, but the reality behind it has been fading. City scandals such as those involving Guinness and Blue Arrow, and the Lloyd's debacle, have now combined to deliver the *coup de grâce.*

"Some years ago," an old Lloyd's hand told me, "we had to insure a ship verbally by telephone over a weekend. On Sunday afternoon, she went down off Scotland. They paid up without a murmur." That would be impossible today, for in place of the gentleman whose word was his bond, we have lawyers. Today no senior figure in the City, industry or commerce would dream of making a compact with his opposite number. He says, instead: "I'm getting our people to have a word with your people ..." This has vastly enriched the lawyers. Few business deals can be sealed without them.

A curious and distinguished exception to this is the foreign exchange market, few of whose operators went to public school. They work mainly by telephone and they deal in millions every day. *Their* word is their bond. But elsewhere in the City, a new breed has come forward, less beholden to a code of ethics than to what lawyers advise is within bounds.

Paternalism is out. The sheer size and compartmentalisation of, say, a modern merchant bank makes it exceedingly difficult for a senior figure to put his stamp on the company, as colonels of good regiments still do. (Oddly, the Army—which we no longer cherish— is one of the few institutions left with a structure whereby leadership can influence standards.) Similarly, relationship banking is out. The banker no longer weighs up the customer but the proposition. He can hardly be expected to weigh the customer, for he is unlikely to know him long. A generation ago, he might have been in the same branch for 20 years or more. Today, three years is probably the limit. He is not there to see his customer through thick and thin.

As for the gentleman in industry, his life expectation is very short indeed. In one of his more notable speeches, Stanley Baldwin spoke approvingly of his old family firm in Worcestershire, where men long past their prime were allowed to sit on the handles of their wheelbarrows and take their pay. The fate of such a company today is hardly in doubt. It would be taken over, the old men and their barrows would vanish, and dividends would rise. The predator prowls, and will pounce on anyone stupid enough to mix gentlemanly instincts with modern business methods.

It is hard to establish precisely when the death of the gentleman in this country occurred. Christopher Hollis wrote a book about it—Death of a Gentleman, the Letters of Robert Fossett (1943). Fossett believed that civilisations met with their catastrophes because the decent people became decadent. "Those who possessed grace, humour, culture, decency and all that made life worth living became also slack and sterile, and the barbarians, who had the 'guts', overran and conquered." Evelyn Waugh delivered his own message on these lines in his wartime trilogy, particularly the last volume, Unconditional Surrender.

Some would place the gentleman's death earlier, linking it to Lloyd George's propensity for selling honours. Some believe, not unreasonably, that the gentleman perished on the battlefields of France in 1914–18. My preferred date is later than any of these. In June 1963 the last Gentlemen v Players match took place at Lord's—a series which had been played regularly since 1806. But in the Sixties it was seen as no longer appropriate for amateurs to leave the Lord's pavilion by one gate and professionals by another.

In that same year I received a severe lecture from William Haley, then editor of The Times, on the deplorable absence of professionalism in public life. The Government, he complained to me, was being run mainly by amateurs who supposed themselves to be gentlemen. The future, he declared, lay with a "meritocracy" through which men rose according to their abilities, not their antecedents. This struck me as stuffy at the time, but Haley had allies. The Sixties was a great time for shaking up the British scale of social values.

*

My mother once warned me to be careful of men who wore signet rings on the little finger of their right hand. By the mid-Sixties one had ceased to pay much regard to signet rings. Nancy Mitford had fun with U and non-U behaviour. David Frost became one of Haley's meritocrats. Harold Wilson was the man of the hour. The gentleman began to look *de trop*.

In reality, nothing in history happens as suddenly as that. A principal architect of our social revolution was the first Lord Beaverbook. No gentleman himself, mistrustful of the breed (it was mutual) and self-made, he encouraged his enormously successful pre-war Daily Express to illustrate in practical ways the truth of Lincoln's proposition, that "all men are created equal". Women too. If Jack bought Jill the right clothes, she could enter the Royal Enclosure at Ascot looking the equal of anyone there. It won a host of readers.

At one time it was modish to blame the gentleman's demise, his code of ethics and his funny ways on Mrs Thatcher. Her doctrine, one or two bishops declared, had created this rat run. They overstated their case. It is true, curiously, that the gentleman has been outmoded more in consequence of Conservative policies than Labour doctrine. But the policies long precede Mrs Thatcher. To pick from a vast miscellany, they go back to Mr Heath's famous Selsdon House gathering in the late 1960s, to the ideas of men like Jim Slater of Slater Walker, to new concepts about competing in Europe and to countless distinguished visitors to the United States who returned declaring that in the American dynamic they had found the key to perpetual prosperity.

Hollis's Fossett thought the true test of a gentleman is a readiness to abandon his privileges without inordinate fuss. The gentlemen of England, he thought (with George Wyndham), must not abdicate but die at their posts. It is their successors who abdicate, in return often for colossal golden handshakes. In theory, the rest of us should have prospered from this rescue of business by professionals from amateur gentlemen. Casting an eye over the condition of our manufacturing industries and the City's state of health, we observe that in reality our gains have been dispiritingly low. Except for those who had the foresight to take their law exams.

December 1994

BRITAIN MAY HAVE BEEN HARD UP BUT THOSE WERE THE DAYS, MY FRIEND

Leading Conservatives are hoping Labour will be embarrassed by the publication this weekend of government papers from 1964, when Harold Wilson came to power with promises of dynamic reform. The documents are to be released on New Year's Day under the 30-year rule and the Tory Party chairman, Mr Jeremy Hanley, expects they will portray government chaos, indecisiveness and confusion. But what is 1964 really remembered for? W. F. Deedes, a Conservative Cabinet Minister in the 1960s, remembers much more . . .

It did not turn out to be all that bad. We were painfully braced on the Tory side, jaws set, knuckles white, for the advent of Harold Wilson to No 10 after the General Election of 1964.

Strutting platforms with heroic confidence, he promised us a Hundred Days of dynamic action, a nation reforged in the white heat of modern technology, and a transformation from the scandal-prone, deadbeat 13-year-old Tory government presided over by a 14th Earl, Sir Alec Douglas-Home.

But the scene which then unfolded, at least to the best of my recollection, was mostly bathos.

It had much in common with one of those old music hall acts, when the comedian, swathed in dignity, enters the stage to a roll of drums and falls flat on his backside. We stopped wringing our hands in order to hold our sides.

For one thing, Labour won power by only a whisker—an overall majority of four. Were it not for a Tory massacre in Scotland, the 14th Earl would have won.

For another, Mr Patrick Gordon Walker, Harold Wilson's choice as Foreign Secretary, had lost his seat at Smethwick—and, amid much Tory heaving of sides, contrived also to lose a subsequent by-election at Leyton.

Then there was Mr George Brown, a man always hard to take altogether seriously. Grandiloquently dubbed First Secretary of State and Minister for Economic Affairs, he was saddled with a National Economic Plan; and thereafter was doomed to be seen as an angry man far out to sea on a raft, not waving but drowning.

Also prominent on the public stage was Mr Ian Smith of Rhodesia. Publicly charged with treason by Harold Wilson, he responded by accusing Wilson of blackmail, and therefore, to the joy of Right-wing Tories, thumbed his nose at the Prime Minister through both Labour's terms of office.

The most serious blow to high hopes came within six weeks of the Government taking office. Some $3,000 million had to be raised by 11 central banks to save the pound, which Wilson refused to devalue.

Were we downhearted? On the contrary, I can think of no period of modern times when politics seemed to matter less, and the world about us seemed a more exciting place to be. What we now call the "feel good" factor ran high.

It was not Harold Wilson, but Mary Hopkin (then 18) who established the mood: "Those were the days, my friends . . ." she sang. "We thought they'd never end, / We'd sing and dance for ever and a day . . ."

An optimistic decade? I inquired years later of a friend born in 1945. "It was not just optimistic," she replied. "It was brilliant."

And so in many ways it was. The Beatles were emerging from their cave in Liverpool. In the dying days of the Tory government I had rashly said something favourable about them, and was abused for populism.

But they *were* popular—so much so that Harold Wilson made them all Members of the Order of the British Empire. Beatlemania stormed the United States and made a better impression than Cunard's QE2.

London was swinging. There was Carnaby Street, and all the joys that young people were able to find there.

Men were thinking of how to dress *well*, rather than to ape tramps. There was Mary Quant.

Private Eye had arrived. *That Was the Week That Was* was going strong. Twiggy, a cockney weighing 6½ stone, arrived.

The unexpurgated version of D H Lawrence's *Lady Chatterley's Lover*—first run of 200,000 copies—had been taken to court, arousing enormous public interest.

Class barriers were coming down. The truth is that the young people were liberating themselves from their parents' generation, which (not without reason) had become pretty gloomy in the aftermath of the second world war. At seaside resorts and elsewhere, Mods and Rockers roamed.

Like it or not, the world buzzed with liberating ideas.

Jim Callaghan's first Budget in the autumn of 1964 is not vividly remembered. David Steel's measure to reform the abortion laws, 1966–67, on which some of us toiled for months, will not soon be forgotten.

The most memorable decision in the first year of Wilson's "dynamic" Government was taken by the House of Commons on the Private Members' Bill of a Labour Left-winger, Sydney Silverman. It abolished hanging.

Labour Home Secretaries, Frank Soskice and Roy Jenkins, set about making racist behaviour a statutory offence.

It was not all joy. Drugs were becoming a serious social issue. Some will insist that the seeds were sown of today's broken families.

Among many of the young, America's war in Vietnam was a cause célèbre. Universities blazed over it. But it provoked political passion, rather than today's disturbing political indifference.

Financially, the nation was in far worse shape than it is today. Yet spirits were higher. The young might act irresponsibly and "sing and dance for ever and a day," yet most of them were more confident of finding a job than they are today.

On the extremely shaky foundations of Harold Wilson's New Order, hopes burgeoned, new music throbbed, confidence thrived, especially among the young.

Bliss it was to be alive . . . in a way not so many feel today.

It lies with those in the Tory Central Office who propose to exploit the Wilson years to explain to us just why this should be.

EAST END PAYS ITS RESPECTS
TO A MYTH

Ronnie Kray buried but gang legend survives

The coffin left the church in Bethnal Green preceded by bearers of a large gilded portrait, proclaiming: "Misunderstood, but simply the best."

Behind walked Ronnie Kray's twin, Reggie, a shadow of his former self in a grey suit and handcuffed to a bearded prison officer.

As the coffin moved towards the funeral coach, drawn by six black horses in funeral drapes, a cheer went up, followed by repeated cries of "Let him out! Let him out!"

"I love him for his magic," Mrs Patricia Gordon exclaimed to me. "I don't care what he's done. I love him."

The burial of Ronnie Kray, which took five hours in all—and fell not far short of Winston Churchill's for grandeur—began before 10am outside the undertaker's premises in Bethnal Green Road, where he had been lying in modified state, guarded by three minders.

Reggie made the arrangements for the funeral by telephone from Maidstone prison and was allowed to visit Bethnal Green under escort last Thursday to see the undertakers and clergy.

There were 40 Daimlers lined up in Pott Street to carry the mourners. Some of them were hard men in thin sharp suits, defying a chilly March wind. Their women wore smart black suits, furs and black lace hats. One ample figure wore a small black mini-dress.

The former south London gangster, "Mad" Frankie Fraser, a one-time enemy of the Krays in the days of 1960s gang war, was among those paying his respects.

Countless wreaths of great beauty were transferred from the undertaker's premises to the Daimler roofs. Reg's huge tribute—To the other half of me—done in white flowers, outclassed them all.

Thousands had come to mourn an East End gangster, who had become a mythical figure. There is no other way of explaining the scenes at yesterday's burial of Ronnie Kray, who had died after collapsing at Broadmoor a fortnight ago.

"There's more out there than there'll be on VE Day," said a butcher in the Bethnal Green Road, which was at a standstill. Of course, there were some for whom it was simply an extraordinary spectacle.

But to most of them, it was the ending of a romanticised chapter in the East End's history. Few of them had met the Krays, but most of those to whom I spoke saw them as legendary figures.

In fact, relating their booty to the time spent behind bars, the Krays were unsuccessful—which perhaps explains Reggie Kray's determination to give his brother a monarch's funeral.

It was the "security" men who caught the eye, some 70 of them, drawn from uncertain backgrounds, with their shaven heads and defiant looks. Behaving with admirable tact, the police allowed them their hour of glory.

The men guarded the undertaker's entrance and the door of St Matthew's Church and, later, the graveside.

The funeral service itself, conducted by Father Christopher Bedford, was designed for catholic tastes. After the opening sentences came Frank Sinatra's *My Way*. An early entry on the Service Paper read: "Charlie and Reg would like to include in this Service friends who cannot be here today, friends from Broadmoor and Prisons, they are young Charlie, Mohammed, Joe, Bradley, Anton, Jim, Rab, Ron, Pete, Lee, Andrew and all others too many to mention, they are with us in spirit."

We sang *Morning has broken*, *Out of the night which covers me*, and, finally, *Fight the good fight with all thy might, Christ is thy Strength, and Christ thy Right.*

There was a special message from Reg: "My brother Ron is now free and at peace. Ron had great humour, a vicious temper, was kind and generous. He did it all his way, but above all he was a man, that's how I will always remember my twin Brother Ron." We closed on Whitney Houston's *I will always love you*.

Between the end of the service at half noon and three o'clock, two and a half hours were spent in moving the extended cortege a few miles to Chingford's ample burial ground. Here it had been ordained that company round the graveside be restricted to family and the news media. "Surely not," I remarked, as we surveyed a crowd of four to five hundred, with many children.

"My daughter," said the woman in front of me proudly, as she lit a cigarette, "has been here since a quarter to nine." Outside the cemetery, Chingford's High Street was lined with those who had been less provident.

In a final gesture, designed to touch hearts, Reg Kray moved round the six weary horses and offered crumbs of comfort. The horses and their coachman had had a long day.

As a resident of Bethnal Green before the war, I saw this event as less bizarre than most will do. These brutal brothers were part of the culture which prevailed in Bethnal Green 50 years ago, before it was bombed to bits and rebuilt.

They combined wickedness with thoughtfulness. It took hard men to survive, let alone succeed. Against that background, the Kray brothers became folk-heroes.

SCOUTS HONOURED

Boys and *girls? In mixed tents? It's not what Baden-Powell envisaged but it's true to his dream. W. F. Deedes joins the jamboree near Amsterdam*

There are aspects of life in Amsterdam which would cause the late Lord Baden-Powell, founder of the Boy Scout movement and advocate of clean living, to turn in his grave. The red-light district is extensive and livelier than in most capitals. There are also cafés where cannabis can be smoked freely—and legally. The Dutch are well advanced in these matters.

A rum part of the world, I reflected, for the 18th World Jamboree of the scout movement, which would draw 25,000 young—and not so young—people from the ends of the earth. "I think," I said to my photographer, Eleanor Bentall, "that if we are to do justice to this great event we should as a matter of duty cast an eye over the temptations of the flesh which may present themselves to these young folk."

From the viewpoint of the scout movement, our experiences in Amsterdam went some way to allay such misgivings. Such is the reputation of the city's red-light district that it attracts the curiosity of thousands of tourists. Like twitchers in pursuit of a rare bird, they descend on Amsterdam's streets of shame and tramp through them in hordes.

Once a red-light district becomes a huge attraction to earnest social-science students in steel-rimmed spectacles, elderly couples and those who might equally well be found in Disneyland, it forfeits eroticism. "The lone man in search of sex in this place," I remarked to Eleanor Bentall, as we sipped a cold beer in the small hours near the Cannabis Connoisseurs' Club and surveyed the scene, "is like a hunted fox."

We were yet more heartened by the place chosen for the World Jamboree camp, which, for those interested in detail, was one-and-a-half miles long and one mile broad. It was on a site so isolated that our professional driver lost his way at every attempt to reach it.

Getting to the flesh pots of Amsterdam from such a camp would require the determination of an escaped prisoner of war.

Most heartening of all, however, are the fundamental changes which the Boy Scouts have undergone in recent years. Renamed the Scout Association, it has become reassuringly heterosexual.

Great Britain, with its *Carry On* films and its *News of the World* and its cockney view of the universe, is probably the only country left on earth which clings to jokes about naughty vicars and choir-boys, scoutmasters and all the rest.

After an inspection of all ranks at the jamboree in Holland, I have to report that the scoutmaster joke is dead. I have never seen so many pretty girls in all my life. I am not talking of Girl Guides; they were girl *scouts* and thoroughly integrated with boy scouts.

"They all sleep in the same tent," Gillian Hughes, scout leader from Folkestone, explained to me, as we shared a beaker at one of the water drinking stations, "and there's no problem whatsoever." Most of Europe is now in line with this. To be precise about our position, Venture Scouts (aged between 15 and 20) have been mixed since 1977. The younger categories, Beaver Scouts (six–eight), Cub Scouts (eight–10) and Scouts (10–15), became mixed after 1991. "An excellent move," I said to Britain's Chief Scout, William Morrison, over another big beaker of water. He cordially agreed.

I joined the Glasgow contingent during supper. There were 34 boys and two girls. I asked one of the girls, Pamela Walls, what had drawn her into the movement. She found it difficult to explain. The fact is, reflecting the age in which we live, the scout movement now attracts a category of girl who would never have joined the Girl Guides and who would thus have been lost to the movement altogether. She will go through exactly the same training as the boys. If they go cliff- or rock-climbing, so will she—and that was her main instinctive reason for joining.

"Are the girls a good idea?" I asked Nicholas Jones, 13, of the Bishop's Stortford contingent. "It depends," he said. "They're not so good at work! Some help, some don't."

"Nonsense!" exclaimed their experienced unit leader from Hertfordshire to me later. "If I had a choice between all girls and all boys, I know what it would be. And since the girls came in, the boys have greatly improved their appearances."

Temptations of the flesh and the English sense of humour aside, this dream of Baden-Powell's in 1908, which now has a worldwide membership of 32 million, has become a highly impressive inter-national organisation. What moves the heart is the extent to which the troubled countries of the world draw strength from it.

"One of our tenets," Baden-Powell wrote in his book *Lessons from the 'Varsity of Life* more than 60 years ago, "is to extend our goodwill and toleration so that we pay no regard to differences of class or country or creed."

"When I was at the jamboree in Canada in 1983," said William Morrison, "the Falklands War was on. The scouts from Argentina went out of their way to be friendly with us."

"We have 100,000 scouts in Lebanon," said Nabil S. Imad, "and 72 of them are here"—the biggest Arab delegation. Hong Kong had also brought in 72 from its ranks of 50,000; Oman had 12 of its 10,000.

Among the more remarkable was the contingent of 19 from Bangladesh, one of the poorest countries on earth, where there are 500,000 scouts in a population of about 110 million. Two of them, their leader Afzal Hossain told me, had cycled to Holland, setting forth in January. The scouts of Bangladesh are not learning to be of future service to their community. It is already part of their duty.

"Our scouts," said Hossain, "save more lives than scouts in any other country. They are trained in rehydration therapy." Diarrhoea and dehydration are big killers of young children in the Third World. The Bangladeshi scouts know all about the salts and glucose and other ingredients needed to deal with them.

The contingent of 97 from Croatia—54,000 in the scout move-ment there—were having supper. The young girls, some not yet in their teens, were intelligent, articulate, funny. Why had they joined? Lots of answers, the main thread being that it might help them to be useful to others later in life.

"Who works the hardest—girls or the boys?" I asked one. "The boys!" she said and clapped a hand across her mouth. Peals of mocking laughter from the young of Croatia. "Sometimes—only sometimes!" she yelled back at them.

How some of these people had financed the journey to this vast camp under Dutch skies remained something of a mystery to me. The British had a presence of 2,500 at £750 a head. Of this, the family, the district and the county had contributed roughly a third each.

These people have come a long way, I said to myself, as the

25,000 moved in their contingents towards the arena where the opening ceremony would be led by the Netherlands' Queen Beatrix. Bands were playing, banners flying, drums beating. There were warm cheers for South Africa's entry, which did a lap of honour behind its new flag. "But you have always brought blacks to these jamborees," I said to their leader. "Always," he said.

The Dutch had spent 12 years preparing for this hour. They had choreographed the pageant that followed and one of their number marked every national flag holder—more than 100 of them—who had had little time to rehearse their performance. Then a thousand silver balloons swept into the sky and everyone was gazing at a spectacle they would remember all their lives.

These young people were there not mainly for learning but for fun and this experience of associating with contemporaries from every quarter of the globe. But the underlying message came through to us all.

It came best from Dr Jacques Moreillon, formerly of the International Committee of the Red Cross, now an outstanding director-general of the World Organisation of Scout Movements. He delivered it without any notes in two languages, English and French. One aim, he said, was to develop the personality of the individual, so enabling young people to make their contribution to society, to be capable of making a difference in the world of tomorrow.

In my experience, many of the young today respond to such a call. I find it in the field of international aid and development. I observe it on school speech days when there is mention of voluntary service. On the whole, this is a more generous generation than was mine or the one that came after mine.

We tend to be suspicious of movements, particularly youth movements with a message. "I could *never* join a movement," Eleanor Bentall told me late one night as we talked of our conclusions. There are many like her. But 87 years on, and after 18 of these quadrennial jamborees, I think the scout movement has won the benefit of the doubt.

There was an echo of John Kennedy at this camp in Holland: "And so . . . ask not what your country can do for you—ask what you can do for your country." To coach the young to be of service to others, regardless of class, creed or country—and this in an adult world so often more concerned with rights than obligations—well, it's not a bad line to take.

TO BE AN ENGLISHMAN

Euro-sceptics can relax, says W. F. Deedes—60 years of social revolution, world war and edicts from Brussels have not dimmed the essentials of Englishness as satirised by A. G. Macdonell in England, Their England

Some people like to set off for the summer break bearing bestsellers newly minted from the publisher. For myself, I find forgotten favourites more relaxing—and sometimes more enlightening. So this year's batch included *England, Their England*, that classic satire on the Englishman—and woman—that A. G. Macdonell wrote in the early 1930s.

Macdonell had a wonderfully sharp eye for English foibles. I came to know him briefly in the mid-Thirties, soon after this book had been published. I was a lobby correspondent at Westminster and he was temporarily employed by the then-*Manchester Guardian* to write parliamentary sketches.

My hat, what a flutter he created! On reading some of his sketches, Members of Parliament rose like a flock of birds at the sight of a scatter gun—which, in the literary sense, A. G. Macdonell was carrying. Shocked by his perception of their pretensions, they vainly implored his editor to employ him elsewhere.

Macdonell also coined, for his circle of acquaintances only, a series of slogans for London clubs. The Athenaeum's, I recall, was "Bring out your dead!" For the RAC he hit upon "But sir, you haven't paid your bill!" At the old, heavily marbled National Liberal Club, it was "Please adjust your dress before leaving!"

My edition of *England, Their England*, has a picture of a village cricket match on the cover; and that is the essay in the book which people who are familiar with Macdonell's work remember best. Based on his experiences with Sir John Squire's cricket side of eccentric, and sometimes tipsy, literary figures, it is funny; but it is, in my judgment, less revealing of English character than several of the other pieces.

Running my eye over these again, roughly 20 years since I last read them, I get a feeling that Euro-sceptics could draw comfort from them. Naturally, much around us has changed in the 60 years since Macdonell was writing the book. There has been another war, and a peaceful but far-reaching social revolution has taken place in this country. Yet in many respects, as one perceives on re-reading Macdonell, much of the English character is essentially unchanged and nothing Brussels does is ever going to change it.

Macdonell made a shrewd choice for the setting of his novel. The tale begins in a pill box on the First World War battlefield where he had served in the Artillery. A young and inexperienced gunner from Scotland named Donald Cameron is discussing lightly with an English publisher named Davies, 15 years his senior, the character of the English: "What do you think of them as soldiers?" asked the older man. "They're such an extraordinary mixture," replied Cameron. He goes on to describe his experience as a liaison officer with an English county battalion:

> "The Colonel wore an eyeglass and sat in a deep dugout all day reading the 'Tatler'. He talked as if he was the 'Tatler', all about Lady Diana Manners and Dukes and Gladys Cooper. We were six days in the Line and he had the wind up all the time, except once, and that time he walked up to a Bosche machine-gun emplacement with a walking-stick and 58 Bosche came out and surrendered to him. What do you make of that? Do you suppose he was mad?"
>
> "I don't know," replied Davies, puffing away at a huge black pipe. "We had an English subaltern once in our battery who used to run and extinguish fires in ammunition-dumps."
>
> Cameron dropped his cigarette. "He used to do what?"
>
> "Used to put out fires in shell-dumps."
>
> "But what ever for?"
>
> "He said that shells cost five pounds each and it was everyone's duty to save Government money."
>
> "Where is he buried?" asked Cameron.
>
> "In that little cemetery at the back of Vlamertinghe."
>
> "I know it . . ."

On the strength of such talk, publisher and Scot form a bond. Cameron experiences shell shock, but both survive. Faithful to his undertaking, Davies commissions Cameron, an aspiring writer, to produce a book about the English character.

Macdonell himself was a Liberal—in the 1923 and 1924 general elections he was a candidate for Parliament. Today he would have been a force in the League Against Cruel Sports—and a thorn in the side of the local hunt and shoot. He had a clear view of the Englishman's attitude towards animals.

"They're the kindliest souls in the world," Macdonell has Davies saying, "but if they see anything beautiful flying in the air or running along the ground, they rush for a gun and kill it." Towards the end of his experiences, Cameron attends a day's fox-hunting. He has a brief and unexpected meeting with the fox, as it emerges "tired, muddy, panting, limping, desperate", from a hedge, and commiserates with it. Then, amid the mud-bespattered black and scarlet of a fashionable hunt, he finds two men in a fast bout of fisticuffs.

> One of the antagonists was a six-foot, scarlet-coated, scarlet-faced young man; the other was a lean, dirty, dark gypsy ... The comments of the ring were clear, and expressed so forcibly and so repeatedly, that Donald had no difficulty in discovering what it was all about.
>
> "The bloody swine was kicking his horse!" said a girl of about 19, with lips like the petals of a rose. "Bloody swine!" said another girl, the perfection of whose fragile face was a little marred by a diagonal stain of mud about six inches long and three inches broad.
>
> A short, tubby man, who looked very rich, shouted out: "Bravo, Ralph! Well done, boy."
>
> Two men on foot discussed the matter in grave undertones. "Thank God it was a gypsy and not an Englishman," the first said. "An Englishman wouldn't do a thing like that," says the second, rather shocked. "If there's one thing that gets me mad," said the first, "it's cruelty to animals. I don't care whether it's a mouse or an elephant, it simply makes me see red."
>
> A horseman, pale with passion and covered with clay from silk hat to orange-topped boots, was staring wildly in front of him and repeated over and over again to the world in general, "I'll report him to the Society for the Prevention of Cruelty to Animals ..."
>
> An old lady of about 70, perched like a sparrow on an enormous black horse, kept on saying plaintively: "Why doesn't someone flog him? I can't understand why no one flogs him."

An unflinching supporter of fox-hunting, I cannot withhold a cheer for the satire. Yet Macdonell, in pursuit of the truth, holds the ring fairly. A few minutes later at the hunt, Donald Cameron is knocked into a hedge by the shoulder of an enormous horse.

The woman riding the horse responsible for this does not even glance in his direction. She is about 50 years of age and "her mouth and jaw were resolute and her eye unwavering". Donald recognises her as one of the nurses in a hospital near Hasebrouck in Flanders in which he had had measles:

> One pouring wet night when the hospital, which by an unfortu-
> nate mischance had been placed immediately beside a large
> ammunition dump, was being bombed by German aircraft, this
> hard-faced Diana carried out seven wounded officers from a
> burning ward into which the stretch-bearers refused to go, and
> rigged up a shelter for them from the rain, and boiled tea for
> them by the light of the blazing huts ... On another occasion
> she had held the icy hand of a dying subaltern for twenty-seven
> hours. And on another she told Matron what she thought of
> her.

They are still among us, these hard-faced Dianas. The fox-hunting crowd remain much as they were. Before he leaves them, Donald hears another little exchange at the hunt which sounds an authentic note: "Look here, Ted, don't touch Moggeridge Ordinaries till they hit half a dollar. We're doing a wangle, see? Weinstein's coming in with us, and so's old Potts and old Finkelberg. Get me?"

Yes, we get him. I am less sure about Macdonell's diplomats. At one point in his odyssey, Donald Cameron secures the post of private secretary to Sir Henry Wootton, a Tory MP with a rosy face, a large white moustache, blue eyes and old-fashioned manners.

He had in his time driven his coach-and-six to the Derby, worshipped the Jersey Lily from afar and nursed a hatred of Lloyd George and his anarchistic theories about land and money. Now he is living the life of a traditional English gentleman—of which there are not a great many left in our current Parliament. The Prime Minister wants Sir Henry to go to Geneva, where the League of Nations is at work. He is assigned to the Committee for the Abolition of Social Abuses.

To keep the old booby on course, three exquisite young men from the Foreign Office work behind the scenes. Mr Carteret-Pendragon, Mr Carshalton-Stanbury and Mr Woldingham-Uffington receive Donald, who is in pursuit of a brief for his master. Eyebrows

are raised in amazement. "My dear Sir," exclaims one of the exqui-
sites, "we don't have policies about things."

"And what about brothels?" asks Donald. "What do we say about
them?" "At the last six Assemblies we've simply said that we don't
know what they are. All you have to do is to say it again."

There is a distinct whiff of pre-war diplomatic manners here;
but, in my experience overseas, diplomatic manners have radically
changed. Not long ago I was visiting a capital in Eastern Europe.
The Telegraph's local correspondent met me on a very cold evening
in a woolly sweater, denims and ski boots. Our first port of call was
the British Embassy. "Why don't you both come to dinner?" our
ambassador asked after our talk. "I have some interesting people
staying here."

Our correspondent made her apologies. Her flat was some way
off, so she would not be able to change in time for dinner. "Come as
you are," said the ambassador. When she returned shyly to the
embassy for dinner, most of the guests were dressed like her.

> And there's another thing, Davies advises Cameron about the
> English. "They're always getting themselves up in fancy-dress.
> They adore fancy-dress. Look at their Beef-Eaters, and their
> Chelsea Pensioners, and their barristers' wigs, and their Peers'
> Robes, and the Beadle of the Bank of England, and the Lord
> Mayor's Show, and the Presenting at Court, and the Trooping
> of the Colour, and all that sort of thing. Show an Englishman a
> fancy-dress and he puts it on."

We no longer present our girls at Court, otherwise all this is
much as it was.

One of the funniest chapters in Macdonell's book relates to the
tyranny of the pre-war country-house weekend. For such occasions
my eldest sister and I went to great pains to pack suitcases with our
modest possessions in order to create the right impression on the
butler or the lady's maid who would unpack them.

Donald Cameron has similar misgivings, until a drunken friend
rushes out and buys a dozen second-hand suitcases, crams them with
Donald's belongings and labels them "Beagling Kit," "Amateur
Theatricals" and so on. "I'll fix that bloody butler," he declares and
is as good as his word. He telephones the butler with a totally false
account of Donald Cameron's eminence.

The Morning Post, on which I began my life in journalism, made its living by holding a near-monopoly of classified advertising for servants needed in the great houses of London and the countryside. The servants had to buy the newspaper in order to find out what was on offer. After the First War, many great houses had their shutters up, and butlers dwindled. After the Second, they became a threatened species.

But some of the dinner-table conversation at Ormerode Towers, where Donald was spending his Saturday to Monday, has a solid ring. The company is the usual mix of politicians, senior officers and young men from the City with a dusting of fashionable authors.

> "Well, Bob," began Sir Ethelred, "and when are we going to get a really decent tariff instead of this footling ten per cent?" "As soon as we've drowned all those poisonous Liberals," replied Mr Bloomer. "It won't be so long now."
>
> "Poisonous crew of traitors," said the Major-General. "I wish I'd had them in my company in the old days at Abbotabad." "Do you think that this Free Trade stuff is lunacy or criminal?" enquired Captain de Wilton-ffallow. "Definitely criminal," replied his senior officer. "They're all in the pay of Moscow."

Later in this conversation he adds: "A man whose judgement I rely on, a sound man, mind you, told me that he knows for a fact that every Liberal candidate at the last election was sent a thousand roubles in gold to help with his expenses."

"Whew!" the Captain whistled. Yes, many of us have quite often heard such claptrap discussed round political dinner tables; and we shall probably be hearing some of it again when the next General Election comes along.

Not all of it is satire. One of the best character sketches in *England, Their England* is the working engineer whom Donald meets on a small steamship sailing between Hull and what was then called Danzig. William Rhodes is taking a machine to Warsaw, which will pump out a 5,000-gallon sewer in 85 seconds. He has been in Hungary with a machine for weeding between rows of fruit trees. He was in Romania with machines for oil-boring. He had been in Russia with dredgers and had dug irrigation canals in Spain.

This talkative but modest figure has spent his life—41 years with the same firm—selling the best of British engineering round the world. He still exists, but in smaller numbers. You will find him in the Club class of most airlines, with a table of figures on his lap and a large pocket calculator in his hand. Mr Rhodes saved enough to send both his sons to Leeds University. One has become a school-master, the second a parson. "A parson! That's queer, isn't it? and him mad on cricket, too. They wanted him to play for Yorkshire, but he wouldn't . . ."

And, finally, Donald in the village pub, talking to the old men. He remarks on the absence of young men, and asks if there is another inn in the village.

> "No, sir," said Mr Davis, smoothing his head with a hard thin hand. "They don't drink here, nor anywhere else, the young chaps. They hardly drink at all." Donald asks why.
>
> Mr Stovold, the violinist, seemed to be the readiest with his tongue, for it was he who answered.
>
> "There's several reasons for it, sir. For one thing there isn't the money about that there used to be; and then beer costs twice as much; and then there's picture houses and sharrabangs and motor-bicycles with girls sitting on behind . . . And then, you see, there's no one between them and old chaps like us."
>
> "All the rest were killed, you mean?"
>
> "Most of them, sir. Forty-two were killed from this village and they'd be men of thirty-five and forty by now."
>
> "Ah! That war didn't do any of us any good," said Mr Stillaway. "Nothing's been the same since . . ."

England, Their England has much in common with some of Evelyn Waugh's novels. The talk is of long ago, yet it strikes an instant chord. Macdonell, like Waugh, had a good ear for light chatter that revealed character. Waugh's *Vile Bodies*, *Decline and Fall* and *Black Mischief*, all of them written before Macdonell's novel, are still widely read. Macdonell's portrait of the eternal England is much less widely read. Well, at least, during my short break, I have redis-covered what others have been missing.

THE BEST OF TIMES, OR THE WORST?

W. F. Deedes compares Our Friends in the North *with his memories of the era*

One difficulty in writing a work founded in the 1960s is that no two people who lived through that decade feel quite the same about it. There was Carnaby Street and the Pill. There was Vietnam and teddy boys and the Beatles and the Krays and the BBC's *That Was the Week That Was* . . . There was also John Kennedy and his New Frontier—"For the world is changing. The old era is ending. The old ways will not do . . ."

As a member of a dying government, I thought the early 1960s hell. It was a time of the Great Train Robbers, of Blake's escape from prison, of Beeching and his railway cuts and Philby and Rachman, the rapacious landlord. All our political stars were awry.

But I have a friend, now 50, who thought the Sixties heaven. "We just felt we were liberating ourselves from our parents' generation, who'd all been rather gloomy after the war. And you just felt you could do everything . . . I think people don't feel that now."

It was also, she pointed out, a time when class barriers fell. "So you would go to parties and you'd find that you might be dancing with a peer or with a barrow boy, and I can remember a party where I did both. I had one at either end of the room, and it was great."

In short, as Charles Dickens had it, it was the best of times, it was the worst of times. Peter Flannery, writer of *Our Friends in the North*, has chosen to show us the worst of times, at least in the early episodes I have seen.

His is a tale of four young friends in Newcastle upon Tyne, who from 1964 onwards go their separate ways; and those of us who stay with them in the weeks ahead will discover what they do with their lives during the next 30 years. But before I start pulling petals off it, I must predict a success for *Our Friends*. My wife, herself a Geordie, thinks it will jolt the other soaps.

This is a striking serial, and it carries one or two outstanding performances, among them Gina McKee as Mary Cox. She is the girlfriend of Nicky (Christopher Eccleston), an intense figure just back from working in America's civil rights movement. We are not shown him there, but we can imagine it. He wants to change the world. He canvasses for Labour in the election of 1964, which Harold Wilson won, becomes disillusioned with conventional politics, and is drawn towards direct action and a housing drive in the hands of an exceedingly shady chairman of Newcastle's housing committee. Shades of John Poulson here, I fancy, though his bubble did not burst until 1972.

Neglected by Nicky, his girlfriend turns to the seductive and appalling Tosker (Mark Strong), a nightclub singer. Nicky's closest friend, Geordie (Daniel Craig), a former pitman, leaves for London and works for a porn baron in Soho. More corruption there, too, with a very senior policeman in the Met reeking of guilt.

Undeniably, Flannery's tale and his characterisations are true to life. For example, both Nicky and Geordie in their different ways quarrel with and part from their fathers. Well, that was a time, as my friend observed, when young people *were* liberating themselves from their parents.

And yes, there was corruption both in cities like Newcastle and in Soho. When Nicky ends one episode by looking us all in the eye and declaring, "The great moral issue in modern British politics is corruption", we feel half inclined to shout, "Bang on!"

Yet I got a twinge of pain out of all this. I go back to a Newcastle 30 years earlier than Flannery's, to the derelict shipyards and the Jarrow marchers, and a time when I wrote: "They really cannot get anything except bread and potatoes, and not enough of those . . ." And later: "The River Tyne stank. Decaying wreckage of its past lay everywhere. Tyneside had the worst-housed population in England and Wales. The amount of tuberculosis was alarming. In South Shields they were living 180 to the acre."

I saw a lot of it, because this newspaper ran a Christmas fund for the children of unemployed in the Distressed Areas, of which Tyneside was one. I went in search of copy, and spent two Christmas Days up there to watch children open a parcel for the first time in their lives. Had I entered politics then, I would have joined the Labour Party, preferably Jimmy Maxton's left-wing Independent Labour Party, the ILP.

Not long after that, these lads from the Tyneside stepped forth for King and Country. Granted a little extra weight from army rations, they became the hardest men in the British Army. None who fought in the last war close to 50th Division with its Tyne/Tees insignia will deny them that. Montgomery used them for most of his main assaults, including D-Day. He used them until there was virtually nothing left of them.

In 1989, I went back for a week's tour with our correspondent there. I told her about the hard men. "They are still here," she said, and after supper took me to pubs in central Newcastle outside which stood young men clad only in trousers and a shirt. It was January and the wind was bitter. "It's their fashion," she explained.

A headline in the piece I then wrote for our magazine in praise of Newcastle read: "The new capitalists of the North work with people more than with other people's money."

So do not fail to watch *Our Friends in the North*. There are one or two scenes to which some will object. But see it, and admire it. It is not untruthful, only incomplete.

When that Newcastle bridge catches your eye, just bear in mind that that great city gave birth to some of the salt of the earth, as well as to naive young men and crooked councillors.

MEMORABLE DAY OF DEFIANCE
AND DESPAIR

*From early morning until dusk W. F. Deedes was with the marchers in
the streets of London. The mood may have been carnival-like, but beneath
it he discovered a deepening sense of desperation*

It began so quietly. Very early on Sunday morning, there were little
knots of people in the back streets of central London, just off trains
or out of minibuses. They were straightening their waxed jackets,
adjusting their badges and squaring their shoulders for a long day on
their feet. Clough's lines came to mind: "... *Far back through creeks
and inlets making / Comes silent, flooding in, the main.*"

By nine o'clock, they were in full spate, moving eastwards down
the Strand towards the march's starting point. A fire engine suddenly
called to deal with a blaze in the Strand was confronted by a torrent
of marchers. "They all seem to be on the same side," said the driver
of my car. "Of course," I said. "But you'd think there might be a few
of the antis around ..." "Not today," I replied. So it was a triumph?
Yes, indeed it was. It was a beautiful piece of organisation. The
numbers who came to London on a March day exceeded hopeful
estimates. The stewards, though sometimes almost swept off their
feet, kept their heads. The countryman is good at organising slightly
unpredictable things like point-to-points—with which this event had
a certain amount in common. Throughout the day, I never saw any
of them in a flap.

"I'm stunned," said a woman from Cheam. "I'm stunned by the
quiet and by the good humour of people." She spoke for many who
witnessed this march. The police were gentle. The weather was mer-
ciful. The whole tone of the day was underlined with good humour.
Nobody made a speech, yet the message was absolutely clear.

The countryside told the Government that it was fed up with
being told what to do and what not to do by people who knew
nothing about it. As a man of around 80 observed succinctly when I
asked him why he was there: "Keep off my grass!"

For much of the time, they marched in silence. When the head of the march reached the Ritz in Piccadilly around 11 o'clock, a small band opened up with *Jerusalem*. There was an occasional cheer; but mostly they were quiet. Two policemen I encountered near Hyde Park found this impressive. They were accustomed, they said, to marchers who like to chant slogans and shout. Many who came were unfamiliar with London and its ways. For some it was the first experience. One woman (who had walked down the Strand) had never seen people sleeping in doorways. "Yes, ma'am," I heard a friendly policeman say at Rutland Gate to an elderly party, pointing towards Knightsbridge station. "That is our Underground Railway. It is quite safe." He then advised her how, eventually, she might arrive at King's Cross.

Yes, in many ways it was a triumph. It demonstrated that, at long last, the countryside has got its act together. It has developed a voice to which reasonable people, even urban people will be paying more attention.

Yet behind the triumph, so it seemed to me, lay a great deal of heartache. The hill farmers, the small farmers were there in force. My guess would be that they outnumbered the fox hunters. And some were marching with a sense of desperation.

The first I spoke to came from north Wales and had his sheep dog with him. It was on a long lead of binder twine. Strictly, dogs were not permitted to join the march. But if you live alone in the Welsh hills and are coming to London for the day, what do you do with the dog? It has to be treated like a small child and brought along.

He kept about a hundred sheep plus a few supplements, and had farmed at a loss for the past eight months. He saw no future for himself at all. Another hill farmer who had come down from Oban told the same story. He had been offered £2 to £3 for his lambs. "What was the price last year?" I asked. "Around £12 to £15," he said. "Now they are stacked up with lambs. They don't want any more lambs. They don't want my lambs."

It is lonely work on a hill farm, and very easy to get depressed. Here, today, a great multitude. There, every day, a great solitude.

Among the small farming fraternity they also wondered anxiously what the children would do. A mother from Hessle, East Yorks, held the hand of her six-year-old son as they passed the finish. "I want

him to have the same choices as his father had. Really, I'm here for
my son."

As the march was ending in Hyde Park at around half past four,
a farmer's wife of about 60 opened her heart about this. "I feel
despairingly for the young people. We've had our time. Will they
get a living out of our farm? Definitely not." She shook her head,
adding with touching inconsequence: "I think it is a great shame we
have to create this chaos in central London." We will come back to
this underlying sadness. The march was full of people who understood, as so many now do not, the inner workings of nature. There
was the naturalist from Lancaster. "The preservation of field sports,"
he said quietly, "leads to a much higher wildlife population. The
foxhunters have opened up the rides in our woods. Now in those
rides wildlife is flourishing."

There was the stalker from the Highlands, who made his living
as a guide to people who wanted to shoot a stag. The trade had
fallen off at one time but was enjoying a revival. He explained to me
why his work was so important to the welfare of the herd. He was
there because he saw the end of foxhunting as the beginning of the
end for all field sports.

"We are here to defend a way of life. If you kill country sports,"
said a woman farmer from Northamptonshire, "you kill the sociabil-
ity of the countryside."

She and her husband didn't go to pubs, didn't holiday abroad.
Their social life consisted of meeting people who engaged in the
same traditional pastimes.

A sculptor from Hereford came wearing a deerstalker to which a
long pheasant's feather had been attached. Other parts of his attire
were equally eccentric. But his mind was clear enough. "Country life
is part of my life. If it is taken away from me, life is not worth living."

"How many politicians have ever seen a fox?" I was asked by a
man who had never ridden, but regularly followed the local hunt on
foot. Hard feelings ran deep over our rulers' apparent lack of interest
in the ways of the countryside. "There are too many new MPs who
don't understand the rural way of life," said one gentleman of my
generation. Labour was seen by many of them as a dictatorial
government, but the Conservatives came in for hard words as well.

My acquaintance had noted that, for the first time, there were
Conservative MPs ready to vote against foxhunting. "That's new,"
he said. "Yes," I admitted sadly. "That's new."

Yet, so the feeling ran on, these rulers had the nerve to interfere. Most of the banners bore that message. "Listen to us." "Say no to the urban jackboot." Much of the language used with me was simple but direct. "People have got to be allowed to do what they want to do without being pushed around." Such language is rather out of fashion these days. Yet it does convey what a lot of people feel but think twice about expressing. The Government will have to use a lighter rein on those who earn their living and take their pastimes from the countryside.

Why, I reflected, are Tory MPs now to be found in the Aye lobby voting for Mr Foster's Bill? It is because their political senses tell them that the urban vote holds sway. If the urban voter finds foxhunting cruel and insupportable, then foxhunting must go. Towards Hyde Park I came across a London family—husband, wife and two little girls—all dressed in Barbour jackets. They lived in Vauxhall, had no connection with country sports, but were there to protect, they thought, precious and long-held freedoms.

"We are fed up with the Government telling us what to do," said the wife. "It is turning into a dictatorship and we're here to defend the freedoms we have for our children's generation."

A young farmer from East Anglia spoke frankly about his protest on behalf of foxhunting. "Lots of things we do are *unnecessary*, but that is no reason to make them illegal." This freedom point, let Labour take note, is not confined to countrymen and women. A surprising thing about this march was the number of younger Londoners who felt moved to join in. I came across a young writer from Kensington who admitted to being very urban, but declared he was there for "libertarian reasons". "If they ban hunting, where are they going to stop?" he said.

Along with all this inspiring stuff, I caught a sense of despondency. Many were there who, looking ahead, saw an end to their way of life—not because foxhunting was threatened, but because this country seemed to have no further use for them.

There were quite a few on the march who belonged to my generation and who remembered a time when, not much more than half a century ago, the life of this nation lay in the farmers' hands. German U-boats knew how to strangle this island, in both world wars. Everything we could grow contributed to victory. In both world wars, we looked to the farmer for salvation.

When the first war ended, the coalition government under Lloyd George abandoned the farmer. Prices collapsed. Farms went back to thistle. After the second war, Labour decided—rightly, in my view— that self-sufficiency in food still mattered. So there came about the Act that guaranteed farm prices, year by year, until Europe's agricultural policy took a hand. Yes, it led to some rapid fortunes, especially among the cereal growers; but now those happy times are drawing to a close. What makes the farmer on Sunday's march feel bitter is knowing that he has not failed (as some of our industries have failed) through lack of efficiency. Our farmers have farmed too well. The more acute of them now have a feeling that they are surplus to requirements.

Any sense of being surplus to requirements digs deep into human dignity. To me, Sunday's march was the most emotional, if not the biggest, show of its kind since the marches of the unemployed on Westminster in the early 1930s. I remember them well. We were in the Great Depression. Millions were thrown out of work; and worse, given the impression that their services might never be needed again.

We are talking of being denied self-respect, which is partly what Sunday's march was all about. When our farmers were found to be producing more than we needed, they were put onto a regime of set-aside. It related to land no longer needed for cultivation. Farmers would be remunerated for keeping it in limbo.

"Set-aside" was an unfortunate choice of phrase, I thought on Sunday. There are some on the march who feel that it applies not only to the land but also to themselves. "I feel badly unwanted," a farmer said to me.

"Not all that long ago, they told us to grow and grow. Now they don't want it." He spoke also of the forms that have to be filled in— "more than there were during the war; we are being legislated out of existence." This feeling of not being wanted and anger about the proposed ban on foxhunting run together. Counting for less, carrying less weight than he did, the countryman can be pushed around. That comes close to the innermost feelings of so many. With this goes an uneasy sense of growing urban dominance. "They're building houses all around us," said a farmer's wife from Worcestershire. "Then people start complaining about what we are doing." The smell of pig, the crowing of cocks at dawn, and the sound of the hunting horn become offensive to those who have fled the town.

To understand what this march was about, it is important not to blame the Government for too much. Their disdain for the country-side and its ways is palpable, deplorable and a source of anger among country folk. But there is also the march of human change which lies outside the range of any government. The coal miners, once counted among the elite of our workforce, know about that.

There is the world of difference between seeing the countryside as an essential agricultural workshop, which it is no longer considered to be, and seeing it simply as a weekend playground in which urban folk should have the right to stroll.

More than once on Sunday I caught a whiff of Goldsmith's melancholic 18th century lament for the rural England that went as our first industrial revolution set in. *"Sweet Auburn, loveliest village of the plain, / Where health and plenty cheered the labouring swain."* Goldsmith believed that the sort of rural England we had then lay at the heart of our survival. He feared lest that essential balance between rural and urban England would be lost. And that was a thought uppermost in the minds of so many who marched.

January 2000

A CENTURY OF CHANGE THAT ENDED IN A BLAZE OF GLORY

It passed off so peacefully. After the kind of century we have been through, that is something for which the world has reason to be thankful. Most of us nurse tension of one kind or another about these great occasions now, and this one, we had been warned, was an obvious target.

So not for nothing were 6,000 policemen deployed to guard the capital and a level of security imposed on approaches to the Dome that led to delays and tears and frustration for distinguished guests, some of whom came close to missing the show.

Yet it was a night on which almost all the world seemed to feel an urge to quieten down. In Ireland peace reigned. Boris Yeltsin, who might well have been fulminating about something or other, signalled his retirement instead. The week's agony for passengers held hostage on the hijacked Indian plane might so well have ended in carnage. Instead, the hostages were released to their rejoicing families.

Thus, as it turned out, this so often harassed world was left free to enjoy a wonderful party clear of the shadows. An invaluable ingredient to such a night is good humour, and in most of the capitals of the world plenty of that seemed to be shining forth.

A pity, of course, about that Ferris wheel which unexpectedly had won so many public hearts. It looked gorgeous in its night dress of laser beams when the Prime Minister unveiled it. But "far better to be safe than sorry", as Chris Smith, our Culture Secretary, put it so perspicaciously. Yet there was something about the inability of the wheel to carry its first eager passengers that was peculiarly ourselves.

The mind turned irreverently to one of those flights when up comes the British Airways pilot's cheery voice: "Sorry about this, ladies and gentlemen. We've had a small problem with the landing gear, but it's coming right and we should be on our way quite soon."

A pity also about the distinguished guests who spent four hours in a queue before joining the party at the Dome. This tension we suffer from is hard to live down. So the police felt it necessary to

search all 10,000 guests for weapons. They also imposed a requirement to pass through a single security scanner. It was, of course,
deplorable, but not nationally uncharacteristic. It spoiled the party
for a lot of people, because queueing for four hours creates the
wrong frame of mind. But it was also a reminder, as the old century
ended, of the way we live now. We have so often to be reminded
that the assassin's hand may not be far away. For many policemen, it
is constantly borne in mind.

Those who eventually made it to the Dome will have a lot to tell
their grandchildren about. Well do we know, those of us who have
had the luck to report some of the memorable events of this century,
there is nothing to equal "I was there . . ." Yet, in this instance, there
was a difficult choice to make. If you were lucky enough to get a
ticket and to reach the Dome in time, well and good; but even then
you might have missed a lot. You might have missed seeing on the
television screen dawn over the remoter parts of the Pacific, where
the new Millennium began and the first celebrations started.

You might have missed the Prime Minister coming off the
Underground at Greenwich and the Queen sailing down the Thames
in a style befitting to majesty.

If you decided to make Trafalgar Square your corner, there was
the indefinable joy of sharing a huge event with thousands of others.
Not everybody's cup of tea, but those who were there and were also
compulsive soap opera viewers, got *EastEnders* on the big screen
added to their night's entertainment.

If you decided to stay in your village or province, there was the
beacon and fireworks and neighbourliness—and a chance to get
home and to bed a degree earlier than the lucky ones in the Dome.

To all of which may be added, there was nothing in the least
derogatory about watching the whole event on television, as millions
chose to do. Television was, after all, an invention of the century
that has just passed. And if you chose the right channel—I am
not disclosing mine—much of the world's rejoicing came to your
door.

Refreshingly, it will seem to many, this long-heralded night—
perhaps "hyped" is a better word—struck one as living up to expectations. It maintained its air of expectancy. Whether you were in the
Dome, or on the banks of the Thames, in the Mall, in Belfast or
Cardiff or Edinburgh, or simply watching the screen, you could
never be sure what was coming next. It may have occurred to some

how well the Queen's face conveyed this air of expectancy. Goodness knows, she has seen more of this kind of thing than most people. Yet there were moments when she contrived to look touchingly uncon- fident about the duties allotted to her.

Her Prime Minister, by contrast, wears a perpetual air of confi- dence, even when travelling on the still slightly grotty Jubilee Line. William Hague looked as if he knew what he was about—though it is open to question whether Ffion should have let him appear with that yellow tie on a blue shirt.

But more than any of them, the Queen had the expression children sometimes wear at their first pantomime. It might have been genuine wonderment. It might have been derived from long experience, and so wariness of what is liable to go wrong on these well-rehearsed occasions. It might—though this is unlikely—have been the earlier bomb warning, which she had put firmly in its place.

As some have reason to know, excessive precautions on her behalf aggravate the Queen. She lives by a rule which requires her to co- operate with all reasonable requirements for her safety. Beyond that, she insists, you take your chance.

She certainly had a struggle to light the obstinate beacon. There were times earlier in the Millennium that has just passed when some minion could well have lost his head for that bungle. As it was, the Queen simply looked puzzled. Starting at the beginning, I found the close of the old Millennium and the start of the new at the other end of the Earth strangely moving. One got that sense of the Earth turning on her axis.

That familiar hymn, *The Day Thou gavest, Lord, is ended*, crossed the mind, with its line: "The sun that bids us rest is waking / our brethren neath the western sky."

The Church was not sidelined, as some of the gloomier prophets had forecast. The Queen and Prince Philip were at Southwark Cathedral, joining a congregation of 2,000 at their New Year's vigil and there they lit a large Millennium candle.

The Prime Minister and his family were at Westminster Abbey's candlelit Service of Light. There was a religious celebration in and around Parliament Square attended by thousands and welcomed by the Lord Mayor Westminster. They switched on with dramatic effect the new Millennium floodlights of Westminster Cathedral where there was a Roman Catholic Mass.

It was a night to think back to our earlier history, a night to reflect upon the enormous change which has come about in relations between the two Churches.

At the right moment, soon after 11pm, the Archbishop of Canterbury took centre stage at the Dome and with three young children from a Barnardo's project around him led the nation in prayer. His explicitly Christian words bear repeating: "For Christians Jesus Christ is the Light of World. Tonight let us thank God for Him and for all He has given to this country and to our world.

"Let us pray for that world and its people. Jesus said love the Lord your God with all your heart and your neighbour as yourself." The children said prayers for the poor, for an end to fighting and for protection of the natural world.

Then they recited in unison: "Lord help those who are sad, or ill, or lonely tonight to know that you love them."

What more was needed? The music was mixed—and what a mixture! *So Young, Let the Bright Seraphim, Let it Be, Cymru Fach, Wave the Old World Goodbye, Amazing Grace* and *All You Need Is Love.* Earlier on they sang, *I Vow To Thee My Country.* But plainly it was a night when Bach or Handel would have seemed inappropriate.

It was not, on the other hand, at all a bad night for Dr George Carey, who had fought very hard for his Church's place in the Dome. And his New Year's Day broadcast will have caught some ears.

It is hard to disagree with his proposition that we have lately been dwelling on the heroes of our day.

So he entered a word for heroic figures in our world who are entirely unknown, for those who never achieve fame but whose influence on their fellow beings may be profound. "Two thousand years ago," the Archbishop reminded us, "Jesus Christ Himself was an unsung hero." There is a disposition by everyone who lives or works in London to suppose that on all such occasions the capital becomes the centre of light and furthermore it is where the light shines brightest. But this was a night when lights shone in every city and village of the land. Edinburgh, which invariably takes the New Year more seriously than southerners, had an atmosphere all its own.

The fireworks that blazed from Edinburgh Castle probably looked as well as any in the world. Some even took refuge there from the south, reckoning that a night of celebration on the streets of Edinburgh would be less punishing than a night in Trafalgar Square.

A candlelit service in St Giles' Cathedral was attended by the Prince of Wales. St Mary's Cathedral offered "three hours of stillness". In the most western quarter of Scotland and its islands, nearly six degrees west of Greenwich, citizens took pride in setting off fireworks 24 minutes *after* midnight.

In Manchester of course it rained, but there was a tremendous party at Castlefield. In Londonderry, scene of so much tension in the past, they gathered to sing *Danny Boy*.

Nowhere, one reflected, can these celebrations have been marked with a deeper sense of relief and tremulous thankfulness than in Belfast.

You had to be a citizen of over 30 in that city to remember a time when New Year could be safely marked by dancing in the streets. There was a plan there to fire a beacon made up of decommissioned arms. It became a very small one. Mr Trimble, Ulster's First Minister, felt moved to say: "The finishing line is in sight, but we are not quite there yet." Yet the candle of reconciliation shone a little brighter than at any time since 1969.

Credit where it is due. It fell to television to remind us that we were not celebrating alone. This was a global feast. Even Red Square in Moscow looked a degree less gloomy. New York has its own style for such occasions. In Rio de Janeiro, beneath that giant landmark, Christ the Redeemer, they thronged on to the Copacabana Beach.

Oddly, it seems, rejoicing in Jerusalem was muted. For reasons of security, there was a ban on public celebrations. Armed police mounted a guard on the Mount of Olives. Some 20,000 police and volunteers were on security duty in Israel. This was one place where tension failed to lighten, which did not quieten down. But the church bells rang out, and, unsurprisingly with such precautions, there was peace on the streets.

In South Africa, when this century opened, British troops were fighting Boers, not altogether successfully.

Women and children were among those living on iron rations in the besieged towns of Mafeking and Ladysmith.

More than a half a century later, apartheid made it a country morally condemned by most of the world. Around 10.30 our time on Friday night, Nelson Mandela was to be seen in his old cell in the Robben Island museum of reconciliation, where he had spent so many years of his life. There the ex-prisoner and ex-President lit a candle and handed it to his successor, who then handed it to a child. Another dramatic scene of reconciliation. Another place where the world had quietened down. Another dawn.

Then, as everywhere else in the world, they set off the fireworks. Among many who regard any firework display as the best of treats there will long be argument about who did best.

In sheer volume, no doubt, we were among the heavy hitters. Barges on the Thames sent up volleys of star-spangled rockets.

The tonnage disposed of was impressive. Much earlier on we had seen that wonderful bridge in Sydney ablaze with fireworks. Auckland in New Zealand, Hong Kong, Hawaii, Moscow and even Beijing had their displays. But then, at 11pm our time, the Eiffel Tower in Paris exploded into life.

Perhaps "exploded" is the wrong word. It simply became suffused with beautiful colour.

"The Eiffel Tower as we have never seen it," someone in Paris remarked; nor ever shall again. The French have their detractors, but when it comes to artistry, to sheer elegance, they hold the palm. Out of this night of a million lights, the Eiffel Tower will hold memory for a long time.

There were other small memories to treasure from this night. I thought how much that satirist Evelyn Waugh would have relished the short interview Lord Falconer (who had inherited some responsibility for the Dome) granted a television interviewer. "Bit of a pile up," he agreed, when asked about the thousands of distinguished guests begging for release from police clutches on their way to the Dome.

Then he spoke eloquently of Peter Mandelson being an "incredibly important midwife for the Dome". Most enjoyable.

It came back to mind a little later when they turned to a hospital in Birmingham full of expectant mothers hoping they might deliver on the stroke of midnight.

"I'd be so proud," said a nurse in a way that touched the heart, "if it were *our* hospital."

There was the moment when our Home Secretary, who rarely looks embraceable, received a smacking kiss from a red-haired television presenter. And towards the very end there was John Prescott's expression when a performer daringly dressed performed a daring act. One could see plainly that he had been properly brought up.

Finally we came to that closing moment when they struck up *Auld Lang Syne*.

That is when, if you feel matey, you cross your arms, grab the hands of your two neighbours and wave arms up and down. When it comes to being matey, our Prime Minister excels. He crossed his arms.

Our Queen, I rejoiced to see, is more selective about matiness. So she didn't fold her arms. She simply extended her hands to her husband and the Prime Minister.

After that, she turned and kissed her husband warmly on both cheeks.

December 2000

LOOKING BACK TO THE FUTURE

"A woman's lot has changed beyond all possible expectations"

Henry Wallace hailed it as "the century of the common man"; and so the 20th century was. But what a price that common man paid!

My first memory is of being wrapped in a blanket by my nurse late one night and taken up to the tower of Saltwood Castle, in Kent, where I spent most of my childhood, to see two German warplanes caught in searchlights as they crossed the south-east coast for London. It must have been 1915 or 1916. And I remember hearing, when the wind blew from France, the rumble of the big gun barrages on the Western Front.

The tomb of the Unknown Warrior in Westminster Abbey marks the common man's sacrifice in that war, which killed eight million of his kind. By the time the son he never saw came of age, the trumpet had sounded again, and he fell on a Normandy beach in June 1944. At the going down of the sun, once a year, we remember them.

One makes too much of the world wars? Oh, no. Those of us born just before 1914 know how much the First World War changed the human landscape. In spring 1945 men died under my command at the battle for the Twenthe Canal. I have felt ever since that they left a gap which those of us who survived must try, however inadequately, to fulfill. The consequences of both wars are still with us, even with those who do not remember them. Yet, undaunted, the common man has made his way towards what Churchill called "the sunlit uplands".

I say the common man, but I mean, of course, the common man and woman. A woman's lot has changed beyond all possible expectations that the suffragettes could have had when, from 1906 onwards, they went to war. Mrs Pankhurst experienced and described the horrors of Holloway prison. At the Derby of June 1913 Emily Davison threw herself under the King's horse and died. They won the vote for women of 30 in 1918 and for 21-year-old women, 10 years later. How many of these pioneers could have foreseen that Margaret Bondfield would be a cabinet minister by 1929? Or that

599

Margaret Thatcher would come forward, fight a hopeless parliamentary seat in Kent—we were candidates in that county at the same time—win a London seat, lead the Conservative Opposition for four years and occupy 10 Downing Street for 11 more. She owed much to women's enfranchisement; but, speaking as one who came to know her fairly well, much more to a singular character.

As a good democrat, the common man affected to despise all politicians but was in debt to some of them, including Thatcher, under whose government hundreds of thousands became homeowners for the first time. Lloyd George was one of the first—certainly the most influential—to perceive the social inequalities that prevailed early in this century.

Britain, he observed in 1906, when the British Empire of 400 million people occupied a fifth of the globe's surface, was the richest country under the sun: "Yet 10 million workmen are living in chronic destitution."

Three years later, as Chancellor, Lloyd George produced "The People's Budget". It levied income tax of nine pence in the pound on those earning more than £2,000 a year. The charge on unearned income became one shilling and twopence in the pound.

The proceeds provided a pension for the common man—and provoked a huge political crisis. The House of Lords threw out Lloyd George's Budget. In the election that followed, Tories and Liberals drew even at 273 seats but—more importantly—Labour, under Keir Hardie, returned 42 Members of Parliament.

A burgeoning Labour party under Ramsay MacDonald took up the struggle for greater equality and won power briefly in 1924. More than half of MacDonald's first Cabinet were of working class origin.

Lloyd George and MacDonald were not the only men to draw destitution to the public attention. In 1936 King Edward VIII visited the Welsh valleys and saw the stricken Dowlais steel works outside Merthyr Tydfil. His judgment has echoed down the years. "These steelworks brought the men here. Something must be done to see that they stay here working."

I was not there, but I heard the words from other journalists who had been on the tour. In 1938 I saw the Great Depression encapsulated in childish form on the hill between Merthyr and Dowlais: a girl of about nine peering longingly into the window of a toyshop, her arm round her much younger brother. She was dressed in a boy's worn jacket far too big for her, and her face was thin and white with faint blue circles beneath her eyes.

Yet this century, begun so harshly, was the one in which the common man was to become a man of property. He acquired some savings; contributed to a state pension, invested in a pension scheme. During its course he became master of the internal combustion engine—while turning it into a monster which now threatens to strangle him. His children no longer walk barefoot to school—he or his wife drives them there. Their rooms are full of mass-produced toys.

In the sitting room the common man has another machine which has changed his life: the television. Since the Second World War the silicon chip has transformed—and goes on transforming—his communications. It has given him a spectator seat in the House of Commons. It has introduced him to the looks and mannerisms of his leaders, and those politicians whose style had popular appeal benefited. I recall a by-election at which I reported an eve-of-poll speech by Macmillan, a supreme exponent of the art, as his "Wind of Change" speech was to prove in 1960. "There are two kinds of progress—the Rake's Progress and the Pilgrim's Progress. My friends, let us be pilgrims!" he said. It went down a treat.

But television, besides helping politicians gifted with the common touch, also made multi-millionaires of those fellows of the common man with a genius for entertainment. In 1956 Elvis Presley, a millionaire at 21, attracted 82 per cent of America's 54 million watchers of television. Tommy Steele at 20 was hailed as the British Elvis.

A new youth market opened up: culturally, much of the century has belonged less to the common man than to his children. The flappers and Bright Young Things who arrived—not altogether unwelcome—in the early Twenties were only the advance guard of what followed. By the end of 1959 it was reckoned that around five million teenagers had £800 million a year to spend. There came Cliff Richard and the Teddy Boys. In 1963, the world experienced Beatlemania: soon after taking office in 1964 Harold Wilson felt constrained to honour all four with MBEs.

Some thought that the new popular culture beamed into the home by television was, to use a phrase from the century's last decade, "dumbing down". But there were other influences at work. Among the century's richest gifts to the common man and his children was the paperback book. It opened the door to almost every classic. He could pick up Wodehouse, Waugh, Buchan, Sayers, Eliot, Greene, Powell and scores of others for a song.

It was the century of the cinema: one that introduced us to Mary Pickford, Charlie Chaplin, to Garbo and Dietrich, to Bogart, to Disney and their successors from the make-believe world of Hollywood. The local Odeon and the BBC and ITV at home competed for the common man's custom with a cornucopia of entertainment surpassing anything seen in earlier centuries.

On the cricket pitch and the football ground sporting heroes came and went, their exploits chronicled first on the large screen, then on the small. Jack Hobbs, Don Bradman and Denis Compton gave joy to millions. Compton's golden summer, with 18 centuries and 3,816 runs scored, was a timely gift to 1947, when we all felt down in the dumps. Alf Ramsey summed it up for all of us, when after some disastrous defeat for the England football side, he observed: "England has no choice but change." From there he led the side to win the World Cup in 1966.

Many of us remember these highlights: countless pioneers in medicine such as Marie Curie and Alexander Fleming have extended the life span of the common man. Medicine, much of it based on art and chance at the beginning of the century, has been transformed into a science.

I recall the day when a maiden Deedes aunt fell ill in her old age. "It would do her the power of good," said the doctor, in all seriousness, to my father, "if you could run to half a bottle of champagne a day."

The advances of the century are almost innumerable. In 1909 Bleriot flew across the Channel. By the end of the century the common man flies across the Atlantic faster than sound merely to reach Florida for his holidays. He has set foot on the moon. But he has also dropped the atom bomb. When it fell on Japan in 1945 it averted a bloody conflict, but it also left man with a moral dilemma. Henceforth, he could use nuclear energy for good or ill.

More and more, as the century went on, the advance of technology in weaponry, medicine, genetics and much else has confronted him with the same hard choice. That dilemma, I believe, will be the common man's greatest challenge as he steps confidently into the next century.

A FLIGHT THAT BRINGS US CLOSER TOGETHER

W. F. Deedes, who as a Tory minister in the 60s helped to get Concorde off the ground, was abroad yesterday for its defiant return to the skies

"I feel," said a pillar of industry sitting next to me, as Concorde charged down the runway, "that we are making a tremendous British statement." Unaccustomed to such a show of emotion from a fellow passenger in any aircraft, I wrinkled my eyebrows.

But then, I reflected, he certainly has a point. This return to the skies of Concorde is a statement, a statement of defiance even. As the plane surged up, the thought took further hold of me.

Much of the world is looking at this take-off. And we are saying to the world: "We're going to New York to consolidate our bond with the United States. We still have the ability to make things happen. Aviation still has a great future."

At that moment, Capt Mike Bannister, flight manager and chief pilot, passed down the aisle, shaking us all warmly by the hand. He has been flying Concorde for 23 years. If we were delivering a message, he is certainly one of the chief messengers.

We were climbing rapidly, but Concorde takes time to hit its stride. Half an hour after take-off, we are at 25,000ft and flying at only 560mph. Then the cabin crew began the cosseting, which on Concorde is impressive.

But I am digging into the past, which I find intoxicating enough. So I give the champagne a miss and think back to some dreary committee room in the Treasury in 1962, where ministers were being persuaded to take this leap into the future.

Now we're at 32,500ft and up to 700mph. I hear Julian Amery, then minister of civil aviation, assuring us in a silky voice that Concorde is the future.

My old friend and adversary, Tony Benn, minister of civil aviation in 1966, was at Heathrow to see us off. We compared notes. He knows all about the $2 billion it cost Britain and France to get Concorde aloft.

By making a compact with France, he reminds me, "you locked us in". The Labour government of 1964 found itself committed to Concorde. "I think," says Benn to me with a flash of intuition, "it appealed to Macmillan."

He's right, I think, as we start to surge and at 49,000ft reach 1,240mph. My mind floats back to the early 1960s when this beautiful aircraft was born.

It was more than Macmillan. Concorde, I remembered, was a concept of the 1950s. Free from the dangers and drudgery of war, we were starting to reach out a little. So many things then seemed possible.

Two hours out of London, and we are at 55,000ft and travelling at 1,280mph. "We're on top of the world," said my companion, "and flying faster than the speed of a bullet." We are in fact on the edge of space. New to these delights, I am impressed.

I think of all the work and patience and determination which has gone into making this day since the catastrophe in France 16 months ago. There's a strong message there for those with doubts about the West.

We glide into New York just after 9am their time, three hours and 20 minutes after take-off.

When we land, the Mayor of New York enters the plane. I have seldom shaken anyone's hand more fervently. "Thanks," he says. "I appreciate your support for New York City. Spend lots of money!" Feet firmly on the ground there, all right.

At Kennedy, where so much of the world goes by unnoticed, our reception was emotional. Another Concorde came in from Paris. Suddenly I feel that it really is a day bringing us closer together.

It is a lovely autumn day in New York with all the colours of America's fall on display. Not an inappropriate day, I reflect, for Concorde is in the autumn of its life.

Yet it retains the power to deliver a strong message: "We're back in business." "This does help," as the New York's mayor put it, "to bind us together."

Maybe that decision we took in that dreary Treasury committee room all those years ago was, after all, the right one. On such a beautiful day in New York it certainly did seem like that.

THE REVOLUTION THAT
NOBODY NOTICED

In the 1930s, ordinary people could buy a decent house for the equivalent of their annual income. W. F. Deedes examines a seismic shift

"Female emancipation has been the biggest social revolution since print," Boris Johnson declared recently in *The Daily Telegraph*. I disagree. The remorseless, post-war rise in the cost of acquiring a home of your own has influenced the lives of more people than the emancipation of women.

This rise has been happening so slowly, and is so easily confused with a rise in the cost of living, that we do not yet see it as a revolution, nor fully grasp its consequences. After all, we reason, the purchasing power of the pound today is one-thirtieth of what it was in 1938. The cost of almost everything has gone up.

But the price of buying a house has soared much higher than the cost of living. Look at it in this light: before the war most people could purchase a house for the equivalent of their annual income.

For those on an annual salary of £350—not bad pay in the 1930s—there were homes available on the new estates rising round London. Someone earning £1,000 a year could reckon on getting a semi-detached house with three bedrooms, a garage and a patch of green for the same amount.

Today, although increases in wages have gone a long way to meet the higher cost of living, a house will cost up to five times more than the income of the principal breadwinner. In London, someone on £25,000 a year will probably have to spend at least four times that amount on buying a home.

When, after the Wall Street crash of 1929, my father sold Saltwood Castle in Kent and a lot of land, he received a cheque for £12,000. It would be hard to find a broom cupboard in London for that amount today.

At the other end of the scale, prime houses in London have moved beyond the reach of all but the most affluent. A house that cost £100,000 in 1976 would today cost £1,750,000. Yet if the price of that house had risen simply in line with inflation, the cost would be a more affordable £446,000.

Many of the houses built between the wars, furthermore, were made of good, solid stuff. There was less of the unseasoned timber and shoddy workmanship that went into some houses built after the Second World War. If you travel round the suburbs of London that were created in the 1920s and 1930s, you will find most of those houses still stand well.

This dramatic shift in the ratio between income and the cost of a home has had far-reaching social consequences. We have come to see married women in the workplace as a mark of social progress. But not every married woman, particularly if she has young children, desires to be working outside her home. How many married women today reluctantly go out to work just to help with the mortgage?

It is easier to identify this housing phenomenon than to explain it. When I touched on this subject elsewhere in *The Daily Telegraph* earlier this year, many of the letters I received came from professionals in the housing business. A lot of explanations were offered, but there was no consensus on why during the last half century the price of a house has got so far out of line.

Someone who had spent his working life as a consulting structural engineer put land at the top of his list. "The continual heaping of planning restrictions on the supply of building land in places where people want to live," he wrote, "reduces the land available and therefore (in a free market) makes it a more valuable commodity."

Before the war, he reckoned, the cost of a reasonable plot of land in Friern Barnet (Finchley) was £5 per foot of frontage freehold— with a 50 ft frontage, say, £250. Today, he would expect the price of a smaller plot to be £20,000.

Another professional wrote from Taunton that until 1960 in that area they allowed £100 a plot plus another £100 for services. "A farmer getting two or three times the agricultural value of his land thought he was doing well. A small builder could purchase land without too great an outlay." As a proportion of the cost of a new house, he declared, land had gone from 5 per cent to 50 per cent.

Another correspondent blamed town and country legislation introduced by the Attlee government in the immediate post-war years, declaring that it severely restricted the supply of building land.

If the demand had remained stable, he added, severe restriction of supply might not have mattered too much. "But demand did not remain stable; it increased substantially for a number of reasons: immigration, marital separations, single parent families and children leaving home earlier than before." On top of that, there had been a considerable migration from the North to the South East.

Several correspondents referred to the amount of residential property acquired as an investment by foreigners, declaring that if they occupy it for fewer than 90 days a year, their income here is exempted from tax. "I am treasurer of a block of 52 flats," someone wrote on this topic. "At least two are kept empty for residents abroad." Foreign holdings of property left empty, he claimed, is extensive.

Also, today we build more expensively than we did, as many point out. Our structures in the 1930s comprised roof, walls, plastering, doors and windows, electricity, gas and water. That was little different from Victorian times. Now, we have more "extras", as well as post-war building regulations—tougher glass, better insulation. There is central heating, double glazing, second bathroom/shower room. There are many more electric points for television, vacuum cleaners and burglar alarms.

Elsewhere, in North America particularly, houses are built faster with much less labour by using timber frame and similar construction. Here we do nearly all of it with brick.

"To wade through the field of glue in which the planners operate," writes another, "you need various consultants—on environmental impact, traffic congestion and the archaeological factor. You are then faced with Section 106, whereby a local authority can gouge out of a developer arbitary sums for 'amenity' purposes."

Many people mention building wages, but I see them as part of the cost of living equation. They do not go far to explain why houses are so far out of line with almost everything else. Nobody expects bricklayers to work for a shilling an hour these days.

It seems to me that those who assert that too much money is chasing a limited supply of housing come nearest the mark. You do not have to be an economist to see the force of that. Unquestionably, borrowing has been made a lot easier. When house prices began to soar in the 1960s, the limits on borrowing were loosened.

At one time it was based on two and a half times salary. Today, it may be four or five times salary and even multiples of joint salaries. Yet how else can a man and his wife expect to buy a house within their lifetime? We seem to have here an inflationary cycle which nobody can break—without breaking hearts.

September 2002

A DAY FOR 815,582 SENSIBLE SHOES

It was to be a march to vent rural wrath. But W. F. Deedes found good humour and politeness along the way as he joined the countryside protesters

It exceeded hopes, was well-organised, so good-humoured, dignified; but at times it conveyed a depth of feeling I found solemn. There were men and women on that march who were not carrying banners or blowing horns, small farmers and their wives from the hills, country craftsmen, blacksmiths and their kind who sense that a way of life is slipping away from them.

It was the life of their fathers and their grandfathers, but it will not be the life of their children and grandchildren. They're for the towns, not for rural penury. A parting of ways is taking place, a severance of family ties, and if you studied some of the sad faces on that account you glimpsed despair.

"But," I heard a BBC lady say rather accusingly to a sorrowful-looking man early on Sunday morning, "this march is also about hunting foxes." Yes, ma'am, no disputing that. You could say it was mainly about foxhunting.

The ban on hunting, threatened mainly by those who know nothing about it, turned out to be the long fuse to Sunday's benign explosion. Don't tell me that 400,000 people would have marched through London to save hill farmers and little country traders.

But the ban held over the heads of the foxhunters has been read as a signal. Countrymen, beware! So those who are fond of shooting, enjoy fishing and love horses joined the march in large numbers.

As one of the march banners put it succinctly, "Guns wound, hounds don't." If hunting is stopped and people discover what happens to foxes left to the mercy of shot guns, *all* those who shoot will provoke outcry. They'll be next for the chop, and, as the march demonstrated, they seem to be well aware of it.

At one point on the march I took a small refreshment outside a pub close to Purdey House, home to gun and rifle manufacturers of renown. I raised my glass to the premises. "Here's all the luck in the world," I said, "and the way things are going, you may need it!"

For this depth of feeling I encountered at times on Sunday has deep roots. In scores of snatched conversations it was expressed in different ways which might be summed up something like this: Foxhunting is an integral part of country life and has been for many years. Okay, we may appear to urban man an eccentric lot, but it is so much part of our lives that if you politicians and your supporters cannot perceive this, then *nothing, but nothing,* in our lives is safe any more. So we choose the business of hunting as ground on which to stand and fight. We see it as symbolic of this great divide between urban man and countryman, between your majority and our minority. And, if after last year's disaster visited on us by foot and mouth disease (coming on top of BSE), you are sufficiently insensitive to snatch away a traditional recreation—for those who follow hunts, as well as those who ride—then we have every reason to fear the worst.

If hunting goes, who among us is safe? That is why some of us, a few from distant parts paying fares they can ill afford, have travelled through the night to make our feelings known. It is pointless for ministers to deny rural poverty. A quarter of those involved in rural employment work at below the Government's poverty line. Yet they are proud of what they do.

There was this man from Ayrshire. I asked him what he did. "I put up fences," he said impressively. So many like him depend on the small farmers' income.

But maybe I have started at the wrong end. Early morning in London under a clear sky, and roads from the mainline railway stations were full of people you hardly expected to see there. Those from the far north may have endured an uncomfortable night, but showed small signs of it.

"Why have you come all the way down here?" I later asked Mrs Proudlock, from Morpeth, in Northumberland. Hers is a small family haulage business. They transport farmers and their beasts to market. The price of diesel has soared. "But I cannot put prices up, because the poorer farmers could not afford it."

Mrs Proudlock speaks for small rural business, smothered in regulations, paying through the nose for fuel, almost wholly dependent on an industry going downhill. So, I suggest to her, more and more who are living precariously will gravitate towards the towns. She nods, then adds: "And there's plenty from the towns who are happy to take their places over; but they don't always see things our way."

A good many townsfolk in this transmigration, I reflect, will naturally feel unfriendly to foxhunting. It has played no part in their lives. That is why the so-called foxhunting issue is all of a bigger piece and why it arouses such emotion.

Knowing my wife, who has hunted much of her life, knowing my youngest daughter, a redundant joint Master of Foxhounds in Scotland, I get shirty with people who tell me that those who hunt enjoy inflicting cruelty on animals.

That feeling was one of the inaudible battle cries of Sunday's march. How *dare* they tell us how to behave towards animals! We live with them. It is those who reside in cities who have lost their touch with the elementary; who, cut off from natural life and death, have been desensitised.

It was touching, by the way, to see how many people up from the country welcomed each other. I was warmly embraced by one or two women I cannot remember meeting—perhaps because I was wearing an old Barbour and carried a walking stick. But there's a serious point here. When you walk down the village street, you do greet people you don't know very well. It goes to the heart of this sense of the community about which Labour in abstract is so enthusiastic. You even dare at my age to smile at other people's small children, which is on the border of becoming an urban offence.

Urban man tends to be altogether more reserved. His is a more cellular existence. At any rate, it was a joy to stand at the foot of St James's Street as they poured through and witness uppermost this instinct to greet your fellow men gladly.

The welcoming instinct seemed to be infectious. We took a look at London Bridge, which never appears to be the most welcoming of London's railway stations. There were hard-pressed officials there fingering lists of trains that were bringing in the marchers.

"I didn't know this number of people lived in this country," one official exclaimed to his colleague as they streamed off three platforms. None of that crowd looked to me the sort of toff which the Labour party supporter, determined to end foxhunting, treasures in his mind's eye.

There were many more children than I recall seeing on the 1998 Countryside March. The schools were there in great force. Well, who wouldn't leave the confines of a boarding school on Sunday for an adventure in London? But not since the great Vietnam demonstration in Grosvenor Square in July 1968 have I seen so many young people looking so involved.

"What brings you and your three children here?" I asked a woman from Norfolk. She didn't say, as she might well have done, "I can't very well leave three young children at home." She said, "they're all seeing a bit of history."

Before I could properly interpret that, a man who told me he lived nearby in Mayfair, introduced himself and shook his head. "You think this will make a difference?" he said, lip curling a little. "I'm a reporter," I explained, "listening to what other people think."

He shook his head again and looked maddeningly wise. "Look," he said, "Labour has an overwhelming majority on which today's event will make no impact at all. They will vote solidly for a ban and the Labour Government will back them to the hilt."

"A valuable corrective to my enthusiasm," I replied coolly, and in order not to look cross fastened my eye on a Jack Russell that was passing by. Such a jolly little chap. The dogs who joined the march, I must say, were a joy to behold—patient and plucky. Imagine being a very small pug and being required to walk all the way from Hyde Park to Victoria Street.

But then, as a perfect stranger in St James's observed to me and to the world at large: "Look at them. None of them overweight . . ." There was truth there. Nearly all the marchers, some of them never to see 70 again, looked enviably fit and slim. And when around tea time a few spots of rain fell, there was little shuffling of umbrellas. They simply marched on. The weather, it has to be said, took the foxhunters' side. "Red sky at night, shepherd's delight," I recalled as my train rolled into London on Saturday evening under a sky flushed red. So it turned out to be.

There was another feeling, buried deep in some of the marchers which came to light when they talked. It was recently well-expressed by the Bishop of London, Richard Chartres. There were, he said, many things he found "morally repugnant" but which he accepted could not be turned into a criminal offence.

That line of thought ran strongly through some of the marchers. Mr John Smithson, who runs a small business in Warwickshire and is a hunt supporter, said to me: "Why single me and my sport out for punishment, when there's so much wrong going on in towns?"

Edward Hall, from Newbury, was there with his three children, Rupert, Phoebe and Eliza. We met on a corner of Hyde Park just before the march got going. "What do you want out of today?" I ask him. "Less inteference in my life," he says simply. He came close to the heart of all this. But before enlarging on it, I think it well to admit that this march had far stronger political undertones than the 1998 affair.

There were some homemade banners addressed to Mr Blair that we did not see on the march four years ago. "Hedge-layers say billhooks to Blair" was one of the milder offerings. You may interpret this as saying that the Conservative Opposition seems not to be hurting Labour severely enough. That cockpit of the nation, the House of Commons chamber, is not a cockpit any more. They run office hours.

Again, you may see it as declaring that politics have become too anaemic by half and more robust attitudes would be welcome. Or you may conclude that this Government *does* interfere a damn sight too much in other people's lives and this lay at the root of the protest. I fancy that last point comes closest to the mark, though it is not necessarily in the best interests of foxhunting.

It leaves it open for stalwart Labour supporters to say, as they enter the Aye Lobby for a ban: "This protest was really a broad-based attack on our party and our Leader and we'll have none of it."

Yes, it *was* in part a political protest. Edward Hall from Newbury got it in five words, but this takes us into another realm of thought. Public feeling for politics is at low ebb. If anyone doubts it, let them ponder the turn-out at the last general election and contemplate the way in which the BBC and other networks are striving to shrug off politics.

Yet in the biggest demonstration ever staged in London, hundreds of thousands of people travelled uncomfortably to make a political point. The march teemed with young people who, we are assured, think politics a pain in the neck. So does the march mean that people, despairing of the democratic process, are moving towards direct action?

I think not. This was not simply a well organised event. It was thoroughly good-tempered and orderly. The policemen on duty looked relaxed, not tense. In Parliament Square a degree of provocation was offered by those opposed to hunting—and was virtually ignored.

As one who has reported most of the big marches in London, from the Great Depression that set the unemployed marching on

Westminster, through Mosley's affrays, the poll tax riots and the miners, I marvelled at the calm. A demonstration on that scale, throughout which people observed the courtesies, made it an epic.

Some blew plastic horns loudly, some carried rather vulgar homemade posters and banners, but it was never an ill-tempered show.

Plainly many of those who marched make a habit of keeping their homes and gardens tidy. Given the numbers and the need to fuel the human frame while on the hoof, the relative absence of litter was astonishing.

The fact remains that the idea behind this march drew the sort of crowd—only far larger—which in the 19th and 20th century might have flocked to hear Gladstone, Disraeli and, later, David Lloyd George. We haven't many politicians today that can attract a hundred to the local market square. Yet this turned out to be of huge public appeal.

"If Labour chooses to ignore it, what then?" asked the cynic from Mayfair. Then, I replied, in what I hoped were measured tones, it will cost them something politically. If they choose to snap their fingers at this, then a lot of people who don't give a rap about hunting will draw certain conclusions and that will do Labour lasting harm. At that, I received a very superior smile and returned one every bit as superior.

Such an event has this in common with foxhunting: it gives rise to all sorts of false scents which divert the hounds from their quarry. This, above all, was a march on which you could hear the bell tolling for a way of life, something that is slipping away from all of us.

This, as a good many of the marchers informed me in their different ways, has been going on for a long time. I spoke with farmers who do not have many thousands a year to live off, given the price of milk and meat, but whose land can still fetch £3,000–£4,000 an acre, because so many people would like to develop it.

We're not exempt in this country from a movement I have witnessed elsewhere in the world. A big exodus from the land goes on in Africa, India and other continents. Towns swell and, sadly, the squalid shanty towns on their fringes swell even faster. The process here could be reversed or at least slowed down, but this is unlikely under a government so out of touch with the earth, so unconcerned with rural needs, so beholden to urban man and woman for their votes.

That is what drew them down on coaches running through the night from the North and the West. That is why some of them stood for hours in the corridors of trains. Before coming to the march, I turned up Oliver Goldsmith's lines on the doomed village of Auburn:

> Princes and lords may flourish, or may fade.
> A breath can make them, as a breath has made.
> But a bold peasantry, their country's pride,
> When once destroy'd can never be supplied.

So it has happened before. And two and a half centuries on, it is happening again. Urban England rolls on over the green fields. That is what quickened their step, why some of their faces looked so dark.

THE TEST OF TIME

When W. F. Deedes took to the roads in 1932, he wasn't required to pass a driving test. Now, more than 70 years later, he has agreed to undergo his first examination.

If you first owned and drove a car as long ago as 1932, as I did, you were spared the need for taking a driving test, because it was not made compulsory until a couple of years later (69 years ago this week, to be precise). So for many years I have been at large on the roads without instruction, guided only by an occasional sharp intake of breath from unhappy passengers or indignant gestures from other motorists.

"It's high time you learned the error of your ways," it was put to me by the people who run the *Telegraph Motoring* section in the interests of all road users. So, under the experienced eye of Bryan Lunn, chief examiner at the Institute of Advanced Motorists, we took a little run together.

A good mix of 30 miles or so, he called it, embracing a length of motorway, some narrow country lanes, a stretch of urban work through Hythe, Sangate and Folkestone, and a few miles of A-class road.

It would be what footballers call a "friendly", they promised me. In other words, Mr Lunn's opinion of my driving would be treated as if it came under the 30-year rule, and so not made available by the Public Records Office until the year 2033. Suffice it, we both returned safely and I heard a sharp intake of breath only once. That was when I accelerated while approaching a green light which had been on some while and which, in the opinion of Mr Lunn, was about to turn. But in his company our journey became a voyage of self-discovery.

Come to think of it, all sorts of professionals such as doctors and magistrates find it necessary to take refresher courses. Motorists, though in charge of a potentially lethal weapon and competing with a lot more cars than there were about in 1932, see themselves as people with nothing more to learn. But as they grow older, Mr Lunn brought home to me, there is more to learn—mainly about themselves.

I received reasonably good marks for observing the speed limits and for keeping a safe distance from the vehicle in front. We had an instructive discussion about this. Mr Lunn carries a chart which shows that if you are travelling at 30mph, you are moving at 44 feet per second. At 40mph, this becomes 58 feet per second and at 70mph it is 102 feet per second. As it will take one second to react to something suddenly occurring in front of you, and the elderly will take 25 per cent longer than that, it is plainly beneficial to keep a substantial gap behind the vehicle in front. At 30mph, says Mr Lunn, you need 75 feet from sight to stop to be on the safe side.

If you draw too close to the vehicle in front, he points out, and a car bumps into you from behind, then three vehicles will become involved because your own will be shunted from behind into the vehicle immediately in front of you. We speculated on what insurance companies must pay out for thousands of such accidents every year.

A principal fault in my driving, of which I was aware but had not taken seriously, was using the gears to slow down instead of the brake. "Gears to go, brakes to slow," said the chief instructor and that has now sunk in. It is, as he incontestably points out, cheaper to renew brake linings than a burned out clutch.

My mirror work came in for criticism and is clearly in need of reform. The correct order before moving off is to look into the mirrors, deliver a signal and then manoeuvre. I occasionally reversed this order, offering a signal, then moving off, "with a final glance in the mirror to see what chaos you have caused," as Mr Lunn put it picturesquely. He was also critical of my method of changing gears when turning. "Complete the turn, then change gear," he said.

The motorway and urban driving was not so dusty, and our merging and work on the roundabouts received favourable comment. I got Brownie points for taking a good wide turn when entering a road on the right. But on the A-class road, said Mr Lunn, I drove a shade too fast, probably faster than usual because I was anxious to appear a confident and not a hesitant driver.

"When you come to a bend," I was advised, "imagine a lorry parked on the left and just out of sight."

"You don't have to imagine it," I told Mr Lunn bitterly, "because the county of Kent, formerly the garden of England, has become a funnel between Great Britain and Europe. There are lorries everywhere." But his advice has taken root, and I now anticipate a stationary vehicle inconsiderately parked on the left before taking sharp bends.

The chief examiner judges a driving performance by three main criteria. Is it safe? I think we got by on that one. Is it systematic? On that, I fancy I heard him murmur, "Not overly." Is it smooth? Ah, there's the rub. I have the same problem with my golf swing.

As we travelled along together, I thought it would be only courteous to let the chief examiner into a secret of my own. "It's rather snobbish," I said by way of introduction. He was intrigued. "Well," I said, "I have devised a way of remaining cool and calm when some villain on the road cuts me up, drives past me on the motorway at 100mph or drives so badly as to put me at risk.

"I say to myself, well, you can afford to behave like that because you are a nonentity. If you get nicked and appear in court, nobody will be any the wiser. If I am nicked, on the other hand, the chances are that it will be reported in the newspapers, because I am better known than you are." I find this wonderfully calming, I told Mr Lunn, who expressed interest in my thinking.

When the chief examiner talks about the progressive decline in our driving skills and performance as we get older, one does well to sit up and pay attention.

After we pass the age of 60, he warns, the risk of being involved in a blameworthy incident increases steadily. By 2031, a third of our population will be above that age—and there will be even more cars on the road than there are now.

Reaction times get slower with age and can be more than 25 per cent longer for the over 55s compared with the under-30s.

"There is no direct correlation between biological age and age in years," he points out, "and the physiological changes that take place as we get older are often gradual and vary greatly from one person to another.

"Nevertheless, even though there is no specific age at which drivers can start to become less safe, the decline is an inevitable part of the ageing process."

Observation errors and misinterpreting information, he points out, are also common factors in crashes involving older drivers. About 90 per cent of the sensory information that we need to drive safely reaches our brain through the eyes.

"If you can't see something, then you can't do anything about it;

and if you can't see something properly, you may do the wrong thing."

There, in my experience, Mr Lunn is on to a solid truth. As we grow older, we not only react more slowly, we take longer to read notices on the road.

When we reached home after our little outing and my mind was turning to a nourishing cup of Bovril to restore lost tissue, our photographer had arrived. So we launched forth again and I was called on by the camera to perform a series of manoeuvres with my car which proved more challenging than anything Mr Lunn had called for.

"I trust we shall be awarded a let for this manoeuvre," I said to him, as I backed the car off a main road down a narrow pathway. I began to feel like a stuntman in a motion picture. Mr Lunn's nerve held up wonderfully well.

"Oh, one other thing," I said as we prepared to part company. "If I come to a crossroads at the same time as another car comes down the road opposite me, how do I safely arrange with him or her who is to make the next move?"

It is best done, Mr Lunn advised, by eye contact and hand signals. Flashing a light is not wholly reliable. It says no more than "I am here". That nugget of information might save a few accidents.

After we had finished our inquest on my driving, Mr Lunn handed me the mock theory test.

Question one goes:

You are following a long, heavy goods vehicle. It approaches a crossroads and signals left but moves out to the right. You should:

(a) pass it on the right
(b) pass it on the left
(c) stay back and give it room
(d) sound your horn to warn of the incorrect signal.

Mark one answer.

I was worn out by then, so I leave the right answer to the reader of this article. Mr Lunn then took a sheet with all the answers, placed it in an envelope and licked down the flap before handing it to me.

I am left to work out whether, after being driven by me for an hour, this last gesture signalled Mr Lunn's confidence or lack of confidence in my reliability . . .

February 2006

WEEKLY NOTEBOOK

"When is she coming back?" shouted the only other occupant of our hospital waiting room at the nurse who looked in to call me to an appointment. He was referring to his wife. "She won't be long, I'm sure," said the nurse tactfully. "Yes, but I've got an appointment at eleven this morning," the man retorted. It was then half-past eight. "She'll be back long before then, I promise you," said the nurse. "Well, find out," said the man. "I can't miss my appointment."

Why do so many people treat the NHS personnel contemptuously? Because it's free? The same attitude is taken towards doctors and nurses of the NHS by some advocates for euthanasia. It implies these professionals don't know how to deal with the mortally sick. In fact they are well acquainted with it. In this imperfect world, we expect them to preserve our lives. Why mistrust them at life's end?

This government's charter for pets will, no doubt, be followed by an official requirement to feed birds during the winter months. All those with gardens of more than one twentieth of an acre will have to install bird tables. Measuring gardens will become part of the reassessment of property values for rating purposes. Supervision of the scheme, the Prime Minister tells the Commons, will not be added to police duties but carried out by inspectors of the Board of Ornithological Betterment (Boob). This body will also guard against bird table makers from forming cartels. To finance the resulting army of inspectors, Gordon Brown ("only the state can ensure fairness to birds") will impose a complicated tax on bird food, favouring finches. There will be penalties for those who dodge the tax by feeding birds with bread crumbs. "But," insists a Downing Street spokesman, "a bread crumbing offence will attract a fine or community service. Only a refusal to pay the fine may result in imprisonment." So we go on.

RACE AND
IMMIGRATION

I was working for the Home Office when the issue of immigration became prominent in the latter half of the 1950s, and it was badly handled by the government from the outset. Mr R. A. Butler's Commonwealth Immigrants Bill, which was designed to restrict entry of Commonwealth citizens into Britain, was knocked about, but when Labour came to power in 1964, they found that they had to repair much of the damage they caused through their heavy criticism of the bill.

Throughout the twentieth century, the world became – very quickly – increasingly mobile, and we failed to realize the powerful impact of the aeroplane. The USA handled this new mobility best, and welcomed the world's poor across its borders where they went on to help enrich the nation. Things were handled rather differently here in Britain.

A parliamentary committee was set up to visit the countries of origin of immigrants, and to advise on where policy was going wrong. I was part of this committee, and know that we failed to think deeply enough about what we were taking on.

At the root of the immigration problem is the reluctance to admit that immigration, as well as enriching society, also poses a major social challenge. For this reason, numbers are of major importance. Citizens need to feel that the government is in control of the number of immigrants entering the country. That is a condition of good race relations.

March 1965

THE WAY INTO BRITAIN

W. F. Deedes, MP, outlines the case for a new approach to immigration policy

Our problem over Commonwealth immigration falls mainly into two parts—controlling the entry of those who wish to come, and integrating the 800,000 who are already here. They are to a great extent interdependent.

Successful integration depends largely on attitudes. Attitudes are influenced adversely by a fear that entry has got out of hand. By contrast, no such attitude has been shown towards aliens, of which we have 500,000 increasing by about 16,000 permanent residents every year.

The twin systems for controlling the entry of aliens and the entry of Commonwealth citizens are rarely mentioned in the same breath. We avoid doing so—or politicians avoid it—to maintain the illusion that there are fundamental differences in our treatment of the two categories. At one time there were, but the distinction, narrowed by the Commonwealth Immigration Act of 1962, is dwindling.

Of course it seemed highly desirable in 1962, when we were ending the traditional right of Commonwealth to free entry, to distinguish Commonwealth from the rest. Circumstances have subtly changed since then.

The need now is less to prove clear distinctions for the Commonwealth than to disprove discrimination against colour. It is more than ever desirable that we associate restricted entry, not with colour prejudice, but with the respectable principles which have governed immigration control since it was first introduced here 60 years ago.

WARTIME METHOD

Politics apart, the administrative case for reviewing and revising our immigration policy as a whole is powerful. As things stand, we are trying to operate two separate machines for filtering Commonwealth citizens and aliens respectively through the traffic of overseas visitors.

This amounted to 16 million in 1964 and increases by at least 10 per cent every year.

The aliens machinery is in any case long overdue for total overhaul. It is based, ludicrously, on a system enforced in World War I and still carries the faint aroma of German spies and tele-scopes. Control is by Orders in Council under the Aliens Restriction Acts of 1914 and 1919.

These orders are renewed every autumn in the Commons. It has become an annual ritual since World War II for the Home Office spokesman to rise, admit that the arrangements are wholly unsatis-factory and to promise permanent legislation as soon as time permits. Time has never permitted, but the moment is coming when it must.

To take a simple analogy, we are maintaining for aliens and Commonwealth citizens two separate schools. We ought to have a comprehensive school. That would not imply that all its members were equal, but it would enable us to deal with all immigrants in streams rather than classes. Is it impracticable? It is worth examining what our controls over Commonwealth and aliens have in common.

A basic principle of alien control is that foreigners may not come here to seek employment. Those who wish to work here must hold on arrival a Ministry of Labour permit for a specific job. That permit is restricted to those able to do jobs for which British labour is not available.

The Commonwealth immigrant must hold a Ministry of Labour voucher proving that he or she has been asked to do a job here (Cat. A) or possesses a special skill (Cat. B). The distinction between Commonwealth citizen and alien is not fundamental. True, the unskilled Commonwealth citizen enjoys the right, denied to aliens, of coming in under Cat. C without a prospective job or special skill. But in practice the first two categories have reduced that privilege to a point where 300,000 are waiting for it in the queue.

Beyond that, students from both Commonwealth and foreign countries are freely admitted and represent common ground. So do visitors who come for holiday, social or business visits. So do those from any part of the world who can satisfy the immigration auth-orities that they have sufficient means to maintain themselves without working.

Wives, dependent children, elderly parents and certain distressed relations of aliens already resident in this country are admitted. An alien will normally be accepted as resident after four years in this country. There is no correspnding qualifying period for the Commonwealth citizen who wants his family with him.

It may be said that the big difference lies not so much in the categories admitted but in the conditions imposed after entry and that this remains an important distinction in principle between Commonwealth and the rest. Even that is less true than it was.

At one time, for example, all aliens were required to register with the police. Since 1960 this condition has not applied to permanent residents, who number over 300,000. To-day about 120,000 "qualifying" aliens are registered with the police.

LANDING CARDS

Deportation carries one minor but important distinction. A Commonwealth citizen who has been here less than five years may be deported—but only on the recommendation of a court after conviction of an offence punishable with imprisonment. Aliens may also be deported on the recommendation of a court but, additionally, the Home Secretary has discretion to make an order without recommendation by a court.

Politically, this is probably the most explosive corner of the aliens field. In reality about 120 aliens are deported every year, barely one-third at the Home Secretary's discretion; and since 1956 there has been a right for all except security and criminal cases to make representations to the Chief Metropolitan Magistrate.

Refusal of permission to land by an Immigration Officer applies to both categories. In the most recent year 3,500 aliens were refused permission out of 2½ million permitted to land—or one in 700. For Commonwealth citizens the figure was one in a thousand. Neither Commonwealth citizen nor alien has any right of appeal against refusal of permission to land.

There remains one significant difference between Commonwealth and the rest, which is the machinery to prevent illegal entry. All foreign visitors must, on arrival, complete and hand in a landing card; on departure, an embarkation card.

Both cards go to the Aliens Traffic Index maintained at Princeton House. The cards are sorted and filed. There may be as many as four million cards a year and surveying them occupies a staff of over a hundred.

In theory, the system enables the Aliens department of the Home

Office to follow the personal movements of every foreigner entering the country and to take action if conditions imposed at the port are not fulfilled. Normally, for example, a visitor is given three months' grace. If, at the end of that time, the landing card and embarkation card are not "married," inquiries are set on foot, usually a policeman's foot.

In practice, as a Select Committee found when examining the system two years ago, it is not as easy as that. It is impossible without a computer—which has never attracted the Home Office—constantly to check four million cards. Spot checks of 10,000 are made from time to time and these, it is claimed, rarely show a discrepancy.

No Record

Foolproof or not, the mesh offers reasonable safeguards against illegal entry which, in the case of the Commonwealth citizen, are non-existent. When the Immigration Act was passed the idea of such a system for Commonwealth was felt to be obnoxious. Without some such system it is hard to see how illegal entry can be checked.

Moreover, such a system not only checks entry but provides a great deal of information about movements which we possess in respect of aliens but not for the Commonwealth. The Home Secretary had recently to admit to the House:

> Since the control (Commonwealth) began nearly half a million visitors have come into the country, but it is difficult for me to inform the Committee what is the number who went out, because Commonwealth citizens leaving the United Kingdom are not, under the present system of controls, classified. When they leave one does not know whether they are workers, visitors or students, because no record is kept to classify them.

It is hard to see how sensible immigration policies can be devised without such essential information. Can it be seriously maintained any more that an efficient system for checking Commonwealth entry and departure would be inimical to Commonwealth relations, even in the older countries?

For half a century immigration has been governed by a careful policy, to which a small overcrowded island is entitled, with spasms of great generosity. In the light of the benefits we have derived, and public tolerance of this policy, it could be described as a success. A big factor has been the maintenance of a reasonably efficient accounting system.

January 1969

HOW MANY MORE IMMIGRANTS?

What Mr. Powell had to say at Eastbourne has involved us in the heat of an emotional, personal and occasionally savage argument. It has not thrown much more light on questions about immigration which a lot of people urgently want answered.

As at least one representative public meeting last week sharply reminded me, there are still very many people far more concerned about our policy on immigration than by Mr. Powell's choice of words. And for all that has been said by Ministers, Mr. Heath and others, they remain far from clear what political policy about future numbers amounts to in firm figures.

Do we, for example, accept that voucher holders, that is male employees, shall continue to enter at the current rate of 5,000 (more or less) indefinitely? Do we accept that dependants must continue to arrive at the rate of something over 40,000 a year until the backlog related to earlier settlers is worked off; thereafter (dependent on the number attached to each new voucher holder) at somewhere between 15,000 and 25,000 a year?

Whether we like it or not, it is *numbers* which trouble most people. There seem to me arguments against both "A" vouchers (prospective employer) and "B" vouchers (special skill).

Undeniably, the reservoir provided by "A" vouchers has enabled us for too long to shirk the urgent task of tackling over-manning in industry and services. In the first 10 months of this year, for example, out of 2,471 "A" voucher holders admitted, 443 came as waiters and kitchen hands and 754 as unskilled factory workers. We should surely examine not the racial but the economic implications of this.

"B" vouchers issued in respect of skills raise a more serious issue. Of the 5,425 such vouchers allowed in 1966, 1,793 went to doctors from India and Pakistan. Last year doctors from those two countries accounted for 1,813 out of 5,370 "B" vouchers for the Commonwealth. In the first 10 months of this year Indian and Pakistani doctors accounted for no fewer than 2,275, or more than half the 4,317 "B" vouchers issued to the Commonwealth—and two-thirds of the 3,739 vouchers issued to those two countries.

This year's rise is due to changes quietly made in the 1962 Act by our Minister of Labour early this year. In effect this substituted as from June 1 for the "first come, first served" principle a policy of relating "B" vouchers "more closely to Britain's economic and social needs."

It must be added that about half these doctors have come for further training and will return to their own countries. They ought to be officially classified as students, not doctors. But Oscar Gish, of Sussex University, has estimated in the *Lancet* that we shall hold about 46 per cent of them or 550 a year—equivalent to the output of six British medical schools and training costs of £1,650,000.

How in the world do we reconcile that to our policy of overseas aid? In effect we are "milking" these countries of their doctors to support our own National Health Scheme—and have, this year, taken steps to raise the milk yield. How do we represent this as charity towards the Commonwealth?

To apply a limited term here to all medical categories would be to the Commonwealth's ultimate advantage. The argument applies in some degree to all "B" vouchers, which in the last 10 months amounted to two-thirds of the total. To trim these vouchers to a trickle would therefore be hardly immoral, but it would radically alter long-term prospects and, I believe, have a considerable psychological effect on the public mind.

There remains the back-log of dependants. Mr. Powell hinted at Eastbourne that their continued entry merged with the issue of repatriation. However, we read that to go back on our word to admit dependants would be indefensible. Would it be indefensible to regulate the flow "more closely to Britain's economic and social needs"? To relate, for example, the granting of entry certificates to these families to the date on which the breadwinner arrived here? Or more practically, to declare that the entry of such families must be conditional upon a unit of accommodation being available; and so avoid their being stacked, as many are, in privately rented house-camps?

There are other variants open to us. Any quota system, I accept, is disputable. The need to inject some further element of control into this influx is not. For the nub of the problem is not just numbers but the concentration of numbers in certain areas which our *laissez-faire* policy dangerously accentuates.

Assuming we continue to admit some voucher holders, are they to continue to drift where they will from the ports—inevitably towards the areas of heaviest concentration? This negative policy seems to me folly; to be creating problems in such areas far more rapidly than such measures as the Bill just announced to finance areas of special need can meet. (We must reckon, incidentally, that forthcoming cuts in civic and social expenditure in the 1969–70 estimates are bound to react on these social programmes.)

Drift or an element of direction? Agreed, it is a harsh dilemma. Is it harsher than the decision taken five years too late in 1962 to restrict entry? The lesson of that experience was that a rational immigration policy does demand hard decisions, the shirking of which gives rise to far more disagreeable situations.

The crux now is whether we are ready to throw our weight behind an enlightened race relations policy for the 1,250,000 in our midst. A fair policy of assisted repatriation—towards which no party has yet put a sum beyond the cost of passage—might marginally, but no more, reduce even these numbers. For the remainder a race relations policy must be made to work.

No one who mixes with people today can fail to recognise that a more restrictive policy on future entry, particularly vouchers, is a prerequisite to public co-operation in this task. This is, or should be, the main argument between Government and Opposition. It is a legitimate one. And it should be conducted not by raising emotions but by exposing and discussing the facts.

April 1970

BUT WILL IMMIGRANTS EVER
BE ASSIMILATED?

Patterns of Dominance
By Philip Mason (Oxford University Press)

We have not thought much about our philosophy of race relations in Britain. We have no such philosophy. It is questionable whether we have even a policy. Race Relations Acts are in the main negative instruments.

The political platforms of Government and Opposition have two main planks—restriction on further entry, and no discrimination against these already here.

A Select Committee explores aspects of immigration and race relations, but perforce selectively. Day-to-day business is left to what Peter Simple calls the "race relations industry."

What nobody is clear about is the kind of society which may eventually emerge, or we might wish to see emerge. A number, perhaps a majority, wish simply to see the immigrants go back home. I doubt if they will. There will be some repatriation, but sooner or later we shall have to accept and think more deeply about a pattern of society incorporating something over a million immigrants permanently living here.

Tight Circles

Philip Mason, for many years Director of the Institute of Race Relations in London, whose new book is a study of patterns of race relations in different parts of the world, suggests that we have two quite different ideas—seldom explicitly stated by either party. One pictures a nation-State, homogeneous in language and custom; the other, a new kind of society, more like America, with approximately equal opportunity for all but with diversity of language and culture, various groups of varied origin keeping their distinctive nature and enriching the whole by their contribution. Homogeneity or diversity?

He has little doubt, and nor have I, that the considerable majority of Englishmen, insofar as they think about it at all, think of the first as their ideal. They speak of West Indians and Asians "rising to our standards' and "learning our ways." Their prototype is the immigrant who becomes more and more English.

Subconsciously, we have led ourselves to suppose this must be the best solution. Good words are "assimilation," "integration" and "harmonisation"—indiscriminately used. Bad words are "ghetto" and "segregation" and "apartheid."

My instinct, after a little exploring with the Select Committee in immigrant areas, leaves me increasingly doubtful whether those who want homogeneity will see their ideals fulfilled. It is instructive in some cities where Asians have settled to discover the marked reluctance of Asian parents to release their young—girls in particular—from the tight family circle for the social delights of our present day society. Ought we to prod them into assimilation? What right have we to do so?

My doubts are strengthened by reading Mr Mason's difficult but rewarding study. He has been a long time, 17 years or so, assembling this historical picture of race relations in places as different as Africa, India, Spanish America, the Caribbean and Brazil. He began with a single thought: Why are black and white relations so different in South Africa from those in Brazil and the West Indies?

AFTER CENTURIES

Between all his examples and our own there is a main difference, that of time. Even South Africa's story goes back a century or two. Our own experience covers less than a generation. Yet the harsh truth which emerges from Mr Mason's work is the degree of inequality remaining in societies where races have co-existed not for tens but hundreds of years. In some respects these inequalities are sharper than our own.

In Brazil, sometimes here regarded ethnically as a unitary society, the distinctions are very wide—and not unrelated to ethnic origin.

The Negro's lot *is* easier than in, say, the United States, but he has certainly not been assimilated. In Bahia, 93 per cent of white students objected to the idea of marrying a Negro; in Sao Paulo, 95 per cent of white students said they would not marry a Negro, and 87 per cent said they would not marry a light-skinned mulatto.

India's hierarchy is more familiar to us. It is, as Mr Mason says, the most ancient, the most highly systematised and the most complex. Caste has lasted 2,000 years. Though it is now in decline it is still strong enough to complicate India's politics and bedevil Mrs Gandhi's Government.

South Africa's system is *sui generis*. There are many other countries, Mr Mason agrees, where something similar does in fact exist, but only in South Africa does the Government legislate to keep people apart. (Some, with Kenya's Asians in mind, might cavil at "only" as applied to South Africa.)

Mr Mason adds: "Two facts feed the resentment felt about South Africa: first, that no conceivable combination of African powers can match South Africa in military strength; secondly, that South Africa's two best trading partners are Britain and the United States and that neither is prepared to forgo their trade."

STILL THE TURBAN

Again, in truth, some may feel there is as strong a case against some African countries. Malawi, with 200,000 of her million or so workers in Rhodesia and 80,000 in South Africa—their return would be economically disastrous—finds compromise with emotion necessary.

Nowhere do we find some of the woollier aspirations expressed about homogeneity in our own "multi-racial" society flowering strongly. Mr Mason goes for limited objectives. Resentment, he thinks, will be kept within bounds if we envisage not a homogeneous mass, but a "system of overlapping circles." We must settle for that expression of diversity, he says, for which the Welsh language and the Sikh turban may serve as symbols.

Accepting such limitations, avoiding provocative doctrines about assimilation and mixed marriages (for which none of Mr Mason's overseas examples offer promise) might have a conciliatory effect on our indigenous as well as our immigrant population.

September 1970

WHY SHOULD THEY "INTEGRATE"?

The Un-melting Pot
By John Brown (Macmillan)

W. F. Deedes, MP on what those who have chosen to come to this country think of our modern culture

British xenophobia, which may yet dish our entry into Europe, was a fact of life long before Commonwealth immigrants began to arrive in the early 1950s. Our fathers, and their fathers before them, believed that "wogs' began at Calais. *Punch* carried a cartoon in 1854: *"First Polite native*—"Who's 'im, Bill?" *Second ditto.* "A Stranger!" *First ditto.* "Eave 'arf a brick at 'im."

So there is a rewarding but difficult study to be made on how far antagonism to blacks, to what Alf Garnett called "bloody coons," is colour prejudice, how far it is British antipathy to all that is not congruous to our own standards.

Colour or culture? Which is the *raison d'être* of the Race Relations Board, the Community Relations Commission and the earnest bodies we are building round them?

John Brown, a discerning academic with a sense of irony, chose the town of Bedford, pop. 70,000, for such a study. Bedford is truly cosmopolitan. There are no fewer than 50 nationalities there—the most numerous being Italians, Indians, West Indians, Pakistanis, Poles, Yugoslavs, Germans, Latvians, Hungarians and Chinese.

It not only affords a magnificent conspectus of British prejudices against foreigners, but exemplifies a root cause of the influx, over most of this century, of immigrants, foreign Irish and Commonwealth: the town's staple industry, brickworks, offers dirty and arduous jobs, unwelcome to many British workers but acceptable to Europeans displaced by the upheaval of World War II, and latterly to other immigrants.

The Heroes' Road

Britain after World War I was to become a "land fit for heroes." After World War II towns like Bedford entertained a good many heroes unawares.

> Poles took many routes to Bedford. None was more terrible than that of their priest, Father Majewski. "I was in Polish underground movement, as chaplain. Going to visit ill persons, I have been taken by Gestapo: first to Birkenau, then to Auschwitz, Buchenwald and at last Dachau . . . In one year in Buchenwald, was called 25 times to come to place for gas chambers."

Brown gives some moving cuts on these lines from the life histories of Bedford's "European voluntary workers."

> Those who to the harvest home would come,
> Expect no harvest, and possess no home.

Bedford's reception of these refugees was predictable, in no way atypical, and nothing is gained by making heavy weather of it. The refugees felt bewildered, at a loss among these cold, northern undemonstrative people. "Not friendly to you, you don't know what they think." They felt keenly the force of British insularity and allusions to "bloody foreigners."

Most of the Europeans were patriots, reluctant to believe in the late 1940s that they had forever lost the country they knew as home. The bulk were country folk, used to the life of the village, the mountains and passes. Recent hardship rendered life in Bedford's brickworks, but not English urban life, supportable.

> On the way from Dover to London, I would have gone back. The flat countryside, the backs of houses, the tiny gardens and yards all dirty and depressing. In Yugoslavia, at least there are open fields, rivers, animals.

How absurd the words we drop so insensitively about "integration' and "assimilation' sound alongside John Brown's picture of the transition from the steppes to the kilns. How equally absurd to talk about "the immigrant problem" or the "alien problem" as if we were one, and they were one. As Brown reminds, few immigrant groups, whether European or Commonwealth, have much in common. Indians and West Indians have nothing in common.

Most of them, aliens and Commonwealth immigrants alike, have even less in common with the commercially based culture of de-Christianised Britain. To that sort of impertinence there will be rude and ready rejoinders. "Then why the hell did they come?" "If they don't like it, why don't they go home?"

Less easily brushed aside are the involuntary reactions of Bedford's immigrants quoted, I have no doubt pretty accurately, by John Brown about the quality of our own life here, of which they had formed a romantic and unrealistic impression.

The Poles, for example, feel that some attitudes and standards of behaviour have changed out of all recognition since they first came here—30 years ago. Pressed beyond the limits of natural courtesy, they admit that the qualities they admired in the British during the war years have fallen into temporary or permanent desuetude. "Might it not be that we can best serve you not by imitating you or by integration, but simply by enacting our own ways?"

When some of us were working with a Select Committee in the cities on coloured school leavers, we discovered the alarm of Asian families at standards of British behaviour; their reluctance to let their children join the permissive—or hedonistic—young mainstream is proving a barrier to "socialising" them. Brown bears this out.

> Discipline, order, authority: these are words often found on the lips of the first-generation immigrants, and surprisingly often among young people of the second generation. There are constant condemnations of British laxity in morals and authority, the weakness of parents and teachers.

For contemporary Britain, alas, they have diminishing regard. That is one sentiment which unites immigrants of all kinds and conditions. By the canons of some aliens' family life, where love and authority go hand-in-hand, family bonds are waning in contemporary English society.

Many of Bedford's West Indians are deeply shocked by the decreasing concern for old people in British society as human responsibilities are shed upon the State:

> In Barbados, where my great-grandmother was very ill, my mother stayed home from work, and I helped her, and we looked after her until she died. Here many old people just seem to be pushed out and forgot about.

A young Indian of 20, successful, a top apprentice out of 24, no chip on shoulder, fond of Bedford, expresses his sense of shock at the changes in Britain since he came eight years ago.

> If you had said then about showing blue films and strip, everyone would have thought you mad. But now it's all changed, it's all corruption. English girls, they seem sex-mad. If they want enjoyment, why don't they get married? England is best country in world for education, but not for other purposes; not for settling down. In fact, I will go home.

These expressions of disaffection will be ill-received in many quarters. A nation whose quality of life is in decline finds criticism of its conditions incredible. The sophisticate will say that these primitive folk, drawn from villages centuries behind the times, are incapable of appreciating the "advance" of Western societies.

I draw my share of letters from correspondents who insist that our fall from grace is largely attributable to these hordes of "bloody foreigners" and "black bastards" in our midst, and they will write to make the point again. At least Brown's book will afford them one consolation. If the large-scale repatriation of aliens and immigrants for which many so devoutly wish takes place, it may be attributed in part to disgust with our society. We must draw what comfort we can from that.

UNNATURAL TRUCE

The knot of what we loosely call race relations is formed not so much by colour or creed or birth or breeding as by "cultural antipathy." As some have perceived and vainly declared for some time, and as John Brown confirms, for all except the West Indians, whose cultural background is quasi-British, the notion of "integration" with British life and culture is irrelevant and degrading.

For a second generation, one senses, there will be some differences. Already round the breakfast tables of a good many immigrant families, perhaps, are being re-enacted the scenes through which so many English middle-class families have already passed. "But, mother, why *not*?" Some will succumb to our happy ways. Many more, at least for another generation, will keep their own system of apartheid.

And what is the race relations industry to make of this? Ostensibly, on behalf of this proud race, they are employed in holding an unnatural truce between reluctant hosts and unwelcome guests. A pity perhaps that the blunt home truths which John Brown has garnered from the visitors' book should not enjoy franker expression. A conspiracy of statutory restraint protects us from the truth.

There is something infinitely saddening in this portrait of an insular race, fearful less an alien horde corrupts its standards—at the same time discarding its standards in a fashion which leaves the aliens fearful lest they themselves be corrupted.

If we can summon the humility—but can we?—a no-nonsense re-examination of ourselves in this context would be salutary. It might help us to get on terms with Europe. As an indispensable preliminary, it would bring us on terms with ourselves.

TIME TO PICK OUR IMMIGRANTS

Quite soon the Conservative Government must make yet another attempt, the fifth in eight years, to design a workable and acceptable Commonwealth immigration policy. There are substantial difficulties, not lessened by the party's undertakings in Opposition.

Our open door policy ended with the Act of 1962. Its passage was so savaged by Labour that its operation became ineffective. Thus Labour, facing realities in 1964, was called on to repair its own mischief and did so, bravely enough, in a policy White Paper of August, 1965.

Fully converted to a restrictive immigration policy, Labour followed this up with the Act of 1968, washing its hands of all but a token number of Kenya Asians. There followed the Act of 1969 which introduced entry certificates, with a system of appeals against refusal of entry as a *douceur*.

With some telling administrative strokes added, of which Parliament took little heed, Labour could meet electors in June declaring in the words of the Home Secretary: "The figures of immigration for the year 1969–70, are the lowest on record."

This indeed is true. It is one of the events which have overtaken Conservative policies. The 1962 Act permitted 20,000 voucher holders or heads of households to enter. The White Paper of 1965 cut this to 8,500. Last year about 6,500 vouchers were issued and something over 4,000 admitted. (The discrepancy will be discussed.) Admissions are running at about the same rate now.

Allowing four dependants to each voucher holder, this represents a gross intake of about 20,000 a year. Dependants admitted to those already here amounted to about 30,000 last year, compared with 42,000 in 1968 and 50,000 in 1967.

Control System

Against this background a Conservative Government has to make its own mark, foreshadowed to the electors in these terms:

> We will establish a new single system of control over all immigration from overseas ... We believe it right to allow an

existing Commonwealth immigrant who is already here to bring his wife and young children to join him in this country. But for the future, work permits will not carry the right of permanent settlement for the holder or his dependants. Such permits as are issued will be limited to a specific job in a specific area for a fixed period, normally 12 months.

These proposals pose awkward questions. In the first place they envisage two classes of Commonwealth immigrant, those already here and those who come in future. But dependants of all those now here will, the undertaking makes clear, remain free to enter as now.

While future holders of work permits are on probation, will their dependants be refused entry? That might be awkward. If they are allowed in—as, for example, are the dependants of students (also limited to a year at a time)—will they be tied to a job for a year or free?

It must be borne in mind that most Commonwealth immigrants come from relatively minuscule areas. In these districts there is close propinquity, if not ties of blood and friendship between them. That makes separation into two classes much more difficult.

A larger difficulty, however, looms over the proposed 12 month rule. Unless the number of work permits is to be greatly increased (most unlikely), controls must be extended to supervise about 4,000 new immigrants a year.

This supervision already imposes an intolerable burden on the police. They must inquire about visitors who have gone astray— about 1,000 cases a year in London alone. They must explore backgrounds for prospective dependants seeking entry certificates. They must chase up Commonwealth students. Under the new scheme they would have in all this work to differentiate between those who came before the new control and those who came afterwards. This is asking a lot—given even police registration for "tied" immigrants (which would be discriminatory.)

It works for aliens? Yes, largely because aliens (who register with the police) are less mobile and easier to trace than a Commonwealth immigrant. The latter can become a needle in a haystack. If illegal immigrants can now cover their traces, as they do, in concentrations of their own kind, so can some of the new, "tied" immigrants.

Assuming the necessary system can be devised (for only 4,000 immigrants a year), what is to be the fate of the immigrant in breach of conditions—if traced? Is he to be sent back? Who will pay the fare? All experience shows that it is far easier to keep people out of this country than to deport them once they are here. Without sanctions, the "tied" scheme would be ineffective. With sanctions, blackmail, which creeps into the affairs of so many irregular immigrants, would have fresh scope.

In sum, the plan for a small number of immigrants would be administratively costly, probably ineffective and certainly damaging to race relations. A more fundamental weakness is that it appears to perpetuate the unselective and now illogical methods by which we admit immigrants.

At the time of the 1962 Act, when the principle of the open door to the Commonwealth was abandoned, we adopted certain conciliatory principles. One was that vouchers should be issued on the basis of first come, first served. The second was that Commonwealth immigrants, when admitted, should be treated not less favourably than aliens. Thirdly, the basic purpose of the Act was to restrict immigration, not to meet our labour difficulties. The fourth was that we should not recruit skills for ourselves of which Commonwealth countries stood in greater need.

Our service to these principles must be judged by the fact that we now have some 8,000 overseas doctors, mainly Commonwealth, who now comprise some 55 per cent of all Registrars and two-thirds of our senior house officers. Until Mr Crossman put the brake on a year ago, we were drawing about 1,000 doctors a year (out of an annual output of 8,000) from India and Pakistan.

The fact is that we have been getting the worst of both worlds. We have not been faithful to our own principles. Nor have we, as America, Canada and Australia have felt free to do, benefited from a stricter selection policy, incorporating certain tests. One reason for the shortfall between vouchers issued and taken up is that the immigrant has also applied to these countries and been accepted.

When entry immediately after the 1962 Act was high, the unselective policy of first come, first served was justifiable. At the level to which Labour have reduced it, a drop in the bucket in terms of Commonwealth populations, it is not.

Nor does it foster race relations. We do not promote racial harmony by admitting teachers on B vouchers whose insufficient grasp of English and our methods eventually relegates them to unskilled work; or by admitting unskilled peasants on A vouchers, who cannot speak English at all. If we want an immigrant population who can hold their heads high, then the time has come for a policy which is not an apology for closing the door, but calculated to improve the immigrants' status.

In rough and ready terms, A vouchers go to those employers who want; B vouchers to those whose skills we need. The elaborate A voucher machine largely recruits unskilled workers to do our dirty work.

B vouchers are more complex. Some, like the doctors, are valuable to us and would be more valuable to their own country, if there were hospitals to employ them (which there are not). Others, like teachers, accountants, engineers, may have paper qualifications which do not correspond to our standards. Thus they disappoint us and themselves. Of late we have become a little more selective, but not nearly enough.

Equal Terms

We are handicapped by a fifth principle which is to treat all Commonwealth countries as equal. Dependent territories are limited to 300 A vouchers a year; and independent territories to 15 per cent of A vouchers. This is inherently absurd, since (as we learned from Kenya) needs change and pressures differ.

The time has come to base a policy on our needs and the immigrants' interests *here*, not on those who may yet wish to come. A main object of the Tory plan to "tie" immigrants is to aid dispersal. In theory (but not in practice) it would steer new arrivals away from concentrations.

Dispersal is a valued objective, but in the long run it will be better served by a policy of more careful selection. Indian doctors, for instance, do not crowd into Brixton and Birmingham. They disperse themselves as the unskilled and the illiterate will never do.

A knowledge of English, an artisan or professional skill in demand—these are keys to that sense of independence and confidence which will free future immigrants from the multiple-occupied housing areas and spread them into new and expanding communities.

Machinery in countries of origin recently set up to grant entry certificates could well be adapted to undertake the process of selection. Applied to a total of only 4,000, such selection would not "milk" the Commonwealth countries. It would spell a better future for the immigrants and ourselves.

THE ROOTS OF ILLEGAL MIGRATION

W. F. Deedes, MP, on how India and Pakistan might discourage their nationals from coming here illicitly

Illegal immigrants don't start their journeys from Calais. They are nearing the end of a long and tangled process which will not be unravelled by Interpol, however clever they are. But until the process is unravelled, it will bedevil race relations and our own administration.

By its nature, illegal immigration is impossible to quantify, but the figures involved are not negligible. They are higher than we have been led to think. A combination of factors makes it unlikely that they will decline. That being so, we shall have to try something more radical than setting policemen to sniff around suspicious ports and ships.

The right place to send a few of them for a start is the sub-continent itself, to observe for themselves the origins of the pressures to come here at almost any cost.

There has always been a strong economic incentive to enter a country with a level of earnings, let us say conservatively, 20 times higher than India's and Pakistan's. Of late, drought, floods and crop failures, higher taxation and local unrest have increased them. So has the recent war and its aftermath which did nothing to raise the low economic status of India, Pakistan and Bangladesh, but rather otherwise.

Ironically, these pressures have coincided with our own determination, expressed in the 1972 Immigration Act, to abolish the right of entry for settlement save for those with blood ties in this country. Taken together, the mounting pressures there and our tighter controls here spell fresh and profitable business for the countless agents and sub-agents in the sub-continent whose trade is to "facilitate" journeys to this country.

It might be supposed that their sails have been trimmed by the controversial House of Lords judgment in June that the 1971 Act does operate retroactively, making those who entered illegally after March 1968 liable to removal.

I doubt it. Agents in places where the text of this will not be read will put their own gloss on it. In any case, as the Home Secretary has made clear, we do not intend to hunt for or chivvy those who have entered illicitly: if they keep out of trouble, they will stay.

Were the Commonwealth communities in this country hostile to illegal immigrants it might be more difficult for them. But generally they are not, and we have done little to persuade their leaders to see illegal immigration as evil as well as criminal and inimical to their interests.

A starting point in this country is to shift the community leaders (when they can be found) from neutrality on illegal entry to hostility—though I dare say that some in the race relations business, who declare (quite wrongly) that we are obsessed with numbers, would challenge that.

But that is peripheral because our basic problem lies not here but in the sub-continent. It springs, again, from standards of public administration as different from ours as our economic circumstances.

If you pay £8 a month to a local official whose duties include certifying particulars about births, deaths and marriages required for entry certificates and passports, certain things will follow.

We take for granted our own local registries and records. It is risky—though not impossible—to fudge such particulars on certificates and travel documents. In the sub-continent such records range from the incomplete to the non-existent. Certainly there are senior officials in India and Pakistan as conscientious as our own, but they have to work within the framework of custom, which does not regard forgery, bribery and corruption as we affect to do.

Nor are the penalties for such offences severe. Defacing a passport in Pakistan, for example, carries a penalty of imprisonment, but the usual punishment is a fine of £10 or £20. To an agent who makes his living by changing photographs or substituting pages (which eliminates British High Commission conditions) in passports, for which the going rate is £750 up, a fine of this order is an occupational risk.

Big Business

In India, when police inquiries lead to a passport being withheld it will be impounded, but it is unlikely that action will be taken against the offender.

Even more remarkably, travel agents can obtain passports on behalf of applicants without restriction—and without any guarantee that it will go to the right person. If we relate the sums involved for "facilitating" travel to this country to the local standard of living we are dealing with big business.

In short, the economic forces behind illegal immigration, both for the agent and the immigrant, are far stronger than the incentives on our side to defeat it. That sounds derogatory of the overworked staff in British posts, wrestling with doubtful applications, and to the 2,000 immigration officers at our ports in this country. If we all did our work as well as they do this country would be humming, but the balance of power is against them.

It cannot be redressed, I am persuaded, until we enlist not only the co-operation of the Asian community in this country but essentially the Governments of India and Pakistan, whose sympathy for our difficulties is stronger than we suppose.

Senior Indian officials in Delhi will privately admit astonishment that our immigration policies have been so generous. In Pakistan they are amazed that Pakistan citizens can still come as Commonwealth citizens, since President Bhutto took Pakistan out of the Commonwealth.

They would understand and accept stiffer restrictions and penalties, provided they did not embarrassingly discriminate between white, black and brown. Furthermore, both Governments have a strong vested interest in helping us to check illegal immigrants. They dislike the traffic every bit as much as we do. One of its side effects is a very large market in illegal currency.

The remittances returned to the sub-continent by immigrants entitled to be here are enormous—perhaps as much as £200 million a year. To avoid risk of detection the illegal immigrant will not send remittances through the usual channels, but with couriers will despatch sterling which attracts a higher rate of exchange.

It would be a major step forward if we could induce the Governments of the sub-continent to accept that if they could stamp out—or at least stamp on—illegal agents in their own countries, they would also reduce the traffic of black market currency which so troubles them.

Nor does the case for attempting to reach a package deal with these Governments rest solely on illegal immigration. As we shall discover, our policy for admitting dependants (which we shall continue to do even under the 1971 Act) is a self-perpetuating exercise.

Upwards of 50,000 Asians return annually to their homeland, where they can remain for up to two years and then come back here. That, to say the least, in the circumstances already described, is a difficult traffic to superintend.

Moreover, young Asian males in this country will not, for traditional reasons, marry their kind resident in this country. Most will return home for their brides, and will have the right to re-enter here with them. In a sense the terms are discriminatory, for women cannot do the same.

For the parents of Asian daughters in this country that is already casting a shadow—and providing a class of young male who will offer his hand to a girl here in return for a dowry from her family.

I have my doubts whether we can solve these complexities single-handed and by fresh regulations, any more than we shall effectively check illegal immigration with policemen.

Attempts to reach a fresh understanding with the Governments in Delhi, Islamabad and Dacca—not without advantages to them— might well fail. But we ought to try it for, in the long term, if we are serious in our declared intention to stop fresh immigrants for settlement, no other course lies open to us.

WHITE LIBERALS AND BLACK CHARGES

Black Britain
(George Allen & Unwin)

W. F. Deedes M.P. on a new attack on Britain's "guilt-ridden" attitudes

What are the chances of black militancy making itself felt in Britain? Is all as peaceful as it seems among our coloured population or might we awake one morning to an explosion? What could spark it off?

Normally these are questions we hesitate, at least publicly, to ask. They are taboo. They could be said to be gratuitously offensive to the two-and-a-half million coloured people here, most of whom wish only to live as peaceably as the rest of us.

But, as Northern Ireland has taught us, the wishes of the majority are not decisive. A small number, sufficiently determined and ruthless, can raise a whirlwind. A writer on Ireland, commenting on Lord O'Neill's first meeting with Seán Lemass in 1965, recalled de Tocqueville's observation that a grievance, while it might be patiently endured so long as it seems beyond redress, "comes to appear intolerable once the possibility of removing it crosses men's minds."

Could it be argued that some aspects of our enthusiastic race relations industry in this country have just that effect? That is another tactless question: but what strikes one about a very angry book which Chris Mullard has written from the standpoint of a black Briton in this country is that the angriest parts of it are directed not at racists but at those who toil for race relations.

In many ways this is a sad book. It will give most satisfaction to those who insist that we were crazy to admit any immigrants at all. It will give least joy to those who seek to foster good race relations. It will disturb a lot of immigrants who do not share Mullard's strident opinions:

> We are still treated as "lazy, immoral, savage, drug-taking, stinking bastards ... the black scum spreading over our fair land." Discrimination has increased. Hatred has crystallised into

a determination to rid the country of us. We are ridiculed. We are forced into ghettos, into menial jobs, and into a life pattern which reflect hopelessness, exploitation, man's inhumanity to man.

Like many of his *genre*, black and white, Mullard has suffered personal experience which shaped his attitudes. Born in Britain, at 16 he suffered humiliation in a café. Later he had a protracted quarrel with the Community Relations Council over his appointment as a community relations officer on the Tyne, where he now is. Though bizarre, his testament can, however, and will be cited as giving us insight into the mind of a black Briton and how it got that way.

If one could feel sure that Mullard was simply a lone eccentric with a chip, this book might be dismissed as irrational as well as inaccurate. Some of its inaccuracies are palpable.

But most of the diatribe has a familiar ring. It reflects much of the material which gets printed and circulated among at least a minority—and the youngest, I suspect—of our coloured population. Since satire is not part of a West Indian's repertoire, it relies on fierce exaggeration.

It is sometimes asked why the more offensive examples are not picked up by the Race Relations Act. The answer, which will not satisfy everyone, is that they are not thought to be worth powder and shot.

Mullard now gives us between respectable hard covers not only the substance of this but its motivation. His principal target is what he calls our patronising approach to race—he wants to see blacks, not whites, in charge of community relations.

The approach, he declares, springs from our sense of guilt for our colonial past. "Deep down they feel ashamed and wish to atone for their guilt by faking a liberal concern for the future of 'second-generation immigrants'." More dangerous than overt racist bigotry, concludes Mullard, white liberalism is an unknown quantity.

ESSENTIAL PARADOX

One wonders how many school teachers, social workers, council officials, housing officers not directly employed in the race relations mills Mullard has seen at work. A year or two back some of us trudged round Brixton with a junior official of the Lambeth housing department, whose unenviable task was tactfully to sort out over-crowding and multiple occupation. In his uncomplaining matter-of-fact, all-in-the-day's-work approach I could find no trace of colonial guilt.

Then we have the routine charge that police in this country, or "the pigs," are used as agents to crack down on blacks. Some of us spent the best part of a year recently pursuing these elusive charges. We traced infrequent episodes of serious police misconduct, which had spread widely and improved in the telling. We also found in many places prodigious efforts by police forces to get on terms with coloured people. You cannot whitewash a few bad policemen. Nor can you blackwash the striving majority.

But, while Mullard is being absurd and unfair to dismiss the collective effort being mustered by a lot of conscientious citizens as guilt-ridden "tea and sympathy," he has of course seized the essential paradox of the race relations business.

It *can* be held to imply the inferiority of its protégés. Not everyone employed is simply coping with numbers. A lot, consciously or otherwise, are trying to redress a balance to make up for deficiencies.

I am ready to go along with Mullard in thinking it might be a very good thing if the "host" community, another term he resents, did rather less for the immigrants and the immigrants did rather more for themselves.

For this they are simply not organised. Even here—a difficult fellow this—Mullard blinks the facts. Lack of organisation, he declares, is not due to the black man's inability to organise. "Organisation is difficult when the Government and the majority of people in the country in which you live dislike you and treat you like modern slaves."

The truth is simpler. West Indians and Asians do not dovetail into the British style of organisation. They do not take naturally to our ritual of committees, subcommittees, elected officers, public meetings, minutes and the rest of it. There is nothing derogatory about that—quite the reverse, some will say—nor is it singular.

Possibly the most urgent task we have is to find a way forward from this. The Jews—I wonder if Mullard in search for his own identity has read the early history of their migration here!—now have their own Board of Guardians.

In religion and culture there has been no question of Orthodox

Jews "assimilating" with us, any more than West Indians or Asians will. But the Jews have established a model for relationships with our community and for identifying themselves with our community's interests.

Mullard would say that their insecurity of tenure makes this impossible. There may be an element of truth in that, but it does not get to the root of it. No one would argue that we should at once start winding down white patronage for race relations. But we should be thinking of a transitional stage when Chris Mullard and his friends, endowed with public funds if need be, are given parity of responsibility for at least some spheres of the coloured population's affairs.

We shall soon have emerging from the schools a generation of blacks able and wishing to do just that. That *is* equality.

Given such responsibility, they will discover some facts of life from which we now protect them. They will discover that the frustrations suffered in some of our cities do not spring solely from having a black skin, but are shared with many whites, particularly young ones. They will discover how impersonal advanced societies become and how many from rural communities, whatever their colour, are driven to despair by it.

They will discover how much harder it is to remedy the social ills of modern cities than to blame them all on ethnocentric prejudices; how much harder it is to build men up than to tear them down.

LAWS THAT INJURE COMMON SENSE

W. F. Deedes on the "total politics" of the new Race Relations Bill, due for second reading in the Commons today

It has sometimes occurred to me that if 25 million English, Scots and Welsh had between, say, 1950 and 1975 settled in India, concentrating mainly on New Delhi, Calcutta and Bombay, the Indians would have seen this as a matter for remark and possibly of concern.

So people who express anxiety about settlement on roughly that scale of Commonwealth immigrants here are not necessarily racist. In not much more than 20 years we have undergone a profound human change, and it is only human to notice it.

As Parliament begins to work today on one more Race Relations Bill we should notice something else, less obvious but relevant: New Commonwealth citizens now settled here have become an electoral force to reckon with. They vote. In a growing number of constituencies their wishes must be weighed. We shall see, as the Bill rolls along, how politicians of all parties take this, and how far it has subtly altered attitudes.

Well, why shouldn't it? This minority is here to stay. They are part of us, and have full rights. Agreed, but in weighing the main chance parliamentarians should not forget, nor allow Ministers to forget, that successive Governments since 1962 have given certain undertakings.

"We accept," they have said (repeatedly), "that there has to be a strict limit on entry; that entry of immigrants (to quote from Labour's White Paper of 1965) 'does not outrun Britain's capacity to absorb them.' We will see to that. But those who are here must be treated fairly, on equal terms, without discrimination."

That was roughly the compact made. Before Parliament gets lost in a thicket of tougher anti-discrimination clauses, it should view the whole scene in proper perspective and then take fresh bearings from there.

When I had finished some years' work with the Select Committee on Race Relations and Immigration, someone asked me for my outstanding impression. "Our tolerance," I said, and I still stand by that. Granted the blemishes inseparable from human folly, which small politicians find hard to live with.

Taking it in the round, weighing it against the experience of minorities through history and in many parts of the world today, the British have precious little to be ashamed of in this 20 years of such profound human change—though it would be uncharacteristic of them to say as much.

Were we in proper balance, we might perceive that more clearly—as they do in Delhi and Bridgetown and Islamabad. But at the moment we are not in balance; so putting tolerance at risk, we embark on a fresh round of extirpating what remains of racist employers, rogue club secretaries and bigoted housing managers.

The new Race Relations Bill is the product not of political wisdom, but of "total politics." No exceptions can be allowed. Given this prevailing itch for totality, in race, in closed shops, in law, in incomes policy, the Bill will go through all right—yet not without doing some injury to the common sense on which all human relations ultimately hinge.

Not long ago a left-wing friend of mine asked one of his constituents in West London why in working men's clubs—the Bill is to sit firmly on top of them—blacks were kept out. "We live in a sea of colour," said the man. "The club is our oasis." "Mind you," said my friend, "he's wrong—but I see what he's getting at."

Then I recall the factory manager in Bradford, who was asked pretty sharply why all his Pakistani labour was in the foundry, the hottest and dirtiest corner of the plant.

"They are there," he said, "because it is the best paid work on offer, and they wanted to be there. If I direct some of them to cleaner and less well-paid work, we *shall* have trouble."

THE LOOPHOLES

Such realities do not invalidate all race laws, but they illustrate the subject's deep complexities and limitations. Employers, no doubt rightly, are made answerable for discrimination at work. But trade unionists, defending skills, differentials—and prejudices—also have something to answer for. And perhaps this time round MPs working on the Bill should have a closer look at this.

But then let us look at the other side of the compact. Has the Government which now declares it cannot trust citizens to behave decently towards colour without more regulation, itself proved wholly trustworthy when we come to control of entry? The impression is not reassuring.

Certainly, the mood of this Government towards immigration has changed since the White Paper of 1965—when Labour Ministers were genuinely alarmed by the loopholes they found (largely of their own making in Opposition) and went to work on them; or since Mr Callaghan remorselessly moved in 1968 against the Asian holders of British passports who were clamouring for entry from East Africa.

As recent studies by Mr Barry O'Brien in our news columns have told us, the relevant figures are elusive—but their elusiveness is suggestive. The truth is that, given the advent of jet aircraft; the enormous movement which now takes place between the United Kingdom and New Commonwealth homelands; the right of entry given to, say, male fiancés; the volume of visitors, genuine and otherwise; and a growing desire not to offend politically an influential minority—given these things, our controls are bound to be unreliable, to put it mildly.

What precise orders have gone to our entry certificate officers in the New Commonwealth, whose job it is to vet dependants claiming right of entry here, I do not pretend to know. Circumstantial evidence suggests that they were told not long ago to cut the waiting queues, giving the benefit of the doubt more often, if need be.

No one is deeply to blame—except Government, which knows that external controls will not work efficiently any more, but also that more effective internal controls, through the identity card, are a political loser.

Compact aside, does it matter any more? Yes, I think it does, and one simple paradox illustrates why it matters. There is something inherently absurd about Government posturing with more legislation against discrimination while with vast carelessness, Government admits unconditionally dependent children of up to 18, with little or no English, and thus handicapped in a way which will forever prejudice their success in an industrial society.

It is no answer to say that the increasing numbers born and educated here will not be so handicapped. It is the *exceptions* which reproach us—is that not supposed to be the message of the Race Relations Bill?

Successive Governments have administered our immigration policy—if that is the word—without grasping the scale of what we have taken on. They have failed to provide for it, and so have left a lot of extraordinarily tolerant and uncomplaining school teachers, housing managers and employers to grapple with the consequences. (And if that looks like hindsight let me add that such words appeared in a unanimous Select Committee report on the subject three years ago.)

What right have they now to tell the citizen that *he* has fallen down?

LESS GUILT OVER RACE COULD IMPROVE OUR RELATIONS

Anti-Racism
By Russell Lewis (Quartet Books)

Britain has always enjoyed freedom of opinion and speech but on the question of race we have learnt to be subdued. W. F. Deedes considers the historical background to this unhealthy situation

In a country given to fairly uninhibited expressions of opinion, where the clergy may question the existence of God, the press may mock Royalty, and school teachers may dwell on the merits of homosexuality, the argument about race is remarkably subdued. This, if we consider it, is not entirely because certain of our laws now govern what we may say but more because of the one-sided way in which we have been induced to think.

If people declare, as Mr Michael Day of the Commission for Racial Equality did the other day, that racial discrimination in this country is still rampant, that we are guilty of harassing blacks, that we need a yet stronger Race Relations Act, then we must accept that scolding uncomplainingly. It has become part of our lot. By contrast, if someone like the Prime Minister uses the word "swamped," as she did a decade ago, it is not readily forgotten.

After some years of experience with a parliamentary select committee on race relations and immigration I came to think that we would never achieve the relations we desire with other races in this country without a good deal more openness and candour. We have since travelled in the opposite direction. The experiences of Mr Ray Honeyford after his article in the Salisbury Review, and of the Brent headmistress, Miss Maureen McGoldrick, to name but two, warn us that even constructive criticism on race matters is best kept to ourselves—if we want to hold on to our jobs.

Many of these aberrations are popularly attributed to the so-called "loony" Left councils, but this is only partly true. We have assembled bit by bit an apparatus aiming not simply to win justice for the Asian and Caribbean people here, but to implant in our minds a perpetual sense of guilt. A far stronger apparatus, it would persuade us, is needed to counter our iniquities.

There is something extraordinarily patronising about some of the attitudes we have been conditioned to accept. Taken too far, as the recent tragedy at Burnage High School has shown, they are also dangerous. The argument, in short, has become far too one-sided. It is time to remark on the emperor's nakedness. In a book published today with the no-nonsense title Anti-Racism, a Mania Exposed, Russell Lewis has made a good start.

The virtue of his book is not the critical analysis of our race relations industry, but its lucid account of how we came to get trussed up in this undignified fashion. It is a long story, starting in 1955 with the failure of the Government (of which I was a member) to take the course of immigration seriously. It failed to control it; worse, it failed to prepare for the social consequences of this neglect.

The critical turn of events, however, came a decade later. A Conservative Government had by then acted to control immigration. Labour had opposed this measure furiously. This was to have awkward consequences when Mr Wilson's Government took office in 1964 and found that, thanks to their ravaging of Rab Butler's Bill, immigration was still out of control. Labour's White Paper of August 1965 proposed severe steps. But, as Mr Lewis observed, Wilson realised how important it was psychologically for Labour to feel superior to their opponents on the issue of race.

Having given way to public demand for stricter immigration controls, therefore, Labour promised a law against racial discrimination and against incitement to race hatred. On these foundations was built what surrounds us today. The strongest measures came after the defeat of the Heath Government in 1974, when Roy Jenkins took over at the Home Office. Eventually, the Race Relations Board and the Community Relations Commission gave birth to the Commission for Racial Equality. A new law sought to prohibit discrimination in employment, training, education, housing and the provision of goods.

That was the first main chapter. After the race riots of 1981, Lord Scarman's report wrote a second. It has, Mr Lewis remarks, become the bible of the race relations lobby. In 1985 came the report of the Archbishop of Canterbury's commission, Faith in the City. One of its messages was that ethnic minorities are the worst casualties of the inner city.

Other influential offerings on these lines included the report of a committee set up by Mrs Shirley Williams in 1979 on attitudes in schools. First under Mr Peter Newsam and then Lord Swann, it produced the conclusions expected of it. One was the abolition of Christian morning prayers on grounds that they are meaningless to Moslem and Hindu children.

It would be wrong, and unfair to these distinguished authors, to imply that what they wrote was nonsense; but at least their conclusions, however wise, should have been open to challenge and serious argument. We have been led to a point when publicly to challenge assumptions about race and the way we are handling it is too dangerous for professionals like schoolteachers.

To take an example, the behaviour of some of our young has become a matter of great social concern. Unquestionably, the West Indian matriarchal extended family leads to a large number of fatherless children. It does not necessarily follow (although Mr Lewis says it does) that the absence of a father harms a child's moral and mental growth; but *whether* it does or not is a legitimate matter for public discussion. In respect of the West Indians there is no such discussion. Indeed, as Mr Lewis reminds us, Lord Scarman saw the fatherless West Indian family not as a source of social fragility and potential unrest but as the consequence of the impact of English social conditions upon it.

We have established a frame of mind in which any issue that appears critical of ethnic minorities, any fact that could be misused by wrong-headed persons, is best kept hidden. This is folly and could harm our chances of living together in peace.

Given our subservience to the race relations institutions, it is not surprising that they have grown too big for their boots. They can call for stronger laws, for more affirmative action—without fear of much public contradiction. We have grown nervous of contradicting them. That is bad for any democratic institution. Mr Lewis is critical of their arrogance. I am less critical because I think our own supine attitudes have encouraged such arrogance.

Vocabulary is a factory. It is easier for Russell Lewis to make the criticisms that ought to be made with precision and without undue offence than it is for those who feel just as strongly but are less articulate.

Ultimately it is a question of balance. There is no call to put the clock back and repeal our race laws. Ethnic minorities should be protected against a minority that will always discriminate if it can. But that does not call for constant reproach of our population at large.

As Enoch Powell remarks fairly enough in a preface to this book: "After the Second World War the British were the victims of an event for which nothing in their history or experience had prepared them." The national response to this challenge over 40 years has not been an ignoble one. It deserves better than the constant scolding which comes from those with a political axe to grind, with a vested interest in the race relations business, or a combination of both.

December 1988

CAN AUSTRALIA AVOID BEING
ASIA'S POOR RELATION?

Singapore's Prime Minister has warned Australia that it can no longer remain isolated from the rest of the Pacific basin. W. F. Deedes looks at the country's immigration debate and argues that its British institutions remain its greatest asset

Australians, at the close of their bicentennial year, are in the throes of determining what their future role is to be in an ocean dominated by Asia. It is not an easy decision for a nation of little more than 16 million people (nearly half of them still with British kith and kin) in a region from which British power has disappeared.

The discussion unfortunately has become entangled with the lesser but more emotional question of how many immigrants—and what kind—are to be allowed to enter Australia. This is exciting a lot of political attention and a certain amount of ill-feeling, but it is not throwing much light on the main question.

From Singapore, Prime Minister Lee Kuan Yew sees the issue for Australia more clearly than Australians themselves. Taking the long view, he sees to the north of Australia a region of around three billion people at one and a half or two per cent growth, with a weight far exceeding that of Europe. If you will not link up with this region, Lee recently told Denis Warner, editor of the Pacific Defence Reporter, you are going to be very poor relations. He added mischievously: "If you don't involve yourselves in trade and development, in culture and social contracts . . . you'll be suppliers of beef, mutton, wool." Singapore's Prime Minister will not be accepted as a reliable witness by loyal Australians, but he is not far wide of the mark. It might be to Australia's advantage if Mr Hawke, for the Labour Government, and Mr Howard, for the Liberal Opposition, could bring themselves to talk to their own countrymen on this plane.

This isolation of Australia in a fast-expanding Asian ocean has come about by mutual consent. We determined that our own future lay with Europe. The nature of the British Commonwealth changed. We have withdrawn our hand from Australia's affairs by its desire. Even now, there is small realisation in Europe of what formidable company the Pacific nations are becoming.

Yet given that Australia must increasingly associate itself with Asian neighbours, there is plenty of room for argument on what sort of a nation it is to become. The modish word running through the immigration debate is "multiculturalism".

It is designed to make immigrants feel thoroughly at home, and many Australians thoroughly uneasy. It blurs the question a lot of Australians take seriously: how far will they be able to maintain racial homogeneity. As we have learned in this country, it is a difficult subject for calm public discussion. One mismanaged sentence and the cry is "racism!"

Opposition leader Howard fell into this trap during the summer, when he spoke loosely about "One Australia". He was accused by a media much further inclined to the Left than our own of exploiting the politics of race, breaking a tradition of bipartisanship, and costing Australia vast sums of money withheld by angry Asian businessmen.

The squabble is misleading. For on the point of main concern to Australians there is no real disagreement. There should be no discrimination between immigrants on grounds of race or ethnic origin; but all immigrants should be called upon to make a commitment to Australia, its traditions, its values and its institutions.

Mr Howard says that. So does Mr Hawke's Immigration Minister, Senator Robert Ray. So, with greater emphasis, did Dr Stephen FitzGerald, on whose impressive report on Australia's immigration policy the Government has just pronounced. FitzGerald wanted less attention paid to ethnic interests and more to Australia's needs. Far from appeasing ethnic minorities—as Ministers hoped he would do—FitzGerald wanted migrants to drop their defensive stance and join wholeheartedly in the creation of a new Australian identity, "hostile to any British cringe", as someone charmingly put it.

FitzGerald's ideas proved too strong meat for Mr Hawke's men, and after some shuffling about, they have compromised. The migrant intake stays at 140,000, roughly divided between the humanitarian (which means refugees) at 14,000; family immigration (with the definition of family slightly narrowed) at 71,000; and the economic category (or good for Australia) at 54,000.

None of this meets FitzGerald's fundamental proposition. To

ease public misgivings about immigration, "seen by many to be a grab-bag of favours", and multiculturalism, "seen by many as social engineering", immigration should involve a firm commitment to Australia's social system.

There seems to be marked reluctance on this score. Something like 43 per cent of migrants eligible to become Australian citizens have not done so; 60 per cent of those are from Britain and Ireland. Refugees from Vietnam and elsewhere are, by contrast, usually eager to get Australian passports. Some from Hong Kong have arrived, taken out Australian citizenship, then returned to Hong Kong having insured their future.

FitzGerald wanted more pressure to be applied, with certain benefits withheld from those who declined to take up citizenship. But this was perceived to be politically far too risky. Safer by far to keep the settler vote sweet by what Professor Geoffrey Blainey bluntly calls "ethnic payola". One source declares that Government funding of ethnic enterprises is now costing about £250 million a year. Mr Hawke, naturally, is thinking less about the future shape of Australia than the shape of Labour's vote in what might be a tight election next year.

In round figures, Australia is accepting each year for settlement about one-tenth of those who wish to enter. A third of those who enter are Asians, another third come from the United Kingdom and Ireland. It is reckoned that Australia, without over-reaching itself, could accommodate 45 million people.

According to the writer Bob Santamaria, himself the son of poor Italian immigrants, challenge is inevitable. The belief, he says, that Australia will be permitted to leave its mineral resources in the ground and, in a region of hungry millions, to waste fertile land with extensive rather than intensive farming practices, is a mirage. That is an uncomfortable view, but like Lee Kuan Yew's it strikes me as close to the mark.

One of Australia's main attractions to the Asian immigrant is the relative solidity of its political institutions. And for that Australia owes much to the British political system which has prevailed there for the past 200 years. I do not think that Australians in their present "no British cringe" mood can lightly set that aside and at the same time meet the Asian challenge. They need a solid foundation on which to build this uncharted future. It is hard to see where it is to

come from if Australians persuade themselves that the British connection, being a mark of subservience, is something to eradicate.

Commenting on the recent inquiry into the Queensland mess,
an Australian journalist observed the other day how much the style
of government there had assisted the growth of corruption and
malpractice. Single-chamber government, a marked absence of clear
separation of powers in the political-judicial set-up, a breakdown in
the rule of law—it was on those counts that Queensland came
unstuck.

We have no reason to sing small about this. Australians need to
be firmly reminded at this juncture that adherence to the British
political system, by which their nation has been guided, is not
subservience at all, but rather a safeguard for their future.

July 1989

ASSIMILATION: AN IDEA WHOSE TIME HAS GONE?

The furore over The Satanic Verses has exacerbated divisions within the Labour party and other liberal circles about racial integration in Britain. W. F. Deedes, a former chairman of the Select Committee on Race Relations, examines the way in which the optimists have become disenchanted

When he put his pen to The Satanic Verses, Mr Salman Rushdie no doubt considered—and seemingly underrated—the impact it would have on Moslem minds. But he could hardly have foreseen its repercussions on our own race relations in this country, for they are only starting to unfold.

Our race relations were founded on liberal ideals, which were given expression in the early Race Relations Act of the 1960s. They have not been seriously challenged—until now, when by an ironic twist we find them threatened by the illiberal attitude of a minority which our legislation is designed to protect. Small wonder our liberal intelligentsia shows signs of mental confusion. It is hard to avoid a wry smile at its dilemma, for it was largely this intelligentsia which confidently formulated the original guidelines on race relations, and made clear to the rest of us how we were to conduct ourselves.

As chairman or deputy chairman of the Select Committee on Race Relations and Immigration in the late 1960s and early 1970s, I well recall the atmosphere which prevailed then. In our very proper determination to make citizens from the British Commonwealth feel at home, we used words like integration and assimilation expansively, without entering too deeply into what they implied or where they would lead.

About that time I entered a protest on this page, which was headed: Why should they "integrate"? "How absurd are the words we drop so insensitively about 'integration' and 'assimilation'," I wrote, and concluded: "There is something infinitely saddening in this portrait of an insular race, fearful lest an alien horde corrupts its standards—at the same time discarding its standards in a fashion which leaves the aliens fearful lest they themselves be corrupted."

Indeed, as the Select Committee travelled around the principal cities of this country, we could not fail to observe how apprehensive many Asians were lest members of the family be drawn into some of our easy ways. We supposed—wrongly—that this little difficulty would have faded away a generation or two later.

But this was totally out of tune with the thinking of those times. The ruling voices spoke about a liberal democratic society, within which our friends from the Commonwealth naturally would be happy to form a close part. Mutual tolerance was our watchword. We enjoined it on our own citizens, and it was not to be entertained that anyone would dissent.

Nor have they until now. We have had our share of racial disorders and of black crime; and there persist strong convictions that the police discriminate unfairly against coloured people—which I doubt we shall ever eradicate. But there has not, until Rushdie, been a fundamental clash over the pre-eminence of our law.

We are dealing with an issue which Rushdie has brought to a head, but which has long been lurking and which extends to much wider ground. There are heavy implications here, for example, for the future of some of our schools in the inner cities. We shall go on resisting separate Moslem schools, but I am not sure how long we shall be able to do so successfully. For one thing we are about to get the worst of both worlds over religious observance in schools. The requirement of the recent Act that such observance must be predominantly Christian is not going to be observed, which will disturb Christian parents; but Moslems and others think that it will be observed, and that increases the demand for separation.

So the Rushdie affair ought to be seen as a watershed, from which we look again at some of our earlier, easy assumptions and think through more realistically the sort of society we are aiming at. Yet we know this is unlikely to happen. As the battle of words going on within the Labour party makes plain, this is an explosive subject. It invariably generates more heat than light. It has become very difficult to discuss objectively. Even research has to tread carefully.

Mr John Patten, the Home Office Minister with responsibility in this realm, has written bravely and at length to leading British Moslems. There is ample room in Britain, he says, for diversity and variety; but not for separation or segregation. At the heart of our thinking, he concludes, is a Britain in which all races can live and work together, "each retaining proudly its own faith and identity, but each sharing in common the bond of being, by birth or choice, British".

That does not touch the heart of Moslem feeling over Rushdie. In the eyes of most Moslems it is intolerable that our law should punish—in theory at least—those who insult Christianity but not those who insult Islam. Do we widen the law on blasphemy to embrace other religions, or do we abandon blasphemy law altogether? Either course would provoke furious controversy; and we can reckon the law will stay as it is.

But among members of the Labour party the controversy swirls not so much around the religious issue as the degree to which a multiracial society, which we now are, can move toward cultural pluralism without the taint of separatism. It is easy enough to condemn apartheid in South Africa; much harder to accept that multiculturalism here is unattainable, and that we may have to edge toward what South African nationalists euphemistically call "separate but equal".

Writing on the subject recently, Roy Jenkins, who as Home Secretary was principal architect of the race relations laws of the 1960s, observed of the Asians: "They have obviously not merged their culture and still less their religion. They were not expected to." Perhaps not, but a great many people devoutly hoped that they would, particularly after a generation or two had lived in this country. That hope, we are sharply reminded by Rushdie, has not been fulfilled. The prospect of assimilation is dead.

Then what, if any, is the common bond to be? There is hardly available to us the American example, whereby those who would become citizens of the United States must swear allegiance to its constitution. And I am sceptical about Mr Patten's formula—"each sharing in common the bond of being, by birth or choice, British". The philosophical emphasis today is on Europe and on being a good European.

One example to which we might look has been set by the Jews in this country. They have been an important minority since at least the turn of the century. They have kept within the mainstream of British life yet with a different religion, culture and, where appropriate, separate institutions—all of which some observe more faithfully than others. And they have been law-abiding, which partly explains the irritation some of them have been showing over Rushdie.

A calming down on the Rushdie issue will not remove our fundamental difficulty—our deep fear of separatism. We are apprehensive lest it leads to segregation. We have built up this idealistic and unreal world in which under our liberal democracy all races must ultimately draw together. We see this prospect for them as irresistible. They see it otherwise.

There can only be one *law* for all in this land. That is ground we must hold at all costs. But it might be easier to hold if we could first rid ourselves of certain cherished delusions, the chief of which is that one day, somehow, we shall become one homogeneous people. We shall not. We may desire it, but they do not. We must bring ourselves to cater for differences; and if that adds to the cost of our schools, as it will, so it must be. We owe the money.

ANOTHER COUNTRY

Ethnic minorities rarely venture into the English countryside—which concerns Julian Agyeman, a black Yorkshireman. In conversation with W. F. Deedes he looks for a way ahead

"Can we begin with Stanley Baldwin?" I say to Julian Agyeman, founder member and chairman of Black Environment Network. He is a Yorkshireman, born of an English mother and a Ghanaian father, who works in London as an environmental education adviser. Foremost among his concerns is what keeps black people away from our countryside.

When English Nature, a Government agency, recently announced that it will no longer describe trees or plants as "native" or "alien", thus felling our native oak, Agyeman's BEN welcomed the decision as a victory against "biological racism".

Armed with a copy of Baldwin's speeches, I invited Agyeman to read one delivered to the annual dinner of the Royal Society of St George in 1924, which established Baldwin in the public's mind as a sort of politicised Lord Emsworth. "To me," said Baldwin, "England is the country, and the country is England".

> The sounds of England, the tinkle of the hammer on the anvil in the country smithy, the corncrake on a dewy morning, the sound of the scythe against the whetstone, the sight of the plough team coming over the brow of the hill, the sight which has been in England since England was a land, and may be seen in England long after the Empire has perished and every works in England has ceased to function, for centuries the one eternal sight of England. The wild anemones in the woods in April, the last load at night of hay being drawn down a lane as twilight comes on . . .

No politician would dare to talk like that now. Agyeman reads the speech thoughtfully. Only in the English language, he points out, does the word "country" mean both nation and countryside. "Which leads to a feeling that the countryside is the place where things are natural, where things are . . ."

"Where the English spirit is buried?" I suggest.

"But it's not. It's alive!"

"With the bluebells in the wood . . ."

"Exactly," says Agyeman. "When you look at it, 90 per cent of Britain is countryside. Only 10 per cent is urban. And the minority groups . . . they're not exactly trapped—that's not the right word. But they live off 10 per cent—or less—of the landscape, and very rarely venture out into the other 90 per cent. Which I find very interesting."

Alone of almost all European societies, Agyeman insists, we don't like urban society. Unlike the Belgians, the Dutch, the Germans, the French, we do not have civic pride. He looks at the speech again. "As Baldwin said, 'England is the country, and the country is England'." There is a pause.

"Look at advertising, Bill. Look at what you see on television. They portray archaic landscape, never-changing landscape—where there are still 'buxom wenches' milking cows. Whereas in fact they factory farm down there! Advertisers like the small field hedgerow."

"The English idyll?"

"Idyll! Yes. So the public is sold the image subliminally. They're told, 'This is really where your heart is; and when you've made your money in the town, in the city, this is where you come back to—where your spirit belongs.'"

One of Agyeman's friends at University College has done some research which shows that the most active people in a village action group are the newcomers. They want to keep the place the way it is—or the way they conceive it should be.

There is a concept in geography, Agyeman explains, called "museumisation", which is often the aim of the newcomers. I confessed that, as president of my county's branch of the Council for the Preservation of Rural England, I had come to much the same conclusion, without the benefit of research.

People, Agyeman goes on, leave the city for different reasons: retirement and so on. "But I suspect that some of the reasons for leaving are perceived links between rising crime, rising poverty, rising homelessness and—there's always a hint of this in the media—the minorities. These minorities occupy a very weak position in society."

*

We branch off into ecology and discuss this debate within the conservation movement about what are called "native" and "alien" species. I had talked to George Barker of English Nature about the death of our "native oak". He argues that the old jargon is lazy and inexact. Guidance to schools or local authorities is better expressed by phrases such as "appropriate to particular areas" or "best suited for the site". Most blacks, he agrees, do not give a hoot about the words "native" or "alien". "Those who take umbrage tend to be local minority leaders."

Native species, Agyeman explains to me, came back of their own free will from the ice ages. Aliens are species introduced by humans. "Among conservationists there's a great dislike of alien species. They seem less worthy in wildlife terms than the native species—because the natives have had time to equilibrate with local ecology. Conservationists accept aliens in confined areas—like gardens, where a lot are introduced. But they want to keep them behind garden walls. We're talking on the sort of mental plane whereby I feel there is a similar desire to keep black people in the cities."

I point out that when Hungarians and Poles and others came to this country during and after the war, there was much muttering in the villages. "You notice," says Agyeman, "I haven't used the word racism. It is not racism. It is xenophobic reaction to the outsider."

We talk about his recent visit to America, to which he carried a mixture of fears and expectations. "I stood in a crowd at a baseball match and looked around at this melting pot of people; and when the national anthem came on, they all stood up, looking proud. They are Americans, because they want to be Americans. Well, I'm English, but I'll never be accepted, despite my accent."

He claims that none of the bodies looking after race relations is much interested in his concerns, but he is impressed by the Countryside Commission. "I've been badgering them. They've turned round."

But none of their publications or policies showed a positive image to black people. "How many rangers, how many Commissioners are black? This isn't racism; it's parochialism." Nonetheless, he is confident that the Commission has "turned the corner". They have treated the subject sympathetically in published material.

I point out that the minorities do not show great enthusiasm for a day in the country. Agyeman accepts this and starts to list the reasons. "Minority groups tend to go for activities they know are safe . . . they have no experience of the countryside.

"There are also cultural reasons for not going to the countryside. When you look at it, most minorities in Britain come from rural areas. The city is associated with progress, with moving forward. To go back to the land is failure."

"So the countryside is seen as something they have escaped from . . . and do not particularly want to go back to?"

"Exactly. The countryside is associated with backwardness, with farming. Nigerian students are all doing business classes or law. Business is the big thing. South-East Asian students, they do engineering." Agyeman adds that in many minds the countryside is associated with spirits—and worse. "You won't see Asian people or West Indian people walking in long grass, because there is a residual fear of snakes."

On the other hand, we recalled, back in the 1960s when the dominant ethos in race relations was "assimilation", local authorities were encouraged to open country homes for foster care and so on. "The kids loved it," said Agyeman. "They helped on the farm. They went out fox hunting. Later they hankered after this childhood in the countryside." I said I thought this had happened to some of the children evacuated during the war. Later they looked back on that existence longingly.

"Today," added Agyeman, "most children think the countryside is boring. You say, 'all right, we'll go for a walk.' 'Where are we going?' 'We're just going for a walk.' 'But we've got to be going *somewhere*!'" Yet there is evidence of landscape linking. "They'd see a field, a wheatfield. 'Look, sir, that's just like home.' Some Asian girls, Kashmiri girls, went to the Black Mountains in Wales, and they said, 'It's just like back home.'"

Julian Agyeman enjoys saying that there were Africans in England before the English. There was, he insists, a black Roman division on Hadrian's Wall in the 1st century AD. It was, he thinks, commanded by a Libyan general. "Let's tell people that." There is a plaque on Harewood House outside Leeds, he insists, claiming that it was built on the proceeds of investments in the West Indies. "What does that mean to you, Bill? Why don't they come up straight and say it was built on the proceeds of slavery? A bit of honesty would go a long way towards getting black people out to see what was there. People like the National Trust could get a lot of sympathy."

I decide this is a bridge too far. "If I made my house over to the

National Trust, and they wanted to put up a plaque declaring that my grandfather was a slave driver ... I would hesitate ... well, I wouldn't give it to them." Agyeman concedes, with a laugh. "All I'm asking for is some honesty. As a teacher in Carlisle, I'm not aware that the kids up there were told there was a black Roman ..." We're back on Hadrian's Wall again, and I am determined to make a point of my own.

"The countryside," I say, "it's the last fort, and it's under fire. The British feel a lot has been taken from it in recent years. Our people in the countryside feel that things are going away from them. Now we're to be Europeanised ... There are two sides to this, nervousness on both sides ..."

"Exactly." Agyeman accepts my point, which pleases me. I feel I should say something helpful by way of conclusion.

As we part, I say to him, "What about Black Environment Network coming out in favour of field sports ...? 'Blacks for Fox-hunting!' That would win them a lot of marks in the countryside just now. Come on!" There is no reply. But Julian Agyeman has a thoughtful look as he leaves.

THE IMMIGRATION NETTLE
THAT NO GOVERNMENT WOULD GRASP

Mercifully for those ministers responsible for the key decisions, the public has never had a full account of the political shilly-shallying that went on over Commonwealth immigration during the decisive years of 1955–75. But they are brought a little closer to it by the release of Cabinet papers relating to 1965, Labour's first full year of office under Harold Wilson.

These uncover one of the most staggering political reversals of modern times. Having furiously opposed the Conservative Government's Bill to limit Commonwealth immigration in 1961–2, Labour found it necessary to impose far more severe restrictions within nine months of taking office. These were first presented to an astonished party through a White Paper, published in August 1965.

Cabinet papers reveal the powerful emotional conflicts that this aroused among Harold Wilson's ministers—and, in particular, for his unhappy Home Secretary, Sir Frank Soskice. For those on the Left, such as Barbara Castle and Dick Crossman, it was a bitter pill.

"This has been one of the most difficult and unpleasant jobs the Government has had to do," observed Crossman in his diary of August 2, 1965. "We have become illiberal and lowered the quotas (*of work permits*) when we have an acute shortage of labour." Yet, in true Crossman style, he goes on to admit that it is politically unavoidable. "Politically, fear of immigration is the most powerful undertow today."

A tremendous row erupted at Labour's party conference that year over the White Paper. An emergency resolution spoke bitterly of "the expression of a surrender, however disguised, to the currents of illiberal opinion". Only the block vote of the trade unions ensured its defeat by a majority of three to one. Yet the tribulations of the Labour Party in 1965 were trifling by contrast with the changes which these political manoeuvres created in this country. What these new papers remind us is that on an issue which would alter our society even more fundamentally than European integration, there was *no* policy.

Commonwealth immigration first became a matter for concern to the Conservative Government in 1956. Citizens from Commonwealth countries could enter as they pleased. We kept no record of their numbers. As late as 1958, we kept no record of who entered by air.

In the mid-1950s the entry figure, mainly Caribbean, was around 45,000 a year. Immigrants were actively recruited by London Transport, our hospitals and other employers, on account of the post-war labour shortage. A group of ministers looked at the possibility of immigration controls. As a junior minister at the Home Office then, I was kept acquainted with their difficulties.

Deeply reluctant to change the long-standing tradition of free entry for all Commonwealth citizens, they strove for inaction. It was not until 1961—when the entry figure had risen to 136,000 (57,000 from the Caribbean; 36,000 from India and Pakistan)—that ministers moved to act. Rab Butler, then Home Secretary, embarked on the Commonwealth Immigrants Bill. It was designed to restrict entry by a voucher system.

Labour tore it to shreds. As if addressing a revivalist meeting, the leader of the Opposition, Hugh Gaitskell, conveyed to his party that the Bill was the embodiment of evil. In face of this onslaught, heavy concessions were made in order to secure the Bill's passage through Parliament. A main fault of the final Act, as I observed at the time, lay not in the rigour of its controls but in their laxity.

So successful was Labour in emasculating the Bill that upon taking office in 1964, the Wilson Government found that there were upwards of a million Commonwealth immigrants already here, and the rate of entry was rising, particularly of dependants of breadwinners. It dispatched Lord Mountbatten round the Commonwealth on a forlorn mission. He returned to report rather fatuously that we needed breathing space and recommended to Wilson that drastic restrictions should be "temporarily" imposed. This would sugar the pill to Commonwealth governments. Sir Frank Soskice realised what was happening within days of taking over the Department. We now learn that he persuaded Wilson—not without difficulty—that "whether we like it or not, we are faced with a very serious social problem in the presence of not far short of a million coloured immigrants". Moreover, he foresaw the prospect of another half million "in months or years".

He called for a complete ban on immigrants without skills, and a ceiling of 10,000 a year for other categories. This was subsequently cut to 7,500. In July 1965, he contrived to push all this through Cabinet. Frank Cousins, then Technology Minister, attacked the proposals. So, from outside the Cabinet, did the Archbishop of Canterbury, Michael Ramsey. Labour's White Paper dwells on such matters as medical checks, housing, schools and the language problem. It advises that about one third of immigrant children in a class should be the maximum "if social strains are to be avoided and educational standards maintained". Today, many teachers in cities where immigrants and their descendants have concentrated will read that with a wry smile.

In reality, Labour's controls were not effective. Illegal immigration, to which the White Paper referred, continued. During two tours with a Select Committee dealing with this subject—to the Caribbean, India, Pakistan and Bangladesh—I learnt a great deal about methods of evading controls.

But even when Labour was replaced by the Heath Government in 1970, there remained a reluctance to push controls beyond a certain limit. Enoch Powell's "Rivers of Blood" speech of 1968 weakened the hand of those ministers anxious to control entry more firmly. The pressures on immigrants to win permanent residence were—and remain—enormous.

These new and embarrassing revelations of Labour's agony in 1965 should fool nobody into thinking that Labour was mainly responsible for the policy of drift, applied ineptly by successive governments. There was a failure to grasp what the party is now on record as reluctantly concluding in 1965—that effective control of immigration is an absolute condition of good race relationships.

Seen in that light, the people of this country have nothing to be ashamed about. It was governments of all parties—starting with Churchill's peacetime ministry of the 1950s—which failed to grasp the scale of the problem. No positive policy was ever produced, and successive ministries were shunted about by events. Yet, notwithstanding these blunders, this country has on the whole proved itself to be pretty tolerant and fair. And nobody will ever persuade me otherwise.

AFRICA

AFTER THE FIRST WORLD WAR, the nations of Europe began to divide Africa between the winners and losers. After the Second World War, a different duty fell to them; they had to prepare for the independence of their separate colonies. I saw a good deal of this, visiting countries like Angola, Mozambique, the Congo—where the transition proved difficult, South Africa—which had a separate problem of apartheid, Rhodesia and finally Sudan.

Looking back on it, the movement towards granting independence to African countries went too quickly. There was no lack of ambitious rulers; what we had not prepared for was the need for the equivalent of our own civil service. There were simply not enough administrators trained to hold things together in the African countries to which we'd granted independence.

I've seen a lot of Africa in the years since independence. I've followed it sympathetically and thought a good deal about how the difficulties may be remedied. HIV and AIDS, which I've studied in various countries, is a problem on its own, but it relates to an area where I see the need for change if Africa is to make progress.

It is critically important to advance the power of women in Africa, for too long subject to the dominant male culture. There are still countries which do not educate girls, but I have discovered through encounters with women who have succeeded—not only in terms of schooling but university training as well—the potential that lies there and must be developed. The future of Africa depends, more than most people think, upon the degree to which we gain independence and greater influence for its women.

NIGERIA'S EXPERIMENT WITH TIME

There are many happy auguries for Nigeria when full independence arrives next year. But much may still depend on Britain's contribution to the Federation and on our understanding of its basic problems.

When they know you in Nigeria, it is said, they will give you three nicknames. There is no secret about the first one—a shrewd but friendly soubriquet. You are unlikely to discover the second, though it would not be a disaster if you did. You will never learn the third.

It is well to keep this little enigma in mind after a festive visit to Maduna, before making prophecies about the future course of a nation whose progress will depend less and less on what we wish, more and more on what they will.

Yet one is reluctant to leave Northern Nigeria's recent celebrations without a reflective glance, if only because in a continent which subjects us to the constant glare of anxiety, Nigeria offers welcome shade. Because we have come thus far in peace and friendship there is a tendency to underrate this giant.

By the time the Englishman has got abreast of constitutional developments in Ghana, the Federation of Rhodesias and Nyasaland, Kenya's new party, apartheid at the Cape and a state of emergency in Buganda he has less mind for the quieter transition of the largest British colony.

I doubt if one in a thousand, without sons or daughters in the West African service, knows exactly what Northern Nigeria has been celebrating. In the roughest nutshell, the much smaller Eastern and Western regions became self-governing in August, 1957. The Northern region, comprising two-thirds of the whole area and possessing just over half its population, followed suit in March. The final stage comes in October, 1960, when all three regions will constitute the independent Federation governed from Lagos.

STROKE OF STATECRAFT

Suffice it Northern Nigeria, three times the size of Britain and with twice Australia's population, will have a massive part to play in the emergence of Africa's biggest State, and it is on this region that last month's limelight has fallen.

This will not only be a new experiment in democracy. It is an experiment with time. Before anyone judges to-day or the unpredictable to-morrow in Nigeria they should ask: how might we have fared had the Reform Bill of 1832 come a few centuries earlier—when feudalism reigned, when barons were to be reckoned with, when power lay not in high office but in land and local suzerainty?

Stimulated possibly by the blaze of colour and the blare of horns, this reflection struck me during the recent Durbar—we shall not see many more of them—while the Emirs led their regional hosts, some five weeks on the road, past the Duke of Gloucester in friendly but apparent rivalry.

The Emir of Kano, they remarked, had pulled a fast one. He appeared on a camel. A day or so later at the Government House garden party the Emir of Katsina, whose great attributes include a polo handicap of 6, spoke disparagingly of camels. "A child can ride a camel," he said pleasantly. At the Durbar Katsina's equestrian contingent had outshone all the rest.

These are men of great possessions and prestige, wielding the kind of territorial power which is now a distant part of our own history; power which had been eclipsed long before we adopted, with far more fuss, the formula—"one man, one vote."

It must be counted among the happier auguries for Northern Nigeria's future that the great Muslim Emirs, Sultans and Chiefs are playing full, consenting and intelligent roles in the democratic régime. Four, the Sultan of Sokoto, the Emir of Kano, the Aku of Wukari and the Emir of Katsina, are Ministers in the Northern Government.

Much is owed for that stroke to the statecraft of the Northern Premier, Alhaji Sir Ahmadu Bello, Sardauna of Sokoto. As an aristocrat and a statesman, he is the keystone of the arch which the Emirs and the politicians must contrive.

In both the Premier and in the Prime Minister of the Federation, Abubakar Tafawa Balewa, also a Northerner, the new State is fortunate. They are men far above the ordinary. I heard four speeches by the Premier and the slightest of them had touches of vision which excited notice.

There was an echo of Asquith and Baldwin in one of them, hinting that the Premier had studied the language, perhaps the methods, of past masters of the English tongue.

LUGARD'S LEGACY

The Sardauna holds a strong affection for the Royal Family and a keen sense for the new mystique of Commonwealth relationships, to which some other nations have shown indifference. There also caught my ear some moving words about Cecil Rhodes and Lugard during a speech he made at a ceremony in Kaduna.

Politicians rarely quote such men to make effective perorations unless they sense that such sentiments will touch certain chords among their followers.

A portrait of Lord Lugard, who made the greatest single contribution to Nigeria, hangs at the entrance of the Northern Region's Parliament, named after him. To America he must appear the archtype of British colonist. To many Nigerians he is an object of gratitude and respect.

It is a fantasy to suggest that his memory has given Nigeria a race of British administrators above those of other territories. It is not fanciful to believe that it has inspired some of the Europeans who governed yesterday and will inspire some Nigerians who will govern to-morrow.

These are an assortment of assets against which to lay the inescapable problems. They abound, and many are common to all such territories: to lift agriculture, the national mainstay, from the primitive to the productive; to choose the right industries; conquest of the tsetse-fly, in which the Institute at Kaduna pioneers for all West Africa. These bread-and-butter problems will need not only money, which is short, but patience, which is shorter.

Greatest of all problems, certainly in Northern Nigeria, will be to find and train administrators at every level. Even if many Europeans are encouraged and willing to remain—prospects are not disheartening—demand must for some years exceed supply. These rulers will face—as we did not so long ago—the demands of patronage, which is the companion of power, and the deficiencies of a qualified Civil Service.

In the course of celebrations we gave Lugard Hall a handsomely bound copy of Erskine May. It is a proud and proper act to hand over your own instruments of government. It is unwise to expect others to wield them precisely as you have done.

"Work and Worship"—that is the motto on Northern Nigeria's new coat-of-arms. Round this unexceptional doctrine convolve historical influences, associations, human impulses, the depth and strength of which no one can predict. Not the least of these influences will be external.

New Spearhead

For centuries what is now called Nigeria has lain, sheltered—or isolated—by desert and swamp from the world's influence. The Stratocruiser has changed that. "Modern communications," Sir Anthony Eden once said, "corrupt good manners." If you consider Cairo radio, that is not the limit of their influence.

Our responsibilities as much as Nigeria's are changing and challenging. The spearhead before Lugard was traders. The spearhead after him should be teachers. For the young school master or mistress with eyes a little above the horizon here is a tremendous call to opportunity.

The children's pageant during the celebrations was less elaborate but far more moving than the Durbar, and caused one to wonder, among other things, what influence the young women of Nigeria may have upon the future. That might still depend upon our contribution.

Beyond that urgent need we shall have to adjust our voice and influence to the new medium of mass communication. We tend to behave sometimes—and not only in Nigeria—like an elderly after-dinner speaker confronted by a microphone for the first time. Nigeria has nearer neighbours more adept and less bashful about using public address equipment.

All Africa's territories differ and so do their anxieties. But success speaks a common language. The Nigerian example, which begins so propitiously, can carry influence beyond even the great sphere of West Africa.

A Nigerian has written: "In my view, the genius of British colonising power will ultimately be judged, not in the vastness of the empire she built up, but in the new nations which she made." That is, historically, a generous verdict upon our work.

Our willingness to give as generous a historical perspective to Nigerian affairs can help to decide whether her future shall continue in peace and friendship; whether this is a meteor or a fixed star over Africa.

May 1960

KARIBA AS SYMBOL OF PARTNERSHIP
IN AFRICA

The Kariba Dam, which the Queen Mother will open on Tuesday, is not only an outstanding achievement of engineering but a symbol of what can be done by inter-racial co-operation to tame the forces of Nature

On a flight between Salisbury and Lusaka there can now be seen, stretching over some 1,500 square miles, what appears to be a flood of disastrous dimensions. In this gigantic basin, the largest man-made lake in the world, are accumulating the waters of the Zambesi River for the Kariba Dam, which Queen Elizabeth the Queen Mother will formally open on Tuesday.

Kariba is a project conceived and achieved on a scale which would have taken the heart of Cecil Rhodes. Its builders have overcome great obstacles, some totally unforeseen. It will supply over 5,000 miles of line electric power to all Rhodesia, from Kitwe in the Copper Belt to Bulawayo. It is a monument not only to engineering skill, but to the work of all races in Africa.

It is just five years since the site was chosen—not without controversy—and the necessary funds, initially £80m, were raised. Kariba was then bush, 100 miles from the nearest town and 50 miles from the nearest road. To this day the nearest railhead is 150 miles away; everything needed has been borne to the site by lorry.

MEN, BEASTS AND NYLONS

A huge African population, some thousands of the Tonga tribes, had to be moved away to make way for the lake. Game wardens trapped and transported 2,000 wild animals and 500 reptiles. Women surrendered hundreds of pair of nylon stockings to tie the legs of the beasts painlessly.

A new town was built in 16 months on the heights above Kariba by an English firm to house 10,000 workers, including 8,000 Africans. Roads, sometimes based on elephant tracks, were built and progressively improved until generators, turbines and transformers could move up on 100-ton trailers.

These were preliminaries. The principal task of temporarily taming the Zambesi and building a dam 420 ft. high and 1,900 ft. long fell mainly into the hands of an Italian consortium of four firms.

The Italians, in common with nearly everyone else on the site, have worked in two 12-hour shifts. That, in the climate of Kariba, is no mean demand on a man's strength. The only hint of labour trouble in the European camp came when doctors advised a reduction of shifts to eight hours for men working above 100 degrees on the vast underground power stations. After protest the Italians continued 12-hour shifts.

To all the natural difficulties was added the behaviour of the river itself. The Zambesi is a temperamental giant. Its flow varies normally throughout the year from 15,000 to 200,000 cubic ft. of water per second. It is to even this out and capture some 84 p.c. of the annual flow for power that the Kariba lake has been formed.

In 1957 the Zambesi produced what they termed a "once in 500 years flood," some 360,000 cubic ft. of water per second. The phenomenon held up work, but for a miraculously short time. In the following year there came the "once in 10,000 years flood"— a volume of 580,000 cubic ft. a second. It delayed work for six weeks. This year the first main phase of the work finished on time.

A story of this kind has facts to attract many professionals. To the financiers it may be of interest to know how the £80m—the final cost will be £113m—was raised: £28.6m from the World Bank, £15m from our own Colonial Development Corporation, £20m from the copper companies, £6m from the Federal Government, and so on.

The engineer may like to take note that 1,400m cubic feet of concrete went into the dam, that the six flood-gates on its face must take a thrust of water of 3,000 tons when the dam is full. The electrician can reflect on a total installed capacity of 1,200m kw, an ultimate annual output of 8,180m kw, and 930 miles of single circuit 330 kv steel tower transmission lines connecting Kariba to transforming stations all over the Rhodesias.

Sporting Prospect

For the sportsman, too, there is a wealth of promise. When I flew over the lake yachts were racing. A single boat brought in 133 fish this month. Kariba Lake will soon rival Victoria Falls as a centre for tourists and holiday-makers.

Its waters, now rising above scrub and forest at the rate of four inches a day, will not reach their full height until 1963. Were this dam situated at London Bridge the tail of the lake would be in Exeter.

There is much also at Kariba—in contrast to many schemes of this kind—in which the architect can take pride. The underground transformer hall, 537ft long, 55ft wide and 60ft high, with its curved roof of blue and white, has not only the distinction of size but the rarer distinction of beauty.

A European who has had a hand at the top in bringing architects and engineers together at Kariba told me he believed this was an outstanding example of co-operation between the two professions.

He had had the pitching of the town, with many of its houses perched or propped precariously on the surrounding hills. Into this, he said, two considerations had entered. The first was that, come hell or high water, the workers' town would be secure. The second was that only on these heights could dwellers catch what little breeze Kariba offers.

A COMMON GOAL

Yet none of these attainments conveys the true nature of Kariba's significance. Left to themselves, unseen by civilisation and untouched by politics, the races of the world—some of them hardly less temperamental than the Zambesi by repute—have worked in harmony.

They had a single goal and spared themselves nothing to achieve it, at the cost of 120 lives. Kariba is an exemplar of race relations in Africa.

It is not inappropriate that the Queen Mother will open this project a few days after Lord Monckton's Commission leaves the Federation. For a long time politics have dominated—or appeared in Salisbury and London to dominate—the future of the Rhodesias and Nyasaland. Kariba helps to restore perspective.

The future of Central Africa will not be shaped by politics alone, whatever the final shape of Federation. Its natural wealth, though far developed since Rhodes's day, still has about it the space, the possibilities and the grandeur which inspired his life work. Kariba is a reminder of them.

CONFRONTATION IN AFRICA

Problems of independence are giving way to problems of administration, and African politicians now face, not Colonial officials, but each other.

On the Comet's longest hop to Africa, Rome-Khartoum, the fretful middle-aged traveller may become aware about 1 a.m. that he has passed the point of no return. The sensation is being widely shared by the future rulers of East Africa.

The curtain is falling on constitution-making, or Act I. Already the slogans that went with its leading actors—"wind of change," "*Uhuru*," ". . . but always as friends"—begin to sound like last year's tunes on a juke box. Act II brings confrontation.

East Africa's politicians no longer face the Colonial Secretary in Lancaster House, but each other. It requires a tremendous effort to change postures, gestures, habits of mind and speech which have been assumed and practised so long as to become conditioned reflexes.

Confrontation brings its little local difficulties in every territory. In Kenya they can be seen at their worst. In Tanganyika Mr. Nyerere faces an early test in his own Parliament with a Citizenship Bill. In Uganda Bunyoro and Buganda dispute the "lost counties." In Nyasaland, where what confronts Dr. Banda is obscure, Sir Roy Welensky has been brought back into the ring for vigorous shadow-boxing.

These issues and not speeches in London now make East Africa's headlines. A new language is emerging, a new kind of politics. Thus, angrily facing an Opposition Member who had demanded on the Citizenship Bill the resignation and departure of non-Africans after independence, Mr. Nyerere declares:

> "My friends talk as if it is perfectly all right to discriminate against Europeans, Arabs and Indians and only wrong when you discriminate against black men. The crime in the world to-day is the oppression of man by man."

Fundamental Issues

Isolated, perhaps, but it carries the authentic ring of Act II about it, which some remarks after an earlier gathering of Nationalist leaders at Dar-es-Salaam lacked. Mr. Nyerere's phrase on that occasion about "ruthless imperialistic tricks" and Dr. Banda's "all of us agreed that imperialism must go" were snatches borrowed from earlier scenes to mask a somewhat barren event.

So Africa's political apprentices turn inwards, some after merely a few months both as Member and Minister.

To spend three weeks with members of two new Legislatures, discussing constitutional problems, brings no answer to any local difficulty; but it suggests one or two fundamental issues which in the longer run will count for much. At the head of a long list stand Civil Service administration and financial responsibility. They are inter-related.

We have laid tremendous stress on the Westminster model throughout Africa's new legislatures; and have excited Africans with romantic, if hazy, notions about it. What of the Whitehall model?

Though few Englishmen acknowledge it, having been brought up on jokes about the fountains in Trafalgar Square, stable rule depends on the experience and behaviour of a Ministry's Permanent Secretary as well as on the Mace and Erskine May. With their love of ceremonial, which Africa shares, the English see a romantic ideal in the Speaker's procession, but not in the mundane habits of the joint head of the Treasury. It is a serious deficiency.

Ultimately some of Africa's Governments are going ahead without the Mace or May and yet they may succeed. They will emphatically not succeed without a good Civil Service.

Confrontation is bringing acute awareness of this home to some Africans. It is striking to find that one or two perceive how much appallingly weak administration contributed to the United Nations' defeat and dishonour in the Congo. In Tanganyika Mr. Nyerere has openly appealed to senior British civil servants to save the government from "making a mess."

That an alarming gap might develop in competent administration after independence has been foreseen in London. There are plans to compensate Europeans and to Africanise provincial and central government.

Our failure is to convince ourselves and Africa that it takes much longer to make a reliable civil servant than a passable politician. Mr. Macleod was a Minister two years after entering Parliament. There can be few Permanent Secretaries in Whitehall who got to their chairs in much less than 20 years.

Fear of Civil Servants

Uganda, where on the whole things go smoothly, is a fair illustration. There are now something like 1,200 expatriate civil servants of which, at a guess, perhaps 20 to 30 per cent will leave when the country becomes independent. Africanisation in the middle and lower reaches proceeds steadily, possibly fast enough to persuade Africans to go easy with the top posts. The crucial point is who will be sitting in the chairs of under-secretaries and above after 1962.

The most experienced Africans count most heavily on the British civil servant and, though they find it a difficult topic to discuss, their anxieties about the future are palpable. The novices—and this is sadly true of Nyasaland—display poignant mistrust of Civil Service control. To them civil servants are not mentors, agents or friends, but dangerous rivals. What of the African head of a Treasury whose African Chancellor sees in him a rival?

In Uganda the prospect, which is not singular in East Africa, is plain enough. There is no African of Permanent Secretary calibre within sight, and they will be lucky to have half a dozen by 1965.

An unpredictable number of civil servants may be persuaded to stay because the political atmosphere is relatively cordial. Elsewhere, grudgingly accepted, publicly pinpricked by a minority, they may elect to pack their bags. Much of Africa's future is being decided now in quiet, anxious family talks about the future among British administrators.

On this standard of administration hangs financial responsibility. The African tends to be vaguer about public money than we are—particularly large sums. Up to now he has not, in all conscience, had great inducement to be prudent, indeed the reverse.

Stricter Accounting

A host of liberal international agencies, apart from the British Treasury and Colonial Development Corporation, appear ready at hand to drop in a million here or there, with surprisingly few questions asked. Such sources offer a reassuring prospect, but they are not conducive to strict accounting.

No doubt we shall have to continue to be reassuring for some time to come. The bill for reassuring Kenya, now blinking at bankruptcy, is in the post. But a new fact confronts us: increasingly the competence or otherwise of Africans in financial administration is going to touch the British taxpayer's pocket. Loans will have to be properly serviced and capital projects at least related to our own principles, if they are to have our money.

Puzzling and painful adventures await some African politicians who, momentarily dazzled by emoluments of £1,000 a year as M.P.s and £2,000 or £3,000 as Ministers, reckon that the future beckons with a golden finger.

In Uganda no African pays income tax. Between the new African Minister with £3,200 a year net, and the British Minister with £3,200 a year gross a world of sad experience lies ahead.

It is not unknown for Russia to enter arguments about finance. "We shall not wish to approach them but failing all else . . ." But the Communists make hard bargains, and, when they do fulfil all their promises, the terms make our financial arrangements look like charity. A few intelligent Africans have discovered this.

Trade, they say, is better than aid and it is not only the rulers of East Africa who will have to awake to the economic facts of life. It is a shock to discover how many British commercial interests seem to think that their performance ended with Act I. They are not even rehearsing for Act II.

It is natural that British boards, surveying Central and East Africa, and after a year of news bulletins from the Congo, should view future investment cautiously. But this is not the root of the difficulty. Because British administration is primarily involved in East and Central Africa, British commerce puts the risk of enterprise higher than any other country. In parts of East Africa British enterprise seems to be conditioned by headlines about Kenya.

"Uncertainty" does not unduly worry Germans, Frenchmen, Italians or Japanese. They are not politically implicated. A little ferreting in commercial circles establishes a disquieting paradox. Our past and present responsibility for Africa is not enhancing but positively diminishing our future commercial prospects.

Meeting Local Needs

Nor is that all. Let it be charitably assumed that insecurity justifies a commercial "freeze," even that to some British manufacturers the markets of East Africa seem a bagatelle. It remains to discover why, for example, the motor vehicles of East Africa are predominantly German, French and American.

The reason is not political, but technical, and since it enters a wider field it is worth noting. Apart from durability—not a bull point in Africa for British cars, excepting the Land Rover—the habit of British manufacturers of changing models annually (for the Jones family?) makes their products in East Africa unacceptable.

Six models in seven years require a reserve of spare parts which few dealers will contemplate and few British firms can maintain. For the unchanging Volkswagen and Peugeot they stock and use the same spares for years. Moreover, firms which do not re-jig for new models annually plough a little more into the value of the model, and that is noticeable on the price tags.

In search of the cause of our poor showing in East Africa many explanations are offered—the dock strike, bad salesmanship, bad servicing—compared with enviable German arrangements. The simple fact emerges that we cannot or will not apply production to local customers' needs.

Some in East Africa declare we have indeed passed the point of no return. I think not. Those whose ears are not too sensitive to noises from the Congo and Kenya are already assembling in the wings with offerings for a consumer market in East and Central Africa which, if not comparable to the Common Market, is not to be sniffed at.

For those with steady nerves it is a prospect to weigh, even with audacity. It is our portion of confrontation.

January 1977

LET RHODESIA CHOOSE

Mr RICHARD's perpetual motion round Southern Africa and the daily reflections of his mood—now surly, now smiling—obscure a stunning and grim reality. The British Government, whose day for shaping overseas events is widely supposed to be spent, now carries more responsibility for Southern Africa's future than anybody else. All Mr RICHARD offers is cynical proposals acceptable to no one except possibly Mr MUGABE and friends. The crux is this. Who, after Mr SMITH, is to be the Black leader of Rhodesia and how is this choice to be made? Mr RICHARD offers no clue, yet there can be no progress in Rhodesia, there can be no transitional stage there—with or without a British High Commissioner and assorted councils—until that is settled.

The five front line Presidents have put their weight (probably with varying emphasis) behind Mr MUGABE. He would not be the popular choice among Rhodesia's Blacks or Whites. Nor would Mr NKOMO. The popular choice appears to be, though it is hard to be sure, Bishop MUZEREWA. Two points may be made here. First, it is dissension between Africans on this crucial choice of leader and not the intransigence of Mr SMITH which is now the stumbling block. Secondly, the greatest single threat to Rhodesia's future is again, not Mr SMITH, but the acceptance of a figure preferred and nominated by African leaders outside Rhodesia which ran contrary to the wishes of the African majority inside Rhodesia. The resultant conflict could well lead to the situation which Dr KISSINGER last summer moved to avert: chaos in Rhodesia and the consolidation of Marxist influence in that region.

It is of course possible that Mr SMITH will try to resolve the deadlock by taking some initiatives of his own, by taking Black Rhodesian leaders into partnership before bowing out. His conciliatory moves taken while Mr RICHARD has been touring could pave the way to this. In many ways it would be the best solution. But any such moves would be rejected at once by the five Presidents, now the ringmasters. No initiative in which Mr SMITH had a hand would be acceptable to them. And that could be decisive because the British Government has allowed the Presidents to secure a dominant role.

When Mr SMITH submitted to Dr KISSINGER's terms he did so believing that the five Presidents had accepted the arrangements. He may have been misled—or have misled himself. What is certain is that the Presidents, astonished by the apparent ease with which Mr SMITH had been manoeuvred into submission, regretted that more had not been exacted from him and determined to exact it. Apprehensive of appearing to side with Mr SMITH, even in equity, the Government encourages them.

The only way now to recover the initiative and to secure a leader of Rhodesia's choice is to test Rhodesia's opinion. Bishop MUZEREWA has called for a referendum. That would take a long time, long enough perhaps for dangerous pressures to develop on sections of Rhodesian opinion. Mr VORSTER is thought at this stage strongly to favour a Commission on the lines of the Pearce Commission as the best means of giving Rhodesian opinion expression. The front line Presidents would oppose that. On its record so far, so would the British Government because it is fundamentally (and wrongly) more concerned with propitiating African opinion outside Rhodesia than inside it. But the choice has to be made.

The hardest and right course is to incur displeasure now in order to secure the right choice and the best chance of an orderly future for Rhodesia—and Zambia too. The easiest course is to continue drift towards dissension or disaster in Rhodesia—perhaps in all Southern Africa.

September 1987

THE WELL OF LIFE

*In the vast, lonely region of south-west Ethiopia, a network of deep wells
has supported man since time immemorial. W. F. Deedes watches the
remarkable daily ritual of the Borana people and the ingenious efforts of
aid organisations to improve the quality of a life lived on the narrowest
of margins.*

We saw the long column of dust a mile away. As we drew closer, it
became not one column but several—countless cattle moving in file
across the arid plain. 'There is activity here today,' said Santha Faiia,
who knows the region, gathering up her cameras. After two days'
travel south from Addis Ababa, down the road that eventually reaches
Nairobi, we had come to the Borana wells.

The Boranas are a pastoral, semi-nomadic tribe, who occupy
6,000 inhospitable square miles or so in south-west Ethiopia. One
feature distinguishes them from all other East African pastoral
societies. During dry seasons, the entire human and livestock population becomes wholly dependent on a network of 40 or so groups of
wells, most of them very ancient indeed. Some are crater wells, some
are shallow wells; but the predominant group, the group which
catches the eye, are the deep (*tula*) wells. It was these astonishing
feats of primitive engineering I had travelled 4,000 miles to see.

It is rare today to come across a scene of human activity that
could well be unchanged since the earliest years of Christendom.
Nobody knows how old some of these wells are. Many were abandoned, buried and lost long ago. Others have fallen into disrepair;
and one of the contributions made by CARE International, working
with the local Ministry of Agriculture and the International Livestock
Centre for Africa, is to get some of these opened up and working
again.

It takes a year, more likely two, to dig a new *tula* well. All work
is done by hand. The men dig, the women carry away the spoil in
sacks. The Boranas themselves believe that the *tula* wells were dug
by the Wardai tribe, who now live in Kenya. When the Borana took
control of the area in the 16th century, so the legend runs, the wells

were divided among their clans. Every well still has a name, which is usually linked to the clan that uses it.

A considerable effort of imagination is needed to grasp the workings of a classical *tula* well. On that first morning, which was spent at the Dubluk group of 16 or so deep wells, it took me a full half-hour on the ground to discover how the system worked. Imagine, first, the deep but irregular shaft (*ella*) of a well, in which the water may lie at a depth of 50 feet. To bring that water to the top, a chain of men is spaced at intervals of roughly six feet down the well. Supported by projections or wooden struts across the void, they rapidly and, it seems, tirelessly pass the water up from hand to hand in small leather buckets (*okoles*).

That is the first stage. Then, at the top of the well the water is tipped from the last man's bucket into a holding pond (*fetchana*) just above his head. Standing in this holding pond, usually the size of a small garden pool, two or sometimes four men or women throw the water one final stage higher into long watering troughs (*nanigas*), while chanting loudly and in rhythm to one another and to the men in the well. From these low troughs a dozen camels, a score of cattle, or approximately 40 small stock can drink at any one time.

These simple, earth-built troughs are set up in large excavated watering areas (*dargula*) which themselves may be 30 feet below the ground. The animals approach them down long, narrow ramps cut from the ground level, their movement controlled by herdsmen standing at the entrance to the ramp.

One must pause and deal with questions which will have occurred to anyone who has read this far. Why are there no engine-driven pumps, or even windmills? Why this enormous expenditure of manpower and endurance—it may take up to 40 men and women in perpetual motion to keep a deep well flowing towards the animals at a peak hour—when modern technology is readily available?

A part of the answer, as the agricultural scientist Noel Cossins observed a few years back after studying these wells, is that the arid regions of Africa are littered with broken-down diesel engines. 'Maintaining pumps and engines in isolated areas where technicians are in short supply is not easy,' he wrote. In this vast, lonely region, there are not many technicians.

Furthermore, at most of these wells the water supply is limited. After a day's watering, it may take a day or two to restore the water levels. There have been signs of wells becoming exhausted. Thus the numbers of livestock that can be kept by the Boranas are to some extent regulated by their capacity to raise enough water. That is important, for even if mechanical pumps were kept working and the wells could feed them, a supply of more water would lead to the keeping of larger numbers of livestock than the surrounding vegetation can support.

The Boranas cherish their cattle. Milk is their staple diet. Prestige is measured by the head of cattle a man possesses. Bullocks are therefore not readily sold for meat—until the need to purchase what little there is of other commodities becomes pressing. So these people and their livestock live on the slightest of margins. Much of the work of CARE International and other related organisations is given to overcoming seasonal shortages of forage as well as water.

Even that is not the complete answer. The working of these wells, the daily marshalling of endless columns of livestock—most of them about two hours' march from a well—enters a certain routine and purpose into the lives of these people. It calls for wisdom from relief workers who are striving to increase the narrow margins to grasp this, and not unduly to disturb a timeless rhythm of life.

What stretches the imagination is the planning and organisation needed among primitive people to bring these innumerable columns of animals to the right place at the right hour—and in the right order. For within the system there are priorities. The horses, which are kept mainly for reasons of prestige, have first place. The camels, most of which are owned, not by Boranas but by the small minority of Gabbras, come last. The camels are sometimes used for their milk, but along with the donkeys, are primarily beasts of burden.

In a dry season, the cattle will normally be brought to the wells once in three days, sheep and goats once in five, horses every other day, and camels at anything between seven and 14 days. One afternoon at the wells in the Medecho crater, I watched the arrival of a column of perhaps 200 camels. Trained by custom, they stood patiently a shortly distance from the ramp of the well. I wondered if they could smell the water.

Figures are hard to come by, but a detailed study was carried out in 1982, covering 23 of the 26 well groups in the Borana area. The total of 168 individual wells was found to be the sole source of water in the dry seasons for 219,000 cattle, 80,000 sheep and goats, 4,000 camels, 14,600 horses and donkeys, and a human population of about 60,000. It was further calculated that to meet these needs, the wells would have to supply about a million gallons in an eight-hour day for up to five months a year, or more than 5,000 gallons per well per day.

This is a formidable task to organise on a daily basis. Because it demands such a high degree of co-operation, it contributes also to the social cohesion of an otherwise rootless people. Each well has an *aba ella* or father of the well, who is responsible for its upkeep and use, and an *aba hirega* appointed by the wells council (*cora ella*) who supervises daily use. Control is in the hands of the wells council, but it rests with the judiciary or *gada* council to punish offenders by excluding them from specific wells. Total exclusion, the harshest punishment available—ponder for a moment the consequences for the animals—is rare.

Without disturbing the timeless rhythm, traditions and organisation of all this, there remains a good deal that international organisations such as CARE can do to help the Boranas. For one thing they can organise the rehabilitation of wells which have fallen into disrepair. When all watering troughs in the wells were composed of dried mud, time and water would be constantly wasted as the trough walls crumbled under the pressure of animals. To replace them with stone or cement increases efficiency and finds favour with the Boranas.

Then, crucial to the wells system, there are the *okoles* or buckets, highly valued objects, skilfully made of buffalo or giraffe hides. A finished *okole* costs about £15, and a good one will last for 10 years or so. There are, however, no buffalo or giraffe in Ethiopia, and in any case hunting is prohibited there and in Kenya. Thus the *okoles* deteriorate faster than they can be replaced and a good deal of water is wasted. It would not be easy to procure sufficient hides for the Borana from elsewhere, but it illustrates the sort of assistance that is most needed.

In such small ways, improvements can be made to the water output. The key is to offer tools or hides for sale, if they are needed, but always to depend ultimately on the efforts of the people themselves. What CARE calls its Sidamo Rangelands project embraces not only the rehabilitation of 25 Borana wells but the installation of a dozen water tanks of about 25,000-gallon capacity, the selling of about £35,000 worth of tools, and the building of a hundred grain stores. Thus are the margins against sudden disaster widened.

The productivity of this predominantly agricultural country is falling behind the growth of its population. Future disasters are already written on the wall. To reverse the trend calls for heroic efforts, diplomacy, patience and, for field workers, constant discomfort. Money matters a great deal, because it can buy lorries, trucks and land cruisers, and finance more expertise in the field. But the lesson to be learned from the wells is that relief in a country like Ethiopia amounts to far more than 'simply throwing things at people', as one field worker put it. 'What would happen if, by some miracle, enough water could be kept flowing through the pipes to save them all this labour?' I asked. 'A great many of them would get drunk,' was the unromantic response. Those who toil unceasingly to make the wells of Borana a degree more productive have to keep their feet on the ground.

March 1988

WHAT SANCTIONS REALLY MEAN
TO SOUTH AFRICA

Liberal orthodoxy continues to insist that trade sanctions and industrial disinvestment will hasten the end of apartheid. But W. F. Deedes, who has just returned from Johannesburg, found evidence to the contrary

It is well that those on Washington's Capitol Hill who are just now calling for a second round in the disinvestment and sanctions campaign against South Africa do not have to present an annual report and accounts to shareholders. They would be found to have issued a false prospectus, to have been trading at a loss and now to be bankrupt.

A fresh look at the present state of South Africa's economy and business confirms that not only are sanctions and disinvestment in South Africa failing to do what was promised of them. They are rapidly bringing about results exactly opposite to those desired.

Disinvestment by American companies had enriched a lot of white South Africans, who took over businesses at bargain basement prices. It destroyed black jobs. It dumped the Sullivan Code which imposed conditions on American companies for treatment of their workers. It killed multi-million dollar social programmes. It removed America's voice from South Africa's affairs and weakened the liberal influence.

Politically, the consequences of this economic war are proving even more disastrous. They led directly to the recent rise in support for the Conservative and extreme Right-wing HNP parties, which have supplanted the Liberals as the principal opposition to Government. The consequence of that has been to put reform into mothballs. The last reformist speech by President Botha was in January 1986.

The cost to America herself has not been light. Her relations with South Africa are now at zero. Japan has moved in behind her to become South Africa's largest trading partner. I discount tales of intense diplomatic activity between South Africa and the

Soviet Union (attributable, I suspect, to a desire to aggravate the State Department), but there is growing commercial traffic between them.

The Japanese are under increasing pressure, particularly from Washington, to stop taking advantage of the situation in South Africa. They will not be easily persuaded. Japanese vehicles, for example, have become part of the blacks' biggest commercial success story—the growth of the South African Black Taxi Association.

Begun in 1979 by 21 taxi drivers, SABTA now represents 45,000 minibus owners, 55,000 other employees and transports half a million passengers a day. It is the largest private-sector consumer of petrol, lubricants, tyres and spare parts in the country.

To damage South Africa to the extent the campaigners desire, it would be necessary to blockade the ports and sever telecommunications. Short of that, I foresee no crisis for South Africa's economy between now and the mid-1990s. More than half South Africa's imports, being high value and low bulk, are in fact unsanctionable. It is impossible to police the export of diamonds.

Adverse winds have actually improved the position of many South African companies. They have led to new disciplines and tighter ships. The dangerous year was 1986, when there was a huge outflow of nervous capital. Thanks to the talents of Dr de Kock at the Reserve Bank, that situation was repaired. There are now positive signs of renewed confidence; indeed a main private anxiety among those commanding the heights of the economy is that the Nationalist Government will take it as a signal that all is well and best left alone.

In the long term, certain adverse consequences will flow. The capital shortage will make itself felt and with American ties severed, South Africa will suffer from being outside the mainstream of modern technology. But that is not going to happen this year or next. So much for Neil Kinnock's most recent and fatuous observation to a South African publication: "The motivation for sanctions is neither vindictiveness nor vengeance, but speedy and certain change."

It will be argued that the importance of sanctions lies not so much in their practical effects as in their symbolic importance. That would ring truer were countries like Canada and Australia, strong supporters of sanctions, not palpably influenced by knowing that South Africa's loss is their gain. Australia is in open competition for South Africa's coal exports. It would ring truer, again, if America's legislators were not so careful to exclude strategic minerals from their hit list.

As some South African witnesses in Washington last week, for hearings on the comprehensive Anti-Apartheid Act, reminded us, every main change for the good in South Africa in recent years has been brought about by economic realities. Economic growth erodes apartheid.

Sanctions have slowed down but not stopped the rise in South Africa's economic life of black owners, managers and above all entrepreneurs. That is where the political leverage will come from.

The campaign against South Africa's economy assists the Government in several ways. It gives them every pretext to centralise power. It offers an excuse for going slow on education, housing and other social programmes for the blacks. And it slows down the dismantling of the apartheid apparatus to meet the demands of industry and commerce. When booming industry called for more skilled black labour, pass laws had to go.

The black trade unions are in a harsh dilemma. Sanctions and disinvestment cost their members jobs. When the Americans left, their South African successors tightened business up and shed labour. Black union bargaining power has been weakened. Yet for political reasons the black unions cannot publicly oppose what they know to be most damaging to their interests.

As America is propelled towards yet stronger measures against South Africa, I see fresh perils arising for the West. My inquiries in South Africa leave no doubt that nations are already cheating on a grand scale. The stronger sanctions become, the more profitable it will be to cheat. It is not difficult. This is a highly sophisticated world economy. Cheating over South Africa, I predict, is going to become progressively more damaging to international relations.

With supreme irony, Botha and his companions in the Government strive to prove that action against them is wholly justified. Just as things calmed down, and some of the world entered second thoughts about this pyrrhic economic war, Botha and company gratuitously banned black organisations, picked a ludicrous quarrel with Archbishop Tutu, and appeared eager to hang six Sharpeville blacks.

It is not wickedness. Cut off from the world, they can no longer follow international winds and tides. Between Western pressures and their own politics they are effectively locked in. We have sterilised political possibilities in South Africa. In the years far ahead of us, historians will look back at this and say of us, this was their silliest hour.

November 1988

JUST LIKE OLD TIMES

In 1935 W. F. Deedes was despatched to north Africa to cover the Abyssinian war for the Morning Post. There he became a model for Boot of the Beast, hero of Evelyn Waugh's "Scoop". Half a century later, he retraces his steps through the shifting sands of Ethiopia

"For lust of knowing what should not be known, / we take the Golden Road to Samarkand." Rather grandiloquently, I thought of Flecker's lines as we climbed the Ethiopian mountain road from Dire Dawa towards the walled city of Harar, for centuries an independent Emirate and a city state.

I had last travelled this road early one morning in November 1935, when some of us believed that Italy's Marshal Graziani, later Viceroy of Abyssinia, was about to roll up the Abyssinian southern front towards Jijiga and Harar. We were wrong. Graziani did not get there until early in 1936, by when most of us had been recalled by our newspapers. But the hospital in Harar, I recollect, was filled with Abyssinian wounded, most of them victims of gas or machine-gunning from the air. Two young Spanish women journalists, who had travelled with the Times, Reuter's and myself, took a look at the hospital and wired their Madrid papers not to expect news for a while. Then they rolled up their sleeves and went to work—not in the wards, but in the corridors into which the wounded had overflowed.

So here we are, 50 years on, in Harar again on a golden afternoon, searching for traces of times past. When Evelyn Waugh first saw Harar at the time of the Emperor's coronation in 1930 he was enchanted by its magic. Returning five years later for the war with Italy, he was disappointed. Much of the old beauty, he thought, had faded. Therefore I did not expect too much, and was well content with what I found.

"Do not walk in the walled city alone," they said at the British Embassy in Addis Ababa. Whether dangerous or not, it is pointless to do so. Harar's remaining treasures, its historic houses and minute bazaars, its mosques and few remaining workshops are found through unpromising chinks and narrow corridors of stone which the casual visitor will not discover without a guide.

I had chosen Harar for a visit, not wholly out of nostalgia, but because I thought it would illustrate the immunity of an ancient and remote people from ephemeral regimes, such as the present Mengistu government which rules from Addis Ababa. Capitals tell us little about a nation; least of all in Marxist states like Ethiopia, where there has to be much outward show of revolutionary slogans, garish arcades, hideous banners and giant pictures of the boss, in order to make clear to visitors who is in charge.

The Mengistu regime will be but a short chapter in the thousand years of Harar, still predominantly Moslem, as it has been since the city was founded by Arabs from across the Red Sea. Some say Islam was introduced there by Sheikh Hussein, after the flight of Mohammed from Mecca; true or not, it was certainly done a long time ago.

We returned to the walled city at dusk, just after the hour of prayer, to see the Hyena Man. It did not seem to me as we drove down the uneven streets through the throng that much could have been changed by Mengistu, or by the British (during our war) or the Italians whom the British evicted; or by the Emperor Menelik II (who in uniting Ethiopia incorporated Harar), or by the earlier Galla hordes or Egyptian invaders.

Except, of course, the Hyena Man. He was a new phenomenon. I remembered hearing in 1935 the nightly chorus from hyenas around Harar, a deeply unattractive sound. We were to hear it again that evening. In an open space, just outside one of the walled city's six gates, there was a man tossing chunks of raw meat to a ring of 20 or more excited hyenas. As a special favour, he threw a gobbet in the dust about six feet from my feet. I felt it would be bad form to move back; the hyenas thought it risky to move forward. Eyeball to eyeball, as it were.

Hyenas are unsuitable pets. It struck me that Hararis might resent this man behaving like a huntsman in kennels. On the contrary, small appreciative groups joined me. When the basket was empty, my guide moved a short vote of thanks. The Hyena Man, he said, had paid for this meat out of his own pocket. This he did to secure foreign currency for his government from visitors. There was something distressingly ironic about forking out cash to keep hyenas in red meat, in a country where one is aghast at the scale of famine. I rewarded him suitably, resolving to give rather more to Unicef on return to Addis.

What else had changed since 1935? The semi-metalled road between Dire Dawa and Harar, which was there (unexpectedly) before the Italian road-builders arrived, is busier, much of it with Army traffic—which perhaps explains why passes to Harar are not given on the nod. The many soldiers I saw in and around Harar were far different from the barefoot warriors we watched marching against Mussolini, brandishing often useless firearms and proclaiming eagerness to get at the enemy's throat. Today's Ethiopian soldier in his olive green drill and ankle boots has a short back and sides and modern arms, which I did not venture to inspect but surmised had come from Russia.

During lunch in the Ras Hotel just outside Harar, the guide became fretful at the waiters' inattention. But I had observed a large screened-off portion of the dining room to and from which there was much bustling service. "Party or Army," I said conspiratorially to my guide, who affected not to hear. Lunch over, a score of smartly dressed officers hurried out—all of them looking good Camberley material.

Ethiopia is bleeding itself to death with its war in the North. Mengistu came close to admitting as much in his speech to the Ninth Plenum of the Central Committee while I was in Addis Ababa. The war against Eritrea, begun in the 1960s, now the biggest in Africa, has pushed up Ethiopia's crippling defence budget to half the Government's total income.

Perhaps the Russians are signalling a desire to spend less in future on equipping Ethiopia to fight this war. Perhaps they will put more weight behind a political settlement. They have spent about £3 billion on arms for Ethiopia, none of which they will see back, in return for this Marxist fiefdom in Africa. They have certainly conveyed to Ethiopia that undiluted Marxism is a medicine which modern experience has shown to be harmful to health; and there are some signs the advice is being heeded.

I do not think that the regime of Comrade Mengistu Haile-Mariam, General Secretary of the Central Committee of the Workers' Party of Ethiopia, President of the People's Democratic Republic of Ethiopia and Commander-in-Chief of the Revolutionary Armed Forces, is going to be isolated from that wind of change which blew through Africa 30 years ago, and is now blowing through the world of Marxism.

*

Such matters, however, lay outside my immediate pilgrimage, and did not unduly distract me from the fading glories of Harar, few of which any of us except Evelyn Waugh bothered to examine in 1935. In one of Harar's small antique shops, there is a list of the 72 Emirs of Harar who ruled these parts between AD 969 and 1886. Waugh declared that the Emir's family showed signs of decadence when Sir Richard Burton—their first white visitor—appeared during the middle of the last century.

"The Hararis," he wrote, "naturally look back to the days of their independence as a golden age, the Bagdad of Haroun el Raschid." The kingdom was savaged by wars that raged during the 16th and 17th centuries and it ended with its capture by the Shoans under Menelik II. The close of the golden age was speeded, too, by the advent of the Franco-Ethiopian railway at the turn of the century.

Originally, this line was to join Harar to the French port of Djibouti—where in 1935 we waited in blistering heat for the bi-weekly train to Addis Ababa. The project faltered, and when it was resumed ran direct to Addis. Harar had flourished because it lay athwart the camel trains from the coast. They made it a centre of trade. They produced people like the young Frenchman, Rimbaud, famous among smugglers. When the railway diverted this rich traffic, as Waugh put it, the Shoan rulers fastened themselves upon the dying body and drained it of vitality.

Nevertheless I found specks of gold. The open markets at all the walled city's gates must have been there for centuries. There are small places which display the finely wrought filigree silver and handcrafted basketry of dazzling colours, for which Harar is famous. There are still one or two workshops where this is done; and there is just one book-binder, remainder of a once flourishing trade. There are marks of grandeur in Rimbaud's house and in the older house of Ras Makonnen, father of the last Emperor, Haile Selassie, who did some of his learning in Rimbaud's house when it was a French school.

This is not a conformist people. How does one explain, for instance, the vast contraband market in Dire Dawa, the so-called Taiwan market, where all imaginable goods are sold? It is Aladdin's cave. What is it doing in a Marxist state? (I suspect, providing jobs which the state cannot find.) Here is the wealth, much of it still borne from the coast by camel trains, that made Harar rich. Here is private enterprise on a grand scale.

Bale upon bale of beautiful materials, radio cassette recorders, shoes and slippers of all shapes and sizes, Johnson's baby powder, cami-knickers, coconut oil, "brandy for the parson, 'baccy for the clerk . . ." all are here in rich profusion.

Fatuously, I tripped round the place, head bowed under the rough awnings, supposing that I was on forbidden territory, that I might well be caught in a raid, to the subsequent embarrassment of our excellent ambassador. There had been such an episode in 1935, when Waugh, Stuart Emeny of the News Chronicle and I had made a dash for the northern front, were arrested and returned to the capital in disgrace. We got a sorrowful rocket from our man in Addis, Sir Sidney Barton. So as we went round this den of sin, I protested loudly that we were only seeking new shoes for my guide— he had split his. Nobody paid any attention to me.

When, for old times' sake, I arranged to return from Dire Dawa to Addis Ababa on the railway, it did not enter my mind that it could be *less* comfortable than in 1935. Formerly a Franco-Abyssinian enterprise, it appears to have lost the French interest. The journey began at 6am with brisk fighting at the station entrance in Dire Dawa between those with and those without tickets. Just like old times.

I held a first-class ticket—so that my guide and I occupied the front two of eight seats, sharing the other six with heavily armed soldiers and their friends. A crate of beer and two of Coca Cola lasted until elevenses time. Thereafter we lived off the land, so to speak, most of my travelling companions preferring to chew leaves of a plant resembling *bhang*. Thus, when we finally reached Addis Ababa at 7.30pm the floor of our compartments resembled a vegetable market after a brisk morning's trading.

One of the main changes in Ethiopia since I last travelled there is the emergence of a middle class; and more, of a thin band of intelligent and professional young men and women, well versed in modern technologies. The tragedy is that so many of them have left the country, and others are eager to go. The total exodus is put at not far short of a million—there are 15,000 Ethiopians in Washington alone. No nation can flourish when so many of its intelligent people want to leave.

The burgeoning talent still there faces formidable obstacles. Ethiopia is in crisis because the population is growing faster than its capacity to support itself. It cannot all be blamed on Mengistu: the man of my time, Emperor Haile Selassie, fell to the revolution because of famine.

Much of Ethiopia's soil has been starved and wasted. Yields are patchy, but in some places down. That is one reason why so many will continue to starve unless we can get more food in there. We shall be in the business of relief there for a long time to come. At the end of 1935, some of us left Abyssinia to its fate in the hands of the advancing Italians. How sad now to leave this beautiful country, and its remarkable people, to a worse fate, wrought very largely by their own hands.

SALVATION IN A DESERT OF DESPAIR

W. F. Deedes shares the struggle of relief workers in Ethiopia striving on behalf of the rest of the world in the cause of humanity to ease the pain of a people who, whether the rains come or not, are dwelling perpetually on the edge of disaster

These are anxious times for governments such as Ethiopia's which lie on the periphery of the Soviet Union's dissolving empire. The Cubans have packed up and gone home. There is an impression of outposts being recalled. The Soviet Union has had enough of Ethiopia's appalling war with Eritrea, on which it has spent millions for arms. So has the United States, which has spent even more millions on relieving the consequent suffering.

Imagine the condition of a country whose gross national product is £63 a head, the lowest in the world—and which has been devoting between 50 and 60 per cent of that meagre product to a war which has lasted for 24 years. It is, furthermore, an agrarian country in which population rises remorselessly and food production falls. Between 1980 and 1987 agricultural production in Ethiopia actually went down by 2.1 per cent.

So these are also anxious times for the world's relief organisations in Ethiopia who battle against heavy odds. Regardless of politics or ideologies or regimes, they must strive in the cause of humanity to reduce the vulnerability of a people who, whether it rains or not, dwell perpetually on the edge of disaster. There are no margins in Ethiopia.

There is room for two views about this relief work. One, to which I have inclined in the past, is that relief resources applied in a country, where the Government seeks so persistently to cut off its nose to spite its face, are better expended elsewhere. The second, to which after recent travels in Ethiopia I now incline, is that those who work uncomplainingly for the relief organisations in such utterly discouraging conditions restore something to the human spirit which, in the relatively affluent West, we seem to have lost.

It was a salutary experience, though not a comfortable one, to

live for a few days with Mr Chaudhary in Yabelo, close to Ethiopia's southern border with Kenya. Mr Chaudhary, lately from India,
is co-ordinator of a project designed by the international relief
organisation CARE to give the semi-nomadic pastoralists in the
Sidamo region a degree more food security through self-help and so
reduce their dependence on food aid.

The worldly possessions of Mr and Mrs Chaudhary—whose
curries at the evening meal were the high point of our day—have
been awaiting clearance in the Addis Ababa customs for three and a
half months. He makes no special complaint of this, murmuring that
work in the field for CARE calls for dedication, but apologising for
any resulting discomforts visited on guests in his humble abode. Mrs
Chaudhary seemed less cheerful, and with reason. I wondered what
she felt about the cold shower and the broken lavatory that has to be
flushed with buckets of water, and the mosquitoes which, at dusk,
pounced through a small hole in the mesh that constituted the sitting
room's window.

In Ethiopia under the overall direction of a self-effacing American, Mr Scott Faiia, CARE has a total of 14 expatriates working
with 560 nationals (75 per cent of them in the field) on six main
projects, at the cost this year of about £9 million. As I watched the
troubled face of Mrs Chaudhary, it struck me that, unless relief work
is to be restricted to celibates, there will often be a partner, not
necessarily dedicated, who must share the strains of work in the field
at remote places like Yabelo.

During our daily travels of 200 miles or so with Mr Chaudhary,
there were other hard lessons to be learned about relief work in such
places. There are, first of all, local officials and administrators to
placate. They are not unco-operative, but they serve an authoritarian
system which often employs people more for their political creden-
tials than for their practical experience. "The Government *is* trying
to do something," a professor at Addis Ababa University later
observed to me, "but not the right things."

The hurdle with the bureaucracy having been crossed or circum-
vented, the relief worker must next seek the cooperation of the
peasant, who represents 85 per cent of Ethiopia's agrarian economy.
In the Sidamo region, CARE is dealing with about 25,000 semi-
nomadic pastoralists, whose livelihoods depend on camels, cattle and
small stock. The immediate aim, after the disastrous droughts of
1984 and 1987, is to improve elementary water supplies, drawn solely

from wells, and to improve forage resources which, in the two dry seasons that occur down there, may run pitiably short.

Hundreds of thousand of acres in Ethiopia have been reduced to dust by over-use. The rate of deforestation—wood being the only fuel available to Ethiopia's 44 million people—alarms everyone, including the Government.

Replanting is a slow and difficult process. The peasant is not drawn to it. "We will plant four million trees," a Minister says. "Let us start with one million and try to get a higher survival rate," say the experts. That is only the beginning of the argument.

Most of us think of relief in terms of doling out grain or milk powder. In times of famine or great movements of refugees, there is no alternative; but in the long term, it solves nothing. The next step, fostered by CARE and kindred organisations, therefore is to give food in return for work. The final step, greatly to oversimplify a highly complex and uncertain process, is to persuade the peasant to work on projects, not because he gets food in return, but because he perceives the benefit to him of what he is doing.

The task, in short, is to wean people from free hand-outs to participation in reviving slender local physical assets. And this has to be done without unduly upsetting cherished local traditions or disturbing the unseen social rhythms of an ancient people. If new work is carried out on water or grain storage, if tools are bought, the community that benefits is called upon by CARE to pay the cost.

That sounds well, and it happens. But to tour a Borana or a Gabbra village in the Sidamo region is to go back to what in our West was the primitive life of centuries ago. These people have *nothing*—save their precarious flocks. In the whole country there is only one doctor to every 65,000 of the population—and there will not be as many as that in the Sidamo region. "Over a thousand miles," said Scott Faiia to me with great wisdom, "we take one step."

Among Ethiopia's teeming refugees—from genocide in the Sudan, from war in the North, from Somalia and elsewhere, the task is more daunting, the wounds harder to staunch. One of CARE's tasks is to truck daily over rough territory a million litres of water to keep refugees in the Ogaden alive.

In Ethiopia now, one rediscovers a serious fact of life. It is often in the darkest vales that we find the human spirit at its brightest. We may, from comfortable chairs before our television screens, find reason to disapprove of aid to a country like Ethiopia. But we should not disparage the spirit of men and women drawn in utterly dispiriting circumstances to serve humanity in need.

As we bumped across vile and apparently endless tracks searching for wells in our robust land cruiser, Flecker's lines entered my head:

> Always a little further; it may be
> Across that last blue mountain barred with snow,
> Across that angry or that glimmering sea.

In New York, I am told, as many as 200 people a week apply to join CARE international. For their sake, that city may be saved.

SOUTH AFRICA'S "LAST CHANCE"

Today Archbishop Desmond Tutu will ask the South African President, F. W. De Klerk, to spell out the "drastic change" he says he wants for the country. W. F. Deedes talks to one of those who says de Klerk should be given a chance. He is Chief Mangosuthu Buthelezi, leader of the Zulu organisation Inkatha—and a man reviled by radicals because he presides over the apartheid statelet of Kwazulu

As I left the Chelsea home of Sir Laurens van der Post, after an hour's talk there with Dr Mangosuthu Buthelezi, Chief Minister of Kwazulu in South Africa and president of Inkatha, an irreverent thought entered my mind. What a pity it is that the world hears so much from Archbishop Tutu, and so little from Chief Buthelezi.

The thought arose after our talk, not because Buthelezi is widely recognised as a force for moderation in South Africa—for which he is mistrusted and frequently reviled by the militants; but because he strikes one as having a far clearer vision of the true difficulties that lie ahead in South Africa than the archbishop and his friends—or indeed than most people in the West.

"Perhaps," says Buthelezi sadly, "the West in the end will prove to be more efficient at protesting about apartheid than actually doing something to assist in the process of ensuring that apartheid will be followed by something multi-party, multi-racial democracy that will *last*." That final word goes to the core of his anxiety about the future. Repeatedly in our talk, Buthelezi referred to the bloodshed in Angola and Mozambique.

His nightmare is the fratricide among blacks which might so easily persist after a settlement in South Africa. "By far the greatest stumbling block to success is now the lack of black unity. Tragically it is the very fluidity of the South African situation and the promise of success that is so divisive." We came back to that later.

In one sense Chief Buthelezi is an optimist—it is hard to see how he could have survived all these years unless he was. He believes that F. W. de Klerk is ready to make a deal with the blacks in a way which his predecessors in office were not. "I met the man, and the thing that struck me very strongly was the sense in which he was so different in his approach from two of his predecessors [Presidents Vorster and Botha] ... there was a note of penitence in it, you know."

"Last chance?" I suggested. "It is the last chance," said Buthelezi slowly. "Mr de Klerk has not got as much time as Mr Botha ... who had a lot of time to fool around. He got himself immobilised by the appearance of the Right."

Is the Right a diminishing factor? "I don't think they can go any further."

I drew Buthelezi's attention to reports of Mrs Thatcher's recent statement in which she said, "I believe in one person, one vote. Any solution has to be based on universal adult suffrage."

"Well," said Buthelezi, "there is no way we can settle for less than one man, one vote; but how we negotiate that is a separate matter altogether. It does not necessarily have to be the British or the American system."

We came to relations between Buthelezi's Inkatha and the African National Congress. Have the prospects of reconciliation improved? "Let me say this: for some time at least the ANC has been committed to making the country ungovernable. Whether they shoot their way to power or whether they are going to buy their way to power because they are so awash with the resources that they get internationally—these are things that bother me very much."

He goes on: "Both sides have to change. That is why earlier this year I sent a letter to Nelson Mandela saying that whatever policies we have are going to be completely ignored unless we get the act together ... that's the crucial thing, because the obstacle is not only the intransigence of the Government, but also the terrifying strife."

I asked if he had an understanding with Mandela. "We get on very well. He has written to me. His message was that he regarded me as a freedom fighter in my own right. There couldn't be any settlement without a role for me and Inkatha. Also in the letter he wrote to me he accommodates the idea that the ANC and Inkatha have the right to separate organisations."

Is it important for them to get together? "It is crucial."

We had referred to the fact that in Natal there had been cruel casualties arising out of feuding between Inkatha and the ANC. "I took the initiative. I went to the places where the violence was taking place. And everywhere I appealed for peace. I read this Mandela letter. And just about that time the Anglican Church was meeting in Durban, and I sent a message to Archbishop Tutu and said that I was very concerned that the Church did not seem to involve themselves in African reconciliation, which I regarded as their job. I also wrote to Mr Tambo, suggesting a date for a meeting, but I have not received any acknowledgement. Yet I regard such a meeting as crucial. It is essential we blacks get our act together." He had already made it clear, he added, that he could not be drawn into negotiations until Nelson Mandela's release.

That would be one symbol. Another would be a declaration that the tricameral parliamentary system was going—"It cannot cater for legitimate black demands." Another would be the repeal of the Group Areas Act, and the Act under which people of different races have to be registered.

The longer we talked, the clearer became Buthelezi's belief that the West will also have to do some fundamental rethinking. I mentioned that on my last visit to Johannesburg it had seemed to me that American disinvestment had made some white South Africans very rich indeed, and many blacks much poorer.

"It is quite true. The West should really look at this policy of isolation. If they want to see negotiations getting off the ground, it is absolutely crucial that Mr de Klerk should be given a chance."

He uttered a warning: "Those who have insisted that violence is the primary means of bringing about radical reform in South Africa now more than ever want to monopolise violence as a factor of success. Those who thought that reform was not possible unless South Africa was made ungovernable through the politics of confrontation now more than ever want to monopolise confrontational tactics."

Then we came to a matter which clearly rankles deeply with Buthelezi. "If we were to declare a South African moratorium on all in-flowing funds for the purposes of electioneering and party political machinery maintenance, Inkatha would be streets ahead of all its rivals. We have danced to nobody's tune."

By contrast, Buthelezi declares with feeling, organisations like the United Democratic Front and the Confederation of South African Trade Unions and even the South African Council of Churches spend millions of rand between them, which they receive from abroad. "The Soviet Union and its allies have annually provided revolutionaries with multi-million-dollar backing. Scandinavian countries in particular have annually provided the ANC with millions for its organisational programmes. Whenever it comes to funding for a group like Inkatha, Western governments become all coy and say they cannot interfere in the internal affairs of South Africa . . ."

So the West must recognise that there will be more than one party to agreement with the Nationalist Government? "Absolutely true." There was a pause and Buthelezi drew his chair back a little. "I don't know if you have ever paused to think what would happen if the white minority in South Africa established guerrilla warfare. Given the strength and mobility they have, it could destroy everything in Africa. So it is vital there should be negotiations.

"They have nowhere else to go . . . It would be terrible . . ."

March 1991

FIVE MILLION STARVING IN
NEW SUDAN FAMINE

*W. F. Deedes first reported from Africa in 1935 when he covered Abyssinia.
Since then he has frequently reported on the affairs of that continent, from
the Nile to the Cape. His latest Africa adventure took him to the famine-
stricken lands of the Sudan. His report below of seven days spent there is
one of the most moving he has written*

Sudan's food crisis, which threatens the lives of at least 5 million
people, is deep-seated and will be long-lasting. The 60-ton lorries,
carrying wheat and sorghum from the world's donors, belatedly
thundering down the long road from Port Sudan to El Obeid in
Kordofan will alleviate suffering; but they will not be able to avert a
human tragedy of grievous proportions.

To starvation is added the threat of acute water shortages in
many of the rural areas. Pumps, some of them going back to British
occupation (which ended in 1956) have broken down. Spare parts
are unobtainable; yet a dozen villages may depend on one such
pump. Donkeys used for moving water across the desert from
wells to villages are dying; and many are too enfeebled to do their
work.

In the hardest hit provinces, such as Kordofan and Darfur, the
seed corn needed for this year's crops has vanished. It has been eaten
by hungry people. If fresh stocks cannot be found and distributed in
time for the rains of June and July, there will be no harvest in 1991.

These are some conclusions I have reached after a week's travel
through the famine area with CARE Sudan (responsible for the local
distribution of relief in Kordofan) and some days of talking with
organisations in Khartoum.

I am haunted by the words of a woman working for World Food
Programme, who had just come back from the Sodiri district in
North Kordofan. "First they watch their animals die before their
eyes, and now they must watch their children die," she said.

There are 120 villages in the Sodiri district with a population of

718

about 300,000. Death from starvation is running at about 240 a month, or two in every village.

For the moment, news that lorries are arriving from the coast in El Obeid has checked a fatal mass movement of population from villages towards the centre. It started, but then checked. In the great famine of 1984–85 some 425,000 people were thus dislocated. Today many of them are still in the grim rescue camps outside Omdurman, El Obeid, Sodiri and elsewhere, in which during the 1984–85 crisis the mortality rate was 17 children a day.

In the rough dispensary of the camp at El Obeid, I saw sick babies who are certainly going to die. There and in the villages, malnutrition is widespread among pregnant and nursing mothers and young children. There is a chronic shortage of drugs and medicine. The only glint of hope I saw for medical assistants were one or two solar panels, given by British charities, which can be used to refrigerate medical chests.

Let me illustrate the plight of these people with a simple episode, not atypical, which we witnessed in the market square of El Obeid early one morning. An old man was pulling at the tail of his donkey to get it up. A second man tugged its ears. Two boys joined them and heaved in the middle. All of them failed. The donkey was dying.

It was all the old man possessed. His cattle had gone in 1984–85, his sheep early in this calamity—for virtually nothing. His wife had died under an operation. He had lost everything. Seeing the expression on his face, Sarah Errington, our photographer, impulsively took his hand. It was battered and calloused by work at the wells, where for a pittance he was winding water for the local council. It is hard to know what to say to people who are dying very, very slowly.

In round figures, 1,200,000 tons of grain are needed between now and November to make up the shortfall. Of this the world's donors have given about 400,000 tons and the government of Sudan is distributing 200,000 tons. The UN has just renewed its appeal for £350 million, which is the inclusive cost.

I reached El Obeid in time to see the earliest lorries in from Port Sudan—a journey of some 800 miles, taking 4–5 days. There was wheat for Darfur from Italy, Germany, Australia, Switzerland, Austria; and sacks of sorghum (which Kordofan prefers) marked "Gift of the British Government through CARE." At first my heart leapt to see swarms of men swiftly shifting 800 of the 56kg sacks off the big lorries, and sending them speeding back to Port Sudan. I had much to learn.

In the first place, El Obeid represents only the first and easier stage of the journey. Non-government organisations (NGOs) such as Save the Children, Oxfam, Concern and CARE have then to find smaller trucks to shift the sacks from the El Obeid base to villages up to 400 miles away. Sudan is the largest country in Africa, but it has no roads off the few main trunk routes and its railway is useless.

If the rains come in June, truck journeys through the desert to villages in Kordofan and Darfur will thereafter become a nightmare. All emergency food—and the seed—must be out before then. My enquiries lead me to doubt whether nearly enough will get through in time.

I take with a grain of salt allegations that the government of Sudan has been diverting the lorries for other purposes; but there has certainly been a tussle over what the trucking companies may keep by way of foreign exchange. Much more disturbingly, at least some village committees engaged in the final distribution of wheat or sorghum to individuals are spreading it too thin. Uncertain of seeing further supplies, they are requiring a month's ration of, say, three and a half kilos per person—against UN recommendation of 12 kilos—to last 45 days.

This is serious because in some of these villages there is virtually no other source of nutrition. Oil, lentils, beans, and like traditional food supplements, have either vanished or cost too much. Many who can afford to buy them cannot find them; others can find them but cannot afford to buy them.

The essential fact to grasp about this present food crisis in the Sudan is that the famine of 1984–85 stripped most rural families of all reserves. They are far worse off than they were. They have little or nothing at their backs. Their animal stocks are down, because they have not been able to build them up since 1985. Without animals to sell, they have no means to buy. They are on the extreme rim of life. Thus any shortfall of staple commodities such as wheat, dura or sorghum (which is dura mixed with millet), even for a short time, may prove fatal.

When I first set eyes upon the rescue camps, I wondered what could have driven rural families from their homes and villages towards such vile conditions. Now that I have seen in villages mothers, whose babies are failing for want of proper food and formerly proud nomads reduced to destitution, I understand why they moved.

As Sarah Errington and I travelled across the desert from Barah back to Omdurman, a journey which took us 11 hours in a land cruiser, we came across a woman with two little girls, a small boy and a baby on her arm. All but the baby clutched bags of food. She bore a jar of water on her head. In burning heat, this little group was walking to Omdurman, 180 miles away.

Amid such turmoil there are inevitably bitter recriminations. Some donors are fiercely angry with the government of Sudan, a military dictatorship, which they accuse of neglecting the emergency by talking lightly about a "food gap" and then obstructing those who want to help. Both donor countries and the NGOs working on the ground know perfectly well that most of Sudan's slender resources are being recruited and lavished on an unending war against the rebellious South.

I can obtain no reliable figures for numbers suffering in the South because of the war; but it cannot be far short of two million. At one time the UN was allowed to help both sides in the South through an operation named Life Line Sudan. But this arrangement, always subject to military considerations, has broken down.

So none can be surprised that between donors and NGOs and the government of Sudan relations are cool, to say the least. That said, all political experience warns me that by one means or another they have somehow to work together to save life. Just before I left Khartoum I had an enlightening hour with a senior source close to the government. "When people see that outsiders have become their main providers," I was told, "the government is done."

That indeed is true. The government of Lt-Gen Omer Hassan Ahmed El-Bashir, chairman of the National Salvation Revolutionary Command Council and Prime Minister, preaches the gospel of self-sufficiency. If such a government is seen to hand over the front seat and the driving wheel to non-government organisations from abroad, it is doomed.

Most of the principal NGOs, such as Oxfam, Save the Children, Concern and CARE—which has been working in the Sudan since 1979—are too experienced to try to push government around; but dedicated people striving to save life get badly frustrated by pettifogging bureaucracies.

Sudan's administration is even weaker than its infrastructure.

Economic deterioration over the years has greatly increased the impetus for emigration. Many able Sudanese are in the Gulf.

As the World Bank puts it in a confidential report, "thousands of Sudan's best-trained labour force have left, leaving once well-functioning institutions, including the civil service, in disarray."

However ill-disposed people may feel towards the present government of Sudan, the present is not alone responsible for the chronically bad performance of Sudan's economy over recent years. Since 1975, real per capita income has declined by almost a fifth.

The total external debt is around £6 billion, which is over 1,500 per cent of exports and represents a debt of £250 for every Sudanese—nearly twice the average debt of sub-Saharan Africa. Nor can it be held answerable for what, I have concluded, is the underlying cause of this food crisis—the remorseless destruction of Sudan's environment. Deforestation, inappropriate farming practices, overstocking of animals are main contributors to Sudan's plight.

Since 1917, one institute for agricultural research showed me, the population of Sudan has multiplied by six, its cattle by 21, camels by 15, sheep by 12, and goats by eight. If things go well and rains come, all this may be sustainable. Sudan, after all, was once the bread basket of Africa.

Today it cannot be sustained because Sudan's ravaged rural environment is creating a vicious cycle. To declare that degradation of Sudan's soil and widespread deforestation has radically altered Sudan's climate may be going one step too far. "But unquestionably," says Dr Yagoub Mohammed, Director of Khartoum University's Institute of Environmental Studies, "trees play a crucial part in rainfall. Trees prolong the process of rain. If you want to stabilise rainfall, you must re-afforest". Millions of acres of Sudan's trees have been lost to mechanised farming—begun in the Second World War—and millions more to charcoal and fuel for cooking.

I commissioned Khartoum's Meteorological Office to produce for me the rainfalls in certain districts between 1970 and 1990. The results need close analysis, but at a glance they support the hypothesis that Sudan's deterioriating landscape is reducing its rainfall.

In most villages visited, I asked men of middle age, not ancients, what they remembered of their surroundings in boyhood. Almost without exception, they spoke of the abundant trees that had gone. Now in some villages the sand dunes are piling up and will soon render them uninhabitable. The desert is gaining.

It is widely put about that the government of Sudan seems not to care whether these people live or die. I would put it rather differently. There is a marked degree of fatalism at every level in Sudan. If it seems to be God's will that many must die, then they will die. The fittest will come through. Sudan will emerge leaner and tougher. Such thinking is unacceptable to the West, but we shall not be able to change it.

If we quarrel about the past, we shall be in danger of losing the future, Winston Churchill once said. If by a united effort—and it will have to be united—the world is going to save some of these lives, it will have to heed those words.

FORGOTTEN FUGITIVES FROM THE TERROR IN MOZAMBIQUE

Far from being tamed by government concessions made in search of peace, the Renamo rebels' terror campaign still preys on large parts of Mozambique and visits desolation on at least a third of the country's 15 million people.

Mozambicans, home-loving people, have been turned into a race of nomads by what may seem to the outside world an unimportant war.

Put it this way. Renamo's primary aim throughout has been comprehensively to dislocate the country. From what I have seen on a long tour, the dislocation is as comprehensive as it has ever been.

Trunk roads are closed to all but armed convoys. It is hard to move stuff out of the ports. Rail is totally inadequate.

The only way to find out what is happening was to take a light plane and fly north from Maputo via Inhambane, Quelimane and Nampula, branching off where Renamo activity is heaviest.

As our pilot put it: "At 3,000 feet you're safe because they have no missiles." With this cheerful fellow, Steven Urquhart, our small party comprising Joe Kressler, CARE's director of operations in Mozambique, Ann Allport of CARE in London, and Harlan Hale, who has worked for five years in the country, flew some 2,000 miles round the country.

To pretend that 16 months of negotiations in Rome has ended the long civil war between the Right-wing Renamo guerrillas and the Leftist Frelimo government seemed to us a joke in poor taste. Not since war ended in Europe have I encountered so many displaced people. The *dislocados*, as they are called, are to be numbered in millions. The sum of human distress is vast.

Here is a snapshot of what life is like in parts of Zambezia province, where a third of the three million population has been displaced.

Our pilot thought it well to spiral round the beleaguered village of Derre twice to make sure Renamo had not moved in overnight, then dropped neatly on to a landing pad surrounded by an armed guard.

I thought this guard an uncommonly civil gesture, but they had mistaken us for the provincial governor. A hundred children greeted us enthusiastically as we were led to the bare office of Derre's administrator.

Flanked by two enormous government soldiers, he told his story in Portuguese, describing how the village had changed hands and was breathing uneasily in Renamo territory. He had some 5,327 people on his books, most of them displaced at one time or another.

Then we moved to the transit camp, where upwards of 100 fresh fugitives from Renamo were penned in. Never in my experience, not even in our war, have I set eyes on such human degradation.

The new arrivals had come with nothing, no possessions, no clothes. Men, women, children, babies at the breast, naked except for bits of sacking, were jammed together while people sorted them out.

They had been living ostensibly under Frelimo control but, constantly raided by rebel gangs, stripped of their property, they could no longer hold out.

Nearly all had lost kin—a wife here, a father there, a nephew, countless brothers, an uncle. Some of the men had been skilled carpenters and masons. Now they had nothing.

They described what Renamo had done to their women, and a man suddenly cried out: "Renamo has forfeited the moral right to rule."

Ann Allport murmured appositely: "How will they ever live together again?"—but here is a mystery of this war.

Over and over again on our journey, we heard from people high and low that they *would* live together again. One listens to endless tales of rape and pillage, of children kidnapped and then trained to return to kill their parents, of what amounts to the destabilisation or depersonalising of children.

Then one hears some senior administrator say gravely: "Yes, we shall come together again, for after all, they are our people."

This is Africa, but my imagination cannot bridge that far. This is war in which during, say, the course of a month, 200 will be killed, 50 severely wounded and 40 kidnapped by Renamo. The sense of insecurity thus engendered will be far more widespread.

Though not easily moved, thousands will be unsettled and either desert their land and homes, joining the ranks of *dislocados*, or, as most of the rural population do, draw into the nearest towns, between dusk and first light. More than a quarter of the inhabitants of the populous provinces of Zambezia and Nampula have been dislocated or disaffected.

Amid these ruins of a nation, poor at the best of times, working alongside Mozambique's Department for the Prevention and Combat of Natural Calamities (founded in 1984), the world's non-government organisations—World Vision, Save the Children, Oxfam as well as CARE, toil round the clock in extraordinarily uncomfortable places like Nampula to bring food and order and comfort into these demoralised lives.

The killing keeps up, the terror persists, plans fail, roads are cut off, convoys are lost, but the work goes on. For there is a spirit behind it which will never die.

I crept into a barn on the outskirts of Nampula, where the *dislocados* were drawing their slender rations. There in the centre stood a young woman in a veil of Mother Teresa's order, a Biro pen pressed to her lips, gazing intently at the 10-litre tin of maize splashing into sacks. She stood there motionless, a figure of mercy in a cruel world.

They show a fine disdain, some of these young women, for disturbance which would send most tourists scurrying for the airport. "So there *was* some trouble out there last night," says Gaye Thompson, a CARE worker in Inhambane, as we assembled after breakfast to look at her water relief scheme.

"I heard the firing during supper," she explained. Then she headed the Land Cruisers in the same direction so that we could examine these exciting wells which local people are being encouraged to dig, with technical assistance. We passed a lot of deserted houses on the way.

The need for this technical assistance springs mainly from the past. The Portuguese in their time did very little to develop skills among Mozambicans—who presumably might then have taken Portuguese artisans' jobs.

The top Mozambican administrators who fought their way through this handicap are first-class. But history's legacy is an acute shortage of skilled Mozambicans at the middle level with experience of responsibility.

The logistics of supply for Mozambicans in the north are daunting. Because the main roads are unsafe for all but armed convoys, the lorry drivers, starting from, say, the port of Beira, must follow a route of some 1,200 miles to the north.

They have to follow the Beira corridor, which is protected, pass through Harare in Zimbabwe, then work their way through Tete in Mozambique to the Malawi border, strike north for Mandimba—the worst bit of the route—until reaching Lichinga.

They say of Lichinga that it may not be the end of the world, but from there you can see where it is.

This chronic insecurity invades and impedes every department of national life. It has driven hundreds of thousands from the lands and cultivation to the relative safety of the towns and cities, the reverse of what an enlightened government, striving to resurrect a market economy, is trying to bring about.

Local authorities cannot cope with the influx. During 1992, almost two million internally displaced people will have to have emergency assistance. It goes without saying that the terror and violence, the constant insecurity and movement have had serious social, emotional and traumatic effects.

The Family Tracing Programme has documented nearly 10,000 unaccompanied children. Restoring to their families children who have been snatched from their homes or lost in this mad world will be a long task for the future, and is unlikely to be totally fulfilled.

More than half, 53 per cent, of the primary schools network is destroyed.

Yet, as one perceives from this journey, there lies just ahead for the Mozambican government the heaviest challenge of all. When peace eventually comes, millions of Mozambican refugees now over-seas will seek to return to a country which is without a social, health or education infrastructure.

Outside the borders of Mozambique there are some 900,000 refugees in Malawi, another 230,000 in South Africa. Zimbabwe is looking after 190,000 more. Tanzania, Swaziland and Zambia add another 125,000. This is a total of around a million and a half people. As the Mozambique emergency programme for 1992–93 makes plain, the country will be called upon to resettle millions of hungry and impoverished Mozambicans in a social and commercial infra-structure devastated by 15 years of war.

They have up against them drought as well. In the north of Mozambique, the prospects are not so bad. Given half a chance, it could become the nation's granary as it has been in the past. South of the Zambesi, there will be very little, and the neighbouring countries, afflicted by the same drought, will not have much to offer.

There is an inclination in the outside world to perceive the plight of countries like Mozambique as a self-inflicted wound, the price of war and the foolish policies. Aid is seen as perpetuating dependence—and the war.

But Mozambicans do not altogether fit this comfortable pattern—comfortable because it excuses others from doing anything about it. They are hardworking, resilient, and for most land on which to work is home.

Christina Kressler, the director's wife, who joined our trip, met one of them, Mandinho Silva, a typical Mozambican. He lives in a small safe area in the Manica province, uprooted from his traditional home by the war.

His face is wrinkled by worry and his hands worn by toil. He had planted four-and-a-half hectares of corn around his hut. Early rains in November gave him hope. No more rain came. His crop failed. Asked what he would do, he shrugged his shoulders and said: "*Fica com fome,*" which means, go hungry. He shrugs in a way which says, "we've done it before and survived. We'll probably have to do it again."

If the war doesn't get them, said Christina, then the climate does. Mandinho Silva has many companions, planting in hope, conditioned to disappointment, watching for a signal of peace which, like a desert oasis, seems perpetually to draw away from them.

March 1992

FOR SOUTH AFRICA, THIS IS THE END OF THE BEGINNING

Against the odds, President de Klerk has fulfilled the world's demands. The West must now consider its debt of honour, says W. F. Deedes

South Africa is back with a chance. Her white population has decided overwhelmingly that, however uncertain the future may seem, they have to go forward rather than back. In an extraordinary turn-out they have rewarded President de Klerk's courageous gamble with a landslide which precious few anticipated. As the polls closed on Tuesday, a shrewd British observer in Pretoria gave me what was then an optimistic forecast. It was that 58.5 of the vote cast would say "yes". As a friend on the Afrikaans newspaper Beeld said yesterday when the surprising Johannesburg result came in: "Something has been happening under our eyes which we have missed."

It is to be borne in mind that this has been an emotional campaign, calculated by both sides to wrench feelings in a way I have never before witnessed in any country. The Right hammered across a warning that a "Yes" vote would mean black dictatorship under Mandela. Former President P. W. Botha declared that his successor was a victim of a Communist plot. He would vote "No" because he refused to contemplate the suicide of his people.

From the National and Democratic parties came a warning that "No" would trigger mass action by the black majority and render South Africa ungovernable. It stands to the credit of South Africa's white minority, which the world has not regarded highly in the past, that through the tumult of this campaign they kept their nerve. They kept their head. Finally, they knew what they had to do.

There have been extraordinary mood swings. Last Sunday, it looked as if the "Nos" might have it. True or false, this seems to have concentrated the minds of normally apathetic English-speaking white voters wonderfully. The big change came in the last 48 hours of this 24-day campaign. It was not so much the Nos turning to Yes as, rather, a great human stirring among normally indifferent voters. This became a vote that had to be delivered.

Amid the euphoria, it is well to bear in mind that this, as Churchill said after Alamein, is only the end of the beginning. "We face a future full of challenge," said President de Klerk, acknowledging his triumph yesterday afternoon; and this is true. Some now believe that the troika of Right-wing leaders—Dr Andries Treurnicht and his Conservative Party, Jaap Marais's HNP and Eugene Terreblanche's AWB—all wounded by this result, will turn more militant, and therefore more dangerous, than ever. I think it more likely that they will break up.

In one sense, their policy lies in ruins. Results from the Orange Free State and elsewhere show that in the Conservative Party's prospective homeland, the majority actually voted "Yes". Unquestionably, the contradictions that have developed between them as the campaign went on influenced the outcome. The more thoughtful elements will join Codesa and the negotiating process. A minority of Conservatives will move towards the extreme Right and Terreblanche. Dr Treurnicht could find himself a general without an army. Fragmentation of the Right seems now inevitable.

The English-speaking whites overcame apathy. The Afrikaner has overcome something more than that: he has become a pragmatist. He has, with this vote, come to terms with the fact that as a minority he can no longer expect to govern an involuntary majority. That decision enters history. The challenge to President de Klerk is now twofold. He and his National Party have to conclude negotiations for the future government of South Africa with a far more confident ANC. Mandela and his friends now know that the whites cannot veto what emerges from Codesa. That is not entirely to President de Klerk's advantage. Because this vote has made him appear politically unassailable by his Right-wing, he has lost an important bargaining counter.

More significantly, these negotiations are taking place in a country whose economy is in decline, and which nevertheless is now called upon urgently to make a colossal outlay in human resource development. There are two million blacks without school places, in a country where fixed investment is down by one third and total farm debts are approaching £4 billion. The cost of abolishing racial disparities in public spending over a decade is put at £15 billion— more than South Africa's 1990–91 budget.

This decline may yet be checked. By the end of the 1980s, South Africa's level of fixed investments was 30 per cent lower than in 1981. The ratio of fixed investment to GDP fell from 28 per cent in 1983 to 19 per cent in 1989. Helen Suzman may have been right to declare of this result, "They voted for investment, not disinvestment. They are sick and tired of economic isolation." Which raises the main question arising from this result: how is the world proposing to respond?

A peaceful outcome in South Africa may now depend heavily on the answer. Mandela's ANC will reward President de Klerk with a new call for an end to sanctions. That will be a step forward, but in this battered economy, only a short step. Since the world chose to disinvest in South Africa, claims on the world's capital resources have multiplied. The question now is not whether America should assist South Africa forward, but whether it should bail out Yeltsin's Russia.

Rightly or wrongly, cynics in South Africa expect little or nothing from the United States. Its concern about South Africa, they claim, sprang from the fact that apartheid impinged on America's own delicate race problems. Now that this embarrassment is being removed, sustained American interest in South Africa is thought to be lukewarm.

Yet the world outside America does need to take stock of this happy result. President de Klerk, against the odds, undertook the task of meeting the world's demands upon South Africa. With this vote he is well on the way to delivering what was sought of him. There have not been many signal acts of statesmanship in this century, but this surely counts as one of them. It is for the world to consider whether a debt of honour has now been accrued here; whether the time has come for the West to stop wringing hands and start searching purses.

President de Klerk's position in South Africa today is not far removed from that of an earlier South African figure, Cecil Rhodes: "So much to do, so little time . . ." As it searches its conscience, after this momentous day in South Africa's history, the world would do well to bear that in mind.

April 1994

THE WAY IT'S GOING TO GO

The new South Africa will not be able to resist the Afrikaner's most dangerous bequest, says W. F. Deedes in Johannesburg

Archbishop Desmond Tutu was "over the moon". So was the Stock Market. So were millions of South Africans. The euphoria sprang from awareness that had Chief Buthelezi's Inkatha Freedom party maintained its boycott of the polls, election week would have been a bloody week. The toll of killings, already horrifying, would have soared.

Inkatha's decision will not end the reign of the AK-47. But it makes the escalation of violence less likely. Violence looms in the public mind here above everything else. It obscures other dangers.

All elections promote rumours, but in South Africa the rumours are running wild: once the election is over, black servants, on orders from above, will take over the houses from their white employers; water and food supplies will be cut off; Jumbo jets are standing by to lift threatened whites out of the country . . . and so on.

It is not altogether surprising. This is the tensest election I have witnessed in any country. Nerves among blacks as well as whites are taut. It is hardly the moment therefore to introduce another dire prediction—but amid all the clamour of this election, one certainty has settled in my mind.

No matter what happens, South Africa's future government will be to many Western eyes distressingly authoritarian. It will resemble more closely what we have witnessed in Eastern Europe than our own kind of democracy.

This is not to accuse the African National Congress of conspiring to impose a dictatorship after an election that it is bound to win. It is to assert that the ANC will inherit from the Nationalists a *dirigiste* political system which will make the imposition of a dictatorship temptingly easy.

The world in recent years has only had room in its head for one main idea about South Africa. It has been obsessed by the evil of apartheid and the injustice of government by a white minority comprising 14 per cent of the population. It has tended to overlook other flaws, foremost among them what has aptly been called "Afrikaner authoritarianism".

"Look at those government buildings in Pretoria!" exclaimed an Afrikaner friend of mine a day or two ago. "They bear a far closer resemblance to some of those buildings in Moscow than anything you will find in Western capitals." It is a fact that earlier in this century South Africa inherited from the likes of Lord Milner and his young men autonomous provinces which are now hardly less subordinate to the centre than were the countries which until recently comprised the Union of Soviet Socialist Republics. What else have Chief Buthelezi and the Kwa-Zulu kingdom been crying out about?

There are four principal reasons for the establishment here of such a heavily centralised state, three of which I have seen in action during the post-war years. It is in the first place bound up with the Afrikaners' nature. Second, the imposition of apartheid demanded a highly authoritarian system. How else were pass laws and the rest of the paraphernalia to be kept in place? Any minority conducting such a system is virtually driven to dictatorship. Third—and consequently—there was the constant threat of insurrection from within, which necessitated imposing states of emergency from time to time.

As if that were not enough, the rest of the world sought to defeat the Nationalist government through sanctions and disinvestment. During that period, which has only recently ended, the Nationalist government had every pretext for putting itself on a wartime footing. It was up against external coercion as well as internal violence.

I recall interviewing President Vorster, in one of his most ferocious moods. He defied the world to do its worst. South Africa, he declared, was a very tight ship and it would not founder. It remains a very tight ship.

One of the few men who saw Afrikaner authoritarianism as self-handicapping was the late Gerard de Koch, Governor of the Reserve Bank and one of South Africa's greatest servants. While battling to preserve the economy against world pressures, he lamented to me more than once the damage he thought was being done by the centrist policies of his masters.

There is already an enormous bureaucracy in South Africa, to which the ANC will be adding numbers of its own. "We are not going to live like fat cats," Nelson Mandela pledged in his recent television debate with President de Klerk. Not fat perhaps, but the cat population is going to grow.

What then is the likely response of an ANC-dominated government to his inheritance? To loosen up? To centralise? I can think of nothing less likely. In one or two directions I see the possibility of more authoritarian developments.

"Who is going to form the opposition?" I asked an acquaintance on one of the Afrikaner newspapers before the IFP's last-minute decision to enter the lists. What effective opposition can be expected against a so-called "government of national unity"?

He thought the media would have a critical role to play. I would like to think so too, but some of South Africa's prospective new masters do not take criticism amiably. Mr Mandela resents cross-examination, and so do most of his colleagues.

It has to be said that if the new government felt driven to imposing restraints on critics in newspapers and broadcasting, it would be taking a leaf out of the Nationalist book of earlier years. After the Muldergate scandals, life became more difficult for journalists who wanted to report freely. And overseas correspondents who overstepped the mark were occasionally invited to leave the country. If the ANC finds it desirable to get rough with the news media, it will have precedents to quote.

It is not in the African's nature to share power. I see no prospect of the ANC and the IFP sharing power for long. Looking across the rest of this great continent, we can observe that almost everywhere only Number One counts.

Some of my friends declare that South Africa will be an exception to the rule because it has a bigger white minority than any other African country. I am not sure this is going to count as much as some hope. Mandela and Co are not saying a great deal about the future white contribution. This may of course be from fear of antagonising some of their own supporters; but my prediction is that they will eventually dispense with much of the top white echelon in government which has been running political affairs here, and work with the middle ranks. There will not be much "creative tension" between black and white at the top.

The ANC will, oddly, have easier relations with the Afrikaner than with the European or the Jew. But when it comes to decision-making there can be no doubting who will prevail—at least after a short while.

As an added bonus, it is already clear that the ANC will enjoy the full support of South Africa's armed forces. Most servicemen are careerists. They serve the government of the day. Any fancy notion that senior military figures now in active service will be found waving swords on behalf of the white right-wing is in the realm of cloud-cuckoo-land.

So, little more than a week from now, the world can expect to be hailing a revolution in South Africa. What it needs to be mindful about is not the weapons which the victors may require, but the weapons which the vanquished have already placed in their hands.

HEALTHY BABIES CRY ... THESE WERE SILENT

W. F. Deedes reports from a feeding centre at Bahr el Ghazal in southern Sudan

It was a melancholy experience to return to a Sudan famine for the second time in a decade. The earlier one was in the North, back in 1991. Supplies, I remember, were slow to come down the long road from Port Sudan to El Obeid. The truckers argued about money. But eventually they came, in abundance.

The famine I have been witnessing in the South is different in that vital respect. This time, there is a war on, and the famine is striking hardest in territory held by the Sudan People's Liberation Army, enemies of the government.

So in the North, ministers in Khartoum deal meanly with attempts to feed their citizens in territory of the South. Clare Short, the International Development Secretary, was timely this week in condemning Khartoum for preventing food going to starving people. I wish I felt it would make much difference.

Babies are dying of starvation *now*, as I have just seen, after reaching Bahr el Ghazal; and many more will die before May is out.

This is a war that has been running for 30 of the last 40 years. The reasoning behind it and the factions involved are beyond my comprehension—and indeed the comprehension of people familiar with the Sudan.

"If you are not confused," they said to me, "you do not understand!"

Fundamentally, between Arabs and tenacious Islam in the North and the Africans and Christians of the South there can be no reconciliation; and within that great divide are factions fighting each other.

In all the civil wars I have witnessed in recent years, there has arisen in one form or another this impasse over bringing relief to the innocent citizens. Every aid organisation in the world is familiar with it. "If you bring in food for the women and children, you leave soldiers opposing us a freer hand to fight."

It is an argument being strenuously advanced in Sudan now—by both sides. To meet it, the United Nations Children's Fund (Unicef) and the UN's World Food Programme devised Operation Lifeline Sudan (OLS), and secured agreement to it from both sides.

Within its severe limitations, OLS struck me as a brilliant operation, though one to challenge stout hearts. From a camp and airfield in Kenya on Sudan's border, Hercules and Buffalo transport planes fly limited supplies to the famished areas of Sudan.

This is harder than it sounds. To travel with them from the Lokichokio base, as I have been doing, is to discover how far determined men and women can triumph over obstacles. The heart leaps. But when you watch the faces of hungry men, women and children who crowd round every supply plane, the heart sinks again.

There are simply too many of them, and they are quietly desperate. These people will walk 10 miles or more through the scorching sun of southern Sudan on a rumour that a plane bearing supplies has landed.

The chances are that they will be disappointed. Not enough planes are allowed to fly under the Sudanese government's restrictions. Donor countries show increasing reluctance to find money needed for basic foods. As many people see it, this famine is simply another of Africa's self-inflicted wounds.

I saw it rather differently, as I stood one morning this week with a huge group of mothers who had come with their babies to a small supplementary feeding centre run by *Médecins Sans Frontières* (MSF) at Panthou, heart of the famine area.

Some of them had walked miles in the heat. They sat there, awaiting a test on their babies which would guide MSF on whether they needed supplementary feeding. As well as the mothers and babies, there were some skeletal figures hanging around in hope.

I could not bring myself to look at them, still less take pictures. Their ribs and legs brought back to my mind a day long ago when some of us stumbled into one of Nazi Germany's death camps.

As for the babies, it struck me with grandfatherly intuition how eerily silent they were. Healthy babies cry. Here were a hundred or more babies, and only one was crying. Walking round, striving not to look intrusive, I saw why they were not crying. They were inert.

Last week, this relatively small centre reported that seven babies

had died. The death toll for April is 40. In all famines, babies die
first.

The mothers know this. You could read it in their eyes, as they
sat under a great tree—waiting. The look they gave conveyed so
many human emotions—patience above all, woe, pleading, resignation.

These people have been living in hell for a long, long time. They
are now at a critical fulcrum of the war. Running away from fighting,
their menfolk cannot sow or reap. So they depend on the host
population, who themselves are lacking.

I have seen famine before, but nothing more desperate than this.
So these women look at you, silently conveying their plight.

This ghastly war is going to impoverish not one, but two
generations. Much of the first went without schooling, having been
kept perpetually on the move.

Now we have a generation of children who will start life chronically short of essential foods. Many, I dare say, will live through it and
survive. The Sudanese are hardy people. Living and working in that
desert, they have to be. But others will not. They will fall by the
wayside, as some are falling now.

The rains are about a fortnight off. That could well lead to more
fighting, and that in turn could bring further restrictions on famine
relief transport. The consequences would be dire, because the last
ditch for this region will be getting enough seed flown in for an
autumn harvest.

Meanwhile, I detect growing unease among Sudan's neighbours.
Much of Africa wants trade, not aid. It seeks investment. The last
thing it wants is a famine caused by an inexplicable war leading to
the death of tens of thousands of innocent people.

"Oh, Africa again!" we shall exclaim despairingly. Countries like
Ethiopia, Eritrea, Uganda and Rwanda know that. There is something of a sea change going on, and Khartoum can feel it.

There, maybe, lies a glimmer of hope for the despairing mothers
I saw under that tree. Just a glimmer.

THE POT HOLES ON SOUTH AFRICA'S ROAD TO FREEDOM

W. F. Deedes reports from Johannesburg on the precarious state of Mandela's new nation

It is winter on the Highveldt, which brings clear blue skies all day but chilly nights. On the National Party, which governed this country from 1948 until 1994, an altogether deeper—and many believe lethal—chill has settled.

In recent days the rand's fall has attracted the headlines—there are now 10 to the pound. But the plunge in popular support for the Nationalists will prove of more lasting consequence.

"There is a strong perception in white people's minds and in the Afrikaners' minds," said one observer to me, "that this lot is finished." All the evidence I have been able to gather points that way.

As our own Tory Party testifies, all political parties suffer for a while when they lose power after a long spell in office. After a year or two they start to recover. There is no sign of that for the Nationalist party. I can think of no precedent for what is happening to them.

One interpretation is that, after 46 years of it their supporters came only to understand political power. They have no experience of, and no appetite for, opposition.

Chris Fismer, former right hand man to F W de Klerk and a minister in the transitional government, believes that the Nationalists should have been more open about the past, more candid about some of the wretched things done in their name before 1994.

Nationalist supporters were horrified by what emerged from the Truth Commission. The Nationalists were damned by their past and doubly damned by pretending it never happened. "We should have said 'we were wrong'," says Fismer. "But we didn't, and we deserve what we got. If you govern, you must know what goes on."

On top of that, many think, de Klerk blundered when, under pressure from the Afrikaners, he withdrew his party from the government of national unity.

However you interpret it, the widely perceived irrelevance of the Nationalist party has serious implications for the future government of South Africa.

With its eye on global opinion, the African National Congress (which holds 240 seats against the Nationalists' 42 in parliament) has so far held a reassuringly moderate course. It has reined in spending. It has a prudent Chancellor and a balanced budget.

It accepts the need to move towards a market economy and acknowledges the virtues of privatisation but (as business is swift to point out) it has done precious little to move in either direction.

"It has failed to deliver," says Helen Suzman, who spent 30 years of her life in parliament upholding liberal principles against Nationalist power. And it is true that the declared growth, economic and redistribution strategy of President Mandela's government has faltered, some would say foundered.

Growth is slow, unemployment remains high and the much sought foreign investment has not been attracted.

Most people here attribute failure to free the economy to pressure from the Left. There are also structural problems. There are grounds for thinking that the ANC simply does not know the best way to set about privatisation. So central control prevails.

More ominously there are signs that the government would like to achieve 66 per cent control of parliament—it now holds 62.3 per cent control—which would enable it to change the constitution. That prospect will do nothing to draw investment from overseas.

What has developed and is still expanding is a huge informal economy. Street trading, or what is known as the cardboard box economy, is the fastest growing sector of the economy. Self-employment on these lines, always desirable in a country like Africa, is proving the life-blood of millions and is reducing the number of totally unemployed. It is rather as if the people, peacefully and profitably, had decided to show their government the right way to go about it.

Other things being equal, tourism could make an enormous contribution to South Africa's economy. But they are not equal. The road to South Africa is rendered attractive to the tourist by the lowly rand. But that also makes promotion of tourism overseas prohibitively expensive.

What discourages the tourist is South Africa's appalling crime rate, the prevailing topic of conversation at every dinner party. As someone put it to me, "there is collective depression about our crime rate".

Fortress homes are small encouragement to tourists. The police are ill paid—a sure road to corruption.

The prisons are crammed and the process of justice clogged by lack of qualified magistrates and judges. One third of all those behind bars is awaiting trial.

Not surprisingly, the white exodus continues. White families do not see a future for their children. Affirmative action is in the early stages, but it will develop. White citizens, who already perceive themselves politically irrelevant are left wondering how long it will be before their children become commercially irrelevant.

Afrikaners are also leaving, but in no great numbers. They are individualists. That is why they have survived and will continue to do so.

With the disappearance of the Nationalists, and the trade union and communist wings of the governing party apparently given notice to co-operate or quit, the question becomes how far South Africa may move towards single-party government.

The party making the best running appears to be the Democrats—who gathered only seven seats in 1994. In the local by-elections seats have been falling to them fast; but that is no true guide to what may happen in the 1999 general election.

The fact is the ethnic factor remains enormously strong. At present one fails to see the growth of any party which is going to attract the hearts and minds of blacks as well as whites. The past, or perhaps it is Africa itself, creates a barrier.

One combination that might achieve it would be the emergence of a Workers' Party. Suzman thinks that is a possibility. She envisages a 1999 election which the ANC will win, but not necessarily overwhelmingly. During the ensuing five years, failure to deliver might lead to a hiving off of trade unions and discontents, in short a workers' party.

In terms of the moral high ground there is much to be said in favour of this government. The prisons may be full, but there is no detention without trial. The press remains free, scolded from time to time but not seriously threatened. The rule of law has been restored.

For the first time in almost half a century, South Africa has become part of the real world and most of its citizens show awareness of this. The government may falter and fumble but it is a legitimate government and everyone feels better for knowing it.

It is in the field of economic policy that doubts arise and that is because there is at the centre a failure to agree on the direction it should take. Business attributes that to politics. I would attribute some of it to inexperience.

So the future is unsure. "Yes, it is the dawn that has come," I wrote, borrowing from Alan Paton's *Cry, The Beloved Country*, on that magical day in 1994 when all South Africa voted together for the first time. It is the sunrise that will take longer to arrive than we hoped.

July 1998

MANDELA: THE HERO WHO
FELL TO EARTH

Nelson Mandela turns 80 on Saturday. W. F. Deedes visited Soweto to find out how black South Africans now regard their president

Among all the revolutionary leaders we have known in this century, Nelson Mandela, who is 80 on Saturday, holds a place of his own.

A number, such as Jomo Kenyatta of Kenya and Jawaharlal Nehru of India, languished in prison—at our hands—before emerging as leaders. But none attained the heights Mandela has reached in pulling together by personal example a country so savagely riven as South Africa was in 1994 after half a century of apartheid.

There have been better administrators. There have been stronger leaders. It is as a figure of reconciliation in a country at war with itself for 46 years that Mandela will be remembered.

"But for how long?" I asked a black South African in the Johannesburg township of Soweto. "The world remembers Gandhi," he replied. Yes, but Gandhi—whom we also imprisoned—was never called upon to answer for the consequences of the revolution he led by means of passive resistance.

What we can say confidently is that no revolutionary who became ruler of his country ever displayed more courtesy towards his former persecutors than Mandela.

"He has such good manners," says Helen Suzman, who fought the Nationalists in parliament for 30 years. She recalled accompanying Mandela in a car after some ceremony and they went past a protective guard of white Afrikaners. "He stopped the car, got out, shook every one of them by the hand and thanked them for taking care of him. They were stunned."

I spoke to a score of witnesses, white and black, some of them outside the Mandela museum in Soweto which attracts about 100 visitors a week. There was the African who said simply, "Yes, I think he's a hero." "Why?" "Because he's a black man like me!" Laughter.

Then I approached another African at the Soweto Country Club,

743

who was hitting scores of golf balls on the practice ground with expensive golf clubs. One of the new class of prosperous blacks, I surmised. "He's not my hero," he said gruffly. "He's joined the elite. He's a traitor to the cause. Whatever happened to the freedom fighter?"

He spoke for those in South Africa who, regardless of their status, believe the armed struggle stopped too soon. We will come back to him and his kind.

There was the businessman from Iowa who said cautiously: "I don't think any one man can carry this country forward. One of anything is not good in business or in politics. But perhaps Mandela can inspire them to hold together."

"His ability to survive in prison was admirable," said the lawyer from Italy who was exploring the Soweto township with his young son. "But this country has to look to the future. The problem is now, not then."

He spoke for many who acknowledge Mandela's singular gifts as a conciliator but have reservations about his failure to fulfil political promises.

"Mandela is a symbol of the new Africa," said one black. "He is a symbol of the end of white power in Africa." That touches an innermost chord in many. "He is the man behind the history," as one put it.

The birthday celebrations, which are extensive, will not pass without criticism. "As an individual, he is a great man," said a black African. "He is a great leader." Then: "It's a lot of money to spend on a birthday." He was referring to Mandela's decision to charge guests for the privilege of attending his official birthday party, with the proceeds going to the president's preferred charities.

"But he is not spending it," I objected. With emphasis. "He is *causing* a lot of money to be spent, and there are a lot of very poor people in this country."

Only revolutionaries, it occurred to me during some of these conversations, draw reverence from their supporters. As soon as they embark on the endless adventure of governing men, they descend to earth and encounter critics.

In this country we see Mandela's former wife Winnie as a woman perpetually in disgrace. In the Mandela museum, I observed, she shares the honours with her former husband.

Prominently displayed in the museum shop are two big pictures of Winnie—"Mother of the Nation". One needs to weigh this lingering feeling for Winnie, notwithstanding all her misdeeds, fully to grasp Mandela's achievement as a conciliator.

We come back to the man hitting golf balls at the Soweto Country Club who thinks Mandela has joined the elite and betrayed the cause. Vain to explain that the cause has been won. There are those in South Africa who believe that some of their former white rulers were guilty of criminal behaviour and want to see them made to pay.

Winnie has much in common with that figure in Dickens's *A Tale of Two Cities* called the Vengeance. Such figures hover around most revolutions and can cause a lot of blood to be spilt. We need to think about such figures and the power they could exercise in a place with South Africa's recent history if we are fully to grasp the achievement of Nelson Mandela.

POOR RULERS TO BLAME FOR POST-COLONIAL WOES

W. F. Deedes analyses the grave mistakes that have led to rapid economic and political decline across the continent, making even rich nations poor

Beyond the conflict now threatening to tear central Africa apart and belying the claims of its leaders lies a hard truth. Politically and economically, much of Africa is going rapidly downhill.

For this, various excuses are advanced—the legacy of colonial rule, irrational boundaries, the scale of African debt, the Cold War and the internal wars that it engendered. But at the root of Africa's plight lies widespread failure of statecraft.

It is seen at its worst in a country like Angola, potentially rich in diamonds, oil and mineral resources, yet crippled by misrule, inflation, and an interminable war which, after smouldering for a short time, has burst into flames again.

Kenya, a country of high promise, produces nothing like its potential. Nigeria has riches, is a major oil producer but is confused by corruption.

Strangely, this centre of the cruel Biafran war in the Sixties does show signs of fresh promise under a new military ruler, who next week will hold discussions with Tony Blair.

One consequence of Africa's failure in statecraft is widespread poverty, and where people possess virtually nothing worth defending, the prospect of war is not something that alarms. It may even represent faint hope of betterment. This can amount to a stimulus to war.

So what we are witnessing now in the Congo conflict is partly tribal, partly related to boundaries, partly also a scramble for diminishing resources.

In fairness, the Cold War did much to sow the seeds of ruin. Both East and West poured money into Africa, much of it unconditionally. In effect, East and West bribed rulers to secure their allegiance.

Nowhere in sub-Saharan Africa has decline in the condition of the people been sharper than in the Sudan. For 30 of the past 40 years this former condominium has been in conflict.

This war has splintered in a score of different directions, which makes any formula for settlement almost unattainable.

In much of the south and some of the north life for the Sudanese has long been reduced to bare necessities; and now these are running out.

Ethiopia was brought to the point of ruin by the barbaric regime of Col Mengistu. His successors have had a hard struggle to repair the ravages he inflicted. In Zimbabwe, President Robert Mugabe has held unfettered power since the end of the Ian Smith rebellion. His Marxist philosophy has done little for the country's betterment.

It is almost half a century since the British Government sought to create a Central African Federation, comprising southern Rhodesia (Zimbabwe), northern Rhodesia (Zambia) and Nyasaland (Malawi). It crumbled because it was seen as an obstacle to black rule.

Had it survived and prospered, it might be offering an element of stability at least in southern Africa.

One consequence of conflict in the Congo is likely to be a much heavier load for United Nations High Commission for Refugees.

At one time South Africa was seen as a possible steadying influence. Today it has too many problems of its own. It sorely needs more overseas investors, but rampant crime has discouraged international companies.

That is where this fire in the Congo will inflict such long-term damage as it will further discourage the investors the continent badly needs.

BOY SOLDIERS WHO ARE TRAINED TO KILL WITHOUT SCRUPLE

W. F. Deedes reports on the trauma and horrors of Africa's civil wars

One of the horrors of Liberia's recent civil war and of the brutal conflict now being waged in Sierra Leone is the extensive use of children trained to kill or mutilate without scruple.

From the age of eight upwards, they are given cursory military training, sometimes beaten into submission and sent into battle. To render them immune from fear they are dosed with amphetamine.

Save the Children Fund, which is striving to rescue some of these children, believes that 6,000–8,000 were used in Liberia's war, about one fifth of the forces deployed by the six factions involved.

Judging from evidence we obtained from a refugee camp on the Liberian frontier, both forces supporting the government of Sierra Leone and the rebels are making equally extensive use of young children as combatants.

Particularly degrading for the children is that both these wars have involved terrorising civilians, who have been and are still being deliberately mutilated.

SCF, which has had 6,000 of Liberia's child ex-fighters through its hands, and is still working to reunite them with their families, now has the task of starting all over again with Sierra Leone.

Restoring these children to their family, their community and their right mind is a complex business. In the Voinjama centre for Liberians, we met two young ex-fighters who had been reunited with what war had left of their families.

One of them, Maikie, displayed strong signs of recovery. His father was dead. He helped his mother, traced by SCF, to run a small shop, and is studying to become a doctor like his father.

The second youth, Musa, who was recruited at 13 and is now 19, is a very troubled young man. He has had no schooling and appears to be interested in nothing except his small cart. The only time he became animated during our talk was when I mentioned a machine-gun. His father, who works ceaselessly to persuade the community to accept him, is constantly embarrassed by his behaviour.

The majority of these Liberian children have been restored to their community and their progress is being monitored. In contrast, some of the children we met in the Sierra Leone camp, relatively fresh from battle, chill the nerve.

We talked with a group of them and interviewed one or two in depth. The smallest of the bunch, still well under five feet tall, had entered battle at nine with an AK 47 on his shoulder.

His parents were dead. His experience of fighting was bringing him under intense pressure from others in the camp to rejoin the war. As both sides run short of soldiers, this pressure on children to return to the battlefield increases.

Removed from family influence, they are malleable, ruthless and, given food, drugs and clothing, can be made to fight without pay. Some are conscripted. Others, who have lost contact with their families, join to get food. This treatment of children breaks every canon of war and human rights; but in some of the dirtiest fighting even Africa has witnessed (with torture, mutilation and cannibalism thrown in) it seems to have escaped the international community's attention.

"Could you really handle an AK 47," I asked Jusu, who joined up at 10 and is now 17. "If I had one now," he replied, "I could give you a demonstration."

Before his teens, he had achieved the rank of first lieutenant. A few in the "small boy units' attained even higher rank.

His companion, Sao Kallon, who had also lost his parents, claimed to have joined the army at eight, got three months training and fought on the government side.

Like Jusu, he had been given regular doses of amphetamine before fighting. He struck me as humorous, highly intelligent and capable of any wickedness.

It became clear to us that children whose parents have been killed or separated make the best cannon fodder. Street children who abound, in particular, can be easily rounded up and prove easier to control than adults.

Mixed up with countless unaccompanied children, pouring into this Sierra Leone refugee camp on Liberia's border, the child fighters are creating havoc.

All supplies have to be moved by lorry up an almost impassable road. When the rains come in May, it will be totally impassable for at least three months.

Given the work of SCF and the local community and the resilience of children, a lot of these ex-fighters will be restored to normal life. But, as our experiences in the camp made plain, many will not be readily reclaimed and will continue to plague their community.

Aid workers discuss in troubled voices what appears to some of them evil on an unprecedented scale. Something very dark seems to have happened; and it is something to which the international community should awaken.

July 2000

REACHING THE UNREACHABLE

Malnourished and suffering from blackwater fever, this six-year-old boy and his mother walked 300 kilometres to the nearest clinic, run by Amref, a pioneering charity whose team of doctors reaches parts of Africa where no one else goes

It would be a long hot day, they warned us, the sort of day you drink a litre of water every hour to avoid dehydrating. By the time we reach the Turkana nomads after 90 minutes on a dirt track, it seems like it. We're not in any place marked on my map, though I know we're close to Kenya's border with Uganda. These Turkana people live just beyond the back of beyond, or what Amref calls the outreach.

Our LandCruiser pulls up as we suddenly come to a hundred of them clustered in the shade of the etesiro trees and they're expecting us, because word has been that the mobile clinic would come when the moon was right; and by some happy chance we arrive at that particular phase of the moon. They're mostly old men, women and children, for the young men are out on the plains guarding what is left of their animals.

Their appearance is striking, taking you back a long way in time. The women's necks are swathed in beads and some of them wear heavy jewellery on their bottom lip. Most of the men are in rags, covered by a blanket, topped up here and there in bizarre fashion with a small English homburg hat. But they are very still and somehow convey a marked dignity.

Some have walked miles to be here, but there are no queues for the clinic, no jostling. Time is of no consequence on the outreach. Most of them are resting quietly on the tiny stools they carry around with them. Where we sport watches, the men wear the abarait, a razor-sharp circular knife like the top of a soup tin. To my unpractised eye nearly all are suffering from prolonged malnutrition. When their blankets slip, you can see that the old men are skeletal. They're normally big meat eaters, but no longer. Kenya's worst drought since 1985 and the death of so many of their animals is hitting them hard.

One of the elders, who is blind, comes up to shake my hand. The man with him says he wants to talk to me about the need for water. How can you answer that? The fact is that as far as Kenya's government is concerned, these Turkana pastoralists are a waste of time. They live solely off their own animals and are otherwise economically unproductive. My medical companions from Amref are the only friends from the outside world they've got.

One four-wheel-drive, coated with dust, has pulled up alongside three small tents. These are the temporary residences of Amref's medical clinic in this corner of the outreach. A few yards on, towards the edge of the wood, the Amref African medical team has established three small posts.

At one of them, sitting at a camp table, the doctor is taking a look at the patients. A second medic nearby is handing out remedies. A third is working a microscope, which can give surprisingly quick returns on what may be seriously wrong. A little further on, a fourth is giving children jabs against polio.

I find that the heat, even in the late afternoon, is blurring some of what I am trying to take in. But according to a note I scrawled down, the mobile clinic is working on the outreach 21 days in the month. The operators seem to know by instinct where to go, and the pastoralists know where to find it.

The serious cases, identified by the mobile clinic, will eventually finish up in one of Kenya's small hospitals, which have doctors and nurses but no resident surgeons. It is to these hospitals that Amref's surgeons fly at regular intervals and on carefully pre-arranged programmes. A Cessna aircraft drops them off for two or three days to perform operations, then picks them up and brings them home for the weekend. All the surgeons know what to expect and carry their instruments with them.

So on another scorching day we go out to take a view of this. The journey from our camp with a surgeon and his anaesthetist to the village of Kakuma takes 90 minutes on Tarmac and another 70 minutes on a dirt track. The handful of patients waiting outside the Catholic mission hospital there have one thing in common. They've all come huge distances. The first one I meet, Lochor-Akalong Lowasa, is a boy of six. He and his mother have travelled 285 kilometres to get here. His badly swollen tummy suggests that he has a hydatid cyst. She's come this way because she has heard of my travelling companion, Dr Zeyhle Eberhard, one of Amref's doctors and a foremost authority on these cysts. Standing in the sun with me,

Eberhard runs a sensitive hand over Lochor-Akalong Lowasa. He suspects that it's not hydatid but malnutrition and blackwater fever.

Kaputuro Adukon, a woman of 43, has travelled 180km. She's another possible hydatid cyst case, but with suspected complications. Eberhard thinks she has multiple cysts in the liver, spleen and abdomen. Lokale Nato, 47, has had the shortest journey, a mere 95km. She has an enormous cyst on the back of her thigh, which we are invited to examine, but there are no complications. I watch her being moved into the small operating-theatre, but excuse myself from watching the operation which turns out to be straightforward and, I learn later, successful. Normally it takes the patient about a week in hospital to recover from these cyst operations. Amref has a place near its local headquarters where they can rest up.

Drought has aggravated a number of maladies, trachoma being one of them. In the persistent hot dry weather, with flies galore, eyes become vulnerable. Among children, trachoma is prevalent. So they need to learn that washing their face twice a day helps to ward off blindness. Water being desperately short, they pour a little into a suspended plastic mug with a tiny hole in the bottom. The trickle is enough for washing.

But here among the Turkana nomads the enemy is the hydatid cyst. It is a condition known in other parts of the world, Eberhard explains, but it is common among these pastoralists because they live so close to their dogs, and dogs eat filth, such as the corpses of animals killed by the drought.

Sanitising Eberhard's somewhat gruesome analysis, the cyst may grow in almost any part of the body, usually the stomach, and it can grow to a progidious size. Amref's surgeons removed from one woman a cyst weighing 12kg. She was, they assured us, much rejuvenated by the experience.

Sometimes it can be dealt with by local treatment, such as massage. More often it grows bigger and calls for an operation. In theory removing a cyst is a straightforward procedure; in practice it is often more complicated. As Eberhard, while patting the protruding stomach of one young patient, explains to me, 'When the liver or the pancreas is involved, then it is another matter.'

Eberhard, extrovert and a wonderful conversationalist, was a lucky find by Sir Michael Wood, who was one of Amref's founders more than 40 years ago. These flying doctors, as they are sometimes known, were the inspiration of Wood, Sir Archibald McIndoe of

New Zealand and Tom Rees of America. They perceived that the only way to cope with casualties and sickness over vast distances was to fly.

With a small fleet of light planes, Amref provides a 24-hour service. Kenyan and Tanzanian surgeons and doctors fly to rural hospitals for monthly surgical and medical circuits. On each one, a doctor treats up to 60 patients over three days. At our little hospital in Kakuma the surgeon worked for 12 hours at a stretch, carrying out six operations.

But for Amref now the big thing is to prevent this chronic drought from inflicting on Kenyans the sort of punishment their animals are suffering. There are some 700 Amref staff involved in this endeavour, pilots, surgeons, doctors, nurses, scientists—and 97 per cent of them are African. Amref enables Africans to look after Africa.

One or two, like Eberhard, have come from overseas. As a medical student in Germany, he studied hydatid. Sir Michael Wood lighted on him as one of five men in Europe with knowledge of the hydatid cyst. After thinking about it for two years, Eberhard took the job. He's been with Amref 18 years and has carried out about 10,000 prognoses.

The second star in the battle against hydatid is Dr John Wachira, a Kenyan reconstructive surgeon, who travelled with us. He graduated in Canada then turned the brain drain back to front and came back to work for Amref in Kenya.

Wachira was inspired by the life and work of Dr Anne Spoerry, one of Amref's pioneers, a doctor who at 45 learnt to fly a single-engine Piper Cherokee Lance PA-32 across a practice that stretched from the Kenya-Ethiopian border to Tanzania. She flew 30 years for Amref, logging more than 8,000 hours flying time. A much-loved eccentric who died last year, she gave her heart to the people of East Africa who called her Mama Daktari. Her little plane is still in the Amref hangar at Wilson airfield.

Amref's staff has to embrace anthropology, education, agriculture and half a dozen other disciplines—but, above all, human psychology. There was this boy I met at the Kakuma hospital who had walked with his mother 150km. His swollen legs suggested to Eberhard that he had oedema. After examining him, they told the mother that they needed to keep him in for a day. No, that would not be possible, she said. There were goats back home which needed attention. Then the question of a charge for treatment arose. It amounted to the equivalent of two goats. She consulted her brother who had come with them. No, it was too much. They walked away with the boy, who will probably die. 'I'd have paid the bill,' Eberhard said later, 'but they walked off.'

Amref has to persuade its flock that nothing is for free. Kenya's government cannot afford—or says it cannot afford—more than a fraction of what is needed for health and education. So, if there is to be the sort of health centre they are planning in the village of Lopiding, where some of the nomads have settled, the local population must be persuaded to contribute something like a third, say, £30,000.

Coming from a country where people expect a totally free health service, the idea of billing nomads for health care struck me as odd but it is, Amref insists, a sound principle. 'The crux always,' says Eberhard, 'is how much the local community will contribute.' They must share in all the decisions taken, and in the cost of what is done for them.

Amref knows that no single discipline, such as medicine or surgery, will suffice. There are many actors on Amref's stage who are not doctors. Lucy and Margaret are anthropologists. They see the problem in the round. They know, for instance, that what is most urgently needed is better livestock management and more sources of water for livestock, so that they do not die in a drought and make a meal for the dogs. As things are, such sources are in never-never land.

Working among these problems demands a robust spirit, proof against setbacks and disappointments, from all Amref staff. They have to know their limitations. 'We cannot solve the problem,' says Eberhard. 'We can only ease it.'

I thought I had seen the worst of Kenya's drought while we were on the Uganda-Sudan border. But around the Masai Mara in the south it was worse. In Nairobi when our Cessna flew out, it was raining stair rods. Eighteen minutes later and a few thousand feet lower, the earth all around us was grey and the scrub was dead. It looked like the surface of the moon.

On this ranch, 70 miles south of Nairobi, there had been 2,000 cattle. Now, after three years without serious rain, they had 100 beasts left, some barely able to stand. The Masai had pulled the weaver birds' nests out of the trees and thatch off the farm roof for cattle fodder. Drought on this scale punishes humans as well as animals. I asked the Amref doctor travelling with me what troubled him the most. 'Malnutrition,' he answered instantly, 'particularly among the young.'

It looks pretty grim, yet there is a glimpse of a better future for Africa here. Working on what looks like a gigantic lake of soda is the Magadi Soda Company. They've built the local hospital, which is among the best I've seen anywhere in Africa. It is a joint venture, shared by the company, Amref and the Kenya government.

There we meet a girl of four, Moinan Moibuko, recovering from burns she suffered while her family slept, exhausted by hunger, and she played by the fire. She lost her arm and part of her face, and is prone to sudden tears, but she is getting better. An Amref surgeon will undertake reconstructive surgery on her face. It was a tantalising glimpse of the future and how so much more could be done with joint ventures like this.

More than once on our long trek, I thought of Christina Rossetti's lines: 'Does the road wind uphill all the way?/ Yes, to the very end./ Will the day's journey take the whole long day?/ From morn to night my friend." In Africa, it takes a little longer.

A GOOD MAN IN AFRICA

The Shadow of the Sun
(Allen Lane)

Ryszard Kapuściński has transformed journalism into literature in his writings about Africa. W. F. Deedes met him

Ryszard Kapuściński, Poland's celebrated reporter and author, has been roaming through Africa on a shoestring for more than 40 years—trying to get himself killed, some would unkindly add. "I think," wrote Salman Rushdie, of Kapuściński's new account of his life in Africa, *The Shadow of the Sun*, "that nobody who puts himself in danger as much as he does is entirely sane."

So I give this robust, 70-something figure a quizzical look as we clink glasses over lunch. Having shuddered a bit over the description in his book of cerebral malaria—"I was two weeks unconscious . . ." followed by tuberculosis on a collapsed immune system, when his weight fell to 42 kilos, I had expected to see a more depleted figure.

He also had a close call with an Egyptian cobra, whose bite is 20 minutes away from death, and was fiercely bitten by a grey scorpion that crept onto his pillow—"they're the bad sort". It got him in the head on the Somalia-Ethiopia border, 500 kilometres away from the nearest hospital at Dirě Dawa and an agony-relieving injection.

What I wanted to discuss, however, was not his brushes with death, but his prose style, his gift of turning poor Africa into literature. Consider this description (translated by Klara Glowczewska) of the mountains of Rwanda—Rwanda, of all places, scene of that grisly massacre in 1997, which we both reported:

"High yet gentle peaks stretch before you into infinity. They are emerald, violet, green, and drenched in sunshine. It is a landscape devoid of the dread and darkness of rocky, windswept peaks, precipices, and cliffs; no deadly avalanches, falling rocks, or loose rubble are lying in wait for you here. No. The mountains of Rwanda radiate warmth and benevolence, tempt with beauty and silence, a crystal clear windless air, the peace and exquisiteness of their lines and shapes. In the mornings, a transparent haze suffuses the green valleys. It is like a bright veil, airy, light and glimmering in the sun . . ."

Here is Kapuściński on Africa itself: "The problem of Africa is the dissonance between the environment and the human being, between the immensity of African space (more than 30 million square kilometres!) and the defenceless, barefoot, wretched man who inhabits it. Whichever way he turns, there is distance, emptiness, wilderness, boundlessness."

And that smell of the tropics: "It is the smell of sweating body and drying fish, of spoiling meat and roasting cassava, of fresh flowers and putrid algae—in short of everything that is at once pleasant and irritating, that attracts and repels, seduces and disgusts . . ."

The way people write often depends on what they have read. "Which authors influenced your writing?" I ask. He misunderstands me. "For my new book, I read 220 books." I shook my head. "Who inspired your writing? Who did you read?"

"Conrad," he responded. Surprise. "Yes, he was a Pole." He named Malinowski, of whom I have never heard, as another favourite author. "And at university?" "At Warsaw University, I read history."

There was, I then suggested, more to it than that. Kapuściński got closer to African life than most Western reporters dream of doing. Much of his time there, he lived as Africans live, claiming that this was all he could afford. "In Africa, you don't need money," he asserts, looking me in the eye. I know better than that. Oh, come on, I say. "Did you live cheaply in Africa because you were short of money or from choice?" Another look. "Both!"

His style of life in Africa entailed other risks. When tuberculosis followed malaria, they wanted him in hospital. He refused. A month in hospital would consume more than his quarterly salary. Then they insisted he must return home.

No, no, he explained to the doctor who became his friend, he had to stay and pursue the chance of a lifetime. Poland had never before had a permanent correspondent in sub-Saharan Africa. So the doctor, the only pulmonary specialist in Tanzania, then arranged for him to become an outpatient in a local clinic for poor Africans. It meant 24 large grey pills and a painful injection in the arse every day.

"There was one syringe for the whole hospital," he says to me cheerfully. "That was in 1963. If there had been HIV Aids then, I would have been killed." But there was a cheery side to it. "Nothing," he writes in his book, "creates a bond between people in Africa more quickly than shared laughter—for example, at a white man jumping up because of a little thing like an injection." As they drove the needle in, he came to share the joke with them.

What Kapuściński writes about Africa is authoritative as well as attractive. His account of how the Hutus and the Tutsis were drawn into that dark night of genocide in Rwanda is the most enlightening I have read anywhere. So is his chapter on Amin, tyrant of Uganda, about whom he once contemplated writing a whole book. Furthermore, he has insight into some of Africa's frailties which perplex me. "Why do African leaders feel the need to stash away so much loot?" I ask. There are three reasons, he explains.

"First, having big money makes a real boss chief. It is part of traditional African culture—someone who can spend fabulous sums.

"The second reason he wants so much money is to satisfy a huge family. And thirdly, if there is a coup d'état, he needs money to escape. Being in power in Africa is very unstable."

He is perceptive on child soldiers too, a subject which closely interests me. As he puts it in his book: "The bloody chaos in which various African countries are plunged has spawned tens of thousands of orphans, hungry and homeless. They look for anyone who might feed and shelter them, and it is easiest to find food where the troops are."

Inevitably, "these armed encounters between youngsters are particularly bloody, because a child does not have the instinct for self-preservation, does not feel dread or comprehend death, does not experience the fear that only maturity will evoke." For these children, he says seriously, being in the Army is the best solution. "Otherwise, they will die of hunger." Yes, they are dehumanised, "but they get food, protection and power."

As a white European, Kapuściński seems always to have carried a sense of guilt in Africa because of colonialism. It was the Second World War, he thinks, that sowed the seed of that system's defeat and demise.

"Africans recruited into the British and French armies in Europe," runs a passage in his book, "observed that white men were fighting each other, shooting one another, destroying one another's cities. It was a revelation, a surprise, a shock . . . all the more powerful because the earlier inhabitants of Africa were not permitted to travel to Europe or anywhere else beyond their continent."

I feel roused to suggest that colonialism has been used for too long to defend a lot of the old Adam in Africa. What of the Cold War? Was not slavery a worse infliction? The slave trade, he agrees, was more serious. "Slavery was much more devastating than colonialism. It gave Africa a thorough complex of inferiority."

We discovered that we knew many of the same places in sub-Saharan Africa. The difference was that my style of travel was beyond his means, and his style of writing is beyond mine. We part amicably, and as I walk away it occurs to me that Salman Rushdie's reflection on Kapuściński's sanity does him less than justice. I thought back to the hair-raising exploits undertaken on our behalf by Poland's armed forces in the Second World War, one or two of which I witnessed. A lot of Poles are happy living as Kapuściński does.

April 2002

INNOCENT VICTIMS OF SUDAN'S FORGOTTEN WAR

W. F. Deedes reports from Lankien on the grim struggle to survive as fighting intensifies

In the oil-rich region of Western Upper Nile, the biggest battle of Sudan's long war is now raging between the government army and the military forces of the south.

Darkness has prevailed there since April 9 when fighting suddenly intensified. Flights by relief agencies have long been denied; and this month the number of flight denials in neighbouring areas were doubled. So the outside world knows nothing of this battle, nor why it is happening.

The most likely explanation is that moves towards a peace settlement in Sudan have driven both sides into a desperate attempt to stake claims in the country's most valuable territory. If so, this is the decisive battle of the war.

Both sides have recently gained strength. A ceasefire in the Nuba mountains has enabled the government to bring down reinforcements from there. The so-called rebel movements of the South, the Sudan People's Liberation Army under John Garang and the Sudan People's Democratic Front under Riek Machar have agreed to fight together and not each other. The senior man in the field from SPLA or SPDF takes command.

But a determined attempt, driven by Britain, America and Norway, to end this 19-year-old war is also moving. Four delegates from each side, the SPLA tell me, will meet next week to draw up an agenda. Certain principles have already been agreed, such as the right to self-determination and separation of religion and state.

That is what is seizing the military minds. For this complex war is partly about power and religion and race, but it is also about resources. And Sudan's most valuable resource is the newly found oil in Western Upper Nile. It is oil, moreover, in disputed territory on the sketchy boundary between north and south. The south knows that by moving the goalposts the government has secured oil that belongs to the south. It is also convinced that $300 million (£210 million) of the $500 million oil has brought in has been used to buy weapons against it.

So it targets the oil wells and the pipeline, in which British companies have had a hand, conveying the oil to Port Sudan. Small wonder the government fiercely defends the region. More cause to wonder, perhaps, how countries like Canada and Sweden, apostles of human rights, have got themselves mixed up in such a nasty business.

For to protect the oil fields of Western Upper Nile, named Unity state by the government, tens of thousands have been driven out of their villages, homes have been destroyed, families scattered.

China holds 40 per cent of the oil concessions, Malaysia 30 per cent. Their oil workers are said to mock the Canadians and the Swedes, who hold the rest, for their liberal scruples.

What exercised Susan Ryan of this newspaper and myself while travelling in Sudan was the vast cost of this conflict in human and financial resources. We met some of the four million people who have been not simply displaced but kept perpetually on the run.

In Lankien, where we flew with the United Nations World Food Programme, people are squeezed between government forces in Malakul and SPLA guerrilla fighters. Some 2,500 people in that area have been driven from home.

Nyaweeh did not know her age, but thought it was around 40. In fighting around Malakul, her husband was shot. She and her three children of six, four and two, fled across the river. The children never made the other side.

We asked if she knew what the fighting was about. "I don't know. I think it is to have a separate state. Oil? I know nothing about oil." The only thing she knew for sure was that life was hard. "You can see it in my body. I have no clothes, no food, no shelter."

You could see it also in her eyes. They were dead. With her was Nyabeh, of about the same age. She had left Lankien to follow a prophet. He told them to cast away their clothes and follow him. But then he started his own army, which led to fighting. Like Nyaweeh, three of Nyabeh's children died crossing the river. The other three were captured in the fighting. "We were deceived, the prophet told us he was God and that God wore no clothes. When I was found, I was naked."

In Lankien, there is not much for them. There are no roads, in or out, no water or electricity, and the ground is unforgiving. Christian Mission Aid offers primary health care in a small compound there and Médecins Sans Frontières copes with such things as kala-azar which, if not treated, kills.

The last food drop there was in June 2001 and was intended to last two months until the harvest but what little they can sow was interrupted this year by fighting. New supplies were due two months ago, but flights were banned. We were there in time to watch WFP drop 16 tons of food on a patch of land cleared of bushes.

It was a stirring sight to see the Hercules C130 plane fly in low and make two runs to discharge its cargo. Each bag of grain has three layers round it. Two burst, but the third survives. As we left the scene, hundreds of women passed us to collect their small ration of grain and oil. For most of them it had involved a walk of between one and six days. Returning home with the grain, they risked attack.

On just such a drop two months ago at Bieh, women and children gathering up the food were attacked, first with rockets and then machine guns. At least 24 people were killed and dozens wounded. Accident? On the contrary, the helicopter gunships flew so low that staff on the ground could distinguish the faces of the gunmen.

As the women of Lankien moved towards the drop we watched; the sky was clear, but there flashed across the imagination a vision of that massacre of innocent women and children ... of the way so many in this tormented land are living now.

For, as was borne in on us, nowhere seems safe for long. Less than 24 hours after we left Lankien, tensions rose over the arrival of a government militia man with water drilling equipment—coupled with instructions to take control of the area. Local chiefs asked him to leave, then started to mobilise and arm their men.

In anticipation of a fight, Operation Lifeline Sudan, operating from the Kenyan air base of Lockichoggio, airlifted out the two WFP staff monitoring food distribution and three Christian Aid workers to whom we had spoken and who treat between 150 and 300 patients a day.

These evacuations, which normally run at 70 a year but amounted this week to about five a day, are a sure signal of increased fighting.

There were other signs of stress. No one in Lankien, we observed, was even trying to provide education. It was the first place I have ever been in where local leaders showed no enthusiasm for the subject. Schools? Everyone is too busy, they told us. They have other priorities in their lives—finding water and food, running away from gunships or soldiers. Staying alive in much of Sudan is a full-time occupation.

We caught glimpses of what it is to be an internally displaced person. First, there are weeks on the run, with little or no food to cook and no pots or pans with which to cook. Eventually, with luck, the displaced person becomes a returnee. Back home, but there is no home left and the family has dispersed.

That's life for many today in Sudan, where in some places 30 per cent of the people suffer malnutrition. So we found the UN agencies and aid organisations at full stretch, insofar as the fighting and the government—which plays ducks and drakes with relief flights—permitted.

The WFP strives to provide enough to avert starvation, but sensibly leaves the rest to human endeavour. Even with that limit-ation, getting food to those most in need in course of a year has meant shifting 178,000 metric tons of food at the cost of £100 million.

If this sorely afflicted people could express a voice, it would be a united cry to end this extravagant war. But in a country with so little infrastructure and non-existent communications, they are denied a voice. There are simply no vehicles for expression.

That is why the world knows so little of what happens in Sudan. Nowhere else have I encountered such unheeded and inarticulate suffering. The only network of communications in Sudan today depends on those who fly, often at risk, to deliver relief from some 225 airstrips.

But when, as is happening now, so many of those strips are ruled out by the government to conceal the flames of war, then some 1.7 million people who are most in need are denied relief, and darkness falls.

We came to share the view of those who know this country best. If there is to be peace, then it must come this year. And if, for one reason or another, this most promising of all recent peace endeavours fails, then Sudan will stay in the dark for a long time to come.

SLAVES OF SUDAN HOLD THE
KEY TO PEACE

W. F. Deedes reports from Bahr el Ghazel on how a barbaric trade is finally ending

Painfully slowly, on the shifting border between north and south Sudan, the cruellest trade on earth is being brought to an end. Some of the thousands of women and children abducted by northern raiders and then enslaved in the north, sometimes for years, are struggling back towards home.

When you talk to parents who have lost children to this trade and to children who have been retrieved, as I have been doing, you grasp the iniquity of it. Some of these children come back totally changed, as if their minds had been stolen. They do not know to whom they belong.

Nobody knows how many have been abducted over the years. Save the Children and the United Nations Children's Fund put it conservatively at between 10,000 and 17,000, but some estimates are higher. Raiding between north and south has gone on for generations. But most of the present victims, a by-product of the civil war, have been seized by irregulars of the government of Sudan.

An international commission of inquiry in Sudan this year declared that abductions in Bahr el Ghazel, where I have been travelling, and Western Upper Nile, continued with the knowledge of the government's military. Some of those abducted, it also found, were held in conditions that amount to slavery.

For a long time the government of Sudan turned a blind eye to all this. In 1999 under intense international pressure, it declared its intention of reunifying all abductees and eliminating the practice in Sudan.

Much is owed to America's decision to tackle this issue at the highest political level. It was seen as a major obstacle to any peace settlement in this interminable war.

But up to now, even with peace talks in progress, the government of Sudan and the Sudan People's Liberation Army have failed to agree on a mutually acceptable way of returning the women and children in the north awaiting reunification.

This means that many children are being held too long in transit care centres, with serious psychological consequences for them. Despairing of agreement, local committees on both sides of the border, assisted by Save the Children, are resorting to their own methods of retrieving some of these children. The key is the market place in Warwar.

There you find Arab traders selling all manner of goods from clothes to cooking pots. They have been trading at considerable risk, for in the eyes of the north they are sustaining the enemy. They compensate themselves by charging three or four times the market price, because their wares are unobtainable elsewhere in the impoverished south.

Through some of these traders an intelligence network operates. They go back to the north regularly to replenish their stocks. They bring back with them names of abductees. So families who have lost loved ones seek for clues in this market place, and sometimes their number comes up.

I talked with a father, Dot Been Dot, whose son was abducted six years ago. One day recently, Save the Children in the south announced some names of abductees sent by their office in the north. One or two of the father's friends recognised the name and told him.

Though badly wounded in a foot, "I danced for joy", he told me. He had then managed to walk two miles to the Save the Children compound in Bahr el Ghazel for more information. There has to follow an elaborate procedure to avoid fraud. Suffice it, the father knows his son is safe. Save the Children reckon it will take another fortnight to get clearance from the government and the SPLA.

Then the boy will be taken to an agreed crossing and flown to the nearest airstrip. The reunion of father and son must be witnessed by the local authority. After that, they are free to go home and become reacquainted.

The first reunifications took place in May when five children were flown back in this way. Because neither side can agree on a road passage from north to south, all reunifications so far have been by air—which is very expensive.

Meeting the joyful father was cheering; meeting Nimari Garang, abducted in 1988 at the age of four and now returned at 17, much less so. Because his mother and father were killed at the time of his abduction, he has returned to an aunt and seems happy with her.

But weeks after his return, his eyes are vacant and occasionally wild. His legs are still scarred and ulcerated, for he was badly treated by his Arab master and often beaten. He has had no education but is reluctant to go back to school, sensing that he will be embarrassed by other children.

He would prefer, he told me haltingly, to take up manual work, perhaps building. When his aunt's small children aged two and three appeared, his face softened and he offered them sweets. He is not beyond reclaiming and, with help, may yet be restored; but to be enslaved between the ages of four and 16 is a crippling experience. There are many more like him.

A wall of hypocrisy and evasion has been built round this crime of abduction and enslavement, which has made countering it more difficult. The word "slavery" is avoided to protect feelings of both north and south.

For this traffic touches the root of what divides them and has fuelled this terrible war. Many in the north *do* view the predominantly African south as inferior folk, in this context as beasts of burden, people to be exploited.

So until this trade is wiped out and its victims restored to their families, there can be no lasting peace. That is why America has put such pressure on the government of Sudan. Sudan's slaves hold one of the keys to peace.

THE DAWN OF A NEW ERA IN AFRICA? DON'T HOLD YOUR BREATH

W. F. Deedes says that, while democracy was the winner in Kenya's presidential election, endemic corruption will continue to hold back the continent

How cheering it would be if we could see in the outcome of Kenya's presidential election promise of a new era in Africa. The power of the Kenyan African National Union Party is ended and the country rid of the despotic and corrupt President Moi. The influence he hoped to maintain after losing power has been nullified.

But does it herald a wind of change for that continent? Not for a while. Do we really suppose that President Mugabe of Zimbabwe will see this triumph for democracy as an example to follow? As one who has successfully clung to power by intimidation and rigging every election, he will see it as a warning.

Will the present rulers of Angola, Sudan, the Congo, Malawi and Somalia see the light and determine in future to "trust the people"? Africa's ruling elite doesn't think along those lines. It treasures power, and knows that, in Africa, great wealth is indispensable to the business of winning and holding power. If the acquisition of that wealth means doing business with gangsters, so be it.

We are easily shocked by this, but, as an old Africa hand observed to me in Nairobi a few weeks ago, it is barely half a century since any African got his hands on real money. When I was travelling in Africa, not long before we wound up our colonial empire, most of the potential rulers I met were poor as church mice.

The tragedy is that this accumulation of wealth as a tool of power in Africa has almost without exception gone hand in hand with gross misgovernment, sometimes leading to rebellion and crippling civil wars. While piling up cash in their overseas bank accounts, the elite has been destroying its own economies. Kenya exemplifies it. A month ago I was looking at very small farmers earning not much more than a dollar a day. That is far below Kenyans' potential.

An earlier generation of Africans has been amazingly tolerant of these abuses—just as many centuries ago, the English peasant tolerated bad barons. He had no real choice in the matter. It is in the minds of those now under 35 in Africa that enlightenment has been dawning, among the younger women particularly. That is where hope lies.

I have been startled in Africa to hear the opinions of younger women who have managed to acquire a better-than-average education. They are not going to overthrow their government, however despotic, tomorrow or next year. But their thinking, developed by awareness of what goes on in the world outside Africa, will lead to change.

As young mothers, aware of what education can unlock for their children, they will not forever submit to schools that, subsisting on a tiny fraction of GDP, leave their children unprepared. This new generation knows why Mugabe sent his soldiers to the disastrous Congo civil war and what he got out of it. Africa today has something in common with the Soviet Union in the 1980s, when its rulers could no longer conceal from the people what the rest of the world was doing.

But if we want to see change for the better, there are contributions to be made from our side of the hill—and it will not be done, as some insist, simply by redeeming Africa's colossal debts.

We need to clear a few delusions of our own. Apologising for the past is politically fashionable, but perpetuating the myth that Africa's failure can be laid at the door of colonialism is no help at all to Africans brave enough to defy Mugabe. He says that, and they know better. Africans are a lot brighter than some of our own ideologues.

Above all, we must insist on greater transparency in the West's commercial dealings with Africa. That would deliver a blow to the heart of corruption in Africa, which is going to be infernally difficult to eradicate. Does anyone seriously suppose that a clean wind will now blow through Kenya? There are too many involved in the racket. Corruption runs from top to bottom. It is institutionalised, endemic.

Corruption, remember, goes hand in hand with government employees being paid a pittance or not being paid at all. During a visit I made to Angola, a wise old bird said to me: "If your vehicle is stopped by the police in Luanda, don't argue or panic. You will be surprised how pleased they are by a currency note of relatively low value. It is, after all, their only source of income."

What urgently needs to be addressed are the colossal sums of money that international oil companies and their kind pay in backhanders to corrupt regimes in return for concessions. Companies should be required to disclose payments they make to governments for the resources they use.

Angola's government has been raking in millions of dollars on that account, while many of its population are destitute and a third of its children die before reaching the age of five. Oil and arms deals are bouquets for the gangsters interlocked with some of Africa's regimes.

Global oil corporations retort: what business is it of anyone else if we make private deals with governments? If we want to reduce the corruption that renders so much of Africa anaemic, it is our business. An end to corporate secrecy in some of these shady deals would contribute as much to the welfare of Africa's people as reducing debt.

Africa's perpetual famines are caused partly by natural causes, partly by political ineptitude, and sometimes by cynical politics. Ethiopia's famine in 1984, which brought Bob Geldof's Band Aid into action, had been aggravated by deliberate inaction. The Marxist Colonel Mariam Mengistu reckoned that hungry people might be less inclined to support expanding guerrilla movements.

He was not the last to exploit food shortages for political purposes. It has happened in Sudan. Mugabe has been caught redhanded manipulating food relief—urgently needed to make good his own follies—in favour of his political supporters.

On hurriedly granting our African colonies independence, we naively left them with the makings of parliamentary democracy, which a ruling elite promptly sought to counter by the weight of power and wealth.

In Kenya, democracy rules again. In due course, other African nations will move that way, but not soon. The closing lines of Alan Paton's *Cry, The Beloved Country* apply:

"For it is the dawn that has come, as it has come for a thousand centuries, never failing. But when that dawn will come, of our emancipation, from the fear of bondage and the bondage of fear, why, that is a secret."

WAR CHILDREN LEARN TO
LIVE IN PEACE

*Education is helping Sierra Leone to heal scars of a brutal conflict, reports
W. F. Deedes in Freetown*

One year after the curtain fell on one of Africa's most brutal civil
wars Sierra Leone is shaking off its nightmare and looking itself in
the face again.

Pointing the way is President Ahmad Kabbah who seems the
right man to pull his country out of the mire of 11 years of savagery.

"What worries you most?" I asked him.

"Security, food, education," he said, and a few days in this country
bears him out.

Though it is only a year since the people made a celebratory
bonfire of weapons and Mr Kabbah declared the war over and
disarmament complete, the country seems unexpectedly calm. But
peace after a long civil war is always fragile.

He is right about food. Too many men have been fighting instead
of sowing and reaping. I have been visiting schools where children
keen to learn falter because they arrive with empty stomachs and
may very well get only one meal in the day.

"Education," says the president, "is a priority area, and you
cannot have education without teachers. I was once permanent
secretary in the Education Department, so this is close to me. There
has been a brain drain from Sierra Leone."

One penalty of long civil wars is that so many of the best brains
leave the country, never to return. Some 40 per cent of the teachers
in the Gambia, the president told me, were trained in Sierra Leone.

Some now express willingness to return. Looking me in the eye,
the president added: "There will be no difficulty in them being
accepted back in their communities. We Africans are very forgiving
and accepting."

That sentence is one of the foundations on which Sierra Leone
is being slowly restored to life. A war which displaced almost half the

population, brutalised thousands of children and left thousands more
without parents bequeaths psychological problems.

Travelling in Sierra Leone with PLAN International, who make
part of their mission pulling war-torn children back from the brink,
I saw consequences of a conflict in which boys and girls were
drugged, armed with machetes and ordered to massacre and maim.
One is the huge camp for war wounded and amputees outside the
capital, Freetown.

With PLAN's help I have been talking to children, still only 12
to 14 years old, who were driven to commit atrocities. I spoke at
length to Kobbe Williams, now 18, who was captured and sent into
battle at the age of nine. "Sometimes," he said to me, "I have to sit
down and think of what I did." For the many children moved to do
that, school is a great healer. It fills the mind with other thoughts.

It is heartening to see the resolution of these ex-warrior children
to catch up with their learning. There was a girl of 18 in class with
girls of half her age. For her pride came second to the will to learn.
"One of the reasons that led to war," Mr Kabbah said, "was poverty.
You cannot address poverty without education."

The girls came off worst in this war, for they had to submit. One
who had been the "wife" of a "brigadier" wept as she recounted her
experiences. The boys had a degree more choice. And it is those over
10 years of age who bear the heaviest scars, for they witnessed more
horrors than the younger ones.

I spent one morning at a Catholic school for 400 girls in
Moyamba, which PLAN helped to restore. Outwardly the school
would dignify any part of London, all the girls in uniform and
beautifully behaved, but looking closely at one or two faces you get
the weird impression that they belong to someone 40 years old.

To cheer some of these children up, I told them that after both
World Wars, Oxford and Cambridge dons declared that young men
who returned from the front made excellent students. Experience
had matured them.

With a United Nations force of some 16,000 peacekeepers and a
more visible police presence than we see in Britain, the country's
internal security feels solid. Where we travelled outside Freetown
there were UN watch towers. Most of the roads are ruinous but
communications are being restored. I crossed more temporary Bailey
bridges than I have seen since the Second World War in Europe.

The country thirsts for reconciliation. That mood is dominant and seems genuine. The heaviest cloud on the horizon is the unavoidable duty of bringing to justice those who were mainly responsible for what amounted to genocide.

A unique criminal court has been set up jointly by the International Court and the Sierra Leone government. According to one of its members with whom I flew to Freetown, it will deem the use of children in war a crime.

None can doubt the necessity of this court, but many fear for the consequences. This country lies still. The sudden arrest of, say, 20 or 30 war criminals, presumably former members of Foday Sankoh's Revolutionary United Front, would undoubtedly create a stir.

The court will be controversial because it may take up positions that the accused challenge. Why disturb peace? Yet how can some of the unspeakable atrocities committed in Sierra Leone in 1991–2002 be brushed aside? It would provoke outrage. Furthermore, the longer evidence is kept in store, the less reliable it becomes.

And if there is to be trouble, let it occur while the UN has a firm grip on security. It aims to reduce its force to only 2,000 by December 2004.

Stability in Sierra Leone may be fragile, but the tales I have heard of what this war did to children, and the faces of some of those children that I looked into leave me in no doubt at all. The criminal court has an inescapable duty to humankind.

A NATION HUNGRY FOR MORE FOOD AND EDUCATION

W. F. Deedes reports from Leku on Ethiopia's famine and its causes

A journey 190 miles south from Addis Ababa to Leku takes you into the heart of the famine that is again plaguing Ethiopia. We stop at a compound there and move into a big tent where a score of mothers have brought their small children for therapeutic feeding.

All these children, the doctor explained to me, are wasting away; that is to say they have fallen more than 70 per cent below the normal weight for height ratio. You can tell when a child is not responding to such treatment, because the gleam in the eye fails. The mothers' eyes which followed us round were dulled by that sense of helplessness you find in famines and refugee camps.

Yet these are women who, given half a chance, would be caring for their children, carrying the burdens of all African women and representing the backbone of the community. This is a country, bear in mind, where by custom the women eat last and least.

Then on to another compound where a huge throng of hungry men, women and children have gathered to draw their monthly allowance of 33 lbs of maize. This is supplementary feeding for pregnant women and children being organised by the children's development agency Plan. These people are not sick but hungry. Men run back and forth humping sacks of grain from the USA.

There is irony in this hunger we see all around us, for this area is green and lush. Nothing of the desert here. Cattle graze off rich pasture. The eucalyptus trees, the cacti and the ensett which resembles banana trees grow high.

So why this destitution? Mainly because the price of coffee, main crop in this region, has fallen from 40 birr (£4) to 10 birr (£1) a kilo. "The future for my children is grim," says Medina Berassa who grows coffee on a plot one quarter the size of a football field. "There are so many and the land is so little. It is in God's hands."

But I witnessed this destitution and therapeutic feeding of children going on in Addis Ababa as well.

This is Ethiopia of 1986 all over again, without Bob Geldof and Band Aid but with an important difference. The aid agencies and big non-government organisations, familiar with Ethiopia's proneness to famine, have been on the alert. That is saving a lot of lives.

But as we drive away from these melancholy scenes in Leku, I reflect on what I have learned as the reasons for this perpetual failure of Ethiopia to feed its own people. Even in a good year six million Ethiopians now depend on grain from the outside world for their daily bread. This year the figure is 13.2 million or a fifth of the population.

Simon Mechale, Commissioner of the Disaster Prevention and Preparedness Commission knows why. Only a 10th of this country, five times the size of the UK, is arable and much of that is hopelessly unproductive. Good soil has been degraded. A million tons of topsoil is eroded every year. Deforestation at the rate of at least 250 square miles a year—wood hewn for cooking and selling—has reduced rainfall, increased drought and devastated much of the environment.

There is a grievous lack of farming skills in a population almost 90 per cent of which lives off the land. Water resources have been neglected. To all of which it is relevant to add this is a country which recently spent almost half its gross income on military readiness.

True, there is an uneasy truce in the wasteful war between Eritrea and Ethiopia; so uneasy that UN Secretary General Kofi Annan has just called upon them expressively to end their "cold peace". Against such a background it is hardly surprising to find half this nation's children ill nourished and one in 10 so badly fed that its body is wasting away.

So what's to be done? Aware that this state of affairs is becoming insupportable, aid donors and the World Bank have been meeting in Geneva to talk.

Marie Staunton, Director of Plan UK with whom I have been travelling, is right in saying that the drought requiring huge dollops of food aid which steadily increase dependency has become a vicious circle. Aid has grossly outstripped development. This year for instance America has given £350 million worth of food but only £3.5 million for development.

A population of 67 million is soaring at 2.8 per cent a year. This is a country crying out for education of women, churches permitting, in family planning.

The most urgent need is policies leading to better use of

resources. In Lalibela a Plan enterprise illustrates what can be done. We visited a model farm, where a typical smallholder, with only half a hectare or half a football pitch at his disposal, has been encouraged to grow onions, garlic, potatoes, tomatoes, cabbage and lettuce. As well as feeding his family he makes £150 a year.

In 2001 this man was on food aid which he has now dispensed with. Better still, some of the 16,500 farmers in the area being advised by Plan visit this demonstration holding and profit from it. Tourism is yielding only a fraction of its potential. No country in Africa has stronger appeal to the tourist than Ethiopia. It is absurd that a country so rich in history, treasure and natural beauty should be attracting more aid workers than tourists.

"We are not making good use of our land," Girma Woldegiorgis, the president of Ethiopia, emphasised to me. "We need better productivity." Then he reminded me that when I first visited Ethiopia in 1935 the population would have been around 15 million, one quarter of today's. No, he went on to assure me, the churches raise no objection to family planning. So there lie perhaps two keys to release Ethiopia from its plight—family planning and far better use of land. In brief, more development, less relief.

HOPE WALKS WITH GHOSTS OF SUDAN'S CIVIL WAR

W. F. Deedes reports on the ceasefire in the Nuba Mountains, a region which for years has been a no-go area for outsiders

To feel the reality of Sudan's 20-year war, and weigh the chances of a lasting peace on which so many are now counting, the Nuba Mountains are the place to go.

Here you learn of the terrible things people do to each other in a civil war, and you breathe the air of mistrust which is the final impediment to peace.

So many have died in this Nuba Mountains region, roughly the size of Austria.

So many have been torn from their homes and tortured. So many ghosts walk here.

All this in a land of startling beauty. From a de-mining compound one glances across the craggy hills in the evening light as the sun goes down.

They look the stuff dreams are made of, not the nightmares so many have experienced.

Yet now, unmistakably, change is sweeping this tormented land. "Everything in this country is normally from the top down," said Colonel George McGarr, the British Chief of Staff to the Joint Military Commission in Kadugli, which monitors the regional cease-fire between government and the Sudan People's Liberation Army rebels which has held for almost two years now.

"Now it is surging up from down to the top. Even among the hardliners in Khartoum there are signs of change, perhaps because they realise they are now up against the will of the world," he said.

If the ceasefire agreement in the Nuba Mountains does turn to lasting peace, much will be owed to Friends of the Nuba Mountains which maintain in the region a small but effective Joint Military Mission costing around £600,000 a month.

The Friends comprise Britain, America, Canada and six Western European countries.

The mission keeps a watchful eye on the ceasefire, deals with violations, grievances and complaints and holds a weekly meeting with the military of both sides to thrash things out. Government forces occupy 70 per cent of the Nuba Mountains region.

The SPLA holds the remnants with probably not more than 2,000–3,000 men.

"This is a martial society," said Colonel McGarr. Indeed it is. In every village I enter to discuss future needs I encounter the military.

"No," they say at one village I approach, "you cannot speak to the people. Your papers are not quite in order."

In the village of Katcha from which I write, all is sweetness and light. I spent 20 minutes discussing with soldiers, military needs—disposal of land mines, water, getting the children back to school. Then I spent 20 minutes with a village elder or two whose wishes are almost exactly the same.

This war has caused a huge displacement of population, not least in the Nuba Mountains. Now they are pouring back. Some 150,000 have returned already to this region. When peace comes that figure will multiply. Then they will face the deadly obstacle of landmines that litter much of this land. Most of the anti-tank mines on the so-called roads were laid by the SPLA. Government forces laid most of the anti-personnel mines. Landmine Action, my hosts in Sudan, are doing heroic work to clear the roads with teams of locally trained de-miners.

But it is slow and hard work in the fierce heat of the day, and in de-mining protective clothing. Travelling over Sudan's infrastructure moreover, takes time to move the de-miners to and from the minefields. Landmines are a particularly sensitive issue for the military in the peace process.

Notwithstanding government assurances, they are reluctant to permit the removal of anti-personnel mines which have been laid defensively round villages.

In every village security and freedom of movement heads the citizens' list of priorities. What else would they seek after being a war zone for up to 20 years?

Then come the humanitarian needs—water and sanitation, starter packs of seeds and so on and, of course, education.

Every school in this region has been laid waste. Some classes are held under the trees, but in the rainy season from May until October that is out of the question. There are teachers, but many of them are inevitably ill-trained. So virtually a generation of young Sudanese have had little or no schooling.

Ask the local farmers their priority and they will talk of ridding them of the nomads. War has destroyed the nomads' natural routes. So they prey on farmers and cattle go missing. Nomads, incidentally, have been creating problems in Sudan for 400 years or more.

No matter what priority the military or the farmer choose, little will get done in this vast land until the rutted tracks that pass for roads are made fit for anything other than a sturdy four-wheel drive vehicle.

When peace comes this will take time and a lot of money before Sudan is anything like in working order again.

Yet Europe and the United States, which will be called on to meet some of the cost, can take heart they are dealing with a resilient and self-reliant nation.

Sudan is not holding out a begging bowl to the world. "We don't want food relief," a meeting of village chiefs, representing tens of thousands, told me. "Our farmers will till their own soil, but they will need some tools and seed."

The bearing of the women tells you something. They walk straight-backed and serene, carrying enormous weights on their heads.

And as one British officer put it to me: "You can greet the children and expect them to return your greeting in a style now almost unthinkable in the UK."

It is in the Nuba Mountains that some of the worst atrocities occurred during this war. There you discover what a forgiving people these are.

"The past is the past," say some of the elders. The wisest among them put it differently: "We won't forget but remember—and learn."

GOOD FENCES MAKE
GOOD NEIGHBOURS

In a small corner of Kenya, where banditry and poaching were once rife, a unique conservation project supported by Tusk Trust has brought hope and security to humans and animals alike

Africa's darkness is often lit by candles we don't see. This is a candle, I thought, as Ian Craig drove us through the Sarara valley in northern Kenya, one of the wildlife conservation areas in the region that he has inspired. It was such a beautiful African evening, sunny, silent, still. Not a leaf stirring.

"It's been quiet here for five years," says Craig. Before that, the bandits had taken charge. "Gangs of 20 or more," he reflects, as we drive past two giraffes that eye us calmly.

"They know they're safe," I murmur.

"They're learning that they're safe," amends Ian.

"The bandits," he resumes, "rendered human and animal life intolerable. Foreign invaders made this area impossible. They stole cattle, killed elephants for their ivory—and anyone who got in the way. They had no hesitation in killing policemen. They were very aggressive."

We drove on through the quiet. There was, in truth, very little large wildlife to be seen that evening, but one felt enveloped by the surroundings. Sometimes a dik dik, one of the smallest antelopes, crossed our path. Very small animals scuttled about. An Egyptian goose resting on a fallen tree made off with a great clatter. Craig went on talking quietly of the bad times past in northern Kenya and how they were changed.

"There were thousands of elephants here in the 1960s," he says. "The 1970s were bad—due to the high price of ivory and corruption in government. Until 1989, it was a wild area." Ivory, before the world ban on transactions, was fetching $150 a kilogram. There were guns galore, lots of AK-47s spilt over from conflict in Somalia and between Ethiopia and Eritrea. A nightmare for man and beast.

Everything changed because Craig set about persuading the local people that sanctuary for human beings and sanctuary for wildlife had become indivisible.

Craig was born in Kenya. His family had farmed one of the big estates, 55,000 acres at Lewa, not far from Mount Kenya, since 1922. I picked up some of what followed, not from him, but from one of the local elders, Kipsoi by name, in the Il Ngwesi community, where the first of the community wildlife projects became established.

It all began with the big drought of 1984, explained Kipsoi. It killed most of the cattle, on which this region of Kenya, with its poor soil, then wholly depended. "We had 20 cattle left," he says. Then they learnt that Craig was selling off his herd. Why? Because, Craig told them, he reckoned wildlife would offer a better, more reliable source of income.

The elder paused here, as we turned another corner in this narrative, and drew on a cigarette which our photographer, Abbie Trayler-Smith, had offered him. Tobacco has its uses. I hoped the cigarette smoke might curb the flies that were pestering us. I had declined to climb a steep slope to the appointed meeting place. So chairs were brought down to us and we were sitting under the trees amid animal droppings that enormously attracted the flies.

It dawned on some of the community of 448 families, the elder went on, that the wildlife belonged to them and not to the government. One step on and they perceived that, if they looked after the wildlife as they had looked after their cattle, the wildlife might well pay a dividend through tourism.

At this point, they went back to Craig for advice. He offered to take three elders to the Masai Mara to see how the people there contrived to run a tourist business in conjunction with wildlife and cattle. The elders returned. "We have seen the light," they claimed. The population of Il Ngwesi stayed unconvinced, believing the elders wanted to sell their land to the government. Another year passed before they could reach agreement among themselves.

Then they sent another party to the Masai Mara, 70-strong, young and old, representing all opinions. That was the turning point. The younger generation won the argument. Wildlife became a new form of land use. Tourists produced money they had never seen before. Some of it went into schools, clinics, water—assets the government of Kenya had never managed to provide.

*

They set up a management committee. They decided they must
build a six banda (cottage) lodge for the tourists. With help from
donors, they raised a beautiful place, named, like the homeland, Il
Ngwesi, at the cost of £60,000. We spent a night there. It's a bit of
a rocky climb from the lounges and dining-room to your bedroom,
at which my legs protested; but there is a sedan chair for ancients,
you are wholly at one with your surroundings, and the view from my
bedroom across a great vale of trees to a pool where the animals
come to drink in the evening is majestic. The staff serve a good wine
for dinner, too.

An airstrip has been built alongside the lodge. In Kenya, they fly
like you take a taxi in London. This was the first lodge in the seven
conservation areas in northern Kenya owned and run by the Masai
community. Building it provided local employment, running it provides more jobs.

By 1990, the Il Ngwesi project had reached a stage when the
government of Kenya felt moved to smile on it. It had reason to feel
satisfied. This is a difficult region of Kenya, with a relatively small
population, unproductive soil and poor cattle and goat farmers.
Government perceives that this outreach idea of a community looking after wildlife and profiting from it is proving a success.

You learn as you move around the conservation areas under the
aegis of Tusk Trust, the first major donor to Lewa and the other six
community conservation projects, what a close affinity there is
between safety for man and animal life. A lawless land is ruin for
both of them. As the bad old days proved, gangs hunting elephants
and rhino for their tusks and other wildlife for their meat will cut
down anything in their path.

Furthermore, as you travel around the tracks in a Land Rover,
encountering here and there a game warden carrying a gun, it dawns
on you that you are physically safer in one of these conservation
areas than you would be in London's Soho after 11pm on Saturday.
"The government of Kenya," says Craig, "has taken a long time to
appreciate the connection between tourism and peace of mind."

Sure, there's truth in that. But now they are willing to arm the
police reservists, who form part of the defence against lawlessness and provide arms for better security. The carrying of arms
outside the law, on the other hand, attracts a sentence of up to seven
years.

There are other factors that have changed men's thinking. In the community project's early days, there was a sudden outbreak of cholera. It began with 10 sick, then it began to spread. Lewa used its powerful radio network to inform the government. Two army trucks were sent to gather the victims. On their way to hospital with the afflicted, both trucks broke down. At this point, 90 people were down with cholera. Another radio call to Lewa instigated a rescue operation. A helicopter was flown to a hospital to collect the necessary drugs and then carried these to the trucks. A lot of lives were saved.

Thus the organisation, through its network of modern communications with a radio range of 80 miles, established a formidable presence. In a serious battle with raiders, the same system of communications enabled the authorities to prevail. Both episodes won respect for what had been established and uttered a warning to poachers. "They know we have the paraphernalia to protect wildlife," says Craig.

Predictably, after the Nairobi bomb blast in 1998 and the turn of events in Mombasa, our Foreign Office felt obliged to issue a warning against travel in Kenya. More up-to-date advice to the traveller might be: "Go where the wildlife is to be seen and feel secure."

You can read off the map in Craig's office where such security is assured. Some 1,000 square miles in northern Kenya have now been given over to conservation of wildlife, embracing a population of about 60,000. There are seven of these conservation areas now at different stages of development. In all of them, the terrain differs, the water factor, which is crucial, varies and so do local inclinations.

But the same doctrines prevail everywhere: when wildlife is made safe, so is the human being; keeping cattle and fostering wildlife are not incompatible. Carefully done, they can run in harness —profitably.

Cattle livestock are still an important part of Masai culture, but they and other livestock are kept in separate fenced-off areas. Thus, both they and the wildlife thrive. The livestock are in less danger from predators, there is room for the wildlife and the destruction over-grazing makes on the land can be controlled.

Craig's family home is situated on the Lewa conservancy, which is the marker, the founding father of this idea. Its 55,000 acres are enclosed by a wire fence more than 80 miles long, electrified by a solar panel. The volcanic soil is dark and rich. After the rains that are ending, the pastures, alight with wild flower, are verdant. I have never before seen grass like it anywhere in Africa.

The animal population at Lewa includes 36 black rhino, 34 white rhino, some 200 elephants, 20 per cent of the world's remaining Grevy's zebra and thousands of smaller mammals. A young giraffe patrols the grounds of Craig's home and a couple of young cheetah are housed there. I was persuaded to make friends with both of them, which wasn't difficult once it became clear that what sounded to me like a growl was in fact a purr. No, one mustn't call them tame, because in six months or so they will be returned to the wild. They can hunt well enough now when they are hungry.

Grevy's zebra is a good example of a breed of wild animal, not widely known, less dramatic than the big beasts, that could very easily slip into extinction within 10 years. In the late 1970s, there were 15,000 of them. Today there are between 2,500 and 3,000 left, a decline of at least 80 per cent.

We set out one evening across the Lewa territory to catch a view of them and, by a stroke of luck, found some mingling with the more familiar zebra—although they are a separate species and never inter-breed. The Grevy's is more finely striped, leaving a white underbelly. You can identify every one of them by looking at the stripes on its right-hand rump, which are the equivalent of our human fingerprint. Extinction is inevitable if the rate of decline through poaching, predation and competition with domestic livestock is not reversed. Community conservation areas are their last hope.

It is easy to see why Prince William, who spent his gap year working on a project at Lewa, fell in love with it and visits frequently. The whole place is rich in glimpses of wildlife behaving unexpectedly. We were out one evening watching a herd of elephants grazing nearby. The adults form a rough protective ring around the young ones. All seemed to be at peace. "Elephants are not really compatible with people," says Craig. "They need their solitude, they need their peace. They know when they are safe."

"How do they know?"

"We don't know."

That goes for other wildlife as well. Something unfathomable to us tells them where they are secure. They will feel drawn from one area to another by such a sense. Tourists do not disturb them. It's the sound of a shot, the sight of children throwing stones at them that alarms.

Doing the rounds of Lewa one evening with Craig in his Land Rover, we came across one of the 36 black rhinos feeding close to the elephants. Suddenly, it got into its head that the elephants were pressing too closely on it and darted at them aggressively. The elephants fled before this show of temper from an animal one tenth their size.

They're clever, those elephants. Some of them have learnt how to deal with an electric fence and they teach others how to perform the same tricks. The simplest trick is to lean on one of the posts and create a gap, but they have also discovered that, if they pull two wires together with their tusks, the system is short-circuited. If they find something looking like a battery in the system, they brush it off with their backsides.

Elephants create problems, the elder Kipsoi explained to me, because, with their rough ways and enormous appetites, they create difficulties for both cattle and wildlife. Their population is increasing by up to 10 per cent a year. The world ban on ivory trading has given them a new lease of life—and they are a huge draw to tourists.

The fall-off in tourism, especially from America, is grievous and a setback. Tourism did provide half the modest budget for all the projects; this year's contribution is down to 15 per cent.

Ian Craig has inspired and fostered an idea whose time has come and is now on the move. A map of the conservation areas put you in mind of a jigsaw puzzle, of which Lewa was the first piece. Il Ngwesi, Namunyak and Lekurruki came next. Three more, Kalama, West Gate and Sera, are in their infancy. They are all being supported by Tusk Trust, which was chosen as one of our Christmas charities, and the newer ones particularly need support to get established.

This is a scheme in which animals, people and Africa can only benefit. Tusk Trust works widely across Africa and has learnt to recognise which projects deserve support. That's partly what moved us into making our first appeal for an animal charity.

Much of the world is beating a track to Craig's door. There have been official visitors from Ethiopia, Uganda and Tanzania. Elsewhere in Africa, wildlife is dying fast. Here, in northern Kenya, something has taken root that may save a lot of wildlife from extinction. Nor is that all. It is plain for all to see that zeal for conservation within the community exercises a very civilising influence.

So the idea will march, but in places where the genius of Ian Craig is not on call it will march more slowly and with more setbacks. Africa does not change its ways readily, nor is it easy to clone pioneers.

June 2004

BENEVOLENT CONSPIRACY BETWEEN AID AGENCIES AND MEDIA BENEFITS EVERYONE

News of world disasters opens the public's pockets, reports W. F. Deedes

Tonight, the One World Media Awards in London throw light on a flickering but influential relationship between the news media and leading aid organisations.

Flickering and slightly shady, I hear some cynic exclaim. For there are those who see the symbiotic relations between news media and aid as a benevolent conspiracy to prise money out of the public's purse.

First, the cameramen and the reporters, who can nearly always travel swifter than aid convoys, uncover and highlight a disaster somewhere in the developing world. Public compassion is aroused. The aid organisations set the wheels turning and address their appeal to the compassionate. The money rolls in.

Well, as Oscar Wilde expressed it, we are all in the gutter but some of us are looking at the stars. It's surely no bad thing that the public should occasionally be jerked into awareness about what is going badly wrong in the world.

Half a century ago, famine, pestilence, plague and tyranny passed unnoticed by most citizens. What the eye failed to see, the heart had no reason to grieve. Today, we live in a much less comfortable world.

What I label the curse of modern communications means that there is no escape from a sight of the world's injustices and catastrophes. We can't keep them out of the house. A thousand babies die from a famine somewhere in Africa, 10,000 children are orphaned somewhere else in Africa or Asia by Aids/HIV—and it's all on the 10 o'clock news.

So we *know*. We can shrug it off, tell ourselves it is of no account, instruct our consciences to lie easy, but we cannot avoid knowing about it. And even if we throw television out of the house, newspaper headlines will ensure that we are kept well-informed.

The smartest of the international aid organisations do not count on rousing public generosity only when disaster strikes. They keep their relations with newspapers and television in good repair by enlisting their interest in the work they do in the field of aid and development year in, year out. There is a useful bargain to be struck here. If, as a journalist, I want to know more of what is going on inside Angola or Sudan—because I smell a good story—I have no alternative but to draw on the resources of an aid organisation involved.

In some African countries, conflict has destroyed all conventional ways of travelling. If you want to know more about the genocide going on in the Darfur region of Sudan, there is no future in taking a taxi from Khartoum. It won't get you there. You will have to ask for the light aircraft and four-wheel drive vehicles of an aid organis-ation there.

I have struck a number of such bargains in recent years. In return for the lift, I make mention in this newspaper of the work being done by the organisation working to relieve the human condition. It becomes part of the story.

A few years back, I thought this newspaper's readers might be interested in how Rwanda was making out after that fearful blood-letting between the Hutus and the Tutsis in 1994. The International Red Cross arranged the journey and took me to warehouses into which countless prisoners awaiting trial had been stacked (the prisons were crammed) and where Red Cross doctors were trying to restore some semblance of humanity.

We went on to meet families in Rwanda who were ashamed of what had occurred in their country and seeking to make amends by giving refuge to countless young children who had been orphaned. It was quite a tale. Our readers were interested. The Red Cross came well out of it. But I would not have got to first base if that organisation had not plotted a way round that chaotic country.

But how much does it all matter? Have we not enough woes in our own country without exploring the plight of people in Africa? That is a good question to ask in the week that a G8 economic summit is meeting in America to discuss, among other things, how to relieve the burden of debt and destitution that falls on so much of Africa.

Our world is being constantly persuaded that the gap between our relatively wealthy West, and the impoverished countries of Africa and elsewhere disgraces us and ought to be narrowed. Some think it is best done by wiping out debt. I have my doubts on that score because unless conditions were strict, not much of the money saved would find its way towards public health and education.

On the other hand, I have seen enough of unsuccessful Africa to know the extent to which the UN relief agencies—working for refugees, for women and children and for the sick—in conjunction with other world organisations in the field of aid and development help positively to narrow this gap.

If those whose consciences are more readily aroused by the plight of sick and starving children in Africa than by the woes of this relatively prosperous island are then encouraged to support agencies doing the work, what fault do we find with that?

There is another elementary factor involved in this symbiotic relationship between news media and overseas charities. It does a newspaper or a television network no harm at all to be seen tapping the charitable instinct of this country. The cynics who declare we have become a selfish people are mistaken. This newspaper's annual Christmas appeal, in which I take a hand, has taught me differently. We are more generous than most of our European neighbours.

Maybe we inherited something from the Victorians, some of whom took the world's scandals—insofar as they came to light—very seriously indeed. Then, the problem was more likely to be slavery; today, it is the scourge of HIV/Aids. Or perhaps it is a legacy of empire which, no matter what some say now, attracted a great deal of unselfish service.

If we can link the needs of this world to the generous spirit that runs unseen through so many of this nation's homes, then at least some of the sins that we, of the news media, commit every day may be forgiven.

July 2004

SHAMEFUL COVER-UP THAT PREVENTS CHARITIES TACKLING A CATASTROPHE

Aid agencies are struggling to help a million people displaced by an Arab militia

Here in the small town of Tawila in Northern Darfur, they show you the burnt-out shopping centre. Then you talk to terrified women and children nearby who experienced the atrocities of four months ago. Some of them now have only a light covering of thorn bush branches for their home.

Look at them, their tiny possessions and sad cooking arrangements sodden with rain, and you stare into the abyss of man's inhumanity to man.

Mercifully, Save the Children, the leading agency here, is about to reach them with blankets, plastic sheeting and cooking pots. They also run a big clinic operation in this stunned town which is saving goodness knows how many children's lives.

What happened in Tawila? The attack by the dreaded Janjaweed militia focused on a 20-mile radius round the town. About 34 villages were looted or burned, a hundred people were killed, women and children raped, and almost the entire population fled to nearby wadis or bushes.

Whether it amounted to ethnic cleansing is hard to say. Counsel for the government of Sudan might argue it sought only, along with other attacks, to teach the Darfurians a lesson they could never forget.

Either way, the outcome which I have been looking at is horrible. Why was the world so slow to react? Why has the rescue of these people taken so long? We're talking of a million displaced people, 700,000 of them in urgent need of food aid, and 150,000 of those likely to be cut off by the rains which are starting now. "We need a thousand more aid workers," a United Nations source says to me, "and it's very late in the day."

But gaining access to this remote part of the world is hellishly difficult. There is no infrastructure. Lawlessness prevails. Aid agencies have found it difficult to get visas for their staff—though that situation, after heavy pressure on Khartoum, is easing. Security is used as a pretext for curbing all movement. It took us four hours of hard negotiating before we were allowed to enter Tawila.

As Kofi Annan, the UN secretary general, discovered recently, there is a strong desire by government to conceal what happened here with its dreadful consequences. Government has established a bureaucracy which has a life of its own. It assists the process.

This reign of terror, mainly designed to drive Africans off shrinking territory that Arabs aspire to possess, has had far-reaching consequences. It has led to a cover-up which impedes access. It has so terrified Darfurians that they dare not leave the refugee camps for home.

I visited a huge camp outside El Fasher where 30,000 of the 40,000 inhabitants are children. The men are seeking work to keep things going. Many of the children are traumatised. The women are scared. Many refugees are occupying other people's houses which greatly adds to the confusion. Listen to them speaking about the simplest and most essential of domestic chores in almost all Africa, which is collecting firewood. "If you send the men, they will be killed. If you send women or girls, they will be raped. If you send old women, they will only be beaten up."

Oh how melancholy is the plight of the refugee who knows that his or her home has probably been destroyed, as many African homes have been, along with every possession.

As we moved through the vast El Fasher refugee camp, they crowded round our vehicle, not begging, not asking for anything but with expectant smiles. Did we bear any prospect of a change in their lives? It is the expectant look that wrenches the heart. From mid-July to mid-August is sowing time, but precious little seed is going into the ground. Schools in the region I have been travelling through have been destroyed, are shut, or occupied by refugees.

There are, as one might expect, an unhealthy number of guns about. Men with guns are highly valued by much of the population for they are thought to keep the Janjaweed at bay. Worst of all, the reign of terror has so scattered the population that they become increasingly difficult to feed. Both Port Sudan and Libya offer main supply routes, but getting those supplies to small pockets of population will need a lot of vehicles, and when the rains get going the vehicles will get bogged down.

There is talk of helicopters, very expensive carriers. On the day Save the Children took us to Tawila, there had been a downpour in the morning.

The problem this created for our four-wheel-drive vehicle struck me as ominous.

And with the rains will come health problems for this displaced population. With people living so close together and chronic mal-nourishment, some think it will be a miracle if these people escape an epidemic. If you say prayers, pray that no epidemic may be added to Darfur's woes.

Plainly, one urgent need in Darfur is a peacekeeping force. The prospect of the government of Sudan deploying its own forces fills people with dread. That is no way forward. The United Nations has its hands full in Iraq. The African Union has promised a 300-strong protection force, which is nowhere near enough; and the government of Sudan has stipulated that it must restrict itself to protecting those monitoring the so-called ceasefire and protection of the Sudanese people is for government alone. Impasse. Yet without some curb on the lawlessness, this urgent rescue operation is going to be severely handicapped. This is a dangerous region in which to engage in humanitarian work.

There is a lot of "maybe" about the future in Darfur. Maybe enough aid workers will be allowed in to augment the work being done by those already on the ground here. But time is short, funds have to be raised, it's not easy to get here and every hand involved has to be professional.

Maybe the government of Sudan will abide by its word and at the insistence of Kofi Annan and Colin Powell, the US secretary of state, call off the murderous Janjaweed.

But Khartoum is masterly at non-compliance. I believe that much of the government, wishing to look well in the eyes of the world, opposed what was done in Darfur. But there are elements in Khar-toum that take a hard line, just as they have over the interminable civil war, and they prevailed.

So close monitoring of undertakings made is imperative if Darfur is to be restored to its right mind. Maybe they will get the trucks and the workers in time before those in inaccessible parts of this vast region starve to death.

Maybe the rains will be light, sufficient to sustain planting— if any gets done—but not heavy enough to bog down the rescue.

Maybe, above all, there will be a peacekeeping force strong enough to restore some sort of order in this land.

But the road will be uphill all the way. I've seen a few emergencies in my time and fine agencies like my companions here, Save the Children, striving to surmount them. Here in Darfur they have mountains to climb.

JOURNALISM

WHEN I BEGAN REPORTING in 1931, the world of journalism was a very different arena to the one with which we are familiar today. Many men and women who pursue a career in news reporting now are those who, in 1931, might have sought a career in public life. University degrees, in the 1930s, were rare amongst reporters. These days, degrees are found everywhere in journalism, suggesting that more talent now flows towards the critics' circle than towards the political stage, and greater material rewards are to be found there.

Reporting has gained a reputation for being more harsh, cruel and cynical to its subjects than before. The discretion shown by the press towards the crisis created by King Edward VIII's friendship with Mrs Simpson, as she then was, was partly due to nervousness about libel, but it also illustrated a deference shown to royalty, and indeed all public figures, that no longer exists. This deference has now been replaced by the industry's pursuit of a story, which has led to a constant watch over all those in the public eye.

We live in a society which has become far more equal than the hierarchical system into which I was born, and the authority of both the politician and the royal family is ever more open to challenge from journalists. In some ways this is beneficial to democracy. Tension between press and politician acts as a safeguard. But if the public are persuaded that their politicians are a poor lot, then we shall run into difficulties. I find myself wondering how far my own profession of journalism has made the downfall of the monarchy more likely.

A CHAPTER OF EXCELLENCE

The former Daily Telegraph editor, W. F. Deedes, reflects on the distinguished career of Lord Hartwell, a "gentleman most deserving of praise", but who would view any tribute as "rather over the top"

One of Lord Hartwell's favourite—and most characteristic—expressions is reserved for journalists and politicians whom he considers to have overstated their case: ". . . rather over the top, I thought". It needs to be borne in mind before reflecting on the chapter which closes today as Michael Hartwell ends 33 years as chairman and editor-in-chief of this newspaper.

I write "chapter" rather than "era" in deference to this tiresome preference for understatement; but if we reckon that his father, the first Viscount Camrose, acquired the Sunday Times in 1915, then the Berry family fully account for an era in Fleet Street.

Michael Hartwell has been guided by his father's example ever since as the younger son he became, after Lord Camrose's death in 1954, his *de facto* successor. So, one has to bring his father into the reckoning. His genius lay in building up the fortunes of The Daily Telegraph, while taking it up-market rather than down. He took it over on Jan 1, 1928 with a falling circulation of 84,000. He modernised it, increased the staff and on December 1, 1930 cut its price from 2d to 1d. On the outbreak of war sales were 750,000.

Physically, and in all his dealings, Camrose was an upright man. He bequeathed that. My links with the family go back to 1937 when Camrose was *invited*—the word is exact—to buy the failing Morning Post. I can remember countless Berry idiosyncrasies, but no occasion on which a member of their staff was called on to act dishonourably. Not a bad memorial, after a life's span in Fleet Street. They even had the gift of being whimsical about their idiosyncrasies.

Soon after the war, Camrose held an office lunch joined by a formidable Edwardian, Hugo Wortham, who ran the Peterborough column and had a fine nose for wine. When the wine arrived, a faint haze could just be seen round the neck of the decanter. "Oh God," exclaimed Wortham, in a silence which often accompanies such remarks, "they've boiled the claret again." Nothing was said then, but later, at a similar lunch, Camrose observed drily but loudly: "I hope the claret is to your taste today, Mr. Wortham."

I enter the tale because one of the burdens of working for the Berry family, and Michael in particular, has been that they are exceptionally attentive listeners. Worse, they *remember* what has been said. When Michael Hartwell could observe: ". . . but I thought you said the other day . . .", he had won the argument.

A most private man, Hartwell has proved a hard subject for profile writers. None of them throws much light on relations with his editors because they all miss an elementary truth. Hartwell's relations with all senior staff were founded on good manners. The ultimate in rebukes would be a bit of paper with the offending passage pinned to it and, in his most difficult handwriting: "This is really a bit much . . ."

A sense of courtesy governed his authority. There might be expressions of distress at what an editorial had said, never an instruction on what an editorial ought to say. Nor has it ever been Hartwell's custom to utter generalised complaints. Like his father before him, he understands the value of drawing attention to specific if minute errors as a means of keeping people up to scratch.

A great time in Hartwell's book for reproaches on minutiae was an evening when an industrial storm loomed over the newspaper. One would enter his room around six o'clock to hear the General Manager's voice on the intercom. "So they are all walking out at eight, sir, unless . . ." "No," Hartwell would say. "I thought I heard you say 'No', sir." "No," Hartwell would repeat enigmatically, ring off, apologise for the distraction and gravely produce the incriminating cutting. It would be Peterborough on a pop star. "Bit over the top, again," Hartwell would say. I came to the conclusion it was a form of therapy.

Hartwell had no need of such therapy. Lord Wavell observed that an essential for generals is "mental robustness". That also seems to have been part of Hartwell's inheritance. The Street has struck its tents. Mrs Thatcher has curbed some trade union excesses. Soon the anarchy of Fleet Street during the last two or three decades will have passed into legend. Yet they were heavy days for a man carrying upwards of 3,000 employees on the back of a family bank account.

Through them, I never saw him shaken, nor his temper raised. Such was the stoicism and reticence that when industrial action by the National Graphical Association stopped the printing of The Daily Telegraph in London for 11 days in 1978, Hartwell's public declaration that the paper "was in danger of bleeding to death" came like a thunderclap. Even those who had never heard of him, sensed that things were seriously amiss.

Another example of Hartwell's personal style appeared in 1980, when The Daily Telegraph became 125 years old and he was persuaded to write a feature. In the course of some 2,000 words he entered this sentence: "In 1961 The Sunday Telegraph was added." Yet, for the only privately-owned newspaper to launch the only new title of those times was a great source of pride to him.

It cost him his weekends; thereafter he worked on Saturdays and took Mondays off. We then, as it were, had two women in the same kitchen. Hartwell remained irreproachably loyal and generous to both; but it was when the younger woman walked into the room that his eye lit up.

Like his martinis, Hartwell's humour tends to be on the dry side; and so, in an age conditioned by television to prefer slapstick to humour, it is incomprehensible to some. Not, however, to the boys of East-the-water primary school in Devon. A few years back these 10 and 11-year-olds made a survey of London newspapers. One of their conclusions was that the percentage of advertising was too high.

Hartwell sent the whole class a long humorous letter on the virtues of advertising, concluding with a cautionary tale about "Mr. Percentage—a very fickle fellow." "When I was at school," wrote Hartwell, "there was a master who was very keen on population control. He said the average parent had 2.8 children. My friends and I thought one of the boys a little soft in the head. As he had two elder brothers, we used to call him 'old point eight per cent'."

Among other Fleet Street publishers, competitive and cantankerous though they are, Hartwell, I think, had no enemies. They have counted on his judgment and respected an ability to settle arguments with great economy of language.

A more difficult question is whether Hartwell, so much in his own world, particularly after the death of his gifted wife, had sufficient regard for his best interests.

The answer to the main question, however, depends on which witness you call. My files of the middle 1980s are full of City comment on where Michael Hartwell had made commercial mistakes. I doubt if they will count much against him at the final judgment. I think that what Paul Johnson has called his "pre-war sense of honour" may count for more.

Hartwell's real achievement has been to run his newspapers for so long and so successfully, while remaining steadfastly the antithesis of what much of Fleet Street has become. Property deals and profit margins have never counted high with him. A product of good report was all. There has not been and nor is there likely to be a man at the head of any newspaper who so undemonstratively made so plain what he wanted his newspapers to be.

"Who steals my purse steals trash; 'tis something, nothing;/ 'Twas mine, 'tis his, and has been slave to thousands;/ But he that filches from me my good name/ Robs me of that which not enriches him,/ And makes me poor indeed." Oh dear, Shakespeare—frightfully over the top again.

DANGEROUS SPORT

For the past 10 years, the British press has been increasingly relentless in its pursuit of the Royal Family. W. F. Deedes looks back over the quality of the coverage—and the reasons behind it

Hounding members of the Royal Family has been sport for the tabloid newspapers for a decade—a period coinciding with Mr Rupert Murdoch's ascendancy in our national press. We are so familiar with it we do not think of the damage being done. Yet we should, for persistent royal bashing is, perversely, shifting some public odium from the tabloids to their royal quarry.

It takes a long memory, or a collection of press cuttings, to grasp the diversity and growing intensity of this harassment. Some of its impetus sprang from the betrothal of the Prince and Princess of Wales in 1980. "May I ask the editors of Fleet Street," wrote Mrs Peter Shand Kidd to The Times, "whether, in the execution of their jobs, they consider it necessary or fair to harass my daughter daily, from dawn until well after dusk?"

Mrs Shand Kidd could not know that her daughter's engagement came when intensifying competition between tabloid newspapers was debasing standards of journalism. A random glance through what has happened since illustrates the pace of the decline—and the consequences for the Royal Family.

It was the People in 1980 who trumpeted the wholly mendacious story about an alleged nocturnal rendezvous on a train in a rural siding between the Prince of Wales and his then fiancee. In 1982 the Princess of Wales felt "totally beleaguered" and the Queen summoned editors to the Palace to reason with them. In the same year photographers from the Sun (Murdoch) and Star (then Lord Matthews, since 1985 Lord Stevens) stalked the Prince and Princess of Wales in the Bahamas to catch the pregnant Princess in a bikini. In 1984 the Queen appealed again to Fleet Street editors to call off photographers and reporters who had been harassing the Royal Family during their New Year holiday at Sandringham. In 1985 the Daily Mirror (Maxwell) discovered that Princess Michael's father had been in the SS, and lashed her for it. In 1986, a News of the World (Murdoch) splash (which led to a writ) accused Princess Michael of spending four nights in a secluded Kentucky cottage with the Earl of Suffolk and Berkshire. In 1987, when for the umpteenth time the tabloids had the royal marriage on the rocks, the Guardian printed an account of the Prince of Wales in Manchester.

"The pack [of journalists]: 'Will you ask about his marriage?' Child care workers: 'No.' 'Aren't you worried about his marriage?' 'No.' 'Go on, everybody is.' 'We're not.' 'Haven't you been reading about it?' 'No.' 'Go on, ask him.' 'No.' 'Why not?' 'It's his own business.' 'So you won't then?' 'No.'"

In 1988 the Sun declared that "a defiant Fergie is at the centre of an extraordinary royal crisis over her disgraced father Major Ron Ferguson." The Queen was quoted as saying: "You really must stop backing your father"; the Duchess of York as replying: "I have to put my dad before royalty."

In 1989 a Sun front page carried "£69,000 for Andy (And Nigel gives the rest of us just £4.35 a week more)". "Fury erupted last night," said the Sun, "after Prince Andrew was given a £1,325-a-week pay rise—while Chancellor Nigel Lawson's Budget left Britain's workers just £4.35 a week better off."

In 1990 the Sun caught the Prince of Wales "clad only in short white bathing trunks' embracing Lady Penny Romsey ("Charles Hugs his Old Flame"). She had just told him (we learnt later) that her four-year-old daughter was suffering from cancer.

And so to 1991 and the richest crop of all. "Separate Rooms" was the Sun's headline in April on the marriage of the Prince and Princess of Wales—founded on the reminiscences of a former police guard at Highgrove.

In February the Sunday Times (Murdoch) charged the Royal Family with shirking the Gulf war, and told the Queen to remedy it. Last month a Sunday Times front-page headline ran: "Queen: tax me and I'll have to sell Balmoral"—though to whom she addressed this was unclear. The story inside bore the headline "Can't Pay Won't Pay". It was not the first attack on royalty in the Sunday Times, but it was a rare attack on the Queen herself in a broadsheet.

Last week the Sun had another royal exclusive, a picture of Prince Andrew bathing in the nude. "Get set to grab a glimpse of the cheeky clown prince."

As one reflects on Murdoch and his editors, Pope's lines spring to mind: *Damn with faint praise, assent with civil leer, / And, without sneering, teach the rest to sneer; / Willing to wound, and yet afraid to strike, / Just hint a fault and hesitate dislike.*

In September 1990, when the tabloids were shrieking about Prince Charles's injured elbow and sneaked a picture of him looking miserably out of a window—"The Window Pain" (Sun)—Today ran an editorial headed "Disloyal Servants". "The deceit of the royal PR men", it declared, "does an injustice to a scrupulously honest and worthy heir to the throne."

Fanning aside the smell of humbug, that editorial is particularly rich. For it is "disloyal servants" on whom the tabloids count heavily for dirt on the Royals. In the royal scandal market, large sums of money are paid to rogues for dirt. A kiss-and-tell girl revealing (or fabricating) goings-on with royalty need never work again.

There are two strands to all this. One, the "Dallas syndrome", relates to growing confusion in the public mind between soap opera and real life. Fantasising about the Royals feeds this bizarre taste.

Some say that the Royal Family has brought this upon itself. By admitting the television cameras, by numbering popular comedians among their friends, by taking jobs, by making jolly speeches, they have—so the argument runs—debased their own currency. Yet not so many years ago, similar pundits were urging the Queen to bring herself and her family into the modern world.

The second strand is more insidious. The Sunday Times headline alongside a picture of the Queen—"Can't Pay Won't Pay"—is intended to convey that the Queen is no different from those refusing to pay poll tax, an offence described in Parliament as tantamount to shop lifting.

Such mendacity cumulatively has damaged the Royal Family, and is intended to do so. It seems a mistake to dismiss the press onslaught upon the Royal Family as mere harmless, circulation-building fun. Cumulatively, its impact is substantial, as The Daily Telegraph Gallup poll seems to confirm. Have those who lap up this stuff grasped this? John Citizen is to have a charter to protect his interests. The Queen and her family enjoy no such protection. The modern Tory party in election year will not lift a finger to defend the Royal Family, if this seems likely to damage its relations with the press. Only the public can decide whether it is happy with a process, heavily powered from overseas, which undermines and could eventually destroy the throne.

FROM GENTS TO JOURNOS

W. F. Deedes, 80 this week, looks at how journalism has changed, for good and ill, since the days when reporters were expected to behave like gentlemen

"Of course," the chief reporter said, with a faint curl of the lip, "you can always hire the stuff from Moss. But here they prefer you to have your own rig." I was seeking advice before reporting my first public dinner for the *Morning Post* in 1931. It would be a white-tie affair, as most public dinners were in those days. It followed that the *Morning Post* representative would be in a white tie and tail-coat, preferably his own. When reporting Ascot, he would appear in a morning-coat, and for informal evening occasions he would wear a dinner-jacket. The lobby correspondent, who had known Gladstone, wore a frock-coat.

I duly purchased all three outfits from Huntsman in Savile Row, at something between £12 and £15 each—slightly reduced prices, due to a long family connection—and because they came from that quarter I can wear them still. The *Morning Post* also expected its reporters to wear suits, a collar and tie, and a hat. This was not out of the way. Those were still formal days. Glance at any group of men photographed in the 1930s; most of them are wearing hats or caps. Hats were usually raised when greeting a woman, and invariably when passing the Cenotaph in Whitehall. When dispatching me to be a war correspondent in Abyssinia in 1935, the editor, H. A. Gwynne, tendered three bits of advice. Please remember a dead correspondent is valueless. A finger of whisky in the water-bottle kills bugs (he had been a correspondent in the Boer War). And get all your kit from a decent outfitter; you are representing *us*.

With such formalities of dress went a certain formality of address. On the *Morning Post* we observed a deference—you might call it old-fashioned courtesy—towards all public figures, which would today be derided as daft. The former Chancellor of the Exchequer, Mr Lamont, was asked last week whether he was "past his sell-by date". No *Morning Post* reporter would have put such a question. My mentor in the reporters' room was Hugh Speaight, brother of a then well-known actor Robert. He would call the secretaries of those whom he sought to interview and conclude by saying: "And please tell him that if he will grant this interview, we shall be sending our very best man . . ." It rarely failed.

Unlike the young women employed by television these days, who can draw public men to the screen at unearthly hours with a crook of their little finger, we did not expect prominent figures to make themselves readily available. Publicity hardly entered their minds; and if it did, it made them shudder. The public relations officer, now ubiquitous, had scarcely been born. Sir Kingsley Wood, later Air Minister and Chancellor of the Exchequer, invented him while he was at the Post Office. Nobody offered news. You dug for it.

This difference in degree between the politician and the journalist was nicely conveyed by that brilliant but aloof laywer Sir John Simon. In 1937, as a senior minister, he made a rare appearance before the lobby correspondents, of whom I was then one. "Gentlemen . . ." he began with just the right ironic inflexion, ". . . I so address you, because I have every desire to be on good terms with journalists . . ." Imagine that from a Cabinet minister today!

It followed that journalists outside the lobby rarely approached senior politicians. Editors and newspaper proprietors dined at the right tables, saw ministers in private, and then conveyed their views and wishes to editorial writers. There came a point in the affairs of King Edward VIII in 1936 when I sought to persuade my seniors at the *Morning Post* that it was incumbent upon us to write an editorial. I had been collecting material from newspapers and magazines published overseas for the editor, who wanted to show them to the Prime Minister. It seemed clear to me that the secret had not long to live. Baldwin told Gwynne that he wanted more time, and that was that. I doubt if Mr Kelvin MacKenzie of the *Sun* would have been so obliging.

This deference by journalists towards public men played its part at the time of Munich. Editors, such as Geoffrey Dawson of the *Times*, had close relations with ministers—Dawson's relations with Lord Halifax, Foreign Secretary, were exceptionally close. Ministers desired above all not to aggravate Hitler. Most editors followed that line. *The Daily Telegraph* was lucky in that Churchill, a hawk towards Hitler's Germany, was a regular contributor in the late 1930s, and on good terms with Viscount Camrose.

Far from being a defender of the deferential system, I judge, with hindsight, that it wrought inestimable damage in the 1930s. Journalists who differed from their editors or proprietors about the nature of Hitler's Germany were ignored or suppressed. Some resigned. Newspapers failed to convey, as they should have done, the appalling character of Hitler's Nazi Germany. They have since then printed countless articles heaping blame on Neville Chamberlain and his kind. Yet, in truth, newspaper editors were themselves among the "guilty men". They failed in their first duty, which was to warn the public of what was going on.

The war and the Labour Government of 1945 shifted the balance appreciably. Journalists and politicians moved towards more equal terms. When I became a junior minister in 1954 they were on equal terms. Churchill, who appointed me, though he had earned most of his living from newspapers, was still mistrustful of journalists. But most of my colleagues in government reckoned the time had come to make terms with them.

Television put the journalists on top. I joined the Cabinet in 1962 after the so-called "night of the long knives", with the odd and unattainable task of improving appearances. At that point a minister had to seek permission from 10 Downing Street to appear on any television programme. It was sparingly granted. Vigorously prodded by Paul Fox, then with BBC's *Panorama*, and others, I loosened the stays a little. From the 1960s onwards, politically, socially and professionally, television began to change the map of politics—and countless youthful ambitions.

For some time many well-connected young men and women of talent, who in the world of 50 years ago might have aspired to a political career, have been looking to the news media as a vehicle for their ambitions. When I visit universities I am asked about short cuts into newspapers, rarely about the prospects of a political career. In 1931, when I joined it, the *Morning Post* was embarking on the novel policy of recruiting reporters with Oxford or Cambridge degrees— though I had neither. Today there is a fair sprinkling in newspaper offices of those who took Firsts.

Thus more talent is flowing towards the critics' circle than towards the stage itself. The columnist Julie Burchill, and others of her genre, earn more than the Prime Minister. Why enter the hazards of public life when such prizes beckon? To put it on the lowest terms, a journalist today can consort with half a dozen bimbos, while at the same time ditching one aspiring to be President of the United States or Prime Minister for alleged association, at some time in the past, with a single bimbo.

There remains one distinction between the politician and the journalist. The former takes decisions, and the latter does not. But the latter increasingly exercises influence on decision-making. I date the start of this from the Vietnam war. We are seeing it vividly illustrated in what was formerly Yugoslavia. And who insisted that Mr Major must carry out his Cabinet reshuffle last Thursday? If we were still in the world of the *Morning Post* it would have taken place when he wanted it, at the end of July.

WHY DIANA DEALT WITH THE ENEMY

The Daily Mail *said that Diana, Princess of Wales colluded with its reporters. W. F. Deedes argues that it was only done in self-defence*

For good reasons of their own, newspapers have not—yet—sought to absolve themselves from the charges made against them by Earl Spencer at the funeral of Diana, Princess of Wales. "Of all the ironies about Diana," he said, "perhaps the greatest was this: a girl given the name of the ancient goddess of hunting was, in the end, the most hunted person of the modern age."

In the prevailing mood, the public does not want to hear excuses from newspapers. It wants to have assurances, for what they are worth, that newspapers have learnt their lesson, have turned over a new leaf and will not offend again.

Well aware of this, the *News of the World*, the *Sunday Mirror* and the *People* have all promised to work closely with the Press Complaints Commission to protect Diana's sons, Prince William and Prince Harry, from media intrusion. They could hardly do less.

We would be grievously mistaken, however, to suppose that matters will rest there for very long. For it did not need Lord Spencer's words to persuade much of the public that his sister, Diana, had had throughout her public life a rough deal from sections of the press. What is alleged to have happened in that Paris tunnel pointed a blazing finger in that direction. There was something of an exorable Greek tragedy about the way her life was ended.

My profession in consequence has been wounded. Whether some sections of it have been damaged by loss of circulation remains to be seen. Personally I very much doubt it, but an unforeseen and still unpredictable public mood is still abroad.

What we can be sure about, however, is that when it judges the moment to be ripe, my profession will seek to defend itself vigorously against charges that amount to brutality against the Princess of Wales. It will try very hard to appease public anger. And in course of this defence, by no means an easy one, it will plead that Diana herself formed friendships with journalists, enjoyed their attentions (when it suited her), encouraged them to support her causes, indeed used them more skilfully than any member of the Royal Family has ever done.

Paul Dacre of the *Daily Mail* declared in the *Guardian* yesterday that Diana was on friendly terms with him and one or two of his journalists. True. She was friendly with one or two of us here as well. Paul Dacre said she often called up journalists on the telephone. True again.

In other words, my profession will claim that there was collusion, that in this balance sheet accounting for her relationships with the news media, the credit side of her account comes close to matching the debit side of our own. There is sufficient truth in this line of argument to require a careful explanation.

First of all, as those of us who were involved in Diana's relations with newspapers from the earliest days know, reasonably or unreasonably she feared photographers. There was no question of a *quid pro quo*. When she first became a public figure, on her engagement to the Prince of Wales, she found their attentions overwhelming and frightening.

Why else, before the marriage, did the Queen invite editors to Buckingham Palace for an informal talk, on her behalf, and beg them to go easy with Diana? As an editor at the time, I listened to this plea with sympathy and attention but no great hope of easement for Diana.

The next phase came when the two Princes were growing up. Diana had by then perforce buried some of her personal fears of the press, but resurrected them all on behalf of her two sons. She saw their chances of growing up naturally put at risk by excessive attention from photographers.

This time round it was felt best that she should deal with the newspapers directly herself. I was one of several editors invited to lunch, one or two at a time, with her and the Prince of Wales at Kensington Palace. Those lunches stand out in my mind as the start of a defensive system which the Princess of Wales felt impelled to create on her own behalf and on behalf of her sons. To put it loosely, if you can't fight 'em, join 'em.

Confronted by what seemed to her an army of reporters and photographers insensitive to her fears, unfeeling about her sons, deaf to pleas from the Queen or herself, she began very slowly and hesitatingly a process of making friends among the enemy.

This policy was first publicly observable as her marriage to the Prince of Wales started to break down. At that point, the world's news media laid siege to the couple. What could not be discovered was, by some newspapers, invented. It was also the beginning of a deep public division of opinion about the Prince and Princess of Wales.

Reckoning that she had very little on her side, and that the hand of the Establishment would be against her, the Princess of Wales began privately to enlarge her circle of journalists, writers and broadcasters, and sought to enlist their support. One outcome was the Morton book. Another was the *Panorama* interview. Nor were the chief offenders, the tabloid press, excluded from this policy. She became pals with one or two who had given most offence.

Now there are two ways of looking at this. People in newspapers, seeking to defend themselves from the sort of charges Lord Spencer delivered with such effect from Westminster Abbey's pulpit, and members of the public who were unfavourable to Diana, will declare her to be guilty of manipulation.

"She wanted to have it both ways," they will argue. She did her utmost to make friends with journalists, rang them up, took meals with them, occasionally flattered them. She cultivated a love-hate relationship with the tabloid press and so had only herself to blame for the consequences.

Having been in on all of this from the start, I take another view. When we were in Bosnia together, some chatty fellow at a dinner party supposed that she, Diana, had by now become accustomed to the cohorts of photographers. "No, you never become accustomed to it," she retorted firmly. "That's the trouble."

We shall never know now exactly what went through Diana's mind, but of one thing I am sure: in all her manoeuvres with people in newspapers the defensive mechanism was dominant. Unquestionably, she consorted with reporters and photographers. She made close friends of one or two of them. She did so in pursuit of self-protection and, sadly, wholly in vain.

"IN 1931 TO BE A REPORTER WAS HEAVEN"

Seventy years after W. F. Deedes became a journalist, he is still reporting from around the world. Here, he recalls a unique career

Bliss it was in the summer of 1931 to have a job—any job; for the number of unemployed had climbed to 2.71 million. But to be a newspaper reporter was very heaven! The world was in turmoil. Within days of my joining the *Morning Post*, Britain faced bankruptcy, Ramsay MacDonald's Labour government fell, and an all-party coalition under pressure from King George V was cobbled together to deliver us.

"Go and watch the crowds in Downing Street," they told me. "Don't write anything, old boy, just useful experience." So it was. I had never reported anything in my life. Why was I there? The *Morning Post*, feeling its age, had decided to recruit a few young reporters. I was among them.

It was three days before I got anything into the paper. Late one evening, the deputy news editor handed me a small newspaper item reporting that the Indian Rope Trick had been performed at Cheltenham before the International Brotherhood of Magicians. He instructed me to ring Jasper Maskelyne, the well-known conjuror and discuss it.

I trembled at the thought of inviting such a celebrity to talk to me, but he was happy to explain at length why the trick was a myth. My story appeared. I was "in".

On a higher plane, the pound was devalued by 30 per cent and all public pay cut, leading to riots in London and a brief mutiny in the Navy at Invergordon, where ratings found themselves down to 25 shillings a week.

In the General Election of that October, an anxious nation gave the new coalition 554 seats and Labour just 56 seats. For my miscellaneous duties during that one-sided event, the *Morning Post* awarded me £5 a week, good pay then for a young chap "on space", which meant being paid only for copy that got into the paper.

Other sensations coloured that summer, such as a violent mutiny at Dartmoor prison, which I longed to cover. More than any other event, it determined me to become the sort of reporter they might send on such a terrific story.

In weeks that followed, reporting duties required me to meet Gandhi—that story didn't get in—and the Prince of Wales. I travelled across the Drury Lane stage in the London bus that featured in Noel Coward's *Cavalcade*, wrote stories about cat shows, Whipsnade Zoo, London fires and riots and the Chamber of Horrors at Madame Tussaud's, where I volunteered to spend a night.

Nothing serious came my way until self-government for India became a big political issue in the early 1930s, and I was required to ferret out the divisions this created within the Tory party. It led to encounters with Winston Churchill, who led Tory opposition to Indian reform, and his irascible son Randolph.

In their kindly way, senior staff at the *Morning Post* sometimes went through my copy with me, rather as tutors treat student essays, so replacing at least part of the university education I lost after my father got caught in the Wall Street crash of 1929.

For major events, such as the stunning Silver Jubilee of King George V, which I reported from the Mall, there was a seat in the stalls. A modest man, the King was bewildered by the cheering. After the marriage of Prince George, Duke of Kent to Princess Marina of Greece, a few of us joined their royal train to report cheering crowds that gathered at every station, as they travelled to Birmingham for the start of their honeymoon at Himley Hall. Yes, those were different days.

One evening in 1933, they sent me down to the House of Commons to hear the tail-end of a debate on the plight of cotton. I met one or two lachrymose Lancashire MPs and took the night sleeper to Manchester. Our cotton mills were shutting down fast, heavily undercut by Japanese competition. It made a couple of splashes in the *Morning Post*. Historically, I was seeing another curtain fall on our former industrial supremacy.

When in the summer of 1935, the *Morning Post* asked if I would report Italy's threatened war against Abyssinia, it was alarming to find how little anyone knew about the country. Anticipating that I might be away for months, perhaps never to return, they lavished me with gear. The chief reporter gave me his compass.

Evelyn Waugh's novel, *Scoop*, about that war, has embalmed some of us who were there in romance. Yet it was a dull war. Addis Ababa was not the capital it is now. A primitive African town, it offered two bars and a cinema. There were other dividends. I was paid £15 a week, good money then, and Waugh taught me to ride a horse.

To save money, because cabling from Addis Ababa cost £5 a word, I eventually sent skeleton dispatches which were converted into elegant prose by our theatre critic, J C Trewin, in the *Morning Post* office and published under my name. My office code included words like ELBA—please cable more money; and SKELETON—following message is much abbreviated, please elaborate. So I would send: "Skeleton stop desertion gugsa italianwards greeted here anger, incredulity, fantasy stop jealousy kassa query."

J C Trewin would convert this into half a column, starting:

Addis Ababa, Oct 14

"The news of the desertion of Dedjasmatch Haile Selassie Gugsa to the Italians has caused much perturbation in Government circles here.

"Although frankly mystified, the Government expresses itself as incredulous of the report, and emphasises the fact that Dedjasmatch Haile Selassie Gugsa is the son-in-law of the Emperor.

"At the same time, it is admitted in some quarters that the defection of the leader of the Ethiopian North-Eastern Army might be accounted for by his known jealousy of Ras Kassa, his powerful neighbour . . .

"The whole attitude of the Government here is to treat the news as a fantastic rumour, to which they are not in a position to give either official denial or official confirmation . . ."

And so on.

Back in England for Christmas, in time to report the lying-in-state of King George V in Westminster Hall and a London food strike, I spent part of the following summer investigating our neglected Territorial Army.

"On the idle hill of summer, / Sleepy with the flow of streams, / Far I hear the steady drummer / Drumming like a noise in dreams . . ." My wisest friends assured me that war was coming.

Nothing appeared in British newspapers, but early in 1936 there was talk of our new King's fixation with a Mrs Simpson. Not without difficulty, I collected clippings from overseas publications about this affair, with which our editor, H A Gwynne, aimed to warn his friend at No 10, Stanley Baldwin. I wanted us to run the story, but was told "Baldwin wanted more time . . ."

Just before he left us, King Edward VIII toured the valleys of South Wales, met the unemployed and declared, "Something must be done . . ."

"Well, let us do something," the *Morning Post* news editor instructed me. We contrived to raise enough money to send anonymously to every child of unemployed parents in the distressed areas a Christmas present by post. The departing King sent a donation.

In the autumn of 1936, Oswald Mosley and his Blackshirts, joined by some odd figures, began rampaging through East London. Reporting most of these affrays, I saw in October of that year some of the nastiest London riots of the last century.

Mosley's aborted march down Cable Street in Stepney, which later provoked Communist countermeasures in Whitechapel, aimed to win recruits by inflaming anti-Semitic feeling. It led to the destruction and looting of Jewish property and drove Parliament into rapidly passing the Public Order Act.

Dispatched to the House of Commons lobby as the *Morning Post*'s political correspondent at the start of 1937, I was there long enough to bid farewell to Ramsay MacDonald, report Neville Chamberlain's arrival at No 10, hear Lloyd George ragging the Government, Churchill demanding faster rearmament, and Baldwin, in his final speech to the Commons, calling on the nation to support the new King and Queen.

MPs' pay was raised from £400 to £600 a year, and in the light of Lloyd George's admissions in his war memoirs, the *Morning Post* was instrumental in securing for General Sir Hubert Gough, sacked for the collapse of his Fifth Army in March 1918, a belated GCB.

Early that year I broke the news that all work on the new Whitehall block that today houses the Ministry of Defence, was to stop. Considered too great a target from the air, it showed where minds were turning.

Lord Camrose, owner and editor-in-chief of *The Daily Telegraph*, bought and incorporated the *Morning Post* late that year. Relieved of the political job, I joined the *Telegraph*'s defence staff and began to report our unpreparedness for aerial war. The bomber would always get through, Baldwin told us. Given our defencelessness, what would then happen to our urban population?

That was the factor that later sent Chamberlain flying to Germany, umbrella tightly furled. I saw him off in a tiny plane from Heston on one of his three visits to Hitler, reported his return from Munich—and thereafter felt driven to write more urgently about our inadequate defences.

For a month before Christmas in 1938 and 1939, I dropped defence, toured the Distressed Areas and ran what became the *Telegraph* Christmas appeal for children of the unemployed. In South Wales, on Tyneside, in Lancashire and in the ports of West Cumberland, conditions were dire. I witnessed much poverty, but also heart-warming generosity among the poorest of the poor. No one has ever had to explain to me why the Tories lost the 1945 election.

After Hitler marched into Prague in March 1939 and we ceased pretending that there wouldn't be a war, Camrose asked me to put together guidance for our readers when the bombers came. We got it on the bookstands a few days before Germany invaded Poland.

With five years of war, 30 years of the Peterborough column which coincided with 25 years in politics, and a further 12 years editing this newspaper, it would be nearly half a century before I became a reporter again. There was ample political travel, watching the end of Empire in our African and Asian colonies. But not until Max Hastings took over from me as editor in 1986 and asked me to stay on and write, did I fully recover the right to roam and report.

So back to old haunts in Ethiopia, where 50 years on, the Emperor Haile Selassie had been replaced by a Marxist tyrant. It would be 2000, just 70 years after his coronation, before his remains received a decent burial, for which I returned once more to Addis Ababa, now a modern city.

To Hanoi, where the United States, alarmed by baseless reports that the Vietnamese were concealing American prisoners-of-war, had resorted to extraordinary measures to find and account for every missing man. To Latin America—"there's a lot going on there," Max Hastings thought. To Mozambique and Angola, where Portugal's imperial exit had provoked ruinous fighting. To Rwanda, bloodiest of all.

Such journeys brought two things home to me. First the hasty end of Empire, predictably followed by inexperienced—and often corrupt—government have made huge demands on the world's aid agencies.

Aid workers, of whom I've seen a lot in recent years, have their critics. If they feed the needy during conflict, they are accused of freeing men to fight and so prolonging conflict. To render help to the afflicted, they have sometimes to reach agreement with villains, so exposing themselves to the charge of supping with the devil. They make mistakes, yet without them, I can testify, countless innocent women and children would have suffered and died the world over.

Second, conflict in Africa and Asia, to say nothing of the Balkans, infested the earth with landmines which, a decade ago, were taking a cruel toll of life, limb and land in poor countries; and nullifying effort in much of the developing world.

Few outside international Red Cross, the de-mining and aid agencies saw this as a scandal until, early in 1996, Diana, Princess of Wales elected to go with the British Red Cross to Angola. Those of us who reported her tour, blessed by some tactless criticism from a Conservative minister, saw how she contrived to throw sharp light on a dark subject.

Days before her life suddenly ended in August 1997, I went with her to Bosnia, where, as if without another care in the world, she listened to tales of woe from the bereaved and the limbless and, as nobody else had managed to do, made the clearing of landmines—"this day"—seem an imperative.

All through history, wars have visited suffering on civilian populations. But as I saw in shattered Sarajevo in 1995, in Macedonia, Albania and Kosovo in 1998 and 1999, modern weapons accentuate this, and innocent citizens suffer many more casualties than the combatants.

Conflict and its consequences apart, important things are happening in the world today. There is a world-wide movement from rural to urban areas, which is moving millions from the soil to the city via shanty towns. I have observed this movement in India, Indonesia, Africa, Eastern Europe, Morocco and elsewhere. Many young of this third Millennium have done with subsisting off the land. Their eyes are on the city, where it all seems to be happening. Who can guess what the consequences of that may be?

In Africa and much of Asia, women are pressing forward. They are getting top posts and outshining the men. They will not quickly be rid of either drudgery or war; but they are on the move. I report it, but briefly, because, though much has changed during my 70 years in journalism, it remains eternally true that good news does not sell newspapers.

April 2004

FASTEN YOUR SEATBELTS, WE HAVE ENCOUNTERED A LITTLE TURBULENCE

This newspaper has taken W. F. Deedes on some rough journeys, but he has always landed safely, he says

If you choose to make a career in journalism or politics then, count on it, your journey through life will sometimes encounter what the airlines call turbulence. The sensible traveller then fastens his seat belt with a sigh and, as the plane jumps about a bit, draws what comfort he can from the imperturbable faces of the cabin staff. As this Conservative newspaper goes through what we hope will be a short spell of turbulence, one tries to convey that same reassuring message: Turbulence? I've been through worse than this in my time.

So, indeed, I have. The dear old *Morning Post*, my first employer, suffered perpetual turbulence. It was not built to fly at 30,000ft along with Rothermere's *Daily Mail* and Beaverbrook's soaring *Daily Express*. The *Morning Post*'s fortunes were heavily dependent on Upstairs, Downstairs classified advertising. If you sought a butler, a footman, lady's maid or reliable cook, you advertised your needs in the *Morning Post*. And if you were in the market for any of those jobs, you bought the newspaper.

But, when that ruinous First World War ended and the shutters went up on the big houses, especially in London, that source of revenue declined. So I joined a beautiful, true blue newspaper, which was in rapid decline and fighting tenaciously with Winston Churchill against granting India independence. (This newspaper more progressively backed Indian independence.)

Within a year of my arrival there, a quarter of the staff received their notices. I was too small to be noticed, but I felt the draught. We staggered on for a few more years, long enough for me to experience the real thing in the way of turbulence, which was the abdication of King Edward VIII.

I was involved there because the British press of those days discreetly published nothing about Mrs Simpson and the King, but my editor sought to persuade the prime minister, Stanley Baldwin, that overseas rumour was rife. I was called on to hunt up press cuttings from overseas about the affair, which eventually found their way to Number 10.

Within a year, the *Morning Post* breathed its last. Viscount Camrose, then proprietor of this newspaper, bought us and in the closing months of 1937 shut us down. That was what airlines call extreme turbulence. Most of the old hands who had taught me something about the craft were retired. One or two of us got offers from other newspapers. We are a rough crowd, but not devoid of generosity. I was lucky because I had finished up as the *Morning Post*'s political correspondent with a good salary for those times and a tax-free entertainment allowance, which this newspaper took on without blinking. But that was like climbing out of an aircraft which has been brought down by storm, and knowing that some are left in the wreck.

Politics, which this newspaper gave me every encouragement to enter after the war, brought turbulence of another kind. My adoption meeting as prospective Conservative candidate for the Ashford division in Kent was chaos. The sitting Member had promised the seat to someone else. He and his supporters raised points of order for two hours before I was able, with a dry mouth and a headache, to deliver my acceptance speech. Useful training.

Being a junior minister under Churchill and number two to his son-in-law, Duncan Sandys, taught me a thing or two about turbulence. Crikey! Even the cabin staff—in this instance the senior Civil Service—looked pale. Then to the Home Office for a spell which coincided with the Suez disaster. My boss, the home secretary, was in Cabinet all day and some of the night. My contribution was to pilot a controversial Bill about capital punishment through the Commons. The plane lost about 10,000ft rapidly while that was going on.

Journalists are unsuitable for ministerial office. We are vagrants, apt to be resentful, as I was, of the essential disciplines of government imposed by the Civil Service. Retiring of my own volition, I rejoiced to return to the easier harness of this newspaper. Then, in the summer of 1962, Harold Macmillan ran into trouble. His plane lost height at an alarming rate. He summoned me and in effect asked me to hand round drinks to the frightened passengers as minister without portfolio or, less enigmatically, minister of information.

All went well for a while, then we ran into big trouble by mishandling the Jack Profumo affair. That bout of turbulence nearly tore the wings off the plane. It did for the pilot, Macmillan, who went down with prostate trouble the same year. There followed the drama of Alec Home's choice as successor, which led to a parting of ways with one or two dear colleagues who thought we were crazy. That was hurtful.

So, narrowly losing the 1964 election to Harold Wilson came as a blessed relief to this vagrant. There followed happy years, flying smoothly at 30,000ft, on the then Peterborough column (don't ask me why it changed to Spy).

My 12 years of editing this newspaper coincided with Mrs Thatcher's term at Number 10 and the rise and rise of militant trade unionism. Mrs Thatcher never sought to change our political line but the print union bosses of those days knew how to create turbulence, and how! Heavens, even the cabin staff were belted into their chairs every night!

It proved altogether too much for the private fortunes of the Berry family, then headed by Lord Hartwell, son of the Viscount Camrose. Vain to say it might all have been done differently. At the height this highly competitive industry aims to fly, the down draught can be fierce.

So, in 1986, Conrad Black stepped in with an offer. We loosened our seat belts; drinks and dinner came up. But you don't settle down to sleep, not on this airline. So here is another spell of rough flying. We'll come out of it. We'll land safely. And, for good measure, we shall uphold those Conservative principles in which we have long believed.

Meanwhile, some of the passengers are looking a bit solemn. Time I took a walk down the aisle. Turbulence? Alongside what I have known, this plane's a rock!

Index

extracts reading groups
competitions books new
books discounts extracts
extracts extracts
competitions discounts
books new events
reading groups events
new books reading groups
extracts reading groups
new books extracts discounts
titles reading groups
interviews
events extracts events new
reading groups discounts books
books interviews
new books events interviews new books extracts
events new events
discounts extracts discounts books
www.panmacmillan.com
extracts events reading groups
competitions books extracts new